Writing Brexit

Drawing from a rich corpus of British cultural production and postcolonial theory, this book positions Brexit in the historical nexus of colonialism, colonial nostalgia, and the rise of narcissistic nationalism in contemporary Europe.

This collection moves away from existing literary discourses framing Brexit as a 'novel' event that ushered in a new genre of British fiction. It challenges the hackneyed public discourses that depict the results of the 2016 Referendum as the catalyst of regional instability as well as sociopolitical emergency in Europe. This book traces and critiques populist myth-making in the current United Kingdom through engagement with a wide range of literary and cultural productions, and reminds readers of the proleptic potential of postcolonial theorists and authors – Paul Gilroy, Austin Clarke, Mohsin Hamid, Ali Smith, to name a few – in identifying the residual ideologies of imperialism in the lead up to and after the Brexit campaign. The articles featured here extend Brexit's figurative geography towards India, Britain, Pakistan, Ireland, Palestine, Barbados, and Eastern Europe, amongst others. They engage with films, media representations, and public discourses alongside more traditional genres such as the novel and stage productions. With a diversified approach to scholarly fields such as postcolonial literary and cultural studies, the book offers new insights into Brexit's diverse histories not only in academic discourses, but also in the socio-political public sphere at large.

The chapters in this book were originally published as a special issue of the *Journal of Postcolonial Writing*.

Caroline Koegler is Assistant Professor of British Literary and Cultural Studies, University of Münster, Germany.

Pavan Kumar Malreddy teaches English Literature at Goethe University Frankfurt, Germany.

Marlena Tronicke is Assistant Professor of British Literary and Cultural Studies, University of Münster, Germany.

‘These excellent essays are an important intervention in understanding the cultural politics of the Brexit phenomenon. Multifarious in their starting points and focus, they hone in on the cultural nostalgias, the politics of race and nation, and the long-term historical forces which have shaped the UK's departure from the European project.’

Colin Graham, *Professor of English, Maynooth University, Ireland*

‘Drawing on fiction, film, theatre and other cultural texts, these twelve postcolonial scholars give unique insights into the resurgent colonialism and nostalgia for Britain's imperial past that underpinned the decision to leave Europe in the 2016 Brexit referendum, and its aftermath.’

Janet Wilson and **Chris Ringrose**, *editors,* Journal of Postcolonial Writing

‘An impressive lineup of young and veteran postcolonial scholars turn the outward colonial gaze inwards, resulting in an original set of perspectives on the (textual) forms and (historical) formations of Britain's exit from the EU.’

Lars Eckstein, *Professor of Anglophone Literatures Cultures,*
University of Potsdam, Germany

Writing Brexit

Colonial Remains

Edited by
Caroline Koegler, Pavan Kumar Malreddy, and Marlena Tronicke

Routledge
Taylor & Francis Group
LONDON AND NEW YORK

First published 2021
by Routledge
2 Park Square, Milton Park, Abingdon, Oxon OX14 4RN

and by Routledge
605 Third Avenue, New York, NY 10158

Routledge is an imprint of the Taylor & Francis Group, an informa business

British Library Cataloguing in Publication Data
A catalogue record for this book is available from the British Library

ISBN: 978-0-367-77587-2 (hbk)
ISBN: 978-0-367-77590-2 (pbk)
ISBN: 978-1-003-17198-0 (ebk)

Typeset in Minion Pro
by Newgen Publishing UK

Publisher's Note
The publisher accepts responsibility for any inconsistencies that may have arisen during the conversion of this book from journal articles to book chapters, namely the inclusion of journal terminology.

Contents

Citation Information

The chapters in this book were originally published in the *Journal of Postcolonial Writing*, volume 56, issue 5 (October 2020). When citing this material, please use the original page numbering for each article, as follows:

Introduction

The colonial remains of Brexit: Empire nostalgia and narcissistic nationalism
Caroline Koegler, Pavan Kumar Malreddy and Marlena Tronicke
Journal of Postcolonial Writing, volume 56, issue 5 (October 2020), pp. 585–592

Chapter 1

Ain't no black in the (Brexit) Union Jack? Race and empire in the era of Brexit and the Windrush *scandal*
Ronald Cummings
Journal of Postcolonial Writing, volume 56, issue 5 (October 2020), pp. 593–606

Chapter 2

Warning signs: Postcolonial writing and the apprehension of Brexit
John McLeod
Journal of Postcolonial Writing, volume 56, issue 5 (October 2020), pp. 607–620

Chapter 3

Brexit literature's present absentees: Triangulating Brexit, anti-Semitism, and the Palestinian crisis
Lindsey Moore
Journal of Postcolonial Writing, volume 56, issue 5 (October 2020), pp. 621–635

Chapter 4

"We are all migrants through time": History and geography in Mohsin Hamid's Exit West
Shazia Sadaf
Journal of Postcolonial Writing, volume 56, issue 5 (October 2020), pp. 636–647

Chapter 5

"Eastern Europeans" and BrexLit
Vedrana Veličković
Journal of Postcolonial Writing, volume 56, issue 5 (October 2020), pp. 648–661

Chapter 6

Imperial pasts, dystopian futures, and the theatre of Brexit
Marlena Tronicke
Journal of Postcolonial Writing, volume 56, issue 5 (October 2020), pp. 662–675

Chapter 7

The Brexit within: Mapping the rural and the urban in contemporary British fiction
Birte Heidemann
Journal of Postcolonial Writing, volume 56, issue 5 (October 2020), pp. 676–688

Chapter 8

Writing back to Brexit: Refugees, transcultural intertextuality, and the colonial archive
Jan Rupp
Journal of Postcolonial Writing, volume 56, issue 5 (October 2020), pp. 689–702

Chapter 9

(Post)colonial friendships and Empire 2.0: A Brexit reading of Victoria & Abdul
Clelia Clini
Journal of Postcolonial Writing, volume 56, issue 5 (October 2020), pp. 703–715

Notes on Contributors

Clelia Clini is Research Associate at Loughborough University London, UK.

Ronald Cummings is Associate Professor in the Department of English Language and Literatures at Brock University, Canada.

Birte Heidemann is Assistant Professor of English Literature at Dresden University of Technology, Germany.

Caroline Koegler is Assistant Professor of British Literary and Cultural Studies at the University of Münster, Germany.

Pavan Kumar Malreddy teaches English Literature at Goethe University Frankfurt, Germany.

John McLeod is Professor of Postcolonial and Diaspora Literatures at the University of Leeds, UK.

Lindsey Moore is Reader in Postcolonial Literature at Lancaster University, UK.

Jan Rupp is an adjunct professor at Heidelberg University and has served as visiting professor at Goethe University Frankfurt, the University of Giessen, and Heidelberg University, Germany.

Shazia Sadaf teaches human rights and social justice at the Institute of Interdisciplinary Studies at Carleton University, Ottawa, Canada.

Marlena Tronicke is Assistant Professor of British Literary and Cultural Studies at the University of Münster, Germany.

Vedrana Veličković is Principal Lecturer in English Literature at the University of Brighton, UK.

Introduction

The colonial remains of Brexit: Empire nostalgia and narcissistic nationalism

Caroline Koegler, Pavan Kumar Malreddy and Marlena Tronicke

Since the formal end of colonialism, perhaps no single political event has been as influential in shaping British narratives of national and transnational identity as the United Kingdom's (UK) departure from the European Union (EU). The elusive, protracted, and unceremonious slew of events – with their vague beginnings in the Treaty of Lisbon and an equally indeterminate ending wagering on the empire's vestigial hold in the Commonwealth – that came to be known as "Brexit" in popular parlance, continues to frame assessments of difference and sameness, freedom and dependence, regional alliances and cultural entitlements, and discourses of national health and viral threat. Brexit has triggered large-scale speculations about social insecurities and national trauma. It has given racism a free pass, and hate speech a broader acceptance in society. It has bolstered populism, prejudice, and homophobia – and yet also instilled a sense of hope and renewal, not least among its apologists, lobbyists, and also sizeable sections of the British population. The convergence of these mutually reinforcing discourses has often been attributed to the turmoil of the British Referendum on EU membership on June 23, 2016 which, for many, was a moment of reckoning – the day when Britain's deep social divisions became visibly manifest. In literary criticism, the ensuing coinage of "BrexLit" (Day 2017; Shaw 2018; Ferguson 2019) as a catch-all phrase to describe what appeared to be a novel body of texts, even a "new landscape of British fiction" (Day 2017, n.p.), similarly implied that the result of the Referendum was entirely unanticipated, triggering a sustained sense of cataclysmic change and sociopolitical emergency. This special "Brexit" issue of the *Journal of Postcolonial Writing* moves away from any such temporal or generic framing of Brexit as a novel, even unforeseeable "event". Instead, it identifies and historicizes Britain's departure from the EU as the result of a long-standing process, rooted in persisting imperial attitudes and, arguably, narcissistic yearnings.

To be sure, Brexit is not a bona fide postcolonial event. But, as the articles in this special issue demonstrate, it represents a moment when anxieties about harnessing and unleashing colonially engineered power structures and cultural hierarchies crystallized. If Britain's departure from its colonies marked the end of colonialism as we knew it, then, for some, Britain's departure from the EU marked the end of yet another kind of colonialism. In his resignation letter as Foreign Secretary on July 9, 2018, Boris Johnson warned that Theresa May's Brexit plan would reduce Britain to "the status of a colony" (Buchan 2018, n.p.). Johnson was not alone in ruminating on the perks of *being* or holding a "colony" – Tory backbenchers, United Kingdom Independence Party (UKIP), and the Leave campaigners repeatedly, at times habitually, tapped into colonial nostalgia, conjuring images of a glorious imperial past of global dimensions. What was formulaic about Johnson's projection was the sheer imaginary bankruptcy: a colonizer assuming the role of the colonized. This is by no means unique to Johnson or the Leave campaign; other populist leaders across Europe – Marine Le Pen of France, Giuseppe Conte of Italy, Geert Wilders of the Netherlands, Björn Höcke and Alice Weidel of Germany – have enjoyed a moderate success in appropriating the language of oppression and victimhood, repeatedly wielding it against EU membership, to advance their own populist agenda. In *Heroic Failure: Brexit and The Politics of Pain*, the Irish critic Fintan O'Toole (2018) reads this doubling act of the Leave campaign as both the victim and beneficiary of a supposed Brussels dictatorship as a play of "the political erotics of imaginary domination and imaginary submission [which] are the deep pulse of the Brexit drama" (25). Sure enough, the *doxa* of Britain-becoming-a-colony was further exacerbated during the interregnum of Brexit, flanked by familiar references to World War II.[1] In their commentary on Brexit and nostalgia, Campanella and Dassù (2019) quip: "having defeated the French and the Spaniards throughout the centuries, having stopped Wilhelm II, Adolf Hitler, Joseph Stalin and Leonid Brezhnev from permanently disrupting global order, London was now primed to roll back Brussels' technocrats" (107). Populist appropriations of the COVID-19 pandemic, too, are rolled into this logic, as in public appeals that Britain should muster warlike endurance to extricate itself from both the clutches of the coronavirus and the grip of the EU. As this confluence of empire imaginary, anti-EU sentiments, and paradoxically deep identitarian investment in European history already indicates, Theresa May's "truly global Britain" may not be all that global in outlook but poised on a selective, if not a skewed, representation of Britain's role in colonial history that postcolonial studies is best equipped to articulate.

Populist campaigns built around the commingled tropes of Brexit, empire, and World War II have proven highly effective across various sections of British society, and have exerted a particular force amongst those who witnessed the gradual crumbling of empire after the war. As John McLeod notes in his contribution to this special issue – "Warning Signs: Postcolonial Writing and the Apprehension of Brexit" – World War II was the last large-scale political and military event affording untainted heroism before the empire collapsed entirely – and with it, if more gradually and more uncertainly, its moral legitimacy. As such, World War II was the last incarnation of a kind of British imperial fortitude that continues to facilitate a safe and legitimate sense of national attachment, particularly in times of upheaval. Given the affective investment in Britain's victory (one that bars critical examination of colonialism up until this day), "devolving power to the EU [has been] experienced as especially destabilizing to nationalists' sense of self-esteem and progression" (Beaumont 2018, 380). In a twist or two, resistance to EU policies has become a way of preserving British exceptionalism, carried over from empire's "last days of innocence". For the populist camps, Britain's EU membership has helped to sustain a victim-like, sacrificial, and defensive position, giving ample opportunity for constructing the country as having to fend off unjust, inferiorizing "onslaughts" of EU bureaucrats, and abject invasions of European immigrants. In the process, as Sarah Franklin (2019) observes, the "recommemoration of lost British soldiers [has been brought] to a reforgetting of how British imperialism, Orientalism, and racism set the stage for the globally catastrophic losses of the two world wars", thereby "displac[ing] the violent legacies of enforced racial hierarchy, military subjugation, and theft of resources from colonized peoples around the globe" (51–52). In its continuing predilection for self-aggrandizing visions of empire, as well as a lack of critical self-positioning in relation to its imperial history, Britain remains vulnerable to "the threat posed by injured white nationalism" (52). Eurosceptic manoeuvring of the EU into the phantasmatic position of the colonizer, and of Britain itself into the position of the resisting and retaliating colonized, is symptomatic of such predilection and lack. It reveals not only the perverse flexibility of populist discourses – to arrogate, appropriate, and even claim the discursive position of the colonized – but also a continuing inability to conceive of transnational cooperation outside the framework of domination and victimhood. Therefore, in more than one sense, and for more than one reason, as John McLeod remarks in his article in this issue, such positionings reflect a "failure of the imagination".

Likening Britain's current, post-Referendum position to the varied and often violent resistance movements in former colonial territories not only makes a compelling case for populist myth-making, but also bespeaks a potent blend of imperialism, narcissism, and exceptionalism. Given its grievances over the perils of domination and perceived victimhood, parts of the Brexit debate are narcissistically invested in hierarchical, controlling relationships ("take back control"), rather than more balanced, inclusive, and socially just models of cooperation. In her essay "The Disaster of Colonial Narcissism", Simone Drichel (2018) fruitfully conjoins clinical thought on narcissism and postcolonial theory, in particular Leela Gandhi's (2006) research on "affective communities". Drichel flags what Gandhi names colonialism's "crisis of nonrelation" (184) and the "antirelational basis of imperialism" (185) which stand in the way of more meaningful (affective) politics based on relationality. Drichel also accentuates Diane Simmons's (2007) study, *The Narcissism of Empire*, which paints a pathological "portrait of narcissism [as] a grandiose sense of superiority alternating with feelings of loss, rage and revenge" (1). According to Simmons, as an antidote to these infirmities of negation, "subject peoples" serve as a psychic mirror to "their conquerors, as they could be compelled in a variety of ways to reflect back to the imperialist a grandiose self-image" (1).

With the loss of its colonies that in many ways shaped Britishness and its cultural boundaries through annexation and exclusion, it seems that empire's narcissistic disposition, as defined by Simmons, has been preserved. In an age of public apologies, colonial reparations, restorative justice, and truth and reconciliation, it may serve us well to read shame and guilt as potentially enabling affects, as opposed to their presumed complicity with passivity, docility, or the politics of victimhood (Malreddy 2019, 311). If shame can be defined as "one's shortcomings" in relation to the social standards a person "identifies" with (Striblen 2007, 478), and guilt as a recognition of one's wrongdoings to others, then, as Wüschner (2017) posits, a shame that does not transform into guilt can effectively lead to a "narcissistic rage that does not really care for the ones who have been wronged but only grieves the loss of social recognition" (99). Applied to the context of imperial demise, Wüschner's reasoning suggests that, for Britain, this rupture in the affective pact between shame and guilt represented an abject loss of its recognition worldwide. Furthermore, resistance movements, equally worldwide, waged an unrelenting campaign against colonial rule to expose its wrongful injuries, wrought in the name of a "civilizing mission". In short, accepting empire's modus operandi as the cause of a "*wrongful injury to others*" (Murphy 1999, 235; emphasis in original) would prove damaging to the narcissistic self. Hence, it comes as no surprise that the appropriation of the colonized position by none other than Britain's current Prime Minister, Boris Johnson, is neither innocent nor premediated, but an unfortunate consequence of his inability to come to terms with empire's injurious past that ultimately shaped the Leave campaign's exceptionalist logic.

In this introduction, then, we wish to frame Johnson's dramatic usurpation of a scenario of "reverse-colonization" as symptomatic of repressed anxieties surrounding empire nostalgia and narcissistic shame. Whilst the narcissistic forces of empire hang in the balance and, eventually, might have been more constructively resolved while Britain was still an EU member, Brexit has for now forestalled any such possibility. Indeed, it has revived those remains of empire's narcissistic nationalism that now militate against the very idea of Europe. Cultural productions concerning Brexit in many ways register the affective upheavals – a sense of doom and relief about the nation's much-anticipated "independence" – that the decision to quit the EU has produced throughout British society. In one peculiar instance, the "Irish Border" (2019) itself has joined forces with literary and cultural productions on Brexit, authoring an autobiography under the rubric of "I am the Border, so I am", as if reaffirming its corporeal presence, territorial absence, and existential erasure – all at once.[2] Other striking examples, some of which are discussed in greater detail by individual contributors, include neo-historical films about particularly "heroic" chapters of British national history such as Christopher Nolan's (2017) *Dunkirk* and Joe Wright's (2017) *Darkest Hour*. Both these films rehearse the empire nostalgia and narcissistic nationalism we have outlined above – or, as Robert Eaglestone (2018) puts it, the "cruel nostalgia" with which World War II as a subchapter of Britain's imperial history is remembered. Sam Mendes's (2019) much-lauded *1917*, though marketed as an anti-war movie, similarly positions Britain in the role of the heroic underdog that emerges victorious over an all too powerful, external (German) aggressor. All these cultural productions feed on both empire nostalgia and apocalyptical scenarios of World War II-type post-war austerity.

In turn, the rich body of novels that either explicitly interrogate Brexit's colonial entanglements, or else are discussed in this context, consist of such wide-ranging texts as Ali Smith's Seasonal Quartet (2016–20), Mohsin Hamid's (2017) *Exit West*, Anna Burns's (2018) *Milkman*, Sam Byers's (2018) *Perfidious Albion*, or Bernardine Evaristo's (2019) *Girl, Woman, Other*. Theatrical works that negotiate the nostalgic notions of long-lost colonial influence as well as the anxieties surrounding migration that have fuelled anti-EU sentiments include Zinnie Harris's (2015) *How to Hold Your Breath* (Royal Court Theatre), Mike Bartlett's (2017) *Albion* (Almeida Theatre), and Sharon Watson's (2018) dance work *Windrush: Movement of the People* (Phoenix Dance Theatre) – as does Billy Bragg (2017) with his album *Bridges, Not Walls* (see Reinfandt 2019). From the field of art and photography, Martin Parr's (2019) exhibition *Only Human* at the National Portrait Gallery and Anish Kapoor's (2019) artwork *A Brexit, A Broxit, We All Fall Down* exhibited at Pitzhanger Manor & Gallery bear testimony to "a garish scar [which] opens as Britain's inner geography is mutilated by violently redrawn borders" (Ghoshal 2020, 3).

The contributions to this special issue do not "write back to the empire", so to speak, but write into, away from, and against the colonial underpinnings of the Brexit discourse. They trace and critique the present day's empire nostalgia and populist myth-making in the UK through a wide range of literary and cultural productions, and remind readers of the proleptic potential of postcolonial writers in identifying the residual ideologies of imperialism in the lead up to and after the Brexit campaign. With their vast geographical as well as diverse linguistic reach – India, Britain, Pakistan, Northern Ireland, Palestine, Barbados, Eastern Europe, and Greece, among others – the articles featured here make a productive contribution to postcolonial literary discourse. A number of contributors employ Paul Gilroy's (2004a) concept of "postcolonial melancholia" as Britain's lingering grief over a lost empire and the "heroic" chapters in British history. If melancholia is a product of the loss of the object of national desire or the erasure of "whole segments of national past […] leaving destructive blank spaces in individual autobiographies" (Gilroy 2004b, 107–108), then nostalgia is best understood as an attempt to retrieve, recreate, and, where needed, reinvent such lost objects through populist myth-making, as evinced in the Leave campaign's promise of a return to past imperial glory in the guise of a "truly global Britain".

Ronald Cummings's article "Ain't No Black in the (Brexit) Union Jack" complicates the question of borders upon which the entire Brexit discourse rests. Through an original reading of Paul Gilroy's *There Ain't No Black in the Union Jack* (1987) and Austin Clarke's *Growing Up Stupid Under the Union Jack* (2005), Cummings offers a critique of the narrow formulations of British national identity in Brexit discourse by delineating the exclusion of black subjects from the Union Jack since the time of HMT *Empire Windrush* and the annexation of colonies as part of empire's cultural heritage. John McLeod's article offers an equally refreshing historical perspective on Brexit literature, arguing that postcolonial literatures have long anticipated the advent of an event such as Brexit. McLeod reads Caryl Phillips's *A Distant Shore* (2003), Zadie Smith's *NW* (2012), and John Lanchester's *Capital* (2012) as prime examples of anticipatory texts that unveil the historical, racial, and socio-economic "origins and depth of a crisis brought by the long formation of Brexit's post-imperium". Within this historicist frame of Brexit, Lindsay Moore's "Brexit Literature's Present Absentees: Triangulating Brexit, Antisemitism, and the Palestinian Crisis" reads two texts – British Jewish author Linda Grant's *A Stranger City* (2019) and British Palestinian author Raba'i al-Madhoun's *Fractured Destinies: A Novel* (2018) – that shed light on Britain's colonial interventions in the Middle East from the 1917 Balfour Agreement to present-day discourses of Zionism and anti-Semitism. Moore contends that the empire's fork-tongued policy "accrues [new] meaning when read in awareness of British colonial intervention in the Middle East and in the context of its divisive departure from Europe".

Shazia Sadaf's "'We Are All Migrants Through Time': History and Geography in Mohsin Hamid's *Exit West*" leaps from historical contingencies to speculative post-colonial futures shaped by Brexit. Sadaf argues that, despite its dystopian setting and the trials and tribulations of its characters through disjointed times and spaces, *Exit West* ends on a hopeful note and gestures towards a seamless assemblage of races, geographies, and technologies that must learn to live together. Vedrana Velickovic's "'Eastern Europeans' and BrexLit" examines the postcolonial vacuum occupied by the Eastern European migrants in Britain. Velickovic's broad corpus – Adam Thorpe's *Missing Fay* (2017), Amanda Craig's *The Lie of the Land* (2017), Carla Grauls' *Occupied* (2012), Andrew Muir's *The Session* (2015) and Agnieszka Dale's short stories – reveals the sites and sources of postcolonial paranoia and the subsumption of Eastern

European migrants to an imperial logic, even if they do not find a place within the history of British colonialism.

Marlena Tronicke's "Imperial Pasts, Dystopian Futures, and the Theatre of Brexit" returns to the contested turf of the British Isles, albeit with a focus on drama. She mediates Mike Bartlett's (2017) country house drama *Albion* and Jez Butterworth's *The Ferryman* (2017), set during the "Troubles" in Northern Ireland, through Gilroy's notion of post-colonial melancholia, suggesting that only through a constructive engagement with the colonial past can a post-Brexit Britain be envisaged. Birte Heidemann's "The Brexit Within: Mapping the Rural and the Urban in Contemporary British Literature" draws on Amanda Craig's *The Lie of the Land* (2017) and Ali Smith's *Autumn* (2016), while reversing the gaze on the inequalities within British society. By linking Raymond Williams's thesis on the discrepancies between "city and the country" to the structural divide between metropolis and the colony, Heidemann reads the two novels as postcolonial commentaries on the multiple entries and exits – across class, culture, and race – within and among British society. Jan Rupp's "Writing Back to Brexit: Transcultural Intertextuality, Refugees, and the Colonial Archive from Chaucer to Kipling" holds that a refraction of the colonial archive helps understand how the refugee figures are both written in and written out of the colonial narratives. Against this, Rupp argues that contemporary accounts of refugee literature, largely occasioned by the Leave campaign's xenophobia and ethnic exclusionism, write back the wandering and vagrant migrant figures into the colonial canon. Clelia Clini's "'We Are Here For a Greater Purpose': Brexit, Britishness and the Re-production of Imperial Fantasies on Screen" turns to the cinematic representations of imperial desires through a close reading of the 2017 historical film *Victoria & Abdul*. The film, drowned in the nostalgic effluvia of Victorian glory, turns a blind eye to the jarring inequalities between its Indian character and Queen Victoria, thereby reaffirming the dated view that colonialism is, at its best, a benign enterprise.

Although the articles featured in this special issue make a strong case for reading Brexit through the lens of colonialism and postcolonial discourse, they do not necessarily exhaust other ways of readings the events leadings up to UK's departure from Europe: the rise of right-wing populism on both sides of the Atlantic; the use of social media technologies in swaying public opinion; the internal inequalities and divisions within the EU; the dwindling fate of regionalisms and local governance structures in the face of global capitalism; and, last but not least, the proliferation of fake news, "alternative facts" and "post-truth" discourses.

Notes

1. A case in point: on the campaign trail for Brexit, Nigel Farage "would ride into town in a purple campaign bus playing the soundtrack from classic Second World War film *The Great Escape*" (Beaumont 2018, 385–386), so as to warm up his audience.
2. The author of this avant-garde enterprise is the same person who founded the Twitter account @BorderIrish, and chooses to remain anonymous.

Disclosure statement

No potential conflict of interest was reported by the authors.

Funding

This work was supported by the Deutsche Forschungsgemeinschaft for Pavan Malreddy [grant number MA 711911-1].

ORCID

Pavan Kumar Malreddy http://orcid.org/0000-0002-4214-1464

References

Bartlett, Mike. 2017. *Albion.* London: Almeida Theatre. dir. Rupert Goold.

Beaumont, Paul. 2018. "Brexit, Retrotopia and the Perils of Post-colonial Delusions." *Global Affairs* 3 (4–5): 379. doi:10.1080/23340460.2018.1478674.

Bragg, Billy. 2017. *Bridges, Not Walls.* London: Cooking Vinyl.

Buchan, Lizzy. 2018. "Boris Johnson warns 'Brexit dream is dying' in scathing resignation letter". *The Independent*, July 09. https://www.independent.co.uk/news/uk/politics/boris-johnson-letter-resignation-latest-theresa-may-brexit-statement-a8439346.html

Burns, Anna. 2018. *Milkman.* London: Faber.

Byers, Sam. 2018. *Perfidious Albion.* London: Faber.

Campanella, Edoardo, and Marta Dassù. 2019. "Brexit and Nostalgia." *Survival* 61 (3): 103–111. doi:10.1080/00396338.2019.1614781.

Day, John. 2017. "Brexlit: The New Landscape of British Fiction." *Financial Times*, July 28. https://www.ft.com/content/30ec47b4-7204-11e7-93ff-99f383b09ff9

Drichel, Simone. 2018. "The Disaster of Colonial Narcissism." *American Imago* 75 (3): 329–364. doi:10.1353/aim.2018.0020.

Eaglestone, Robert. 2018. "Cruel Nostalgia and the Memory of the Second World War." In *Brexit and Literature*, edited by Robert Eaglestone, 92–104. Abingdon: Routledge.

Evaristo, Bernardine. 2019. *Girl, Woman, Other*. London: Hamish Hamilton.

Ferguson, Donna. 2019. "From Epic Myths to Rural Fables, How Our National Turmoil Created 'Brexlit'." *The Guardian*, October 27. https://www.theguardian.com/books/2019/oct/27/brexlit-new-literary-genre-political-turmoil-myths-fables

Franklin, Sarah. 2019. "Nostalgic Nationalism: How a Discourse of Sacrificial Reproduction Helped Fuel Brexit Britain." *Cultural Anthropology* 34 (1): 41–52. doi:10.14506/ca34.1.07.

Gandhi, Leelia. 2006. *Affective Communities*. Durham, NC: Duke University Press.

Ghoshal, Somak. 2020. "Thresholds and Borders: Reflections on the Art of Brexit." *Wasafiri* 35 (1): 3–10. doi:10.1080/02690055.2020.1683284.

Gilroy, Paul. 2004a. *Postcolonial Melancholia*. New York: Columbia University Press.

Gilroy, Paul. 2004b. *After Empire: Melancholia or Convivial Culture?* London: Routledge.

Hamid, Mohsin. 2017. *Exit West*. London: Penguin.

Harris, Zinnie. 2015. *How to Hold Your Breath*. London: Royal Court Theatre. dir. Vicky Featherstone.

Irish Border. 2019. *I Am the Border, so I Am from the Twitter Hit @ BorderIrish*. London: HarperCollins.

Kapoor, Anish. 2019. *A Brexit, A Broxit, We All Fall Down*. London: Pitzhanger Manor & Gallery. Exhibition, April 3–August 18.

Malreddy, Pavan Kumar. 2019. "Imperialist Shame and Indigenous Guilt: George Orwell's Writings on Burma." *European Journal of English Studies* 23 (3): 311–325. doi:10.1080/13825577.2019.1655249.

Mendes, Sam, dir. 2019. *1917*. Los Angeles, CA: Dreamworks Pictures.

Murphy, Jeffrie G. 1999. "Shame Creeps through Guilt and Feels like Retribution." *Law and Philosophy* 18 (4): 327–344.

Nolan, Christopher, dir. 2017. *Dunkirk*. Burbank, CA: Warner Bros Pictures.

O'Toole, Fintan. 2018. *Heroic Failure: Brexit and the Politics of Pain*. London: Head Zeus.

Parr, Martin. 2019. *Only Human*. London: National Portrait Gallery. Exhibition, 7 March 7–May 27.

Reinfandt, Christoph. 2019. "Brexit and the Lost Cause of Progressive Patriotism: Some Thoughts on Billy Bragg." *Journal of the Study of the British Cultures* 26 (2/19): 207–220.

Shaw, Kristian. 2018. "Brexlit." In *Brexit and Literature*, edited by Robert Eaglestone, 15–30. Abingdon: Routledge.

Simmons, Diane. 2007. *The Narcissism of Empire: Loss, Rage, and Revenge in Thomas De Quincey, Robert Louis Stevenson, Arthur Conan Doyle, Rudyard Kipling and Isak Dinesen*. Eastbourne: Sussex Academic Press.

Smith, Ali. 2016-20. *Seasonal Quartet (Autumn, Winter, Spring, Summer)*. London: Hamish Hamilton.

Smith, Zadie. 2012. *NW*. London: Hamish Hamilton.

Striblen, Cassie. 2007. "Guilt, Shame and Shared Responsibility." *Journal of Social Philosophy* 38 (3): 469–485.

Watson, Sharon. 2018. *Windrush: Movement of the People*. Leeds: Phoenix Dance Theatre.

Wright, Joe, dir. 2017. *Darkest Hour*. London: Working Title Films.

Wüschner, Philipp. 2017. "Shame, Guilt, and Punishment." *Foucault Studies* 23: 86–107. doi:10.22439/fs.v0i0.5343.

Ain't no black in the (Brexit) Union Jack? Race and empire in the era of Brexit and the *Windrush* scandal

Ronald Cummings

ABSTRACT

This article examines Brexit and the *Windrush* scandal as twin manifestations of the border anxieties that have structured questions of belonging in contemporary Britain. It discusses Paul Gilroy's *There Ain't No Black in the Union Jack* and Austin Clarke's *Growing Up Stupid Under the Union Jack* as two texts which attend to questions of race and empire in the mid-20th century in relation to British national identity. Both Clarke and Gilroy situate the reterritorialization of Britain in the wake of the globalizing history of British Empire which made possible, for instance, the widescale solidarities and conscriptions of World War II. In their attention to the role of empire in the making of Britain, these texts effectively complicate easy demarcations of Britishness and borders and allow us to historicize the conditions under which national boundaries have come to be so central to narratives of British identity.

Race and British border politics: Notes towards a (pre)history of the present

In an interview published in the *Tribune* in January 2019 titled "Still No Black in the Union Jack", the cultural critic Paul Gilroy, in reflecting on the contemporary moment and its cultural-political manifestations of Brexit and the *Windrush* scandal, argued that the "story has been frozen in the mediascape. It needs to be given a history and the continuing problems of the 'hostile environment' held up to proper scrutiny" (Gilroy 2019, n.p.). If media debates, as Gilroy notes, have foregrounded the anxieties of the present, in this article I seek to extend the cultural history of this moment and to examine the long unsettled interrelations between race, nation, and empire in Britain and how these reveal a history of border anxieties and complexities. I examine Brexit and the *Windrush* scandal as twin manifestations of border anxieties that structure debates about citizenship and belonging in contemporary Britain. In locating the *Windrush* scandal and Brexit alongside each other and within this longer historical framework, this discussion not only positions race as central to each of these current cultural and political instances of British reterritorialization, but also unsettles the ground of the present as the singular space from which to understand these events. This critical move subverts a straightforward teleological rendering of history by attending to connections and resonances across time, as well as co-occurrences as a way of thinking about the unfolding present.

In 2018, two years following the June 2016 Brexit referendum, the *Windrush* scandal came to public attention through a series of investigative newspaper reports. These news stories documented in stark detail how changes and restrictions in immigration laws (set in motion over previous decades) and an unfair culture of punitive enforcement of immigration legislation and procedure, had resulted in migrants of the *Windrush* generation and their children being detained, refused access to social benefits, and in many cases forcibly expelled from the UK to countries where they had never lived or where they had few or no sustained ties. The scandal resulted in an immediate public outcry and the resignation of the then Home Secretary, Amber Rudd, in April 2018. Yet while the public narrative record of these events structure a particular temporal chronology, as Amelia Gentleman (2019) has shown, the timelines are not straightforward but also have deep connections to the past. Gentleman's work, for instance, attends both to a larger historical context by returning to relevant colonial laws and to histories which are implicated in the present crisis, and also traces personal narratives such as that of the late activist Paulette Wilson, whose personal accounts of being detained in 2015 and marked for deportation refuse and reorient the temporal specificity of 2018 as the moment for recounting the scandal of British immigration exclusions. Examining Brexit and the *Windrush* scandal together also has key implications for how we might understand Brexit and its unfolding as part of a longer state doctrine and practice of border control. In placing these events together, we might come to understand Brexit, and its border foreclosures not as exceptional, but rather as part of a longer process of border policing. Brexit might then be understood only as an exception in so far as Europe, in this instance, becomes visibly framed as the object of immigration anxieties.

This article turns to two texts which explore the unsettled histories of border, race, and empire in the mid-20th century in relation to British national identity. I examine Paul Gilroy's (1987) *There Ain't No Black in the Union Jack* and Austin Clarke ([1980] 2005) *Growing Up Stupid Under the Union Jack* as two books that effectively complicate the easy demarcations of Britishness and borders that have become so central to debates about Brexit. They also, at the same time, allow us to historicize the conditions under which national boundaries have come to be so central to narratives of British identity.

Both Clarke and Gilroy situate the reterritorialization of Britain in the wake of the globalizing history of the British Empire that made possible, for instance, the widescale solidarities and conscriptions of World War II in the mid-20th century. Clarke's text offers one account of World War II, tracing an understanding that what happened in Britain was not separate from what was taking place in colonial Barbados and indeed other locations in the British Empire. This understanding is articulated in Clarke's description of his childhood and his experience in Barbados in *Growing up Stupid Under the Union Jack*. His work then, I would argue, pushes against narrow mappings and understandings of British borders and territoriality to recall a necessary context of empire.

Alongside the discussion of Clarke's work, I also examine Paul Gilroy's *There Ain't No Black in the Union Jack* as part of an important political and theoretical critique of the ways in which race and borders have become so entrenched in contemporary understandings of Britishness and in the political rhetoric of Brexit Britain. Gilroy not only articulates what he terms a "profound antipathy towards nationalism in all its unwholesome varieties" (Gilroy 2019, n.p.), but he also situates its current manifestations within an important historical context of post-World War II nationalist rhetoric; this is most spectacularly archived in Enoch Powell's speeches, including but also beyond his infamous 1968 "Rivers of Blood" speech in which he warned of the prospect of racialized civil war due to increasing numbers of migrants in Britain. Powell's speeches reflect the view that the rise of multicultural Britain was instead a "process of national decline […] coinciding with the dilution of once homogenous and continuous national stock by alien strains" (Gilroy 1987, 46). The trenchant racism resulting from this "racist logic" (46) has been amply documented in a range of historical and literary narratives including the writings of E.R. Brathwaite (1959), Andrew Salkey ([1960] 2009), Samuel Selvon ([1965] 2020, [1975] 1991), and Andrea Levy (2004) among others. Four years after his "Rivers of Blood" speech, Powell would notably leave the Edward Heath-led Conservative Party in protest at its support of Britain joining the European Economic Community (EEC). These punctuations in time, which continue to reverberate in the present, reveal the ways in which Black Atlantic diasporic histories and British–European border politics have long been interlinked in the popular and political sphere and in the making and remaking of British border politics.

Building on Gilroy's work, I argue that some attention to this longer history meaningfully extends and complicates our understandings of contemporary Brexit Britain beyond our current political scene of encampment. As Gilroy importantly notes in his 2019 interview, which draws a line of connection between the current moment and Britain's notorious Powellian past:

> Let's not forget that New Labour did their best to ape the populist postures of the Tory right and sprinkle some Powellite pixie dust on the uncertain edges of their electoral bloc. Blunkett's bluff Yorkshireman bluster and Gordon Brown parroting the BNP line on "British jobs for British workers" are also implicated in bringing about the bleak predicament we're in. (Gilroy 2019, n.p.)

Here Gilroy traces the echoes of one recurring phrase in his mapping of the calls from various political corners for fortifying border Britain. Gilroy implicates both Tory *and* Labour politicians as participating in what he terms the "the populist postures" that have incited the contemporary political climate. He notes how the phrase "British jobs for British workers", which has been part of the logic of Brexit discourse, re-emerged for forceful public discussion in the 21st century in the context of Gordon Brown's first speech as Labour leader at the party's conference in 2007 in which he invoked that phrase to much criticism at the time. Gilroy is keen to remind us that that slogan was also touted by extreme nationalist quarters such as the British National Party (BNP). We might also attend to its longer history and echoes across time. This rhetoric was also mobilized in previous generations as part of the popular and political opposition to *Windrush* migration and settlement and, as Rachel Shabi (2019) recalls, this has an even longer but no less troubling history: "Go back to the 1930s and you find Oswald Mosley, leader of the British Union of Fascists, declaring: 'No more admitting of foreigners into this country to take British jobs.' At that time, the foreigners he meant were Jews" (n.p.). In turning to this longer history, I draw attention to how British anxieties about borders in the present connect to a history of British racial discourse set against the backdrop and context of empire. In making this link, I conclude by briefly turning to Gilroy's (2004) work in *After Empire* in order to raise further questions about what postcolonial studies and a view towards the long operations of empire might offer to an analysis and critique of the contemporary crisis of identity and relations at the heart of British cultural life and nationalist politics today.

Narratives of arrivals and borders: The world the British Empire made

In 1939, George Orwell remarked that "the overwhelming bulk of the British proletariat does not live in Britain" (Orwell 2000, 397. Recalling Orwell's observation, Gilroy has poignantly noted that "empire itself [has] remained unrepresentable" in the Brexit debates (Gilroy 2019, n.p.). Britain's nationalizing narratives, we might then argue, have produced denials and active forgetting. The very immediate concern with borders that structures visions of Brexit, in effect, cuts off at the border not just political and economic ties with Europe, but also a longer history of entanglements (the story of Britain from the story of empire). Hazel Carby (2019) describes these entanglements as imperial intimacies – "the everyday ties, relations and intricate interdependencies of empire and colonialism" (17). Turning outwards to the geography of the sea beyond the terrain of land and in terms that recall Paul Gilroy's (1993) well-known book *The Black Atlantic*, Carby notes, "The story of imperial relations is as restless as the Atlantic surging between the islands" (2019, 18).

For Gilroy, the foreclosed mapping of British territoriality belies the presence of empire as a condition of the history of modern Britain (Gilroy 1993). While a particular romance of British colonial greatness, or what Gilroy (2005, 52) theorizes as "postcolonial melancholia" makes space for the acknowledgements of Britain's "contributions" to the modern world, empire's contributions to Britain are often displaced within and by this nationalist narrative. Taking Danny Boyle's 2012 Olympic pageant celebration of British cultural history, with its narrative of belated Black British arrival, as one key example for discussion, Gilroy critiques persistent demarcations of Britishness that rely on a strictly bordered understanding of the relationships between nation and empire. In Boyle's territorialized vision of Britain, Gilroy observes,

> [t]he energetic, tropical immigrants with battered suitcases were effectively being visited on the green nation from the outside. Of course their carnivalesque appearance could be spun positively. They were exotic, exciting and in some ways attractive. But they were conceived essentially as an addition, an extra rather than a basic condition of the country's modern phase. (Gilroy 2019, n.p.)

This foregrounding of the *Windrush* arrival story as part of the British performance of national history and as a starting point for emplotting the complex interrelations between blackness and Britain obscures a long history of "imperial intimacies" (Carby 2019). As Gilroy further notes, this vision of a putative arrival from beyond the nation's borders structures an understanding of Black labour, resources, and presence as "an extra rather than a basic condition" for the making of modern Britain (Gilroy 2019, n.p.). The profound effects of this narrative and conceptual positioning can be marked in the tangible ways in which the foreclosing of British border politics in the context of Brexit has so neatly coincided with the exclusions and deportations of people of the *Windrush* generation and their descendants as seen in the ongoing *Windrush* scandal.

In contrast to this vision of nation, the opening of Austin Clarke's *Growing Up Stupid Under the Union Jack* reminds us how Britain was in the habit of routinely dispatching a steady line of colonial administrators to distant regions of the empire. Clarke's opening chapter sets the scene of colonial governance in Barbados with his descriptions of Black civil servants "walking up and down the corridor of the Old Public Buildings on the second and third floors, with huge important files of all colours – blue, red, white", but also he refers to "the white Colonial officers who ruled and ran the country and who had the knack of looking important" (Clarke [1980] 2005, 3). Clarke's work additionally recounts the arrival of a line of school headmasters and other administrators to Barbados, all as part of the colonial "civilizing mission" and as part of the mobilities of empire. He offers one important supplement to the writing of Black Britain which emphasizes the iconic story of the *Windrush* arrival dramatized in Boyle's Olympic opening ceremony pageant. His work reminds us of the fact that, as Joan Anim-Addo (2018) notes, "many of the new [*Windrush*] migrants replied when questioned on landing in Tilbury, or arriving later at Victoria Station, […] that they were, 'British subjects' " (n.p.). They were arriving from elsewhere in the British Empire.

Empire's mobilities and remains: In the wake of *Windrush*

World War II and its aftermath was characterized by migrations from different parts of the British Empire. British subjects were conscripted to aid the war effort and subsequent post-war recovery effort in Britain. There was no small irony to the reversal of the routes of mobility within the circuits of empire. The counter-directional mobilities of the post-war moment are highlighted by Joan Anim-Addo when she argues that

> [t]he irony of the *Empire Windrush*'s homecoming to the mother country is that World War II had forced Britain to break with its practice of keeping its colonised black people at a safe distance away – 'beyond the seas' – from the seat of Empire. (2018, n.p.)

Anim-Addo's description of a *Windrush* "homecoming" here is not accidental and represents one attempt to unsettle a bordered narrative of British national history. British subjects, she notes, arrived as members of empire, and with British passports in hand offering a promise of entry and settlement. As the journalist Gary Younge (2020) puts it, in describing the border politics of his mother's own migration from Barbados to Britain: "My mother didn't cross the border to come to Britain – the border crossed her" (n.p.).

In narrating her story, Younge unpacks the complexity of British immigration histories and border politics by turning to the archives of personal history that constitute empire's remains. He begins with a poignant, personal narrative of finding his mother's first passport which he describes in careful detail, attending to its materiality:

> It's blue and hardbacked, with a lion and a unicorn perched on Latin and embossed in gold […] above the crest it says British Passport and below, in the same gold lettering, it reads Barbados. It was issued by the governor of Barbados "in the name of Her Majesty", and cites her nationality as "British Subject: Citizen of the United Kingdom and Colonies". (Younge 2020, n.p.)

Younge's description of, and attention to, this document is significant in two key regards. Much like Austin Clarke's writing, discussed below, here he renders the wider geopolitics of empire in detailed, intimate, personal terms. Second, this document allows him to draw a connection between the materiality of the British passport as empire's remains (linked to a British imperial past) and the promise of the British passport (as opposed to the European Union [EU] passport) as a symbol of Brexit's future. Younge specifically describes his mother's passport as British: "The kind the Brexit types bang on about. The kind we will have when we get our country back." At the same time, he notes, with some degree of irony, that these are "[t]he ones that will be made in France", simultaneously locating globalization – an aftermath of 1492's colonial restructuring of relations – as an almost inescapable feature of contemporary global geopolitics (Younge 2020, n.p.).

Younge's specific detailing of his mother's passport as British is significant for revisiting post-war migration histories. In mapping the imperial cataloguing of belonging in this period, Robert Miles (1989) points out that: "the world [...] continued to be divided into British subjects and aliens, but the former category included those who were citizens of the United Kingdom and Colonies" (426). Yet, even in the context of these legal distinctions, Gilroy notes that "blacks [were] systematically excluded" (1987, 12). He both adds to, and complicates, a straightforward understanding of the legal instantiations of the categories of *alien* and *subject* when he argues that the Black subject in Britain has been consistently understood as an "alien presence visited on Britain from the outside" (11). For Gilroy, the British nation is consistently imagined and constructed in terms that are not simply geographical, but also "simultaneously biological and cultural" (45). He cuts to the heart of this question when he argues that "[w]hat must be explained then, is how the limits of 'race' have come to coincide so precisely with national frontiers. This is a central achievement of the new racism. 'Race' is bounded on all sides by the sea" (46).

In historicizing this question, Gilroy tracks articulations of British national anxieties about borders in the mid-20th century. Similar anxieties have arguably re-emerged constituted through "new forms and [...] new antagonisms in different situations" in the context of Brexit (Gilroy 1987, 11). Yet at the same time, these anxieties connect the current "hostile environment" of the *Windrush* scandal with the previous hostile scene of *Windrush* arrival. As David Olusoga (2018) notes:

> Even before the Windrush had left Jamaica, the prime minister, Clement Attlee, had examined the possibility of preventing its embarkation or diverting the ship and the migrants on board to East Africa. After the vessel had arrived at Tilbury, the colonial secretary, Arthur Creech Jones, is said to have reassured his cabinet colleagues that, although "these people have British passports and must be allowed to land there's nothing to worry about because they won't last one winter in England" (n.p.; see also Hansen 2000).

Recalling this history demonstrates ways in which Britain has long relied on the environment being a hostile one for racialized immigrants.[1] While the cultural memory of *Windrush* arrival, etched into the collective consciousness, has been of the Calypsonian Lord Kitchener singing "London Is the Place for Me" on the docks of Tilbury in that now-famous Pathé newsreel, H. Adlai Murdoch (2018) also reminds us that *Windrush* arrivants disembarked to a London in which "it was not uncommon to see signs in the windows of rooming houses that read, 'No blacks, no Irish, no dogs', and leaflets and wall slogans that urged, 'Keep Britain White' " (n.p.). In others words, the terms of articulating anti-immigration concerns and arguing for the policing of borders have long been aligned with the politics of race and with racism. Gilroy further recalls: "It has been revealed that, at the suggestion of Churchill, a Conservative cabinet discussed the possibility of using 'Keep Britain White' as an electoral slogan as early as 1955" (1987, 46). The recent political shoring-up of borders in many ways reflects what we might read as a resurgence of a similar kind of border logic, marked by what Sally Tomlinson (2018) calls "The doctrine of 'Powellism' – a combination of demand for national sovereignty and anti-immigration plus residual beliefs in an Empire" (5).

As Gilroy and others like Joan Anim-Addo (2018) have noted, while colonial subjects were taught to view themselves as part of the British Empire, Britain by contrast framed identity narratives and politics in more narrow terms through "conceptions of national belonging and homogeneity which not only blur the lines between 'race' and nation, but rely on that very ambiguity for their effect" (Gilroy 1987, 45). Matthew Mead (2009), for instance, notes how despite an understanding of the world of the British Empire as extending beyond the borders of Britain, in the period between the 1940s and 1960s, there was a notable

> disjunction between what were ostensibly open immigration laws for colonial and post-colonial migrants, on the one hand, and, on the other, unofficial governmental policy which acted to discourage immigration and encourage the swift departure of those who had already settled in the United Kingdom. (144)

Gilroy's work additionally shows how an attention to this period facilitates an examination of some of the mechanisms through which the terms of belonging were consistently and systematically revised in striking ways. He notes, for example, how the Immigration Act of 1968 "codified [the] cultural biology of "race" into statute law as part of a strategy for the exclusion of black settlers" (Gilroy 1987, 45). The revised Act "specified that immigration controls would not apply to any would-be settler [if ...] one of their grandparents had been born in the UK" (Gilroy 1987, 45).

codified [the] cultural biology of "race" into statute law as part of a strategy for the exclusion of black settlers. The revised Act "specified that immigration controls would not apply to any would-be settler [if] one of their grandparents had been born in the UK". (Gilroy 1987, 45)

The foreclosing of migration in these terms enacted a racializing control through what Gilroy calls the "legal concept of partiality" (45). Attention to this historical period demonstrates contrasting views of imperial relations that might best be summed up through referencing the titles of both Gilroy's and Clarke's respective texts. Indeed, while colonial subjects saw themselves as growing up under the Union Jack, for many Britons there was no black in the Union Jack.

Remember (Little) England was an island in the Caribbean

In calling for more attention to this longer history, it is also necessary to introduce a wider geographical framework in order to engage the history and complexity of British border politics. As Stuart Hall (1999) remarked, 50 years after the historic *Windrush* journey: "The fate of Caribbean people living in the UK, the US or Canada is no more 'external' to Caribbean history than the empire was 'external' to the so-called domestic history of Britain, though that is how contemporary historiography constructs them" (1). In turning to Austin Clarke's *Growing Up Stupid Under the Union Jack*, we might note the complex and even paradoxical ways in which both annexation and exclusion have simultaneously structured relations between Britain and its empire. Clarke's work, I argue, serves as one site at which we might reflect on the unsettled border histories of colonial Britain as well as note how some present anxieties are linked to the colonial past, the residues of which, as Gilroy also notes, persist in the present.

In demonstrating these intertwined histories of Britain and its empire we might note how stories of World War II, like Austin Clarke's *Growing Up Stupid Under the Union Jack*, signal the complex networks of solidarities and distance that were all part of British colonial relations. The historical period narrated in Clarke's work is contemporary with the period that Gilroy discusses when he remarks on Churchill's suggestion of a Conservative election slogan of "Keep Britain White" (Gilroy 1987, 46). Clarke's book opens in 1944, the year before the end of the war and closes in 1950, two years after the sailing of the HMS *Empire Windrush* to Britain. It narrates, among other things, events of World War II which helped cement Churchill's place as a central figure in the British consciousness. Clarke's narrative focuses primarily on his experiences as a colonial schoolboy in Barbados but situates these events within the wider context of the war.

Clarke's work contains several references to Churchill. For instance, he tells us that "(e)very night on the BBC World News we listened to the voice of Winston Churchill" (Clarke [1980] 2005, 42). Clarke notes how colonial institutions, including the BBC, functioned in the making of empire and fostering a sense of belonging to Britain for those beyond England's physical boundaries by spreading the sounds and narratives of events across the empire. In attending to these interconnections, Clarke's work, like that of Gilroy, maps historical and geographical disjunctures in British border discourses and narratives. Rather than beginning with a naturalized sense of rigid borders or a defined separation between here and there, Britain and colony, Clarke's work uses Barbados as a location on the margins of empire through which to contest and rethink the relationship between nation and empire.

In the first instance, Clarke unsettles the border logic of separation between Barbados and England by pointing to the increased in/security inside Barbados that structured the experience of the war years, just as it did in Britain. He also notes how the interrelations between these two places ultimately culminate in the declaration of Barbados as "Little England":

> All of a sudden we had an army. The police were put in alert. Sea scouts became important, as they were taken deeper out into the harbour and told a few things about spotting enemy ships by the harbour police. And we heard our leader Grantley Adams, sent a cable up to the King, His Britannical Majestical George the Sixth, King of England, Northern Ireland and British Possessions Beyond the Sea, and told the King, "Go on England, Little England is behind you." And from that day we were known with pride or embarrassment as "Little England". (Clarke [1980] 2005, 43)

In Clarke's account of this christening of Barbados as "Little England", he marks colonial loyalty not just as a form of relation, but instead as consolidation of Britishness. He also satirizes this through a hyperbolic linguistic performance of imperial deference, deploying humour in his reference to George VI. Yet, while this episode operates as humour, it also allows us to deconstruct and unsettle naturalized discourses and imaginings of nation and belonging. British borders are unsettled. In other words, the textual humour found in this moment relies on as well as interrogates a discontinuity in the articulation of race and nation (in the context of both Barbados and Britain). This functions to transform England into an island in the Caribbean sea in as much as this "renaming" rhetorically accomplishes what has been ongoing and operational – the British annexation and colonization of Barbados. The absurdities of colonial relations and the complexities of (non-)sovereignty are exploited by Clarke to raise serious questions about imperial relations.

Chapter 2 of Clarke's book also addresses questions of interconnectedness, distance, and disavowal across spaces of empire in the context of war. The chapter focuses on World War II and situates Barbados within the wider context of the British military campaign. It opens with these sentences:

> Beyond us, in the meantime the Second World war was raging on the high seas and on battlefields in strange countries. In the magazines which trickled through the blockades of ships and reached us, in the pages of *Life* and *English Country Life, Punch* and *Reader's Digest*, we would see the war in pictures. We would see American GI's, stronger than Charles Atlas, drinking cans of grapefruit fruit and overturning German tanks with their bronzed bare hands [...] we lived through the defeats and victories of the British Empire and her Allies. (Clarke [1980] 2005, 11)

This passage simultaneously maps a sense of being both distant and involved. The opening phrase "beyond us" captures this tension and signals a kind of cognitive ambivalence about whether the people in Barbados saw themselves as a central part of this narrative or not. The next sentence then performs a significant representational shift in which narrative accounts of the war become filtered through British publications (*Life*, *English Country Life*, *Punch*, and *Readers Digest*). But we might also read this passage as reflecting the politics of historical construction. Those who exist in the narrative locations that the writer Jamaica Kincaid (1988) has termed "a small place" seem doomed to be outside or on the margins, not constructed as active participants. History becomes understood as what happens in particular places, such as London. The politics of this also plays out along racialized lines through which Britain is able to construct Black subjects as outside its national history.

Clarke's representation significantly reorients our sense of centre and margin to show these men in Barbados as participating in British history. Even more so, the stories of their lives and deaths serve to upend the grand narratives of history and empire. Clarke calls attention to a variety of circumstances, not just patriotism or honour, that enlist and constrain their participation in the war. He at once invokes and undermines the appeal to patriotism as their defining motivation when he notes:

> (s)ome were men who had walked about our streets a few months before, unemployed and barefooted, whistling the last hit tunes; men whom we had remembered passing us along streets that had no paving, no macadam, streets which kicked up the dust of these men's former cocky independence. These men were now names on a folded newspaper page.
>
> Men from our village and from neighboring villages had gone to sea, not to fight the Germans whom they did not know, not to die for the Empire, as the headmaster told us [...] They left to make a living. Unemployment or "no work" as we called it in our village, was as prevalent as the dust in the public road. ([1980] 2005, 12)

In Clarke's account of their lives and deaths, he refuses a straightforward romance of war that valorizes a sacrificial or noble death. Rather, he shows these men as variously constructed as disposable according to the pre-existing circumstances of their lives including colonialism, racism, and poverty, all of which render them "the wretched of the earth" (Fanon 1963). Unemployment and suffering are represented "as prevalent as the dust in the public road" (Clarke [1980] 2005, 12)

In addition to situating the circumstances of their lives within the wider political narrative of colonialism, Clarke, at the same time, situates their deaths within a wider history of the Black Atlantic. Throughout the chapter he narrates the brief public memorials that accompanied the remembering and recounting of the dead:

> For three silent minutes we stood in respect for the dead of our village "lost at sea." Our eyes filled with tears at the unfairness of it all, and at the frightening images of men falling out of ships, in seas higher [...] than any building in our island-country, higher than any wave we had seen off the Gravesend Beach, and blacker too. (Clarke [1980] 2005, 12)

The loss of these men at sea becomes linked to an ongoing count of Black lives lost to the Atlantic, in particular those who died on the transatlantic slave voyages between Africa and the New World. We might once again connect Clarke's work to Paul Gilroy's work and his later book *The Black Atlantic* where Gilroy turns to "the image of ships" (1993, 4) in his attempts to situate Black lives within modernity while at the same time offering a counterpoint to histories of modernity structured through the modern nation state. Yet Clarke's move beyond the nation, in this instance, is not so much an abandonment or a rethinking of the symbolic and representational force of the nation state per se; rather, in this turn to the Atlantic, Clarke asks us to think of the islands of Barbados and England as not so much separated by water but as connected by deep Black Atlantic histories and by waves, the waves ruled by Britannia. This discursive and imaginative move forms a contrast with the intensified faith in borders so central to the politics of Brexit.

In another narrative turn towards an articulation of interconnected relationality through Atlantic histories (Glissant 1997), by the end of this passage Clarke specifically references an idea of Black Britishness not specifically located within the island context of Britain. In talking about the ongoing experience of war, Clarke's narrator declares: "And now the Germans were ruling these same waters and waves and killing fathers, brothers, and uncles from our village. And as black Britons we wanted to do something about it" (Clarke [1980] 2005, 12). In describing Barbadians at war (and indeed those at home through the pronoun "we") as Black Britons, Clarke keenly positions histories of blackness within Britain and the war, not as outside the bounds of nation but as a rethinking of the discourse of British borders. This narrative moment, rather than situating Barbados as auxiliary to British history, remaps this history. Additionally, if Brexit as political discourse has been preoccupied with border anxieties between Britain and Europe, it is striking that not just the relationship between Britain and Barbados is rearticulated here. Barbados and indeed the Caribbean become imagined as a frontier for European tensions. This recalls an even longer history of how British–European border wars have been fought and restaged in the Caribbean with different outcomes for and annexations of particular island spaces.

A similar repositioning of Barbados as a part of what Clarke calls the "theatres of wars" is also seen later in the text in the narration of a series of blackouts in Barbados:

> At a certain time of night, we had to turn down our kerosene lamps. Black-outs reached us from up in the Mother Country from various "theatres of war". The Germans, the British said, were now in Caribbean waters. We got scared. *Sireens* sounded throughout the night,

> throughout the country. Searchlights would point in the sky at nightfall; we would follow the line and imagine German planes in it. (Clarke [1980] 2005, 42)

The narratives of the Blitz, emergency blackouts, and food rationing have been well documented in the histories of World War II and have become almost synonymous with representations of London in this period. Here Clarke offers another supplement to that history, remapping the stories told in popular films such as *Tonight and Every Night* (Saville 1945) and *Mrs Henderson Presents* (Frears 2005). Additionally we might read the moment later in the text (in chapter 16), when it is rumoured that German submarines are spotted off the coast of Barbados (which sends the community into panic) as another moment where Clarke expands and complicates the hitherto mapped geographies of war.

Clarke's work might then be read against the backdrop of attempts to elide blackness as part of the memorialization of the war. In his text, he narrates how silences and absences structure the memorials led by the headmaster of the local school:

> The headmaster brought the proceedings to a close by leading us into the singing of *Rule Britannia, Britannia Rule the Waves.* And in all the singing, nobody remembered to pray for the families of the Barbadian seamen lost or dead at sea. (Clarke [1980] 2005, 13)

Clarke dramatizes not simply an absence or erasure of presence but rather a complex process of obscuring that, in turn, serves to negate and complicate the fact of presence. We might read these narrative moments in relation to what Gilroy (1987) describes in the opening pages of *There Ain't No Black in the Union Jack* as a field of representation marked by "the invisibility of race within the field", but also in terms of his descriptions of "the forms of nationalism [which] tends towards a morbid celebration of England and Englishness from which blacks are systematically excluded" (12). Clarke's narrative calls attention to the way in which the history of British nationalism fails to contain the narratives of Black lives and deaths. They are written out even as the losses of the war are remembered.

The text itself, in intervening in this process, comes to serve as its own mode of memorialization in lieu of physical monuments as well as calling attention to how local narratives and oral tellings potentially recuperate what national and colonial narratives obscure. The significance of the question of scale in the process of attending to different historical narratives is underlined in Clarke's narration of the moment in which Barbados is christened as "Little England". His mention of Grantley Adams's telegraph to Churchill situates the story at the level of state and national politics. However, this moment also coincides in the community with the arrival of a new schoolmaster at Combermere College, a figure described as "a drill sergeant of a man" (Clarke [1980] 2005, 43), wearing "the suit of British officers' khakis, without pips" (44). The narrator adds: "He was an Englishman sent down to us by the King or our leader or Churchill" (44). The inscription of Barbados in British history (its christening as Little England) is thus paralleled by an arrival that situates a visible embodiment of British annexation within the very landscape of Barbados. The schoolmaster's presence and representation additionally demand that we read Barbadian–British intimacies and relations not just in friendly or cordial terms as might be suggested by Grantley Adams's telegraph, but within the framework of colonial histories of subordination. The description of the headmaster foregrounds the language of war and he becomes an embodiment of colonial conquest dressed in his military regalia. Clarke's writing of the complexities and asymmetries of colonial power is also signalled at the very start of the text and potentially serve to frame our reading of the work. On page 9, in his description of the beatings administered to school boys under the governance of colonial headmasters, the marks on the Black boys' bodies made by the belt used to administer punishment are described as mirroring the "various crosses on the English flag" (Clarke [1980] 2005, 9). Clarke importantly does not position the Black body here as alien to the image or representation of the Union Jack; rather, these bodies come to symbolize the history of colonial subjugation by which England was built. Clark writes an intimate personal retelling of the complex colonial relations between Britain and its empire that shows the impossibility of extricating one history from another.

Histories in the shadow of empire

In many ways we might read Brexit as one kind of afterlife of empire. The making of Brexit Britain with the discourses of bootstraps and self-sufficiency is arguably fuelled by memories of Great Britain – that large British Empire on which the sun never set. Clarke attends to the feelings of pride that marked empire in his recounting of a lesson taught by one of the school headmasters in Barbados:

> The headmaster would still be smiling; and running his chalk-covered hand with the tuning fork [...] over the wide expanse of the millions of square miles painted in red.
>
> "What is my hand passing over now, boys?"
>
> "The British Empire, sir!"
>
> The headmaster is still smiling [...] as if he is the owner of this vast empire of land [...] "That is why the sun can never set on the British Empire!" [...]
>
> And we would see only the red of the British Empire with our unbelieving eyes. (Clarke [1980] 2005, 45–46)

In his narration, Clarke attends to the geographical expanse of empire but also its function as a source of pride. More recently, Paul Gilroy in *After Empire: Melancholia or Convivial Culture* has observed that there persists a tendency to romanticize the colonial past. According to Gilroy, "the life of the nation has been dominated by an inability to face, never mind actually mourn, the profound change in circumstances and moods that followed the end of the Empire and consequent loss of imperial prestige" (2004, 98). In this regard, it is noteworthy that the current historical moment of Brexit has also been marked by a somewhat nostalgic recalling of relations with the Commonwealth as seen in popular representations such as the television series *The Crown* (Morgan 2016) but also in governmental and social rhetoric. Boris Johnson, when he was foreign secretary, famously talked of Brexit as an opportunity for strengthening relations with the British Commonwealth (see Plummer 2015). These sentiments engage a nostalgia for empire, its loss and possibility. If postcolonial studies has often tended to focus on the process of decolonization in the context of the various domains that were held by the once-Great British Empire, Paul Gilroy's texts, including *There Ain't No Black In the Union Jack* (Gilroy 1987), *After Empire* (Gilroy 2004), and *Postcolonial Melancholia* (Gilroy 2005) have been particularly useful for their insistent explorations of the afterlives of empire within Britain itself. Gilroy's (2005, 52) concept of "postcolonial melancholia", for example, calls attention to the feelings, insecurities, and anxieties that have marked the necessary restructuring of British narratives of identity and narratives about itself in the wake of empire and the critical interventions of postcolonial studies.

We see evidence of these ideological anxieties in the public rhetoric of Enoch Powell's "Rivers of Blood" speech in the post-World War II moment. Gilroy's work has also sought to connect this to his explorations of the enduring appeal of Churchill as well as the rise of Margaret Thatcher (Gilroy 1987, 2004). While *There Ain't No Black in the Union Jack* offers rich attention to Thatcherite Britain, it also, at the same time, traces connections across different historical moments (the decades from the 1950s to the 1980s). In this regard, Gilroy's work models the attention to a longer history that he has recently advocated for and demonstrates how it might unsettle a sedimented present. This opens up a potential for denaturalizing the politics of the present to show continuities, shifts and afterlives. Gilroy's (1987) examination of "*how* the limits of 'race' have come to coincide so precisely with national frontiers" (46; emphasis added), I am arguing, might be read as methodologically dependent on a critical mobilization of this strategy that proves useful to contextualizing and exploring Brexit and the British public's insistent concern with the foreclosing, policing and the remaking of borders. As a methodological strategy, a longer historical view proves fundamentally useful for rethinking the ground of the present, the afterlives of empire and Brexit.

Note

1. The concept of the hostile environment might be linked to Christina Sharpe's (2016) discussion in *In The Wake* of how anti-blackness is the weather: "In what I am calling the weather, anti-blackness is pervasive *as* climate" (106; emphasis in original).

Disclosure statement

No potential conflict of interest was reported by the authors.

ORCID

Ronald Cummings http://orcid.org/0000-0001-6375-3913

References

Anim-Addo, Joan. 2018. "Windrush Anniversary Reflections: Hauntings and the Longer View." *LW Blog*, July 18. https://www.lwbooks.co.uk/blog/windrush-anniversary-reflections

Brathwaite, E.R. 1959. *To Sir, with Love*. London: Bodley Head.
Carby, Hazel. 2019. *Imperial Intimacies: A Tale of Two Islands*. London: Verso.
Clarke, Austin. [1980] 2005. *Growing up Stupid under the Union Jack*. Toronto: Thomas Allen Publishers.
Fanon, Frantz. 1963. *The Wretched of the Earth*. New York: Grove Weidenfeld.
Frears, Stephen, dir. 2005. *Mrs Henderson Presents*. London and Parik: BBC Films and Pathé Pictures.
Gentleman, Amelia. 2019. *The Windrush Betrayal*. London: Guardian Faber Publishing.
Gilroy, Paul. 1987. *There Ain't No Black in the Union Jack*. London: Routledge.
Gilroy, Paul. 2004. *After Empire: Melancholia or Convivial Culture*. Abingdon: Routledge.
Gilroy, Paul. 2005. *Postcolonial Melancholia*. New York: Columbia University Press.
Gilroy, Paul. 1993. *The Black Atlantic*. Cambridge, MA: Harvard University Press.
Gilroy, Paul. 2019. "Still No Black in the Union Jack?: An Interview with Paul Gilroy [with Ben Thompson]." *Tribune*, January 26. https://www.tribunemag.co.uk/2019/01/still-no-black-in-the-union-jack
Glissant, Edouard. 1997. *Poetics of Relation*. Ann Arbor, MI: University of Michigan Press.
Hansen, Randall. 2000. *Citizenship and Immigration in Post-War Britain*. Oxford: Oxford University Press.
Kincaid, Jamaica. 1988. *A Small Place*. New York: Penguin.
Levy, Andrea. 2004. *Small Island*. London: Headline Publishing Group.
Mead, Matthew. 2009. "Empire Windrush: The Cultural Memory of an Imaginary Arrival." *Journal of Postcolonial Writing* 45 (2): 137–149. doi:10.1080/17449850902819920.
Miles, Robert. 1989. "Nationality, Citizenship, and Migration to Britain, 1945–1951." *Journal of Law and Society* 16 (4): 426–442. doi:10.2307/1410329.
Morgan, Peter. 2016. *The Crown*. London and Culver City, CA: Left Bank Pictures and Sony Pictures Television for Netflix.
Murdoch, H. Adlai. 2018. "Enoch Powell, Stuart Hall, and Post-Windrush Caribbean Identity in Britain." *sx salon*, October 29. http://smallaxe.net/sxsalon/discussions/enoch-powell-stuart-hall-and-post-windrush-caribbean-identity-britain
Olusoga, David. 2018. "The Windrush Story Was Not a Rosy One Even before the Ship Arrived." *The Guardian*, April 22. https://www.theguardian.com/commentisfree/2018/apr/22/windrush-story-not-a-rosy-one-even-before-ship-arrived
Orwell, George. 2000. "Not Counting Niggers." In *George Orwell: An Age Like This, 1920-1940*, edited by Sonia Orwell and Ian Angus, 394-397. Boston, MA: Nonpareil Books.
Plummer, Robert. 2015. "Commonwealth Dream Looms in Brexit Campaign." *BBC*, November 26. https://www.bbc.com/news/business–34855940
Salkey, Andrew. [1960] 2009. *Escape to an Autumn Pavement*. Leeds: Peepal Tree.
Saville, Victor, dir. 1945. *Tonight and Every Night*. Culver City, CA: Columbia Pictures.
Selvon, Samuel. [1965] 2020. *The Housing Lark*. London: Penguin.
Selvon, Samuel. [1975] 1991. *Moses Ascending*. London: Heinemann.
Shabi, Rachel. 2019. "How Immigration Became Britain's Most Toxic Political Issue." *The Guardian*, November 15. https://www.theguardian.com/politics/2019/nov/15/how-immigration-became-britains-most-toxic-political-issue
Sharpe, Christina. 2016. *In the Wake: On Blackness and Being*. Durham, NC: Duke University Press.
Stuart, Hall. 1999. "Thinking the Diaspora: Home-Thoughts from Abroad." *Small Axe* 6 (9): 1–18.
Tomlinson, Sally. 2018. "Enoch Powell, Empires, Immigrants, and Education." *Race, Ethnicity, and Education* 21 (1): 1–14. doi:10.1080/13613324.2017.1365055.
Younge, Gary. 2020. "The NHS, Windrush and the Debt We Owe to Immigration." *The Guardian*, June 22. https://www.theguardian.com/commentisfree/2018/jun/22/honour-nhs-built-on-immigration-windrush?fbclid=IwAR3y_GrI0SbG4_zDxiO2otXVnFOKjrb-HXHsbHKkCjsqO8XwKZd_-KSdFQ4

Warning signs: Postcolonial writing and the apprehension of Brexit

John McLeod

ABSTRACT

This article considers how postcolonial fiction anticipated, apprehended, and critically explored the political and cultural milieu which facilitated the outcome of the 2016 European Union (EU) referendum. In suggesting that "Brexit Literature" existed before Brexit was formally pursued, it understands Brexit as driving an English nationalism that unnervingly appropriates the history of the British Empire and World War II. It uncovers the representation of these manoeuvres in a number of key texts. Caryl Phillips's *A Distant Shore* both logs and challenges the malevolent imagining of newcomers that has deep roots in notions of war and empire. Zadie Smith's *NW* represents post-crash austerity as proleptically exposing the complex politics of race and class which fuelled the pro-Brexit populism that lies latent in the novel. Ultimately, the article calls for a post-Brexit postcolonialism that harnesses the power of critical thought to continue the long-standing contestation of the prevailing political orthodoxy.

It is the spring of 2008, and on an innocuous London street, at around 11:00 a.m., a Zimbabwean traffic warden, "Kwama Lyons", decides not to issue a parking ticket to the owner of a Land Rover. The driver has parked temporarily by an electronics shop and appears to be unloading boxes from the boot with his daughter. Parking for the purposes of unloading is fortunately permitted, and, after all, "Kwama" thinks that the man has an honest face. But one passer-by takes a different view of the scene. An unnamed woman in a tracksuit, with "flushed indoor skin and crinkly, angry hair" (Lanchester 2012, 212), blocks the traffic warden's path and complains about the discrimination she is witnessing. "Let those snobs park anywhere they like", she complains:

> Ordinary people, you stick a ticket on them without looking twice, don't care if they're in the bay they belong in or not [...], only got your job in the first place because of positive discrimination, ordinary working people pay the price. (212)

When "Kwama" politely reminds her that parking for the purposes of loading is permitted, the woman's disdain is brutal and ugly: "Why don't you just fuck off back to nig-nog land, go eat your fucking bananas in a tree and die of Aids [...]? What the fuck are you doing here anyway?" (213).

Although the scene is set a full eight years before the United Kingdom (UK) European Union (EU) membership referendum of June 23, 2016, it seems, when read in retrospect, a distinctly Brexit tableau: the posh, waxed-jacketed Land Rover driver; the racially abusive "ordinary" passer-by speaking up for white disenfranchised Londoners; the maligned and racialized migrant trying to make an honest living by taking on humdrum work, her presence in the postcolonial metropolis still a mystery to those who consider themselves rightfully native. And there is an additional twist: "Kwama Lyons" is a pseudonym for Quentina Mkfesi, a graduate of the University of Zimbabwe, who is seeking asylum due to the brutal Mugabe regime and working illegally. Such subdivisions of race and class, austerity and wealth, and legitimate citizen and migrant trespasser have come to define and defile "Brexit Britain" today. They underwrite the social inequalities and cultural imaginaries that have increasingly structured and corrupted Britain's political fortunes in this century. As such, "Brexit" names not so much a "democratic" decision or bureaucratic process – leaving the European Union – but the grim, glum, political, and cultural milieu epitomized by the referendum result, one which has long historical antecedents.

The novel in which this scene appears – John Lanchester's (2012) *Capital* – consciously positions itself as a reflection on the global financial crash of 2008 and its local consequences, and, for one critic at least, constitutes an example of "Crunch Lit" (Shaw 2015, 7): an emergent literary engagement with high finance, austerity, and the neoliberal world order. Along with the other works that I shall discuss in this article, I want additionally to situate *Capital* as a Brexit novel, and for at least two reasons. First, it points explicitly to one of the most important contributing factors to the enthusiasm for Brexit – namely, the financial crash of 2008 – and implicitly to another: the perception and fortunes of migrants and their descendants in the UK which have deep roots in postwar decolonization and, as we are witnessing more and more, the refurbished legacy of World War II. The recent and ongoing "*Windrush* Betrayal", to borrow Amelia Gentleman's (2019) uncompromising term, is ample evidence of the tryst between colonial past and present, while a recent opinion poll has revealed that 30 percent of Britons believe the colonies were better off as part of the British Empire (Booth 2020). Second, the novel takes its place amidst other works that we should collectively consider as Brexit fiction – one genuinely hesitates to say "BrexLit" – that appeared not after the referendum but before it. (In this regard, very recent novels of Brexit, such as Jonathan Coe's (2018) marvellous *Middle England* and Ian McEwan's (2019) acidic *The Cockroach*, mark the beginnings of a post-Brexit fiction.) There has been gathering for quite some time in literary fiction the signposting and critique of the political, social, and cultural entanglements that have directly contributed to the Brexit imbroglio. Postcolonial writers have contributed significantly to this activity, and over many years, not least by exposing and exploring the calcification of prejudice, the intensification of malevolence, and the growing disparities of wealth and impoverishment that have characterized Britain's hostile environment since at least the turn of the century – to the extent that the result of the referendum should not have come as a great surprise to readers who had been paying proper attention. To be blunt: we were warned.

Zadie Smith admitted to feeling surprised the morning after the result was known, in an essay which first appeared in the *New York Review of Books* in August 2016. "Throughout the day I phoned home", she recalls in "Fences: A Brexit Diary", "and emailed and tried to process, along with much of London – or at least the London I know – our enormous sense of shock. 'What have they done?' we said to each other" (2018, 25). Her article both attends to and exorcizes a degree of self-confessed liberal middle-class guilt, and sounds a distinct note of mea culpa in its cognition of a cellular, cloistered vision of London's diverse and divided demos, one at odds with the blithe and naive cliché of Britain as "Happy Multicultural Land" (Smith 2000, 398), softly satirized in Smith's (2000) well-known debut, *White Teeth*. Amidst its self-critical head-shaking and hand-wringing, her essay makes two especially sharp observations. The first concerns Smith's awareness of Britain's socially striated terrain, the geographical distinctiveness of the nation's disunity amidst which the dynamics of class, race, and culture observe different chronologies. Away from London's societal dissonance, in other parts of the country, multicultural transformation has yet to be clocked or have its time, or has been timed out. Within the capital, too, "Londoncentric solipsism" (Smith 2018, 26) is itself increasingly fenced in by the subdivisions, at once imaginative and very real, of economic privilege and racialized perception that make a mockery of the cheerful and utopian cosmopolitanism presumed to be at large in the postcolonial metropolis. "For many people in London right now", she writes, "the supposedly multicultural and cross-class aspects of their lives are actually represented by their staff – nannies, cleaners – by the people who pour their coffees and drive their cabs, or else the handful of Nigerian princes you meet in the private schools" (27). Brexit is both the product and the evidence of these inequities. It has granted legitimacy to prejudicial responses to inequality not least by attempting to normalize the rancid racism that Lanchester's "Kwama" experiences while going about her business on an ordinary London street.

Secondly, and significantly, Smith's essay reminds us that, while the referendum result (and, as we have seen since, the battle over attempts to implement it) is era-defining news, Brexit per se is nothing new at all. "One useful consequence of Brexit", she hazards, "is to finally and openly reveal a deep fracture in British society that has been thirty years in the making" (Smith 2018, 27). One responsible way for horrified middle-class readers to respond to it, she suggests, is to realize its tentacular and tuberous roots:

> we might also take a look at the last thirty years and ask ourselves what kind of attitudes have allowed a different class of people to discreetly manoeuvre, behind the scenes, to ensure that "them" and "us" never actually meet anywhere but in symbol. [...] We may walk past "them" very often in the street and get into their cabs and eat their food in their ethnic restaurants, but the truth is that more often than not they are not in our schools, or in our social circles, and they very rarely enter our houses – unless they've come to work on our endlessly remodelled kitchens. (31)

Brexit fiction, too, is nothing new. Postcolonial writing has long been taking a look at the unwholesome attitudes, the imaginative and economic austerities that culminated in the confected demand for Brexit, even if that demand was not fully considered by some of those who voted for it. Smith makes mention of the fact that large numbers of Britons were "googling 'What is the EU?' in the hours after the vote" (30) and reports an anecdote heard from a friend concerning one Leave supporter whose vote was motivated primarily by her desire to see the then Health Secretary, Jeremy Hunt, sacked.

As Ben Wellings (2019) has demonstrated in his superb forensic dissection of the political landscape of Brexit, obfuscation and occlusion are crucial to its ideological mechanics. Wellings shows how Brexit is the product and passion of a distinctively English nationalism that secretes its aims through a strategically British register. The masochistic isolation risked by its secessionist ambitions to leave the EU is offset by its integrationist tactics, first and foremost its supposed support of the Union of the four British nations, but also its wider commitment to "the Anglosphere" (5), those English-speaking nations created as a consequence of imperial expansion and still considered as intimately related, often (but not exclusively) through ideas such as the Commonwealth. In these terms, Brexit is not at all a parochial affair but decidedly global in its aims of seeking to reorient its international trading ambitions beyond the existing trading bloc of the EU towards a new "old" raft of predominantly English-speaking international partners, such as Canada, New Zealand, Australia, India, and the United States. In Wellings's view, "resistance to European integration revitalized English nationalism as a defence of British sovereignty whilst the Englishness of this worldview inclined Britain away from the EU and towards the Anglosphere" (14). The protection of British sovereignty was the guise behind which an elite right-wing English nationalism both built and occluded its decidedly England-centric ideology – a fact borne out by the markedly divergent voting preferences of the four British nations. With matters regarding British sovereignty and border controls pushed to the centre of a primarily English perception of the EU, Brexiteers played upon the fears of many who, rightly or wrongly, felt disenfranchised by the consequences of globalization, especially the perceived negative impact of migrant labour on domestic jobs and wages. Such nationalism has depended upon "an awkward but decisive alliance between sections of the electorate disaffected by the effects of neoliberal globalisation and elites attempting to expose Britain to more of the same" (7).

Culturally, this alliance depended upon additional sleights of hand, particularly as regards the conjoined remembering of two key elements of British history: the British Empire and World War II. If England, embedded in the UK, "lay trapped between the receding memory of empire and the waking reality of deepening European integration" (Wellings 2019, 96), then revitalizing the former was essential to rescuing England from the latter. Brexit's advocates promoted the EU as the most tangible evidence of the nation's post-imperial humiliation and post-war demise, suggesting that Europe's perceived wartime saviour had unforgivably become the slavish subordinate of the Eurocrats' crackpot whims.

As a number of critics have explored, the entangled appropriation of each of these historical phenomena – empire and war – has long serviced a reactionary response to Britain's post-war domestic and global transformation. Writing in the year when the UK Independence Party (UKIP) secured 2.6 million votes and won 12 seats at the 2004 European Parliament Elections, Paul Gilroy (2004) commented upon the "neurotic [...] citation of the anti-Nazi war" as a "privileged point of entry into national identity and self-understanding" that seeks to "get back to the place or moment before the country lost its moral and cultural bearings" (97). This sense of loss has firm connections to the slow erasure of Britain as an imperial power on the world's stage, the melancholic disavowal of which impacts upon attitudes to migrants and presumed foreigners who come "not only [to] *represent* the vanished empire but also refer consciousness to the unacknowledged pain of its loss and the unsettling shame of its bloody management" (110). In a similar multi-directional mood, Bill Schwarz (2011) has wondered if the popular cultural indulgence of the "mythic properties of the war" in the post-war years strategically shielded a more painful sense of English diminution and served to "screen other historical realities, not least the end of empire" (7). That said, empire and war have also been previously articulated in a different, dissident manner. As Matthew Whittle (2016) has fascinatingly shown, a distinct confluence of literary activity in the immediate post-war years, one not often remembered today, mobilized "a critique of the ideological assumptions of the Empire [...] as a means of interpreting the atrocities of the Second World War and the realities of decolonization" (29). Such post-war endeavours were part of an important critical re-imagining of Britishness firmly in the light of decolonization in Asia, Africa, and the Caribbean, with writers often "reject[ing] past conceptions of an imperial identity in favour of a unified post-imperial conception of Britishness" (12). It is precisely this critical trajectory, one that also helped open a space for subsequent postcolonial literary explorations of the metropolis towards the end of the last century, that Brexit has hoped to stymie by determinedly remodulating conceptions of both British imperial identity and the legacy of World War II to serve reactionary not radical ends. For the Brexiteer, post-war post-colonial melancholia is triumphantly medicated by the miraculous return to life of the lost empire in the guise of Brexit's promise of national liberation from the EU. Whittle's "post-imperial" is gazumped by Brexit's post-imperium: Britain is ascendant once more amidst the Anglosphere and unshackled from Europe, with migrants and refugees, old and new, freshly perceived (yet again) as a threat to British sovereignty and ample evidence of the lapse of border "control" created by the EU's commitment to free movement.

Fintan O'Toole's (2019) witty and excoriating dissection of Brexit in *Heroic Failure* conveys this compounding of colonial and EU migrants as central to the refurbishment of the foreigner as the tangible evidence of the nation's subordinated sovereignty, when noting the "large overlap between pro-Brexit and anti-immigrant sentiment. [...] The black and brown Other fused with the European Other" (20). Like Wellings, he recognizes the centrality of the memory of empire to the malevolent machinations of Brexiteering and its politics of pain: indulging in strangely masochistic memories of imperial glory that often eulogized fortitude in defeat (the Charge of the Light Brigade, General Gordon at Khartoum, et al.), presenting the UK's membership or dealings with the EU in terms of a Powellite fantasy of post-war British vassalage and subordination, the proud colonizer now abjectly colonized by a German-dominated Brussels. This ideological reconstitution of Brexit as a route back to the finest hours of imperial grandeur and British self-determination, reborn at the centre of a grateful, global Anglosphere, points to the very real and thoroughly sinister consequences of recolonizing the narrative of empire. As Stuart Hall (2017) remarked when prompted by his memories of wartime and mid-century Britain, "[w]henever the British began to imagine themselves as lovers of liberty they also conceived of themselves, at one and the same time, as the imperial lords of humankind" (180). For these reasons, Wellings regards Brexit as a "back-to-the-future reorientation" where a combination of the neurotic celebration of Britain's unconquered, stand-alone persistence in the face of the Nazi threat has been fused with the resculpting of empire as "one of history's 'good things' to allow Britons to imagine themselves distanced from, or completely outside of, the EU" (2019, 106). The empire was in ruins; but, after Brexit, the empire remains.

In seeking to embellish post-EU futurity through a myopic requisitioning of the past, Brexit is both a triumph and a failure of the imagination. It is a triumph (for Brexiteers) in successfully securing a hegemonic position for empire as laudable legacy not shameful heritage, a (re)usable past which rewrites the history of British colonialism as a document of civilization rather than barbarism. Brexit cheerfully obscures the darkness of colonial exploitation, resource extraction, genocide, environmental catastrophe, impoverishment, underdevelopment, and social and psychic immiseration by illuminating instead the exalted model of democratic sovereignty selflessly gifted by Britain to the (Anglospheric) world through the "mission" of imperial expansion. It is a failure of the imagination, of course, for precisely these reasons too, and for keeping at a remove or under wraps contrary ways of imagining England, Britain, the UK, the EU, and the globe – past and present – as well as the multitude that traverses these spaces. Following Wellings's lead in presenting Brexit as a means of both imaginative and political distancing, we should think further about the politics of proximity it instals – both spatial and historical, regarding that which is considered near or far – not least because such thinking returns us to those Brexit fictions that critically narrate a worried prequel to Brexit's electoral success. What warnings do these texts sound of the nation to come? What distances and proximities do they discern, and how did they get forged?

As its title suggests, matters of proximity preoccupy Caryl Phillips's (2003) novel, *A Distant Shore*. Its well-known opening line, "England has changed" (3), routes us into the unsettling zeitgeist of the early 21st century at least for those whom stasis is always preferable. O'Toole has noted that Brexit's voting pattern entrenched England "as a divided thing, bitterly split, not just between Leavers and Remainers but between the England of the big multi-cultural cities on the one side and the England of the villages and towns on the other" (2019, 178). As a contemporary "condition of England" novel, *A Distant Shore* deliberately eschews an engagement with Britain for a sharper English focus, while the predominant setting – the English North – is alert to the uncommon chronologies that render English transformation uneven and distinctive in the provinces, sticks, and suburbs. In this book, selective memories of World War II and the ruinous presence of colonial remains haunt the horizon of the everyday, as Phillips shows how each is dangerously immanent within the undemonstrative, quiet streets and cul-de-sacs of England's turn-of-the-century peace and quiet.

Europe is nearer than one might think. To the newcomer Dorothy, the elderly white former teacher who lives in a new development called "Stoneleigh" just up the hill from the village of Weston, the area seems unexceptional and historically void. But a road-sign by its entrance

> announces the fact that we are twinned with some town in Germany and a village in the south of France. In the estate agent's bumf about "Stoneleigh" it says that during the Second World War the German town was bombed flat by the RAF, and the French village used to be full of Jews who were all rounded up and sent to the camps. I can't help feeling that it makes Weston seem a bit tame by comparison. Apparently, the biggest thing that ever happened in Weston was Mrs Thatcher closing the pits, and that was over twenty years ago. (Phillips 2003, 4)

Weston's proximity to wartime Germany and France is subtly rendered. The conflict is evoked through a patriotic memory of the triumphant Royal Air Force (RAF) that brings to the fore the nation's military achievements in Europe, while also keeping Europe at a distance from English shores – "I can't help feeling that it makes Weston seem a bit tame by comparison" – not least due to the fact that the two mainland European villages are not named. Europe is embraced at a comfortable remove with reference to the war, conjured cosmetically through vague advertising copy or diminutively named on a road-sign that postures equanimity through the quaint confection of civic "twinning".

This contradictory signposting of Europe in relation to England – beckoned in terms of the victories of the 1939–45 war, but remote from post-war England – is strengthened by Dorothy's account of her late father, whose antipathy to Europe is well remembered. Having lost his own father during the conflict in Belgium in World War I, he rarely ventured outside of England and remained hostile to the other European nations: "whenever he swore", Dorothy remembers, "which he seldom did, he was always quick to say 'pardon my French', which, of course, made no sense unless one viewed it through the prism of contempt" (11). His post-war parochialism is manifest in his geriatric grumbling on his allotment, where Dorothy often found him

> bemoaning the fact that we were giving up our English birthright and getting lost in a United States of Europe, or the fact that one never sees men in collars and ties on Sundays, or expressing his continued astonishment that ordinary folk could have any respect for the memory of Churchill, a man who during the 1926 General Strike had, as Dad had been telling me since I was a small child, referred to the workers as "the enemy". (27)

Phillips's depiction of Dorothy's father is slight but sharp, and acutely alive to the contradictions he epitomizes. His disdain for a post-war "United States of Europe" as threatening his "English birthright" anticipates the hardened 21st-century perception of the EU as a betrayal not a guarantor of democracy and peace. In Wellings's words, if World War II was an apogee of British greatness, then "membership of the European Union came to be seen as an eclipse of great power status and an institutionalisation of British decline" (2019, 112). Dad's contempt for Churchill is instructive here, as it was Churchill who first used the phrase "United States of Europe" in 1946 with a relatively positive inflection as a way of re-imagining the continent beyond the carnage of destruction. It is also voiced squarely in the terms of class conflict, as the reference to the General Strike suggests: as a Conservative politician, Churchill was no special friend to working-class interests and was ousted at the 1945 General Election to make way for Clement Atlee's Labour administration. Dad's socialism would seem to put him at odds with Churchill's Conservative Party; yet socially and culturally Dad is conservative, as his liking of proper male attire attests. His socialist politics are scrupulously national not internationalist, turning on a vaguely biogenetic myth of "English birthright". Victory in Europe has come to mean the victory of Europe over the English, a pyrrhic triumph which associates war with a sense of loss felt in national terms (another reason, too, for Dad's lack of post-war Churchillianism) ultimately symbolized by the death of Dad's father in wartime Belgium. With European locations framed in terms of a threat to English identity, sovereignty, and survival – significantly, Dorothy's Mum suffered a minor stroke on the family's only foreign holiday in Majorca – there is no room in this closed circuit to accommodate England's newcomers. Dorothy's regular visits to her parents' graves reminds us that these attitudes remain spectrally extant in the novel's present.

If Brexit successfully realized the refurnishing and fusing together of memories of war and empire, with the recall of empire profoundly rehabilitated as a benign affair,

Phillips's novel grimly exposes the resultant consequences. Their confluence structures the ordinary world of Weston's suburban milieu, which is deeply suspicious of any kind of newness and keen to adhere to chauvinist and racist attitudes when policing the borders of the "foreign". As a newly arrived elderly single woman living in the posh development up the hill from the "small village" (Phillips 2003, 23), Dorothy is already a figure of suspicion amongst Westoners, as she learns from the mother of one of her new piano students: "these people, they talk, you know" (23). Into the parochial, prejudicial milieu of "these people" arrives Solomon from mainland Europe. A refugee from an unnamed African nation, previously known by the name Gabriel, he works as a handyman and occasional driver for Dorothy. Gabriel/Solomon's presence brings to the surface the latent racism of village England: not before long he begins to receive hate mail which includes razor blades, and his life is ended in the canal by the Waterman's Arms, killed by racist youths. It also exposes the installation of those spacings and distancings crucial to Brexit's rewriting of history by effectively collapsing them. His story originates in a brutal civil conflict presumably in sub-Saharan Africa, where as a soldier he witness the killing of his family and is forced to flee; it follows him to a refugee centre near the French coast that recalls the Sangatte refugee camp (that existed between 1999 and 2002), and on his journey to England, clinging to the side of a ship; it captures his rough living and eventual incarceration in London, before he heads north in the company of a kindly truck driver; and it portrays his eventual arrival, employment, and murder in Weston. This spatial trajectory pulls into proximity the local English village with the global "small wars" of the contemporary that are themselves indebted to the advent of colonialism across Africa and to the continent's neocolonial fortunes amidst globalization's ascendancy. It also exposes the coming "refugee crisis" as neither a mainland European nor a British metropolitan affair safely remote in the cities or on the South Coast, but just as large in northern English village life.

In revealing the uncomfortable proximity of these unvarnished historical phenomena to the daily business of Weston by his very presence, Gabriel/Solomon is an embodied reminder to "these people" of all they would like to forget and keep at bay, such as the malign consequences of the nation's colonial conduct on the world's stage and the "free" movement and dwelling of the migrant stranger whose very visibility is perceived as a threat to an "English birthright". Gabriel/Solomon's characterization, too, acts as a meta-textual link to the long history of murderous anti-migrant prejudice that is no stranger to the English North. His arrival from Africa by sea, short incarceration, and death by water recall the hounding of David Oluwale, a Nigerian migrant to Leeds who died in 1969 in the River Aire while fleeing racist officers from the Leeds City Police, and who is the subject of Phillips's moving chapter "Northern Lights" in *Foreigners: Three English Lives* (Phillips 2007). In recent years, Oluwale's murder has concerned historians as well as local activists keen to protect his memory from civic and popular elision, and as part of their wider contestation of the "hostile environment" doggedly pursued by recent Conservative governments.[1] To borrow his character's words, Gabriel/Solomon is a figure "burdened with hidden history" (Phillips 2003, 300) at once real and imagined. His killing is the product of the entangled tryst between the anti-migrant sentiment rooted in empire's end and the conservative-nationalist Englandism which murderously seeks to uphold the fragile distancing of Europe's perceived threat to English "birthright". No wonder, then, that Brexit so successfully secured populist support in feeding (on)

English fears of the EU's post-war ascendancy, symbolized by the figure of the migrant from once-colonized spaces whose ability to access England from the European mainland came to be perceived as epitomizing the EU's failings.

Importantly, *A Distant Shore* does more than merely log the emerging political domain that would stimulate Brexit. As I have suggested elsewhere (McLeod 2018), Phillips pursues a poetics of proximation in his intercalating of Dorothy's and Gabriel/Solomon's narratives and the complex chronologies that unfold in each. In seeking to entangle the narratives of a retired English white teacher and a black refugee by suggesting proximity where others instal distance due to the particulars of race, culture, or gender, Phillips challenges received assumptions of human incongruity – the other has nothing to do with me – as an excuse for ethical inaction. In putting these lives narratively in touch, Phillips hopes for the possibility of forging resistance and ethical steadfastness through quotidian human contact. "This is a woman to whom I might tell my story", thinks Gabriel/Solomon: "If I do not share my story, then I have only this one year [since arriving in Weston] to my life" (Phillips 2003, 300). And although he does not last long in racist England, his brief relationship with Dorothy is instrumental in helping her bring his killers to the notice of the police and also offers her a refuge from her own crippling loneliness. In shaping things in this way, we might retrospectively read *A Distant Shore* as an anti-Brexit novel, one that does more than simply register an unpalatable habitus but mediates it distinctively, strategically, and critically, as well as keeping a degree of faith in the survival of meaningful human relations across divisions and fencings.

To my mind, such glints of hopefulness in such a dark tale also index the novel's moment of appearance at the turn of the century rather than amidst the turmoil compounded by the global financial crash of 2008 that entrenched and widened the kinds of suspicions displayed by Phillips's Westoners. The financial crash and its subsequent austerity measures pursued by successive British governments arguably played into the hands of Brexit's advocates, who could point to the presence of migrants old and new as ultimately responsible for the increasing precarity of work and welfare, rather than this being caused by the global financial system and its unimaginably wealthy proponents. Written in the shadow of the 2008 crash, as was Lanchester's *Capital*, Zadie Smith's (2012) *NW* contends with the precarity wrought by globalization and capitalism in the 21st century.[2] In James Arnett's words, "[t]here is no question that *NW* marks out the complex sociopolitical environment of Britain on the brink of Brexit" (2018, 1). Smith's novel depicts a contemporary postcolonial London neighbourhood characterized by the degree zero of its polycultural populus that pulls the lineages and lingo of other times and places into an entangled present. "[T]he streets turn European", the narrator tells, when an uncomfortably hot sun shines: "there is a mania for eating outside" (3). Its vernacular cosmopolitanism, to use Homi K. Bhabha's (1996) well-known term, is conjured through the complicated family lineages and friendships indebted to migrations from Ireland, Jamaica, Algeria, Trinidad, and more besides, yet sharp divergences in class and wealth cross-cut such cultured convivialities and bring fences and frictions into play. Childhood chums Leah Hanwell and Natalie (once Keisha) Blake meet up regularly as adults, but not equitably: Irish-descended Leah knows that her visits to the dinner parties held by Jamaican-descended Natalie and her Italian Trinidadian husband, Frank, serve their hosts' illusion of metropolitan liberality: "she and [her migrant husband] Michel are invited to provide something like local colour. Neither of them knows what to say to barristers and bankers, to the occasional judge" (Smith 2012, 75). Older possibilities of class- or race-based solidarities seem long gone in this liquid postmodernity wrought from neo-liberal aspirations. These aspirations are epitomized by Natalie Blake's determination to rise from her modest social beginnings through education and middle-class careerism (she trains and works as a lawyer) and by Michel's amateurish nocturnal participation in the stock market online. The normalization of neo-liberalism's approval of bourgeois individualism and self-centredness is eerily captured on the novel's opening page as Leah reclines in her council-house garden, fenced in, and hears on the radio "a good line": "I am the sole author of the dictionary that defines me" (3). But the heteronormative designs of others prove ultimately more definitive. Natalie's quest to leave Keisha behind by being "crazy busy with self-invention" (183) flounders as her legal career is beset by the constraints of sexism and racialization that prohibit her transformation and position her as a diversity hire, forever subject to the entrenched gaze of white male authority, to the judges who regard her performances in court as "aggressive hysteria" (210). Leah's determination not to have a child contends endlessly with the views of her husband and her mother, Pauline, who fail to understand her abortive attitude towards heteronormative aspirational maternity. This vexed, striated urban enclave is thrown into particularly sharp relief by the appearance of two disruptive characters – Nathan Bogle and Shar – whose treatment at the hands of the others seems all the more instructive when viewed from the vantage of Brexit.

Shar's irruption into Leah's home at the novel's beginning appears a confidence trick, one which turns on her distressed and histrionic request for money to visit her allegedly sick mother. Leah's decision to call a taxi and give Shar £30 is received with incredulity by Pauline and Michel. Yet Leah's gullibility has significance in terms of Brexit. Consider her literacy (and, behind it, Smith's) in metropolitan austerity. From Leah's slightly more socially elevated point of view, Shar bears all the hallmarks of social depravity which are read off in terms of pitiable vulgarity. She smokes and smells; her "familiar" face wears a crooked smile; her skin is "papery and dry"; she wears "rolled-down jogging pants, the little downy dip in her back, pronounced, sweaty in the heat" (Smith 2012, 6). Shar speaks unguardedly about personal upset and difficulties – her abusive husband, her single motherhood – and conveys "a dark look" as she "grins satanically" (10). From the point of view of Leah, Shar is a known unknown, a figure "seen many times in these streets. A peculiarity of London villages: faces without names" (6). This queasy rendition of a proximate Londoner, witnessed regularly but rarely encountered, marks the predicament with which Smith is concerned: the attempt to engage sympathetically with those perceived unsympathetically at large. Leah's migrant mother, Pauline, is unmoved by Shar's seeming desperation and argues that the £30 will be used for drugs, while Michel declares Leah "an idiot" (15) – there is little attempt by either to think even briefly how austerity may have propelled Shar into her mendacious performance. The novel's neo-liberal milieu and cognition of austerity's underclass is presented through Leah's distinctly liberal quandary: how should I deal with the seemingly vulgar lives of others? With solidarity voided in the neighbourhood's brittle commons of snobbish suspicion and self-regard, populated by passers-by not participants in a confluent multiculture, Brexit's pernicious rhetoric of blame can quickly take root. Neo-liberalism's stimulation of an unseemly precariat despised for its crudity, condemned for its deceitfulness, and held liable for its own immiseration acts as the perfect preparation for Brexit's populist disdain for the most vulnerable as a threat to the neo-liberal dream of successful self-determination and "sole authorship" – of the entrepreneurial (migrant) subject, of the sovereign self, of the affluent nation – and not as evidence of its political and ethical atrophy, of the cellular social milieu fractured by proliferating imaginative and actual fences. But crucially, as Smith's novel exposes, such populism is not the primary product or possession of a disenfranchised and maligned underclass, but of those – amateur stockbroker Michel, pious Pauline, even liberal Leah – who appear a little better off and seem not unhappy to participate in rather than question capitalism's entrepreneurial values of hard work and money-making.

Nathan Bogle's presence in *NW* is especially penetrating and revealing in these terms. Leah's shocked recognition of him in Kilburn Underground Station – "familiar [...] unknown" (Smith 2012, 40) – recalls Shar's inscrutable proximity, as does his down-trodden demeanour as he stands near the ticket machines illegally selling travelcards at knock-down prices:

> The Afro of the man is uneven and has a tiny grey feather in it. The clothes are ragged. One big toe thrusts through the crumby rubber of an ancient red-stripe Nike Air. The face is far older than it should be. (40)

The decrepit sportswear seems all the more unkind, given Nathan's youthful ambitions to be a successful footballer. But for every Freddy Kamo, the migrant Senegalese Premier League footballer in Lanchester's *Capital* whose brief career gains him more money than Nathan will ever know, there are 100 Nathan Bogles. Just as Nathan receives no chapter of his own in *NW* but squats amidst the tales of others, so too does his neighbourhood open little accommodation for his precarious and itinerant presence. While Phillips's Gabriel/Solomon is the migrant figure freighted with antipathies wrought from the contexts of empire and World War II, Smith's Nathan Bogle is the contemporary black British subject whose racialized disenfranchisement is weighted further with the populist disdain for the wasted lives created by the Brexiteers' beloved globalization. Late in the novel, Natalie attempts to respond to witnessing such pain in proximity, but the gulf is too large, as Nathan vituperatively tells:

> What do you know about my life? When you been walking in my shoes? What do you know about living the way I live, coming up the way I came up? Sit on your bench judging me. [...] Talking out your neck about me. "How does it feel to be a problem?" What do you know about it? What do you know about me? Nothing. Who are you, to chat to me? Nobody. No one. (276)

What is to be done? If Leah's awkwardly charitable response to Shar, offering her money to salve an upset caused by an encounter with impoverishment, suggests the prohibitive distancings which Brexit will deepen and exaggerate as it reorganizes domestic politics in terms of populist antipathy not popular solidarity, Natalie's response is distinctly sinister. Both one-time pupils at Brayton High School, Nathan represents all that Natalie has worked hard to leave behind – not least the constraints of race and class – in her quest for upward mobility and suburban security. Yet their proximity as she wanders the neighbourhood in his uncomfortable company in the novel's dramatic finale suggests the circularity of her journey and the failure of her quest for sole authorship through neo-liberal self-determination – it is not for nothing that her new initials, NB, are the same as Nathan's. Nathan's presence is so unbearable because it threatens to reveal the illusion, from which Natalie worryingly cannot let go, of identitarian sovereignty, of taking (back) control of who you want to be.

So Nathan must be purged. When Leah asks Natalie why Nathan has lived the life of a "poor bastard" (Smith 2012, 292), Natalie's "instinct for self-defence, for self-preservation" keeps her locked inside a post-Thatcherite entrepreneurial standpoint as she admonishes the victim for his vagabondage, just like a good Brexiteer:

> We were smarter and we knew we didn't want to end up begging on other people's doorsteps. We wanted to get out. People like Bogle – they didn't want it enough. [...] This is one of the things you learn in a courtroom: people generally get what they deserve. (293)

Nathan's apparent complicity in the murder of Felix (the young black man whose story preoccupies the novel's second section) is one reason why Natalie, with voice disguised, shops him to the police as the novel closes. But there are other matters at work too, not least the demonization and pernicious erasure of those whose local presence evidences the failures of neo-liberalism's global schematics. Smith's novel of austerity models the machinations of Brexit with bleak, studied prescience.

As Natalie stands suicidal on Hornsey Lane Bridge, near the novel's end, she sees through the railings a "cross-hatched" vision of the city: "St Paul's in one box. The Gherkin in another. Half a tree. Half a car. Cupolas, spires. Squares, rectangles, half-moons, stars. It was impossible to get any sense of the whole" (Smith 2012, 281). As serving as a reminder of Natalie as forever fenced off from her dreams of betterment symbolized by the city in the distance – a reminder which she fails to notice, it seems – the inhibited cross-hatched view, neither whole nor sensible, anticipates the infinitely receding subdivisions of Brexit Britain. This disintegrating vision of the whole proleptically metaphorizes the uncoupling of those cultural and social connections required to sustain a pluralized popular politics of solidarity, as well as the prising open of those fractures in which the pious plaints of self-righteous grievance take root. Importantly, Smith exposes the complex class particulars at play here, in making the intemperate and impious partisan not the disenfranchised figure of Nathan but the entrepreneurial upwardly mobile Natalie, "crazy busy with self-invention", whose disdain for the downtrodden pushes her away from the popular towards a potentially populist politics. In so doing, Smith importantly gives the lie to Lanchester's brief and cliched characterization of the tracksuited woman with "indoor skin" (whose demeanour recalls Shar's), who racially abuses "Kwama" on behalf of "ordinary" people. These will not be the primary harbingers of Brexit, perhaps, as much as those neo-liberals who aspire, like Natalie, keenly to secure their status amongst the bay-windowed, safely gated middle class.

NW offers little sense of a way out of, or a way to contest, the coming crisis. If *A Distant Shore* retains a quiet faith in the progressively ethical possibilities of innocuous human contact and tale-telling, no matter how dark or hopeless things are, Smith's novel seems unable to find even piecemeal solace. Its entangled narratives of the chief characters' fortunes do not enable anything like Phillips's progressive poetics of proximation. By its close, Natalie is still compliant with the (by no means impartial) rule of law and the precepts of neo-liberal self-centredness in turning in Nathan; while

Leah's several frustrations – familial, political, sexual, professional – are silenced rather than settled as she joins Natalie's vendetta against Nathan. What, if anything, has changed for the better? "Let's talk about something else" (Smith 2012, 293), Leah says to Michel and Natalie, as she reaches for a welcome glass of wine as the book winds to its end.

Elite neo-liberals found in austerity the perfect opportunity to deflect blame for its primary causes – globalization, international finance, the reckless money marketeering of millionaires and their minions – towards the presence of those living most precariously. Austerity was fertile ground indeed for Brexit's reconstitution of empire's memory and World War II's legacy. But Brexit's fractures and fault lines are not new and run deeply, and, I would hazard, have been articulated in many more postcolonial texts than I have had occasion to mention. The warning signs have long been in evidence.

So, what is to be done? Lanchester's *Capital* ends with the newly redundant banker Roger Yount promising that "I can change change change" (2012, 577). It is a hideously ironic conclusion, voiced by a one-time high-flying City financier who has himself become part of the expendable slurry and small change of the global money markets. In our current bleak moment, and in the modest domain of literary and cultural critique, we need all the more the critical imagination of postcolonial thought – writing and reading – to remind us of the origins and depth of a crisis brought by the long formation of Brexit's post-imperium, as well as its continued investment in the necessity and possibility of political transformation and meaningful change. Here, one hopes, postcolonial writing might play a fundamental role, in a number of ways: in its contribution to a "BrexLit" that sustains and advances the long-standing ethical and political refusal of the newly nostalgic nation's hostile environment; in mounting a determined cultural challenge to the triumphant political orthodoxy now nakedly at large; and in imagining and protecting the enduring, equitable transpersonal relations that refuse every day the fencings fundamental to Brexit's malevolent politics of plunder.

Notes

1. For more on these local activities co-ordinated by the David Oluwale Memorial Association (DOMA), visit https://rememberoluwale.org/. Caryl Phillips is a patron of DOMA.
2. My discussion of *NW* is highly indebted to the critical imagination of my students at the University of Leeds, with whom I have studied the novel as part of my undergraduate module, "Postcolonial London". In particular, my comments about Natalie Blake's initials and Nathan Bogle's lack of a chapter to himself are inspired by the insights of my students, several of whom saw such things long before I did.

Disclosure statement

No potential conflict of interest was reported by the author.

References

Arnett, James. 2018. "Neoliberalism and False Consciousness before and after Brexit in Zadie Smith's NW." *The Explicator* 76 (1): 1–7. doi:10.1080/00144940.2017.1416329.

Bhabha, Homi K. 1996. "Unsatisfied: Notes on Vernacular Cosmopolitanism." In *Text and Nation*, edited by Laura Garcia-Morena and Peter C. Pfeifer, 191–207. London: Camden House.

Booth, Robert. 2020. "UK More Nostalgic for Empire than Other Ex-colonial Powers." *Guardian*, March 11. https://www.theguardian.com/world/2020/mar/11/uk-more-nostalgic-for-empire-than-other-ex-colonial-powers

Coe, Jonathan. 2018. *Middle England*. London: Viking Penguin.

Gentleman, Amelia. 2019. *The Windrush Betrayal: Exposing the Hostile Environment*. London: Guardian Faber.

Gilroy, Paul. 2004. *After Empire: Melancholia or Convivial Culture?* Abingdon: Routledge.

Hall, Stuart, [with Bill Schwarz]. 2017. *Familiar Stranger: A Life Between Two Islands*. London: Allen Lane.

Lanchester, John. 2012. *Capital*. London: Faber.

McEwan, Ian. 2019. *The Cockroach*. London: Jonathan Cape.

McLeod, John. 2018. "Wards and Rewards: Adoptability and Lost Children." In *Uncommon Wealths in Postcolonial Fiction*, edited by Helga Ramsey-Kurz and Melissa Kennedy, 229–248. Leiden & Boston: Brill/Rodopi.

O'Toole, Fintan. 2019. *Heroic Failure: Brexit and the Politics of Pain*. London: Apollo Books.

Phillips, Caryl. 2003. *A Distant Shore*. London: Secker and Warburg.

Phillips, Caryl. 2007. *Foreigners: Three English Lives*. London: Secker and Warburg.

Schwarz, Bill. 2011. "Introduction: End of Empire and the English Novel." In *End of Empire and the English Novel since 1945*, edited by Rachael Gilmour and Bill Schwarz, 1–37. Manchester: Manchester University Press.

Shaw, Katy. 2015. *Crunch Lit*. London: Bloomsbury Academic.

Smith, Zadie. 2012. *NW*. London: Hamish Hamilton.

Smith, Zadie. 2018. "Fences: A Brexit Diary." In *Feel Free: Essays*, edited by Zadie Smith, 20–34. London: Hamish Hamilton.

Smith, Zadie. 2000. *White Teeth*. London: Hamish Hamilton.

Wellings, Ben. 2019. *English Nationalism, Brexit and the Anglosphere: Wider Still and Wider*. Manchester: Manchester University Press.

Whittle, Matthew. 2016. *Post-War British Literature and the "End of Empire"*. London: Palgrave Macmillan.

Brexit literature's present absentees: Triangulating Brexit, anti-Semitism, and the Palestinian crisis

Lindsey Moore

ABSTRACT

This article addresses a blind spot in Brexit literary criticism: Britain's relationship to the Middle East, particularly its historic responsibility for the plight of Palestinians. Although fiction that directly engages both Brexit and the Israeli–Palestinian crisis has not yet appeared, oblique connections can be illuminated. Shared conceptual fields, albeit ones only partially brought into view in contemporary British fiction, emerge from intersecting historical experiences. The article considers a range of recent literary texts, with an emphasis on *A Stranger City* (2019) by British Jewish author Linda Grant and *Fractured Destinies: A Novel* (2018) by British Palestinian author Raba'i al-Madhoun. When viewed in a certain light, Brexit motifs of enclosure, displacement, and propinquity limn the Palestinian crisis as well as the spectre of anti-Semitism, revealing Britain's role in the shaping of the modern Middle East as part of contemporary British literature's political unconscious.

On Friday, January 31, 2020, Britain officially commenced withdrawal from the European Union. That week began, on Monday, January 27, with International Holocaust Remembrance Day, marking 75 years since the liberation of Auschwitz. On Tuesday, January 28, Donald Trump, flanked by Israeli Prime Minister Benjamin Netanyahu but no invited Palestinian representative, formally announced "Peace to Prosperity: A Vision to Improve the Lives of the Palestinian and Israeli People". This article explores unsounded connections in British literature between the events of that week. Critiquing citations of "9/11" as singular event, Jacques Derrida argued that

> [t]o mark a date in history presupposes [...] that "something" comes or happens for the first and last time, "something" that we do not yet really know how to identify, determine, recognize, or analyze but that should remain from here on in unforgettable: an ineffaceable event in the shared archive of a universal calendar, that is, a *supposedly* universal calendar. (quoted in Borradori 2003, 86; original emphasis)

The near simultaneity of "Brexit Day", Holocaust Remembrance Day, and Trump's so-called "Deal of the Century" should remind us of Britain's historic relationship to the Middle East as well as to Europe. Brexit hubris has been identified as a late convulsion of imperial nostalgia (inter alia Eaglestone 2018b, drawing on Gilroy 2004). Anshuman

Mondal (2018) pinpoints that invoking "independence" from Europe allows Britain's colonial history to be "at once evoked and obscured" (83). Its role in the shaping of the modern Middle East has received scant attention in "BrexLit" criticism to date. However, this history, too, is immanent in fictional engagements with the 2016 referendum and its uncivil aftermath.

In order to tease out the historical connection between Britain, Israel, and Palestine specifically, we need to circle back: first to the centenary of the Balfour Declaration, made in 1917, to "view with favour the establishment in Palestine of a national home for the Jewish people" (Thompson 2019, 72). Gardner Thompson (2019) cites a July 5, 2017 commemoration of this Declaration in the House of Lords in which "the prevailing tone [...] was one of unadulterated pride, and prejudice" (xiii–iv). A week earlier, Prime Minister Theresa May had also articulated "pride" in the Declaration in the House of Commons. Thompson reports "many expressions of loyalty to, and praise of, Israel" and "an understated anti-Arab sentiment (though for the most part the Palestinians' experience was ignored)" (xiv).

Thompson strongly qualifies the Balfour legacy. The Declaration was made, following minimal support for Zionism and low prioritization of Palestine as imperial asset, "in a time of crisis, as a loosely worded, no cost, short-term appeal" to international Jewish communities for financial support in a war that Britain might lose (Thompson 2019, 74). "World Jewry" was an arguably anti-Semitic projection and even American Zionism a peripheral cause (73–74). The British endorsement of the Zionist project for Palestine is "a tale not of inevitability or necessity" but rather "of coincidence and contingency", in which "disregard for Arabs" as well as "anti-Semitism and nimbyism" inhered (72, 141). In the face of expertise on the ground and the British experience in Ireland, Whitehall consolidated its Balfour commitments in a 1922 White Paper that would define the terms of the League of Nations Mandate for Palestine. Leaving aside, temporarily, the injustice done to the indigenous population, the Balfour commitment turned out to be an "act of self-defeating mischief" by the government of the day (112, 135).

This assessment of historical documentation pertaining to the Balfour Declaration precludes the possibility of reading the Holocaust, anachronistically, as a motivating British principle. The governmental platitudes of 2017 cited above, like the "British exceptionality" of Brexit "independence" discourse, are hypocritical. In the late 1930s, Britain partially sought to remedy the unworkable principles of Balfour, prompting Zionist resistance to mandatory rule. While European Jews faced an increasingly existential threat, the British in Palestine were turning away Jewish refugees, a further incitement to paramilitary groups (as captured in Channel 4 television drama *The Promise*, directed by Peter Kosminsky [2011]). In 1947, Britain handed responsibility to the United Nations. In the words of Foreign Secretary Ernest Bevin, "the obligations undertaken to the two communities in Palestine" had proven – as they were always going to be – "irreconcilable" (Thompson 2019, 257–258).

The Zionist project in Palestine was colonialist in articulation from the late 1890s and exclusionary and exploitative in practice by the 1920s. Indeed Zionism, despite its distinctive attributes, "emerges as colonialism in one of its more unyielding forms" (Thompson 2019, 290). The ongoing settler colonial situation in Palestine/Israel is now widely acknowledged. For Paul Gilroy (2006), who dedicates *Postcolonial Melancholia* to Rachel Corrie and Thomas Hurndall (activists killed in Gaza in 2003 by the Israeli Defence Force), the global response to Israel in the 21st century reveals "[c]osmopolitan solidarity from below and afar" with

Palestinians (89). This is spurred by several brutal wars on Gaza as well as prominent rights and justice campaigns: the Boycott Divest and Sanction (BDS) movement initiated by Palestinian civil society, but also older initiatives, including Israeli groups such as B'Tselem, Israeli Centre for Human Rights in the Occupied Territories, and Breaking the Silence, veteran Israeli Defense Forces combatants against the occupation. There have also been prominent British Jewish campaigns: notably, Independent Jewish Voices (2007) published "A Time to Speak Out" with signatories such as Mike Leigh and Jacqueline Rose.

Testimonies to Palestinian besiegement, territorial fragmentation, and disenfranchisement continue to emerge despite the chilling effect of the International Holocaust Remembrance Alliance's (IHRA) expansive "Working Definition of Antisemitism" adopted in 2016, which attempts to define what can be said about Israel.[1] Former UK opposition leader Jeremy Corbyn's initial demurral about the IHRA definition and his purported reluctance to tackle anti-Semitism in the Labour Party may have been factors in the 2019 electoral result that ended more than three years of Brexit prevarication.[2] Accusations of Labour anti-Semitism are compromised by several factors: efforts to deflect attention from the Conservative government's anti-immigration policies; amplification by supporters of Israel (Sabbagh 2018)[3]; and, as a leaked internal report of April 2020 suggests, the impeding of its investigation by anti-Corbyn factions within Labour. It seems likely that anti-Semitism was weaponized. Nevertheless, a *perception* of Labour anti-Semitism informed the Brexit conversation (and endures).[4]

Guardian journalist Hadley Freeman says that she wrote *House of Glass* (Freeman 2020a), the biography of her grandmother Sala Glass,

> in the shadow of the Brexit referendum and Donald Trump's election. Neither of these political shifts were about keeping out the Jews, but they were about keeping out immigrants, and the story of the Glasses was one of immigration, from Poland to France, and France to America. Alongside that, antisemitism was on the rise throughout Europe in a way I never thought I'd see in my lifetime, on both the right and the left. (Freeman 2020b, n.p.)

This is a telling entanglement of anti-Semitism with hostility towards immigration. As I show, contemporary British literature also cites the Holocaust as a template for what exclusionary Brexit policies could lead to. However, this carries a double risk: of reducing racism to anti-Semitism and occluding ways in which the Holocaust already prevails over Palestinian history. Teasing out these differences does not mean denying the persistence of anti-Semitism, sometimes under the alibi of Palestinian advocacy.[5]

Let us remember that trenchant critiques of Israeli policy and practice are also expressed by British and other Jews. An editorial in *Jewish Quarterly* in the wake of the 2008–09 Israeli war on Gaza suggests that "Zionism was at one time the unifying force of Anglo Jewry and is now the most divisive" (Alderman 2009, 52), as is reflected in Howard Jacobson's (2010a) *The Finkler Question*. The novel lampoons British Jews, notably Libor Sevcik, with his reverence for "Issrrae", and Sam Finkler, who publicly condemns the "Israyeli" state (putatively pronounced the Arabic way) and leads high-profile group the ASHamed Jews. This debate is refracted via luxuriously philosemitic (so appropriately monikered) Julian Treslove, who euphemistically refers to Jews as Finklers. Jacobson reserves the most excoriating criticism for anti-Zionists and exposes persistent, sometimes violent British anti-Semitism. However, his novel also self-satirizes via moderate convert Tyler (Finkler's wife and Treslove's lover), who is tired of British Jews "endlessly falling out in public" (Jacobson 2010a, 121).

The eponymous difficulty with names, in this novel, implies the persistence of anti-Semitism and also illustrates that, for many, "Israel exists only poetically, in the imaginations of those who cannot adequately describe themselves without it" (Jacobson 2010b, 22). Ruth Gilbert (2013) sees *The Finkler Question* as displacing British Jewish domestic anxieties onto Israel (92), though the risks of being overtly Jewish in Britain itself are also illustrated. Jacobson has described Israel as a figure of speech for "emotions which originate somewhere else entirely" (2010b, 22) – in unresolved tensions in British Jewish identity – articulating a defining extraterritoriality in British Jewish literature (Cheyette 1996). Such outsourcing, however, presupposes a narrow lens. Israel is not a metaphor for several generations of Palestinians whose defining experience is dislocation, not least due to toponymicide.

The Finkler Question portrays a growing crisis of multiculturalism (in which Jews have figured oddly)[6] commonly understood to have contributed to the Brexit crisis. The exclusionary, indeed racist, rhetoric of the Brexit referendum and its aftermath is historically triggering for minority communities that include British Jews. However, British "colonial remains" pertaining to Middle Eastern contexts, notably to Britain's historical relationship to Palestine/Israel, have still only partially been broached in contemporary literature.

Circling a Brexit blindspot: Other others in contemporary British literature

The British–European relationship historically operates in relation to wider geopolitical imperatives that include the need to maintain stability in, if not control over, the Middle East. The longevity of this entanglement is captured in Justin Butcher's (2018) *Walking to Jerusalem: Blisters, Hope and Other Facts on the Ground*, which reconstructs the performative activism of the "Just Walk" Butcher initiated with human rights charity Amos Trust. This involved, "in the year of Brexit" (following the referendum of 2016), "traversing the [European] continent from west to east" (Butcher 2018, 35). The long walk passes through sites that testify to the forging of European identity in relation to Jerusalem in particular, through Crusading, then colonial history. This culminated between the two world wars. Butcher observes whilst in France that, in the aftermath of the 1917 Battle of Arras, the British General in command – Edmund Allenby – was reassigned as leader of the Egyptian Expeditionary Forces (69–71). Allenby would lead the British takeover of Jerusalem later that year.

Introducing *Walking to Jerusalem*, Robert Cohen suggests that the Balfour Centenary was "an anniversary likely to be little remembered by the general public in the UK" but was "hugely significant to Palestinians who date their suffering from this act of British imperial hubris" (quoted in Butcher 2018, xiii). A touchstone of the book is Edward Said's (1999) reference to the Palestinians as "the victims of the victims, the refugees of the refugees" (n.p.). Butcher recasts Balfour as also "precipitat[ing] a century of dispossession, conflict and suffering" (Butcher 2018, 3). The Just Walk is conceived as "penance for Britain's historic responsibility" for the violent establishment of the State of Israel in 1948, as solidarity with Palestinians for whom a right of return has since then been denied, and as a call for equal rights in contemporary Palestine/Israel (3). *Walking to*

Jerusalem underlines Britain's relationship to the modern Middle East, a history echoed more subtly in other literary attempts to grapple with British withdrawal from the European Union, as we will see.

Life-writing genres are amenable to an alignment of literary and political representation due to their authenticating and witnessing strategies. However, as Gilbert points out, life writing is replete with fantasy and affect, reflecting "highly charged associations and disassociations" (2013, 85). Jacobson's *Roots Schmoots: Journeys Among Jews*, for example, distinguishes between Jewish–Arab "family quarrels" and a more complex enmity towards "enemies of my soul": British critics of Israel (1994, 339). Fiction also unfolds on both explicit and less conscious relational ground, exploring and expanding collective structures of feeling and memory. "BrexLit" has thus far tended to track national complexes, including the "untimely traces" of racist and colonial history (Gardiner 2018, 110). We might expect it to project alternative alignments, whether with an idealized version of Europe that ostensibly "translates cosmopolitanism's universal abstracts into pragmatic practices" (Shaw 2018, 16) or on a planetary scale. Kristian Shaw suggests, however, that "the first wave of post-Brexit fiction largely seems to be detailing the specific frailties and parochial trivialities of an insular and diminished small island" (28).

John Lanchester's (2019a) *The Wall* provides a corrective to this insularity, also unmooring readers from relatively familiar dystopian "pleasures". In Part I, a young Defender narrates, in quotidian detail, national service on a Wall that runs the length of the North Sea, brutally dividing British subjects from "the Others". Part II reveals that Defenders are indeed the outer edge of the nation; they are expendable, marginally differentiated from Others enslaved by the state as "Help". Although the Wall turns out to be infiltrated, its (in)operative binary logic predetermines the narrator's fate: in Part III, he is cast out to sea. This novel starts to map precarious life beyond the nation state, dwelling with fragile floating communities that offer hospitality in the most reduced of circumstances. Lanchester says:

> One of the things about the wall in the book is that it is not a metaphor for anything else. [...] We had this period when walls were coming down around the world and now, just as an empirical fact, they are springing up all over the place. (2019b, n.p.)

One fact on the ground is a wall begun in 2000, variously known as the Israeli West Bank barrier, separation fence, security wall, and apartheid wall and described in al-Madhoun's (2018) *Fractured Destinies* as the "nine-meter wall that fed on [Palestinian] land" (103), that will eventually stretch 440 miles. This wall may also inform the electrified fence erected on common land that features in Ali Smith's *Autumn*. That fence encloses "a piece of land that's got nothing on it" (Smith 2017, 55), echoing discourses about *vacuum domiciliation* exported from England to the New World from the late 16th century and evident in Zionist maps which "render Palestinians as absentees on the land where they lived" (Fields 2017, 14–15). Resistant villagers in *Autumn* are described as "bombarding [the] fence with people's histories" (Smith 2017, 255), recalling uses of the West Bank Wall as canvas for written and graphic protest.

Such (non-)citations of the Israeli–Palestinian context are symptomatic. Although *Brexit and Literature: Critical and Cultural Responses* (Eaglestone 2018a) emphasizes a critical humanism cognizant of histories of anti- and postcolonialism, it draws less than one might expect on Edward Said and makes only passing reference to the Middle East. Lyndsey Stonebridge (2018) does cite human rights lawyer Philippe Sands's argument that the path to Brexit began with Iraq in terms of a loss of public trust in the British government (9). Stonebridge connects the Profumo scandal of the early 1960s that forms a sub-narrative of Smith's *Autumn* to the "dodgy dossier" underpinning the allied invasion of 2003 and subsequently debunked by the Chilcot Inquiry. But what of Britain's longer history of bad faith in the Middle East?[7] Ankhi Mukherjee (2018) also approaches relevant ground in her analysis of Rawi Hage's (2008) *Cockroach* as an unassimilable, "underground" alternative to racist representations of dispersed populations exemplified by David Cameron's 2015 reference to "swarm[s]" of (notably Syrian) migrants coming across the Mediterranean (Mukherjee 2018, 76–77). However, further Mediterranean connections could be pursued. Hage's (2006) *De Niro's Game* is also concerned with undocumented migrancy, but underpinning his corpus is the Lebanese war of 1975–90, key ingredients of which were Palestinian militancy and Israeli invasion. Hage frames this as a pathological, dehumanizing, collective regional trauma, as do many writers from the region.

By impressionistically engaging "the greatest refugee crisis since World War II", Mukherjee (2018) risks occluding that the Sykes–Picot Agreement of 1916 – defining modern Syria, Lebanon, Jordan, and Palestine/Israel – set in motion crises we see in those countries today (73). Israeli historian Avi Schlaim (2015) argues that

> [m]uch of the Middle East has been living with a chronic condition for almost a century which I term the post-Ottoman syndrome. Its symptoms are turmoil, instability and a deficit of rights for the peoples of the region. A major cause is the lack of legitimacy of the new political and territorial order that emerged in the wake of the First World War and the collapse of the Ottoman Empire. That state system, in the lands formerly controlled by the Ottomans, was largely the creation of colonial powers and designed to serve their interests. (17)

At the heart of the Sykes–Picot and Balfour legacy is the Palestinian catastrophe (*al-nakbah*) of 1948 which produced approximately 800,000 refugees, descendants of whom still inhabit camps across the region. The contemporary Palestinian diaspora – populations that have been multiply exiled, including from Syria – tallies in the vicinity of five million people. This refugee crisis has not overtly been represented in "BrexLit" or its criticism to date.

Stranger cities: Pockets, portals, and propinquities

In *When I Lived in Modern Times*, Linda Grant (2000) returns to Mandatory Palestine as a landscape onto which British "domestic anxieties and fantasies are projected" (Gilbert 2013, 81). The novel also anticipates "BrexLit" critiques of defensive nationalism, championing a heterogeneous (albeit stratified) community and mobile affinities, and critically reflecting on constructions of individual and national identity. I return to *When I Lived in Modern Times*, but first consider Grant's (2019) *A Stranger City*, set in London during the Brexit transition.

A Stranger City is achronologically organized, formally fractured, and uses multi-perspectival, free indirect narration to represent provisionally intersecting London lives. It highlights the proleptic and analeptic potential of events – history as repetitive and anticipatory – and privileges chance (and failed) encounters as axes of potential intervention into wider processes of inclusion and exclusion. One of its cast of minor characters is a downwardly mobile interior designer, part-Jewish by birth, named Francesca. We are introduced to her on the Tube in July 2015 with her husband Alan, who is observing a man verbally abuse an Irishwoman named Chrissie. Later Chrissie, a nurse, will befriend someone traumatized by the London Bridge attack of June 2017. In February 2016, Chrissie unknowingly walks past a woman, known as DB17, who drowns and is buried anonymously in the opening scene.

Grant (2019) says that "the origins of the novel go back to 1992 when I stood at the grave of an unknown woman who had drowned herself in the Thames" (323) and who became the subject of a documentary that Grant reviewed for *The Times*. *When I Lived in Modern Times* testifies to the author's long-standing interest in anonymous, performative, and other-defined identities. But Grant chooses to update the setting in *A Stranger City*, which clearly alludes – indeed makes explicit reference – to Brexit (Grant 2019, 318). The drowned woman is eventually named as Valentina Popov, a woman born just "the wrong side" of the border between Moldova and Romania: on the Russian, rather than European side (308). Popov was an "illegal" who worked as a cleaner for wealthy Russians "unconcerned about legalities" (308).

A Stranger City is not only about emblematic strangers on the cusp of Brexit; it estranges London. Francesca and Alan move into a house in gentrifying Wall Park, "a forgotten enclave behind the railway line" and "a tiny sequin in the fabric of London" in which Dutch, Cypriot, British Asian, and white Britons live, though this diversity decreases as the Brexit years unfold (Grant 2019, 77, 76). In one episode, Francesca is guided by two elderly neighbours to a crease within this urban fabric (219). They pass through a house that both freezes time and acts as a portal. A back room smells of bacon fat, grocery deliveries comprise "[l]uncheon meat, spam, peas, baked beans, cling peaches, condensed milk" (218), and the front parlour contains old board games and craft items in "biscuits tins bearing the faces of the newly engaged Prince Charles and Lady Di" (219, 220). The old people describe these as "the old ways, how we used to live and what we had to make do with", even as they undercut the promise of generational identification with this version of Englishness. "There were never any Jews here", they demur; "we wouldn't have been tolerated" (220).

When Francesca exits the other side of the house, she finds five streets known as the Island, "a geographical anomaly" in which families over several generations have stabled circus animals – disconcertingly, an elephant resides in a garage – and worked as bin collectors (Grant 2019, 221). This urban oddity, invisible on Google Maps, gives on to a space in which "wetlands lay deep under the deposited rubble from thousands of bombed houses of the Blitz" (225). Looking out on a bleak vista punctuated by football posts, Francesca recalls a childhood trip to another space of exception: a concentration camp in Poland, probably Auschwitz, in which "a formless dun-coloured wilderness under a lowering sky" features "hundreds of brick structures" (226).

The unverifiable cartography of the London locale suggests an uncanny zone haunted by the future as well as the past. Francesca's musings raise possibilities akin to the secret concentration camps that feature in Russell T. Davies's 2019 BBC series *Years and Years*, which accelerates forward from 2019 to 2034. In one of *A Stranger City*'s closing scenes, Pete Dutton – who leads the DB17 investigation – rows up the Thames past prison ships that hold deportees "to be transported [...] back to chemical weapons and nerve gas and aerial bombardment" (Grant 2019, 303). "Nor was it just refugees from war zones", he thinks, "but anyone whose visa had run out or had the wrong paperwork" (303). These are portals at the service of an exclusionary state: "Next, [Pete] thought, they'll pour concrete through the Channel Tunnel" (303–304).

The scene on the Island (a metonymical designation) suggests repeatable historical precedent for a murderous extension of a logic of exclusion. Once again, in the aftermath of the Brexit referendum, "[t]he country was being emptied of its unwanted population" (Grant 2019, 257):

> As [Francesca] stood there, a faint hallucination rose in her mind: grey, misty, vague in form in which she saw the whitened grassland covered in temporary structures, a wooden city of sheds housing people no more solid than wraiths dressed in modern clothes, wheeling luggage, holding children, talking on phones, checking screens [...] She could see they were deportees, hemmed in on all sides awaiting arrangements for their future departure. (227)

Francesca describes the scene as a palimpsest, "a surface such as a canvas bearing the traces of many layers of record, re-inscribed over time" (227). She also compares it to a "hypnagogic image [...] rising up in the border between waking and sleep" (228). Post-memory is at stake: the cross-generational collective trauma of European Jews in the wake of the Holocaust. The spectre of anti-Semitism is one sign that "time was spooling backwards" (210). The point is linked, uncomfortably – given an often hasty conflation of anti-Zionism with anti-Semitism – to conspiracy theories about a prolonged winter, ascribed by some as "an attempt by Israeli scientist to seed clouds with rainfall to irrigate the Negev desert, permanently affecting the climate" (211).

Alan is somewhat cognizant of the philosemitic flipside of his attraction to Francesca's "sultry dark polished looks" (Grant 2019, 68). The racialization of this desire is (knowingly) troubling, on one level, but also hints at this novel's assertion of expansive Jewishness. Francesca's grandparents are exiled *Persian* Jews, a fact that invites us to see beyond the coding of the Island scene above in relation to *European* Jewish history. Her desire for upward mobility is influenced by the general experience of "what it felt like to be the child of an immigrant family whose only purpose was to do better than the previous generation" (28). But we also learn, specifically, that Francesca's grandparents, Younis and Amira, speak Farsi only under the "protective fleece" of night (105). Younis "could smell that life here in England was going through a process of transmutation into something different" although racism is the couple's long-standing experience: upon arrival in Britain 40 years previously, they expected genteel sociability but were greeted, instead, by neighbourly "complain[ts] about the smells of our cooking" (105, 106).

Timing suggests that Younis and Amira migrated due to the 1979 revolution that established the Islamic Republic of Iran. A double unhoming precedes ethnic and religious minority status in the UK: "there was no longer a home for them in Persia and no Persia either, except in the memory of its exiles" (Grant 2019, 107). Grant critiques the convulsive exclusions that define the nation on historical cusps – Iran, Germany, Moldova, and Ireland are cited – including this (British) nation at this (Brexit) juncture. Jews in Iran are "barricaded into their synagogues" just as the lives of Middle Eastern exiles in London are "contracted down" to a "little flat [in] a sheltered housing block" (107). *A Stranger City* qualifies Zadie Smith's (2016) memories of London as a convivial "outward-looking city" (n.p.). Its specification of diverse Jewish experience, however, aligns with Grant's wider exploration of multicultural propinquity and individual self-remaking in migrant settings.

When I Lived in Modern Times follows a first-generation British Jew, Evelyn Sert, who travels from London to Palestine in the final years of the Mandate. Evelyn's facility for shape-shifting is an inherited trait: "What could an immigrant child be, except an impersonator?" (Grant 2000, 27). Palestine in the 1940s is imagined as a place where Jewish identity might cohere but which is, in reality, a society in flux in which Eastern European "ghetto" Jews (Oestjuden), Middle Eastern Jews (Mizrahim), North African Jews (Sephardim), pioneering Jews of the first Aliyah (return), hardy *sabra* of the kibbutzim, "tough Jews" fighting the occupiers, British administrators, and Muslim and Christian Palestinians uneasily coexist (166). Evelyn is compelled by specific circumstances to assume a range of avatars: she enters Palestine as a religious pilgrim, is briefly a Kibbutz worker, passes as a Gentile hairdresser, and is a reluctant spy for the Irgun. In this "raw, strained" society, she identifies most with the British "oppressive power[,] the enemy", due to an internalized, civilizational sense of modernity (106). The British, however, eventually expel her – she may be perceived as less than British but she is certainly not the right kind of (compliant) Jew in the eyes of the mandatory powers.

Grant's novel is attentive to prior affiliations which puncture an artificially created community and to its classed, linguistic, and ethnic hierarchies. *When I Lived in Modern Times* also illustrates that the promise of Balfour did not cancel out British anti-Semitism. Evelyn's militant lover "Johnny" summarizes British antipathy towards Jewish modernity that is widely evident in the novel: "Tel Aviv is just a city with too many Jews making a mess in their precious desert. They don't want anything here but picturesque Arabs" (Grant 2000, 157). This reminds us that the Balfour promise was consolidated despite objections by British representatives in Palestine. The pro-Israeli governmental commemoration of the Balfour centenary cited earlier (Thompson 2019) reflects a post-9/11 paradigm shift in British attitudes towards Arabs conflated with Islam.

Evelyn's naive perspective also exposes, albeit through emphatic representational absence, the growing marginalization of the indigenous population, "invisible men and women, [sinking] into the landscape" (Grant 2000, 46). She returns, more informed, to Israel 50 years later although, with no proof of Jewish identity, she can only get a tourist visa. Perhaps because of this lack of paper evidence, she asserts that Zionism is premised on stories, whereas for "the Arabs of Palestine" – she still stops short of saying Palestinians – history is embedded in the land and, without that, "they're not just DPs [Displaced Persons], they're an abstract idea – a cause. That's not a human being. This is the great wrong we did them" (239). She attempts to return to the Arab neighbourhood of Manshieh in which she hid from the British as a young woman, to discover it was razed to the ground in the 1948 war. Evelyn's investments in Israel are reframed by her more mature critique of its practices of settler colonial power.

Elderly Evelyn also reflects on the merits of "dirty and chaotic" Tel Aviv. In a pointed allusion to Israeli participation in the Lebanese war, she thinks: "Now that we've destroyed Beirut [Tel Aviv] is the only city on this far Mediterranean coast that can really be called the Levant, a mongrel metropolis of aliens among aliens" (Grant 2000, 254). The term "Levantine" originated in the 16th century to describe those who lived on the Mediterranean coast and served as intermediaries between European merchants and

Ottoman subjects. It became associated, in colonial discourse, with racial impurity and threatening borderline identities and in Israel continues negatively to adhere to Arabs and "Oriental" Jews (Hochberg 2007, 46). A divergent tradition, however, to which Evelyn implicitly subscribes, deploys Levantinism as cosmopolitanism, to describe something "not exclusively eastern or western, Christian, Jewish, or Moslem [sic]" but "more like a prism whose various facets are joined by a sharp edge of differences" (Kahanoff 1951, 247). One negative characteristic of "post-Ottoman syndrome" (Schlaim 2015) is the propagation of ethnic, cultural, and religious homogeneity. Critical Levantinism is a conceptual alternative, notably to the "ethno-nationalist" politics of memory that underpins Israel's "logic of partition" (Hochberg 2007, 3, 141).

When I Lived in Modern Times suggests ways of triangulating British, Israeli, and Palestinian history and of leveraging cosmopolitan alternatives to the nation. Robert Young (2012) has suggested that postcolonial critics disinter the "diversity that preceded nation formation", citing the Ottoman Empire as "a long-lasting system of comparative tolerance of diversity and cultural syncretism that was only destroyed by European imperial greed" (33, 34). Young urges attention to the heterogeneity "hidden beneath the surface of modern national states" as "postcolonial remains" (33, 32). In *When I Lived in Modern Times*, Evelyn's alignment with "a mongrel metropolis of aliens among aliens" (Grant 2000, 254) occludes peoples who have lived continuously in the region for millennia. However, Grant's repeated focus on diverse cities composed of pockets, portals, and provisional propinquities implies "a cultural and political stance, operating within and against the current reality of separatist homogeneous nationalism" (Hochberg 2007, 45). Her work, whether set historically or in the Brexit present, champions untidy diversity and reveals the dangers of performative national homogeneity.

Connected histories, re-imagined futures

What remains is to approach the nexus of Brexit, Israel, and Palestine from a British Palestinian angle. Raba'i al-Madhoun's (2018) *Fractured Destinies* was originally published as *Masa'ir: kunshirtu al-hulukust wa-l-nakba* (2015), literally "Destinies: A Concerto of the Holocaust and the Nakba". Although published before the 2016 referendum, its 2018 translation bestows "BrexLit" post hoc resonance. The novel's emphasis on (re)connection and remaining despite the historical fault line of the Holocaust/Nakba accrues meaning when read in awareness of British colonial intervention in the Middle East *and* in the context of its divisive departure from Europe.

The four "movements" of *Fractured Destinies* track, non-chronologically, a British Palestinian couple's trip to Israel in 2012. Primary narrator Walid Dahman, ghosted by the author who arrives simultaneously at Tel Aviv airport,[8] returns with his wife Julie to fulfil her mother's wishes that her ashes be scattered in Acre, erstwhile Palestine. Walid is described as "a British man [...] who had sown Palestine in the cells of his body and made them into pools of mint" (al-Madhoun 2018, 14). His Muslim family fled Jaffa for Gaza in 1948 and are now scattered across the world. Julie is a British Palestinian of mixed Christian heritage: her mother Ivana Arkadian, a Palestinian Armenian, met her father John Littlehouse, a British medical officer, in Mandatory Palestine. Ivana was expelled by her own community in 1948 for marrying "a hated British colonizer" and her parents fled two months later: they die in camps in Lebanon during the 1975–90 war (16).

One possible model for the novel, given its original title and polyphonic style, is Joaquín Rodrigo's "Concierto de Aranjuez", intended to transport the listener to another time and place (and sampled by both Lebanese icon Fairuz and Israeli star Rita). Before they leave, Walid and Julie hear a group playing this concerto as they walk along London's South Bank, amidst "comings and goings of every kind, with men and women of different ages and nationalities sharing their happinesses and their griefs on the river's wide banks" (al-Madhoun 2018, 27). The fact that pre-Brexit London is sketched as a hospitable, multi-ethnic alternative to Israel provokes unanticipated pathos in readers invested in British cosmopolitanism.

This novel structurally entwines histories of bicultural heritage and exile. It also explores the implications of "remaining" and complicates the notion of return. Ivana's dying wishes are "to reserve myself a place in the [Resurrection Day queue] before the heavens are filled with settlers who have forced the Palestinians out in this world and want to appropriate their places in the next" (23). Her bespoke urn is inscribed "She died here … She died there", equating Palestinian life with terminal displacement.[9] Walid's cousin Jnin – a writer, as will become significant – is a Palestinian born in Ramla (now Israel) who refuses to leave Jaffa. Her husband Basim, a Palestinian from Bethlehem (in the West Bank), has no employment or social security rights in Israel – their story reveals the fatuity of the category "Israeli Arab" as well as the divide between "1948ers" (Israeli-resident Palestinians) and Palestinians in the Occupied Territories.

The category of the "present absentee", peculiar to Israeli law, refers to internally displaced peoples (IDPs) and their descendants who still live within Israel/Palestine; it relates to property acquisition laws that made the existence of an Israeli state viable (see Erekat 2019, chap. 1). Walid's family home is inhabited by the descendants of Yemini Jews who occupied it in the 1950s. Julie attempts to return Ivana's ashes to a house requisitioned for a Jewish family, originally Holocaust refugees. As local guide Fatima puts it: "Your mother died in London a stranger from Acre? Well, just look at us here, strangers and refugees in our own country" (al-Madhoun 2018, 8). Partial returns show that national identity, citizenship, and residency are precariously articulated. These categories are rigidly separated for Basim who defines himself as "a virtual citizen", even "absent absentee" (91). They have also come apart for vulnerable British residents: recall the "unknown woman" of *A Stranger City* (Grant 2019, 323) and the Windrush scandal that broke in 2018.

Al-Madhoun's novel is centrally concerned with the politics of historiography that define insiders and outsiders. When Walid visits Yad Vashem, the World Holocaust Remembrance Centre outside Jerusalem, his response to the Hall of Names is affective and haunting:

> I studied the names, and examined the features of the victims – who continued to scrutinize me as I looked at their faces – and tried to gauge their feelings at the moment the pictures had been taken. Moments that would no longer be there for people who had been reduced to skeletons or whose corpses had disappeared entirely. I lifted my head to follow the names upward until my gaze reached the hall's circular extremity, open to the sky. (al-Madhoun 2018, 230)

The implications of the scene then change:

> I felt like the faces of thousands of Palestinians – some of whom I knew, but most of whom I did not – gazed down on me. They were pushing and shoving, as if they wanted to come down into the halls of the museum, spread through them, and take their places as victims. (230)

Walid "cried for those who were crowded together in the sky, looking for a place to assemble their names" (231). He takes a cable car to the (imagined) Zikhron ha-Filastinim or Museum of Palestinian Memories, named in Hebrew but flying the Palestinian national flag (234). This impossible *lieu de mémoire* is the centrepiece of an alternate reality in which the 1993 Oslo Accords created a "homeland for everyone" (234). It is built on the site of Deir Yassin, site of a 1948 massacre disavowed by Israelis for whom everything before Independence is "a void" (235). At Deir Yassin today, one really sees only "forests and a distant settlement" (239).

Al-Madhoun's novel is a testament to this occluded tragedy, refracted through a draft novel that Walid is reading: Jnin's story of her uncle The Remainer – a freighted term in the post-Brexit reading context. Walid recalls that The Remainer, his father, would travel every Friday to the Deir Yassin ruins "until he had written the names of more than a hundred and sixty victims, each name on a piece of stone, which still exist in the form of a small pyramid near the cypress tree" (al-Madhoun 2018, 239). The use of *mise-en-abyme* suggests literature's capacity both to retain history and to transcend it because Jnin's novel is given two endings. In her manuscript *Filastini Tays* ("A Stubborn Palestinian"), The Remainer carries placards of peace in Arabic and Hebrew to a Jaffa square, sings the Internationale, and is mortally wounded by the security forces. However, in the final scene of *Fractured Destinies*, Walid directly addresses the reader:

> [In *Filastini Tays*] Mahmoud Dahman died, the man who was my father and who played his own part in this novel [*Fractured Destinies*,] the stubbornest Palestinian in the book. [...] But The Remainer didn't actually die. I rebelled against my closing scene of the novel you have read, a probable scene of death, in the light of the rise to power of the Israeli right. (250)

Al-Madhoun's emphasis on enlaced histories rejects an ethno-nationalist version of the state, exemplified by the "Basic Law", adopted in 2018, that defines Israel as the nation state of the Jewish people. The novel's ethical humanism similarly strikes a chord, particularly in translation, with the Brexit dispensation.

Literature "is able to articulate the powerful effects of [the] past whilst also drawing on the complexities of the present" because it can "stand at a slight distance from polemic" and transmit "subtle emotional complexities" (Gilbert 2013, 3, 88). While British Jewish history "produces a rich generative tension" (10), *Fractured Destinies* invites capacious Palestinian identifications. This article calls for a more consistent triangulation between British, Jewish, and Palestinian reckonings with history. As I finish writing it, BBC Radio 4 is airing a serialized version of Colum McCann's (2020) *Apeirogon*. I would not advocate a "balanced" view of a crisis in Palestine/Israel that is the product of both settler colonialism and imperialism. However, an apeirogon – a shape with an infinite number of sides – is an apt figure for the ways in which creative literature performatively complicates ways in which we "mark a date in history" (Derrida in Borradori 2003, 86). Britain's exit from Europe should be considered in tandem with the events almost simultaneously commemorated in January 2020.

Notes

1. The IHRA definition begins: "Manifestations might include the targeting of the state of Israel, conceived as a Jewish collectivity. However, criticism of Israel similar to that levelled

against any other country cannot be regarded as antisemitic" (https://www.holocaustremembrance.com/resources/working-definitions-charters/working-definition-antisemitism?focus=antisemitismandholocaustdenial).

2. This is supported by a poll conducted by Conservative Lord Ashcroft in early 2020 but has not definitively been proven.
3. Attempts to reduce legitimate criticism of Israel to anti-Semitism have historical precedence: Zionist ideologue Eyal Weizmann commented in 1921 that "Zionist ideals may have upset some Arabs and some British anti-Semites", in Thompson's view "casually conflating [...] anti-Zionism and anti-Semitism [in] a shameless rhetorical tactic that was to take root" (2019, 123).
4. Corbyn was criticized in the mainstream press as well as prominent Jewish newspapers: Sabbagh (2018) cites examples from *The Times of Israel*, *The Guardian*, *The New Statesman*, and *The Independent*.
5. British charity Community Security Trust (CST) cites 1805 anti-Semitic incidents in 2019, including a 25 percent rise in violent assaults. Five hundred and five incidents referred to Israel, the Middle East, or Zionism, of which "63 directly compared or equated Israel with the Nazis" (Sherwood 2020, n.p.).
6. Due to lack of clarity about whether Jewishness is defined by religion, ethnicity, or cultural identity, and a tendency towards assimilation, the British Jewish community has "failed to get a place at the table of multiculturalism" despite "lessons its diasporas story might have for a multicultural nation" (Kuhn-Harris and Gidley 2010, 7).
7. Philippe Sands spoke about the need to leverage human rights law against Israel at the 2019 Edward Said London Lecture, "Is Justice Still Possible? Palestine, International Law, and Public Discourse" (Sands, Akram, and Jabareen 2019).
8. Walid Dahman shares biographical characteristics with al-Madhoun and is also the protagonist of his *The Lady from Tel Aviv* (Al-Madhoun [2009] 2013).
9. Although uncited, the quotation echoes Palestinian poet Mourid Barghouti's ([2009] 2011) memoir *I Was Born There, I Was Born Here* (*Walidtu hunak, walidtu huna*).

Disclosure statement

No potential conflict of interest was reported by the author.

References

Alderman, Geoffrey. 2009. "Debating the Debate." *Jewish Quarterly* 213: 50–54.
Al-Madhoun, Raba'i. 2018. *Fractured Destinies: A Novel [Masa'ir: Kunshirtu Al-hulukust Wa-l-nakba]*. Translated by Paul Starkey. Cairo: Hoopoe.

Al-Madhoun, Raba'i. [2009] 2013. *The Lady from Tel Aviv [Al-sayyida Min Tal Abib]*. Translated by Eliott Colla. London: Telegram.

Barghouti, Mourid. [2009] 2011. *I Was Born There, I Was Born Here [Walidtu Hunak, Walidtu Huna]*. Translated by Humphrey Davies. Bloomsbury: London.

Borradori, Giovanni. 2003. *Philosophy in a Time of Terror: Dialogues with Jürgen Habermas and Jacques Derrida*. Chicago: University of Chicago Press.

Butcher, Justin. 2018. *Walking to Jerusalem: Blisters, Hope and Other Facts on the Ground*. London: Hachette.

Cheyette, Brian. 1996. "'Englishness and Extraterritoriality: British-Jewish Writing and Diaspora Culture." *Literary Strategies in Contemporary Jewry* 12: 21–39.

Eaglestone, Robert, ed. 2018a. *Brexit and Literature: Critical and Cultural Responses*. Abingdon: Routledge.

Eaglestone, Robert. 2018b. "Cruel Nostalgia and the Memory of the Second World War." In *Brexit and Literature: Critical and Cultural Responses*, edited by Robert Eaglestone, 92–104. Abingdon: Routledge.

Erekat, Noura. 2019. *Justice for Some: Law and the Question of Palestine*. Stanford, CA: Stanford University Press.

Fields, Gary. 2017. *Enclosure: Palestinian Landscapes in a Historical Mirror*. Oakland, CA: University of California Press.

Freeman, Hadley. 2020a. *House of Glass: The Story and Secrets of a Twentieth-century Jewish Family*. London: 4th Estate.

Freeman, Hadley. 2020b. "I Could Never Understand My Grandmother's Sadness - Until I Heard Her Tragic Story." *The Guardian*, February 22.

Gardiner, Michael. 2018. "Brexit and the Aesthetics of Anachronism." In *Brexit and Literature: Critical and Cultural Responses*, edited by Robert Eaglestone, 105–117. Abingdon: Routledge.

Gilbert, Ruth. 2013. *Writing Jewish: Contemporary British-Jewish Literature*. New York: Palgrave Macmillan.

Gilroy, Paul. 2006. *Postcolonial Melancholia*. New York: Columbia University Press.

Grant, Linda. 2000. *When I Lived in Modern Times*. London: Granta.

Grant, Linda. 2019. *A Stranger City*. London: Virago.

Hage, Rawi. 2006. *De Niro's Game*. London: Penguin.

Hage, Rawi. 2008. *Cockroach*. London: Penguin.

Hochberg, Gil. 2007. *In Spite of Partition: Jews, Arabs, and the Limits of the Separatist Imagination*. Princeton, NJ: Princeton University Press.

Jacobson, Howard. 1994. *Roots Schmoots: Journeys Among Jews*. New York: Overlook Press.

Jacobson, Howard. 2010a. *The Finkler Question*. London: Bloomsbury.

Jacobson, Howard. 2010b. "Anti-Zionism – Facts (And Fictions)." *Jewish Chronicle* 30: 22.

Kahanoff, Jacqueline. 1951. *Jacob's Ladder*. London: Harvill Press.

Kosminsky, Peter, dir. 2011. *The Promise*. London: Channel 4.

Kuhn-Harris, Keith, and Ben Gidley. 2010. *Turbulent Times: The British Jewish Community Today*. London: Continuum.

Lanchester, John. 2019a. *The Wall*. London: Faber.

Lanchester, John. 2019b. "Interview: John Lanchester [With Lisa Allardice]." *The Guardian*, January 11.

McCann, Colum. 2020. *Apeirogon: A Novel*. London: Penguin.

Mondal, Anshuman A. 2018. "Scratching the Post-Imperial Itch." In *Brexit and Literature: Critical and Cultural Responses*, edited by Robert Eaglestone, 82–91. Abingdon: Routledge.

Mukherjee, Ankhi. 2018. "Migrant Britain." In *Brexit and Literature: Critical and Cultural Responses*, edited by Robert Eaglestone, 73–81. Abingdon: Routledge.

Sabbagh, Karl. 2018. *The Antisemitism Wars*. Oxford: Skyscraper.

Said, Edward. 1999. "The One-State Solution." *The New York Times Magazine*, January 10.

Sands, Philippe, Susan M. Akram, and Hassan Jabareen. 2019. "Is Justice Still Possible? Palestine, International Law, and Public Discourse." The Edward Said London Lecture. The Royal Geographical Society, 2 May.
Schlaim, Avi. 2015. "The Post-Ottoman Syndrome." In *Shifting Sands: The Unravelling of the Old Order in the Middle East*, edited by Raja Shehadeh and Penny Johnson, 17–32. London: Profile.
Shaw, Kristian. 2018. "Brexlit." In *Brexit and Literature: Critical and Cultural Responses*, edited by Robert Eaglestone, 15–30. Abingdon: Routledge.
Sherwood, Harriet. 2020. "Antisemitic Incidents Hit New High in 2019, according to Study." *The Guardian*, February 6.
Smith, Ali. 2017. *Autumn*. London: Penguin.
Smith, Zadie. 2016. "Fences: A Brexit Diary." *The New York Review of Books*, August 18.
Stonebridge, Lyndsey. 2018. "The Banality of Brexit." In *Brexit and Literature: Critical and Cultural Responses*, edited by Robert Eaglestone, 7–14. Abingdon: Routledge.
Thompson, Gardner. 2019. *Legacy of Empire: Britain, Zionism and the Creation of Israel*. London: Saqi.
Voices, Independent Jewish. 2007. "A Time to Speak Out." *The Guardian*, February 5.
Young, Robert J. C. 2012. "Postcolonial Remains." *New Literary History* 43 (1): 19–42. doi:10.1353/nlh.2012.0009.

"We are all migrants through time": History and geography in Mohsin Hamid's *Exit West*

Shazia Sadaf

ABSTRACT

Exit West reflects a progressive shift in Pakistani anglophone literature from the familiar framework of postcolonial writing back to writing *beyond* the 9/11 era. Set in a post-Brexit–Trump world, this speculative fiction seeks to democratize the future by re-imagining the relationship between history and geography, aligned with the dimensions of time and space. In Hamid's view, the present wish of humanity to go back towards past greatness poses a grave danger to the imagining of a progressive future. His novel therefore presents a radical future of global migration imagined through the magical portals that allow instant access to destinations around the world, challenging border divisions. This article argues that this turn towards speculative post-colonial fiction opens literary doors into cognitive spaces of contestation as well as meaningful dialogues in a *post*-post-9/11 world of global insecurity and anti-immigration sentiments that have contributed to far reaching events like Brexit.

> To call the current Economic Union "Europe" is [...] to claim a name for a place whose boundaries will shift in the future, as other countries join, or even leave, its membership. But more interesting than the delimitation of its boundaries are the attempts to define the character of this place. All of the attempts depend on a reading of both history and geography: what is at issue here is space-time. And each attempt at identity-definition depends on a particular reading of that history. (Massey 1995, 189)

Brexit is paradoxically aligned with the idea of progress because it looks to the future by seeking a return to a past identity. In the literary response to this event, aptly called BrexLit, two openings for the novel are identified: a "gleeful, frenzied dystopianism", or an opportunity for "speculative, and slightly hysterical, world-building" (Day 2017, n.p.). Both of these choices reflect an urgent attempt to make sense of the Brexit event by presenting pessimistic or optimistic viewpoints on the future of globalization. Mohsin Hamid's (2017) *Exit West* is a deliberately ambivalent reflection of both responses. Additionally, from its postcolonial positionality, the novel adds complex layers of race, religion, immigration, and national identity to this subgenre.

However, *Exit West* is more than just an echo of postcolonial resistance in BrexLit. The novel represents the transactional relationship between postcolonialism and globalization that are both powerful movements of social change. Although generally regarded as contradictory, according to Simon During (2000),

> in practice, colonialism, postcolonialism and globalism are reductive, often internally divided, names for forces which work, and long have worked, in transaction with one another. More importantly, contemporary world unification is simultaneously reconfiguring the past in its own image and renewing colonial struggles which keep old pasts alive. (394)

Like other contemporary Pakistani anglophone fiction writers in the post-9/11 period, Hamid's early writings hover between a traditionally classed retaliatory postcolonial stance and a more progressive reconciliatory postcolonial position (Sadaf 2018, 115–117). In *Exit West*, Hamid's postcolonial ambivalence is tempered by globalization theory based in time-space distanciation/compression (Harvey 1990; Massey 1994). Space-time compression is any alteration in the way we understand the relationship between time and space, caused by faster means of transport, speed of electronic transmission, and Internet communication that is changing the pace of the world. The most significant effect of globalization is that "the world is being reconstituted *as a single social space*" (Brennan 2004, 123; emphasis in original), conditioned by the instant availability of images and information through similar commodities such as cellular phones and computers, and, as a result, "social theory itself has undergone a spatio-temporal reformulation in which earlier modes of analysis are no longer tenable" (124).

In response to this, although Hamid's protagonists move in actual geographical locations, their time-sped journey through magical doors becomes a symbol of the redundancy of traditionally understood migrations. As everyone becomes a "migrant through time" (Hamid 2017, 209), no one is really a migrant, and geographical fragmentation means no one is really "native" to a place. Rather, abstract spaces created through social structures replace what would otherwise be concrete places with protectable physical borders. Within these spaces the history of colonization can be simultaneously dismantled and continuously redefined. In other words, Hamid is emphasizing in his novel the importance of a new collaborative space where postcolonial enquiry can move beyond the restrictive processes of historicization and expand into time-space detachment that globalization theory offers. As During puts it:

> the distinction between postcolonialism and globalism is finally a distinction between a theory of de-historicization (postcolonialism as the loss of progressive, teleological time as a master-narrative and the recovery of 'non-modern' relations to the past and future) on the one side, and, on the other, a theory of de-territorialization (globalism as the retreat of geographical determination and the gradual transmutation of objects, styles, work into exchangeable and replicable resources within a fragmented but unified world-system in which new cultural-economic routes, zones or regions proliferate). (2000, 389)

According to theorists like During, in order for postcolonial writing to maintain relevance vis-à-vis the inevitable reality of globalism, a more constructive realignment between postcolonial and globalization theories is required. Hamid is of the opinion that recent times have seen a failure of imagination and that around the world people are facing difficulties in "imagining a future" (Brown 2017, n.p.). This, he believes, has happened because everywhere there seems to be a call for going back towards past greatness, going to the pre-European Union (EU) era in Britain, making America the great country of its past again, and for the Islamic world to go back to the time of the Caliphates. Hamid believes that the appeal of past glory, based on only one version of history, presents a real danger in today's world because it bars us from "imagining something where we can go to that's different and progressive", and it is in part the responsibility of a novelist to encourage the imagining of those futures (Brown 2017, n.p.). In this sense, Hamid's novel seeks "to radically reimagine the future" (Milo 2017, n.p.), in an effort to push back against the allure of constructed histories for the present global consciousness.

One means of addressing the threat of the Brexit–Trump era in the postcolonial literary domain is to gain control over the crafting of humanity's collective future. Young Pakistani authors are taking their cue from Indian science fiction writers, like Anil Menon who claims that new South Asian speculative fiction has "as much a shot at manufacturing the future as do the Americans" and has thus democratized the imagining of a future (Basu 2016, n.p.). Usman Malik (2015), an award-winning young science fiction writer from Pakistan, even suggests that science fiction "*has the potential to alleviate or fix many of Pakistan's problems*" because Pakistan has become "the perfect dystopian setting", and perhaps speculative "fiction is one way to regain hope, mutual tolerance and empathy" (n.p.; emphasis in original). For Hamid, the value of Pakistani literature lies in its potential to tackle global divisions as well as local ones. In an interview conducted in Waterstones, Hamid stresses that, with its violent history of partitions, "Pakistan has lessons for the rest of the world, and this novel has some of those lessons" (Hamid 2018a, n.p.), one of which is in curbing the dangers of a similar "partition impulse in Britain" with its tendency towards purity and segregation. From Pakistan's history can be learnt that

> pessimism is a deeply conservative and reactionary position. It tends to lead towards deference, towards the strong and powerful, towards powerlessness and a kind of surrender [...] Putting forth an optimistic vision like [*Exit West*] makes that vision, in some small way, more likely to come true. (Hamid 2018b, n.p.)

In other words, the power of imagination can possibly change the larger dystopian reality of our present time.

Although it may be true that the ability of a writer to imagine Utopia disappeared in the 20th century in the face of war, genocide, and totalitarianism, Edward James (2003) is of the opinion that Utopia has not died but has re-emerged in a mutated form in the science-fiction genre. The criticism that caused utopian visions to perish in the 20th century was based on the argument that

> in reality many such utopias would turn out to be 'dystopias', that is, oppressive societies [...] because of the tyranny of the "perfect" system over the will of the individual [or] the difficulty of stopping individuals or elites from imposing authority [...] over minorities. (James 2003, 220)

However, James contends that today's science fiction Utopia is antithetic to the classic utopian ideal of Thomas More in that it shows "a better world" rather than "a perfect world" (222). Science fiction writers, he thinks, object to the earlier idea of perfection because it shows a "largely static society" without any conflict, where there is "a denial of adventure, of risk-taking, of the expanding of spatial or technological horizons", which is why they reject it "in favour of continued struggle and progress" (222). Finding hope in continued struggle is a topic that resonates more with modern readers' reality.

Although not classed among mainstream science fiction writers, several established Pakistani authors are incorporating speculative elements in their fiction to cultivate such hope through struggles against widespread discord. Like Hamid, Nadeem Aslam's (2017) recent novel *The Golden Legend* is also set in a fictional place called Zamana in a dystopian future, although it is a harsh and dangerous one where Islamic extremists have taken control, violent mobs lawlessly attack the weak, and US military drones fly overhead targeting civilians below. Despite its dark and cruel setting, the story still projects a future, one that is ultimately transformed by the resilience and cooperation of a group of people who believe in change.

The future presented in Hamid's *Exit West* offers a more fantastical means of escape from turmoil. It tells the story of Saeed and Nadia, who are citizens of an unknown country (yet quite identifiable as Pakistan) which is being taken over by unspecified militants (yet recognizable as the Taliban). In their fictional war-stricken city, mysterious black doors appear that allow instant access into previously visa-bound locations without having to undertake illegal journeys across dangerous oceans or barbed borders. The journey-less destinations are only accessible through Narnia-inspired wormholes across time and space. The novel revolves around the experiences of the two escapees as they migrate from one location to the next in a rapidly transforming world. Because his focus is more on migrant–native contact than on the journey of his characters, Hamid explains that the doors in the novel not only provide him with a way to avoid the journey, but are also "emotionally true to our current technological reality" and therefore almost believable (Inskeep 2017, n.p.). The strong presence of technology in the novel, from the frequent mobile phone communication between the main characters to satellites and sub-oceanic fibre-optic cables, follows the trend of the "science fictioneers" in fashioning a better world by offering "alternate possibilities" through technological rather than political revolutions (James 2003, 222). For Hamid, "technology works a bit like magic [in that it] is obliterating geographic distance. And so, the doors in a way give life to that" (quoted in Brown 2018, n.p). Hamid's comment clearly echoes the optimism of globalization theory which, as During explains, is based in "the effects of geosynchronous communication technologies and massified transcontinental mobility, to the formation of collectivities (cultures, audiences, market niches, coalitions, etc.) bound together by neither history nor geography" (2000, 389).

It is not surprising that *Exit West*'s worldscape disrupts the relationship between two established markers of national identity – history and geography – that align with the dimensions of time and space. Of these, the temporal dimension reflects a continuity with the past, and the spatial dimension represents the importance of physical locality. It has been established that these two elements are of key interest in both postcolonial studies and globalization theory. At the very start of *Exit West*, readers are reminded that, according to historians, "[g]eography is destiny" (Hamid 2017, 9), and that holds true in the case of the postcolonial struggle for de-mapping the colonies from the political boundaries of empire, which was also a fight for cultural preservation. In *Culture and Imperialism*, Edward Said (1994) asserts that the "slow and often bitterly disputed recovery of geographical territory which is at the heart of decolonisation is preceded – as empire had been – by the charting of cultural territory" (209). Even today's deterritorialized, technological world touting globalization as progress is still stymied in many ways by the multivocal history of colonization.

Prominent social scientist and geographer Doreen Massey (1995) points out that the identity of places is highly influenced by the dominant versions of history associated with them, and how those histories are told. Massey believes that power structures controlling the way history is to be interpreted must be challenged because

> debates over how to think the relationship between past, present and future can help us to reinvigorate the way in which we conceptualise geographical places [... and] to think of them as temporal and not just spatial: as set in time as well as space. (186)

The superiority of western culture that formed the basis for imperialist expansion across the globe is also the reason for the enclosure of national borders against foreign contamination in a Brexitian world. In present times, when colonizers of the past are fearful of being reverse colonized by the "Other" and wish to protect their identity by controlling geographical boundaries, Massey's query is a pertinent one: "Is it not possible for a sense of place to be progressive; not self-enclosing and defensive, but outward-looking? A sense of place which is adequate to this era of time-space compression?" (1994, 147). At the very least, the literary imagination can suggest such possibilities. Without downplaying the importance of the postcolonial struggle – indeed, there are deliberate reminders of the sociopolitical legacies of colonization in the novel – *Exit West* ends with an optimistic destination called "Marin" for its protagonists; this is a place of the future with a "radical" history, defined by neither a "simple temporal continuity [n]or only spatial simultaneity with no sense of historical depth", but as that "conjunction of many histories and many spaces" that Massey describes (1995, 191). Marin is, quite obviously, a future new-world vision of Marin County in the San Francisco Bay Area which at present, according to the current United States Census Bureau (2019), has a predominant 85.3% white population.

While the word "*Exit*" in Hamid's title is clearly a direct nod to the exit of Britain from the European Union, "*Exit West*" appears to point to a unidirectional movement through the doors from poor countries to the affluent west. The characters observe

> that the doors out, which is to say the doors to richer destinations, were heavily guarded, but the doors in, the doors from poorer places, were mostly left unsecured, perhaps in the hope that people would go back to where they came from. (Hamid 2017, 101)

Even a fictional failure in securing physical borders, and the possibility of timeless travel within this worldscape, invokes the cultural fears of the Brexit world. There is a general understanding that Brexit was the result of a cultural argument, and Benedict Anderson's concept of "imagined communities" tells us that culture plays a pivotal role in the formation of a national identity (Eaglestone 2018, 1). Where a culture is threatened by external influences, the defence of a national identity is underlined by suspicion. A good example of this can be seen in one of the largest ever studies on public belief in conspiracy theories that was carried out by Cambridge University's "Conspiracy & Democracy Project" in collaboration with YouGov, which shows that a significant sample number are suspicious that their government is not revealing the truth about immigration, and that Brexit and Trump voters are more likely to believe in a range of theories including a fear that "Muslim immigration to this country is part of a bigger plan to make Muslims a majority" (Rogers de Waal 2018). The British association Tell MAMA (Measuring Anti-Muslim Attacks) also suggests that Brexit might "be connected with a specific understanding of British identity that excludes Muslim minorities as 'other' to UK culture" (Taylor 2019, n.p.).

Understandably, *Exit West* is interspersed with symbols of Islamophobia and suspicion such as Nadia's "black robe" (burqa) and Saeed's beard that represent Islam. What is more interesting is the way in which Hamid reconstructs these symbols. Nadia wears jeans under her "conservative and all-concealing black robe", does not pray, and says the burqa is a practical choice "so men don't fuck with [her]" (Hamid 2017, 15). The robe also becomes a comic disguise for Saeed who pulls the hood of the burqa "furtively" over his head while entering her apartment to have sex, looking like a "stage play robber" given away easily by his "mincing gait" (25). Saeed's incongruous disguise downplays the paranoia around reports of men carrying out terrorist attacks disguised in a burqa, one of the security risks cited by the UK Independence Party (UKIP) leader Paul Nuttall's call for a burqa ban in 2017 (Williams 2017, n.p.). Similarly, Saeed grows out his otherwise fashionable chin stubble to show the militants in the unnamed Pakistan that "he was bearded in accordance with the rules on beards" (Hamid 2017, 83). However, after crossing into London through one of the mysterious doors, he finds the "nativist extremists" who are forming legions to "reclaim Britain for Britain" (132) to be no different from the militants back home. Saeed lets himself be increasingly influenced by another bearded refugee from his own country who advocates

> a banding together of migrants along religious principles, cutting across divisions of race or language or nation, for what did those divisions matter now in a world full of doors, the only divisions that mattered were now between those who sought the right of passage and those who would deny them passage. (152)

The bearded refugee's comment about control over passage is a good example of the "power geometry" (Massey 1994, 149) in space-time compression theory. This is apparent in the resistance of the British nativists whose boundaries are invaded by the appearance of these doors, clearly an unwelcome circumstance for them. In its traditional sense, the degree of mobility has always been influenced by power and capital, which is why the west has opened doors into the world easily, without much fear that the doors could also provide a two-way access. The connection between power and the flow of movement is manifested in the history of colonization itself and of the predominant western control of trade and communication routes sustained for centuries. Although globalization appears to have removed the limitations to free movement, structures of power are still maintained by differentials that control who benefits from the movement. According to Massey,

> [d]ifferent social groups, and different individuals, are placed in very distinct ways in relation to [mobility] flows and interconnections. This point concerns not merely the issue of who moves and who doesn't [...] it is also about power in relation to the flows and the movement. Different social groups have distinct relationships to this anyway differentiated mobility: some people are more in charge of it than others; some initiate flows and movement, others don't; some are more on the receiving-end of it than others; some are effectively imprisoned by it. (1994, 149)

The most important thing about *Exit West* is that the power geometry of time and space has been dislodged. In this fictional future, the doors eliminate any discrimination between those who have access and those who do not. Indeed, some scenes in the novel show that migrants arriving through the doors into rich cities are clearly all non-white: a man with "dark skin and dark, woolly hair" (Hamid 2017, 6) and "two Filipina girls, in their late teens" (27) emerge from black doors into Sydney and Tokyo. With the erasure of this disparity between those who possess or lack the means to move, anyone can pass through the doors, and the doors can appear in any place, even in poor and previously exploited countries. Therefore, the novel is imagining a future in which entrances into both spaces and places are not the privilege of only the powerful. *Exit West* might also, in this sense, stand for the exit of the west from its hegemonic position in the power equation of a time-space compressed world.

The word "door" occurs more than 80 times in a 250-page novel, averaging once in fewer than three pages, and clustering in a maximum of nine times on one page (Hamid 2017, 70). Through the symbol of a "door", Hamid alters the connection between time and space, history and geography. Stepping through the first magic door, we are told, Nadia was "struck by its darkness, its opacity, the way that it did not reveal what was on the other side, and also did not reflect what was on this side, and so [it] felt equally like a beginning and an end" (98). Seeing the doors as both beginnings and endings supports a circular rather than single view of history. Beginnings and endings are also a metaphor for the cycle of birth and death. When the travellers pass through these portals, they emerge from the other side "trembling" and "spent" (98), struggling to draw breath, "like newborn foal[s]" (7). Nadia and Saeed's metaphoric twin birth through the door changes their identity and, as a result, their relationship. Having drawn comfort from each other's closeness in the past and finding solace in their similarity based on the geography of their initial nascence, they slowly drift apart in time, and form their own new lives, as their love changes to something like a fondness between siblings. The agent who facilitates their passage speaks softly to Saeed and Nadia as he instructs them about the doors, resembling a whispering "poet or a psychopath" (84). In either case, he is a "seer" of the future; through power of the imagination in the case of the former, and because of a distortion of accepted reality in the latter case. It is not too far-fetched to think that Hamid sees himself as the much-needed agent who opens the doors for readers into a realm of untapped realities through his novels.

The doors also distort national identities, as actual borders become almost redundant dividing markers. The crossing has an uncanny similarity to Lewis Carroll's character Alice's passage into Wonderland. The magical, almost slippery access across geographical space blurs cartographic boundaries, and, as the narrator observes, "without borders nations appeared to be becoming somewhat illusory, and people were questioning what role they had to play" (Hamid 2017, 155). Within the fictional reality of the novel, there are different reactions to the discovery that these doors exist. While this situation is "being discussed as a major global crisis" by world leaders (83), and is bitterly opposed by nativists, it is not a wholly devastating development. There is hope in the presence of a few visionaries who demonstrate "migrant compassion" and are wearing badges of "a black door within a red heart" (105), in support of the refugees. Although the doors bring hostilities out into the open that were in the past kept in check because of political correctness, the feelings are eventually overcome, ending first in resignation, then acceptance, healing, and the possibility of a lasting change. After all, when "everyone was foreign, [...] in a sense, no one was" (100). Also, because regarding the futility of border control, authorities finally realize that "the sheer number of places where there were now doors had made it useless to fight in any case" and that "the doors could not be closed, and new doors would continue to open" (164).

Having crossed through the door Saeed finds himself afloat, and to Nadia it seems as if "the further they moved from the city of their birth, through space and through time, the more he [Saeed] sought to strengthen his connection to it, tying ropes to the air of an era that for her was unambiguously gone" (Hamid 2017, 187). The two polarized reactions of Saeed and Nadia represent the ambivalence that can be seen in Hamid's own writing. Saeed demonstrates a yearning for coherence by clinging to the past which reflects the general "geographical fragmentation, the spatial disruption, of our times" as he faces the "defensive and reactionary responses – certain forms of nationalism, sentimentalized recovering of sanitized 'heritages' " and outright antagonism to newcomers and "outsiders" (Massey 94, 147) – in the nativist backlash in the London of *Exit West*. He starts praying whereas he never did before, and he desperately seeks people who speak his language, and belong to his birth city. Nadia, on the other hand, wants to look to the future, even as she staunchly and stubbornly wears her black robe throughout the geographical journey, a robe that disrupts all the stereotypical symbolism attached to the covering as an identity marker. Having it on and keeping it on as a sign of her agency, Nadia finds a new confidence in her identity and refuses to be labelled immutably by her choice of clothing. In other words, she keeps her robe on, but liberates her identity to new experiences. Unlike Saeed, who is still nostalgic about the physical location in which his identity is anchored, her journey is not through "areas on maps, but as constantly shifting articulations of social relations through time" (Massey 1995, 188). Nadia's black robe is an interesting modern replacement for the "monastic habits" (James 2003, 220) worn by men and women in More's classic utopian society. In an ironic twist, while the habits in More's Utopia reflect a happy uniformity, Nadia's robe is a celebration of diversity.

In the novel, as national borders are lost, cities and streets become cramped with "walls" (Hamid 2017, 46), "fences" (71), "cordons" (134), "sand-bagged checkpoints" (48), and "razorwire" blockades (49), reinforcing eerily reminiscent migrant/native identities that loop a future vision into the colonial past. However, this is an inverse view, a mirror image: the native is the migrant; the migrant, native. All identities seep into one another: militant, native, military, migrant. The novel is riddled with references to monitoring technology: "helicopters", "drones", "surveillance balloons", "flying robots" (83), "quadcopter drones" (86), "drones no larger than hummingbirds" (204), "lasers peering from the sky" (88), and "aircraft that bomb from the heavens" (81). There is never a decisive line between who does the watching and who is watched; or who is the militant and who the refugee. In London, confined inside a building by angry mobs of True Brits outside, "the fury of those nativists advocating wholesale slaughter was what struck Nadia most, and it struck her because it seemed so familiar, so much like the fury of the militants in her own city" (Hamid 2017, 156). If everyone is both a militant and a refugee, then the definitions become fluid and interchangeable.

The concept of relativity is persistently reinforced in the novel by anchoring geographical positions in points of time where past, present, and future coalesce. Some passages in the novel very deliberately guide readers' attention to this: for example, sitting on the steps of a building in London, a startled Nadia thinks she saw a photograph of herself sitting on the steps in the news on her phone:

> and wondered how this could be, how she could both read this news and be this news, and how the newspaper could have published this image of her instantaneously [...] and she had the bizarre feeling of time bending all around her, as though she was from the past reading about the future, or from the future reading about the past, and she almost felt that if she got up and walked home at this moment there would be two Nadias, and one would stay on the steps reading, and one would walk home, and two different lives would unfold for these two different selves. (Hamid 2017, 154–155)

Parallel universes suggest possibilities of making better choices, and, in this way, offer consolation and hope. The text consistently paints images of light from different planets and stars falling on places and cities, skewing the concept of a singular present, and uses time-tropes like seeing "light from other centuries" falling on cities (14) or seeing "Mars from another moment" (15). This is what Saeed's father calls "time-travel" (14). At one point, looking at photographs by a French photographer of famous cities set against computer-imposed starry skies that Saeed shows her on his mobile phone, Nadia cannot tell "under their stains of stars, images as though from an epoch before electricity, but with buildings of today. Whether they looked like the past, or the present, or the future" (55). Through Saeed and Nadia's conversation, Hamid introduces readers to French artist Thierry Cohen's work series *Villes éteintes* (Darkened cities, n.d.) that underline the imaginative possibilities suggested by his novel. Cohen says of his photographs: "By combining two realities, I am making a third that you cannot see . . . but it exists! [...] I am not showing you post-apocalyptic cities [...] merely bringing back the silence" (quoted in Brook 2014, n.p.), much like Hamid's wish of combining competing realities into a newer outlook on the future.

Time is important in *Exit West*, not in its horizontal linear passage, but in its static, vertical dimensional quality. As a manual worker making roads in London Halo (the new name for migrant habitation), Saeed feels himself suspended between the past and the future. His physical labour has an element of the past, almost like muscle-memory, but the emerging road is a symbol of future destinations, as he realizes the "unimaginable scale of what they were undertaking [...] they were remodelling the earth itself" (Hamid 2017, 177). In this timeless world of past mistakes and future bondings, migrants in London Halo barter with time instead of goods (131), rather like selling a better future as a commodity that is much in demand. And there is also a "time tax that [has] been enacted, such that a portion of the income and toil of those who had recently arrived [...] would go to those who had been there for decades" (168). This gives time a boxed, concrete quality that can be weighed and valued in spatial terms.

Besides the direct use of words like "hope" and "optimism" that convey Hamid's optimism in a literal sense throughout the novel, the story does provide an ending that anticipates a better future. The choice of names for the protagonists appears to be deliberate. The name Nadia means "hope" and a "caller; announcer". Saeed means "fortunate" and "lucky". Despite the dystopian setting, these characters symbolize an optimism and a belief in a social Utopia. Before they leave on their journey, Saeed's father's words are portentous: "Let us hope" (Hamid 2017, 85), he says. The journeys through "doors" are hinged on hope and optimism against despair. Stark binaries, like dark, white; migrant, native; terrorist, military; doors, walls, are foregrounded but slowly recede into an acceptable grey normalcy. Marin, where Saeed and Nadia end their migratory journey, is the real glimpse of a collective future, where "plausible desirable futures began to emerge, unimaginable previously, but not unimaginable now" (216). The readers go on the same journey with "both of them [...] filled with hope" (189) about Marin, in which can be seen "all kind of ensembles, humans with humans, humans with electronics, dark skin with light skin with gleaming metal with matt plastic, computerized music and unamplified music" (216), in a *Star Trek*-style mingling of humans and machines. Languages meld too, and the migrants learn to make sense of the "cacophony that was the languages of the world, what one might hear if one were a communications satellite, or a spymaster tapping into a fibre-optic cable under the sea" (100). One interpretation of this novel can be that the migrants in Marin have become transmitters through whom disparate global communication can be received and decoded into a single coherent message about the possibility of unity in diversity.

Speculative fiction constructs cognitive spaces that are concerned with borders and transgressions; these metaphors are useful in analysing present-day geographies, their construction, reproduction, and contingency, and in theorizing a range of concepts such as space, nature, subjectivity, and reality (Kneale and Kitchin 2002, 9). *Exit West* is not just the story of one journey, but a palimpsest of all historical migrations, from slow colonial movements over the oceans to instantaneous digital connections through fibre-optic cables under the oceans, that have changed the way we understand human interaction in time and space. Similarly, Nadia and Saeed are not just one refugee couple, but a future vision of all humanity as migrants in a technological world that changes rapidly around them. Although technological advancements in surveillance apparatus and border control correlate with the segregation in society exemplified by Brexit, Hamid's future is based on the hope that in time humanity will come together to use technology in overcoming divisions and drawing the world closer together, so that physical migrations are not really necessary. The only danger to avoid would be inequality in the access to technology, because as Hamid says in the Waterstones interview, "competing nation-states threatened by each other will tend to allow technology to unfold in a completely unregulated fashion" (Hamid 2018a, n.p.). Despite such caveats, *Exit West*'s hope is clearly articulated in Hamid's strong assertion:

> I'm optimistic about our species [...] we are descended from refugees, all of us. Our people have migrated. Everybody comes from the mother continent of Africa [...] So I think that we will find a way. Human beings do. And the current fear that we have of the future, I suspect we will overcome it. (Brown 2018, n.p.)

Although Hamid's optimism might not be shared by many, his novel opens up a space in which perhaps authors and readers can reflect upon the changed nature of geo-historical productions of identity and how the future can be manifested through the power of the imagination.

Disclosure statement

No potential conflict of interest was reported by the author.

References

Aslam, Nadeem. 2017. *The Golden Legend.* New York: Alfred A. Knopf.
Basu, Samit. 2016. "The South Asian Diaspora and Speculative Fiction." *Samitbasu.com*, July 4. https://samitbasu.com/2006/07/04/the-south-asian-diaspora-and-speculative-fiction/
Brennan, Timothy. 2004. "Postcolonial Studies and Globalization Theory." In *Postcolonial Literary Studies*, edited by Neil Lazarus, 120–138. Cambridge: Cambridge University Press.
Brook, Pete. 2014. "What Cities Would Look like if Lit Only by the Stars." *Wired*, November 13. https://www.wired.com/2014/11/thierry-cohen-darkened-cities/
Brown, Jeffery. 2017. "Magical Novel *Exit West* Explores What Makes Refugees Leave Home: An Interview with Mohsin Hamid." Transcript. *PBS Newshour*, March 16. https://www.pbs.org/newshour/show/magical-novel-exit-west-explores-makes-refugees-leave-home
Brown, Jeffery. 2018. "Exit West Author Mohsin Hamid Answers Your Questions." Transcript. *PBS Newshour*, March 30. https://www.pbs.org/newshour/show/exit-west-author-mohsin-hamid-answers-your-questions
Day, Jon. 2017. "Brexlit: The New Landscape of British Fiction." *Financial Times*, July 28. https://www.ft.com/content/30ec47b4-7204-11e7-93ff-99f383b09ff9
During, Simon. 2000. "Postcolonialism and Globalization: Towards a Historicization of Their Inter-relation." *Cultural Studies* 14 (3–4): 385–404. doi:10.1080/09502380050130392.
Eaglestone, Robert. 2018. "Introduction: Brexit and Literature." In *Brexit and Literature: Critical and Cultural Responses*, edited by Robert Eaglestone, 1–6. Abingdon: Routledge.
Hamid, Mohsin. 2017. *Exit West.* London: Hamish Hamilton.
Hamid, Mohsin. 2018a. "On Hope for the Future: An Interview." *YouTube video*, 9:20.Posted by "Waterstones", February 13. https://www.youtube.com/watch?v=NOu7eM42jY4
Hamid, Mohsin. 2018b. "'It's Important Not to Live One's Life Gazing Towards the Future': An Interview with Mohsin Hamid [With Alex Preston]." *The Guardian*, August 11. https://www.theguardian.com/books/2018/aug/11/mohsin-hamid-exit-west-interview
Harvey, David. 1990. *The Condition of Postmodernity: An Enquiry into the Origins of Cultural Change.* Cambridge, MA: Blackwell.
Inskeep, Steve. 2017. "Mohsin Hamid's Novel *Exit West* Raises Immigration Issues: An Interview with Mohsin Hamid [Transcript]." *KRWG-FM*, March 6.
James, Edward. 2003. "Utopias and Anti-utopias." In *The Cambridge Companion to Science Fiction*, edited by Edward James and Farah Mendlesohn, 219–229. Cambridge: Cambridge University Press.
Kneale, James, and Rob Kitchin. 2002. "Lost in Space." In *Lost in Space: Geographies of Science Fiction*, edited by Rob Kitchin and James Kneale, 1–16. New York: Continuum.
Malik, Usman. 2015. "Rockets, Robots, and Reckless Imagination." *Herald*, July 3. https://herald.dawn.com/news/1153167/rockets-robots-and-reckless-imagination
Massey, Doreen. 1994. *Space, Place, and Gender*. Minneapolis, MN: University of Minnesota Press.
Massey, Doreen. 1995. "Places and Their Pasts." *History Workshop Journal* 39: 182–192. doi:10.1093/hwj/39.1.182.
Milo, Jeff. 2017. "'We Are All Migrants': Mohsin Hamid Talks His New Novel, *Exit West*." *Paste*, March 7. https://www.pastemagazine.com/articles/2017/03/mohsin-hamid-exit-west.html

Rogers de Waal, Joel. 2018. "Brexit and Trump Voters are More Likely to Believe in Conspiracy Theories." *International YouGov-Cambridge Centre*, December 14. https://yougov.co.uk/topics/international/articles-reports/2018/12/14/brexit-and-trump-voters-are-more-likely-believe-co

Sadaf, Shazia. 2018. "Human Dignity, the War on Terror, and Post 9/11 Pakistani Literature." Special Issue. "Global Responses to War on Terror." *European Journal of English Studies* 22 (2): 115–127. doi:10.1080/13825577.2018.1478255.

Said, Edward. 1994. *Culture and Imperialism*. New York: Vintage.

Taylor, Ros. 2019. "#islamexit: Islamophobia and Twitter after Brexit." February 28. https://blogs.lse.ac.uk/brexit/2019/02/28/islamexit-islamophobia-and-twitter-after-brexit/

United States Census Bureau. 2020. "Marin County, California (Quickfacts)." Accessed 7 August 2020. https://www.census.gov/quickfacts/fact/table/sanfranciscocountycalifornia,marincountycalifornia,CA/PST045219

Williams, Martin. 2017. "Is the Burqa Really a Terror Threat?" *Channel 4 News*, April 27. https://www.channel4.com/news/factcheck/is-the-burqa-really-a-terror-threat

"Eastern Europeans" and BrexLit

Vedrana Veličković

ABSTRACT

This article examines the representations of "Eastern European" migration in contemporary BrexLit, focusing on Adam Thorpe's *Missing Fay* (2017), Amanda Craig's *The Lie of the Land* (2017), Carla Grauls's *Occupied* (2012), Andrew Muir's *The Session* (2015), and Agnieszka Dale's short stories. Drawing on Paul Gilroy's work on postcolonial melancholia, and extending Kristian Shaw's "BrexLit" definition by focusing on stereotyping, it shows how the figure of the Eastern European migrant exposes unresolved anxieties around a presumed British cultural superiority, race, and empire. The arrival of Eastern Europeans and the increasing Brexodus of their "cheap labour" enables a reflection on the health of the nation – something is, indeed, rotten in post-Brexit Britain – as well as on unresolved legacies of empire that underpin the Brexit crisis. The article also analyses several promising responses from Polish British writers who interrogate the problematic staleness of these representations and take them into a much-needed new direction.

> We closed the borders, folks, we nailed it.
> No trees, no plants, no immigrants.
> No foreign nurses, no Doctors; we smashed it.
> We took control of our affairs. No fresh air.
> No birds, no bees, no HIV, no Poles, no pollen.
> (Kay, 2015)

In 2017, *Guardian* journalist John Harris asked a timely question: "if eastern Europeans leave Britain after Brexit, what happens?" (2017, n.p.). Harris visits Peterborough and Wisbech in East Anglia and interviews business owners and workers in the United Kingdom (UK)'s agricultural and food processing sector that heavily depends on flexible Eastern European labour. He juxtaposes the realities of food rotting in the fields with an almost utopian post-Brexit vision of British workers returning to these jobs, despite his conversations with the leave-voting locals who acknowledge that "most UK-born people wouldn't be interested in the kind of jobs that might soon be available". This vision – or better, illusion – was recently espoused by Home Secretary Priti Patel and the government's new immigration policy. Patel suggested that "businesses ought to enlist the 8 million 'economically inactive' " British people to fill in labour shortages after Brexit (quoted in Mason and O'Carroll 2020, n.p.). Proposed changes to the immigration system also reportedly stipulate that "UK borders will be closed to non-skilled workers and all migrants will have to speak English." It will be more difficult for self-employed and low-skilled workers, such as Polish plumbers or Romanian builders, to come into the UK without a job (Mason and O'Carroll 2020, n.p.). These "newly" arrived Europeans have been predominantly represented in recent British literature and culture as *the* unskilled manual labour from the expanded European Union (EU): with a poor command of English and audibly "Other" with their strong accents, they are willing to do the low-paid jobs that British people won't do, and they are willing to work for lower wages – in short, they are portrayed as an economically useful but disturbing presence on UK shores.

As I have shown in *Eastern Europeans in Contemporary Literature and Culture* (Veličković 2019), such literary examples are numerous and depressingly similar – Eastern Europeans *are* builders, plumbers, agricultural workers, nannies, au pairs, care workers, trafficked and exploited women in need of rescuing and educating, unruly and sexist men. They frequently appear as token characters or a minor "exotic" addition to the narrative. I was recently mistaken for a Polish gardener as I was tidying my own front garden by a white British passer-by who was attempting a conversation and wanted to know where my accent was *really* from. Indeed, it is increasingly difficult not to reflect on the peculiarities of this lived experience and (un)belonging as an Eastern European, even when one writes about literary representations, because those are the parameters according to which Eastern Europeans are knowable in the cultural imaginary. The category "Eastern European" is a construction, and the long history of stereotypical representations and Othering of Eastern Europe and the Balkans has been the object of numerous academic studies (Wolff 1994; Todorova 1997; Goldsworthy 1998; Kovačević 2008). As a result of the EU's enlargement in the 21st century, many of those Eastern Europeans, young and old, educated and less educated, privileged and less privileged, have made their way to Britain, making the most of their freedom of movement as EU citizens, given the British government's decision not to impose transitional work restrictions.

In this article, I consider the ways in which the above-mentioned stereotypical representations of Eastern Europeans feature in recent "BrexLit" (Shaw 2018). As Kristian Shaw argues, BrexLit encompasses works that "anticipate the thematic concerns such as anxieties surrounding cultural infiltration, and a mourning for the imperial past" as well as those that "directly respond or imaginatively allude to Britain's exit from the EU, or engage with the subsequent socio-cultural, economic, racial or cosmopolitan consequences of Britain's withdrawal" (2018, 18). I extend Shaw's definition by placing these representations at the forefront of BrexLit and show how the figure of the Eastern European migrant, when represented in this particular way, exposes unresolved anxieties around a presumed British cultural superiority, race, and empire. I also include here a few, but promising, responses from Polish British writers who interrogate the problematic staleness of these representations and take them into a much needed new direction.

Invading Eastern Europeans

Dubravka Ugrešić (2011) observes astutely that the Polish plumber is the new "colonial bogeyman" or "the new European phantom [...] who wends his way around Europe in overalls, with a wrench, terrifying the local working class" (232). Alongside numerous scaremongering tabloid press titles about Eastern Europeans taking over jobs, benefits, and school and NHS spaces, eating swans, and soiling public spaces, another example that I often cite further highlights anxieties around their presence on British shores, even several years before the UK's referendum on EU membership. It is the question that Rochdale's pensioner Gillian Duffy asked then Prime Minister Gordon Brown in 2010: "all these Eastern Europeans what are coming in, where are they flocking from?" (Veličković 2019, 35). Replace Eastern Europeans with German or French and it would be clear where they are coming from, or replace Eastern Europeans with Muslims or refugees and the liberal alarm bells would certainly not fail to ring as they did in the case of Eastern Europeans. As Larry Wolff (1994) has shown, Eastern Europe's indeterminate and shifting geographical borders are a legacy of the cultural mapping of Europe since the Enlightenment, and the resulting imaginary and real divisions are embedded even in contemporary perceptions. Yet beyond Labour's failure to reconnect with its traditional working-class voters, exemplified by both Duffy's concern about immigration and Gordon Brown's description of her as "bigoted" (2010, n.p.), and the dangers of homogenizing the white working-class revolt in opposition to multiculturalism and immigration, these racist sentiments should not remain unchallenged. While Eastern Europe has always been seen as an exoticized or threatening unknown before and after the Cold War, despite Britain's much longer history of migration from different parts of Europe, such as the Jewish exodus from Eastern Europe from 1881 to 1914, to name only one example, Duffy's anti-European sentiments were mobilized again in 2016 in the service of English nationalism. Just before the British referendum on EU membership, Duffy appeared on the BBC's *Newsnight*, lamenting how "we'll never get England back to how it was" and expressing her concerns about "losing our English identity". "I love being English and I don't want to be a European", she concluded (Duffy 2016, n.p.). This deeply melancholic response and attachment to an assumed, past English greatness with its parochial sense of identity (why cannot one be both English and European?) carries all the elements of Paul Gilroy's analysis of Britain's "postimperial melancholia" (2004, 98) and the nation's inability to work through the loss of empire. These melancholic attachments to past imperial greatness continue to shape contemporary attitudes to migration and strangers across the class spectrum. As Gilroy notes, "even if today's unwanted incomers – from Brazil or Eastern Europe – are not actually postcolonials, they may still carry all the ambivalence of the vanished empire with them" (2006, n.p.). I will return to this ambivalence in my analysis below of the perceptions of Eastern Europeans in recent British BrexLit.

Echoing Gilroy's argument, a number of critics and commentators have emphasized the links between Brexit, migration, and empire nostalgia, dispelling these neocolonial fantasies with factual information. David Olusoga (2017) and Kehinde Andrews (2017) have both criticized the historical amnesia and arrogant hubris that have been a predominant feature of the government's proposals for potential post-Brexit free trade deals with African and other Commonwealth nations under the offensive and delusional banner "Empire 2.0" (see Bayliss 2017). As Andrews reminds us, while "the leave campaign was based on a yearning for the days when Britannia ruled the waves", Brexit also provides an opportunity for Britain "to understand its place in the world; a small island desperately reaching out to countries it formerly ruled in order to try to maintain its relevance" (2017, n.p.). Olusoga puts it even more forcefully – former colonies "don't want to be part of Empire 2.0, any more than most of them wanted to be part of Empire 1.0" (2017, n.p.). It is even more ironic that the former colonial power has been using the language of oppression and liberation in the context of Brexit. Right-wing politicians and the populist press, even Boris Johnson, have repeatedly described Brexit as a "victory for democracy" and other European nations were called to "follow the United Kingdom and 'free [them]selves from the *shackles* of the dying European Union' (*Daily Express* 2016)" (quoted in Bell 2017, 52; my emphasis).

Other critics focused on exploring how experiences of "Eastern Europeans" fit within a wider history of race and migration in Britain. Gary Younge (2016) made an important investigation into how prejudice and stereotypes have affected Eastern European migrants after Brexit in his BBC film *Eastern Europeans in Brexitland* (see also Veličković 2019, 154–157). Anshuman Mondal (2018) is one of a handful of scholars to note "certain continuities in discourse and rhetoric between arguments against EU migration and post-war immigration from formerly colonised countries" (85). He argues that "anti-EU immigration sentiment [...] principally directed at obtrusively *white* migrants from Eastern Europe" was "a displaced proxy for still embedded antipathies towards non-white migration from outside the EU" (86; original emphasis). Mondal is right to point out that their whiteness has provided an outlet for the many unresolved tensions of the past couched in the assumption that one cannot be racist towards Eastern Europeans as they are white. In the same edited collection as Mondal, George Szirtes (2018) also writes about the dormant "demons" of empire that had been "successfully suppressed after Notting Hill in 1958" but were now resurfacing through a new outlet in the referendum campaign (204). Indeed, in the aftermath of the referendum, both EU and Black and ethnic minority British citizens were being told to go back where they came from (Veličković 2019, 140). However, Mondal fails to note that not all Eastern Europeans are "obtrusively" white (think about the Eastern European Roma and other ethnic minorities) and Eastern Europeans whiteness does not occupy the same position. They are constructed as not-quite as white or not-quite as European as their western counterparts. Using Etienne Balibar's (1997) notion of "racism without race" (23) or cultural racism, and building on the existing work on the shifting racial designations of Eastern Europeans (Wolff 1994; Goldsworthy 1998; Kovačević 2008), I have discussed elsewhere how western representations of Eastern Europeans range from an exaggerated whiteness (recalling a distant Dracula imagery) to dirty whiteness (an emphasis on poverty and outdated clothes, for example; see Veličković 2010, 2019). I have also looked at the complexity of Eastern European self-identifications with whiteness via the claims to racial/cultural closeness to Europe and the unresolved legacy of racism in Eastern Europe, as exemplified in the conflation of Romanians with the Roma in recent British journalistic and media accounts of migration from the expanded EU (Veličković 2019). In homogenizing narratives of Eastern Europeans these intersections and differences are often ignored so it is important to highlight them.

"Now let's see if you can work like a Pole": Eastern Europeans in BrexLit

In what follows, I concentrate on works that either anticipate or directly engage with the anxieties surrounding recent EU migration. Recent literary representations often tend to reinforce stereotypes about Eastern Europeans, even when they try to deconstruct them. Adam Thorpe's (2017) novel *Missing Fay* is set in pre-Brexit Lincoln, which would later record the UK's highest Brexit vote with other parts of Lincolnshire

(BBC News 2016, n.p.). The characters are loosely connected by the disappearance of the local young girl Fay, and a sense of claustrophobia, alienation, and small-town mentality permeates the novel. As documented by Tim Samuels in his two BBC documentaries, *The Poles are Coming!* (2008) and *The Great Big Romanian Invasion* (2014), East Anglia and Lincolnshire saw a particular increase in Eastern European migration due to their relative proximity to Stansted and Luton airports (with new, cheap flights from the expanded EU) and the availability of picking, packing, and factory work. The arrival of Eastern Europeans in the novel is registered both as a generic threat, with racist graffiti – "Paedos go back to Poland" (Thorpe 2017, 28) – appearing in town, and through its Romanian character Cosmina, who is a care worker. Howard, a retired steel worker who plays pub-crawl Monopoly, often has to listen to the anti-immigrant sentiments expressed by his friends Ian, Don, and Gary who complain about too many "Polacks or Lithanians" and "whatnot" (71, 72). A survivor of the Kindertransport, Howard seems to possess the knowledge that not all "Eastern Europeans" are the same, but he does not challenge the racism of his friends out loud. He quietly observes the changing demographics of the town, but is far from nostalgic for the old days. We learn that he "quite likes smoked sausage and pickled Herring out of the Baltic" (56) and does not mind Eastern European grocery shops springing up across the town. As a Jewish child refugee, he recognizes that the current calls to save "the nation from intruders" and "floods of immigrants" (56) are part of a much older discourse, but the novel does not explore further potential affinities between the new migrants and those who were once fleeing persecution.

The novel's Romanian character is all too predictable. We are introduced to Cosmina after she has a bike accident near the possible place of Fay's disappearance. She is treated by a doctor from New Delhi who is curious to find out about Romania and whether she is "ever confronted here in England by racist types" (Thorpe 2017, 82). Cosmina disagrees with this sentiment and is presented as another typically racist Eastern European. She notices a photo of the doctor's mixed-race child whom she describes as "a bit like a Roma kid but cleaner" (83), and her perception of Roma people from her home village as thieves with filthy children (80) is equally racist. Ironically, when she is wrongly accused of attempting to steal Nurse Bronwen's bag in the care home where she works, Bronwen sees in her a thief and a Roma (102). Cosmina tries to explain that she is Hungarian Romanian, but this matters little even to the Spanish matron Esperanca, who, in the end, refuses to give Cosmina any more shifts (103) and calls her a "stupid whore of a Romabitch" (105). The only character who tries to get close to Cosmina is a second-hand bookshop owner, Mike, whose mother is in the care home suffering from dementia (Banerjee 2007). However, this proximity is achieved through what Mita Banerjee describes as a fascination with Eastern Europeanness as the "new exotic" and "the new erotic" (317). Cosmina is the first Romanian Mike has ever met; he sees her as "unbelievably foreign and glamorous" (220) and finds her name incredibly attractive (209). He becomes obsessed with her and reduces her to sexual allure. While Mike is more welcoming than others, he displays a patronizing attitude to Cosmina and the Romanians: "We're all as one in Europe: he's looked it up, and in January 2014 – in less than two years – Romanians won't even have to have a work permit. They'll be a proper part of the family" (193).

There is a sense that Europe is "out there" and Eastern Europe is an even greater unknown, generalized as a poor place without prospects through brief snapshots of Cosmina's parents back in Romania (Thorpe 2017, 206) and Mike's assertions that Cosmina's "country is very poor" (223) and having to deal with "endless struggles" (226). This is a familiar stereotype of post-communist transition as an eternal predicament (Horvat and Štiks 2015, 16) and of poor but sexy Eastern Europe, to use Agata Pyzik's (2014) excellent phrase. As expected, Mike also wants to help Cosmina improve her English and suggests "some excellent books" from his bookshop (Thorpe 2017, 223). In the end, no one learns or benefits from these encounters and we can read this representation as a paralysis of the imperialist imagination.

Cosmina's journey to the UK is told through familiar tropes of migrant hardship. Although she has a university degree, she has to start from the bottom, "in the fields cutting cabbages and broccoli all day with the Poles and Latvians under Ted the gangmaster (who wasn't bad, when he wasn't eyeing her bottom)" (Thorpe 2017, 102), because of her poor command of English. She shares a flat in Lincoln with Anca from Timisoara and tries to save enough money to "go to journalism classes, to make contacts, to push upwards", but she remains stuck in low-paid jobs. In the care home, she is given "a lot of responsibilities, but she is treated as if she is slow and stupid" (81). Rather than moving upwards, her only option after she is sacked from the care home is to consider doing an even worse job with the 2 Sisters Food Group fish packing in Grimsby (106). Her future uncertain, she dreams of going home and exits the narrative.

A similarly tokenistic representation of Eastern Europeans can be found in Amanda Craig's (2017) *The Lie of the Land*, described as a "novel that exposes the fault lines in post EU referendum Britain" (Alfree 2017, n.p.). The novel explores the divisions between the rich and the poor, urban and rural areas in contemporary Britain, as it follows a dysfunctional middle-class family that must relocate from London to the fictional village of Trelorn in Devon, having lost their jobs in the recession and no longer being able to afford a house in London. Quentin and Lottie Bredin's marriage is in crisis and so is the country. Their son Xan manages to find a zero-hours job at the Humbles pie factory, "the only big employer in Trelorn" (Craig 2017, 121), where he works among the dissatisfied locals and "Eastern European" migrants. Some of the locals see them as hard working and useful, but also as a threat. Xan's supervisor Maddy cannot decide whether to scapegoat them for their apparent readiness to work long hours and for lower wages or for coming to take what "rightfully" belongs to the locals. She tells him that

> "[a] little British baby is what they want, and benefits. [...] I'm not saying they're not good workers, but nobody does this job for long. Free health care, child benefit, who wouldn't jump at it? Plenty of little Polish kids in local schools". Xan doesn't like this kind of talk, which sounds pretty much like racism, but he knows nothing. (74)

There is a strong sense of being "left behind", an easy byword for the north–south divide that, instead of attempting to account for the long-term inequalities, stagnating wages, and deindustrialization suffered by the north, is directed at scapegoating the migrants. Maddy complains about the lack of school and social places and tells him that at the next election they'll vote to leave Europe and for "UKIP because nobody else cares" (160). Xan, who is mixed-race, is uneasy about the anti-immigrant rhetoric, "but out here he can, reluctantly, see that it might be different" (160). If he is then only beginning to understand the divisions of contemporary Britain, his relationship to migrant Eastern European workers is rather problematic. Xan is fascinated with Eastern European women in the factory who are "pretty, slim and he suspects Polish, for they have those smooth, wedge-shaped faces, heavily made up. Even in overalls, they are seriously fit" (72). He has a brief fling with a Polish girl, Katya, who lives in a cramped house with other fellow migrants. Xan romanticizes the struggles of the Polish and their willingness to live "in what would be slum conditions if they weren't so scrupulously clean" (122) in order to save money. He admires the Poles' "almost military sense of how to behave", clean, cook, and make bread (123), and romanticizes their way of creating a sense of home in the communal space of the tiny kitchen "painted with bright stencils and pots of herbs in the window". He finds "the immigrants' willingness to not only work for the minimum wage but save from it [as] both impressive and depressing" (211). If the precarious locals bemoan the loss of communal spaces, Xan's attitude towards "Eastern Europeans" only emphasizes his middle-class privilege. There are other passages that read like a liberal Marxist manifesto as Xan learns about the vicious cycle of exploitation:

> The Poles not only earn all their income from Humbles, but also rent their cramped and shoddy homes from them [...]. They all know that farming work is the worst work of all [...]. The work goes to the Romanians and Lithuanians [...] who dream of getting a job at Humbles. Everything to do with food seems to be built on a pyramid of exploitation and unhappiness. (210–211)

The novel reveals deeper fractures between the characters as they often feel out of touch with each other, providing another useful metaphor with which Craig can diagnose the nation's current predicament. Katya feels that the British "don't want to work hard like Polish people" (122) and is aware that she is also seen as a migrant who is taking "jobs and homes from English people" (210–211). She also fetishizes Xan as the only "black person" she has ever touched and he has to educate her to stop saying "that his skin is smooth like wood" (213). Growing differences between them are further emphasized by Katya's objections to Xan's lack of cooking skills and his wasting of money on ready meals, while Xan does not appreciate her complete lack of interest in literature and reading, and as a consequence their relationship breaks down.

The last time we hear of Katya is when Maddy informs Xan that she has left the pie factory. She is on her upward journey opening a Polish bakery in Trelorn and outrunning the Brits. Katya is too one-dimensional (exoticized, uncultured, racist, only interested in making money), and Eastern European men are also a generalized and threatening presence in the novel. They are clearly different from Xan: "larger, tougher, more pale and more male than he, with their giant sausage-fed muscles, clipped heads" (214). The novel abounds in other stereotypical passages about them:

> The men have pale, broad faces and small dark eyes; they can look like angry scones until suddenly they smile. They turn their hand to anything: building, joinery, plumbing, electrics, decorating, mechanics [...] most seem to be employed by an especially Big Pole called Arek, who is some kind of master-builder. (123)

The men rarely speak, but are described here by Xan. Of course, one is tempted to read these descriptions in the context of the novel's broader concerns with various class, racial, geographical, and other divisions in contemporary Britain. Craig was inspired to write the novel when a local councillor visited her at her doorstep in Devon. He was begging them "to give work to someone he knew" and told her that he was so desperate because "people don't realise, but in this part of the country we are poorer than Romania" (Kean 2017, n.p.). However, after encountering similar representations of Eastern Europeans over and over again, one can also argue that the divisions between the left-behind Devonians and the new migrants are only perpetuated by these damaging stereotypes. In this context, I cannot help but think of Chimamanda Adichie's (2009) powerful reflections on the "dangers of the single story" that creates stereotypes and make "one story become the only story" (n.p.). If, let's say, another ethnic group of people was represented and generalized through such recurring images, it would certainly be considered problematic. Such depictions of Eastern Europeans, then, reveal the unresolved anxieties towards race, migration, and belonging in post-imperial, post-Brexit Britain, rather than offering any kind of "truthful" representation. Ugly racism and xenophobia from both sides is a barrier that prevents British and Eastern European workers in the novel from finding any common ground. Xan, the local Devonian poor, and the newly arrived Eastern Europeans are all exploited and equally devoid of any political awareness of their own conditions of precarious flexibility and utility in the system. A perfect capitalist tactic that promotes the atomization of individuals rather than collective unity and leaves very little room for resistance and solidarity. In other words, there is a need for more progressive BrexLit that moves away from the state-of-the-nation novels that offer a diagnosis of the pre- and post-Brexit crisis, but fall short of imagining new solidarities. Whether this also reflects the current state of the Left in Britain and Europe is worth pursuing, but it would require another article altogether.

Before I move on to recent works that are taking BrexLit and the representations of "Eastern Europeans" in new directions, rather than using them as token characters, I would like to focus on two more examples that reflect this state of paralysis and thread a thin line between stereotyping and caricature – Carla Grauls's (2012) play *Occupied* and Andrew Muir's (2015) *The Session*. Muir's play is about the breakdown in communication between a married couple, Lena Bayle, who is Polish, and her English husband Robert, as they are struggling to cope with grief after their son Freddy, a lorry driver, was killed in a traffic accident. Spoken alternately by Lena and Robert, the play raises questions of identity and ownership as we learn that the relationship was uneven from the start. There is a language barrier between them in the beginning and Lena also struggles to come to terms with her newly found otherness in Britain. She feels like a "human alien" and imagines that Robert would have been welcomed and not seen as different had he been in her land (Muir 2015, 10–11). Lena idealizes England as "this tiny country that stood with its head high looking down on most of the world", without questioning its colonial history, and thinks that she has found her "prince" (23) in Robert. He is, however, more anxious about their cultural intermixing and often patronizes her ("she needed this country so that she could realise her potential" [37]). As Lena's command of English improves, Robert refuses to learn Polish and feels that English was making Lena "more critical" (46). He also does not want her speaking to their son "in a language I don't feel he needs to know" and marginalizes his Polish heritage ("he's English" [46]). Grief brings them together towards the end of the play, but their identity crises and uneven power relations are far from resolved, as Robert announces that he will look after Lena who is in need of rescuing.

The notion of an identity crisis is also at the heart of Carla Grauls's Beckettian play *Occupied.* Set in a derelict Victorian public toilet, the play presents a conglomerate of stereotypes about Eastern Europeans on almost every page and proves uncomfortable for readers and audiences alike. Tom, an Englishman, has been abducted by the 30-year-old Alex who appears on stage with a copy of the *Daily Mail* announcing the Romanian invasion and occupation of English gardens sheds, abandoned houses, and toilets (Grauls 2014, 4). The play references similar tabloid headlines (23, 57), but often fails to challenge them. Alex has a broken-tooth smile and is wearing a dirty tracksuit, a leather jacket, a fur hat, and a gold crucifix around his neck (3), conforming to the familiar stereotypes of unruly Eastern European men with an outdated fashion sense. Alex has been raised on "potatoes and cabbage, beautiful women, drinking, corruption" (14) which creates a reductive image of his country. He was a taxi driver in Romania, but has now come to England to "become rich" (32) and his other aspiration is to get an English girlfriend, an "English Rose like Kate" who knows that he is "the boss" (33). He wants Tom to teach him about English life, but just like Alex's own illusions about England as "the country that has always been a boss and a place where you are supposed to be nice to foreigners" (49), Tom explains that his having all the "nice things" (43) will not make Alex happy. The English way of life, he tells Alex, is an empty capitalist dream: "get yourself a flat, a mortgage, gadgets, live on credit, work in a job that profits from others, that's the English life" (49). The play further enacts anxieties around masculinity, identity, gender, and race through Alex's altercations with Tom, who is bound, gagged, physically assaulted, and powerless throughout the play, yet speaks with more knowledge and confidence than Alex, despite also feeling empty and suicidal. The play clearly tries to address a number of stereotypes about Eastern Europeans but does not quite manage to challenge them successfully. Alex is mistaken for a Roma (to which he strongly objects), a Pole (when he is abused and assaulted in a pub), and a vampire from Bulgaria (34). He is also racist and sexist throughout the play. His crisis of belonging as not capitalist enough and not English enough is never resolved and he remains a repulsive and pathetic caricature as the play ends with his own death and with migration as a symbolic death rather than a positive experience – "we the immigrants pull the ropes around our necks because English life is still better here than what we have" (82). If the aim of the play is to foreground the post-communist existential crisis in a Beckettian manner, as we learn towards the end that Alex witnessed the Velvet Revolution as a boy and saw his mother commit suicide, it does so by falling prey to another stereotype of post-communist transition as "the catching up revolution" (Buden 2010, n.p.).

If Alex is unable to make sense of his alienation and dislocation, the two women in the play, Elena and Andreea, are also in limbo. Elena is another surreal character reminiscent of Beckett's Nell from *Endgame*, as she often emerges from the dump scavenging through rubbish for food. She is also an undead ghost of Elena Ceausescu haunting Alex. As expected, Andreea is a young Hungarian Romanian woman, possibly underage and trafficked as we learn that Alex found her "in a flat on Holloway Road where they take the girls from Eastern Europe" (Grauls 2014, 67). She is begging and stealing in London and is controlled and often abused by Alex. Even though he is unable to escape himself, Tom often offers to become her saviour. If the purpose of Beckett's plays is to create a profoundly unsettling effect, the characters in this play, who are "occupied" by various sources and unable to overcome mental and physical slavery, suggest an unsettling codependency of post-communist Eastern Europe on the capitalist west and they are locked in stereotypes. As Alex summarizes crudely:

> Every time Romania stands up, some other fucking country come in and make her his whore. But you see we are part of EU now, we Romanians we can go anywhere, we can have better life and better jobs and much more money. (49)

Their experience of the UK shows that this is far from the truth. While Alex imagines towards the end of the play how he will be a car mechanic and Andreea a teacher (80), that alternative, future representation is denied to them. Andreea is a more elusive character and there are hints that she counters Tom's objectification of her as broken and in need of saving. However, the fact that she is being sexually exploited in order to survive in London suggests that she is, indeed, that "one thing" (52) when it comes to the representations of Eastern European women.

Conclusion: Where do we go from here?

So far I have discussed representations that emphasize lack of understanding and divisions between Eastern Europeans and the British, and fall into reinforcing stereotypes about the new migrants as scapegoats for Britain's unresolved social and historical ills, as well as its "left behind" people as narrow and racist.[1] If we have recently witnessed the Brexodus of real Eastern European migrants, although in the midst of the coronavirus pandemic we hear that Romanian fruit pickers are being flown to the UK to help (O'Carroll 2020), in this concluding section I show how recent works by Eastern European British writers have halted their untimely exit in literature. Polish British writer Agnieszka Dale is one of them. In her dystopian short story "A Happy Nation", the narrator literally refuses to leave, even though all the immigrants have gone away and the shops are closing down. She is another Eastern European migrant "we" think we know, a certain Krystyna Kowalska from Gdansk whose father resembles Lech Walesa (Dale 2017, 68). While she speaks to, or rather speaks back to, an immigration officer, the story is a wider conversation with her adopted nation. The post-Brexit vision of Britain is one in which holidays now mainly happen in Wales and she is asked to show her ID. She came to Britain during the EU enlargement not for the benefits or the work possibilities, but "to mix [her] blood" with a Brit who is "one-fifth Spanish. And a little Irish" (70). It is clear that Dale speaks back to a number of stereotypes about Eastern Europeans here (vampires, job stealers, trafficked women) as well as about their hosts, as her narrator reveals that she still loves it here – "I feel loved, just loved by everyone: neighbors, colleagues, shopkeepers, and maybe that's why I'm refusing to leave" (67). The story also tackles issues of racial and cultural purity and historical hierarchy. She is aware of the changing conditions of cultural visibility in Britain and explains the anxieties around Eastern Europeans as a visible and audible presence in 21st-century Britain in the following way:

> You don't like our delikatesy. Not so much the sausages and the bread but more the design of the shop signs. The fonts we use … yes, you can tell we don't study art and design in schools the way you do in Great Britain. And your signs are great. But how come you don't mind the Indian corner shops any more, or the Jamaican fruit and vegetable market on a Monday morning? Or Chinatown? Why us? Why me? (71)

It is refreshing to see an Eastern European character with a better awareness of cultural racism than is usually the case in various narratives about Eastern Europeans who are usually being spoken for and represented as a culturally lagging cheap labour force, as discussed in the first part of this article. By referencing previous histories of migration, the narrator also echoes Gilroy's argument about today's unwanted incomers from Eastern Europe carrying all the ambivalence of the vanished empire with them. The narrator suggests that the presence of "Eastern European" white others is disrupting the hegemonic version of whiteness and comments on her ability to pass by staying silent or being able to "speak English like a British person now" until they can no longer tell the difference (72). While Brexit is never named in the story, the narrator's sense of being perceived as a threat and the references to losing control are clearly a direct critique of nationalism and claims to cultural and racial purity evident in the Leave calls to take back control. Rather than explaining where she is from and who she is, she poses the questions to the officer, and the imaginary collectivity: "How would you define British? Do you know who you are? Did you learn about Great Britain in your history classes? The history of colonization? (70). She uses the UK's White Other ethnic category to gouge a hole in the fortification of post-imperial whiteness after Brexit and carve her own sense of belonging within a new category that she describes as "*whitish*" (69; original emphasis). The suffix "-ish" in "whitish" reminded me of Afua Hirsch's book *Brit(ish)*, an identity under constant renegotiation and a reclaimed, powerful space. She may not be quite white, but neither is the immigration officer. The story ends with a turning point as it is revealed that the officer who questions her is called "Adam Michalowski, born in Lambeth, White British" (73). While the narrator decides to leave in the end, sensing a more hostile atmosphere from the immigration official, Dale's story shows that what we are now witnessing in post-Brexit Britain (new racisms, the resurfacing of post-imperial nostalgia) can be better understood within a longer history of race and migration.

Polish British poet Maria Jastrzebska has recently written a blog reflecting on the racism and xenophobia after Brexit and her growing up in England in the late 1950s when she would be told, alongside her Polish mother, to go back to where she came from. She also writes how, as a young Pole, she was empowered by terms like "Black British" that made her "feel Britain could be multi-racial, multi-cultural, inclusive, welcoming – where someone like me could be Polish British, somewhere that could be called home" (Jastrzebska 2020, n.p.). That there is a renewed call for new alliances and anti-racist activism is, I hope, an emerging trend that will take BrexLit in new directions.[2] There are still so many unexplored stories of Eastern Europeans in BrexLit that are waiting to be told other than the clichéd narratives of Eastern Europeans coming back to the UK to work during the pandemic and undergoing yet another cycle of exploitation. Or perhaps a post-Brexit, COVID-19 version of Marina Lewycka's *Two Caravans* might emerge out of this context. Eastern European writers settling in here and writing their own stories about the experience of Brexit might be another emerging phenomenon that would shape the future landscape of BrexLit. Agnieszka Dale's work is certainly a welcome contribution to these debates.

In another story from Dale's collection, entitled "What We Should Feel Now", Brexit is again not mentioned, but the unnamed narrator clearly addresses its affective afterlife – how it felt to her and to the people around her. The narrator is trying to make sense of different feelings and acts of hostility without being resentful: "because why? Who did what to me? Thugs?" (74). Ethnic and racial markers on both sides are absent – people are just different people and those who were violent to her are denied a voice. Avoiding the "us" versus "them" mindset, she keeps asking people around her: " 'Do you not like me here?' I ask shopkeepers, doctors, policemen, politicians, and friends. 'Of course, don't be silly. We love you. You are like us, part of us, you know' " (75). Faced with the realities of food rotting in the fields and an uncertain future, a small antidote to the Brexit crisis and the rise of populism and racism may be a kind of BrexLit that moves away from all kinds of stereotypes and opens up other ways of understanding and community. As I have argued in this article, representations of Eastern Europeans as economically useful but disposable token characters have limited a deeper engagement with a number of unresolved legacies of empire that underpin the Brexit crisis. The powerful final lines of Dale's story suggest one way in which the divisions might be repaired and a communal/national "we" imagined otherwise: "We'll grow new apples together [...] and then we'll eat together. Our apples. Apples that do not rot" (75).

Notes

1. For an interesting discussion of framing the white working class as racist and disconnected from politics, see Beider (2015).
2. For an emerging queer BrexLit, see, for example, Waidner (2019).

Disclosure statement

No potential conflict of interest was reported by the author.

ORCID

Vedrana Veličković http://orcid.org/0000-0003-2948-8479

References

Adichie, Chimamanda Ngozi. 2009. "The Danger of a Single Story." *TED*, July. https://www.ted.com/talks/chimamanda_adichie_the_danger_of_a_single_story/transcript?language=en

Alfree, Claire. 2017. "*Metro* Review: *The Lie of the Land.*" June 12. https://www.amandacraig.com/books/the-lie-of-the-land/#

Andrews, Kehinde. 2017. "Building Brexit on the Myth of Empire Ignores Our Brutal History." *The Guardian*, March 7. https://www.theguardian.com/commentisfree/2017/mar/07/building-brexit-on-myth-of-empire-ignores-history-at-our-peril

Balibar, Etienne. 1997. "Is There a 'Neo-racism'?" In *Race, Nation, Class: Ambiguous Identities*, edited by Etienne Balibar and Immanuel Wallerstein, 17–28. London: Verso.

Banerjee, Mita. 2007. "Postethnicity and Postcommunism in Hanif Kureishi's *Gabriel's Gift* and Salman Rushdie's *Fury*." In *Reconstructing Hybridity: Post-colonial Studies in Transition*, edited by Joel Kuortti and Jopi Nyman, 309–324. Amsterdam and New York: Rodopi.

Bayliss, Charlie. 2017. "EMPIRE 2.0: UK to 'Improve Trade Links with African Commonwealth Nations' after Brexit." *Daily Express*, March 6. https://www.express.co.uk/news/uk/775399/empire-2-uk-improve-trade-links-african-commonwealth-nations-after-brexit-theresa-may

BBC News. 2016. "Lincolnshire Records UK's Highest Brexit Vote." June 24. http://www.bbc.co.uk/news/uk-politics-eu-referendum-36616740

Beider, Harris. 2015. *White Working-class Voices: Multiculturalism, Community-building and Change*. Bristol: Policy Press.

Bell, Emma. 2017. "Brexit and the Illusion of Democracy." *Socialism and Democracy* 31 (3): 52–73. doi:10.1080/08854300.2017.1368888.

Buden, Boris. 2010. "What to Do with the Question: 'What Will the Balkans Look Like in 2020?'" *WUS Austria*, n.d. http://www.wus-austria.org/25/news/324/what-to-do-with-the-question-what-will-the-balkans-look-like-in-2020

Craig, Amanda. 2017. *The Lie of the Land*. London: Little, Brown.

Dale, Agnieszka. 2017. *Fox Season and Other Short Stories*. London: Jantar Publishing.

Duffy, Gillian. 2016. "I Don't Want to Be a European." *BBC News*, May 25. http://www.bbc.co.uk/news/uk-politics-eu-referendum-36373649

Gilroy, Paul. 2004. *After Empire: Melancholia or Convivial Culture*. London and New York: Routledge.

Gilroy, Paul. 2006. "Multiculture in Times of War." *LSE* Lecture, May 10. http://www.lse.ac.uk/PublicEvents/pdf/20060510-PaulGilroy.pdf

Goldsworthy, Vesna. 1998. *Inventing Ruritania: The Imperialism of the Imagination*. New Haven, CT: Yale University Press.

Grauls, Carla. 2014. *Occupied*. London: Bloomsbury Methuen Drama.

Harris, John. 2017. "They Say after Brexit There'll Be Food Rotting in the Fields. It's Already Started." *The Guardian*, August 5. https://www.theguardian.com/commentisfree/2017/aug/05/brexit-uk-food-industry-eu-fruit-veg-pickers

Horvat, Srećko, and Igor Štiks, eds. 2015. *Welcome to the Desert of Post-Socialism: Radical Politics after Yugoslavia*. London: Verso Books.

"How Gordon Brown 'Bigot' Jibe Row Unfolded." 2010. *BBC News*, April 28. http://news.bbc.co.uk/1/hi/uk_politics/election_2010/8649448.stm

Jastrzebska, Maria. 2020. "My Generation." *Maria Jastrzebska: Poetry, Patter and Politics*, February 10. https://mariajastrzebska.wordpress.com/2020/02/10/my-generation/

Kay, Jackie. 2015. "A Climate Change Poem for Today: 'Extinction' by Jackie Kay". *The Guardian*, May 15. https://www.theguardian.com/environment/2015/may/15/a-climate-change-poem-for-today-extinction-by-jackie-kay

Kean, Danuta. 2017. "Vanguard of Brexit Fiction Set to Appear in 2017." *The Guardian*, January 9. https://www.theguardian.com/books/2017/jan/09/vanguard-of-brexit-fiction-set-to-appear-in-2017-mark-billingham

Kovačević, Nataša. 2008. *Narrating Post/Communism: Colonial Discourse and Europe's Borderline Civilization*. London: Routledge.

Mason, Rowena, and Lisa O'Carroll. 2020. "Immigration: Firms Will Need to Train More UK Workers, Says Priti Patel." *The Guardian*, February 19. https://www.theguardian.com/uk-news/2020/feb/19/immigration-firms-will-need-to-train-more-uk-workers-says-priti-patel

Mondal, Anshuman. 2018. "Scratching the Post-imperial Itch." In *Brexit and Literature: Critical and Cultural Responses*, edited by Robert Eaglestone, 82–91. London and New York: Routledge.

Muir, Andrew. 2015. *The Session*. London: Bloomsbury Methuen Drama.

O'Carroll, Lisa. 2020. "Romanian Fruit Pickers Flown to UK amid Crisis in Farming Sector." *The Guardian*, April 15. https://www.theguardian.com/world/2020/apr/15/romanian-fruit-pickers-flown-uk-crisis-farming-sector-coronavirus

Olusoga, David. 2017. "Empire 2.0 Is Dangerous Nostalgia for Something that Never Existed." *The Guardian*, March 19. https://www.theguardian.com/commentisfree/2017/mar/19/empire-20-is-dangerous-nostalgia-for-something-that-never-existed

Pyzik, Agata. 2014. *Poor but Sexy: Culture Clashes in Europe East and West*. London: Zero Books.

Shaw, Kristian. 2018. "BrexLit." In *Brexit and Literature: Critical and Cultural Responses*, edited by Robert Eaglestone, 15–30. London and New York: Routledge.

Szirtes, George. 2018. "Epilogue: The Immigrant at Port Selda." In *Brexit and Literature: Critical and Cultural Responses*, edited by Robert Eaglestone, 196–206. London and New York: Routledge.

Todorova, Maria. 1997. *Imagining the Balkans*. New York: Oxford University Press.

Thorpe, Adam. 2017. *Missing Fay*. London: Random House.

Ugrešić, Duravka. 2011. *Karaoke Culture*. New York: University of Rochester Open Letter Books.

Veličković, Vedrana. 2010. "Balkanisms Old and New: The Discourse of Balkanism and Self-Othering in Vesna Goldsworthy's *Chernobyl Strawberries* and *Inventing Ruritania*." In *Facing the East in the West: Images of Eastern Europe in British Literature, Film and Culture*, edited by Barbara Korte, Eva Ulrike Parker and Sissy Helff, 185–203. Amsterdam: Rodopi.

Veličković, Vedrana. 2019. *Eastern Europeans in Contemporary Literature and Culture: Imagining New Europe*. London: Palgrave Macmillan.

Waidner, Isabel. 2019. *We are Made of Diamond Stuff*. Manchester: Dostoevsky Wannabe Originals.

Wolff, Larry. 1994. *Inventing Eastern Europe: The Map of Civilization on the Mind of the Enlightenment*. Stanford, CA: Stanford University Press.

Younge, Gary. 2016. "Eastern Europeans in Brexitland." *BBC Radio 4*, September 5. https://www.bbc.co.uk/programmes/b07sy81f

Imperial pasts, dystopian futures, and the theatre of Brexit

Marlena Tronicke

ABSTRACT

Even though traditionally a major analyst of the status quo of the British nation, British theatre has barely responded to Brexit. Two recent plays that seem to have captured the Brexit zeitgeist particularly well look towards the past: whereas *Albion* (2017), Mike Bartlett's take on the country house drama, depicts an Englishness nostalgically mourning its long-lost colonial prowess, Jez Butterworth's dissection of the Troubles in Northern Ireland, *The Ferryman* (2017), appears dystopian as anxieties surrounding the Good Friday Agreement in a post-Brexit scenario resurface. Both plays, this article argues, situate Brexit as firmly rooted in Paul Gilroy's notion of "postcolonial melancholia". They suggest that it is only through confronting its imperial past that Britain can begin to address vital questions concerning the current state of the nation: constructions of selfhood versus Otherness, and the intertwinement of the domestic and the political, as well as the mythical nature of national identities.

Introduction: The stage of the nation?

Without doubt, theatre plays a major role in the British state-of-the-nation debate, with playwriting functioning as a concomitant annalist and engine of societal reform (Middeke, Schnierer, and Sierz 2011, vii–viii). As Aleks Sierz (2011) puts it, "theatre is part of a widespread conversation about who we are as a nation, and where we might be going" (1). The question of whom exactly this "we" refers to acquires special significance in the case of the National Theatre (founded in 1963). Such questions are equally addressed by the National Theatre of Scotland (1922) and the National Theatre Wales (2009), which frequently negotiate regional identities that are subsumed under, but often formed in opposition to, hegemonic constructions of Britishness that posit Englishness as the norm. Though a distinct counter project to formations of Britishness, this similarly applies to the Abbey Theatre as the National Theatre of Ireland (1904), with its prime role in the Irish Literary Revival and conflict over Irish Home Rule. Mark Fisher (2019) notes: "put the word 'national' in your name and you become a receptacle for a country's values. In what you do, the nation will seek to see the very definition of itself; a definition perhaps vaguely articulated, but intensely felt" (n.p.). Arguably, during a national disruption on the scale of Brexit, this maxim extends beyond the context of the National Theatres to all new British writing for the stage at least.

And yet, after a couple of lukewarm forays into the psyche of post-Referendum British society and politics, critics feel that British theatre still "has its head in the sand over Brexit" (Trueman 2019, n.p.). As if to justify the absence of such material, veteran playwright Tom Stoppard suggested that Brexit was too big and multifaceted a debate and therefore inherently unsuited to the stage (Dickson 2017, n.p.). However, given new writing's distinctly political outlook,[1] plays that fall within this category appear ideally suited, if not obliged, to engage with Brexit. The first play that dared to tackle Brexit was then Poet Laureate Carol Ann Duffy and Rufus Norris's verbatim piece *My Country; A Work in Progress: In the Words of People Across the UK*, produced for the National Theatre in 2017. As the National Theatre's artistic director, Norris felt it was the institution's obligation to heed what weighed on people's minds to bridge the diametrically opposed political camps of Leave and Remain (Citizenstheatre 2017, n.p.). He sent a team of researchers all across Britain – provocatively excluding the Remain heartland of London – to record people's views on the Referendum and their motivations for voting either way. Duffy later translated these responses into monologues that revealed deep fissures along the lines of ethnicity and class, juxtaposing crassly divergent and often outright bizarre views on migration, patriotism, and an assumed dictatorship by Brussels bureaucrats. Although envisioned as a cutting-edge project with the capacity to feel the pulse of the nation, the play received mediocre reviews at best. Whilst Trueman (2019) called it "well-meaning, but misjudged" (n.p.), Sierz (2018a) felt *My Country* had "a good claim to be the worst new play of that year" (62). David Hare's highly anticipated *I'm Not Running* (National Theatre, 2018), a dramatic dissection of the current state of the British Labour Party, proved similarly disappointing; its tiptoeing around all things Brexit and the factors that led to Labour's disastrous performance in the Referendum as well as subsequent national elections puzzled both critics and audiences (Sierz 2018b, n. p.). But what, one may ask, would a successful dramatization of Brexit have to entail?

One major strand of new British writing that has long vigorously investigated the state of the nation – that is, what "Britishness" means in the first place – scrutinizes Britain's postcolonial legacies. In various ways, plays by Roy Williams (*Clubland* [Royal Court, 2001]; *Fallout* [Royal Court, 2003]), debbie tucker green (*born bad* [Hampstead Theatre, 2003]; *random* [Royal Court, 2008]), or Kwame Kwei-Armah (*Elmina's Kitchen* [National Theatre, 2003]; *Statement of Regret* [National Theatre, 2007]) debate, amongst other themes, negotiations of Britishness outside normative Whiteness. Many of these examine the racist onslaughts resulting from an ostensible unwillingness or outright inability to consolidate notions of Blackness with Britishness. Similarly, writers such as Hanif Kureishi (*Borderline* [Royal Court, 1981]; *Birds of Passage* [Hampstead Theatre, 1983]), Tanika Gupta (*The Waiting Room* [National Theatre, 2000]; *Fragile Land* [Hampstead Theatre, 2003]), or Alia Bano (*Shades* [Royal Court, 2009]) have dramatized tensions in British South Asian communities in terms of, for instance, female (sexual) emancipation or cross-cultural relationships. All dramatic responses that take seriously Brexit's colonial underpinnings have to be understood vis-à-vis the works of playwrights such as the above, all of whom, in some shape or form, have been writing about Brexit-related issues for years.[2] This article addresses the question of why both critics and audiences nonetheless seem to crave such labels as "BrexLit" (Shaw 2018) or "Brexit theatre", which convey a sense of novelty rather than legacy. I suggest this need to label long-lived processes and realities as novel developments brings to the fore what Paul

Gilroy (2004) has identified as "postcolonial melancholia". As the two plays addressed in this article, and particularly their critical reception, imply, within large parts of the (White) British population an awareness of colonial crimes and the resulting racist violence still lies dormant.

In addition to the rich body of work by Black British and Asian British writers that illuminates Brexit's rootedness in racism, empire nostalgia, and so on, a number of pre-Referendum plays have identified Brexit's pungent (post)colonial undercurrents through staging the multifaceted paranoia regarding migration that has fuelled anti-EU sentiments in all parts of the UK. Zinnie Harris's *How to Hold Your Breath* (Royal Court, 2015), for one, anticipates a mass exodus of Europeans fleeing from a crumbling Europe to the African continent. However, as Tom Cornford (2018) rightly points out, it "seeks not to expose the condition of migrancy so much as the structural violence of privilege" (104). Stef Smith's *Human Animals* (Royal Court, 2016), by contrast, envisions the dystopian scenario of an ecological disaster that leaves London infested with various animal species, to the extent that societal (infra)structures break down. Smith thus depicts society's coping strategies in a state of emergency that allegorizes the ways in which populist discourses have framed migration as a form of natural catastrophe.[3] Another pre-Brexit play, in fact one that predates the Referendum by some 14 years, is Roy Williams's (2014) *Sing Yer Heart Out for the Lads*, first performed at London's National Theatre in 2002. Tellingly, Williams's depiction of the violent eruption of White nationalism in a pub during an England–Germany football match was revived at Chichester Festival Theatre in October 2019 to great acclaim. That all three of these plays anticipate anxieties concerning migration and deeply rooted xenophobia as the predominant issues at the heart of Brexit only confirms that the theatre of Brexit dates back far longer than June 23, 2016; as Sierz (2018a) suggests, it can in fact be traced through the entirety of post-war British writing for the stage (68). By extension, this also highlights that ostensibly neat, event-based generic labels such as "BrexLit" have to be approached carefully as they bear the potential to streamline diverse experiences, subjectivities, or power structures and condense multifaceted processes into singular events.

Two post-Referendum plays which seem to have captured the Brexit zeitgeist particularly well look towards the past: Mike Bartlett's (2017) *Albion* and Jez Butterworth's (2017) Olivier Award-winning *The Ferryman*. Both received enthusiastic reviews and excelled at the box office. *Albion*, which premiered at the Almeida in October 2017 (directed by Rupert Goold), secured the award of *The Telegraph*'s "Play of the Year". It was revived at the same venue in February 2020 and subsequently broadcast as part of the BBC's *Culture in Quarantine* programme during the coronavirus pandemic in August 2020. *The Ferryman* premiered at the Royal Court in April 2017 (directed by Sam Mendes), becoming the fastest-selling production in the theatre's history; it transferred to the West End in June 2017 where it ran until May 2018 and opened on Broadway in October the same year. These productions have no doubt been so successful because they engage with prevalent themes of Brexit discourse. Whereas *Albion* depicts a sense of Englishness nostalgically mourning its long-lost colonial influence and independence, Butterworth's play about the Troubles[4] appears suitably dystopian. In a post-Brexit scenario, the situation in Northern Ireland – *already* a spatially and temporally liminal place – becomes aggravated, as anxieties surrounding the Good Friday Agreement resurface.[5] The apparent absence of "present voices" in the British theatre of Brexit, I argue, can be termed as indicative of Britain's ill-processed and largely unacknowledged imperial history, whose continued virulence manifests itself as this very absence. I therefore explore the ways in which both *Albion* and *The Ferryman* make legible "the chokehold of a nation's past on its present" (Brantley 2018, n.p.) and situate Brexit as firmly grounded in Gilroy's notion of postcolonial melancholia. As both works and their reception suggest, it is only through critically confronting its imperial past that Britain can begin to address vital questions concerning the current state of the nation: constructions of Self versus Other, and the intertwinement of the domestic and the political, as well as the mythical nature of British (and Irish) national identities.

Mike Bartlett's *Albion* and Britain's imperial past

When first staged in October 2017 at London's Almeida, *Albion* was immediately understood apropos of the nation's cataclysmic split that became all too palpable in the Referendum. As Paul Taylor (2017) wrote, "it's a Brexit drama without the word ever being mentioned" because it "explores why some folk, such as the protagonist, are passionately intent on turning the clock back to some imagined golden era" (n.p.). In a similar vein, Toby Lichtig (2017a) felt "this may be the England of Brexit – parochial, petty, thwarted, turned in on itself" (21). It is unusual for the Almeida, or indeed for any smaller London venue, to revive a play so shortly after its initial run. The theatre's decision to include it in their Spring 2020 season therefore has currency. Questioned about his motivation for bringing *Albion* back, artistic director Rupert Goold (2019, n.p.) referred to the increased topicality and emotional pull the text had gained in the two-and-a-half years since its first production, qualities that were also noted by critics reviewing the revival. According to Claire Allfree (2020), *Albion* "remains the only play in recent years to properly probe the competing visions of Britain that make up our fractured isle" (n.p.). Brexit is ever-present throughout the play; in Audrey's casually racist suspicion of everyone and everything that is not English; in the elderly English cleaner, Cheryl, being substituted for by the young Polish Krystyna; in Audrey's novelist friend Katherine, whose cosmopolitan, overt Remain stance and patronizing disdain for Leave voters is juxtaposed with Audrey's contrary sentiments; and in the overall theme of being "rooted", of questions of identity, belonging, and their eclectic interweaving with place. That Bartlett resists the sensationalist lure of using the word "Brexit" eschews the danger of subordinating these larger debates and processes to the "eventness" of the Referendum and its incisive results.

The play's overall atmosphere can best be characterized as elegiac and nostalgic. Indeed, its entire premise is nostalgic, as the protagonist Audrey Walters returns to her childhood home not only to reconnect with her memories, but also, in a poignant metaphor of imperial demise, to restore the estate's historic and now withered garden to its former splendour. In so doing, she epitomizes the nostalgic outlook of Brexiteers – after all, Fintan O'Toole (2020) reminds us, the Leave campaign was built upon the wistful yearning to "take back control" (14). Anna, Audrey's almost-daughter-in-law, cannot let go of the past either, obsessively (to a worrying extent) mourning her dead boyfriend (Audrey's son James), who was killed in Iraq. Similarly, Audrey and Katherine's professed friendship is exclusively grounded in what they may have shared in the past; in the present, they have nothing to say to each other. But in the first place, *Albion* – through its positioning of Audrey as lynchpin for all the characters and actions to revolve around – comments on the reinvigorated empire nostalgia traceable in, and licensed by, current political discourse. Paul Gilroy (2004) famously speaks of "postcolonial melancholia" resulting from the loss of empire as the anchor for imaginations of Britishness.

Since the inexorable decline of the British Empire after World War II, Gilroy argues, the British nation has shown "an inability even to face, never mind actually mourn, the profound change in circumstances and moods that followed the end of the empire and consequent loss of imperial prestige", fuelled by the multilayered anxieties surrounding the radical economic, political, and sociocultural changes the demise of imperial prowess brought with it (90). As a "source of discomfort, shame, and perplexity" the history of empire was silenced and suppressed, which foreclosed any critical accounting for the past (90). Bartlett's play depicts a nation grappling with, or numbed by, this postcolonial melancholia, which in the case of Audrey results in a grotesque misremembering and restaging of the past.

As can be inferred from the title *Albion*, the island of Britain's ancient, romanticized name that translates as "white land" and is used almost exclusively in connection with England, images and afterimages of empire structure the play. This, the title implies, is a drama about a mythical, White Englishness, the longing for an imagined, past "national grandeur" that is mourned by many; a "used-to-be that arguably never was and that certainly is not going to be restored" (O'Toole 2020, 14). The metaphor of a garden is hardly subtle either, as Bartlett here calls upon a tradition that conceptualizes England as a rural idyll that shaped English identity. Such imaginings of England as a second Eden can be traced back to the pastoral poetry of Edmund Spenser or Sir Philip Sidney and became fully pronounced in William Blake's 1804 poem "And Did Those Feet In Ancient Time", later adapted to Hubert Parry's 1916 patriotic hymn "Jerusalem". Critics have furthermore noted *Albion*'s indebtedness not only to the works of Anton Chekhov, but also to more recent "garden plays", as, for instance, Stoppard's *Arcadia* (National Theatre, 1993) or Butterworth's *Jerusalem* (Royal Court, 2009), in which Englishness is negotiated against the backdrop of country settings (Akbar 2020, n.p.). Beyond the title, imperialist chords are next struck in *Albion*'s prologue. Accompanied by David Elgar's "The Spirit of England, Op. 80 No. 3 – For the Fallen", the prologue cuts back to the alleged creation of the titular garden, as it depicts the fictitious army officer Captain Weatherbury, returning home from World War I. He finds an unoccupied plot of land, bends down, and grabs a handful of soil. This potent linkage of war, soil/place, and identity is fully explicated in Audrey's later explanation as to why the particular section of the larger garden in which the play is set is called the Red Garden. As she remarks, Weatherbury created the garden as a war memorial to all those "who made the ultimate sacrifice for England. [...] it's about blood" (Bartlett 2017, 45). To emphasize this link between the personal and the political, between past and present, Audrey scatters her son's ashes in the garden. Not least because of this personal attachment, Audrey insists on solid fences. Prior to her arrival, the villagers had used the space for their annual country fair. Audrey, however, refuses to reopen the garden for this purpose because "the numbers of people would destroy the young plants" (58), a statement that echoes the paranoia of Britain frantically closing its borders for fear of an inrush of migrants.

For Audrey, reinstating the garden's former grandeur is far from a private endeavour, and one in which she cleverly involves the audience. She speaks of "something of national importance, to restore this vital part of our heritage" (Bartlett 2017, 20) – a conviction which provides the character's ideological backbone and confronts audiences with the potentially uncomfortable questions of what "heritage" might mean in this case and who "our" refers to in the first place. Miriam Buether's stage design for the Almeida increased this effect by creating proximity, seating the audience around a naturalistic garden on an oval platform that extended into the auditorium. That way, patrons were made complicit with Audrey's project by their very co-presence inside the titular garden.

On a textual level, collusion with Audrey's neo-imperialist mission is established through the character itself. A London (more precisely, Muswell Hill) owner of a chain of Laura Ashley-like homeware shops, Audrey has no contact with working-class people (Bartlett 2017, 68), let alone migrants. As Katherine remarks sarcastically, "everything is white in her shop. That's her thing. [...] Even the customers" (Bartlett 2017, 36). Whereas her business ethics is progress- and profit-oriented – she lays off 60-year-old, long-serving Cheryl without batting an eyelid simply because Krystyna is more efficient – in all other respects she dwells in the past. In true fashion of the country house drama with its nostalgic looking backward at the "good old times", this romanticizing of the past, for Audrey, includes entertaining by holding lush garden parties. The Agatha Christie-themed murder mystery she hosts for her family and guests Anna labels "obscene" (62) on account of its glorification of a past that was even more illiberal than the – in many ways still illiberal – present. Such ritualized and commodified misremembering of the past bespeaks Audrey's conscious instrumentalizing of temporality in the same way as her peculiar credo "if we do [live in the past], it won't just be the past, it'll be now, and the future. It'll be new and full of opportunity" (92). In her distorted projection of the past-as-future, she sounds jarringly similar to Theresa May's paradoxical vision of a "truly global Britain" heralded on January 17, 2017, a vision that predicts a "glorious" future if Britain remembers its former (read: imperial) muscle and thus wilfully rejects any critical interrogation of imperial legacies.

Audrey is an obnoxious character; surely, her narcissistic bigotry, classism, and xenophobia provide little to no anchor for identification, at least not for the average, left-leaning theatregoer. And yet it seems much of the play's efficacy rests on the audience being simultaneously repulsed and yet reluctantly charmed by her. A well-written, contradictory character, this is a role that makes for compelling drama, particularly if paired with a charismatic actor. Victoria Hamilton, who created the role at the Almeida, received applause and accolades for her Audrey Walters. Across the board, reviewers praised her performance, with Goold (2019, n.p.) going so far as to name her acting turn possibly the best he witnessed during his star-studded artistic directorship of the Almeida. Without wanting to downplay Hamilton's artistic achievement, it therefore appears that something about the character struck a chord with audiences. As Michael Billington (2017) puts it, "in her mixture of romanticism about the past and restless hunger for change" – and, one may add, her inability to listen to others, let alone have a conversation – "she seems to epitomise the nation's neurotic divisions" (n.p.). Whereas Duffy and Norris's attempt to bring London Remainers face to face with the views of Leave voters proved Othering and only hardened pre-existing fronts, Bartlett's protagonist confronts audiences with the enduring hold of the postcolonial melancholia Gilroy describes. *Albion* unpacks a deeply rooted nostalgia for Britain's "glory days", the loss of which has not yet been processed and maybe even more importantly, whose potency many now seem to realize for the first time – otherwise the enthusiastic responses towards the play's heavy, patent allegorizing could not be explained.

The dystopian future of Jez Butterworth's *The Ferryman*

The Troubles in Northern Ireland are an exemplar of Britain's ill-processed imperial history, and so Butterworth's *The Ferryman*, similarly to *Albion*, studies the present through the lens of the colonial past. Despite a large body of Northern Irish plays investigating the legacies of the Troubles,[6] Helen Lojek (2006) describes Northern Ireland as "the forgotten branch of British and Irish theatre, fully integrated neither into the Irish Republic's theatrical scene (developed as a way of investigating and shaping Irish culture) nor into the British theatrical scene" (329). And yet recent London stage history has showcased a number of plays about the effects and after-effects of British rule in Ireland. These include, but are not limited to, the 2017 production of David Ireland's *Everything Between Us* (Solas Nua, Washington, D.C., 2010) at the Finborough Theatre, which explores the Troubles from a Protestant perspective, and the National Theatre's 2018 revival of Brian Friel's classic *Translations* first performed in 1980. Despite its relative marginalization in both British national memory and postcolonial discourse (of which more below), Anglo-Irish history thus seems to be a virulent theme and hot ticket on the post-Referendum London stage.

The Ferryman is set during the height of the Troubles in 1981, in a farmhouse kitchen in Northern Irish County Armagh. The Carney family is just about to bring in the harvest – note the underlying metaphor of "you reap what you sow" – when Father Horrigan, the family's confessor, arrives to tell Quinn and Caitlin Carney that Seamus, Quinn's brother and Caitlin's husband who has been missing for ten years, has been found dead in "a bog across the border" (Butterworth 2017, 47). Both Quinn and Seamus are former members of the Irish Republican Army (IRA), and it is made clear that they were involved in Seamus's killing. Father Horrigan and particularly IRA member Muldoon, therefore, enforce the family's silence about the IRA's involvement in Seamus's death. With the recovery of Seamus Carney's body, Butterworth dramatizes the real-life events surrounding the abduction of the so called "Disappeared", 16 people who were murdered and buried in remote places by IRA paramilitaries. Like Caitlin and her son in the play, the missing people's families were strategically kept in the dark about their relatives' fates, with false clues as to their alleged whereabouts planted by the IRA. Until 1999, the IRA's involvement remained unacknowledged, and, even then, they only took responsibility for ten of the missing individuals (see Peake and Lynch 2016, 453).[7] Through the prism of a domestic tragedy, *The Ferryman* portrays a society in limbo which seeks but does not find closure, neither personally nor politically.

Perhaps surprisingly, given that it broaches a topic which is not exactly new in sometimes rather plain ways, *The Ferryman* opened in London to exuberant reactions, with almost all theatre critics awarding five-star ratings. Much of this excitement can certainly be explained by the combination of star director Sam Mendes and Butterworth himself, especially the hype surrounding his Olivier Award-winning hit *Jerusalem*. With its mythological borrowings, the play employs elements of both Irish folk tale and Greek tragedy (see Teraie-Wood 2018), and so critics highlighted its larger, abstract implications. According to Lichtig (2017b), this is a play about "the cycles of the seasons echoed by the rituals of cultural memory, the tit for tat of political conflict by the rhythmic persistence of unrequited love" (n.p.), and Ben Brantley (2018) deemed it a celebration of "the addictive power of artfully unfolded narratives" (n.p.). In the first place, however, it is a restaging of the Troubles, in their original occurrence between 1968 and 1998 as much as in their possible post-Brexit resurfacing. For Patrick Lonergan (2019), it is Butterworth's prime achievement that he literally puts centre stage a conflict which in British cultural memory is all too often dismissed as dry textbook history. Lichtig, too, stresses the play's renewed contemporaneity. "In terms of festering wounds", he writes, "Butterworth's play could hardly be more timely", and he refers to the apprehensions surrounding the future status of Northern Ireland that surfaced in the Brexit negotiations (Lichtig 2017b, n.p.). Among the many dystopian scenarios projected by both politicians and the media, a potentially violent resurgence of ethno-nationalist tensions in Ulster was the most imminent and threatening. Here, the frequently conversational and trivializing ways in which the word "backstop" was used as a catchy metonym for the larger conflict betrayed a great deal of ignorance about Anglo-Irish history on all parts of society. It speaks volumes about Britain's ability to confront its colonial legacies in Ireland that such a "festering wound" which has existed unnoticed in plain sight all along only gains attention once it threatens to be ripped open again. In a telling metaphor, the murdered Seamus Carney has been found pickled in acidic peat with his body remarkably intact (Butterworth 2017, 8), in the same way as the conflict at the heart of the Troubles has been conserved and simmering under the surface. And when Shane, the Carney children's newly radicalized cousin who has just started working for the IRA, claims that "[t]his is not history. This is happening now" (104), he eerily gestures to the play's foreshadowing of a dystopian scenario – one that only two years after the play's premiere turned into reality when journalist Lyra McKee was killed in the Derry shootings of April 18, 2019.

In delineating the Troubles' precarious settlement and their unrelenting impact on the present, *The Ferryman* recentres a conflict that is not only marginalized in British cultural memory, but also tends to fall outside the "mainstream" of postcolonial criticism (Heidemann 2016, 19–20), which can partly be explained by Ireland's fraught status as a simultaneously colonizing and colonized nation.[8] Yet even within postcolonial criticism, Ireland has been approached in different, and sometimes conflicting, ways. Clare Carroll (2003), for instance, considers Ireland a classic case of a country that was colonized by Britain. As Britain's first colony, Ireland, Ulster in particular, served as a "training ground" for colonial discourse and practice (3). Moreover, the suppression of the Irish language, the long-standing imaginings of the Irish as a racial Other, the partitioning of the island along ethnic or sectarian lines, and the lasting global importance of the Irish diaspora all render Ireland conspicuously postcolonial. At the same time, Carroll points out, a large number of Irish men and women participated in the colonization of non-White peoples around the world, either as settlers and slaveholders in the Caribbean and North America or as soldiers in the British Army (4). Birte Heidemann (2016) diverges from Carroll's conceptualization of British colonialism in Ireland in that she emphasizes the peculiarly liminal status of Northern Ireland. Following her argument, the "post" in "postcolonial" with all its implications of non-closure and continuity still applies (49); especially in the eyes of Catholics living in either the Republic of Ireland or Northern Ireland, British colonial rule remains in place.[9] I suggest that this scholarly divide over how to best understand (Northern) Ireland also helps make sense of *The Ferryman*'s somewhat paradoxical critical reception, much of which bespeaks the Troubles' dual status of being simultaneously unrecognized, because supressed by postcolonial melancholia in Gilroy's terms, *and* deemed exceptionally virulent.

This paradoxical, liminal status equally defines the Troubles' presence in the contemporary cultural landscape. Whereas knowledge of the imperial politics behind the Troubles forms a relative blind spot, "the fuller integration of Ireland than other British colonies into English culture [...] has also meant a particularly daunting process of cultural and intellectual decolonization" (Carroll 2003, 5). Such intellectual decolonization acquires special importance in the case of *The Ferryman* and its process of composition. Butterworth is an English playwright (albeit of Irish Catholic descent), and so the power dynamics resulting from his positionality have to be looked at more closely. In an act of Anglo-Irish ventriloquism, he dramatizes the family history of his partner Laura Donnelly, whose uncle Eugene Simons is among the Disappeared and who played the role of Caitlin Carney in the original London production as well as its Broadway transfer. Butterworth admits to having been aware from the outset that, for him as an Englishman, writing a play about this particular colonial conflict would be a risky undertaking (Gilbert 2017, n.p.). He virtually exhausts the list of canonical, clichéd representations of mythical Irishness: there is a nostalgic celebration of Irish country life, whiskey-drinking, storytelling, singing, jig-dancing, the invocation of a banshee, and even an untrustworthy Catholic priest – an arsenal of "paddywhackery" (O'Hagan 2017, n.p.) tropes that non-Irish critics noticed but deemed successfully translated into "caustic comedy" (Clapp 2017, n.p.).

Commenting on the play's constructions of Irishness, Gerard Lee (2017) recounts his own experience as an Irish audience member and dismisses accusations of stereotyping. As he remembers, English patrons to whom he talked during the interval "were thoroughly absorbed, genuinely engaged with a world that is utterly unknown to most of them" (n.p.). Given that the violent struggle over a reunion with the Republic is neither located far away from the UK – in fact, various bombings during the 1980s and early 1990s even brought the conflict to the nation's capital – nor long-resolved, this ostensible obliviousness on the part of a mostly English audience seems odd. As if anticipating their lack of knowledge, the play re-narrates and authenticates key stages of the British rule in Ireland, going all the way back to Oliver Cromwell's conquest of the island. Aunt Pat vividly recalls her own memories of the Easter Rising of 1916, which she witnessed close to Dublin's General Post Office (Butterworth 2017, 58). In addition to this run-through history lesson, the playtext weaves in original radio footage of Margaret Thatcher denying the Republican hunger strikers in the Maze political status. Aunt Pat, however, silences her mid-sentence by turning off the radio and curses: "If she was standing here I'd fuckin' take a knife from that drawer and I'd disembowel that smirking, sanctimonious, stone-hearted sow right here on this table, so I would" (37). For Lee, "to be Irish and hear that in a theatre in the heart of London creates a very particular sensation" (2017, n.p.). At the same time, however, an English audience might perceive this scene in another way. In England, too, Thatcher is an ambivalent figure, to say the least, but for markedly different reasons. In conflating Irish and English national memories and afterimages of Thatcher, the play's critique of her ruthless colonialist stance on Northern Ireland might be lost on a predominantly English audience for whom the sound on tape may not trigger personal memories and whose knowledge of the Troubles, if any, may be by and large transmitted via (pop-) cultural mediations thereof.

Whilst Lee positively emphasizes the play's critical awareness of British colonial rule in Ireland, others are more sceptical. As Sean O'Hagan (2017) points out, Irish people living in the UK may be made aware of their perceived Otherness in subtle rather than overtly confrontational ways, but still they are Othered routinely. For him, attending *The Ferryman*'s opening night marked such an occasion. Like Lee, he recalls the audience's ignorance, if not celebration, of stereotypical formations of Irishness on stage, which is why he concludes that the play reveals "more about English attitudes to Ireland than it did about Northern Ireland" (O'Hagan 2017, n.p.). The simplistic depiction of IRA paramilitaries as sinister gangsters he cites as particularly problematic because "[a] great part of the IRA's enduring power, as well as the tacit support they depended on, came from the fact that they were embedded in local communities" (n.p.). Whilst the play does show their embeddedness in the community, the IRA appear much more immediate a threat than the equally villainized Thatcher, whose presence is only perceptible at a remove. They are little more than cardboard characters with opaque political motives. Loyalties and dependencies are simplified, therefore, which blurs the reality that the Troubles did not simply arise out of Catholic or Protestant communities themselves but in reaction to, and fuelled by, an external, armed colonizing force. As such, the play's appropriately dystopian vision is at least partly detached from its colonial origins, and the thrill of imminence emphasized at the cost of a more nuanced unravelling of British responsibilities – a vision which both reflects and perpetuates the curious, liminal position of a perceived threat and simultaneously unacknowledged presence the Troubles hold in contemporary British sociopolitical discourse.

Conclusion: Postcolonial melancholia continued

To return to the question of what state of the nation, post-Brexit, the two plays discussed here envision, it is worth taking a look at their respective endings. Like a Greek tragedy, *The Ferryman* ends with the stage covered with bodies: when Caitlin's son Oisin expresses the wish to avenge his father by joining the fight against the British, Shane suggests he start by murdering the English recluse Tom Kettle.[10] Oisin tries to kill the sleeping Kettle, but the latter strangles Oisin in self-defence. In retaliation, Quinn then kills IRA members Muldoon and Magennis. Most critics expressed disappointment with this convoluted ending, calling it "rushed, implausible and wanton" (Lichtig 2017b, n.p.). At the same time, Lichtig points out, the feeling of having been "cheated, as if the dramatic resolution were no resolution at all [...] is thematically appropriate" (n.p.). He is right in that the ending is dissatisfying, but aptly so. Its dramaturgical messiness corresponds to the "messiness" and persistence of imperial forms of dominion, particularly in the case of the Troubles. "Have you forgotten your *own* history there, Quinn Carney? Good luck with that, is all I'll say. Good luck forgetting *that*" (Butterworth 2017, 38; original emphasis), Aunt Pat says at one point. Attempts at silencing the past, the play indicates, will lead to continued injustice and new bloodshed. To avoid such a dystopian outlook, colonial legacies – which for British audiences are a vital part of *their* history – need to be interrogated honestly at last.

By the final act of *Albion*, Audrey has alienated all of her family and friends. The garden, now withered beyond reclaim, has been sold and is about to be converted into a housing complex, each flat with its own garden patch. As Audrey and her husband are about to leave, she suddenly changes her mind. "This is everything. Myself. My family. James. My past. My future. I don't want anything else but this piece of land" (Bartlett 2017, 122), she says and begins replanting some of the uprooted plants. The play ends with her sitting in the midst of the stage, whilst the house is being dismantled in the background and the garden decomposes entirely. Again, the implications are clear: attempts at reinvigorating the past will inevitably lead to isolation and destruction. A future shaped by empire nostalgia, in other words, is dystopian in itself. Reconsidering the aforementioned definition of the genre's confrontational political agenda, both plays are certainly successful examples of new writing for the stage. However, what may seem a radical insight for predominantly White, English audiences is both common knowledge and painful personal experience for others. If empire nostalgia is the defining feature of British nationalism right now, then it does not suffice, as Anshuman Mondal (2018) aptly puts it in the title of an essay, to "scratch the post-imperial itch" from time to time. The glance backwards that both Bartlett and Butterworth (be it in different ways) undertake is what must be the first step towards understanding Britishness in the 21st century, towards untangling constructions of selfhood and Otherness. If this is the most poignant comment on Brexit that drama can make at the moment – and at least this is what the critical receptions of both *Albion* and *The Ferryman* suggest – the postcolonial melancholia identified by Gilroy remains as paralysing as ever.

Notes

1. New British writing is notoriously difficult to pin down, in terms of both thematic foci and aesthetics. Though frequently understood as denoting plays by emergent authors, the term "new writing" is misleading. Rather, as Middeke, Schnierer, and Sierz (2011) explain, new writing should be conceptualized as "a genre characterised by plays which are contemporary in their language, contemporary in their subject matter and often contemporary in their attitude to theatre form" (ix). Whilst some of these plays can be characterized as "confrontational and provocative", all new writers position themselves "in opposition to the populist and commercial West End theatre" (x).
2. For a more comprehensive overview of post-war Black British drama, see Brewer, Goddard, and Osborne (2015); on British Asian theatre, see Hingorani (2010).
3. On further recent productions dealing with issues of migration, see Cornford (2018). Besides *How to Hold Your Breath*, he also discusses the South African Isango Ensemble's production of *A Man of Good Hope* (The Royal Opera and Young Vic, 2016) and Zodwa Nyoni's *Nine Lives* (West Yorkshire Playhouse and Òran Mór, Glasgow, 2016).
4. I use the common expression "Troubles" because it is more established than the official "Northern Ireland conflict". However, the term "Troubles" has been deemed problematic, particularly if ascribed externally. Not only has the term been applied to a number of different conflicts in Irish history, but it has also been criticized for its somewhat euphemistic connotation. "Troubles" avoids the allocation of blame to one particular party, yet its dodging of the term "war" (the phrase preferred by IRA paramilitaries) downplays the involvement of armed British forces.
5. On Northern Ireland's pre-existing status of "negative liminality", see Heidemann (2016, 17–62, especially 18).

6. On earlier dramatic portrayals of the Troubles, see Lojek (2006); on post-agreement Northern Irish drama, see Heidemann (2016, 191–249).
7. Peake and Lynch (2016) specify that "as of 2015, the Provisional IRA (PIRA) has admitted responsibility for thirteen, and the Irish National Liberation Army (INLA) one; the remaining victims have not been officially recognised as disappeared" (453).
8. For a more nuanced discussion of the contested status of Ireland in postcolonial theory and criticism, see Flannery (2009) and Cleary (2003).
9. For a more comprehensive analysis of the "fused postcolonial" status of Northern Ireland and its location in postcolonial discourse, see Heidemann (2016, especially 17–62, especially 22); see also Storey (1998).
10. If coincidental at all, it is certainly unfortunate that the play's simple-minded Englishman bears the name of the famous academic and Irish nationalist Thomas Kettle (1980–1916), a leading figure in the political fight for Home Rule.

Disclosure statement

No potential conflict of interest was reported by the author.

References

Akbar, Arifa. 2020. "*Albion* Review: Mike Bartlett's Thorny Study of Politics and Patriotism." *The Guardian*, February 6. https://www.theguardian.com/stage/2020/feb/06/albion-review-almeida-mike-bartlett-rupert-goold

Allfree, Claire. 2020. "*Albion*, Almeida, Review: An Incisive and Unforgettable Allegory of Our Divided Nation." *The Telegraph*, February 6. https://www.telegraph.co.uk/theatre/what-to-see/albion-review-almeida-incisive-unforgettable-allegory-divided/

Bartlett, Mike. 2017. *Albion*. London: Nick Hern Books.

Billington, Michael. 2017. "*Albion* Review: Mike Bartlett Captures Nation's Neurotic Divisions." *The Guardian*, October 18. https://www.theguardian.com/stage/2017/oct/18/albion-review-mike-bartlett-almeida-london

Brantley, Ben. 2018. "Review: A Thrilling *Ferryman* Serves up A Glorious Harvest Feast." *The New York Times*, October 21. https://www.nytimes.com/2018/10/21/theater/the-ferryman-review-broadway-jez-butterworth.html

Brewer, Mary, Lynette Goddard, and Deirdre Osborne, eds. 2015. *Modern and Contemporary Black British Drama*. London: Palgrave.

Butterworth, Jez. 2017. *The Ferryman*. London: Nick Hern Books.

Carroll, Clare. 2003. "Introduction: The Nation and Postcolonial Theory." In *Ireland and Postcolonial Theory*, edited by Clare Carroll and Patricia King, 1–15. Notre Dame, IN: University of Notre Dame Press.

Citizenstheatre. 2017. "My Country; A Work in Progress 28 Mar - 1 Apr - Citz.co.uk." *YouTube*, March 8. https://www.youtube.com/watch?v=1GKiqSHGxL0

Clapp, Susannah. 2017. "*The Ferryman* Review: Jez Butterworth Pulls Another Rabbit from the Hat." *The Guardian*, May 7. https://www.theguardian.com/stage/2017/may/07/ferryman-royal-court-jez-butterworth-review-magic

Cleary, Joe. 2003. "Misplaced Ideas? Colonialism, Location, and Dislocation in Irish Studies." In *Ireland and Postcolonial Theory*, edited by Clare Carroll and Patricia King, 17–45. Notre Dame, IN: University of Notre Dame Press.

Cornford, Tom. 2018. "Experiencing Nationlessness: Staging the Migrant Condition in Some Recent British Theatre." *Journal of Contemporary Drama in English* 6 (1): 101–112. doi:10.1515/jcde-2018-0014.

Dickson, Andrew. 2017. "Tom Stoppard: Brexit Is Too Big for the Stage." *The Guardian*, February 10. https://www.theguardian.com/stage/2017/feb/10/tom-stoppard-interview-rosencrantz-and-guildenstern-old-vic-travesties

Fisher, Mark. 2019. "Stage of the Nation: What Does It Mean to Be a National Theatre?" *The Guardian*, January 15. https://www.theguardian.com/stage/2019/jan/15/national-theatre-england-scotland-wales-ireland

Flannery, Eóin. 2009. *Ireland and Postcolonial Studies: Theory, Discourse, Utopia*. London: Palgrave.

Gilbert, Sophie. 2017. "*The Ferryman*: Jez Butterworth on the Legacy of Hate." *The Atlantic*, September 5. https://www.theatlantic.com/entertainment/archive/2017/09/the-ferryman-jez-butterworth-on-the-legacy-of-hate/537984/

Gilroy, Paul. 2004. *Postcolonial Melancholia*. New York: Columbia University Press.

Goold, Rupert. 2019. "ALBION | February 2020." *YouTube*, October 24. https://www.youtube.com/watch?v=sQ1dIK5DZ1c&feature=youtu.be

Heidemann, Birte. 2016. *Post-Agreement Northern Irish Literature: Lost in a Liminal Space?* Basingstoke: Palgrave Macmillan.

Hingorani, Dominic. 2010. *British Asian Theatre: Dramaturgy, Process and Performance*. London: Palgrave.

Lee, Gerard. 2017. "In Defence of *the Ferryman* by Jez Butterworth." *The Irish Times*, August 1. https://www.irishtimes.com/culture/stage/in-defence-of-the-ferryman-by-jez-butterworth-1.3173470

Lichtig, Toby. 2017a. "Green Unpleasant Land: Mike Bartlett's Vision of England." *TLS*, November 10. https://www.the-tls.co.uk/articles/mike-bartlett-albion/

Lichtig, Toby. 2017b. "Home to Roost: Jez Butterworth Explores Cycles of Family Life, Politics, History and Violence." *TLS*, May 12. https://www.the-tls.co.uk/articles/jez-butterworth-ferryman/

Lojek, Helen. 2006. "Troubling Perspectives: Northern Ireland, the 'Troubles' and Drama." In *A Concise Companion to Contemporary British and Irish Drama*, edited by Nadine Holdsworth and Mary Luckhurst, 229–340. Malden, MA and Oxford: Blackwell.

Lonergan, Patrick. 2019. "Au Contraire: Exploring Brexit in English and Irish Theater." *The Clyde Fitch Report*, March 18. https://www.clydefitchreport.com/2019/03/brexit-theater-english-irish/

Middeke, Martin, Peter Paul Schnierer, and Aleks Sierz. 2011. "Introduction." In *The Methuen Drama Guide to Contemporary British Playwrights*, edited by Martin Middeke, Peter Paul Schnierer, and Aleks Sierz, vii–xxiv. Bloomsbury: London.

Mondal, Anshuman A. 2018. "Scratching the Post-Imperial Itch." In *Brexit and Literature*, edited by Robert Eaglestone, 82–91. London and New York: Routledge.

O'Hagan, Sean. 2017. "Critics Loved *The Ferryman*. But I'm from Northern Ireland, and It Doesn't Ring True." *The Guardian*, July 16. https://www.theguardian.com/commentisfree/2017/jul/16/jez-butterworth-the-ferryman-irish-stereotypes-sam-mendes

O'Toole, Fintan. 2020. *Three Years in Hell: The Brexit Chronicles*. London: Head of Zeus.

Peake, Sandra, and Orla Lynch. 2016. "Victims of Irish Republican Paramilitary Violence: The Case of 'The Disappeared'." *Terrorism and Political Violence* 28 (3): 452–472. doi:10.1080/09546553.2016.1155931.

Shaw, Kristian. 2018. "Brexlit." In *Brexit and Literature*, edited by Robert Eaglestone, 15–30. London and New York: Routledge.

Sierz, Aleks. 2011. *Rewriting the Nation: British Theatre Today*. London: Methuen.
Sierz, Aleks. 2018a. "British Theatre after Brexit: One Year On." *PAJ: A Journal of Performance and Art* 40 (3): 60–70.
Sierz, Aleks. 2018b. "David Hare's *I'm Not Running* at the National Theatre." *The Theatre Times*, October 13. https://thetheatretimes.com/david-hares-im-not-running-at-the-national-theatre/
Storey, Michael. 1998. "Postcolonialism and Stories of the Irish Troubles." *New Hibernia Review/ Iris Éireannach Nua* 2 (3): 63–77.
Taylor, Paul. 2017. "Carol Ann Duffy Brings a Major's Poet's Ear to the Music of the Text." *The Independent*, March 13. https://www.independent.co.uk/arts-entertainment/theatre-dance/reviews/my-country-a-work-in-progress-dorfman-national-theatre-review-carol-ann-duffy-rufus-norris-a7626791.html
Teraie-Wood, Hana. 2018. "Buried Politics: *The Ferryman*, the Troubles, and the Disappeared." *Moveable Type* 10: 64–87.
Trueman, Matt. 2019. "British Theatre Has Its Head in the Sand over Brexit." *The Stage*, January 21. https://www.thestage.co.uk/opinion/2019/matt-trueman-british-theatre-brexit/print/?login_to=https%3A%2F%2Fwww.thestage.co.uk%2Faccounts%2Fusers%2Fsign_up.popup
Williams, Roy. 2014. *Sing Yer Heart Out for the Lads*. London: Methuen.

The Brexit within: Mapping the rural and the urban in contemporary British fiction

Birte Heidemann

ABSTRACT

Just as the 2016 referendum results had spiralled into a full-blown crisis, it became increasingly clear that Britain's push to leave the European Union (EU) concealed another crisis: a "Brexit within". This term refers to the entries, exits, and enclosures that course through a dominant narrative of English national identity: countryside versus city life. Drawing on Raymond Williams's *The Country and the City* (1973), this article argues that the rural and the urban serve as a template to diagnose other forms of division in Britain – racial, social, cultural, and economic – that the Brexit vote brought to the fore. The reading is based on two works of fiction published in the immediate aftermath of the referendum: Ali Smith's *Autumn* (2016) and Amanda Craig's *The Lie of the Land* (2017). Both narratives continue a larger literary tradition of Condition-of-England novels, as they map out new sites of marginalization and precarity in the post-imperial nation.

Introduction

In her essay "Fences: A Brexit Diary", Zadie Smith moves beyond the familiar terrain of North London that features in much of her writing and shares her very personal perspective on the 2016 Brexit referendum. Just like her fictional portraits of modern urban life, which some critics have compared to Dickensian depictions of London,[1] Smith's essay starts off in Britain's capital to explore why the majority of voters cast their ballot in favour of "fencing" themselves off from the rest of Europe:

> The profound *shock* I felt at the result – and which so many other Londoners seem to have experienced – suggests at the very least that we must have been living behind a kind of veil, unable to see our own country for what it has become. (Smith 2016, n.p.; my emphasis)

Once the referendum results sink in, she begins to see how the "material realities" (Smith 2016, n.p.) she increasingly encounters in London – from fenced-off schools to security-patrolled, gated neighbourhoods to the occasional chat over the garden fence – have become mere symbols of Britain's divisive push to leave the European Union (EU). For Smith, then, the only "useful consequence" (n.p.) of the Brexit referendum is to reveal a rupture along lines of class, education, and generation, a rupture that has continually yet covertly been widening within the last 30 years. After all, Smith concludes, the shock waves that a predominantly young, educated, and urban demographic – like herself – had felt at the outcome of the referendum only *camouflaged* a crisis "that was always there" (n.p.). Thus, while the result of the referendum undoubtedly "produced one of the biggest shocks in modern British politics" (Fox and Pearce 2018, 19), the lines of division had been in the making long before the big revelation of June 2016. Almost four years later, with Britain formally, albeit not fully, exited from the EU, one may even concede that "it's deep in our animal nature [...] not to see what's happening right in front of our eyes" (Smith [2016] 2017, 175); this is something that 101-year-old Daniel Gluck – one of the protagonists of Ali Smith's *Autumn* and central to my reading here – has come to realize at the end of his long life.

Taking its cue from the wisdom (and wit) of a centenarian, this paper explores both the material and symbolic fencing of communities that has remained conspicuously absent from public discourse: a Brexit *within*. By "Brexit within", I refer to the entries, exits, and enclosures that one encounters in the rhetoric used by political commentators, politicians, and journalists alike. Among these, the trope of the "divided nation" has been the most prominent, if not dominant, ever since the referendum results were announced. What came up in the immediate aftermath of the referendum – perhaps to make sense of such results – quickly evolved into Brexit parlance par excellence, whether online, in print, on television, or in academic articles (see, for instance, Ford and Goodwin 2017; Hobolt 2016; Newall 2016; Curtice 2016). And while the trope of the divided nation may be related to a largely demographic analysis that reads the outcome of the referendum as "a symptom of longer-term social changes" (Ford and Goodwin 2017, 17), it restricts such diagnosis to the exits, and to some extent the enclosures, of the debate. It is for this reason that the article has chosen to focus on the less discussed entryways that allowed these divisions – demographic and otherwise – to become Britain's Brexit within. Drawing on Raymond Williams's ([1973] 1975) seminal study *The Country and the City*, which links social formation in England to the economies of imperialism in select works of fiction, the article considers the discrepant dynamics between the rural and the urban as *one* route towards mapping out new sites of division in post-imperial Britain. Thus, my reading extends its gaze from the largely demographic debates on the Brexit vote to a more elaborate treatment of the legacies of empire, particularly in relation to its multipolar immigrant situation. It is here, at the intersections of the local, the national, and the global, that Williams's "structural understanding of the British empire as a spatialised history of rural exploitation" has yet to be addressed by postcolonial literary studies, as Lucienne Loh (2013, 2) reminds us.

Just as Williams moves beyond reading the city's relation to the country as a mirror of the relationship between the imperial metropolis and the subject colony (Williams [1973] 1975, 279; Viswanathan 1995, 192), the present discussion will move beyond the normative empiricism of social science approaches that tend to read the rural and the urban as diametrically opposed categories in the aftermath of the referendum (Becker, Fetzer, and Novy 2017; Jennings, Stoker, and Warren 2019; De Gruyter 2016).[2] Rather, in line with Robert Eaglestone's claim that literature "supplements and deepens the social sciences" (2018, 1), this article contends that representations of the rural and the urban in recent British fiction provide readers with rhetorical cues into a political imaginary that reveals the constructed nature of the divisions at hand. Although the body of literature on Brexit produced after the referendum of 2016 has been growing exponentially, the following reading will be based on two works of British fiction that were published in its immediate aftermath: Amanda Craig's ([2017] 2018) *The Lie of the Land*, whose protagonists from London move to a remote countryside cottage after having lost their jobs in the recession, and Ali Smith's ([2016] 2017) *Autumn*, in which the non-linear narration shifts between the post-referendum musings of 30-year-old Elisabeth and the post-war memories of her former neighbour, centenarian Daniel. Both books, the article suggests, map out the entryways into a "Brexit within" along (colonial) lines of migration, movement, and Othering. While both narratives are set in the countryside, they redress the rigid binaries of rural versus urban as poor versus rich, margin versus centre, colony versus metropole and Other versus Self to lay bare other structural and societal divisions of the Brexit within as part of a larger literary tradition of Condition-of-England novels.

Beyond Brexit: Contemporary Condition-of-England novels

Given their shared context of production and reception, it is surely tempting to categorize the crop of novels published since the Brexit referendum as representative of a new subgenre, like the catchy "BrexLit", a term coined by Kristian Shaw (2018) in his essay of the same title. Shaw defines BrexLit as a set of novels that "either directly respond or imaginatively allude to Britain's exit from the EU" (18). Such generic categorization, however, does not come without its shortcomings, as Shaw himself remains inconsistent in the terminology he uses. Instead of making a case for BrexLit only, he synonymously refers to the same set of texts as "post-Brexit fiction" (18) or as belonging to a "post-Brexit literary landscape" (25). And while this may have to do with the sense of urgency with which Shaw's essay was written – arguably the first attempt to compile and categorize such an emergent body of texts – Petra Rau (2018) reminds us that the "conflation of the referendum as a democratic iteration with its [...] consequence (exit from the European Union)" (36) is symptomatic of how the literary response to the referendum has been framed. Ali Smith's *Autumn*, for instance, was praised by critic Sophie Gilbert (2017, n. p.) as a "post-Brexit masterpiece" (see also Rau 2018, 36) although it is set only days after the vote. Perhaps it is precisely the uncertainty around Britain's eventual exit from the EU that prompted such a terminological time lapse. Even in early 2020, at the time of writing this article, there is nothing "post" about Brexit at all. The UK has indeed left the EU on January 31, but finds itself in a transition period until the end of the year while the United Kingdom (UK) and the EU negotiate additional arrangements, the UK Government website proclaims (GOV.UK 2020, n.p.). Thus, to "Get Brexit Done" – the mantra-like motto of Boris Johnson's 2019 election campaign – ends up reiterating the suspensive moment created by the referendum rather than putting the proverbial end to it.

Scottish novelist Ali Smith's "ultra-of-the-moment seasonal quartet" (Preston 2019, n. p.) constitutes a counter-narrative to such ploys of political suspension. In 2015, Smith set out to write four novels "at breakneck speed" (Preston 2019, n.p.) to respond to a time of political transition, if not turmoil. The temporal composition centred around the seasons advocates a natural progression of time that implies renewal as much as return. Just as prime ministers came and went, and negotiations with the EU faltered and flourished again within a sea of political suspension (and, at times, suspense), Smith's serial project, once completed, will read as a perpetual transformation from one state to another while relentlessly moving towards Brexit, and perhaps beyond. Opening with *Autumn* in 2016, the quartet was followed by *Winter* in 2017 and *Spring* the year after, and is due to end with *Summer* in July 2020. Although not conceived as sequels to plot and setting, the books continue to "converse vociferously" with each other, "as they revise each other's signs and symbols" (Harris 2017, n.p.) – fences being the most prominent – either randomly erected (*Autumn*), chained onto fences in protest (*Winter*), or built around an immigration centre (*Spring*). And while all three books are teeming with literary references, Smith shows a particular penchant for Charles Dickens, as some of her characters seem to "jump right out of" the latter's literary imagination (Huets 2018, n.p.). As early as her first instalment *Autumn* (Smith [2016] 2017), which starts off with a rendition of the opening in *A Tale of Two Cities* (Dickens [1859] 2000), Smith draws on the divisive national imaginary in Dickens's work. *Winter* (Smith [2017] 2018) takes its cue from *A Christmas Carol* and turns it into "a subtly crafted post-referendum allegory" (Pittel 2018, 64). Indeed, what all three instalments have in common is a rather bleak portrayal of present-day Britain suffering from austerity, climate change, and casual racism. Except for *Spring* (Smith [2018] 2020), however, none mention Brexit explicitly. While *Autumn* merely refers once to "the referendum" (Smith [2016] 2017, 196), Smith was granted one month of editorial extension to update the narrative with the latest political developments: the results of the referendum. She explains the sense of urgency with which she completed *Autumn*: "I knew the book had to [...] square up to what was happening if the notions of contemporaneousness [...] were to mean anything at all" (Smith quoted in Anderson 2016, n.p.). Such mediated immediacy notwithstanding, Smith affirms, the scope and content of her seasonal quartet come "on their own terms" (Armitstead 2019, n.p.). Similarly, in response to her post-referendum novel *The Lie of the Land*, Amanda Craig concedes that "Brexit gave us the best excuse for a plot since World War 2", while maintaining that her book is about "the widening division between the country and the city" rather than the political event per se (Craig quoted in Self 2020, n.p.).

Following Jon Day (2017, n.p.), who suggested that "novels about contemporary events written before the political ink has dried can feel like barely padded polemics", I suggest that both books are not necessarily bound to a *specific* contemporary event. Rather, they diagnose an innate yet imminent sense of emergency that, among others, may *also* be read as the underlying cause for all things Brexit. This is why I remain reluctant to classify the two novels under discussion along the temporal trajectories of an event. Generic labels such as "BrexLit" or "post-Brexit fiction" purport a certain degree of finitude or closure, when in fact they are symptomatic of a continuing sense of crisis. If one were to locate them within a literary *tradition*, however, both books may be read as contemporary versions of State-of-the-Nation novels or, more specifically, as Condition-of-England novels that seek to sift out the social divisions of their time. While I do not wish to compare the current "condition" of Britain with the poverty and inequality of the Victorian era – the pinnacle of the Condition-of-England novel – the two novels are acutely aware of an *almost* never-ending Brexit narrative that invites novelists to tackle "the 'now' " (Rau 2018, 31). For Smith, this has largely to do with fiction's formal possibilities, because stories, she points out, provide us with "everything we need to know about the contemporary world" (Armitstead 2019, n.p.). In Victorian England, it was writers of fiction who set out to confront their middle-class readership with a world utterly at odds. The industrial or Condition-of-England novels of the 1840s and 1850s – most notably the work of Dickens, Disraeli, and Gaskell – have served as templates for Edwardian novelists such as E.M. Forster or contemporary authors such as Martin Amis, William Boyd, or Ian McEwan (Ross 2008, 75). It is here, in the fold of the Condition-of-England tradition, that Raymond Williams's pioneering study *The Country and the City* places the rural and the urban into "an ever-present grand narrative" of "Englishness" (Tronicke 2017, 127), namely that of the "two nations". Williams does so by substituting what Disraeli's *Sybil; Or, The Two Nations* (1845) originally defined as the dyad of rich versus poor to map out England's literary landscape along regional, moral, and cultural axes. The rigid nature of such "predetermined horizons" (Tronicke 2017, 127) notwithstanding, the "two nations" topos – and the many intersecting factors it entails – remain "in constant flux and metamorphosis that reproduces itself in ever new (and old) forms" (127). Perhaps the most recent rendition is the trope of the "divided nation" that has been dominating the debates on Brexit. And while Williams's roadmap for reading canonical English fiction as an "unresolved and constantly morphing conflict between country and city" risks the dangers of reproducing the same reductive tendencies of the "two nations" topos, it succeeds in situating its roots in a colonial "tension" of city versus country that "is never arrested" (Brennan 2017, 38–39). It is this very tension, if not suspension, that conceives the "formidable crucible of countryside, empire and immigration" (Loh 2013, 9) as the locus of a Brexit within. In what follows, my reading of the two texts – *The Lie of the Land* and *Autumn* – engages with how literature's rendition of the rural and the urban may serve as a marked-out route towards locating Britain's current moment of crisis within the legacies of empire. As the reading will reveal, both post-referendum novels play with – and often pun – a (post-)imperial entitlement to the "land" through various modes of Othering, migration, movement, and racial stereotyping.

Of entries and exits: Brexit(s) within in *The Lie of the Land* and *Autumn*

"A gloom lies over the world" – this is how Craig's ([2017] 2018, 2) *The Lie of the Land* verbalizes the sense of emergency that looms large throughout the narrative. Despite its reference to the *global* ramifications of such "gloom", Craig's narrative is firmly set within the fissures of what has become a crucial component in the construction of England's national imaginary: countryside versus city life. As early as the Romantic period, with the onset of industrialization, writers such as Coleridge and Wordsworth ([1798] 2007) in their *Lyrical Ballads* began to explore the ever-expanding gulf between country and city. "Although well stocked with imagery that depicts rural England as stable, serene and prosperous" (Frawley 2017, 467), the literary landscapes of Victorian England – particularly those of the Condition-of-England novel – became a potent site of social critique, diagnosing not only urban desolation, crime, and disease, but also the plight of the rural population that was on the very margin of its existence. Set against an urban scenario of hardship, the recurrent trope of the rural idyll as a place of hope, Williams argues, was nothing more than "a myth functioning as a memory" ([1973] 1975, 43) that forgets about the suffering of peasant workers, the old and sick, or the abandoned women. Craig's concern with the internal rifts between the rural and the urban is largely inspired by these literary traditions, as her novel deals with "people moving between rich and poor and the struggle to be a decent human being despite poverty" (Craig quoted in Galton 2017, n.p.). Within this, various modes of movement – and the restrictions thereof – expose her characters' struggle with either entering or exiting the structural divisions of post-recession Britain which, on a narrative level, are cloaked in a murder case. The rundown cottage rented by Craig's London protagonists hides a dark secret that only adds to the dystopian character, if not caricature, of the Devon setting, as "there is much comedy to be had from the juxtaposition of metropolitan and rural lives as the family get increasingly entangled with the indigenous population" (Woodward 2017, n.p.). At the beginning, however, the latter encounter the newcomers with a great deal of suspicion reminiscent of a rhetoric of racial Othering that often resurfaces in times of (domestic) crisis.

"[They] must have been escaping from something […]? Why else do incomers come here?" (Craig [2017] 2018, 228), the Devon locals wonder after protagonists Lottie and Quentin have moved into their remote cottage. Living in a part of Devon that is arguably "poorer than Romania" (105), it is only the local characters, battling with unemployment, malnutrition, and drug abuse, who make explicit comments on "the hated EU" (94). And while Brexit is only mentioned verbatim once (272), Craig cannot deny that it was "the lightning rod for the rage of so many people" in provincial towns (Craig quoted in Galton 2017, n.p.). A part-time resident somewhere in rural England herself, she could sense "so much frustration" among the population "and the EU and immigration were blamed" (Craig quoted in Galton 2017, n.p.). Yet, given their mutual reluctance to get to know each other, the villagers in her novel remain unaware of the fact that the "refugees from London" (Craig [2017] 2018, 258), as they refer to Lottie, Quentin, and their children, similarly suffer from existential fears. In fact, Lottie's hastily planned move to the countryside – to rent out their London property and save up for divorce – plunges her adulterous husband Quentin into an identity (or perhaps midlife) crisis, despite or perhaps precisely because he was born and bred in Devon and only moved to London as an adult. He laments "far more than any woman" the loss of "the love of his life" (80) – London. Quentin's weekly column for the newspaper he once edited becomes his outlet for complaining about the countryside. Thus, it is in his *writing* that Quentin turns into a true local patriot whose unrequited love affair with London makes him forget why they fled the city in the first place. In an ironic twist of editorial intervention, Craig refuses Quentin the rhetorical space for cultivating such bias, as he sees himself confronted with a continual cutback of his column's length. Indeed, the shame and stigma that come with unemployment do not leave them much choice but to abandon their Hampstead home. With the socio-economic crisis at its peak, Quentin seeks refuge in a rhetoric that reminds one of the new round of imperial nostalgia forged by Brexit. While Quentin does not come across as the "average" Leave voter, he invokes one of the most committed imperialists of the 19th century when asking Lottie: "Remember Cecil Rhodes said, that if you're English, you have won first prize in the lottery of life? Well, it's even more true if you're a Londoner" (332). Curiously enough, for Williams, it is precisely "the system we now know as imperialism" that was modelled on "the traditional relationship between city and country" at home ([1973] 1975, 279), including the myths and misconceptions surrounding these sites of habitation. Thus, it may come as no surprise that even Quentin's young children unwittingly echo their father's false patriotism, as they keep asking their puzzled mother – the only one in the family who seems to settle in fairly quickly – when they will be "going back to England". " 'London isn't England', Lottie says. 'This is England, too' " (Craig [2017] 2018, 53).

Given the novel's title, the pun on the "land" was certainly intended by Craig. "The lie of the land", one may infer, not only relates to the rural England in which the novel is primarily set. Rather, it refers to the many misconceptions – lies, as it were – that lay bare the "[d]ouble articulation of the country and the city" (Loh 2013, 16) which is yet to be extended from a postcolonial to a post-imperial context. Just as Craig's many characters dip in and out of the narrative, the novel reveals the many points of convergence between country and city, between local and global, and between progress and regress, all of which have been restricted to how the postcolonial city and country "continue to serve as the global hinterland of the metropolitan centres" (Skurski and Coronil 1993, 232). In Britain, far from being places apart, there is constant movement, if not migration, in and across the two sites: by "refugees" from London who escape the city's economic precarity, by immigrants from Eastern Europe flocking to rural factories, or by those who settled in urban centres as early as Britain's imperial days. If rigid regional divisions have become increasingly porous, with new sites of marginalization in and across city and country, then it is characters like social worker Sally who lived in London before settling back into farm life, or rock star Gore Tore who tours the world but always returns to his rural home, who populate the narrative's layered landscape. And there are, too, a number of characters, rural and urban alike, who turn out to be related to one another or whose paths have crossed in the past. These observations also correspond to the very misconceptions that, as Williams would have it, "fail to expose – and indeed obscure – deeper historical dynamics whereby the country and the city have actually been produced and reproduced in interrelation with one another" (West 2014, 74). What may come across as clear-cut divisions, Craig's character constellation reveals, always leave room for dialogue, albeit one that is rarely responded to in public discourse.

In Ali Smith's *Autumn*, the dyad of rural and urban is reinforced by a narrative form that both visualizes and verbalizes the divisions (if not dialogues) at hand. Unlike Craig's straightforward focalized narration that alternates between four main characters, *Autumn*'s narrative is infused with magic realist elements and a reduced use of punctuation, which only reinforces the provisional nature of the political context in which it was written. The narrative strands are divided between the dream sequences of 101-year-old Daniel, who finds himself in an increased sleep period in an old people's home, and the flashbacks of Elisabeth to the flourishing of their unlikely friendship as neighbours in the 1990s. The present context of the plot, however, is set "just over a week since the vote" (Smith [2016] 2017, 53), which leaves London-based lecturer Elisabeth with a profound sense of dislocation, even despair. Elisabeth's life in London is referred to only fleetingly, for much of the narrative is set somewhere in rural England where she is visiting her mother. But what one can gather from the text's many parentheses is that life in a "metropolitan centre" is far from "living the dream", as her "no-fixed-hours casual contract" at university means "having no job security" when "almost everything [is] too expensive" (15). But in the immediate aftermath of the vote, life in "provincial" Britain is an equally "sullen" (53) affair where people, Elisabeth notices, "either look down, look away or stare her out" (53). And when she is visiting the shops, they "speak with a new kind of detachment" (54). Elisabeth, having left for London to study more than a decade ago, is encountered by the locals with a similar kind of suspicion as Craig's protagonists. Like Lottie and Quentin, she becomes yet another Other who challenges the "authentic" claim to the "country" that is "crucial not only to constructing national consciousness, but also to determining self-identity within a globalized, postcolonial world" (Loh 2013, 1). For instance, just as racist graffiti begins to stain the walls of the cottages in her mother's village, Elisabeth notices a three-metres-high fence with razor wire and security cameras erected along a stretch of land where "there are no people [...] no buildings [...] just fence, then landscape" (Smith [2016] 2017, 142). As if the random and rigorous act of fencing were not intimating enough, then Elisabeth's encounter with a security officer, who threatens to take a sample of her DNA for "trespassing" (142), becomes the epitome of a Brexit within, however absurd the scene may seem.

The most prominent episode of Othering takes place in a countryside post office where Elisabeth's attempt to renew her passport quickly turns into an ordeal of Kafkaesque proportions. While the Check & Send service is supposed to be speeding up the process, the man behind the counter – a postal clerk – rejects Elisabeth's application form purely on racialized grounds. He begins by questioning Elisabeth's last name – "Is your surname really Demand? [...] A name you live up to [...] Only joking" (Smith [2016] 2017, 21) – before challenging the non-standard spelling of her first name: "That's not the normal way of spelling it. [...] It's people from other countries that spell like that. [...] But this [her outdated passport] does say you're UK" (22). As the man moves on to check Elisabeth's new passport photographs, it is the size of her head that becomes another bone of contention between them. When measuring her head on the picture, the man remarks that it does not correspond to the racial phenotypes expected from UK citizens: "Yours falls short by 5 millimetres" (24). Before sending her off, he notes down "in a box next to the word *Other*: HEAD INCORRECT SIZE" (25). And while Elisabeth tells him that such bullying, if not Othering, reminds her of a television drama – perhaps one on immigration – the man responds rather fittingly that he prefers "box sets" (25). Indeed, in his racial profiling of a fellow citizen, the postal clerk camouflages as a ruthless immigration officer who reveals a post-referendum political rhetoric that challenges notions of belonging and national identity. If you don't fit the (racial) frame of what is stipulated as "UK citizen", then your life in Britain will bristle with obstacles.

What Elisabeth encounters in a small-town post office, Smith's narrative reveals, is not necessarily restricted to a particular place or region but reflective of the many *internal* divisions the vote had brought to the fore. In fact, Smith dedicates an entire chapter, albeit only three pages long, to how differently the referendum had been perceived by the population:

> All across the country, there was misery and rejoicing. [...] All across the country, people felt they'd done the right thing and other people had done the wrong thing. All across the country, people looked up Google: what is EU? [...] All across the country, people looked up Google: Irish passport applications. [...] All across the country, people felt legitimized. All across the country, people felt bereaved and *shocked*. [...] All across the country, the country was divided, a *fence* here, a wall there, a line drawn here, a line crossed there. (Smith [2016] 2017, 59–61; my emphasis)

Similar to the "land" in Craig's title, Smith's "country" refers "most evidently to Britain, as a country per se in the most conventional sense" (Loh 2013, 1). Given the anaphoric, mantra-like repetition "*All* across the country", it clearly challenges the demographic factors that were used to analyse the referendum's results. Instead, no matter where voters were situated – in rural or urban regions – what they *all* had in common was a general confusion over the definiteness that is a "yes or no" decision. And while Smith does not shy away from playing with the divisive rhetoric surrounding the referendum, she does so without taking sides, blurring the boundaries of *where* to draw the line.

The perspective of Smith's second protagonist, Daniel, is a compelling counterpoint to Britain's current moment of crisis. Though entirely channelled through his dreams, Daniel's passive interventions made from a bed in an old people's home actively guide the present context of the plot. As they dwell entirely on the past, his dreams cover major historical events of the 20th century – most notably the two world wars – and Daniel's involvement in them: his internment by the English, his sister's round-up by the Nazis somewhere in the South of France, or his portrayal of (and participation in) Swinging Sixties Britain. These recollections are not just a reminder of "the cyclical nature of history" (Gilbert 2017, n.p.) but, on a narrative level, they push the slow and often stifling plotlines set in post-referendum Britain continuously forward. It is perhaps the unlikely friendship between the protagonists, which flourished in the 1990s as one between an elderly neighbour and a curious child, that keeps holding the various narrative strands together. Daniel's comatose condition lets his memory disintegrate into dreams that are sometimes hard to make sense of, either through intertextual references to canonical works, ranging from Shakespeare's ([1611] 2011) *The Tempest* to Huxley's ([1932] 2006) *Brave New World* to Ovid's ([8 AD] 2004) *Metamorphoses*, or by means of magic realist episodes. The most powerful one is of a Shakespearean beach scene with dead bodies scattered along the shore, including a swollen father with a swollen baby resting its dead head on the man's chest. The latter, however, are less disturbing than the undisturbed tourists who continue to bathe in the sun (Smith [2016] 2017, 12). And while this may simply be a harsh commentary on Europe's current policies towards asylum seekers allowing preventable deaths, it, too, resonates with Daniel's own response to both political and personal turmoil. Most of his dreams, however fragmented, depict utopian moments of cheerfulness that stem from Daniel's unabated joie de vivre in one of the darkest periods in western history.

What we do *not* encounter in Daniel's dreams are references to Britain's colonial legacy and the rise of institutionalized racism in the 1960s. Considering that he spent his most vibrant years in London of the Swinging Sixties, it may come as a surprise that the anti-immigration rhetoric by prominent politicians like Enoch Powell remains conspicuously absent from Daniel's recollections (as opposed to the washed-up bodies of today's asylum seekers). The celebration of life, art, and music might have been Daniel's refuge in coping with his own experiences of Othering as a Jew in Nazi-occupied territory. At that point in time, the discrimination against "other" immigrants might have fallen off his own racialized radar; too recent are the memories of his family visits to "the continent" (Smith [2016] 2017, 99) in the 1930s. On one such occasion, teenager Daniel is travelling across continental Europe, and all he can think of is that "the people on the train can see from his clothes he's not from here" (99). Nobody is approaching him, but he can overhear a conversation – whose tone resembles that of a flirtation – in which a man tries hard to impress the woman next to him by talking about "developing a scientific and legal means of gauging exactly who's what" (99). The man turns out to be a professor who, in a curious conflation of time and place, resembles the postal clerk Elisabeth would encounter 80 years later somewhere in rural England. He claims that "[t]he measurement of parts of the body, most especially of the features of the head area, can tell you quite succinctly everything you need to know" (100), something that he himself traces back to the racial anthropometry of the colonial era: "It's been done before, but never so expertly" (100). No matter the time, temporality, or historical circumstances, the novel's constant back-and-forth opens up dialogues across the decades, if not centuries. And just as the various narrative strands transcend the boundaries between the realist and the surreal, or the utopian and the dystopian, they are bound to reveal how "history, that other word for irony, went its own foul witty way" (99), as comatose Daniel, witty as ever, concludes.

Conclusion: Sites of global connectivity

By tracing the "foul witty way" of history, Ali Smith's *Autumn* responds with a reasonable amount of irony to the initial shock reverberating from the referendum results. Although literally absent, as he is sleeping almost the entire narrative, it is through Daniel's view of the world, having lived through an entire century, that the current state of the nation may be read as a mere continuation of historical moments of migration, movement, and Othering that return, just like the seasons, to a different time and space. If a sense of crisis has indeed become a normative experience, then Smith's protagonists Daniel Gluck – a rendition of the German "Glück" – and Elisabeth Demand – a composite of the French "de" and "monde", meaning "citizen of the world" – subtly challenge a politics of self-imposed isolation. And this is despite the fact that Elisabeth repeatedly encounters restrictions, particularly in terms of movement, that foreshadow a post-Brexit future. A cosmopolitan with a strong pan-European spirit, Daniel does indeed owe a modicum of luck to some European countries that enabled him to escape from others. And while the rural and the urban are defining features of the novel's temporality – the former largely related to the post-referendum period and the latter to the metropolitan culture of the Swinging Sixties – it is through *Autumn*'s uneven pair of protagonists that the "model of city and country", as Raymond Williams reminds us, "has gone beyond the boundaries of the nation-state, and is seen but also challenged as a model of the world" ([1973] 1975, 279).

The character constellation in *The Lie of the Land*, on the other hand, invites us to read the failed marriage of its protagonists as mimicking "the fragile patchwork of national identity" (Gilbert 2017, n.p.) that led to the severed ties between the EU and the UK in the very first place. Although it seems as if life in "exile" in the English countryside has made them grow closer towards the end of the novel, Quentin and Lottie's patched-up marriage is not meant to last, for Lottie insists that their divorce go through. Yet while Britain's exit from the EU is imminent, Lottie eventually decides to settle for life in rural Britain for better or worse, as she has bought their rented cottage, much to Quentin's dismay. "We've had the best of times, and you're going to have the worst" (Craig [2017] 2018, 243), Lottie declares with the vengeance of a scorned lover. While it may not be obvious at first, Lottie's concluding remark on their marriage is a reversal of the opening of *A Tale of Two Cities* – "It was the worst of times, it was the best of times" (Dickens [1859] 2000, 1).

In fact, the discussion of Dickens's urban fiction in *The Country and the City* continues to "speak to our present condition" (Hunt 2016, n.p.) – be it Englishness, empire, or the rural/urban divide in Brexit. As such, Williams's work provides "a compelling preamble" to contemporary writers like Zadie Smith whose "mix of metropole and colony, race and urban identity" (Hunt 2016, n.p.) engages with some of the major concerns of the Condition-of-England novel. Among them are the material realities that reveal a rift *between* and *within* country and city, something that Smith so eloquently rendered in her post-referendum piece discussed earlier in this article. The literary readings that followed are testament to how recent British fiction continues along the same lines (of division) that have long been in the making. Both novels diagnose the *current* condition of England as one suffering from a Brexit within, while suggesting some of the ways out and, more importantly, tracing some of the ways in. In the process, they frame the many fissures in the national fabric, not simply around the rural and the urban as fenced-off spaces, but as sites of connectivity (*The Lie of the Land*) that gesture towards a more global understanding of national identity (*Autumn*). More precisely, "as metonyms for collective identity, 'city' and 'country' are not simply opposites", Loren Kruger (1999) reminds us, "but both mutually reinforcing and mutually repellent" (69). The rhetorical cues given in both books reveal how this "double articulation" is rooted in a colonial nostalgia that has permeated much of the political and public debates on Brexit. Lastly, just like Craig's novel, Smith's novel, too, includes a slightly but significantly altered take on the opening of *A Tale of Two Cities*. Yet, compared to Dickens's novel, it is the first few lines of *Autumn* that are all the more befitting in concluding the article: "It was the worst of times, it was the worst of times. *Again*" (Smith [2016] 2017, 3; my emphasis). History repeats itself, not least in the realm of English literary traditions.

Notes

1. See, for instance, Ged Pope's (2015) study on suburban London and also Simon Joyce's (2007) analysis on how Zadie Smith's writings show "a recognizable stylistic inheritance from Dickens" which is "overlaid onto a postcolonial politics [...] to foreground the repressed connections between Britain and its imperial possessions" (141). Smith herself considers Dickens an early influence on how she grew into the idea of becoming a novelist. Dickens, she recounts in a recent essay, "had a name for his condition: novelist. Early in my life, this became my cover story, too" (Smith 2019, n.p.).
2. It is nevertheless important to note here that, only one year prior to the referendum, an EU survey revealed that regional inequality in the UK – in terms of average household income – is the worst in Western Europe (Inequality Briefing 2015, n.p.).

Disclosure statement

No potential conflict of interest was reported by the author.

References

Anderson, Eric Karl. 2016. "Ali Smith on *Autumn*, Brexit, and the Shortness of Life." *Penguin*, October 12. https://www.penguin.co.uk/articles/in-conversation/interviews/2016/oct/ali-smith-on-autumn

Armitstead, Claire. 2019. "Ali Smith: 'This Young Generation Is Showing Us that We Need to Change and We Can Change'." *The Guardian*, March 23. https://www.theguardian.com/books/2019/mar/23/ali-smith-spring-young-generation-brexit-future

Becker, Sascha O., Thiemo Fetzer, and Dennis Novy. 2017. "Who Voted for Brexit? A Comprehensive District-level Analysis." *Economic Policy* 32 (92): 601–650. doi:10.1093/epolic/eix012.

Brennan, Timothy. 2017. "On the Image of the Country and the City." *Antipode* 49 (S1): 34–51. doi:10.1111/anti.12186.

Coleridge, Samuel Taylor, and William Wordsworth. [1798] 2007. *Lyrical Ballads*. London: Penguin.

Craig, Amanda. [2017] 2018. *The Lie of the Land*. London: Abacus.

Curtice, John. 2016. "EU Referendum: Polls Reveal Divided Nation." *BBC*, May 23. https://www.bbc.com/news/uk-politics-eu-referendum-36345750

Day, Jon. 2017. "Brexlit: The New Landscape of British Fiction." *Financial Times*, July 28. https://www.ft.com/content/30ec47b4-7204-11e7-93ff-99f383b09ff9

De Gruyter, Caroline. 2016. "The Revenge of the Countryside." *European Council of Foreign Relations*, October 21. https://www.ecfr.eu/article/commentary_the_revenge_of_the_countryside7156

Dickens, Charles. [1859] 2000. *A Tale of Two Cities*. London: Penguin.

Eaglestone, Robert. 2018. "Introduction: Brexit and Literature." In *Brexit and Literature: Critical and Cultural Responses*, edited by Robert Eaglestone, 1–6. London: Routledge.

Ford, Robert, and Matthew Goodwin. 2017. "Britain After Brexit: A Nation Divided." *Journal of Democracy* 28 (1): 17–30. doi:10.1353/jod.2017.0002.

Fox, Stuart, and Sioned Pearce. 2018. "The Generational Decay of Euroscepticism in the UK and the EU Referendum." *Journal of Elections, Public Opinion and Parties* 28: 19–37. doi:10.1080/17457289.2017.1371180.

Frawley, Maria. 2017. "The Victorian Age, 1832–1901." In *English Literature in Context*, edited by Paul Poplawski, 403–518. Cambridge: Cambridge University Press.

Galton, Bridget. 2017. "Amanda Craig: 'Brexit Is a Lightning Rod for Rural People'." *etcetera*, July 3. https://www.hamhigh.co.uk/etcetera/books/amanda-craig-brexit-is-a-lightning-rod-for-rural-people-1-5089899

Gilbert, Sophie. 2017. "Ali Smith's *Autumn* Is a Post-Brexit Masterpiece." *The Atlantic*, February 15. https://www.theatlantic.com/entertainment/archive/2017/02/ali-smiths-autumn-is-a-post-brexit-masterpiece/516660

GOV.UK. 2020. "The Transition Period." GOV.UK. https://www.gov.uk/transition

Harris, Alexandra. 2017. "*Winter* by Ali Smith Review: Wise, Generous and a Thing of Grace." *The Guardian*, October 27. https://www.theguardian.com/books/2017/oct/27/winter-by-ali-smith-review-second-part-seasonal-quartet

Hobolt, Sara B. 2016. "The Brexit Vote: A Divided Nation, A Divided Continent." *Journal of European Public Policy* 23 (9): 1259–1277. doi:10.1080/13501763.2016.1225785.

Huets, Jean. 2018. "Things Fall Apart: On Ali Smith's 'Autumn' and 'Winter'." *The Millions*, January 16. https://themillions.com/2018/01/on-ali-smiths-autumn-and-winter.html

Hunt, Tristram. 2016. "From Jane Austen to Zadie Smith: The City V the Country in Literature." *The Guardian*, March 12. https://www.theguardian.com/books/2016/mar/12/raymond-williams-the-country-and-the-city-rural-versus-urban

Huxley, Aldous. [1932] 2006. *Brave New World*. New York: Harper Perennial.

Jennings, Will, Gerry Stoker, and Ian Warren. 2019. "Brexit and Public Opinion: Cities and Towns - the Geography of Discontent." In *UK in a Changing Europe*, February 1. https://ukandeu.ac.uk/brexit-and-public-opinion-cities-and-towns-the-geography-of-discontent/

Inequality Briefing. 2015. "Briefing 61: Regional Inequality in the UK Is the Worst in Western Europe." *Inequality Briefing*, June 26. http://inequalitybriefing.org/brief/briefing-61-regional-inequality-in-the-uk-is-the-worst-in-western-europe

Joyce, Simon. 2007. *The Victorians in the Rearview Mirror*. Athens, OH: Ohio University Press.

Kruger, Loren. 1999. *The Drama of South Africa: Plays, Pageants and Publics since 1910*. London: Routledge.

Loh, Lucienne. 2013. *The Postcolonial Country in Contemporary Literature*. Basingstoke: Palgrave Macmillan.

Newall, Sally. 2016. "How to Heal a Country Divided by Brexit." *Independent*, June 30. https://www.independent.co.uk/voices/how-to-heal-a-country-divided-by-brexit-a7110851.html

Ovid. [8 AD]. 2004. *Metamorphoses*. Translated by David Raeburn. London: Penguin.

Pittel, Harald. 2018. "Fiction in Dark Times: The Brexit Novel and Ali Smith." *Hard Times* 101 (1): 58–67.

Pope, Ged. 2015. *Reading London's Suburbs: From Charles Dickens to Zadie Smith*. Basingstoke: Palgrave Macmillan.

Preston, Alex. 2019. "*Spring* by Ali Smith Review: Luminous and Generous." *The Guardian*, March 19. https://www.theguardian.com/books/2019/mar/19/spring-ali-smith-review

Rau, Petra. 2018. "*Autumn* after the Referendum." In *Brexit and Literature: Critical and Cultural Responses*, edited by Robert Eaglestone, 31–43. London: Routledge.

Ross, Michael L. 2008. "On a Darkling Planet: Ian McEwan's *Saturday* and the Condition of England." *Twentieth Century Literature* 54 (1): 75–96. doi:10.1215/0041462X-2008-2004.

Self, John. 2020. "How Brexit Has Reshaped the British Novel." *Penguin*, January 31. https://www.penguin.co.uk/articles/2020/jan/how-writers-responded-to-brexit-in-novels

Shakespeare, William. [1611] 2011. *The Tempest*. London: Arden Shakespeare.

Shaw, Kristian. 2018. "BrexLit." In *Brexit and Literature: Critical and Cultural Responses*, edited by Robert Eaglestone, 15–30. London: Routledge.

Skurski, Julie, and Fernando Coronil. 1993. "Country and City in a Postcolonial Landscape: Double Discourse and the Geo-politics of Truth in Latin America." In *Views beyond the Border Country: Raymond Williams and Cultural Politics*, edited by Dennis L. Dworkin and Leslie G. Roman, 231–259. New York: Routledge.

Smith, Ali. [2016] 2017. *Autumn*. London: Penguin.

Smith, Ali. [2017] 2018. *Winter*. London: Penguin.

Smith, Ali. [2018] 2020. *Spring*. London: Penguin.

Smith, Zadie. 2016. "Fences: A Brexit Diary." *The New York Review of Books*, August 18. https://www.nybooks.com/articles/2016/08/18/fences-brexit-diary

Smith, Zadie. 2019. "Fascinated to Presume: In Defense of Fiction." *The New York Review of Books*, October 24. https://www.nybooks.com/articles/2019/10/24/zadie-smith-in-defense-of-fiction/

Tronicke, Marlena. 2017. "What Condition of England? Re-Imagining the 'Two Nations' in David Lodge's *Nice Work*." *Neo-Victorian Studies* 10 (1): 110–132.

Viswanathan, Gauri. 1995. "Raymond Williams and British Colonialism." In *Cultural Materialism: On Raymond Williams*, edited by Christopher Prendergast, 188–210. Minneapolis, MN: University of Minnesota Press.

West, Harry G. 2014. "Bringing It All Back Home: Reconnecting the Country and the City through Heritage Food Tourism in the French Auvergne." In *Food between the Country and the City: Ethnographies of a Changing Global Foodscape*, edited by Nuno Domingos, José Manuel Sobral, and Harry G. West, 73–90. London: Bloomsbury.

Williams, Raymond. [1973] 1975. *The Country and the City*. Oxford: Oxford University Press.

Woodward, Gerard. 2017. "*The Lie of the Land* by Amanda Craig Review: The Country Idyll Turned on Its Head." *The Guardian*, June 17. https://www.theguardian.com/books/2017/jun/17/lie-of-land-amanda-craig-review-devon-hostility

Writing back to Brexit: Refugees, transcultural intertextuality, and the colonial archive

Jan Rupp

ABSTRACT
This article deals with the role of transcultural intertextuality in writing refugees and Brexit, arguing that refracting the colonial archive has served contemporary accounts of refugee migration to interpret current scenarios, revise lingering colonial imaginaries, and forge new bonds of solidarity. It draws on recent work in transcultural memory studies to explore how emergent bodies of refugee writing have remembered and actualized canonical works by engaging and adding to their relational mnemohistories. A multilateral account of the transcultural travel of memories, including of literary texts, relational mnemohistory allows one to rethink the constellation of source-text and actualization in intertextuality theory. While by no means reducible to writing back to Brexit and the canon, recent literature of the Calais "Jungle" migrant camp, such as the play *The Jungle* (2017), as well as works like the multi-volume Refugee Tales, performs important cultural work, retrieving historical entanglements and envisioning a much-needed relationality for the present.

Refugees, alongside migrants, were infamously cast as a threat of foreign invasion to help engineer Brexit (Mayblin 2017, 19). They have featured prominently in writing about Brexit, too. While refugee literature (Gallien 2018) or contemporary asylum narratives (Woolley 2014) date back earlier than the 2016 referendum, the United Kingdom (UK)'s vote to leave the European Union has exacerbated ever more precarious conditions of migration as registered in 21st-century refugee writing. Brexit has capped an ominous turn of events from the UK Home Office hostile environment policy, first announced in 2012, to the 2016 Immigration Act, impacting new as well as older arrivals, as recent disenfranchisement of the *Windrush* generation has scandalously shown. Under these dire circumstances, and either explicitly or implicitly, writing refugees and writing Brexit frequently overlap.

Like the larger landscape of "BrexLit" (Shaw 2018), new bodies of refugee writing share a quotidian focus on the here and now, such as the paradoxical dynamic of globalization, xenophobia, and resurgent nationalism of which developments like Brexit are a symptom. Simultaneously, recent accounts of refugee migration have seen a characteristic mobilization of temporally distant archives. From ancient Greco-Roman epics like *The Aeneid* or *The Odyssey* to Geoffrey Chaucer's *The Canterbury Tales* and

Rudyard Kipling's *The Jungle Book*, a large number of western and colonial classics have been drawn on to interpret and negotiate the current situation. To name but a few examples, Kipling looms large in recent literature of the Calais "Jungle" migrant camp; Chaucer in the multi-volume project *Refugee Tales* (Herd and Pincus 2016, 2018, 2019); and Homer in works like Patrick Kingsley's (2016a) bestselling account *The New Odyssey: The Story of Europe's Refugee Crisis.*[1] Reading novel developments and experiences through the lens of existing narratives may be an all too familiar move. But just what have canonical works got to offer in this particular instance – how have they been used to write stories of refugees and Brexit, and how have they been transformed in turn?

In what follows, I will explore such cases of transcultural intertextuality in Murphy and Robertson's (2017) drama *The Jungle*, in recent productions of plays such as John Gay's *The Beggar's Opera* (Carsen 2018), and in the stories of *Refugee Tales*. As I shall argue, this renewed interest in the canon on the one hand bespeaks global precarity and division in the 21st-century as legacies of colonialism, crystallized by Brexit and its widely mooted post-imperial pathology – and contested by accounts of refugee migration. Here, refugee writing is part of a substantial revival of politics in trajectories of Brexit literature, of an effort to challenge resurfacing fantasies of a buccaneering island nation that translate into withdrawal from Europe, austerity at home, and a lack of compassion for vulnerable strangers.[2] On the other hand, writing refugees and Brexit can also be seen to extend counter-discursive modes and to invite conceptions of transcultural intertextuality in terms of "relational mnemohistory" (Erll 2018, 283). Aiming for a multilateral account of the transcultural travel and reuse of memories, including of literary texts, relational mnemohistory provides a model to rethink further the often static constellation between hegemonic source-text and actualization in intertextuality theory. Thus, I will draw on recent work in transcultural memory studies to demonstrate how invoking the colonial archive has served, almost in spite of itself, to include rather than exclude refugees.[3] This intertextuality is part of a larger cultural intervention to juxtapose the divisive logic and national retrenchment of Brexit with new forms of solidarity. Adopting a perspective of relational mnemohistory will help to elucidate how canonical works have been revised and reread for transcultural entanglements, in a dynamic process that "bring[s] into relation diverse (mnemo-)histories, thus enabling new or transformed memories to emerge" (Erll 2018, 283). While by no means glossing over fraught legacies, I will show how transcultural intertextuality has served to enlist and actualize sometimes unexpected connections from within the colonial archive, inscribing refugees and migrants in writing back to Brexit.[4]

From "writing back" to relational mnemohistory

Current writing about refugees offers a particular perspective on Brexit's colonial remains in that it has revisited some central texts to the colonial imaginary and its afterlife. Accounts of refugee migration write back to Brexit in a similar fashion to earlier postcolonial projects of canon revision, if only because debates surrounding Brexit have seen such a shocking resurgence of colonial and racist stereotypes. Epitomized by the master trope of animal anarchy in the (colonial) jungle, dehumanizing rhetoric and imagery abound in public and media discourse, prompting manifold attempts to rewrite the jungle as a site of human creativity and expression. Importantly, however, the "inverted" or "negative intertextuality" (Plett 1991, 19) of "writing back"[5] does not account fully for stories of refugees and Brexit. Conceptual impulses may be derived from recent work in memory studies, which has foregrounded convergent as much as competitive dimensions to assess how acts of memory, including of literary texts, unfold transformative potential along transcultural travels.[6] This will help build on the long-standing critique of "writing back" and show that – rather than a binary split between colonized and colonizer, or refugee and (hostile) host – accounts of migration, Brexit, and the rewriting of canonical works frequently foreground transcultural, generative, and relational dimensions of intertextuality.

As a founding concern of postcolonial inquiry, "writing back" is a dated paradigm in more than one sense. Its limitations consist in viewing postcolonial literatures as derivative of the western canon, while conceptually eliding other interests that may well (and frequently do) feature. The view of intertextuality as a "historically prolonged family quarrel" (Schulze-Engler 1998, 6) would severely limit its potential, especially in a postcolonial context. With little hope of actually challenging "imperial textuality" (Brydon and Tiffin 1993, 53), those most familiar with it would be privileged yet again, while effectively silencing historically disenfranchised groups.

Clearly, recent accounts of refugee migration do not write back to Brexit and the canon as their sole purpose. The conspicuous return of references to the colonial archive at issue concerns a segment of current refugee writing.[7] Moreover, many of the works discussed below reflect critically on the status of their pre-texts, as well as on the problematic question of whether and how to use these texts to represent refugees and the refugee experience. There can be no question of identifying refugee stories squarely with intertextuality, and I also follow critics of writing back in arguing that its binary, holistic, and homogenous conception of literary traditions and hermeneutic communities is ill-conceived. Rather than juxtaposing the western canon and postcolonial bodies of writing in this way, it is important to recognize the level of exchange "to be called transcultural in so far as it passes through classical cultural boundaries" (Welsch 1999, 197), interweaving multiple lines of tradition as a transcultural intertextuality all along.

In addition to the transcultural nature of writing refugees and Brexit through the prism of literary colonial remains, two further dimensions of the intertextuality involved deserve attention – generative and relational. For these I build on Astrid Erll's discussion of relational mnemohistory via the example of Homer's *Odyssey*, a key reference for accounts of Europe's refugee situation. There clearly are "cues in the present situation that elicit memories of the *Odyssey*, most obviously the refugees' dangerous sea journeys across the Mediterranean" (Erll 2018, 275). However, "strictly speaking, Odysseus is no refugee figure at all", and so "[u]sing him as a paradigm for today's refugees [...] is a highly selective actualization of *one* epithet that the Homeric epic associates with Odysseus: *polytlas*, 'much-enduring' " (275; original emphasis). The *Odyssey* is by no means a neat fit for the current situation, but what counts are certain parallels and relations that do exist, as well as the way in which these are used to generate new memories in the present.

Kingsley's account in *The New Odyssey* is only one example of how Homer and the *Odyssey* have "become a kind of global heritage" (2016a, 278), a transcultural memory that qualifies lingering associations of Homer with western or European culture. This is true of both the present and the past, for Homer's epics were constituted as transcultural texts from the very time of writing, drawing on "Near and Middle Eastern, and possibly Egyptian influences" (278), not to speak of textual settings and reception histories that extend well beyond Europe. However, rather than forwarding a vague universal claim that "Homer is 'everybody's heritage' ", actualizations of Homer are to be analysed "in the texts' creation as well as in their transmission and re-uses – within transregions as well as across time" (278). They are subject to relational mnemohistory as a highly dynamic and multilateral narrative.

Perspectives of relational mnemohistory are most conducive to studying the critical inspection and reuse of colonial texts in recent accounts of refugees and Brexit. For one thing, where writing back tends to imply a still-dominant, hegemonic source-text, and a rather static, binary constellation of discourse and counter-discourse, relational mnemohistory foregrounds reciprocal and constantly evolving entanglements between texts, writers, and readers already on a terminological level. It is a framework that can be impacted at any point, given the principle of relationality as "an ongoing connectivity among diverse elements, which creates meaningful structures and at the same time transforms all elements involved" (Kingsley 2016a, 278). Viewed in this way, transcultural intertextuality can be engaged by different parties – "partners, neighbors, strangers, or even enemies" (278) – and serve a range of functions: to reject and critique the canon as well as to re-evaluate its use and, perhaps, its adaptability to current scenarios.

Transcultural intertextuality in the Calais "Jungle" and beyond

Segueing to a number of close readings, it is important to recognize the immense diversity of texts engaged in writing refugees and Brexit while simultaneously rewriting the canon. They comprise all manner of poems, plays, and narrative fiction, as well as non-fictional genres of oral history and testimony. My own selection will be similarly eclectic and by no means exhaustive, but representative of some major ways in which canonical works have been taken up to invest in relational mnemohistory. In reverse literary-historical order, I will move from Rudyard Kipling to John Gay back to Geoffrey Chaucer – writers who, to be sure, hold very different places in the colonial archive. Unlike Kipling, with his reputation as the Poet of the Empire, Gay's *The Beggar's Opera* (1728) stands only at the beginning of imperial expansion, and Chaucer's late-medieval *Canterbury Tales* date back to pre-colonial times. However, as the "father" of English poetry, Chaucer's work became a central export disseminated throughout the colonial world (Barrington and Hsy 2018, 2). Productions and transcultural adaptations of *The Beggar's Opera* have circulated widely almost from the outset. If his ballad opera has a rather domestic focus, Gay radically enlarged it himself by setting the 1729 sequel *Polly* on an island in the West Indies. While representing and intersecting with the colonial archive each in their own way, all three writers and their work have been intimately involved in histories of colonialism and imperialism.

Turning to recent accounts of the Calais "Jungle" first, colonial undertones already reverberate in the camp's infamous name – "called the 'Jungle' first in French media, but later by its own inhabitants and by the global media" (Godin et al. 2017, 2). Refugees and migrants headed for the UK have gathered in and around Calais since the 1990s at least. In 2015, a larger unofficial camp began to be built on a landfill site just outside the town. Almost 10,000 refugees were living in the Calais "Jungle" when the local French authorities decided to demolish it in the autumn of 2016. The camp's period of existence coincided with and, in fact, became a central "emblem of the impact of forced displacement within Europe" (3), including fast-growing populist backlash through Brexit and similar developments across the continent.

As Ibrahim and Howarth (2018) note, the "jungles of Calais are a referential in the migration crisis not because they have any distinctive material realities" (22), but rather because of the "'colonial leitmotif' of the jungle" and its association with "a distinctively Western social imaginary" (22). This imaginary is "rooted in a colonial construct about the spaces inhabited by the 'other'", co-produced by formative colonial texts like Kipling's late-19th-century collection of stories in *The Jungle Book*. Ever since, there has been "an ongoing fascination for the Western mind with the 'jungle' " (23), attested by the metaphor's unbroken currency in popular culture, not to mention a plethora of racist media images and political discourse. In all these forms, the jungle, and by association the migrant camp, are constituted as a "pre-modern space of degradation, debasement and barbarism, the antithesis of Enlightened Europe" (Ibrahim and Howarth 2018, 24), involving a "distinct 'othering' of migrants as lesser humans" (25).[8]

It is not by coincidence that the jungle looms large as a reference in literature of the Calais "Jungle", too – both as a form of protest against the camp's abject living conditions and as a critique of lingering colonial imaginaries. Refugees "adopted the name 'Jungle' because, many said, humans could not live in such conditions" (Godin et al. 2017, 2). With the metaphor turned on its head, the camp was indeed pictured as a jungle, though not because of its inhabitants, but because of the "ineffectual efforts of European countries" (3) in (not) attending to the refugee situation. Similarly, conventional images are rejected by placing the jungle in scare quotes in publications like *Voices from the "Jungle": Stories from the Calais Refugee Camp* (Godin et al. 2017), which "bring into view the personal stories of people who lived as refugees during 2015 and 2016 in the Calais camp [...], just 26 miles from the UK" (2). Writing, reading, and performing stories was a central element of cultural life in the Calais "Jungle", and it went a long way towards rehumanizing refugees and debunking colonial stereotypes. Apart from restaurants and small shops, the camp was home to a mosque, a theatre, and a library called Jungle Books, in another playful allusion to Kipling and the colonial tradition. Quite in contrast to tropes of barbarism, multiple activist projects in the camp produced a significant and highly varied creative output.

Like asylum narratives as a whole, the literature of the Calais "Jungle" covers a broad spectrum, ranging from testimonial accounts to more literary and intertextually complex works. Both ends of the spectrum come together in the 2017 drama *The Jungle*, a collaboration between Joe Murphy and Joe Robertson, two British playwright-activists, based on their cultural work in the Calais migrant camp. Murphy and Robertson set up the so-called Good Chance Theatre in 2015, as a space of expression, art, dance, and music. Their play is a "fictional account", yet "inspired by the writers' work in the Jungle", as per a disclaimer prefacing the published play in book form (Murphy and Robertson 2017). Many of the roles are clearly modelled on the camp's inhabitants, and performances have featured migrants as actors. *The Jungle* premiered in London in 2017, as a co-production between the Young Vic and National Theatre with the Good Chance Theatre and co-directed by Stephen Daldry and Justin Martin. A year later it was staged the Playhouse Theatre in London's West End. This production history is symptomatic of an intricate intervention in cultural institutions and archives, revealing a larger network of relations between the UK, Calais, and present-day refugees.

As may be expected from the title, *The Jungle* essentially stages the life and times of the Calais migrant camp from its beginnings in 2015 to its eviction in 2016. In this theatrical recreation, a first intriguing piece of intertextual relationality consists in contemplating transcultural alternatives to the camp's name. As the audience learns, the refugees' own and earlier term of choice was "Zhangal!", a "Pashto word, which means forest" (Murphy and Robertson 2017, 27). This suggests parallels with the etymology and pre-colonial use of the word "jungle", which "originated from the Sanskrit *jangala*" (Ibrahim and Howarth 2018, 23) and on the "pre-colonized Indian sub-continent had both a normative and descriptive meaning of 'culturally desirable' savanna". It was only later that these pastoral connotations "morphed into the Anglo-Indian word jungle where flora and fauna were reconstructed as 'feral', as were the people who lived in or near the jungle" (23). Murphy and Robertson's fictionalized account clearly writes back to this notorious semantic shift, with one of the play's characters protesting: "Jungle for animal, not human" (Murphy and Robertson 2017, 51). However, the camp's residents importantly also reconstruct an earlier transcultural intertextuality, as a way of compensating for the dire reality of migrant life by imagining a habitable forest.

As well as retrieving transcultural entanglements, *The Jungle* envisions new forms of solidarity which equally come to overwrite colonial imaginaries. Generative and relational aspects are particularly pronounced when a group of humanitarian helpers from the UK arrive in the French camp. One of them readily recites Kipling's proverbial musings on the forbidding jungle – "Now this is the law of the jungle, and the Law runneth forth and back" (Murphy and Robertson 2017, 41) – only for one of the refugee characters to interject some comic relief and reply: "You must be very tired." This is the beginning of an intricate meditation on mutual needs and reciprocal roles in the camp, with residents helping the helpers as well as vice versa. While tensions remain throughout, the helpers are portrayed as refugees of sorts, too, having become thoroughly alienated from a forbidding jungle of their own, the UK as their home. All have fled social isolation, poverty, and cultural insularity in search of a sense of community in, of all places, the refugee camp: "Community. I've found things here that have all but disappeared in Britain" (45). As the helpers introduce themselves and tell their story, each time the residents shout "Refugee!" (45–46) in turn.

While the play does not gloss over differences or minimize the plight of refugees in any way, both helpers and residents share in a similar struggle. They are united in protest against hard-hearted immigration regimes – epitomized by then UK Home Secretary Theresa May: "Mother-fucking Theresa is fighting in the courts" (Murphy and Robertson 2017, 89) – and lament the erosion of European values more broadly: "It's only a crisis because we're calling it that. A million people, Europe shits her knickers [...]. European governments need to stop breaking their own laws" (91). The fact that this collective European failure happens against the backdrop of Brexit and is viewed from Calais carries a particular significance. Until the Siege of Calais in 1558, the town was "England's last overseas possession on the European mainland" (Hicks and Mallet 2019, 56). It is a loss immortalized by Queen Mary's last words, as one of the refugee characters in *The Jungle* reminds the audience: "Another quotation for you. 'If you open me up when I am dead you will find Calais engraved on my heart.' One of your queens said that. Is it true for you?" (Murphy and Robertson 2017, 25) At the same time, withdrawal from Calais "was a key moment in the emergence of new oceanic geographies of empire" (Hicks and Mallet 2019, 56), laying the "foundations for the transition from English exploration to overseas settlement, for the Acts of Union in 1707, and thus for the British Empire" (56). Today, the majority of refugees heading for the UK come from the former empire (Mayblin 2017, 5). Calais is thus a most symbolic location, referencing entangled European and imperial pasts, together with resulting moral obligations that, in the 21st-century present, all too often remain unacknowledged.

It should have become clear that Murphy and Robertson's *The Jungle* goes a long way towards writing refugees and Brexit by working through the colonial archive. In taking up Kipling, the play powerfully demonstrates how lingering colonial imaginaries translate into the sorry status quo of European division, resurgent nationalism, and hostility against strangers. What deserves particular emphasis is the way in which *The Jungle*, rather than a simple act of writing back to a colonial text, goes back to before Kipling to retrieve alternative transcultural tropes in place of the colonial jungle. Adding a complex chapter of relational mnemohistory, Murphy and Robertson's play is a "jungle book" of sorts, too. But it contains a very different set of stories, offering new and transformed memories – both for and far beyond the new-found community of helpers and residents stranded in the Calais migrant camp.[9]

Critique of global precarity in a modern *Beggar's Opera*

As for a shorter but no less telling case study, my next example is a modern production of John Gay's *The Beggar's Opera*, directed by Robert Carsen (2018), which premiered at the Bouffes du Nord theatre in Paris in 2018 and toured Europe, including the Edinburgh Festival, for almost two years. Billed as "a beggar's opera for our own turbulent times" (Molleson 2018), it featured conspicuous commentary on Europe's refugee situation and Brexit. Even before the first curtain, it presented the audience with the image of a homeless refugee, both setting the scene and framing the action. One may wonder why Gay's 18th-century play was able to speak to these 21st-century developments. Part of the reason is its own satirical refraction of the canon (of 18th-century opera), and the fact that it has long been subject to a complex relational mnemohistory. Postcolonial versions have included Wole Soyinka's *Opera Wayo* (1977), P.L. Deshpande's *Three-Paisa Entertainment* (1978) and Chico Buarque's *The Malandro's Opera* (1978). Ever since its performance, Gay's ballad opera has circulated widely across time and space, with countless instances of adaptation, translation, and transculturation.

While Gay's satire of bourgeois morality has a more circumscribed target in England, global relations and forms of merchant capitalism are present throughout. Right away from Peachum's famous opening song, the play is suffused with a language of trade and of accounts being settled (Kaul 2009, 59). Gay offers a fairly sceptical take on Britain's emerging trading empire, which is even more pronounced in Gay's sequel *Polly* (first staged, posthumously, in 1777), in which Peachum's daughter is the central character. In a larger scenario of transatlantic capitalism, it is set on an island in the West Indies, unnamed yet recognizably shaped by the early colonial plantation economy. The island is home to wealthy plantation owners, extending prodigal luxury and rampant greed from the metropolitan centre to the outposts of empire. Another, complementary group of British expats are transported criminals turned pirates, who raid trade ships for their own share of wealth.

In this scene of capitalism with the gloves off, Gay's heroine Polly embarks on a quest to be reunited with Macheath, which has brought her to the West Indies in the first place. Macheath has morphed from London's top highwayman to a New World pirate captain, and moreover appears in blackface, his pirate gang conspiring with slave insurgents against the island's plantocracy. Macheath's blackface and the overall context of slavery and empire have led to a number of readings around the question of whether Gay's sequel can be considered an early anti-colonial text (Petzold 2012, 107–108). *Polly* leaves little doubt that the English are as corrupt abroad as they are at home, a moral charge that is now directly levelled at imperial exploits: "Gay's play is not an abolitionist appeal, nor does it offer an enlightened perspective on slavery or race relations. *Polly*, however, is bitingly critical of English empire as a manifestation of human vice and folly" (Frohock 2017, 158). Even if the imperial scheme of the plantation economy ultimately remains in place, it by no means emerges unscathed. *Polly* may not be a radical challenge to colonialism, but it clearly elaborates on transatlantic relations already contained in *The Beggar's Opera*. Gay's New World sequel provides more than a mirror image to criticize social morality back home. The corrupt business practices of pirates and plantation owners are targeted as a material reality in their own right. Both parts of Gay's opera thus open up a global perspective, prefiguring contact zones and routes of transcultural exchange along which *The Beggar's Opera* and its later incarnations have proved to be a highly versatile grid of social critique.

The extent to which Gay's model is able to reflect on social change and accommodate transformed memories is equally borne out by Carsen's (2018) actualization. This production's central prop was a massive wall of cardboard boxes, suggestive, perhaps, of today's delivery economy and its twin effect of spiralling consumerism and an ongoing erosion of workers' rights. It is against this wall that Peachum makes his entry by introducing himself as a present-day salesman running an import-export business. From an 18th-century bounty hunter and metaphorical accountant in Gay's original he has turned into an actual tradesman in this 21st-century version.

Even before Peachum's first appearance, however, Carsen's production inserts a powerful comment on repercussions of capitalism on a global scale. As mentioned before, the very first image presented is a homeless refugee in a sleeping bag at the foot of the monumental cardboard wall. As Carsen acknowledged, the image was a deliberate reference to both the time and place of the production: "I was aware that constructing the image of a homeless person on stage would have added resonance, given the situation in Paris right now" (quoted in Molleson 2018). The Bouffes du Nord in Paris is located only a stone's throw away from inner-city refugee camps as existed at the time. By incorporating this real-life reality into its scenery of commerce and trade, the production drew a pertinent parallel between capitalist exploits and evermore precarious forms of global migration in the 21st century; in Arundhati Roy's (2019) words, between capitalism's "gratuitous wars and sanctioned greed" and the world's multiple refugee crises. In the modern production, Gay's meditation on early capitalist immorality turns out to be highly topical, offering a warning reminder in the light of new fantasies of global trade and nostalgia for bygone pirate glory in current Brexit times.

New networks of solidarity and Chaucerian storytelling

With as many as three volumes of stories to date, *Refugee Tales* is arguably the most extensive updating of a canonical work and its relational mnemohistory. Barrington and Hsy (2018) characterize Chaucer's *Canterbury Tales* as "a text – or an assemblage of texts – that simultaneously reflects and constructs an entire world" (2). They thoroughly extend Chaucer's role as a national English poet, highlighting Chaucer's extra-European settings and characters as well as his "wide world of cultural influences" (2). Moreover, they emphasize "how pervasively his influences were filtered and reprocessed through layers of translation as they moved around the Mediterranean" (2). Like Homer's *Odyssey*, the *Canterbury Tales* emerges as a highly symbolic template, conducive to inscribing present-day refugee experience.

The BBC adapted the *Canterbury Tales* in a six-part series of television dramas as early as 2003. One episode, based on "The Man of Law's Tale", features a Nigerian refugee among its modern-day cast of characters. As for literary adaptations, Patience Agbabi's (2014) *Telling Tales* is a major book-length reworking to take up Chaucer, which assembles a polyglot set of modern storytelling voices, highlighting characters and settings that gesture beyond England or Europe in Chaucer. Abgabi also reproduces the tales' cross-cultural content in her fictive cast of storytellers, complete with flamboyant names and far-flung author biographies. In principle, the same is true of *Refugee Tales*, though it might be considered an even more telling example of updating and transforming the canon.[10] For all its imaginary cross-cultural poet-pilgrims as extradiegetic storytellers, Agbabi's *Telling Tales* remains a single-authored text. By contrast, *Refugee Tales* relies on a collaboration between British-resident writers and refugee testimony. The stories collected are effectively co-produced, further extending multiperspectivity from the level of narrators to the level of authorship. The complex mediation of testimony in *Refugee Tales* engages an intricate transcultural intertextuality. In the process, Chaucer is thoroughly repositioned, as echoed by Marion Turner's (2019) tellingly subtitled biography *Chaucer: A European Life*. Turner rejects a number of conventional associations of Chaucer as "a figure of Englishness" or as "father" of "a national literature" (508). Instead, she stresses his European travels and influences, a relational network newly retrieved "as the starting point for *Refugee Tales*, a collection [...] that brings together contemporary politics, current writers, and Chaucer's *Canterbury Tales*" (508). The *Refugee Tales* project was first carried out in 2015, slightly ahead of that year's historical curve of migration into Europe. It consisted not only in recording, but also in performing refugee stories on historic ground. The tales were read out while walking along the North Downs Way in Kent, which largely coincides with the medieval Pilgrims' Way from London to Canterbury.

Facilitated by well-known multi-ethnic as well as mainstream writers in the UK, *Refugee Tales* protests against indefinite immigration detention – a practice unique in Europe, which allows the UK to hold migrants without a time limit. The stories collected mediate direct individual experience of this policy. Their complex constellation of telling is signalled by the title of the first volume, which is worth reproducing in full: *Refugee Tales, as Told to Ali Smith, Patience Agbabi, Abdulrazak Gurnah, Inua Ellams and Many Others* (Herd and Pincus 2016). Both title and subtitle have the same structure in all three volumes of *Refugee Tales* (although differing sets of contributors). In a complex mediation of refugee testimony, the tales have been told to a go-between writer, in order to be retold and expanded by them in turn. The original storytellers remain unnamed because they were too traumatized or did not want to be identified for fear of reprisal, and so were protected by activists and writers serving as community gatekeepers. Significantly, *Refugee Tales III* (Herd and Pincus 2019) for the first time includes a number of first-person narratives, written by former detainees themselves. Again, however, their identity is protected, with only initials, such as "A", "J", or "F", being provided as author names.

As in Chaucer's stories, the writers of *Refugee Tales* thus mediate life-stories of others and give expression to what otherwise might not get heard. They perform an important function as interlocutors, witnessing and corroborating the refugees' experience. Paradoxically, the fact that the refugees' names are textually absent might in fact help to authenticate their accounts: "by signposting their names, the contributing writers make themselves accountable [...] for the accuracy of the *telling* of the story" (Wiemann 2018, 73; original emphasis). Helen Barr (2019) emphasizes that "*Refugee Tales* is also a physical, bodily realization of *The Canterbury Tales*" (105), in which refugees have a visible presence as part of the project's walks and readings. All this feeds into a relational act of Chaucerian storytelling – "re-humanising some of the most vulnerable and demonised people on the planet" (blurb).

Alongside Chaucer's dialogical narrative, *Refugee Tales* draws heavily on his role in popularizing the English language and establishing the vernacular as a new literary idiom. As signalled in the first volume's prologue, *Refugee Tales* seeks to use "this new language we ask for" to help construct "networks of visitors and friends" (Herd and Pincus 2016, viii). While it certainly cannot make up for the dim realities of immigration policy, the project nevertheless launches a powerful commentary, juxtaposing the practice of indefinite detention with an alternative vision of convivial culture.

Just as much as it references language, *Refugee Tales* capitalizes on Chaucer's intersection with international geographies and tales of journeying. Several of the project's stories draw on "The Man of Law's Tale" in Chaucer, which resonates presciently with itineraries of current refugee migration. Constance, the story's central character, is the emperor's daughter in Rome. She is married off to a sultan in Syria, but the sultan's mother has him killed for turning his back on Islam. Brutally widowed, Constance flees across the Mediterranean and is eventually washed up on English shores. In *Refugee Tales*, Constance is invoked several times. "The Migrant's Tale, as told to Dragan Todorovic" is based on a conversation with Aziz, a young political refugee from Syria. In alternating sections, Todorovic retells Aziz's ordeal and constantly interweaves Costance's original story: "For days, for years floated this creature across the eastern Mediterranean, and into the Strait of Gibraltar – such was her fate. Often she expected to die" (Herd and Pincus 2016, 7). Today, a similar kind of suffering has violently inscribed itself on Aziz, as Todorov observes: "He holds his upper arms and rocks back and forth. Slow and steady, waves in the bay. I've seen this same movement, this same posture, in other times and other cultures" (4).

Refugees like Aziz have little to expect from the law, as other stories make clear. "The Lawyer's Tale, as told to Stephen Collis" shifts attention from Constance's story to its narrator, the eponymous Man of Law. In a combination of critical commentary and lyrical passages, Collis reflects on the Man of Law as a curious blank space in the canonical pre-text: "Chaucer's Man of Law tells us precious little about the law, or himself. [...] It is not clear what Constance's story means to him, either personally or professionally" (108). The Man of Law is an enigmatic figure, just as legal representation or even basic human rights will prove elusive for many present-day refugees in indefinite detention.

Significantly, the voices featured in *Refugee Tales* include not only migrants and refugees, but representatives of the host society, too. Readers get to hear, among others, "The Migrant's Tale", "The Chaplain's Tale", or "The Lorry Driver's Tale" – all of whom are important figures in the refugee process as well. Diverse social groups are bound together, working towards a viable community: "In creating a space of appearance, and a polity out of the structural model of Chaucer's *Canterbury Tales, The Refugee Tales* project reads back into Chaucer's work a community of fellowship and common purpose" (Barr 2019, 103). Refracting Chaucer yields important connections and a reciprocal account of refugee migration, in a nuanced revision of relational mnemohistory that acknowledges lingering challenges but gestures towards common effort.

Conclusion

Throwing into relief the fraught relationship between refugee migration and Brexit, all three case studies demonstrate invariably complex interaction with the colonial archive. While arguably coming closest to a counter-discursive critique, even recent literature of the Calais "Jungle" is not limited to a retaliatory act, instead using its deconstruction of colonial imaginaries to forge novel bonds of solidarity between asylum seekers and estranged Europeans. Gay's *The Beggar's Opera*, actualized in view of inner-city refugee camps, has been shown to offer pertinent commentary on global precarity and capitalist excess today, drawing on the versatile satirical tradition of Gay's highly canonized and yet subversively critical work. *Refugee Tales*, eventually, goes to great length to retrieve a historical transculturality and proto-cosmopolitan vista from Chaucer, in a sustained effort of relational storytelling that gestures beyond the nation and Europe.

On a conceptual level, as I hope to have shown, transcultural intertextuality as staged by these recent accounts of refugee migration, Brexit, and the canon is profitably studied in terms of relational mnemohistory. Rather than representing a stand-off between ever-dominant and derivative traditions, relational mnemohistory brings into view a dynamic and ever-shifting constellation between writers, readers, and texts. This perspective allows for accommodating competitive as well as convergent readings (such as of Chaucer as a European poet), and it will typically shift focus from the source-text to its actualization, leaving the former thoroughly transformed. Insights in memory studies into the travel and transcultural recall of texts no doubt offer important critical purchase for studying asylum narratives and other postcolonial traditions of writing.

Of course, there is much more to refugee writing than Brexit and the colonial archive. Narratives of migration and asylum pursue multiple other concerns and deserve to be appreciated away from European references. And yet, for present purposes, it bears repeating that writing refugees via canonical texts performs significant cultural work – if only not to yield ground to Brexit's own historical recourse in the wider, ongoing debate about how to remember the past and the major literary works that had a role in shaping it. For newly divided Europeans and those arriving to their shores, refracting the refugee experience through colonial archives stands to envision a much-needed relationality.

Notes

1. In his article "Top Ten Refugees' Stories", Kingsley (2016b) selects *The Aeneid* and the Gospel of Matthew as numbers one and two respectively, a choice not unlike many other "best books" lists compiled on this topic.
2. See Wally (2018) and Wiemann (2018) on the trend of politicizing Brexit literature.
3. In a broad understanding, I include not only writers like Kipling in the colonial archive, but also western classics that were central to the colonial curriculum and continue to be drawn on as interpretive models, such as Chaucer and *The Odyssey*.
4. I follow Claire Gallien (2018) and others in arguing for a "new encompassing category" (723) of "refugee". Even where I refer to refugees only, I include (undocumented) migrants to accommodate "eco-refugees and environmental factors in the displacement of persons" (723).
5. For the "writing back" paradigm, see, for example, Brydon and Tiffin (1993) and Thieme (2001).
6. On this reorientation of memory studies, see also Michael Rothberg's (2009) concept of multidirectional memory.
7. For the scope of refugee literature see, inter alia, the articles in Sandten (2017), Gallien (2018) and Gilmour and Chambers (2018).
8. This discursive violence manifested itself in actual harassment and violence suffered by the camp's residents, as previous articles on the Calais "Jungle" have pointed out. While I focus on tropological and intertextual interventions, see Rosello (2016), Koegler (2017), and Sanyal (2017) for more immediate forms of resistance on the ground, including new forms of urbanism and home-making.
9. Analysing rewritings of Kipling in Calais (and other references to the colonial archive) in terms of relational mnemohistory can be compared to Edward Said's (1993) practice of "contrapuntal reading": "contrapuntal reading must take account of both processes, that of imperialism and that of resistance to it, which can be done by extending our reading of the texts to include what was once forcibly excluded" (79).
10. See my discussion of *Refugee Tales* and new diasporic traditions of world literature (Rupp 2020).

Disclosure statement

No potential conflict of interest was reported by the author.

References

Agbabi, Patience. 2014. *Telling Tales*. Edinburgh: Cannongate Books.

Barr, Helen. 2019. "Stories of the New Geography: *The Refugee Tales*." *Journal of Medieval Worlds* 1 (1): 79–106. doi:10.1525/jmw.2019.100005.

Barrington, Candace, and Jonathan Hsy. 2018. "Editors' Introduction: Chaucer's Global Orbits and Global Communities." *Literature Compass* 15 (6): 1–12. doi:10.1111/lic3.12457.

Brydon, Diana, and Helen Tiffin. 1993. *Decolonising Fictions*. Sydney: Dangaroo.

Carsen, Robert, dir. 2018. *The Beggar's Opera*. Paris: Théâtre des Bouffes du Nord. April 20 (premiere).

Erll, Astrid. 2018. "Homer: A Relational Mnemohistory." *Memory Studies* 11 (3): 274–286. doi:10.1177/1750698018771858.

Frohock, Richard. 2017. "John Gay's *Polly* (1729), Bernard Mandeville, and the Critique of Empire." *Studies in Eighteenth-Century Culture* 46 (1): 147–162. doi:10.1353/sec.2017.0013.

Gallien, Claire. 2018. "'Refugee Literature': What Postcolonial Theory Has to Say." *Journal of Postcolonial Writing* 54 (6): 721–726.

Gilmour, Rachel, and Claire Chambers, eds. 2018. *Refugees, Migrants, Border Security*. Online Special Issue of *The Journal of Commonwealth Writing*. https://journals.sagepub.com/page/jcl/collections/refugees_migrants_border_security

Godin, Marie, Katrine Møller Hansen, Aura Lounasmaa, Corinne Squire, and Tahir Zaman, eds. 2017. *Voices from the 'Jungle': Stories from the Calais Refugee Camp*. London: Pluto Press.

Herd, David, and Anna Pincus, eds. 2016. *Refugee Tales, as Told to Ali Smith, Patience Agbabi, Abdulrazak Gurnah, Inua Ellams and Many Others*. Manchester: Comma Press.

Herd, David, and Anna Pincus, eds. 2018. *Refugee Tales II, as Told to Jackie Kay, Helen Macdonald, Neel Mukherjee, Kamila Shamsie, Ali Smith, Patience Agbabi, Abdulrazak Gurnah, Inua Ellams and Many Others*. Manchester: Comma Press.

Herd, David, and Anna Pincus, eds. 2019. *Refugee Tales III, as Told to Monica Ali, Bernardine Evaristo, Patrick Gale, Gillian Slovo and Many Others*. Manchester: Comma Press.

Hicks, Dan, and Sarah Mallet. 2019. *Lande: The Calais Jungle and Beyond*. Bristol: Bristol University Press.

Ibrahim, Yasmin, and Anita Howarth. 2018. *Calais and Its Border Politics: From Control to Demolition*. London: Routledge.

Kaul, Suvir. 2009. *Eighteenth-Century British Literature and Postcolonial Studies*. Edinburgh: Edinburgh University Press.

Kingsley, Patrick. 2016a. *The New Odyssey: The Story of Europe's Refugee Crisis*. London: Guardian Faber.

Kingsley, Patrick. 2016b. "Top Ten Refugees' Stories." *The Guardian*, May 18. https://www.theguardian.com/books/2016/may/18/top-10-refugees-stories

Koegler, Caroline. 2017. "Precarious Urbanity: 'The Jungle' (Calais) and the Politics of Performing the Urban." *Postcolonial Text* 3/4: 1–15.

Mayblin, Lucy. 2017. *Asylum after Empire: Colonial Legacies in the Politics of Asylum Seeking*. London: Rowman & Littlefield.

Molleson, Kate. 2018. "Brexit Gags, Catsuits and Coke-snorting Cops: A *Beggar's Opera* for Our Times." *The Guardian*, August. 15. https://www.theguardian.com/stage/2018/aug/15/the-beggars-opera-robert-carsen-edinburgh-international-festival

Murphy, Joe, and Joe Robertson. 2017. *The Jungle*. London: Faber.

Petzold, Jochen. 2012. "John Gay's *Polly* and the Politics of 'Colonial Pastoral'." *Zeitschrift für Anglistik und Amerikanistik (ZAA)* 60 (2): 107–120.

Plett, Heinrich F. 1991. "Intertextualities." In *Intertextuality*, edited by Heinrich F. Plett, 3–29. Berlin, New York: De Gruyter.

Rosello, Mireille. 2016. "The Calais Jungle: Mediations of Home." *NECSUS – European Journal of Media Studies* 5 (2): 89–106.

Rothberg, Michael. 2009. *Multidirectional Memory: Remembering the Holocaust in the Age of Decolonization*. Stanford, CA: Stanford University Press.

Roy, Arundhati. 2019. "Literature Provides Shelter. That's Why We Need It." *The Guardian*, May 13. https://www.theguardian.com/commentisfree/2019/may/13/arundhati-roy-literature-shelter-pen-america

Rupp, Jan. 2020. "21st-Century Refugee Writing as a Refraction of World Literature: Rerouting Multicultural Canons." *Anglistik: International Journal of English Studies* 31 (2): 35–51. doi:10.33675/ANGL/2020/2/7.

Said, Edward. 1993. *Culture and Imperialism*. London: Vintage.

Sandten, Cecile, ed. 2017. *Representing and Narrating Flight, Refugeeism, and Asylum*. Special Issue of *Postcolonial Text* 12 (3/4).

Sanyal, Debarati. 2017. "Calais's 'Jungle': Refugees, Biopolitics, and the Arts of Resistance." *Representations* 139 (1): 1–33.

Schulze-Engler, Frank. 1998. "Cross-Cultural Criticism and the Limits of Intertextuality." In *Across the Lines: Intertextuality and Transcultural Communication in the New Literatures in English*, edited by Wolfgang Klooss, 3–19. Amsterdam: Rodopi.

Shaw, Kristian. 2018. "BrexLit." In *Brexit and Literature*, edited by Robert Eaglestone, 15–30. London and New York: Routledge.

Thieme, John. 2001. *Postcolonial Con-texts: Writing Back to the Canon*. London, New York: Continuum.

Turner, Marion. 2019. *Chaucer: A European Life*. Princeton, NJ: Princeton University Press.

Wally, Johannes. 2018. "The Return of Political Fiction?" *Arbeiten aus Anglistik und Amerikanistik* 43 (1): 63–86.

Welsch, Wolfgang. 1999. "Transculturality: The Puzzling Form of Culture Today." In *Spaces of Culture: City, Nation, World*, edited by Mike Featherstone and Scott Lash, 194–213. London: Sage.

Wiemann, Dirk. 2018. "Make English Sweet Again! *Refugee Tales*, or How Politics Comes Back to Literature." *Hard Times* 101 (1): 68–76.

Woolley, Agnes. 2014. *Contemporary Asylum Narratives: Representing Refugees in the Twenty-First Century*. Basingstoke: Palgrave Macmillan.

(Post)colonial friendships and Empire 2.0: A Brexit reading of *Victoria & Abdul*

Clelia Clini

ABSTRACT

A 2018 report published by the British think tank Demos claims that, in Britain, "nostalgic rhetoric clearly played a significant role in the Referendum campaign, in particular, emphasising particular tropes around the Second World War, empire and the 're-instation' of British sovereignty". Indeed, these tropes feature heavily in popular culture, with several films and TV series centred on Britain's imperial past. Taking on board Nadine El-Enany's suggestion that "Brexit is not only an expression of nostalgia for empire, but it is also the fruit of empire", this article discusses the role of imperial fantasies in the debate over Britain's membership of the European Union and draws a connection between these fantasies and recent re-presentations of Britain's imperial past on screen. Focusing in particular on Stephen Frears's *Victoria & Abdul* (2017), it argues that the film offers a sanitized version of the empire, which contributes to the reproduction of nostalgic imperial fantasies in post-European Britain.

> If books and films could be made and consumed in the belly of the whale, it might be possible to consider them merely as entertainment, or even, on occasion, as art. But in our whaleless world, in this world without quiet corners, there can be no easy escapes from history, from hullabaloo, from terrible, unquiet fuss. (Rushdie [1984] 1992, 101)

It has been more than four years since the 2016 referendum over Britain's membership of the European Union (EU). Several analyses of the referendum campaign have highlighted the strong nationalistic sentiment that underpinned the Leave campaign, which was very much structured around the rhetoric of "taking back control" (Cain 2016; Gaston and Hilhorst 2018; Hobolt 2016). And yet, if the idea of recovering a sovereignty lost to the EU featured heavily in the public debate promoted by the Leave side, it was not related solely to Britain's role within Europe: it was also predicated on a feeling of nostalgia for a sense of past greatness, in turn rooted in "fantasies of a lost empire to reclaim" (Cain 2016, 1). Indeed, Nigel Farage's comparison of the referendum to the Battle of Britain (British Elections Study Team 2016), and Boris Johnson's (2016) criticism of former US President Barak Obama, whom he accused of having removed a bust of Winston Churchill from the Oval Office because of his "ancestral dislike of the Empire", are just two examples of how the empire, as a signifier of a glorious past that could be regained through the referendum, entered the campaign's discourse. The significance of a "nostalgic rhetoric" in Britain, especially in the discourses that led to the referendum, was also observed by a 2018 report on recent election campaigns in Europe conducted by the British think tank Demos, which noted especially the prominence of "particular tropes around the Second World War, Empire and the 're-instation' of British sovereignty" (Gaston and Hilhorst 2018, 16).

These findings are not surprising if we consider the popularity of these same tropes in popular culture, among others in Channel 4's TV series *Indian Summers* (2015–16), ITV's *Victoria* (2016–) and *Downton Abbey* (2010–15), and films such as *Darkest Hour* (dir. Joe Wright, 2017), *Churchill* (dir. Jonathan Teplitzky, 2017), *Dunkirk* (dir. Christopher Nolan, 2017), *Their Finest* (dir. Lone Scherfig, 2017), *Viceroy's House* (dir. Gurinder Chadha, 2017), and *Victoria & Abdul* (dir. Stephen Frears 2017). It thus becomes clear that the divorce from the EU has been accompanied by films and televisual products that on the one hand proposed a glamorous take on imperial achievements around the world, and on the other celebrated the role of Britain in the Second World War and the myth of British courage and exceptionalism. To be sure, these tropes are not new to British popular culture, but they become of particular significance when they are reflective of the political atmosphere of the period.

Taking on board Salman Rushdie's observation that "the works of art, even works of entertainment, do not come into being in a social and political vacuum; and [...] the way they operate in a society cannot be separated from politics, from history" ([1984] 1992, 92), this article is concerned precisely with the re-presentation of the imperial past on screen in relation to the resurgent nostalgia for the empire embedded in the Brexit rhetoric. Following Nadine El-Enany's (2017) observation that "Brexit is not only an expression of nostalgia for empire, but it is also the fruit of empire", the first part of the article frames the imperial fantasies which have inhabited the Brexit campaign within a longer tradition of revisionism that, as Paul Gilroy (2004) has argued, is the expression of a melancholic reaction to the loss of the empire. The second part focuses on cinematic narratives of empire and colonialism which have been released in the run-up to, and following, the Brexit referendum campaign. Specifically, the article discusses *Victoria & Abdul*'s representation of colonial relations and the monarch as the expression of a more general, romanticized, and benevolent perspective on colonialism – a sentiment which, according to recent data (see the 2014 and 2020 YouGov surveys), seems to pervade the national public. While Stephen Frears's film is not immediately related to Brexit, it is nevertheless embedded in the nostalgic conjuring of imperial Britain and its bygone glory and should therefore, as Rushdie suggests, be read in this very context. My analysis will focus on the film's representation of the Queen's relationship with her servant-turned-teacher, Abdul, in relation to revived myths of colonial grandeur which permeated the 2016 referendum campaign.

Brexit and the empire

In an interview about the cultural legacy of the empire in Britain, published in the *Evening Standard* on September 11, 2019, writer and historian William Dalrymple claimed that "the British still have this ridiculous view of our own imperial history", and he warned that "the idea that the Empire was this great civilising mission, as we were taught at school, is historical nonsense" (Law 2009, 22). Historically inaccurate as it might be, the perception of the empire as a positive force in the world continues to hold sway among a sizable portion of the British population: a YouGov poll published in March 2020 reveals that 33 percent of the British people believe that former colonies "are better off" because of their colonial past. The same poll also revealed that a quarter of Britons wish Britain still had an empire (Smith 2020). Interestingly, the survey breaks down results according to respondents' attitude towards Brexit, exposing "a deep political divide over the Empire between Remain and Leave voters": according to the data collected, 51 percent of Leave voters think that former British colonies are better off because of their inclusion in the British Empire, compared to 22 percent Remain voters (still a significant figure), while 50 percent of Leave voters believe that "the Empire is something to be proud of", compared to 20 percent Remain voters (Smith 2020).

These figures point to the long-lasting legacy of the empire in the social, cultural, and political life of Britain and its continuing appeal for a significant portion of the population. Indeed, as mentioned in the introduction, references to the British Empire abounded in the public debates surrounding the referendum, especially in the discourses championed by the Leave movement, where "empire" became a signifier of greatness, pride, and, ultimately, a lost sense of identity regarding the country's place in the world (El Enany 2017; Martill 2017). As Gaston and Hilhorst (2018) note, in fact, the "take back control" slogan of the Leave campaign in itself discloses the nostalgic longing for an earlier era of greatness, with the word "back" reinforcing the suggestion that the Leave movement would lead the country towards "the restoration of a previous era of supreme sovereignty" (50).

Making a case for Britain's membership of the EU being the reason for Britain's loss of a "special relationship" with Commonwealth countries, the Leave campaign openly framed Brexit as the political move that would allow Britain to break free of the yoke of European rule and rekindle its relationship with the Commonwealth – whose roots lie with the British Empire. As Eva Namusoke (2016) observes, "the Leave campaign presented the Commonwealth as a viable economic alternative to the EU, with an added bonus of working with an organization that already had historical connections to the UK" (468). This was not a new argument, as, in fact, the supposed rivalry between the EU and the Commonwealth has long been a key campaigning point of the conservative group Anti Common Market League (ACML), which has opposed British membership of the EU since the 1960s (Namusoke 2016, 464).

By stressing the historical connections with other Commonwealth countries, the Leave movement promoted an understanding of "the UK's international identity as lying not with Europe but with its former empire and its settler-colonies" (Davis 2018a, 153), paving the way for the emergence of a "Global Britain narrative" which imagined Britain "transcending the EU to recommit to its former imperial possessions" (154). As the majority of the British people voted for Brexit, the new government led by Theresa May embraced the imperial fantasies that had nurtured the Leave campaign, promising to deliver the Global Britain project (also known as "Empire 2.0") via a reconnection with the country's "old friends", namely British former colonial possessions (see Davis 2018a, 153; Law 2009, 21–22). The image of a country that was set to reclaim an identity grounded in its "achievements" around the world was projected by the then prime minister in the Brexit speech that she delivered at Lancaster House in London, on January 17, 2017. As May explained:

> Britain's history and culture is profoundly internationalist. We are a European country – and proud of our shared European heritage – but we are also a country that has always looked beyond Europe to the wider world. [...] The opportunity ahead – is to use this moment to build a truly Global Britain. A country that reaches out to old friends and new allies alike. A great, global, trading nation. (Department for Exiting the European Union 2017)

By defining Britain's history as "internationalist", calling former colonies "old friends", and by vowing to build a new "Global Britain", May carefully fashioned the image of the empire around "warm collective memories of a now lost world where Britain was the global hegemon of the capitalist world economy" (Virdee and Brendan 2018, 1805). As such, these memories promoted a very sanitized version of Britain's imperial past, like that advocated by the Leave campaign, and that never acknowledged the exploitative and violent character of the empire but, on the contrary, emphasized the "goodness" that the British Empire had done around the world (Andrews 2017; see also Tharoor 2017).[1] As we shall see, this sanitized version of the empire finds ample correspondence in a "wave of period films released in the aftermath of the 2016 referendum" which "revisit the days of the (waning) imperial greatness" (Korte 2018, 1).

Nostalgic feelings towards an empire "domesticated as something to be celebrated" (Merriman 2018, 4) did not emerge with the Brexit campaign, though: as Salman Rushdie ([1982] 1992) notes, celebration of imperialism has never really left British society (131). References to it abounded also in Thatcher's nationalist rhetoric (Rushdie [1982] 1992, 129–131), especially in her appeals to restore British greatness, and, Gilroy warned, they "did not vanish with her" but continued, in a mutated form, during the New Labour era – emerging most significantly when the government appealed to the public to support the 2003 war against Iraq (2004, 95). As Edward Said (1994) famously wrote in the opening chapter of *Culture and Imperialism*, "appeals to the past are among the commonest strategies of interpretation of the present" (1), and, especially at times of national crisis, they can serve the purpose of restoring a lost sense of identity. Indeed, Rushdie has drawn a connection between "the refurbishment of the Empire's tarnished image" ([1984] 1992, 91) and the "continuing decline, the growing poverty and the meanness of spirit of much of Thatcherite Britain [which] encourages many Britons to turn nostalgically to the lost hour of their precedence" (91–92). More than 30 years after Rushdie's poignant remarks – and after years of austerity, growing class inequalities, and the general "structural decline that Britain has undergone during the neoliberal era" (Virdee and Brendan 2018, 1804) – the Brexit referendum has, once again, turned the spotlight on a carefully selected image of the empire, one which paves the way for rekindled fantasies of Britain's greatness.

The imperial nostalgia embedded in both the Leave campaign and in the government's post-referendum politics can be read as the expression of Britain's inability to come to terms with the loss of its empire – and the global standing that came with it – and shows a country living in a protracted state of what Gilroy has aptly defined as "postimperial melancholia" (2004, 90). Following German psychoanalysts Alexander and Margarete Mitscherlich, Gilroy analyses Britain's obsession with its imperial past (and with its role in the Second World War) as the melancholic reaction "to the loss to a fantasy of omnipotence" (2004, 99). Of course, this is not an innocent fantasy. Imperialism thrived on violence, looting, slavery, exploitation – aspects of the empire which, even if tamed into a narrative of civilizational "greatness" and imperial "good-will" bestowed upon the colonies, continue to affect the social, cultural, and political make-up of postcolonial Britain. As Rushdie points out, "one of the key concepts of imperialism was that military superiority implied cultural superiority, and this enabled the British to condescend to and repress cultures far older than their own; and it still does" ([1982] 1992, 131–132). Indeed, this sentiment persists within British society, emerging more evidently in the racism met by immigrants and Britons with family roots lying in the former colonies (131–133).[2] To the extent that "memories of imperial greatness" are embedded in the language of British nationalism (Gilroy [1987] 2002, 79), the inability to acknowledge the violent nature of the empire spells a continuous failure to come to terms with the diverse character of Britain's postcolonial society.[3] An example of this failure is the Windrush scandal, which unravelled during Theresa May's term as prime minister and was connected to the "hostile environment" policy started under her mandate as home secretary.[4]

It is in this context that popular culture's re-presentations of the empire will be analysed in the next section.

Imagining the empire on post-Brexit screens: Raj Nostalgia 2.0?

If the empire has occupied a central position in the referendum debate, as well as in post-Brexit politics, it also occupies, as previously mentioned, a prominent position in popular culture, with a significant number of TV programmes and films focusing on the Second World War as well as on colonialism and its legacy, especially in India.

This strong interest in the Second World War and in the British Empire in popular culture deserves some attention. Indeed, as Stuart Hall famously observed, "popular culture [...] is partly where hegemony arises, and where it is secured" (1981, 239); therefore it is imperative to understand what politics of representation lie behind popular reconstructions of the empire. This is especially relevant if we consider that the project of imperialism was not solely concerned with material gains, but also structured as a discourse and a regime of representation which, in order to provide a moral justification for its enterprise, constructed colonial subjects as naturally inferior. This discursive strategy, as Said remarked, was instrumental in leading normal citizens to "accept the notion that distant territories and their native peoples should be subjugated and [...] think of the imperium as a protracted, almost metaphysical obligation to rule subordinate, inferior or less advanced peoples" (1994, 10). It is this investment in culture that has made the ideology of imperialism so resistant to the passage of time, as it was ingrained into the everyday life of Britain.

The much-celebrated victory of the British in the Second World War and (white-washed) narratives of the British colonial empire are two interconnected phenomena, which can both be inserted within Gilroy's aforementioned concept of "postimperial melancholia" (2004). Britain's "melancholic attachment" to its lost (and unmourned) empire relates, as Gilroy explains:

> both to Nazism – the unchanging evil we need to always see ourselves as good – and to a resolutely air-brushed version of colonial history in which gunboat diplomacy was moral

> uplift, civilising missions were completed, the trains ran on time and the natives appreciated the value of stability. These dream worlds are revisited compulsively. They saturate the cultural landscape of contemporary Britain. (2005, n.p.)

In light of this reflection, it is difficult not to read the film productions released around the unfolding of Brexit as symptomatic of the current British political climate. Much has been written especially about *Darkest Hour* and *Dunkirk* in relation to Brexit (see Korte 2018 for an analysis of the reviews received by these films in the British and German press). As two films that focus on the role of Britain in the Second World War, upon their release they were read by politicians and the press alike in relation to the very narratives of empire and war that have been permeating the political debate around Brexit (Davis, 2018b; Jack 2018; Knight 2019; Moore 2018; Williams 2017). One of the most prominent examples of this reception was perhaps Nigel Farage's posting of a photo of himself in front of the *Dunkirk* poster on his personal Twitter profile, which he used to invite all young people to go and see the film – possibly so that they could grasp the roots of British exceptionalism and courage, as remarked by James Cooray Smith (2017) and Zoe Williams (2017). Similarly, Brexit-supporter Charles Moore (2018) published an article in *The Spectator* titled "*Darkest Hour* is Superb Brexit Propaganda", forging an explicit connection between this film and Brexit (see Knight 2019 for a comment on this article). Even though both films had in reality been conceived before the referendum (Jack 2018), the timing of their release, and their uncanny resonance with the tropes used by the Leave campaign and Brexit supporters in the public discussions that followed the referendum, inevitably dragged them into the Brexit debate. As Barbara Korte notes, both films "transport viewers back to a time when Britain, instead of being a part of Europe, was Europe's saviour" (2018, 3), thus feeding into the myth of British exceptionalism, bravery, and an ability to endure – all of which reinforces the Brexit narrative of a restored, post-European, greatness.

And if the public discourse surrounding Brexit has been dominated by tropes relating to the Second World War and the supposed "greatness" of the British Empire, it does not come as a surprise that films focused on the empire would be received in a manner similar to *Darkest Hour* and *Dunkirk*. Stephen Frears's *Victoria & Abdul*, for example, released in 2017, was seen by critics as basking in the same imperial nostalgia that has characterized much of the Leave campaign's rhetorical strategy and which still lingers on in British society (Brooks 2017; Hans 2017; Qureishi 2017). Heeding Rushdie's ([1984] 1992, 92) aforementioned observation that cultural products should not be analysed independently from the political and historical context within which they arise, I will consequently look at Frears's film against the backdrop of imperial nostalgia that has dominated the political discourse around Brexit.

A period drama, *Victoria & Abdul*, while not set in India, tells the (true, albeit fictionalized) story of the unlikely relationship between Queen Victoria (played by Dame Judi Dench, who reprised the role 20 years after *Mrs Brown*) and Abdul Karim, an Indian servant-turned teacher, or munshi, who befriended the Queen during the last 15 years of her life. The film opens in Agra with Abdul, a prison clerk, being recruited to travel to Britain for the Queen's Golden Jubilee (1887), in order to present Her Majesty with a *mahor*, a ceremonial coin. He sets off to Britain with fellow Indian Mohammed Baksh, with whom he will present the gift, and who is far less enthusiastic than him about their task, having been forced to go. Upon seeing Abdul during the Golden Jubilee celebrations, the Queen takes an instant liking to him and hires him as her personal footman, quickly promoting him to munshi (secretary or teacher) and Indian clerk to the Queen. Abdul thus settles in England, and so does a reluctant Mohammed, who becomes Abdul's servant. The munshi becomes a personal confidant to the Queen, much to the disapproval (and hostility) of the entire royal household, and remains in England until Queen Victoria's death, after which he is unceremoniously sent back to India. The film closes with an older Abdul who, back in Agra, visits the statue of Queen Victoria and kisses her feet as the camera moves to reveal that the statue is in front of the Taj Mahal, no less.

Based on Shrabani Basu's (2010) book *Victoria & Abdul: The True Story of the Queen's Closest Confidant*, the film is set against the backdrop of Britain's colonization of India. It focuses in its entirety on the personal relationship between Queen Victoria and Abdul, which is portrayed as a testimony to the power of friendship and its ability to transcend age, class, and racial lines. Despite being set during the heyday of the British Empire, the film does not offer any in-depth engagement with, let alone critical scrutiny of, the politics of empire and colonialism in India. Occasional references to political events in the subcontinent, and the monarch's very own admission that she is "hated by millions of people all over the world", do little to counterbalance this. Moreover, these hints at self-reflexivity are quickly redressed by Abdul, who reminds the Queen that they are there "for a greater purpose"; that is, serving the empire. Even the household's hostility towards Abdul is not contextualized within the ideology of racial superiority championed by the empire. Rather than being read as the direct product of the hierarchies of races championed by imperialism and colonialism, their resentment is portrayed as the consequence of the self-interests of Queen Victoria's petty entourage, family included, who are not pleased with the Queen's newly found enthusiasm for life after Abdul's arrival.

Abdul's arrival is portrayed as a life-changing event for the monarch. Before his arrival, Queen Victoria is depicted as a lonely, bored, and tired woman. Her "misery at court life before Abdul's arrival" (Bryant 2017, 696) is clearly conveyed in the opening scene, when, taken out of bed by her servants, she sits in silence and motionless like a doll, while they dress her and inform her of her engagements for the day. Things change after Abdul, contravening protocol, catches her eye when presenting the Queen with the *mahor*. Abdul's and Mohammed's return trip to India is thereafter cancelled as they are requested to wait at another royal banquet. Once again, Abdul defies the orders received, kneeling down and kissing the Queen's feet when presenting the Queen with a jelly – much to her delight. The relationship between the two afterwards quickly develops into a very intimate (but strictly platonic)[5] one, as Abdul becomes the Queen's "closest friend", teacher, and companion, and he follows her to Scotland and Italy, having become the most important member of her entourage. The film suggests that Abdul's presence instils in the monarch a great curiosity for India, as she asks him to teach her about the country she rules and starts taking lessons in Urdu and learning about the Koran.

The interest that the Queen displays towards India and towards Abdul's religion strongly resonates with Theresa May's description of Britain as "a country that has always looked beyond Europe to the wider world" (Department for Exiting the European Union 2017), reducing colonialism to a sort of innocuous interest in other countries and cultures. The Queen's curiosity towards India, and towards Abdul's culture, come across as the Queen's desire to respectfully learn more about the territories she reigns over, and it is quite in contrast with the cultural politics of the empire, effectively stated in Macaulay's ([1835] 1979) famous "Minute on Indian Education". It is also worth observing that, in the representation of Queen Victoria's friendship with Abdul, the film omits to mention "Victoria's first Indian fascination" (Bryant 2017, 696); that is, Maharajah Duleep Singh. Exiled from his Punjab kingdom when he was just a child, Duleep Singh met Queen Victoria in 1854 (Axel 2001, 49) and he, too, became a close friend of the Queen. And yet his history of exile, his conversion to Christianity, and his much-opposed reconversion to Sikhism, let alone his thwarted plans to return to Punjab to reclaim his kingdom, tell a very different story of empire compared to that of Abdul, one that would certainly challenge this image of imperial tolerance and inter-cultural understanding (see Anand 1996; Axel 2001).

Abdul's encounter with the Queen changes his life and his fortunes too, as he moves from being a prison clerk to suddenly spending most of his time in the company of the Empress of India. Abdul is portrayed as an enthusiastic young man, very much devoted to Queen and empire, and forever grateful to have had the honour to travel to England and be admitted into the Queen's inner circle. If the film offers some insights into the Queen's affection towards Abdul – that is, the fact that when she first meets him she is feeling very lonely and in need of a friend – nothing is revealed regarding Abdul's thoughts about his own situation, not even his feelings regarding the wife whom he has left behind in India (and who gets no mention until halfway through the film). And yet, even though represented mostly as genuinely affectionate to the monarch, his naivety, selflessness, and devotion are at times cast into doubt. There are hints, disseminated throughout the film, that Abdul might not be entirely transparent in his demeanour towards the Queen, but that he instead might be playing the part for his own personal advancement – for example, when he makes her believe that the 1857 Mutiny was carried out by Hindus and not by Muslims. His subtle ambition is outed by Mohammed, as he tells the Prince of Wales that Abdul simply does "what everyone else does: he looks for preferment, he curries favour, he crawls up the stinky greasy pole of the shitty British, making fools of all of you because he is a servant. An Indian, Muslim servant" (Frears 2017). But even though there are moments in the film that suggest that his "happy-go-lucky" appearance might be an act, such hints are mostly played down in the narrative. They are also finally dismissed by the end of the film, when Abdul is shown kissing the feet of the Queen's statue in India, a sign of his devotion to the Empress and her empire. As much as the Queen's interest in Abdul and his culture complies with the revisionist views of Britain as a country always interested in the wider world, the representation of Abdul's devotion towards the Queen and the empire nurtures contemporary fantasies of an empire which was not only benevolent towards its subjects, but was indeed beloved by them. His aforementioned reference to the "greater purpose" he and his Queen are meant to fulfil feeds into the perception that the empire was, overall, a positive force for good, not only in Britain, but in its colonies, too.

The only reflections on the political reality of colonialism in the film come from Mohammed, whose blunt criticism of the empire and the British – whose habits he often describes as "barbaric" – is perhaps supposed to balance Abdul's devotion. It is Mohammed who, by describing Abdul as "crawling up the pole of the empire", exposes the elephant in the room: as endearing as it might seem, this cross-class and cross-racial friendship cannot simply be isolated from politics. Despite the fact that Queen Victoria develops a genuine affection for her munshi, the relationship between the two rests on a very strong power imbalance and, even though he always happily and respectfully accepts his Queen's orders, Abdul (and certainly not his wife) is never asked for his opinion over the most important decisions regarding his own life. The influence of the munshi on the Queen is bemoaned by the household but the film never sees Abdul suggesting to the Queen to take any action regarding himself (for example, making him a Commander of the Royal Victorian Order) or the empire. The action is thus completely led by the monarch, while Abdul remains, to paraphrase Rushdie ([1984] 1992, 90), a "bit-player" in his own history.

Mohammed's remarks raise critical social, cultural, and political issues, but he is mostly ignored, both by the English and by Abdul. His function in the film recalls the figure of the Shakespearean fool – he speaks truth to power, but his insights are mostly aimed at the audience. In the story of Mohammed, the film shows the ruthlessness of the empire: not only is he forced to go to England against his wishes, but he is never allowed back to India, dying ill and alone in a country he has never recognized as his own home(land). But by the time of his death, his on-screen time has already been significantly curtailed, and not even Abdul seems to care very much for him (if he ever had, he probably would have sent him back to India). The potential of the character to provide a critique of the empire is thus significantly tamed. With only the occasional criticism provided by Mohammed, the re-presentation of the relationship between the Queen and Abdul is effectively emptied of its political meaning. This is because, by situating what was indeed the fruit of colonial relations – the friendship between the Queen and her Indian servant – into the private domain of life, the film shifts the focus of the narrative away from the structural inequalities of empire and uncritically celebrates the friendship between the Queen and "her" munshi.

In line with contemporary tamed versions of the British Empire which have been thriving in the pro-Brexit discourse, *Victoria & Abdul* offers the portrait of a rather progressive monarch who is at odds with the pettiness of her entourage. Indeed, the film's characterization of Queen Victoria as a harbinger of tolerance and anti-racism heavily contrasts the very role that she occupied within the empire. Even though the Queen indeed defended her munshi from the racialized attacks of her household (Visram 2002, 45–49), the fact that she was the leader of a political, economic, social, and cultural system that was inherently racist is at odds with her representation as the harbinger of multiculturalism. The fact that the film fails to address this massive paradox ultimately reinforces a revisionist perception of colonialism centred on the idea that "we, the British, weren't as bad as people make out" (Rushdie [1984] 1992, 101), while the focus on the Queen's service to her people, and her benevolence towards Abdul, suggest that there was indeed something noble about the empire, thus feeding into the feeling of postcolonial nostalgia which has re-emerged strongly in British public culture during the referendum debate.

Conclusions: Re-imagining the empire in the Brexit context

Writing about the cultural legacy of imperialism, Edward Said wrote that "the meaning of the imperial past is not totally contained with it, but [...] its existence as shared memory and as a highly conflictual texture of culture, ideology and policy still exercises tremendous force" (1994, 11). The central position of the empire in the debate that preceded and followed the referendum over the British membership of the EU, and the aforementioned results of the 2020 YouGov poll, demonstrate that memories of the British Empire still exercise a strong influence on the cultural and political life of Britain. Considering that "for every text [there is] a context" (Rushdie [1984] 1992, 92), it is inevitable that a film like *Victoria & Abdul* will be interpreted within the framework of postcolonial nostalgia (see Gleiberman 2017; Qureishi 2017). Indeed, had a similar film been made 20 years ago, it would probably have been interpreted within the framework of British multicultural politics of the time. But at this particular time in history, the very theme of the friendship between the Queen and her munshi seems to speak to Brexit fantasies according to which, as Dalrymple put it, "now that we were in trouble in Europe, our friends in India would fill in because they love us so much and were so grateful for the railways" (Law 2009, 23).

Even though *Victoria & Abdul* has the merit of bringing to the screen the story of the friendship between Queen Victoria and her munshi Abdul, still largely unknown to the wider public, the uncritical celebration of this friendship, which only marginally tackles the politics of imperialism and colonialism at the base of their relationship, precludes a closer scrutiny of the impact of colonialism as well as of its present-day legacy. Moreover, the portrayal of the Queen as the harbinger of multiculturalism, together with Abdul's devotion to the Queen (especially in *that* last scene), and to the empire, perpetuates the very myth, popular amongst some Brexiteers, and scrutinized by William Dalrymple, that colonialism wasn't that bad after all (Law 2009, 22). The scene in which Abdul explains to the Queen how the point of carpets is "to bring all different kinds of thread together and weave something we can all stand on" sounds like a metaphor for a very much sanitized version of the empire and what it stands for, echoing contemporary re-imaginings of imperial Britain, that, as seen in the first part of the article, populate political discourses around Brexit and Britain's relationship with the Commonwealth (Davis 2018a, 153).

And yet Stephen Frears himself does not think of the empire in such nostalgic terms. In an interview about the film with *The Big Issue*, he in fact argued that "nobody thinks that stuff [the empire] was any good. Only some idiots for Brexit" (Frears 2018, n.p.). Nevertheless, as Rushdie observed, "no matter how innocently the writers and film-makers work [...] they run the grave risk of helping to shore up the conservatism, by offering the fictional glamour which its reality so grievously lacks" ([1984] 1992, 92). *Victoria & Abdul* might not directly address the Brexit debate, but the tame, and glamorous, representation of the empire that it offers inevitably speaks to the same imperial fantasies that have dominated the Brexit debate and which are still rife in (soon-to-be) post-European Britain.

Notes

1. Writing about the British presence in Africa, for example, Boris Johnson (2016), countering Blair's declaration that Africa was "a blot" on the British conscience, wrote in *The Spectator* that "the continent may be a blot, but it is not a blot upon our conscience. The problem is not that we were once in charge, but that we are not in charge anymore" (n.p.).
2. It is not surprising, then, that the Leave campaign's references to the empire were, as Virdee and McGeever (2018) explain, accompanied by a racist approach to migration which, without ever acknowledging its imperial past as the main cause for the current multicultural character of Britain's social texture, pointed the finger at the EU's "open borders" policy,

portraying immigrants simultaneously as "a threat to the working class" and as "a security threat to the British population" (1806).

3. A recently published report by the Office for National Statistics shows that people from BAME backgrounds, and in particular those of Bangladeshi heritage, are paid significantly less than their white counterparts (Siddique 2019).
4. As Ruth Craggs observed, the scandal was the proof of the fact that "while many might be tempted to see the British Empire as a thing of the past the *Windrush* scandal demonstrates the ongoing impacts of colonial policies, histories and ideologies in the present day" (2018, 362).
5. The potential sexual interest of the monarch in Abdul is hinted at in the banquet scene, as he presents the Queen with a wobbling, phallic-shaped jelly (see Hans 2017), and yet this suggestion is never directly addressed in the film, which remains ambiguous regarding the nature of the Queen's affection for Abdul.

Acknowledgments

The author wishes to thank the anonymous reviewers for their helpful comments, and the editors of this special issue – Caroline Koegler, Marlena Tronicke, and Pavan Malreddy.

Disclosure statement

No potential conflict of interest was reported by the author.

Funding

This work was supported by the Leverhulme Trust under Grant RL-2016-076.

ORCID

Clelia Clini http://orcid.org/0000-0003-0841-9714

References

Anand, Sushila. 1996. *Indian Sahib: Queen Victoria's Dear Abdul*. London: Gerald Duckworth and Co.

Andrews, Kehinde. 2017. "Building Brexit on the Myth of Empire Ignores Our Brutal History." *The Guardian*, March 7. https://www.theguardian.com/commentisfree/2017/mar/07/building-brexit-on-myth-of-empire-ignores-history-at-our-peril

Axel, Brian Keith. 2001. *The Nation's Tortured Body: Violence, Representation, and the Formation of the Sikh "Diaspora"*. Durham, NC: Duke University Press.

Basu, Shrabani. 2010. *Victoria & Abdul: The True Story of the Queen's Closest Confidant.* New Delhi: Rupa & Company.

British Elections Study Team. 2016. "Brexit Britain: British Election Study Insights from the post-EU Referendum Wave of the BES Internet Panel." *British Election Study*, October 6. https://www.britishelectionstudy.com/bes-resources/brexit-britain-british-election-study-insights-from-the-post-eu-referendum-wave-of-the-bes-internet-panel/#.Xp2qiplCRPY

Brooks, Xan. 2017. "Victoria & Abdul Review: Judi Dench Class Act Can't Compensate for Lazy Raj-era Nonsense." *The Guardian*, September 3. https://www.theguardian.com/film/2017/sep/03/victoria-abdul-review-judi-denchs-stephen-frears-venice-film-2017

Bryant, Julius. 2017. "Mrs. Abdul? from Fake News to Fake History." *The Round Table: The Commonwealth Journal of International Affairs* 106 (6): 695–696. doi:10.1080/00358533.2017.1405532.

Cain, Ruth. 2016. "Post-truth and the 'Metropolitan Elite' Feminist: Lessons from Brexit." *Feminists @law* 6 (1): 1–8.

Cooray Smith, James. 2017. "Nigel Farage's Love for *Dunkirk* Shows How Brexiteers Learned the Wrong Lesson from WWII." *The New Statesman*, July 26. https://www.newstatesman.com/politics/brexit/2017/07/nigel-farages-love-dunkirk-shows-how-brexiteers-learned-wrong-lessons-wwii

Craggs, Ruth. 2018. "The 2018 Commonwealth Heads of Government Meeting, the Windrush Scandal and the Legacies of Empire." *The Round Table: The Commonwealth Journal of International Affairs* 107 (3): 361–362.

Davis, Alexander. 2018a. *India and the Anglosphere: Race, Identity and Hierarchy in International Relations.* Abingdon: Routledge.

Davis, Richard. 2018b. "Brexit and the Lessons of History." *The Conversation*, March 30. https://theconversation.com/brexit-and-the-lessons-of-history-93513

Department for Exiting the European Union. 2017. "The Government's Negotiating Objectives for Exiting the EU: PM Speech." January 17. https://www.gov.uk/government/speeches/the-governments-negotiating-objectives-for-exiting-the-eu-pm-speech

El-Enany, Nadine. 2017. "Things Fall Apart: From Empire to Brexit Britain." *IPR Blog.* University of Bath. May 2. http://blogs.bath.ac.uk/iprblog/2017/05/02/things-fall-apart-from-empire-to-brexit-britain/

Frears, Stephen, dir. 2017. *Victoria & Abdul.* London: Focus Features.

Frears, Stephen. 2018. "Stephen Frears: 'Brexit Lunatics Seem Determined to Put the Clocks Back. [Interview with Stephen McKenzie]." *The Big Issue*, January 25. https://www.bigissue.com/interviews/stephen-frears-brexit-lunatics-seem-determined-to-put-clocks-back/

Gaston, Sophie, and Sacha Hilhorst. 2018. *At Home in One's Past: Nostalgia as a Cultural and Political Force in Britain, France and Germany.* London: Demos. https://www.demos.co.uk/wp-content/uploads/2018/05/At-Home-in-Ones-Past-Report.pdf

Gilroy, Paul. [1987] 2002. *There Ain't No Black in the Union Jack.* London: Routledge Classics.

Gilroy, Paul. 2004. *After Empire: Melancholia or Convivial Culture?* London: Routledge.

Gilroy, Paul. 2005. "Why Harry's Disoriented about Empire. The Chronic Pain of Loss Feeds Our Melancholic Attachment." *The Guardian*, January 19. https://www.theguardian.com/uk/2005/jan/18/britishidentity.monarchy

Gleiberman, Owen. 2017. "Film Review: *Victoria & Abdul.*" *Variety*, September 3. https://variety.com/2017/film/reviews/victoria-abdul-review-judi-dench-1202545919/

Hall, Stuart. 1981. "Notes on Deconstructing "The Popular." In *People's History and Socialist Theory*, edited by R. Samuel, 227–240. London: Routledge.

Hans, Simran. 2017. "*Victoria and Abdul Review* - Rather Funny in a Royalist Way." *The Guardian*, September 17. https://www.theguardian.com/film/2017/sep/17/victoria-and-abdul-review-rather-fun-in-a-royalist-way

Hobolt, Sara B. 2016. "The Brexit Vote: A Divided Nation, A Divided Continent." *Journal of European Public Policy* 23 (9): 1259–1277.

Jack, Ian. 2018. "*Dunkirk* and *Darkest Hour* Fuel Brexit Fantasies, Even if They Weren't Meant To." *The Guardian*, January 27. https://www.theguardian.com/commentisfree/2018/jan/27/brexit-britain-myths-wartime-darkest-hour-dunkirk-nationalist-fantasies

Johnson, Boris. 2016. "Africa Is a Mess but We Can't Blame Colonialism." *The Spectator*, July 14. https://www.spectator.co.uk/article/the-boris-archive-africa-is-a-mess-but-we-can-t-blame-colonialism

Knight, Robert. 2019. "Brexotic Mythmaking and Imperial Legaciesin *Darkest Hour*." *History Workshop*, January 18. http://www.historyworkshop.org.uk/brexotic-mythmaking-and-imperial-legacies-in-darkest-hour/

Korte, Barbara. 2018. "In the Brexit Mood: Film Critics and British World War II Cinema after 2016." Paper given at the conference "Writers and Intellectuals on Britain and Europe, 1918–2018. Northumbria University. https://d-nb.info/1193921953/34

Law, Katie. 2009. "William Dalrymple: I Regret Laughing at Boris's Jokes about the EU Now." *Evening Standard*, September 11, 22 –23.

Macaulay, Thomas. [1835] 1979. *Speeches of Lord Macaulay with His Minute on Indian Education. Selected with an Introduction and Notes by G. M. Young*. Oxford: Oxford University Press.

Martill, Benjamin. 2017. "Brexit and UK Foreign Policy: 'Keeping Britain Great' or 'Putting the Great Back into Great Britain'?" *UCL Brexit Blog*, November 3. https://ucl-brexit.blog/2017/11/03/brexit-and-uk-foreign-policy-keeping-britain-great-or-putting-the-great-back-into-great-britain/

Merriman, Victor. 2018. "Oh, to Be in England/Now that Brexit's There." *Third Text* 23 (5/6): 605–610.

Moore, Charles. 2018. "*Darkest Hour* Is Superb Brexit Propaganda." *The Spectator*, February 3. https://www.spectator.co.uk/article/darkest-hour-is-superb-brexit-propaganda

Namusoke, Eva. 2016. "A Divided Family: Race, the Commonwealth and Brexit." *The Round Table: The Commonwealth Journal of International Affairs* 105 (5): 463–476.

Qureishi, Bilal. 2017. "Why Does Hollywood Keep Churning Out Racist Fantasies like *Victoria & Abdul*?" *The Washington Post*, October 9. https://www.washingtonpost.com/news/postevery thing/wp/2017/10/09/why-does-hollywood-keep-churning-out-racist-fantasies-like-victoria-abdul/

Rushdie, Salman. [1982] 1992. "The New Empire Within Britain." In *Imaginary Homelands, Essays and Criticism 1981–1991*, edited by Salman Rushdie, 129–138. London: Granta Books.

Rushdie, Salman. [1984] 1992. "Outside the Whale." In *Imaginary Homelands: Essays and Criticism 1981–1991*, edited by Salman Rushdie, 87–101. London: Granta Books.

Said, Edward. 1994. *Culture and Imperialism*. London: Vintage Books.

Siddique, Haroon. 2019. "Britain's Ethnic Paid Gap: Workers of Bangladeshi Heritage Paid Least." *The Guardian*, July 9. https://www.theguardian.com/inequality/2019/jul/09/ethnic-pay-gap-bangladeshi-workers-earn-fifth-less-white-britons#maincontent

Smith, Matthew. 2020. "How Unique are British Attitudes to the Empire?" *YouGov*, March 11. https://yougov.co.uk/topics/international/articles-reports/2020/03/11/how-unique-are-british-attitudes-empire

Tharoor, Shashi. 2017. *Inglorious Empire: What the British Did to India*. London: Hurst and Company.

Virdee, Satna, and McGeever Brendan. 2018. "Racism, Crisis, Brexit." *Ethnic and Racial Studies* 41 (10): 1802–1819.

Visram, Rozina. 2002. *Asians in Britain: 400 Years of History*. London and Sterling, VA: Pluto Press.

Williams, Zoe. 2017. "*Dunkirk* Offers a Lesson – But It Isn't What Nigel Farage Thinks." *The Guardian*, July 30. https://www.theguardian.com/commentisfree/2017/jul/30/dunkirk-lesson-nigel-farage-brexiters-war-stories-british

Index

For Product Safety Concerns and Information please contact our EU representative GPSR@taylorandfrancis.com
Taylor & Francis Verlag GmbH, Kaufingerstraße 24, 80331 München, Germany

www.ingramcontent.com/pod-product-compliance
Lightning Source LLC
LaVergne TN
LVHW080656011026
849160LV00014B/1456

* 9 7 8 0 3 6 7 7 7 5 9 0 2 *

W. C. McKern and the Midwestern Taxonomic Method

R. Lee Lyman and Michael J. O'Brien

The University of Alabama Press
Tuscaloosa and London

The University of Alabama Press
Tuscaloosa, Alabama 35487-0380

Manufactured in the United States of America

Typeface: Janson Text

∞
The paper on which this book is printed meets the minimum requirements of American National Standard for Information Science–Permanence of Paper for Printed Library Materials, ANSI Z39.48-1984.

Library of Congress Cataloging-in-Publication Data

Lyman, R. Lee.
W. C. McKern and the Midwestern Taxonomic Method / R. Lee Lyman and Michael J. O'Brien.
p. cm. — (Classics in southeastern archaeology)
Includes historical documents by W. C. McKern and others.
Includes bibliographical references and index.
ISBN 0-8173-1221-8 (alk. paper) — ISBN 0-8173-1222-6 (pbk. : alk. paper)
1. Indians of North America—Middle West—Antiquities—Classification.
2. Archaeology—Middle West—Methodology. 3. McKern, W. C. (Will Carleton), 1892– 4. Middle West—Antiquities. 5. Archaeology—United States—History.
I. O'Brien, Michael J. (Michael John), 1950– II. McKern, W. C. (Will Carleton), 1892– III. Title. IV. Series.
E78.M67 L96 2003
977'.01—dc21

2002007554

British Library Cataloguing-in-Publication Data available

Contents

Illustrations

Tables

Preface and Acknowledgments

Beginning late in the nineteenth century, archaeologists in North America found increasing evidence of a diversity of prehistoric cultures. Given their anthropological training and exposure to ethnological theory and ethnographic data, it is not surprising that many of the archaeological collections they generated and studied after the turn of the century were called "culture X" or characterized as representing the "W culture." There were no standards or algorithms for specifying when one had a culture distinct from or identical to someone else's culture in an adjoining or distant region. As a result, by the late 1920s there was a plethora of prehistoric cultures that displayed disparate geographic and chronological distributions. Given the rapid growth in terminology that accompanied the discovery of these cultures, it is not surprising that someone would eventually raise a red flag because he was getting lost in the classificatory confusion.

That someone was Will Carleton McKern of the Milwaukee Public Museum, who in 1929 began to work on what he thought might comprise a solution to the problem. It became known as the midwestern taxonomic method (MTM). At the suggestion of one of his assistants McKern chose a particular model for his solution: Linnaean biological taxonomy. He chose that model because he wanted the ability to monitor relationships, particularly historical and cultural relationships, among the various identified archaeological cultures. His reasoning was simple: Because the Linnaean taxonomy implied historic and genetic relationships among biological taxa, a cultural taxonomy no doubt would reveal similar sorts of relationships among cultures. As simple as this reasoning was, it belied the rough waters that lay ahead as McKern and his colleagues tried to put the method into practice. After several fits and starts they abandoned it in favor of a method based more on intuition than on methodological rigor.

McKern was the chief architect of the MTM, but he did not work alone—a point overlooked for the most part in previous essays on the MTM. In particular, Carl E. Guthe of the University of Michigan was not only a major source of good ideas; in his role as chairman of the Committee on State Archaeological Surveys of the National Research Council, he ensured that various of the early statements on the method were distributed to a wide audience for comment. Thorne Deuel of the University of Chicago helped McKern and Guthe write one of the early statements, and he applied a version of the method in his dissertation. Deuel also wrote two significant but previously unpublished papers on the method. James B. Griffin and William A. Ritchie also made notable contributions to the development of the method—the former attempting an early application of it, the latter proposing some critical terminology that became a significant part of the final published version. These and other aspects of the history of the development and use of the MTM have not received the attention they deserve. One result has been that when modern archaeologists comment on the method, they often discuss how people other than McKern applied it rather than on how the method itself was intended to be used. In addition, previous commentators on the MTM, ourselves included, have variously suggested that the method is analogous to one of three rather particular methods of biological classification. Such claims, however, have been made with little attendant analysis of either the pertinent literature on biological systematics or the relevant archaeological literature.

It is our goal in this volume to fill these voids, but more than that we want to show that many of the thought processes that McKern and his colleagues went through were parallel to, and in some ways anticipated, the thought processes that biologists and paleontologists went through in the decades following the evolutionary synthesis of the early 1940s. The ontological and epistemological issues with which McKern, Guthe, and Deuel wrestled are not unique to archaeology but underlie any attempt to classify segments of the natural world. McKern and his colleagues were apparently not aware of the debates in biology and paleontology, but the method they eventually proposed was remarkably similar to one that would cause a stir in biology when it was introduced in the late 1950s. That method was phenetics, sometimes referred to as numerical taxonomy. Pheneticists might have been interested in knowing that a handful of archaeologists several decades earlier had wrestled with such issues as identifying characters and character states and attempting to understand how various characters were linked. The method used by that small group of archaeologists was nowhere near as sophisticated as that developed by the pheneticists, but the basic approach was the same: Use any and all available characters to determine relationships among taxa, irrespective of the origin of those characters.

Perhaps not coincidentally, both methods ultimately fell into disuse for the same reasons: They left time, and by implication genealogy, out of the equation. And if anything unites archaeology and biology it is an emphasis on chronological and genealogical ordering. Any classification that does not place primary emphasis on those two facets of the organic world is bound to fail. That, perhaps, is the take-home message of our look at the MTM. Its architects had the best of intentions when they started out in the early 1930s, but within a few years even they jettisoned it in favor of a culture classification built around time. In biology, phenetics had its moment in the sun, but it, too, fell prey to other classificatory methods that were based at least in part on genealogical ordering. Time simply plays too important a role in our attempts to understand both culture and organisms for it to be left out of the game.

Our archival research was aided by a number of people and institutions. Jay Satterfield of the University of Chicago's Regenstein Library, Special Collections, provided access to the papers and correspondence of Fay-Cooper Cole. Pat Burg of the Illinois State Museum provided access to the papers and correspondence of Thorne Deuel. Daniel Barbiero of the National Research Council arranged for us to use the archives of the Committee on State Archaeological Surveys. Dan Glover sorted through the papers of W. C. McKern archived at the Milwaukee Public Museum. Interlibrary Loan personnel of the University of Missouri-Columbia's Ellis Library were most helpful in obtaining several critical documents. Lyman thanks his relatives (Jay, Karen, Gracie, Thomas, and Claire) and friends (Jim and Sue Scott) for their hospitality when the book was nearing completion but still lacked certain critical bits of information.

We thank Dan Glover for producing the line drawings and Robert D. Leonard, Charles McNutt, and E. J. O'Brien for reading the manuscript in its entirety and providing numerous comments on how to improve it.

Permission to publish the archived materials was provided by Bruce McMillan (Illinois State Museum), Patricia Zimmerman (Illinois State Academy of Science), Alex Barber and Susan Otto (Milwaukee Public Museum), Daniel Barbiero (National Research Council), the Delaware Archaeological Society, the American Anthropological Association, and the Society for American Archaeology.

PART I
W. C. McKern and the Midwestern Taxonomic Method

1
Introduction

> [T]here is no better method for scientists of one period to bring to light their own unconscious, or at least undiscussed, presuppositions (which may insidiously undermine all their work) than to study their own subject in a different period. (A. J. Cain 1958:144)

Early last century Franz Boas (1902:1) indicated that "in the study of American archaeology we are compelled to apply methods somewhat different from those used in the archaeology of the Old World." Although he was not clear about *why* this was so, part of the reason appears to have been that the then generally accepted time depth of the American archaeological record was much shallower than that of the Old World. By the middle of the nineteenth century, European paleontologists had found archaeological evidence that humans had walked the earth alongside large mammals that even then were known to have become extinct at the end of the Pleistocene (Grayson 1983; Van Riper 1993). No such evidence was then available for the Americas, and the only well-understood and generally accepted evidence of prehistoric people in the New World pointed to a human occupancy that was only a few thousand years old (Meltzer 1983, 1985; Stewart 1949). That would change in the 1920s and 1930s with the discovery of human tools in association with extinct bison and mammoth at several localities in eastern New Mexico (Meltzer 1983, 1985, 1991).

The problem that arose after the New Mexico discoveries was identified by A. V. Kidder (1936a) as one of filling in the cultural gap between late Pleistocene archaeological materials and late prehistoric materials. The problem was in how best to classify the myriad archaeological cultures that lay in that large tract of time. Kidder addressed this problem in the Southwest by founding the annual Pecos Conference (Kidder 1927), at which chronological issues could be debated. The early conferences resulted in a proposed chronological sequence of cultural manifestations for that region, but the sequence was limited in geographic extent. No such framework existed for the Southeast or Midwest, two regions that were beginning to witness more and more attention from professional and avocational archaeologists (O'Brien and Lyman 1999a, 2001).

Will Carleton McKern of the Milwaukee Public Museum addressed this issue in the early 1930s, producing what eventually became known as the midwestern taxonomic method (MTM). As we document in later chapters, the method attracted considerable attention throughout the 1930s as archaeologists, primarily those working in the Midwest, worked to refine the method to suit their needs. No one was ever completely satisfied with it, and few other than McKern really understood how it operated. Unlike the southwestern classification, the MTM explicitly excluded time from consideration, and it was this feature that contributed to its demise. Perhaps because of its short life span, roughly from 1932 to 1940, the MTM has been treated as little more than a historical curiosity in recent textbooks (Fagan 1997). Or, as is more common, it is not mentioned at all (for example, Sharer and Ashmore 1993; Thomas 1998). We have a different take on the matter. In our opinion, what McKern attempted to do with the MTM has important lessons for all archaeologists. McKern and his colleagues wrestled with many of the same issues facing archaeologists today. One of these is how to classify archaeological remains in order to analyze them. Archaeologists are not the only natural scientists who classify the phenomena they study, and McKern borrowed a biological model of classification as the template for the MTM.

This volume is divided into two parts. Part 1 contains six chapters that explore select aspects of the MTM. The remainder of chapter 1 presents a brief biography of McKern. Chapter 2 examines the epistemology and ontology of taxonomic classification and describes biological taxonomy. Chapters 3 and 4 examine the historical development of the MTM based on published information and extensive correspondence between McKern and his collaborators. During the 1930s and 1940s, several archaeologists attempted to apply the method in their geographic areas of concern, and they often published comments on the method, prompting responses from McKern. Various applications and statements are discussed in chapter 5. In chapter 6 we place the MTM within the context of broader classification systems that attempt to order the natural world.

In part 2 we reprint the several versions of the MTM penned in the 1930s and also several published addenda and comments and unpublished discussions of the method. There is much to be gleaned from reading these statements, and throughout part 1 we make extensive reference to them. We use several conventions in the following text. Papers that are reprinted in part 2 are signified by a chapter number in brackets within a standard citation (for example, McKern 1932[7]). Throughout part 1 we use "MPM" to denote the archives of the Milwaukee Public Museum; "NRC" to denote the archives of the National Research Council, Washington, D.C.; "ISM" to denote the archives of the Illinois State Museum, Springfield; and "UC" to denote the Special Collections, Regenstein Library, University of Chicago.

W. C. MCKERN

There is no obituary for McKern in *American Antiquity*, the leading archaeological journal in the United States. Instead, a short notice appeared in the March 1989 issue of the *Bulletin of the Society for American Archaeology*. It read simply:

> Society Founder Dies
> At the age of 96, Will Carleton McKern, one of the founders of the Society for American Archaeology, died in Waukesha, Wisconsin on November 20, 1988. He was the first editor of *American Antiquity* from 1935 to 1939, and President of the Society in 1940. Until his death he was Emeritus Director of the Milwaukee Public Museum.

A bit longer obituary was published in the American Anthropological Association's *Anthropology Newsletter* in January 1989 (Anonymous 1989), and McKern's colleague Alton Fisher (1988) published an even longer one in *The Wisconsin Archeologist*, a journal in which McKern regularly published in the 1930s and 1940s and for which he served as editor in 1931–32 (Overstreet 1999).

McKern (figures 1.1 and 1.2) was born in Medicine Lake, Washington, on July 6, 1892. He seldom used his full name, preferring to be identified as W. C. McKern professionally and to be addressed as "Mac" by his friends. He earned a B.A. in anthropology under A. L. Kroeber at the University of California, Berkeley, in 1917. He received a fellowship to support his studies of California Indians but was inducted into the military and sent to France in 1918. After serving in World War I, McKern married Clara Florence on October 22, 1919. He taught anthropology at the University of Washington in 1919 and conducted ethnographic (McKern 1922, 1923, 1924) and archaeological (McKern 1929) research on the island of Tonga in Polynesia as part of the Dominick Expedition of

Figure 1.1. Will Carleton McKern, 1939. Courtesy of Milwaukee Public Museum (negative number 423187).

the Bernice P. Bishop Museum in Honolulu from 1920 to 1922. He then served as an assistant archaeologist for the Bureau of American Ethnology from 1922 to 1924, working with J. Walter Fewkes at Mesa Verde in southwestern Colorado (Basile 2000; Fisher 1988).

McKern became head of the anthropology department of the Milwaukee Public Museum on January 1, 1925, and held that position until November 27, 1943, at which time he became director of the museum. He was awarded the Wisconsin Archeological Society's Lapham Research Medal in 1930 (Overstreet 1999) and served as president of the American Anthropological Association in 1933 and as president of the Society for American Archaeology in 1940–41. McKern received an honorary doctorate from Marquette University in 1956 "in recognition of his many contributions to anthropology, Wisconsin, and the City of Milwaukee"

Figure 1.2. Will Carleton McKern, 1925, in archaeological field camp at Green Lake Mounds, Wisconsin. Courtesy of Milwaukee Public Museum (negative number 118255).

(Fisher 1988:208). He retired from the Milwaukee Public Museum in 1958, having ensured that a new museum building would be constructed.

McKern was the founding editor of *American Antiquity*, serving from 1935 to mid-1939. On assuming the editorship from McKern, Douglas S. Byers (1939:1) noted that "To Mr. McKern who has prescribed the formula that has brought the [journal] through the trying years of infancy is due not only credit, but also the heart-felt thanks of the Society. As a new Editor attempts timorously to take over his duties he realizes only too well the debt that the Society owes its first Editor who founded its editorial policies. Mr. McKern has made of *American Antiquity* a journal that is above all readable; while keeping the pages open to all who wish to contribute he has maintained a standard for contributions that holds the journal high in the rank of scientific publications."

McKern penned numerous editorials for issues of *American Antiquity*, often encouraging readers to send in letters "pertinent to the subject of archaeology, factual or controversial, as may reflect your interests and experience" (McKern 1935:2). If the topic was controversial, McKern warned that the correspondent should be prepared to see a response published because "science thrives on criticism, and languishes on an exclusive diet of indulgence" (McKern 1935:2). He perceived the value of contributions made by avocational archaeologists as well as professionals, but he also recognized that the former would benefit from training by the latter. In his editorials McKern wrote about the importance of classification and whether or not collections generated by nonprofessionals should be purchased by museums, noting that a collection was valuable only if "the exact origin of [the specimens] is positively known to the purchaser of materials, and [further that] the placement of such specimens in a well catalogued collection, renders a valuable direct service to all students who may have occasion to examine these materials in the course of research" (McKern 1936:179). These topics were still being discussed by members of the Society for American Archaeology in the 1990s.

THE MIDWESTERN TAXONOMIC METHOD

Of all his accomplishments, McKern is best remembered as the chief architect of the MTM, designed to classify archaeological remains from the upper Midwest. This is the reason for the name "*midwestern* taxonomic method" rather than, say, "*archaeological* taxonomic method." Fisher (1997) presented a revealing paper about the origins of the MTM at the Second Indianapolis Archaeological Conference in 1986, noting that by 1929 McKern's archaeological fieldwork in Wisconsin was sufficient for him to suspect that there were relationships among the materials he had excavated. There was, however, "no comparative system in general use in the Midwest at that time to facilitate analysis of subtle as well as overt culture traits so as to suggest possible relationships among them" (Fisher 1997:118). Fisher had joined the Milwaukee Public Museum staff early in 1927 at McKern's invitation, and he remained there until September 1933. During that time, he and McKern often ate lunch together and discussed various archaeological matters. Fisher (1997:119) reported that late in 1929 these lunchtime discussions "began to concentrate on how a cultural classification system could be designed to serve the archaeological needs of the Wisconsin area." Because no means was available for ascertaining the age of much of the archaeological material they had collected, they agreed that "temporal considerations would have to be ignored," at least until chronological information became available. They believed that hypothetical evolutionary sequences would not suffice as either a classificatory or temporal framework and finally decided that "the system that was needed so urgently would have to be based on morphological or typological considerations alone" (Fisher 1997:119). Fisher by that time had recently completed courses in biology, and he later stated that he

> had become quite familiar with the taxonomic system of Linnaeus. It was based primarily on relationships of form. . . . If that classification system could show morphological relationships between animal forms as diverse as mastodons and earthworms, might it not be possible to show some relationship between the creations of man as demonstrated by form or structure alone? When this suggestion was proposed to McKern he was interested but he was not convinced that it would work. After considerable discussion and thought on the matter, however, he began to test the idea with data he had collected, and he was pleased to find that it often was successful. This encouraged further testing and more successes followed. When it became evident that there might be a reasonable prospect of success at designing different levels or degrees of relationship between lithic and bone artifacts, pottery, earthworks, and burials and between complexes of such cultural manifestations, the need to become specific in defining the various proposed categories of relationship claimed Mac's attention. He worked almost alone on this phase of the development of the method, bringing the results of his thinking and writing to me every few days for criticism. There was no need to be fussy about terminology as long as there was no duplication of the Linnaean nomenclature and each term that was chosen had a reasonable connotation of the scope of inclusiveness of the class of relations that was implied. (Fisher 1997:119–120)

This statement indicates that it was Fisher who suggested to McKern that the Linnaean biological taxonomy might serve as a good model for building a system of archaeological classification. McKern may have been amenable to such a suggestion because he minored in paleontology during his undergraduate education (McKern to Julian H. Steward, December 15, 1939 [MPM]). Whether it was Fisher's suggestion or McKern's idea initially, perhaps later reinforced by Fisher's suggestion, will likely forever be unknown.

The proposed levels of relationship mentioned by Fisher would become the focus, aspect, phase, pattern, and base units of the final version of the MTM (McKern 1939[15]). McKern obviously did not duplicate the Linnaean nomenclature of species, genera, families, and so on. Whether he did in fact "duplicate the scope of inclusiveness of the class of relations" among the units composing the various levels is difficult to assess. As we point out in chapter 2, the scope of inclusiveness is still debated among biological taxonomists. Further, the morphological relationships denoted by the Linnaean nomenclature implied several kinds of relationships between mastodons and earthworms to biologists after 1859. These multiple and not necessarily complementary relationships were recognized by McKern, but he seldom spoke of them in explicit terms. When he mentioned relationships between his cultural units, it was generally with ambiguous phrasing such as "focus A is related to focus B and both are subsumed under aspect 1, but A and B are not related to focus C which is subsumed under aspect 2" and the like.

DISCUSSION

McKern was working at a time when explicitly worded explanatory theory was not part of archaeological discussion (Lyman et al. 1997). Rather, as he noted in some of his correspondence, the archaeology of the 1930s had few standardized field and laboratory methods. Writing the history of cultures was, however, an analytical goal that many Americanist archaeologists actively sought throughout the first six decades of the twentieth century (Lyman et al. 1997). They developed and perfected stratigraphic excavation, seriation, and interdigitation as ways to measure time's passage (Lyman and O'Brien 1999; Lyman et al. 1998; O'Brien and Lyman 1999b), and they operated under the assumption that typological similarity reflected the "historical relatedness" (Willey 1953) of archaeological phenomena (for example, Rouse 1939). They were not explicit about what *historical relatedness* meant, but by implication it meant some linkage resulting from contact and information exchange, often glossed as diffusion or enculturation. They did not acknowledge the fact that mere historical succession, such as could be demonstrated with a stratified sequence of artifacts, was not necessarily the same as succession along a lineage of information transmission. Nor were Americanist archaeologists often explicit about cultural transmission as the mechanism of heritable continuity within a cultural lineage (Lyman 2001).

Transmission of information, whether genetic or conceptual, as in teaching an individual how to decorate pottery, is what results in *heritable continuity*—a particular kind of historical continuity—because characters or character states are replicated. Heritable continuity and the phylogenetic histories of his cultural units were what McKern in part sought via application of the MTM to archaeological materials, but these were minor goals. His contemporaries did not disagree; they themselves were seeking such nonexplicit relationships among cultural units (see chapter 4). Without the attendant explicit development of an explanatory theory that could account for various sorts of relationships, discussion of the MTM reduced to endless squabbles over the method itself rather than what its results might signify. Those discussions reflected the "typical methodologizing of the period" (Dunnell 2000:371).

McKern was explicit and vocal about the purpose of the method and what its intended results would accomplish. First, the MTM was intended to produce a terminology for a set of classificatory units that would enhance communication between archaeologists working in different areas. Second, it was supposed to facilitate comparative analyses and thus help archaeologists decipher culture history, particularly "cultural affinities" (McKern 1939[15]:303). Ignoring the ambiguity of cultural affinities, McKern's contemporaries protested that the method itself was flawed because it ignored critical variables, particularly time and geographic space, and was qualitative rather than quantitative. What McKern's contemporaries displayed by such arguments was the lack of agreement on the purposes and analytical goals of the MTM. In turn, that lack of agreement reflected the ambiguity of cultural affinities. If they could not agree on what *those* were, then how could they possibly agree on a method supposedly aimed at finding them?

Gordon Willey, a graduate student in the 1930s when the MTM was under discussion, recently described what he and James A. Ford took to be some of the central problems with the MTM:

> Jim was uneasy with the way many eastern archaeologists used the various categories of cultural affiliation, and I was too. As an example, should the Louisiana Troyville period and complex be grouped under the same classificatory category as the obviously Hopewellian-related Marksville period and complex? Troyville pottery had clear antecedents in Marksville; in other ways, however, as in the presence of what appeared to be temple mounds, Troyville's relationships appeared to go in other taxonomic directions. In our opinion the Midwestern taxonomy ran too fast toward conclusions, building up, which [James B.] Griffin had done [in 1935], the big picture of cultural relationships for the whole of the East before we had local situ-

> ations, especially local chronologies and sequences of development worked out. (Willey 1999:x)

McKern, of course, thought he had the algorithm for finding cultural affinities: Build a cultural classification modeled on the Linnaean taxonomy, and those affinities would be self-evident. The affinities supposedly reflected by the Linnaean taxonomy in the 1920s and 1930s were debatable, so it is little wonder that McKern's effort failed. Because it was the Linnaean taxonomy that served as the model for the MTM, we begin our discussion with a consideration of taxonomic classification in general and biological classification in particular.

2
Taxonomic Classification and Biological Taxonomy

> To know is one of the fundamental human appetites and classification is the method whereby apparent flux and chaos of the external world are reduced to quiescence and unity and become the object of intellectual contemplation. (W. R. Thompson 1952:2)

The conceptual structure of what became known as the midwestern taxonomic method originated with Swedish physician and botanist Carl Von Linné, better known as Carolus Linnaeus. Understanding the Linnaean biological taxonomy—how it was built and what it might signify—is critical to grasping why the MTM took the form it did. As implied in chapter 1, understanding why the MTM failed to accomplish the tasks it was intended to necessitates understanding the ontology and epistemology of the Linnaean taxonomy and how Darwin's (1859) ideas influenced interpretations of that taxonomy. Because the Linnaean biological taxonomy is hierarchical in structure, to make sense of the MTM requires a basic understanding of classification in general and taxonomic classification in particular.

CLASSIFICATION

Although we suspect most people would agree that one purpose of classification is to place similar specimens together and then separate them from dissimilar specimens, the terminology of classification is diverse. We initially use *category* and its derivatives as a generic term for the results and processes of sorting phenomena into piles such that like goes with like.

Terminology

Categorization has several purposes, not the least of which is to simplify variation by reducing it to a small, manageable number of kinds more easily discussed than is each individual specimen. Categorization occurs in virtually all endeavors. A librarian must decide if a newly published book is a work of fiction, a work of history, or a work of historical fiction. Astronomers must decide if a newly discovered celestial body is a star, a planet, a moon, an asteroid, or something else. Pedologists must decide which category of soil occurs in a particular area. The systems, processes, and results of categorization are referred to by a plethora of terms that often have no common meaning, even within a discipline. For example, classification, systematics, and taxonomy are some of the most discussed terms in the biological literature. Sometimes any two of these might be defined as synonyms. Borgmeier (1957:53), for example, equated systematics and taxonomy as "that branch of biological science which explores the order existing in the Plant and Animal Kingdoms and represents it by means of a system of concepts (the categories). . . . [It is] the science of order . . . a pure science of relations [based only on] a simple juxtaposition of different conditions of form." Not all biologists equate systematics and taxonomy, but a sample of definitions for the terms given by biologists (Table 2.1) shows that they also do not agree on the definitions. Standard dictionaries do not clarify things because their included definitions present ideals rather than the meaning of the terms as they are used in particular real-world situations. *Webster's Third New International Dictionary* (1993) defines *classification* not only as a verb—"the act or a method of classifying," where classifying comprises "distributing into groups" and "grouping or aggregating in classes that have systematic relations, usually founded on common properties or characters"—but also as a noun—"the results of classifying: a system of classes or groups or a systematic division of a series of related phenomena." Note that the process of the first definition demands the categories of the second definition. This same dictionary defines *taxonomy* as "the study of the general principles of scientific classification: systematics," which itself is defined as "the science of classification, usually the classification and study of organisms with regard to their natural relationships: taxonomy." Definitions of terms we present in the next several paragraphs are those we use in the remainder of the book.

Classification involves the creation of new units and the modification and revision of old units by stipulating the necessary and sufficient conditions for membership within a unit (Dunnell 1971). The necessary and

Table 2.1. Definitions of Classification, Systematics, and Taxonomy from the Biological Literature

classification

— "a practical application of some particular set of taxonomic principles. . . . the aspect of taxonomy involved in sorting and labeling" (Simpson 1945:1); "consists of grouping things according to their characteristics or properties, placing them in a system of categories, and applying a designation to each group thus established" (Simpson 1945:3)

— "the grouping of species and higher categories—the actual building of classified systems" (Blackwelder and Boyden 1952:26)

— "zoological classification is the ordering of animals into groups (or sets) on the basis of their relationships, that is, of associations by contiguity, similarity, or both" (Simpson 1961:9)

— "the product of the activity of the taxonomist" (Mayr 1969:4); "the delimitation, ordering, and ranking of taxa" (Mayr 1969:400)

— "the name of a logical activity, that of ordering concepts into classes (categories in the sense of biologists)" (Griffiths 1974:90)

— "the ordering or arrangement of objects into groups or sets on the basis of their relationships" (Sokal 1974:1116)

— "arrangement of organisms into hierarchic groups; modern biological classifications are *Linnaean* and classify organisms into species, genus, family, order, class, phylum, kingdom, and certain intermediate categoric levels" (Ridley 1993:632)

— "the tabular or hierarchical end result of [taxonomy]" (Padian 1999:357)

systematics (from the Greek word *systema*)

— "the entire field dealing with kinds of animals, their distinction, classification, and evolution" (Blackwelder and Boyden 1952:26)

— "the scientific study of the kinds and diversity of organisms and of any and all relationships among them" (Simpson 1961:7)

— "the scientific study of the kinds and diversity of organisms and of any and all relationships among them" (Colless 1967:6, after Simpson 1961)

— "the science dealing with the diversity of organisms" (Mayr 1969:413)

— "that branch of science which deals with the systematic structure of the world" (Griffiths 1974:89-90)

— "a near synonym of taxonomy" (Ridley 1993:641)

— "the philosophy of organizing nature" (Padian 1999:357)

taxonomy (from the Greek words *taxis*, meaning arrangement, and *nomos*, meaning law)

— "the science of arranging the myriad forms of life" (Simpson 1945:1)

(*continued*)
— "the descriptive, discriminatory, and nomenclatural phase dealing mostly with species and lower categories, the data accumulated about them, and their names" (Blackwelder and Boyden 1952:26)
— "the general process of sorting things out into groups containing things of the same kind and of establishing a hierarchy between such groups" (Thompson 1952:3)
— "the theoretical study of classification, including its bases, principles, procedures, and rules" (Simpson 1961:11)
— "the design and construction of classificatory systems" (Colless 1967:6)
— "the theory and practice of classifying organisms" (Mayr 1969:2, 413)
— synonymous with systematics (Griffiths 1974)
— "the theoretical study of classification, including its bases, principles, procedures, and rules" (Sokal 1974:1116)
— "theory and practice of biological classification" (Ridley 1993:641)
— "the use of sets of organic data guided by systematic principles, which sort of sets will differ among taxa" (Padian 1999:357)

sufficient criteria for membership are the *definitive* criteria of a unit. They define the members of the unit and at least partially describe those members; thus it is important to emphasize that other characters and character states are simply descriptive and not definitive of a unit. A *unit* is a conceptual entity that serves as a standard of measurement (Lyman et al. 1997; O'Brien and Lyman 2000). A centimeter is a unit constructed explicitly to measure linear distance; the degrees on a compass are units constructed explicitly to measure direction or orientation.

As conceptual entities, units must be explicitly defined to be useful for measuring (characterizing, describing, categorizing, defining) phenomena. Units can be specified at any scale. Phenomena to be classified can comprise discrete objects such as projectile points or organisms; they may comprise *characters* (attributes) of discrete objects, such as the bits of temper in pottery or the genes in organisms; or they may comprise sets of discrete objects, such as aggregates of tools variously termed assemblages or tool kits, or populations of organisms variously termed faunas, floras, or communities. Phenomena are classified on the basis of the characters they display, such as size, shape, color, frequency, and material. Characters used to classify phenomena occur at a finer, less-inclusive scale than the phenomena themselves. They are mutually exclusive properties of phenomena, and each character can take any of several values, which are termed character states. The character weight, for example, can have the states 1–5 grams, 6–10 grams, 11–15 grams, and so on; the character length can have the states 1–3 cm, 4–6 cm, 7–9 cm, and so on.

Taxonomy concerns theories of classification, their bases, principles, procedures, and rules (Simpson 1961). *Systematics* is the study of diversity of the phenomena of interest, irrespective of the scale or kind of phenomena, and involves sorting that diversity into sets such that like goes with like according to some principle of sorting. The goal of systematics is to classify phenomena into sets of individuals that are in some sense similar. Each set should be internally homogeneous such that within-group variation is analytically meaningless and between-group variation meaningful, where a *group* is an empirical unit comprising one or more specimens. Similar phenomena are often, but not always, conceived of as being not only formally similar but similar in other ways as well. *Affinity* refers to the particular relation of analytical interest between formally similar specimens within a group or between groups of formally dissimilar specimens. Multiple kinds of things may be affines because they are close in form, in time, in function, in ancestry, or in terms of something else. Measuring a particular kind of affinity is the ultimate goal of classification, irrespective of discipline, and thus specification of that affinity comes from some principle of taxonomy. Classification is generally problem oriented; it is geared toward some larger goal than simply measuring how similar particular phenomena are to one another. The problem takes the general form: *Why* are phenomena A and B similar to one another (what is their affinity) whereas they are dissimilar to phenomenon C? Answering such why questions demands an explanatory theory, or taxonomic principles.

Ontological Framework

Artifacts are classified so that we can conduct analytical work. There are three important implications of that goal. First, a set of phenomena can be classified in a virtually infinite number of ways. There is no assumption that natural groups exist, and in this sense all classification is arbitrary. This does *not* mean that classification is capricious or willy-nilly; rather, it means that specimens are sorted into groups for some analytical purpose, and as the purpose varies, so, too, will the groups and the units used to categorize them. Second, the analytical validity of the units produced by classification must be testable. Do the units measure the kind of affinity sought? Third, how do we know which characters we should measure and how we should measure them? There must be some *theory*—explanatory statements—that guides analysis, because it is theory (taxonomic principles) and its derivative propositions that suggest which characters are relevant and at what scale they should be measured. The theory one chooses to follow depends in part on the particular analytical problem one seeks to solve. Problems concerning change in culture over time demand some form of evolutionary theory; problems concerning how artifacts work or function demand theories of mechanics, engineering, and physics.

Different theories rest on one of two different ontologies. In the fourth century B.C., Aristotle sought the underlying essence—the essential characteristics—of each kind of organism (Hull 1965). In the twentieth century his ontology came to be known as *essentialism*, or *typological thinking* (Mayr 1959). Typological thinking holds that types *are* real and fixed—a statistical average comprises an essence—and variability between individuals within a kind has no analytical importance. Essentialism influenced all classifications until Charles Darwin (1859) proposed an alternative, today termed *materialism*, or *population thinking*. Darwin focused on the uniqueness of phenomena. Although the basic form of individuals within a set of similar phenomena can be captured by, say, a statistical average, Darwin realized that such measures of central tendency are abstractions and in no sense real (Padian 1999).

Either the ontology of essentialism or that of materialism underpins all classifications (Dunnell 1980; Mayr 1959; O'Brien and Lyman 2000, 2002). This can lead to a misunderstanding of the meaning of a particular classification, but it does not mean that one ontology is always preferred over the other. Essentialism is advantageous when we want to predict how kinds of things interact regardless of their positions in time and space. The periodic table is founded in essentialism, and it serves its intended purpose well. However, when history is the focus of study, materialism is preferred because each particular event is unique in terms of its potentially critical characters, despite the fact that we can construct a classification that places all international conflicts in one group, plagues in another group, and droughts in yet another group. Materialism holds that things are constantly in the process of becoming something else. In biological evolution, a population of interbreeding organisms representing a species can (but might not) constantly evolve via mutation and differential reproduction into another species. Each species is a spatiotemporally unique entity and, unlike a chemical element, does not exist forever.

Under the ontology of materialism, there is a parallel between the biological evolution of a lineage of multiple, temporally successive species and the cultural evolution of a lineage of multiple, temporally successive cultures, tool traditions, and the like. As we will see, McKern was hesitant to say it explicitly, but it is precisely the evolutionary (phylogenetic and genealogical) affinities of the cultural units constructed using the MTM that he thought might be revealed.

Epistemological Issues of Systematics

Because theory is the source of our ideas on causes of affinity, it has to be the final arbiter of which units are applicable for which kinds of analytical jobs. Theory and an analytical problem dictate which characters out of the almost infinite number that could be selected are actually chosen by the analyst for measurement, and theory in particular specifies the values (character states) of those characters. The characters and values chosen are the units used to construct types, and as such they are conceptual, or *ideational,* units (Dunnell 1971, 1986). The specimens we classify are phenomenological, or *empirical,* units. Ideational units, or *classes* (Lyman et al. 1997; O'Brien and Lyman 1999b, 2000), can be descriptional units, used merely to characterize or describe a property or a thing, or they can be theoretical units, which are created for specific analytical purposes. For example, in light of a proposed causal relation between function and edge angles of stone tools, edge-angle units such as 1–30°, 31–60°, and 61–90° could be constructed as theoretical units. A *theoretical unit* is an ideational unit that has explanatory significance specifically because of its theoretical relevance for the solution of an analytical problem.

Ideational units can be constructed or defined in either of two ways. An *intensional definition* comprises the necessary and sufficient conditions for membership in a unit; it explicitly lists the definitive characters that a phenomenon must display in order to be identified as a member of the unit (Buck and Hull 1966; Dunnell 1971). Importantly, there is no necessary reference to a particular set of real, empirical specimens when the unit is constructed other than to specify that, say, projectile points rather than pottery comprise the phenomena to be classified. The basic procedure is to write a set of intensional definitions and then to identify each specimen as a member of a particular class.

An *extensional definition* also comprises the necessary and sufficient conditions for membership in a unit and is derived by enumerating selected characters shared by the unit's members. That is, the definition is based on observed characters of the existing members of a unit. As Buck and Hull (1966:105) put it with respect to biological taxa, "a taxon is thought of as simply the collection of its members," and a taxon's name "is defined extensionally rather than intensionally." The definitive characters of extensionally defined units are not theoretically informed in any explicit manner because the group of specimens was formed by some murky process prior to the specification of the (extensional) definition. One common result of extensionally derived definitions is the conflation of definitive characters and descriptive characters. Most types traditionally employed in archaeology are extensionally defined units formed when an analyst subdivides a collection of artifacts into smaller piles based on perceived similarities and differences. A summary of the central tendencies of the members of each pile, or a statement on the normal appearance of specimens in each pile, comprises the definitive criteria of a type. Because the definitions depend entirely on the specimens examined, we cannot know if such extensionally defined units are comparable in terms of the kind of affinity we hope they measure.

Taxonomic Classification

Paleontologist George Gaylord Simpson (1945:14) argued that "any practical system of classifying a large number of things . . . involves a hierarchy by which minor units are progressively gathered into groups of increasingly greater scope." Although this begs the question of practical for what purpose, it may reflect a tendency of the human mind to generalize at successively more inclusive levels as an efficient information storage-and-retrieval system (Mayr 1981, 1995), particularly with respect to complex phenomena such as organisms (Simon 1962). All German shepherds are dogs, but not all dogs are German shepherds; all dogs are mammals, but not all mammals are dogs. These are commonsensical observations, and the resulting taxonomic classification provides a useful communication system as well as a readily understood framework for organizing such observations. More important, a taxonomy generally not only means a hierarchical arrangement of units—a particular architecture—but also carries an evolutionary implication. This implication originates in the modern connotation of the Linnaean biological taxonomy, as we discuss below. We use the term *hierarchical classification* or *taxonomic classification* to denote a particular structure of classification without any such connotation.

A taxonomic classification sometimes is referred to simply as a taxonomy. Such a classification comprises a hierarchical arrangement of nested sets such that less-inclusive, lower-rank units are included in more-inclusive, higher-rank units (Valentine and May 1996). The hierarchy is a system of units of various ranks, each rank comprising what we will call a *taxon.* Taxa of a particular rank are symbolized as T_j; each particular taxon comprises one or more taxa of rank T_{j-1} and is itself a member of rank T_{j+1}. Multiple taxa of rank T_j are parallel taxa, taxa of rank T_{j+1} are superior taxa, and taxa of rank T_{j-1} are subordinate taxa relative to taxa of rank T_j. In nested taxonomies no two taxa of rank T_j have any T_{j-1} member in common. The specimens comprising the lowest, least-inclusive rank are of rank zero and are themselves not a taxon but a population(s), or aggregate, of individuals. Populations are the "operational units" of classification (Buck and Hull 1966:98). The lowest-ranking taxa are called terminal taxa. Taxa of rank T_j are said to be nested within taxa of ranks T_{j+n} because the latter comprise *all* members of lower ranks.

Several important properties attend the nestedness of biological taxa in a hierarchy. First, although it sometimes is said that empty taxa are not possible (Kay 1971)—each taxon must have at least one empirical member—we find this untenable because taxa are classes and thus their membership can be zero. Knowing which taxa/classes have members and which do not could be important in some analyses (see below). Second, as noted in the preceding paragraph, no parallel taxa T_j can include the same member taxon T_{j-1}. There is no partial overlap between parallel taxa. In extreme form, this attends the fact that a taxon of rank T_j is a member of a taxon of rank T_{j+1}, but the reverse cannot be true (Buck and Hull 1966). Third, not all terminal taxa will be at the same level. This means that terminal taxa will not always be distinguished from each other in like ways or to similar degrees. Fourth, nestedness is a result of the fact that the definitive criteria of a T_j taxon are also present among its member T_{j-1} taxa. In particular, superior classes have fewer and/or more-general definitive criteria, whereas subordinate classes have more and/or more-specific definitive criteria.

There are two methods of building a taxonomic classification. One is to work from the top down. The classifier starts with some specified field of phenomena and then divides those phenomena into successively more internally homogeneous groups. Often this involves dividing a taxon into two or more subordinate groups on the basis of two or more characters. Terminal taxa are attained when no further divisions are made. The order in which characters and character states are chosen influences the nature of the terminal taxa. Many identification keys follow a top-down protocol, which results in the *identification* of individual specimens as members of particular taxa. The alternative means of building a taxonomic classification is to work from the bottom up. Individuals are grouped on the basis of numerous similarities to form the lowest-rank taxa; those taxa are grouped to form the next higher-rank taxa on the basis of fewer and/or more general similarities; and so on until all taxa are grouped into one taxon.

The results of top-down and bottom-up classification procedures can be quite similar, but their epistemologies are obviously different. Differences in their ontologies are more subtle. Both procedures presume an underlying hierarchical structure to the phenomena being classified. The subtle difference is found in the argument that a top-down procedure assumes the classification will produce the taxa; a bottom-up procedure assumes the taxa will produce the classification (Mayr 1969). Here is where theory must be called on to account for which procedure is more valid. Some biologists argue that the bottom-up procedure is preferable because taxa—in particular species—are real biological units and thus are the building blocks that give the classification. This is a slippery issue, which we return to below.

Architecture of Taxonomic Classifications

A taxonomic classification can take one of several forms. It may be symmetrical, such as in Figure 2.1, where each member of a taxon is equivalent to every other member of the taxon in terms of the number of definitive characters. Thus the least-inclusive, or terminal, taxa—F1aA, F1aB, F1bC, and so on—are defined by three characters. Let's say that the field of phenomena to be classified comprises pottery; thus the first-place character (F) is not definitive of the classes within the field. In level II, the second place (Arabic) number denotes temper (1 = shell, 2 = grit). In level III, the third-place (lowercase) letter designates vessel-wall thickness (a = 0.4–0.5 cm, b = 0.5–0.6 cm, and so on). Finally, in level IV, the fourth-place (uppercase) letter designates surface treatment (A = cord marked, B = stamped, C = plain, and so on). All taxa making up each level have the same number of definitive characters. But note as well that there is no possibility of having a grit-tempered vessel with a wall thickness of 0.4–0.5 cm; that is, there is no class F2a. Thus the *kinds* of characters defining a particular class reflect both the order of character inclusion constructed by the analyst and a suspicion regarding the significance of a particular character or character state for classification purposes. In Figure 2.1, character states a and b of level III are deemed important to class F1 of level II, whereas character states c and d are deemed important to class F2 of level II. Here the definitive characters and character states are said to be weighted.

Because characters and character states can be weighted, a taxonomic classification may be nonsymmetrical, as in Figure 2.2. A nonsymmetrical hierarchy is created by selective omission of certain characters from various taxa. Thus, in Figure 2.2, among the terminal taxa comprising level IV, one is defined by two characters (F1), another by three characters (F2a), and five by four characters. The level IV taxa not only have various numbers of definitive characters, two taxa (F1, F2a) have the same definitive characters in level IV that they do in the more-inclusive level III, and one taxon (F1) has the same definitive characters in level II that it does in levels III and IV. Thus, taxon F1 is defined by the same set of characters at three levels in the hierarchy, and taxon F2A is defined by the same set of

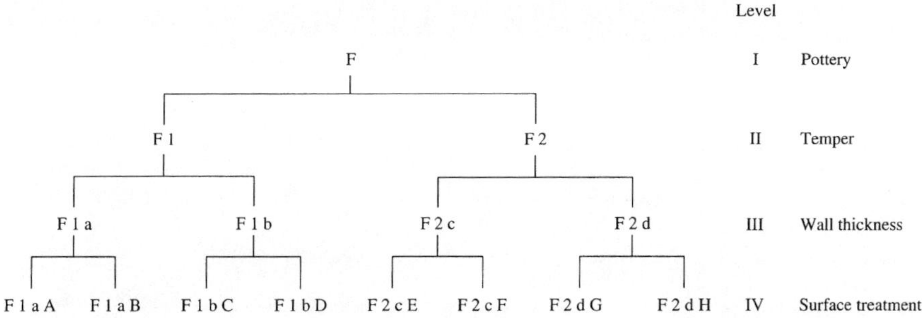

Figure 2.1. A symmetrical hierarchical classification producing eight classes. Note that (1) each class in a particular level/taxon is equally distinct from every other class in that level in terms of the number of definitive characters and (2) the classes (taxa) in level IV are nested within classes in level III, those in level III are nested within classes in level II, and those in level II are nested within classes in level I.

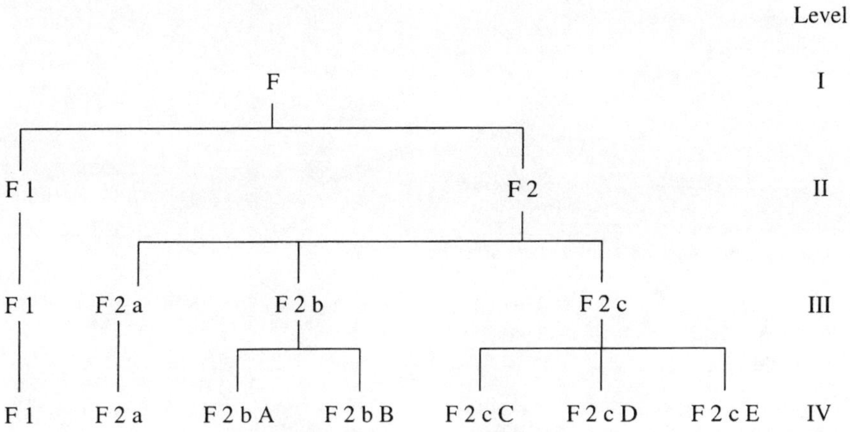

Figure 2.2. An asymmetrical hierarchical classification producing seven classes. Note that five of the classes (taxa) in level IV are distinguished by four characters, one class by three characters, and one class by two characters. Therefore, each class in either level III or level IV is not equally distinct from every other class in that level.

characters at two levels of the hierarchy. Taxa within each of the two least-inclusive levels—III and IV—are not all equivalently different from one another in terms of the number of their definitive characters. This can result in a lack of unit comparability. There are other, potentially more serious, problems.

Figure 2.3 shows an example of a five-level hierarchical classification of a fictitious collection of projectile points. As in Figure 2.2, the three taxa that occur in level V are each defined by four characters and are thus

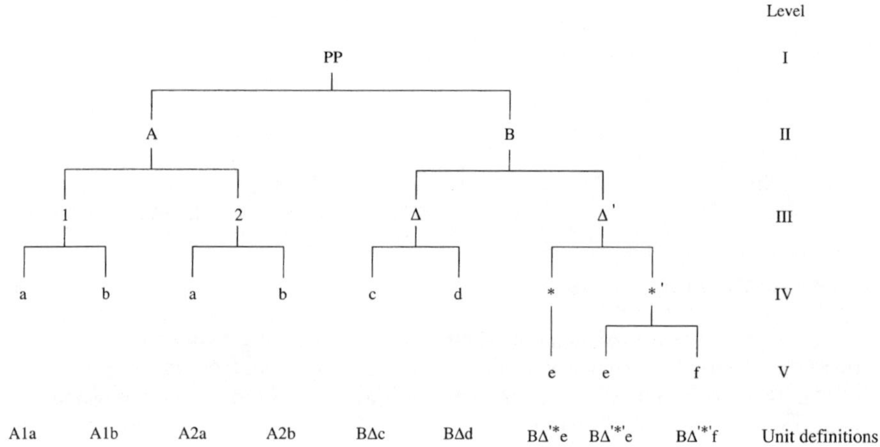

PP = Projectile point

A = Notches present
B = Notches absent, stemmed

1 = Side notch
2 = Basal notch

a = Shallow notch
b = Deep notch

Δ = Constricted stem
Δ' = Straight stem

c = Curved base
d = Pointed base

* = Short stem
*' = Long stem

e = Straight base
f = Convex base

Figure 2.3. A hypothetical five-level taxonomic classification of projectile points. The leftmost six units are each defined by three characters; the rightmost three units are each defined by four characters. The exclusion of a fourth definitive character for the six units on the left indicates either that base shape does not vary or is analytically insignificant, but it is unclear which applies or if both apply. Identifying specimens as members of a particular unit must consider character levels II–V in that order, as reversing the order of levels II and V would significantly alter unit definitions.

equally different from each other in terms of the number of definitive characters. The six other taxa distinguished in level IV are equally different from each other in these terms but are not as different from each other as those in level V in terms of the number of definitive criteria. Thus all terminal taxa are not equivalently different from each other. Note that in

Figure 2.3 the particular weighting of characters reflected by the order in which they are considered influences the nature of the resulting units. The character states signified by c–f concern the character base shape. The problem is that they are distributed across both levels IV and V because stem length is deemed more important for defining straight-stem points than it is for defining constricted-stem points. That's why stem length is listed in level IV prior to base shape in level V among members of taxon BΔ' (level III) but is not considered in taxon BΔ. Differences between units may comprise both differences in the number of definitive characters and the kinds of characters or character states making up the class definition. How might such a difficulty be avoided?

Note that in Figure 2.1 there is no possibility of a taxon F2bC, although such a taxon could be accommodated by adding a third branch, F2b, to the F2 taxon. There is yet a simpler way to contend with this, a way that in fact reveals potentially important information regarding formal variation within a sample. A hierarchical classification need not be asymmetrical nor weight characters. An example is given in Figure 2.4. Here, unlike in figures 2.1–2.3, all possible character combinations are included because each character is added at only one level and each character state possible is included under the next-higher taxon. The result is that the set of terminal taxa listed in level IV includes all possible combinations of character states—all possible terminal taxa are rendered as classes. Perhaps only some of those will have empirical specimens present in a given collection. In such a case, knowing which classes comprise empty morphospace—classes without empirical members—might represent important information for some analyses (for example, Gould 1991).

An example may help clarify some of the preceding points. Figure 2.5 shows twelve phenomena to be classified. Some of them are similar on the basis of shape and might be grouped on that basis; another combination of groups could be derived based on size; yet a third combination would result from the presence or absence of shading. Borrowing this example from philosopher Karl Popper (1968:421), entomologist G. C. D. Griffiths (1974:89) stated that "things are similar *in different respects;* any two things which are similar from one point of view may be dissimilar in another; similarity in general presupposes the adoption of a point of view or interest; and some similarities will strike us if we are interested in one problem, others if we are interested in another problem." Thus, "many different hierarchical arrangements can be made even of these simple geometrical figures, and no one such arrangement can adequately represent the overlapping (non-hierarchical) distribution of similarities" (Griffiths 1974:89). In

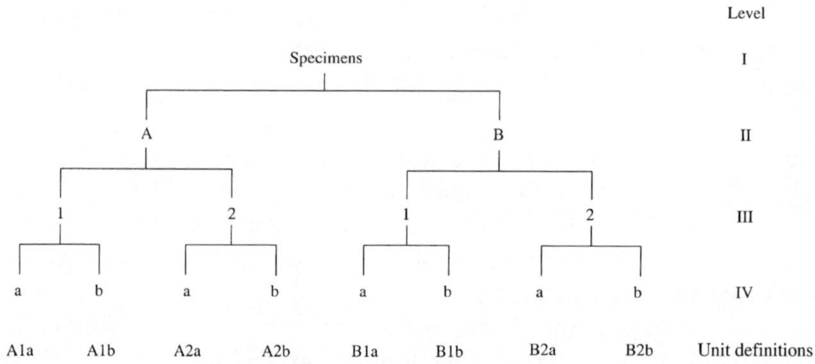

Figure 2.4. A hypothetical taxonomic classification in which characters and character states are unweighted. Note that all characters are part of each unit's definition and that all possible combinations of character states comprise the eight defined units.

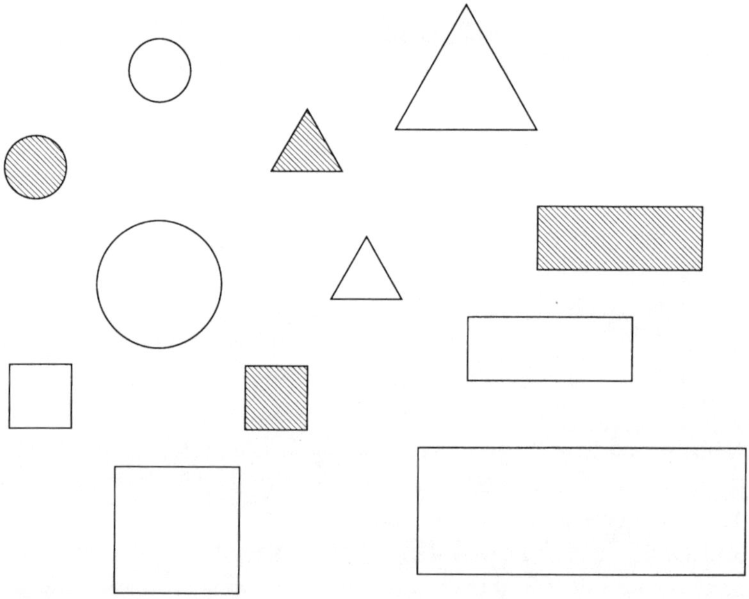

Figure 2.5. Twelve entities that differ in shape, size, and shading (after Popper 1968). Were two individuals independently to build extensionally derived hierarchical classifications of these specimens, it is highly probable that the classifications would differ considerably.

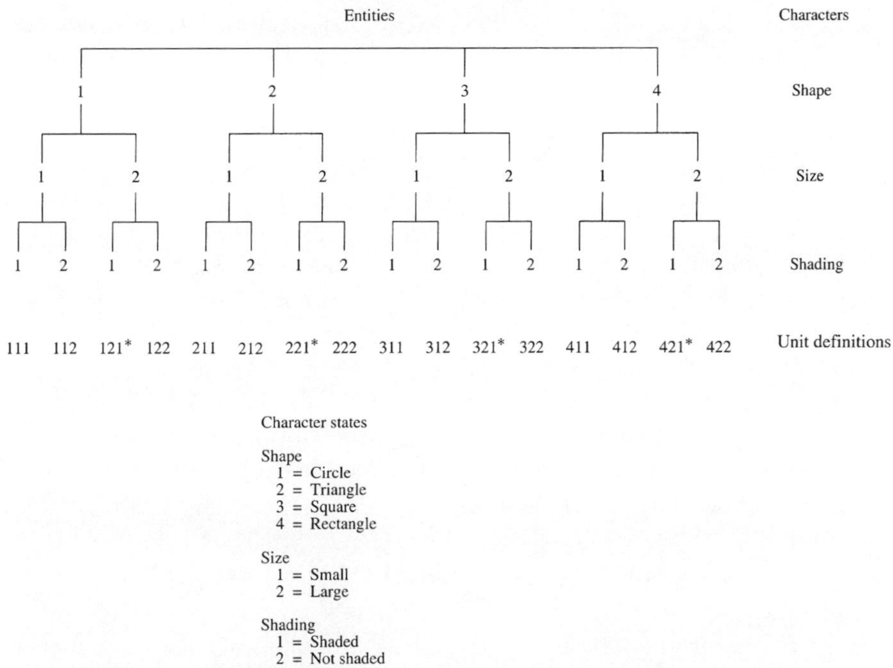

Figure 2.6. An unweighted, symmetrical taxonomic classification for the twelve entities shown in Figure 2.5. Note that only twelve units (classes) have members; units without members designated by *.

our view, the important point here is that were two individuals to independently derive extensionally defined, hierarchically arranged units from Figure 2.5, the odds are good that the two classifications would differ, perhaps dramatically.

If an unweighted, symmetrical taxonomy were to be constructed for the entities in Figure 2.5, it would take the form of the tree in Figure 2.6. Importantly, the resulting terminal taxa comprise classes, each of which is constructed using the same definitive characters, even if the characters were added in a different order. Identifying the entities in Figure 2.5 according to this taxonomy, we find that one entity exists in each of only twelve of the sixteen classes. The four empty classes—those without empirical members—compared to the twelve represented classes—those with a member—tells us something about the diversity of morphospace represented in the sample of twelve entities. But much more important, the taxonomic classification in Figure 2.6 is constructed using all the obvious characters and character states displayed by the twelve entities in Figure 2.5. In light of Griffiths's remarks above, this raises the question of whether such a classification will allow any analytical work to be done. In order to be analytically useful, the characters and character states comprising a classification must be pertinent to the goals of analysis. The taxonomic classification in Figure 2.6 provides a relatively complete description of the twelve entities, but the analytical utility of the sixteen classes is not at all clear for want of a theory and an analytical problem. Further, a hierarchical classification such as that in Figure 2.6 is not necessarily natural but rather "an organizational model and as such, it is a human conceptual construct. [It] is an abstraction" (Knox 1998:3). A taxonomic classification *can*, however, in light of a theory or taxonomic principle that guides its construction, show "inter-level relationships" (Knox 1998:3). The biological taxonomy we are familiar with today has not always shown the same "inter-level relationships" because taxonomic principles have changed. When McKern used it as the model for the midwestern taxonomic method, its modern connotations were being debated.

LINNAEAN BIOLOGICAL TAXONOMY

Prior to the origins of Linnaeus's system of biological taxonomy, there were numerous methods of classifying organisms (Mayr 1969; Simpson 1959, 1961; Thompson 1952). Linnaeus's *Systema Naturae*, which was "first published in 1735 and repeatedly revised and expanded, redefined the study of the living world, and even seemed to put natural history on a par—or at least in the ballpark—with the more prestigious and mathematically oriented pursuits grouped under the rubric of natural philosophy" (Ritvo 1997:15). "Natural" comes from the Aristotelian viewpoint that things have an "essence." Linnaeus "was looking backward to the scholastic philosophy of the Middle Ages and Aristotle" (Mayr 1969:58); thus, for Linnaeus a "natural system" of classification was one based on the "inherent qualities" of organisms rather than on "criteria external to the organisms being classified" (Simpson 1959:294). Although Linnaeus employed few characteristics for classifying organisms, his approach was "empirical" (Mayr 1969:58). Simpson (1959:294) argued that because Linnaeus's classification was based on an "evaluation" of group similarities and differences, "there must [have been] some theoretical basis for the evaluation." That theory was divine creation, and in this sense Linnaeus's system was "natural." Natural classification was founded on the belief that if nature were divinely dictated, the classification itself—the divine plan—might be discoverable (Gilmour 1951; Hull 1965). In Linnaeus's view, classification involved searching for the natural affinity among organisms (Ereshefsky 1994). Natural affinity was not explicitly defined by Linnaeus or anyone else, although morphological resemblance was typically taken as evidence of such affinity (Gilmour 1951; Simpson 1945).

Linnaean taxonomy was in another sense "artificial" (Mayr 1969; Stearn 1959). It was based on characters "selected only for their convenience in identification" of unknown organisms (Simpson 1959:294). As Cain (1958:150) noted, the process of logical division that Linnaeus adopted resulted in definitive criteria being those attributes that were the "most striking" and the "most easily described in words." One result of this was to weight certain characters as more important than other characters for assessing natural affinity (Cain 1959a; Gilmour 1951; Mayr 1969).

Linnaeus proposed a hierarchy comprising five ranks, or levels of inclusiveness. From most to least inclusive these were kingdom, class, order, genus, and species. By the middle of the twentieth century the number of ranks had grown to twenty (Ereshefsky 1994, 1997, 2001; Mayr 1969), largely because it became increasingly difficult to determine which level of the original taxonomy was represented by a particular group of organisms above the species level (a problem that McKern and his contemporaries would have with the MTM [chapters 3 and 4]).

Linnaeus's achievement "was to take systems of procedure which his predecessors had used incidentally or piecemeal or on a very small scale, to analyse and evaluate them from the standpoint of their practical usefulness, and then to apply them consistently, methodically, and on a large scale to the whole living world as then known" (Stearn 1959:6). His proposed system replaced a cumbersome diagnostic polynomial system that described taxa with an easily memorized binomial system that designated and named taxa. The tenth edition of the *Systema Naturae* was published in 1758 and is generally taken to be the initiation of modern biological taxonomy because it is in that edition that Linnaeus first applied his taxonomic method consistently and thoroughly throughout the volume.

Linnaeus began with the taxonomic rank of genus and divided the members of each genus into species. The genus name was a general and collective category, such as "owl," whereas the species name designated kinds within the genus category, such as "screech owl," "barn owl," "burrowing owl," and the like. Hence "the custom of putting the generic name first" (Cain 1956:97) in the taxon's name. All members of a genus hold certain characters in common—virtually all owls have large flattened faces—allowing people to recognize and distinguish them from other genera (for example, ducks, eagles). Genera were "separate, distinct entities with distinct names, and [they were] natural so that all would agree on their limits" (Cain 1959b:235). Linnaeus reasoned that it was difficult for a layperson to distinguish among the particular species observed, so the genus

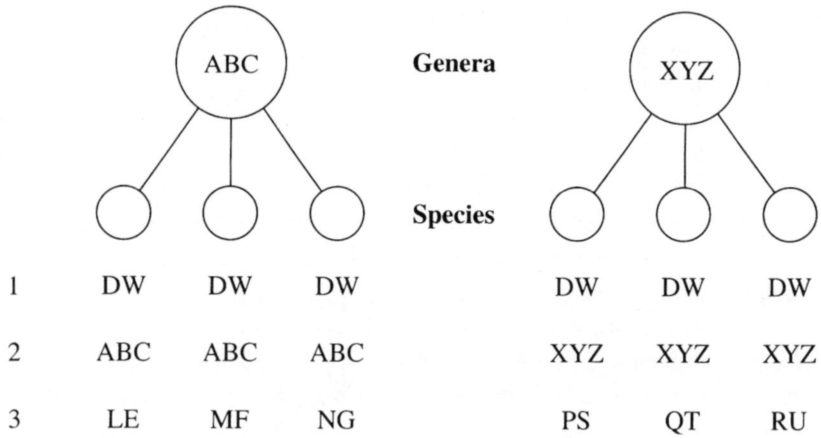

Figure 2.7. A model of the differentia and other characters of two genera (large circles) and six species (small circles). Each capital letter denotes a particular character and the numbers a kind of character: 1, characters shared by members of multiple genera; 2, characters shared by species members of one genus (genus differentia); 3, characters shared by members of a single species (after Stearn 1959).

category was necessary. He also wanted a readily learned system of classification that made finer-level distinctions between groups of organisms (Stearn 1959). His binomial system served both functions.

How were the species of a genus distinguished? Known and named genera did not change when new genera were recognized. Species, like genera, were viewed as "definite entities, clearly separable eventually from each other" (Cain 1959b:235). The word *eventually* is critical because the criteria used to distinguish species within a genus were "liable to alteration whenever new species belonging to that genus were discovered" (Cain 1959b:236). As modeled in Figure 2.7, the characters that the species possess are of several kinds: (1) those that every member of the genus possesses but that are also possessed by members of other genera; (2) those that every species member and only a member of the genus possesses; and (3) those that only a given species member possesses (Stearn 1959). The "*definition* [of a genus comprises] those characteristics which the species shares with other member-species of its genus which [are] implied by giving it and them the same generic name, and those characteristics which distinguish it from these other members [are] its *differentiae*" (Stearn 1959:16).

Linnaeus used the genus as his primary classificatory unit and employed Aristotelian "*logical division* and certain *a priori* ideas of what must be important" (Cain 1959b:234) to distinguish among species within a genus. Following Aristotelian logic, "*[g]enus* refers to the *class* in which the subject is included; the subject is a *species* belonging to this class" (Thompson 1952:3). According to Aristotelian logic, "the genus should not be regarded merely as a collection of species. The genus and the differentia taken together are the definition of the species, the statement of its essence" (Cain 1958:145).

Development and use of the Linnaean taxonomy was enhanced by the notion that taxa were immutable and did not evolve. Linnaeus "believed that all species could be grouped into genera between which there were definite discontinuities of attributes. The final definition of each genus as a natural group would have to wait until all the species in it were known. Presumably the genera which seemed separate only through ignorance would then be duly interconnected by newly discovered species, and exactly which attributes were merely shared by a few species and which were indeed characteristic of particular genera could then be determined" (Cain 1956:98). One result of beginning with the genus taxon was that "unless there are more species than one in a genus it is not possible to know what are generic and what [are] specific attributes" (Cain 1958:158–159). Importantly, the preceding makes it clear that the differentia of Linnaeus's genus and species taxa were extensionally derived from specimens at hand.

Biological Taxonomy between 1758 and 1859

The century between publication of the tenth edition of Linnaeus's *Systema Naturae* in 1758 and publication of Charles Darwin's *On the Origin of Species* in 1859 was characterized by ornithologist Ernst Mayr (1969:59) as involving an "empirical approach" to biological taxonomy, which at the time comprised a tautology (Cain 1959a, 1959b). Characters that were thought to be constant—shared, or held in common—across taxa were used to designate taxa, but to establish that some characters were in fact constant required that the groups be formed "before any particular characters [could] be checked" for constancy (Cain 1959b:237). This circularity began prior to Linnaeus's efforts and involved the search for a structural plan common to members of a natural group. As Simpson (1959:295) put it, "the problem was in defining the plan, which consists of characters in common within a group. In short, the group gives the plan, the plan gives the group."

Linnaeus sought a "natural" classification that reflected *the* divine plan. Thus, one of his famous aphorisms was that "the characters do not make the genus but the genus makes the characters. In other words we do not know *a priori* what characters will define a group but observe them as common to the group once [the group] is given" (Simpson 1959:295).

This is merely another expression of the tautology identified above and comprises the central problem of extensionally derived differentia: Those differentia depend on the specimens polled, and thus it is quite probable that they will change as the sample of specimens examined changes.

Many systematists of the late eighteenth century classified organisms by characters held in common in the same way that Linnaeus had, and thus they fell prey to the tautology. It also became clear that the fewer the characters held in common, the more inclusive the taxonomic unit: "The lower [less-inclusive] taxon, having *fewer* individuals as members, requires *more* properties to meet the qualifications for membership. The higher taxon, having *more* individuals as members, requires *fewer* properties to meet its qualifications for membership. . . . Reducing the number of qualifications increases membership; increasing the number of qualifications decreases membership" (Buck and Hull 1966:107). Hence, during the early nineteenth century many more characters were used than previously, not only to help classify increasingly greater amounts of variation but also to determine which rank within the hierarchy was represented. There were, however, no rules for how many definitive characters were required for a given taxonomic level.

Each unit was seen as an *archetype*, a term introduced by English naturalist Sir Richard Owen in 1848 (Padian 1997). It "represented a model organism, the sum of the features shared by a group of organisms" (Hall 1996:217). As reported by Padian (1997:447), "Owen began by using the archetype as a groundplan, or basic model, with no real existence apart from being a useful concept, but it soon took on more idealistic overtones, as a plan that existed in the mind of the Creator." For Owen, his concept of archetype "created a rational basis for understanding homology" (Padian 1997:448). Owen defined a *homolog* as "the same organ in different animals under every variety of form and function" (Panchen 1994:40). It did not have its modern meaning of designating shared ancestry but rather was taken to mean representative of a common, or archetypical, plan. In the first half of the nineteenth century the biological conception of homology "did not imply anything more than purely formal relation" (Szarski 1949:124).

Archetypal classification commonly involves morphological criteria derived from the archetype and is sometimes called morphological classification or typological classification. An archetypal classification has a particular basis for grouping organisms:

> Its basis is the grouping of animals according to the number, and to some extent the kind, of structural characteristics that they have in

> common. Each grade in a hierarchy corresponds with certain fixed characters possessed by all the animals included under a given rubric at that level. The lower the hierarchic rank, the more characters held in common by the included forms. At one end the highest category is organic creation, with only life common to all its members, and at the other end are minimum units, each including individuals alike in all their hundreds or thousands of characters except for incidental, random fluctuation. Each group of the system has a fixed model, an archetype, consisting of a given set of morphological characteristics, and any animal that agrees, in this set of peculiarities, with the archetype belongs to that group. (Simpson 1945:3)

Darwin's Influence on Biological Taxonomy

Darwin's (1859) *On the Origin of Species* provided an explicit scientific conception of both natural affinity and natural group. In chapter 13 of the first edition, Darwin specified a reason why various sets of organisms were more, or less, similar. It was not a reflection of some divine plan but rather "propinquity of descent,—the only known cause of the similarity of organic beings" (Darwin 1859:413). In general terms, those organic beings that were quite similar had a recent common ancestor, whereas those that were not so similar had a remote common ancestor. We say "in general terms" because Darwin was well aware that processes such as convergence could produce similar organisms that were not closely related through descent. Darwin reasoned that although formal similarity and other lines of evidence such as ontogeny and fossils would be suggestive of phylogeny, they might not reflect it perfectly.

Descent with modification makes evolution dualistic because two mechanisms are involved: genetic mutation, which is "prospectively blind," and natural selection, which is "retrospectively capable of organic improvement. This dualism produces a time-extended historical entity that displays genealogical continuity and phylogenetic discontinuity" (Knox 1998:4). Note that Darwin used the phrase "descent with modification," not descent *and* modification. Descent has "conceptual priority over modification such that modification is best viewed within the context of descent" (Knox 1998:4). This dualism was initially, however, largely overlooked, and as a result the postulate after 1859 was that "structural similarity is indicative of common phyletic origin, and as a rule its degree is proportional to the nearness of the common ancestry" (Simpson 1945:7). In one stroke *natural affinity* came to denote common ancestry, and *natural group* came to mean related by shared ancestry.

After publication of Darwin's *Origin*, a change took place in how organisms were classified: "The important characters were now those least likely to be altered in the course of evolution. . . . The most constant characters were [used] to define groups. They were now explained as primitive, where previously they had been called 'more essential' and the groups were said to be monophyletic rather than just natural" (Cain 1959c:306; see also Simpson 1945:4). What was happening, then, was more of an attempt to accommodate what was thought to be implied by the Linnaean taxonomy—evolutionary descent with modification—than to alter how that classification system was implemented. As Simpson (1945:4) perceptively noted, "the superficial aspects of classification do not necessarily change when the underlying meaning [of the classification] changes." Similarly, Mayr (1969:61) noted that "[a]ccepting evolution did not necessitate any change in the [classificatory] technique. No longer did the [systematist] have to 'make' taxa, evolution had done that for him. All he needed to do was to discover these groups." The discovery process was, however, far from simple.

The procedure of discovering taxa and their phylogenetic relationships was unclear, and between 1859 and the middle of the twentieth century no one developed a specific methodology for determining common descent. Rather, systematics continued to be similar to previous archetypal classifications. In particular, during the several decades preceding and following the end of the nineteenth century, systematists often denoted each particular form of organism as a separate species. This was known as the "typological species concept" (Mayr 1969; Simpson 1961). This concept fell from favor in the late 1930s as McKern and his colleagues were haggling over how to operationalize the MTM. However, it is the typological species concept and how one used it in the field that seem to have influenced McKern. Typological species were recognized on the basis of the morphological similarities of organisms, and higher taxa were simply groups of morphologically similar lower taxa (Bather 1927; Lull 1917; see also the discussion and references in Engstrom et al. 1994). The structure of the classification was still hierarchical and aggregative.

The aggregative nature of the Linnaean biological taxonomy is shown in Figure 2.8. The taxonomy comprises a set of nested units (taxa), with each higher level encompassing greater inclusiveness than the ones below. Thus each level is an aggregate of the units making up the adjacent lower level. After 1859 the taxonomy was thought to reflect not only such varying degrees of inclusiveness but also something else. This something else was spelled out by Simpson (1961:191), who defined higher taxa as follows: "A T_{j+1} is a taxon including one or more T_js of inferred common phylogenetic origin and separated from other T_{j+1}s by a decided gap." T_j denotes

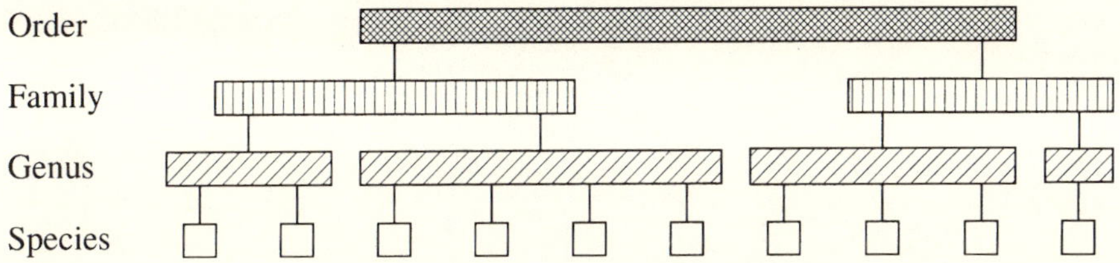

Figure 2.8. The nested (aggregative) structure of the Linnaean biological taxonomy (after Valentine and May 1996).

a taxon of some rank, T_{j+1} denotes the adjacent higher rank, and "decided gap" denotes the degree of formal dissimilarity between T_{j+1}s.

After 1859 the procedure for aggregating low-level taxa into the adjacent higher-level taxon was morphological, but it included two new considerations. First, the more recent the common ancestry of members of a taxon, the more characters they hold in common (irrespective of rank); gaps between lower taxa are small when they hold many characters in common. Second, the greater the gap between taxa of the same rank, the greater the remoteness of their common ancestor. Morphological difference was thought to denote the degree of phylogenetic affinity between taxa. During the first half of the twentieth century, biologists realized that this was but a general rule of thumb and that it did not account for parallelism or convergence. "*Parallelism* is the development of similar characters separately in two or more lineages of common ancestry and on the basis of, or channeled by, characteristics of that ancestry. . . . *Convergence* is the development of similar characters separately in two or more lineages without a common ancestry pertinent to the similarity but involving adaptation to similar ecological status" (Simpson 1961:78–79). As should be obvious from Figure 2.6, simply because entities can be classified within a taxonomic architecture does not mean the results reflect phylogeny. But there is as well a more subtle distinction.

Valentine and May (1996:26) used the Linnaean taxonomic system as shown in Figure 2.8 to illustrate that in an aggregative hierarchy "the fundamental units in the structure are species [and] at each successively higher taxonomic rank, new entities are formed by the aggregation of phylogenetically related species. Nestedness in this hierarchy results from the aggregation of units of equal rank." Individual organisms comprise the basal units of the Linnaean hierarchy. Sets of individual organisms that are reproductively interactive and isolated from other such sets make up a local population, or deme, of a species; multiple demes that are reproductively isolated from other demes make up species (the biological species concept).

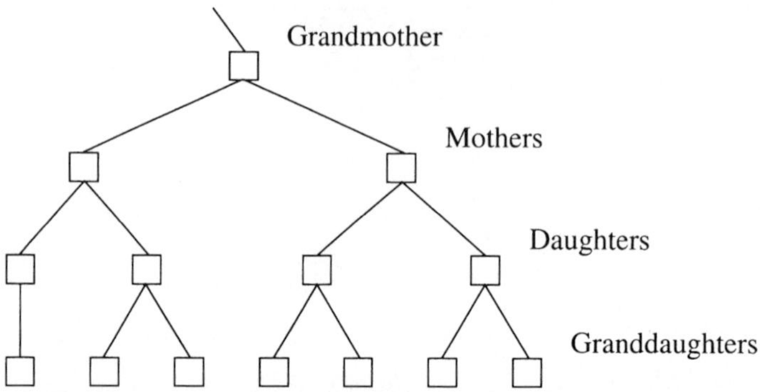

Figure 2.9. A positional-structure hierarchy of descent for four generations of related women (after Valentine and May 1996).

The units of different rank in the Linnaean hierarchy each display different properties. Individuals do not evolve, for example; rather, populations and species evolve as the individuals comprising their memberships change over time. Because of these differences in the properties displayed by the different ranks, interactions within and between units within a rank are typically the subjects of study. What many systematists are interested in, however, is evolutionary descent and phylogenetic history.

An example of evolutionary descent is shown in Figure 2.9. This is a "positional structure" (Valentine and May 1996), the basis of which is merely priority of appearance. In positional structures, all positions are occupied by the same sort of entity. There are no ranked collectives, and the position of particular entities is specified by the order of their appearance. Each positional structure "has a founding entity, and subsequent entities may be positioned in a single series or in branches that form a tree-like structure" (Valentine and May 1996:29). In an aggregative hierarchy, "the units are collected from the bottom up into more inclusive units. In a positional structure they are established from a founding entity and proceed so to speak from the top down. That is, a tree has a trunk first and then branches. [The included entities] are not ranked [so] nesting cannot involve the grouping of entities of equal rank. Rather, nesting involves the inclusion, within a group, of the founder of that group and of subsequent members of the series of entities along its branch and along any branches therefrom. Thus, in principle, each entity has nested within it all the subsequent entities" (Valentine and May 1996:29).

The Linnaean taxonomy does not and cannot trace the phylogenetic tree because it is an aggregative hierarchy (Figure 2.8) rather than a positional-structure hierarchy (Figure 2.9). Simpson (1961) made a similar point when he noted a common confusion between a phylogenetic tree and taxa of different ranks. Our rendition of his illustration of this confusion is shown in Figure 2.10. There, the incorrect reading of the tree is given in Figure 2.10a. What Simpson (1961:191) referred to as the "correct relationship of temporal-spatial taxa to the phylogeny" is given in Figure 2.10b. Importantly, Simpson (1961) also included a third illustration in his discussion. That illustration, Figure 2.10c, shows relationships among terminal taxa rather than phylogeny. There is no temporal or spatial variation included in the graph, only morphological characters. The relationships among taxa are determined *only* by phenotypic characters (Simpson 1961).

Population (New) Systematics

What is variously referred to as the "new systematics" (Huxley 1940) or "population systematics" (Mayr 1969) replaced the typological species concept with the concept of "the polytypic species composed of different populations in time and space" (Mayr 1969:64). That a species can be polytypic simply means that it can comprise more than one formal type. Thus, it is of no great consequence "when a species lacks some of the diagnostic characters of the higher taxon to which it belongs or when an individual lacks the diagnostic characters of its species" (Mayr 1969:76).

As the typological species concept was replaced by the polytypic concept, the biological definition of species was simultaneously popularized (Mayr 1942; Simpson 1944). That definition is the one with which most people today are familiar. The biological species concept defines a species as reproductively isolated populations of (generally, morphologically similar) organisms. Describing a species, however, involves formal properties that have nebulous relationships to reproduction. Further, description can be based on a sample of organisms of a species that does not completely represent the variation within that reproductively defined unit (Shenefelt 1959). Cain (1956:100) suggested that the "justification" for using formal data "in delimiting species and genera is that (i) it allows the inclusion in the taxonomic hierarchy of forms known only from a few [formal] characters (the absolute minimum of taxonomic evidence) and (ii) [formal] criteria are the main example of the only class of criteria available at all in grouping asexual forms at the species level, and in classifying all phyletic lines into the higher taxonomic categories." But not just any formal criteria are used. Only those suspected to have "*taxonomic importance*" (Cain 1956:100) are used, such that the employed formal criteria "are always selected, weighted and interpreted" (Simpson 1951:287). Which characters have taxonomic importance?

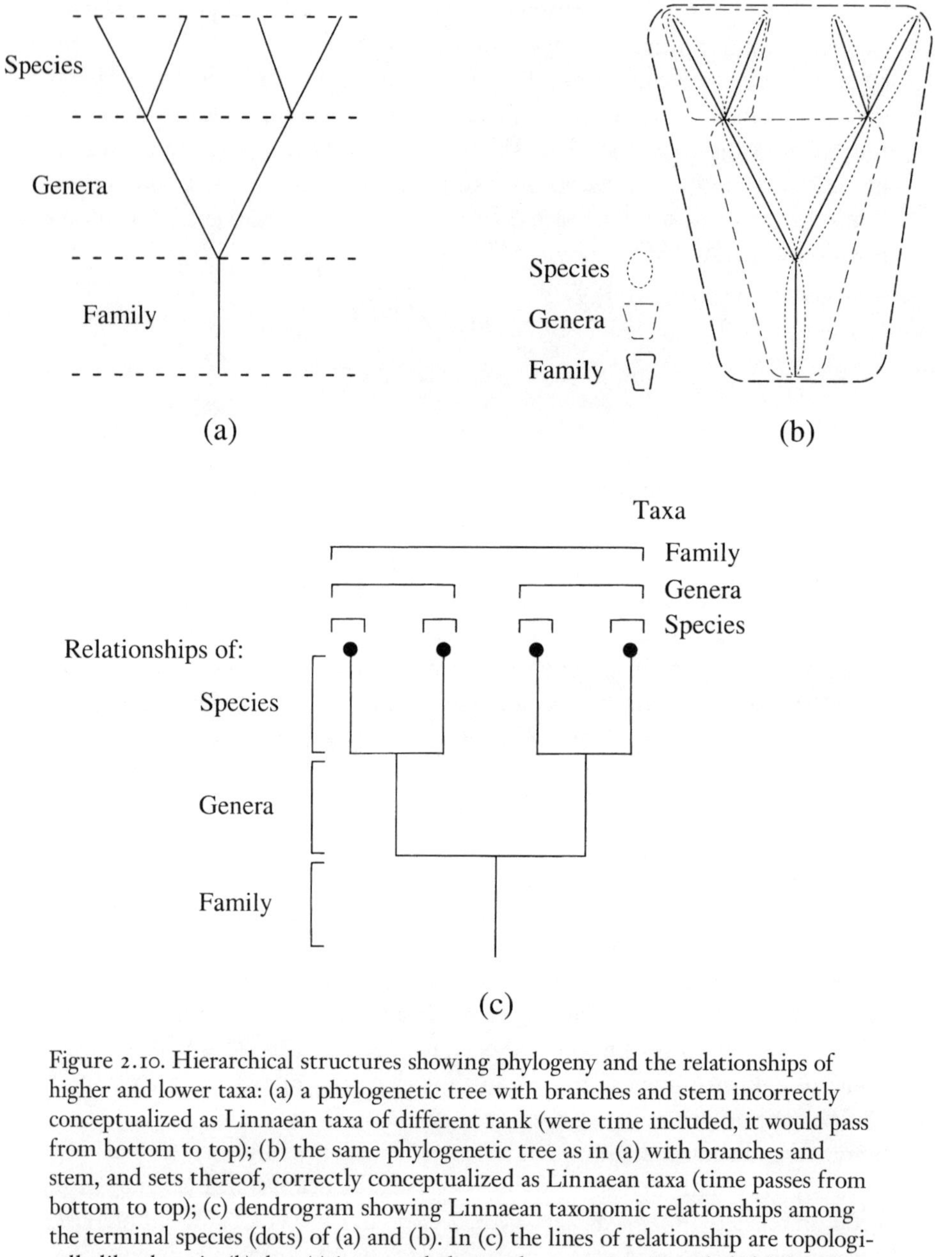

Figure 2.10. Hierarchical structures showing phylogeny and the relationships of higher and lower taxa: (a) a phylogenetic tree with branches and stem incorrectly conceptualized as Linnaean taxa of different rank (were time included, it would pass from bottom to top); (b) the same phylogenetic tree as in (a) with branches and stem, and sets thereof, correctly conceptualized as Linnaean taxa (time passes from bottom to top); (c) dendrogram showing Linnaean taxonomic relationships among the terminal species (dots) of (a) and (b). In (c) the lines of relationship are topologically like those in (b), but (c) is not a phylogeny because time is excluded (after Simpson 1961).

As a paleontologist, Simpson (1945) argued that homologous characters had taxonomic importance. Simpson (1945:11) called on time as one variable that could provide a test of hypothesized homologous characters: "In the ideal case, in [a paleontological] sequence the morphological variation of each population overlaps that of the next."[1] Multiple characters shared by temporally successive and adjacent assemblages imply heritable continuity (descent) but not modification. From that same paleontological perspective, Simpson (1945:14) and his contemporaries (for example, Sylvester-Bradley 1956) fully recognized that they had to assume "that there exists in nature a morphologically definable unit that tends to correspond with the . . . genetic unit" of biological heritability if one sought to classify organisms or fossils on the basis of their formal variation in such a manner as to reflect their phylogenetic history.

The choice of characters and character states as possible homologues is a critical determination. Figure 2.11 shows sixteen fossil species as numbered circles graphed in two ways. The evolutionary relationships of the species are shown on the left; stratigraphic boundaries denote time. Dashed lines surrounding various sets of species denote species grouped within a common genus. The degree of morphometric similarity of the sixteen species (each represented by sets of fossils) is graphed on the right, where the greater the horizontal and vertical distance between each species, the less the formal similarity of the sets of fossils representing each species. As well, dashed lines surrounding sets of species denote marked formal similarity within the group of species. Phylogenetic relationships between species are included in the graph on the right to emphasize one simple point: Using formal similarities and differences to classify entities might not reveal the phylogenetic relationships of the entities classified. Typological affinity, in other words, is not necessarily a valid reflection of phylogenetic affinity. It was for this simple reason that numerous biologists hesitated to ascribe phylogenetic significance to the Linnaean taxonomy (for example, Bigelow 1958; Borgmeier 1957; Gilmour 1937; Griffiths 1973). It was perhaps for similar reasons that McKern was simultaneously optimistic yet skeptical of the phylogenetic implications of the MTM.

For nearly a century after the *Origin* appeared, taxonomists were "unanimous in their endeavor to establish classifications that would reflect 'degree of relationship'" (Mayr 1981:51). Here, relationship signified either

1. This is simply the principle of overlapping common to archaeological tools, such as the direct historical approach and seriation, which simultaneously monitor heritable continuity (descent) and modification as characters come and go and characters change states (Lyman and O'Brien 2000, 2001a; O'Brien and Lyman 1999b, 2000).

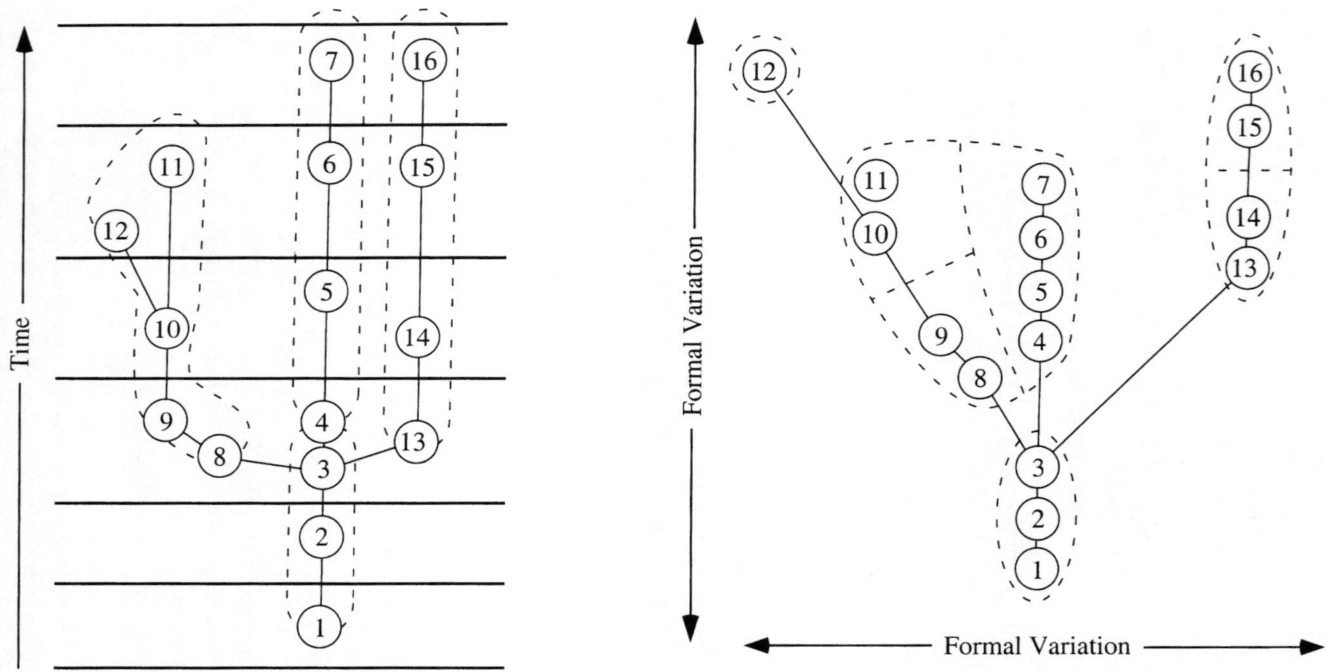

Figure 2.11. Differences and similarities between *(left)* a model of phylogenetic relationships among sixteen fossil species (numbered circles) and *(right)* a model of the degree of formal similarity of those species. On the left, phylogenetic relationships are denoted by lines connecting circles, horizontal lines represent stratigraphic boundaries, and each group of species denoted by dashed lines is a genus. On the right, greater distance between species denotes less formal similarity, and dashed lines group species that are more similar to each other than any of them is to a species in another group (after Cain 1956).

genealogical or phylogenetic affinity. *Genealogy* is a line of evolutionary descent from an ancestor through one of its particular descendants and on through succeeding individual descendants. *Phylogeny* is evolutionary descent from an ancestor through *all* its descendants. A genealogical relationship can be of only one form—that between an ancestor and a direct descendant. A phylogenetic relationship can be between an ancestor and a direct descendant, between two sister species that descended from a common ancestor, or between multiple taxa of various ranks, as long as they share a common ancestor. Thus, genealogical relationship is a particular kind of phylogenetic relationship.

Classification methods were not well formalized until the middle of the twentieth century when three methods crystallized. Each method dictated the kinds of characters that should be chosen. It is critical that we describe each of these methods for two reasons. First, at least two of them have been said to make up the MTM (phenetics and cladistics; see chapter 6). Second, elements of all three methods were being discussed and debated at the time that McKern chose biological taxonomy as his model for the MTM. Interestingly, he seems to have adopted one technique for building the architecture of the classification and the theoretical significance (such as it was) of that technique (phenetics).

As we discuss the three methods, keep in mind that they differ dramatically in purpose. There is a relatively simple, straightforward reason for this: Darwin's evolutionism focuses on descent *with* modification as opposed to descent *and* modification. As a result, "there are two independent sets of criteria responsible for the grouping—*similarity* and *sameness of causation* (lines of descent)—on the basis of which organisms can be assembled into taxa. . . . [T]hese two sets of criteria are frequently in conflict, and their application is controversial. . . . [The] most important difference among the three major current schools of taxonomy lies in the relative weight they give to these two criteria" (Mayr and Ashlock 1991: 115). The two kinds of criteria must be given different relative weight during classification because there is no well-tested method for simultaneously considering similarity and descent in the process of classification. Thus, one chooses one criterion—formal similarity *or* genealogical affinity—or if both are chosen, the use of one criterion must precede the use of the other. These are the only options.

Evolutionary Taxonomy

What came to be called evolutionary taxonomy was the goal of many biologists after the publication of Darwin's *Origin*. Simpson (1945) published the first statement on protocol, and shortly thereafter the two other methods developed as competitors, which prompted the evolutionary taxonomists to explain in detail how their method worked (for example, Mayr 1965a; Simpson 1951, 1959, 1961). Evolutionary taxonomy results in the classification of organisms according to their phylogenetic relationships *and* their subsequent evolutionary divergence. The two criteria of classification—descent and modification—are both considered. The classification procedure is accomplished in two steps, each involving various substeps. The first step involves sorting individual specimens into species such that within-group formal variation is minimal relative to between-group variation. Each group is "recognizable and internally homogeneous," and there are "constant differences between such groups" (Mayr 1969:9–10). Each resulting group is a *phenon*, defined as "a sample of phenotypically similar specimens; a phenotypically reasonably uniform sample" (Mayr 1969:408).

The construction of phena involves the determination, "by comparison, [of] what the unique properties of every species and higher taxon are. [Then,] determine what properties certain taxa have in common with each other, and what the biological causes for the differences or shared characters are. Finally, [determine the] variation within taxa" (Mayr 1969:3). Once these things have been accomplished, the second step is undertaken: "put the species in order . . . [by] group[ing] them into smaller and larger arrays of related species, taxa, and higher taxa, and plac[ing] these into a hierarchy of categories" (Mayr 1969:14), where the categories are families, orders, and so on. Finally, test the taxonomic groups for monophyly. This means omitting from group definitions characters that are shared as the result of convergence and parallelism, which is done by considering all available biological data—morphology, behavior, physiology, genetics, biogeography—in an effort to make the classification reflect phylogenetic affinity.

An evolutionary classification is inferred to reflect genetic and thus phylogenetic relationships between the included taxa based on their phenotypic similarity: "Characters that are shared by most species of a higher taxon are believed to be the expression of a complex genotype, particularly when the given character is not directly correlated with utilization of the adaptive zone of the taxon" (Mayr 1969:80). This follows Darwin (1859: 414), who noted that "the less any part of the organization is concerned with special habits, the more important it becomes for classification." Evolutionary taxonomists state that " 'relationship' is not used in a narrow phylogenetic sense, but is broadly conceived to include all biological relationships among organisms" (Mayr 1969:2). Thus, evolutionary taxonomists emphasize that "presumed relationships have to be tested again and again with the help of new characters, and the new evidence frequently leads to a revision of the inferences of relationship" (Mayr 1981:510).

Evolutionary classification produces the familiar taxonomic tree, or *phylogram*, which records both the branching points and the degrees of subsequent divergence of taxa. This is a result of the fact that both classificatory criteria—formal (phenotypic) similarity and shared ancestry—are included in the classification (Bock 1973). Some argue that the former, although measurable, provides an unsatisfactory measure "for our intuitive concept of evolutionary divergence" (Griffiths 1973:340). This is the problem illustrated in Figure 2.11. In several respects evolutionary taxonomy is a more or less best-guess enterprise, with the results of those who have been the most deeply immersed in their specimens being favored over the results of neophytes. It is in part for this reason that a more objective—so characterized because a mathematical algorithm produces the groups—classification procedure (in the sense defined earlier) was developed. That procedure is phenetics.

Phenetics

One method of classification had been around in various guises since the days of Linnaeus (Gilmour 1937, 1940, 1951). It was formalized in the middle of the twentieth century when computer technology became available for analyzing large sets of phenotypic data (Sokal 1966). The new method came to be known as phenetics. Discrete organisms or sets thereof are grouped together based on their phenotypic similarities. One of the techniques by which the grouping can be implemented is numerical taxonomy (Sokal and Sneath 1963), although it is not the only technique (for example, DuPraw 1964). The method was formalized by several individuals more or less independently and simultaneously (Cain and Harrison 1958; Michener and Sokal 1957; Sneath 1957; see Hull 1988). Early statements on the method and its techniques were synthesized and expanded in a single, landmark volume (Sokal and Sneath 1963) that was later revised in light of various criticisms (Sneath and Sokal 1973). The method was meant to provide an operational approach to taxonomy that was both objective and replicable (Sokal and Camin 1965).

The phenetic method exploits only one of the two criteria of classification—formal, or phenotypic, similarity. It begins by recording numerous *unit characters*, defined as "those that cannot be subdivided into logically or empirically independent characters" (Sokal 1966:110). A particular state of a character should not itself have varied states, which Griffiths (1973:342) pointed out was logically impossible save perhaps at the atomic level, forcing pheneticists to presume that the chosen character states were "relatively atomic." The various techniques of implementing the phenetics method involve an assessment of the phenetic distance (dissimilarity) between the phenomena to be classified, which are termed *operational taxonomic units* (OTUs). OTUs can be individual organisms or aggregates thereof, such as higher taxa (Sokal 1966). An OTU "is simply the lowest level taxonomic unit employed in a given numerical taxonomic study" (Sokal et al. 1965:241). OTUs not only are what are classified; they are the units produced by the classification procedure. OTUs are polythetic, meaning that they comprise multiple characters, although individuals within an OTU will not necessarily share every character of that particular OTU (Sokal 1966). Pheneticists argue that the "adoption of polythetic principles of classification negates the concept of an essence or type of any taxon. No single uniform property is required for the definition of a given group nor will any combination of characters necessarily define it" (Sokal 1974:1117).

Because phenetic classification is based solely on overall resemblance, a pheneticist defines natural classification as yielding "taxa whose members are in some sense more similar to one another than they are to members of other taxa" (Sokal 1966:109). The subjective element of measuring similarity that characterizes evolutionary taxonomy is replaced by an operational and objective measure of similarity (Colless 1967). OTU A can be said to be more similar to OTU B than it is to OTU C because A and B share more unit characters than A or B does with C. Clearly, as the number of shared characters decreases, the level of similarity decreases and the more inclusive an OTU is.

Characters are given equal weight in phenetics. They can be randomly selected, or they can be chosen if they are "taxonomically useful" and comprise "OTU-characters" (Colless 1971:74). OTU characters are those that do not vary over the study group and thus cannot indicate intragroup structure (Colless 1971:74). The character of four limbs, for example, would not be a good OTU character for distinguishing among different taxa of mammals. Pheneticists note that their method is theory free; that classifications that have but a single purpose are "useless" with respect to other purposes; and that the purpose or purposes of a classification must be explicit (Sokal et al. 1965:240).

Pheneticists are quick to point out that the classificatory results of their analyses might reveal something about phylogeny (for example, Camin and Sokal 1965; Colless 1970; Sokal and Camin 1965). Sokal and Sneath (1963:48) defined phenetics as "the numerical evaluation of the affinity or similarity between taxonomic units and the ordering of these units into taxa on the basis of their affinities. The term may include the drawing of

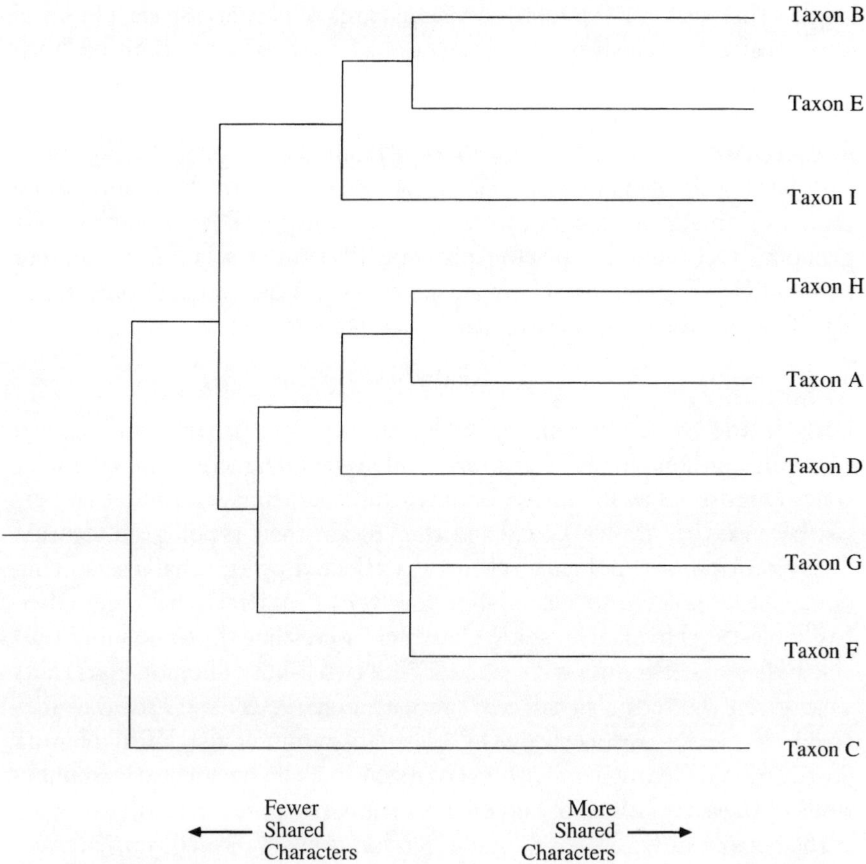

Figure 2.12. A fictional phenogram showing the arrangement of nine taxa. A clustering algorithm (Hintze 1999) was used to produce the phenogram. The more characters shared by any combination of taxa, the farther to the right those two taxa are joined. Each combination of taxa makes up an OTU.

phylogenetic inferences from the data by statistical or other mathematical methods to the extent to which this is possible." For a pheneticist *affinity* and *relationship* mean phenotypically similar, which in turn might (or might not) be caused by shared heritage. Thus shared heritage is a kind of affinity and relationship.

The results of various phenetic techniques make up what is called a phenogram, which displays the overall degree of phenetic similarity within (and difference between) groups. The structure of the classification is one of hierarchical, nested, and nonoverlapping units (Figure 2.12). Each branch of a phenogram denotes an OTU of some level of inclusiveness and implies that within the hyperdimensional area of phenetic space, OTUs of lower scales of inclusiveness will emerge as clusters rather than be "randomly or uniformly distributed" (Sokal 1974:1120). Such results refer "only to the observed properties of entities, without any reference to inferences that may be drawn *a posteriori* from the patterns displayed.... [To] be strictly phenetic [such classifications must] provide nothing more than a summary of observed facts" (Colless 1967:7). Phenetics, then, is a grouping technique for placing phenetically similar specimens together into OTUs of varying levels of inclusiveness. What those groups might signify other than formal similarity is a separate issue.

Cladistics

Early in the twentieth century, biologists began to distinguish between two kinds of homologues—*primitive* and *derived* characters and character states (Figure 2.13). Primitive, or ancestral, characters are those that persist because they evolve slowly and thus retain their typological identity. The retention of typological identity is affected by the characters being nonadaptive relative to more labile (derived) characters that were adaptively plastic. This is why static characters were thought to be more reliable indicators of common ancestry. These two kinds of homologous traits were given the terms *plesiomorph* (ancestral character) and *apomorph* (derived character), respectively, by German entomologist Willi Hennig (1950, 1966). Hennig explicitly recognized that the phylogenetic implications of these two kinds of homologous traits are quite different, as shown at the bottom of Figure 2.13. Shared plesiomorphs—termed *symplesiomorphies* by Hennig—are found in an ancestor, in all of its immediate offspring, *and* in at least some third-generation offspring. Shared apomorphs —termed *synapomorphies* by Hennig—are found in an ancestor and its *immediate* (second-generation) offspring. The same character can be a synapomorphy (derived character) at one time and a symplesiomorphy (ancestral character) at a later time.

Hennig believed that "recency of common ancestry must be considered a criterion of ranking" (Hull 1970:24). In fact, phylogeny should be the *only* criterion underpinning the classification and thus efforts must be made to exclude all characters that do not track phylogeny. Hennig termed his method "phylogenetic systematics," which has come to be known as *cladistics.* Cladistic phylogeny consists of a sequence of dichotomies, or branching events, each representing the splitting of a parental species into two daughter species. The ancestral species ceases to exist at the time of the dichotomy, and the sister groups it produces must be given the same

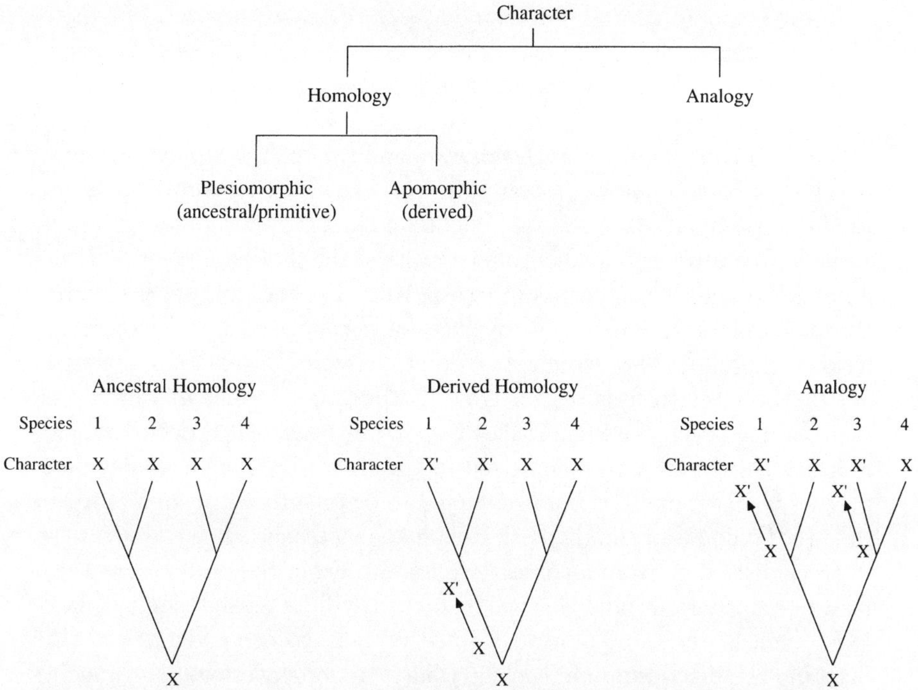

Figure 2.13. Kinds of characters and their relationship to determination of phylogenetic history: *top*, a taxonomic classification of kinds of characters; *bottom*, three phylogenies showing the definitions of symplesiomorphic (shared ancestral) characters, synapomorphic (shared derived) characters, and analogous (as a result of convergence) characters. In all three diagrams, X is the ancestral character state, X' is the derived character state, and arrows denote when the character state changes.

categorical rank. Mayr (1969:213) provided one of the earliest nonjargon-laden descriptions of the method:

> After a phyletic line has split into two separate lines, the subsequent retention of ancestral characters and the acquisition of new, derived characters occur independently in the two lines. The basic rationale of all cladistic methods is that the more recent the common ancestry of two species (or other taxa), the more characters in common they should have. The same thought, expressed in terms of taxonomic characters, is that the occurrence of a relatively new character will be limited to the descendants of the particular species in which the new character originated. A careful study of the distribution of characters

in the taxonomic hierarchy should therefore give information on the grouping and ranking of taxa. The determination of the phyletic age of characters is the key operation in this method.

The splitting is known as *cladogenesis*, and the relative age of characters is referred to as *character polarity* (Stevens 1980). Two additional terms need to be defined. *Autapomorphy* denotes a character that was acquired by a single line after it branched off from its sister group(s). *Homoplasy* denotes a character that appears in two or more lineages that do not share a common ancestor. Sometimes instances of homoplasy can be detected by following Dollo's Law, which states that character states do not recur in *exactly* the same form at a later time. Rather, the manner in which phenomena have been classified makes it *appear* as if a reversal occurred. Homoplasy that cannot be recognized in the light of Dollo's Law regularly plagues cladistic analysis but is assumed to be of sufficiently small magnitude that it does not totally mask the phylogenetic signal.

In cladistics, synapomorphies "are nested. From the point when a feature first appears in phylogenetic history, it will be passed along in some guise (i.e., in the same or transformed version) to descendant taxa. [By] mapping the distribution of such attributes, monophyletic taxa—branches of the tree of life—are delineated, defined, and recognized" (Eldredge and Novacek 1985:67). Cladists believe that monophyletic taxa are "actual historical units" (Eldredge and Novacek 1985:66). Cladistic analysis produces a *cladogram*, which shows the relative sequence of lineage-splitting events. A cladogram represents a hypothesis regarding phylogenetic descent, nothing more. To date, most cladograms incorporate only formal characters of organisms, although biogeographic data and temporal data are becoming more frequently incorporated (see references in O'Brien et al. [2001, 2002] for a more detailed discussion of the basics and an archaeological application).

DISCUSSION

A taxonomy can be constructed from the top down (beginning with the most-inclusive taxon and working down to the terminal taxa by division) or from the bottom up (beginning with the terminal taxa and grouping them into successively more-inclusive taxa). Linnaeus's procedure of logical division began with the genus and worked down to the species; it also involved a bottom-up procedure of grouping genera into higher-rank taxa. Evolutionary taxonomists prefer the bottom-up procedure for two reasons. First, the terminal taxa (species) are conceived of as real entities that can be discovered by observation. Second, higher taxa are real not because they can be observed but because they reflect at least approximately the reality of the phylogenetic relationships of species as well as their divergence subsequent to speciation. As we will see in chapters 3 and 4, McKern preferred to build his cultural classification from the bottom up, whereas Thorne Deuel preferred to work from the top down. The latter, of course, presumes that the largest, most-inclusive groups are already known. One then progressively divides those groups into less-inclusive ones. The issue of where those most-inclusive groups come from brings up another point.

Early naturalists had particular notions about archetypes and basic structural plans. Although explanations of the types varied, there was a shared notion that only a limited number of basic body plans existed. Another term for basic plan is *Baupläne* (pl.; *Bauplan*, sing.), a German word introduced into zoology by Joseph Henry Woodger in 1945 (Hall 1996: 223). For many biologists today this term "represents the basic organizational plan common to higher taxa at the level of the phylum, order, or class" (Hall 1996:225), although there is no generally agreed-on definition of the term (Wray 1999). As proposed by Woodger, the concept signifies a suite of characters, often homologous characters, that unites members at higher taxonomic levels. Some of those characters may change states over time as a result of evolutionary processes, but some will persist in unaltered states. Thus "*Baupläne* consist of a mix of ancestral and derived characters" (Hall 1996:228). If the analyst has a concept of *Baupläne*, then it is likely he has a concept of higher taxonomic categories, meaning that he will start at the top and work down. This may not explicitly address the issue of where particular *Baupläne* such as vertebrate or carnivore come from, but it should be apparent that they are suites of characters shared across otherwise distinct organisms.

The Linnaean biological taxonomy was, for all intents and purposes, the model that McKern used to build the MTM. The fact that this model epitomized for many early-twentieth-century biologists "a pure science of relations, unconcerned with time, space, or cause" (Borgmeier 1957:53), is what caught McKern's attention and prompted him to use a hierarchy of nested taxa as the model for his classification method. That evolutionary descent with modification *might* be reflected in the Linnaean biological taxonomy and also in his own taxonomy was of less importance. Most biological taxonomists of the late 1930s believed their taxonomies reflected evolutionary descent, but they were hesitant to argue strongly in this direction for a number of reasons. These included the lack of a generally accepted and well-understood mechanism for the process of heritability and the fear that convergence would obscure the phylogenetic signal (Mayr

1982). Thus, their taxonomies reflected "relations" (Borgmeier 1957), but those relations were as much phenetic as they were phylogenetic. This was the intellectual milieu in which McKern was educated.

As we will see in the following two chapters, McKern selected particular kinds of characters—ones that he thought reflected "relations" among cultural taxa irrespective of their spatiotemporal positions. As with many biologists, McKern thought these characters *might* show the phylogenetic relationships of those taxa, but this was not at all a sure thing. The Linnaean biological taxonomy had, after all, been built with no knowledge of evolutionary descent (Ereshefsky 1994, 1997, 2001). Rather, that taxonomy provided independent evidence that Darwin's theory was correct (Brady 1985; Brower 2000). McKern did not exceed the thinking of his time and thus did not suggest that a taxonomy of cultures would provide evidence of their evolutionary descent. This was not only *not* a sure thing in biology, such phylogenetic implications were anathema among anthropologists of the early twentieth century (Lyman and O'Brien 1997).

Given this state of affairs, it is not surprising that McKern did not distinguish between homologous and analogous culture traits, although, as we will see in the next chapter, he and his contemporaries were apparently aware of the two kinds, if only in a theoretically unsophisticated way. What is interesting is that McKern and his collaborators grappled with some of the very same problems that biological systematists were grappling with at the same time. Nested taxa *might* reflect an evolutionary process, but they might not. Darwin's postulating a cause for the structure of the Linnaean taxonomy raised that taxonomy to the status that it enjoyed in the 1940s and for several decades afterward. As will become clear, McKern had some good ideas, but his failure to postulate a theoretical cause, together with the sometimes contradictory statements he made and the unclear protocol for operationalizing his classificatory method, resulted in it having a short life span. Above we focused a bit more heavily on phenetics than on evolutionary taxonomy or cladistics. We did this because McKern's taxonomic method is best characterized as phenetics, although without the benefit of statistical and/or mathematical measurements of similarity.

3
Developing the Midwestern Taxonomic Method, 1930–1935

> The most basic postulate of science is that nature itself is orderly. In taxonomy . . . the aim is that the ordering of science shall approximate or in some estimable way reflect the order of nature. (G. G. Simpson 1961:5)

McKern began thinking in 1929 about a means of allowing comparative analyses of the myriad archaeological manifestations of the upper Midwest (Fisher 1997). Later that year his colleague Alton Fisher suggested that the Linnaean biological taxonomy might prove to be a good model for a classification method. McKern cited no biological or paleontological publications in his several articles on the midwestern taxonomic method, so the sources he used for inspiration and guidance are difficult to determine. McKern told Julian Steward in a December 15, 1939, letter (MPM) that he had "minored" in paleontology, and in various letters of correspondence with other archaeologists he occasionally referred to "paleontological method" and "paleontological classification." McKern might have consulted then-current articles on biological taxonomy (for example, Matthew 1926, 1929, 1930) while drafting various versions of the MTM, although there is no direct evidence that he did so. As we point out in chapter 6, however, there is at least indirect evidence that he had more than passing knowledge of published statements on biological taxonomy.

McKern continually downplayed the phylogenetic implications of his taxonomy, but this is not surprising in light of the general feeling in anthropology that biological evolution was a poor model on which to base cultural evolution. For McKern to have consulted the Darwinian version of evolution for ideas about how to detect relationships between cultural units would have pitted him against some of the leading figures in anthropology (Lyman and O'Brien 1997), including A. L. Kroeber, who had been McKern's adviser at Berkeley. Kroeber was one of the most vocal opponents of a biological model, writing that "the designation of anthropology as 'the child of Darwin' is most misleading." (Kroeber 1923:8). This point was made by many of McKern's contemporaries (for example, Boas 1932; Gladwin 1936).

The critics, however, were not always consistent in their admonitions against using a biological model. Paradoxically, McKern had started building his method when Kroeber (1931) published a statement in which he pointed out two things that would have been critically important had McKern been attempting to classify cultures on the basis of their phylogenetic relationships. First, Kroeber noted that biologists of the early twentieth century used a particular method to determine whether organisms were related by shared ancestry or were simply phenotypically similar. They differentiated between homologous and analogous characters and character states. Not only did Kroeber use these two terms correctly in the sense of their modern evolutionary meaning—something not regularly done in the biology of the 1920s and 1930s (see Lyman [2001] for details and references)—but the significance of the distinction was clear in his discussion. Second, Kroeber argued that precisely this same method should be used by anthropologists interested in distinguishing between such things as independent invention and diffusion (for example, Steward 1929) and by those interested in writing the history of a culture's lineage. McKern, as far as we can tell, never cited Kroeber's paper. Instead, he and his collaborators followed basic anthropological and archaeological practice and recognized formally similar archaeological materials as being "culturally" or "historically" related (Lyman 2001). The terms *phylogenetically* or *genealogically related* were never used by McKern or any other anthropologist or archaeologist with respect to cultures; the term *genetically related*, when it was used at all, was used metaphorically.

McKern accepted Fisher's suggestion of using the architecture of the Linnaean taxonomy as a model for his archaeological classification. McKern would take the simple notion of nested sets of biological taxa and modify it for application to sets of archaeological materials. One major modification involved proposing a set of terms for the taxonomic categories, and this turned out to be a contentious modification. The other modification was less contentious, perhaps because it was rather less well understood. It took place midway through the development of the MTM and involved the distinction among certain kinds of characters. These were not the homologues and analogues of biologists, and they were not meant to serve the same functions, although they could have in part. The history of how

Table 3.1. Evolution in Names of Units in the Midwestern Taxonomic Method

McKern 1932[7]	Guthe 1932[8]	McKern et al. 1933[10]	McKern 1934[11]	NRC 1937	McKern 1939[15]
Base	F [Base]	Basic Culture	Basic Culture	Base	Base
Phase	E [Phase]			Pattern	Pattern
Habit	D [Aspect, Pattern, Habit]	Phase	Phase	Phase	Phase
Aspect	C [Frame, Aspect, Pattern]	Aspect	Aspect	Aspect	Aspect
	B [Specific, Gradient, Aspect]		Focus	Focus	Focus
Locale	A [Locale]	Component	Component	Component	Component

McKern developed the method, and the contributions of others toward that end, is the subject of this and the next chapter. To help the reader follow the discussion, the evolution of the terminology used for the various units of the taxonomic hierarchy is summarized in Table 3.1. We note that the focus of our discussion is on the development of the method rather than on substantive empirical results produced during its ontogeny.

EARLY DEVELOPMENT: 1930–1932

Within a few years of his employment at the Milwaukee Public Museum in 1925, McKern worked at several sites in different parts of Wisconsin. Fisher (1988:207–208) reported that McKern "began to recognize distributional patterns of individual [cultural] traits, and, somewhat later, of complexes of traits. These perceptions, or suspected perceptions, became a powerful stimulus to intensive thinking about how to design a classification system of cultural traits that might show cultural relations between prehistoric populations and also the geographic movements of those populations over extended periods of time." We suspect another powerful stimulus was provided in 1929 when Henry C. Shetrone (National Research Council 1929:60), director of the Ohio State Museum, pointed out that archaeological manifestations of Hopewell culture varied somewhat across space and that study of those variations "might very well give us ultimately information bearing on the very interesting questions of the migrations, chronology and interrelations of these various Hopewell developments in the entire area."

On August 31 and September 1, 1931, McKern attended "The Vermillion Conference" at the University of South Dakota (National Research Council 1931). There McKern presented "a synopsis of the four principal Wisconsin cultures known at present: namely, the Lake Michigan, the basic Hopewell, the Aztalan-Cahokia, and the Upper Mississippi," and he suggested "that the first and last appear to be related to known historic cultures" (National Research Council 1931:1). Although we have not been able to locate a copy of this paper, the description at least approximates the contents of McKern (1933[9]). After the formal presentations in Vermillion, there was some discussion of terminology and also of the method that was shortly to become known as the direct historical approach. "The consensus of opinion was that a tribal name should be associated with a site or culture only when historic occupation of the site is known, or when the material obtained from an undocumented site proves to be identical with that from a documented one. In those cases where sites and cultures are not correlated with documentary data, they should be named by geographical or descriptive terms, and not by tribal or linguistic terms. This applies equally well to individual traits and complexes, such as architecture, pottery, or stone implements" (National Research Council 1931:2). We assume that McKern participated in this discussion and that he knew well what the direct historical approach comprised (Lyman and O'Brien 2000, 2001a). Later correspondence between McKern and others cited below indicates we are correct in our assumption. There is no indication in the National Research Council (1931) report on the conference that anyone discussed classification methods.

McKern (1931) published a short paper on the pottery of Wisconsin in *American Anthropologist* shortly after the Vermillion conference. Early in his discussion he stated that, given that Wisconsin pottery "represents more than a single basic type," the first task "is one of classification; the next relates to type distribution" (McKern 1931:383). He then described several major types of pottery found in Wisconsin, noting the formal variation and known geographic distribution of each. McKern used the term *culture* somewhat indiscriminately, but he also noted that one or more pottery types, together with other artifacts, such as particular forms of mounds, beads, projectile points, and burials, appeared to be "culture markers." Interestingly, McKern noted that because a pottery type can be diffused from one ethnic group to another, he preferred to use nonlinguistic terminology for naming the pottery types.

A letter McKern wrote to Carl E. Guthe, chairman of the Committee on State Archaeological Surveys of the National Research Council (O'Brien and Lyman 2001) on October 27, 1931 (MPM), reveals that McKern at that time was working on a solution to the classification problem:

> To me one of the outstanding characteristics of American archaeological research is its total lack of standards. Not only are there no accepted standards for field equipment and field work in general, but the same is true for laboratory equipment and procedure, classification and terminology, publications, and the detailed methods that these involve. As a matter of fact, archaeology is in its birth throes as a field science and does not exist as yet as a laboratory science, or so it seems to me. That is why I consider it other than a waist [*sic*] of time to grapple with the problem of culture classification, on which subject I expect to have a report ready for the next A.A.A. meeting. Not that I expect to cram my classification method down the throats of all present, but I hope that my effort will start a row that may serve to produce a method acceptable to all. I don't care whose it may be so long as it works.

Guthe responded on October 30 (MPM) that "[It] is certainly nice to get news from a colleague which gives every indication of complete understanding and similarity of outlook. I like your emphatic statements regarding lack of standards." Guthe went on to refer to the efforts of the Committee on State Archaeological Surveys: "The general policy of cooperation which the Committee is fostering does not mean, in my opinion, the hiding of differences of scientific opinions. The very fact that we all know one another is all the more reason why individual men should be able to express themselves frankly and forcefully, as you are planning to do, without incurring personal animosities which did so much to delay developments in former years. I may disagree with your opinions, but I am shoulder to shoulder with you on the principles involved."

McKern had planned to present his paper on culture classification at the April 1932 meeting of the Central Section of the American Anthropological Association in Ann Arbor, Michigan, but was unable to attend because of illness (Griffin 1943:327). Fay-Cooper Cole and Thorne Deuel (1937:33) indicated McKern's paper was titled "Culture Type Classification for Midwestern North American Archaeology" (McKern 1932[7]). A. R. Kelly of the University of Illinois invited McKern to attend the Twenty-Fifth Annual Meeting of the Illinois State Academy of Science held in Chicago in May 1932 (McKern letter to Deuel, April 1, 1932 [MPM]). Griffin (1943:327) reported that McKern "proposed [his idea] to a group of archaeologists in Chicago after [the] archaeological symposium at the Illinois State Academy of Science meetings" and that this presentation was the "origin" of the MTM. The paper that McKern published in the proceedings of that meeting in 1933 (McKern 1933[9]) makes only minimal mention of classification method. The paper published by Deuel (1933) in those proceedings contains the terms *component* and *phase*, two of the terms that appear in a paper McKern coauthored with Deuel and Guthe that was issued as a circular by the Committee on State Archaeological Surveys (McKern et al. 1933[10]) but that do not appear in Guthe (1932[8]) (see Table 3.1). R. M. Snodgrasse (1933:88) stated that with respect to his own paper published in the proceedings, "the terminology of culture classification employed here is that suggested by the Committee on State Archaeological Surveys, National Research Council, Circular Letter, April 4, 1933." This undoubtedly was the source of Deuel's terms *component* and *phase*.

James B. Griffin (1943:327) indicated that the papers presented at the Illinois State Academy of Science stimulated McKern's efforts because "the promiscuous use of the word 'culture' emphasized McKern's belief that the term had ceased to have meaning for scientific purposes in an archaeological discussion." Although McKern did not explicitly address the classification problem in his published paper, it represents a fine example of the problem. In some places in McKern's discussion, an archaeological culture comprises the remains from a single stratum at a single site; in other places a culture comprises several stratigraphically delimited yet similar assemblages from several sites distributed over a relatively small geographic area; and in still other places a culture comprises a plethora of assemblages and sites distributed over several contiguous states.

Griffin (1943:327) reported that during the May 1932 Illinois State Academy of Science symposium, McKern "proposed that a system be devised by which the degree of relationship existing between sites or groups of sites could be indicated by the terminology employed." There is no such proposal in McKern (1933[9]), nor have we found any notes or correspondence summarizing discussions that might have accompanied McKern's and others' papers. A letter from Guthe to McKern (see below) does indicate, however, that McKern's classification was discussed at the Illinois meeting. Based on McKern's providing Guthe with a copy of his original paper (McKern 1932[7]), Guthe issued a statement on just such a system in October 1932. Guthe asked for McKern's help in putting this statement together, and McKern answered him on July 30 (MPM):

> I am not sure that I can do any better as a beginning towards helping you in the doping out of a circular letter on archaeological culture-type classification than to send you a copy of the paper on that subject which I had planned to read at the last meeting of the Central Section, changed to omit the so-undesirable term "habit," which, by the way, I still prefer. This paper at least sets forth my ideas on the subject as clearly as I know how to state them, and gives us something to start with. As to the terms I have used, you will find that I do not consider them as my children for whom I am prepared to fight to the death. It is the general plan rather than the specific terms that I am definitely out to battle for, against all foes, if any, and at all costs (job excluded!).

Guthe put together a draft statement in early September and wrote to McKern on September 14 (MPM), asking for his comments on the draft. With that letter, Guthe returned the copy of McKern's revised Central Section paper and included a draft of his own statement. In his letter, Guthe told McKern the following:

> I have taken your idea and adjusted it in several ways, which I feel I should explain. In the first place, I find most people prefer to have a manuscript almost in outline form, in order that they may get its high points with the least amount of mental effort. This accounts for the general set-up of the manuscript and for the elimination of some of your introductory and closing remarks. I have separated the problem of the classification from that of the names to be given the several types, because if I remember correctly, the difficulty at the hotel conference in Chicago [May 1932] was due to confusion in the minds of the persons present about these two problems.
>
> You will note that I have included a few of my own ideas. The principal one is the addition of a new type between your "locale" and "specific." I have also taken the liberty of re-wording both your definitions and the limiting considerations for the names. My reasons for including the extra type will become apparent in the table at the end of the manuscript. I am including an extra, unnumbered sheet which contains a list of synonyms, which is the result of several hours study of a thesaurus.
>
> Now please understand one thing. I have no intention of trying to impose any of these changes upon you. I am anxious to have the idea remain essentially yours. I am trying to give you the benefit of my mental attitude and my experience in dealing with many individu-

> als. Therefore, please do not hesitate to slash and disagree with the manuscript I have prepared. Since the Chicago crowd has worked out a somewhat similar scheme, and are applying it, I feel that [Thorne] Deuel should be included in this committee of three which is trying to work out a statement.

Note that the last sentence of the first paragraph in Guthe's letter suggests McKern discussed his proposed method during the May meeting of the Illinois State Academy of Science in Chicago. This indicates that Griffin's (1943) statement that the method was first publicized at that meeting is correct. McKern responded to Guthe's draft of the proposed method in a letter of September 23 (MPM):

> I am one-hundred-percent satisfied with the scheme for culture-group classification which you have developed from our idea, and with your clear, concise statement thereof. You have my unqualified support in any attempt to sell the plan to the archaeological powers that be in the involved provinces. My sincere congratulations upon the lot you have accomplished.
>
> As for the terminology, I shall agree with whatever other students may endorse. I have no objection to "pattern," although the word has been worked to death by psychologists and others. It is, nevertheless, a good term. I object to the use of "variant" because I should like to see the word retained for general usage. Before specific classification is possible for a given complex of determinants, A, it is convenient to say that A appears to be a variant of B, without implying the specific pigeon-hole in our classification cabinet into which it fits. Later, with accumulating data, it may turn out to have the relationship of "Aspect" or "Specific" to B, as the case may be. However, if the consensus of opinion favors "variant," variant it shall be. So far as I am concerned, there will be no difficulty in reaching an agreement on terms, although I may fight for certain words until I see that the battle is lost.

McKern went on to point out that he disagreed with a few of the relationships that Guthe suggested were evident between archaeological units as shown in a chart Guthe included at the end of his manuscript. This disagreement highlights the fact that the scheme was not yet operational. For example, the number and kinds of traits that had to be shared by multiple archaeological manifestations in order for them to be related in a particular way were unclear. McKern used the term *determinant* in the letter, but he did not specify what a determinant was or how one was to be recognized. Importantly, McKern also noted that Guthe had violated his own rule that "geographical distribution . . . is always secondary to the similarity of determinants." Historically, McKern usually is attributed with omitting time and space from the method. The exchange between Guthe and McKern quoted above suggests such attribution is correct.

On October 3 (MPM), McKern responded not only to a September 27 letter from Guthe (MPM) but also to comments sent to Guthe by Deuel (September 24, 1932) that Guthe had forwarded to McKern. Guthe (September 27, 1932 [MPM]) was "very much pleased . . . to know that [McKern] approved so wholeheartedly of the revised text" of September 14 and noted that "if Deuel is satisfied, I can have the text itself mimeographed." McKern (September 23, 1932) had suggested using the term *specific* for *B* and *frame* for *C* (Table 3.1), and Guthe agreed. On October 3, McKern told Guthe, "I am entirely in accord with your text as it stands." Deuel had asked about using *level* as a subdivision of *locale*. In response, McKern first fulfilled a request from Deuel regarding information on the use of a "biological system of classification for pottery tentatively agreed upon by some Southwest students." McKern noted that he was unsure of the correct references but suggested that Deuel consult the bibliography in Hargrave (1932) because "there may be something there" (see chapter 5 for discussion of what is there). With respect to using the term *level* as a subdivision of McKern's *locale*, McKern noted, "I do not think that you [Deuel] understand our idea of what a locale should be. . . . According to my conception, the cultural level, stratigraphic or otherwise, is the locale."

Deuel wrote to both Guthe and McKern on October 11 (all letters referenced in the next few paragraphs are from the MPM), proposing that they get together in Chicago to discuss during an "informal evening meeting" with Fay-Cooper Cole (University of Chicago) and A. R. Kelly "the matter of classification system." McKern responded on October 15, noting that he was "all for it" but would like to have Guthe "broadcast" his text first. On October 6 Guthe wrote to McKern that A. V. Kidder (Carnegie Institution) had stopped by. After Guthe told him what they were doing, Kidder "not only approved of the scheme in general, but had no suggestions to make on the text." Guthe also noted that William Duncan Strong (Bureau of American Ethnology) and Frank Setzler (U.S. National Museum) had approved the general "principles involved" in the classification scheme in June 1932. Guthe concluded his letter with the remark that "indications are that there is likely to be quite a bit of misunderstanding concerning the use of the division which we call locale." Guthe wrote to Deuel on October 12 and indicated that the text was mimeographed and ready for distribution but that it would not be sent out until a table showing cultural relationships that was agreeable to him, McKern, and Guthe could be appended.

McKern wrote to Guthe on October 14, noting that the "introductory letter" to accompany the draft manuscript required "no improvement or correction." He went on to remark, "I note that you ask that criticisms should be sent to me. Well, I don't blame you, and in consideration of the work you have already put into this project, I am perfectly willing to be the one to stand with his back to the wall at sunrise if it will give you a temporary breathing spell." Guthe responded on October 20, telling McKern that "the idea is really your own and you are the logical man to defend it and profit by the suggestions of the other men." The cover letter, the manuscript, and the accompanying table were, Guthe indicated, to be sent out on October 24. The manuscript was given the title "A Suggested Classification of Cultures" and attributed to Guthe by Griffin (1943). We have been unable to locate a copy of the cover letter, but we did find a copy of the manuscript and accompanying table in the Illinois State Museum archives. We refer to the manuscript and table as Guthe (1932[8]).

THE FIRST CIRCULATED VERSION: LATE 1932

Guthe began the manuscript with the following statement:

> Archaeological evidence indicates the existence of culture relationship areas of greatly varying size, many of which show correspondingly varying degrees of cultural similarity in their component parts. The uncritical application of the term "culture" to a variety of types of determinant-complexes, ranging from the essentially simple to the specifically complex, has led to an improper and undefinable generalization of its meaning. This creates confusion between the several degrees of cultural relationships and obscures the necessity for comparative research.
>
> A system of classificatory terms is needed in order to distinguish between these various types of determinant-complexes.

At 957 words, the first circulated statement on the taxonomic method is terse, and there are several key terms and concepts that are not defined. They require definition if we are to comprehend the problem Guthe identified in the manuscript. First, a "cultural relationship" denotes a linkage of transmission, whether that linkage be affected by diffusion, migration, enculturation, descent, or some other process by which information is passed from one archaeologically delineated culture to another (Sapir 1916:30). Second, a "determinant-complex" could be one of two things, given the literature of the time. It could be a set of culture traits that are typically found associated but that are functionally independent of one another. Melville Herskovits (1926:231), for example, suggested that a culture complex comprised a set of culture traits that merely "go together." Alternatively, a complex could be a set of culture traits that are functionally interrelated. Edward Sapir (1916:29) indicated that a trait complex comprises an "assemblage of specific elements [or traits that are] functionally unified, as a rule." This seems to be the definition of a trait complex preferred by Kroeber (1931). Sapir (1916:52) also noted that "the greater the specialization of function, the more neatly are the parts of a complex apt to be bound together." The distinction between the two possibilities of what a trait complex comprises was not clear in the relevant literature until Deuel (1937b[12]:2) distinguished between a determinant complex as a "cluster of mutually related traits" and a determinant series as "a group of traits or complexes, not necessarily possessing any common or mutual relationship among themselves other than association." The term *determinant* remained vague until McKern et al. (1933[10]:1) provided a definition: "those particular traits of a material culture which, because of their individuality, serve to differentiate it from other cultures." Virtually everyone would confuse a *determinant* trait with what came to be called a *diagnostic* trait.

McKern had referred to "the basic complex of traits which tie our subcultures together" in a January 4, 1932 (MPM), letter to Cole. Sapir (1916:30) had noted that traits and complexes were at the very least analytical units and the fact that the traits comprising a complex were typically "associated" reflected their "cultural transmission" as a set. Perhaps what McKern had in mind was that the traits comprising a complex were functionally related and that the probability that those related traits would be independently invented in the same combination was so remote that when found together they must signify transmission as a complex. Such reasoning helps explain why McKern and others would think a complex of traits would link cultures together. Sapir (1916) had written his monograph at the urging of Kroeber (Darnell 2001), and Kroeber was McKern's adviser at the time, so McKern no doubt knew what Sapir (1916) had said and why he said it.

Guthe (1932[8]) designated six types of relationship by using capital letters and suggested terms for each of the units that designated each of the relationship types (Table 3.1). Importantly, he noted that "in the archaeological field, our first contact with cultures are, figuratively, at the tips of the branches rather than at the roots" (1932[8]:1). That is, much like biologists who advocate evolutionary taxonomy, archaeologists begin with individuals or demes—Guthe's *A* type units—and proceed to group them into more-inclusive units—first, terminal taxa—based on their similarities. The procedure of grouping subordinate groups into successively larger and more-inclusive superior groups progresses through five levels, designated *B* through *F* by Guthe (1932[8]). The highest-ranking, most-inclusive unit was characterized as "the primary cultural foundation, determined by a few fundamentals of widespread importance and influence, such as the agriculture-pottery complex" (1932[8]:2).

The "informal evening meeting" to discuss "the matter of classification system" proposed on October 11, 1932, by Deuel apparently was quickly agreed to by all correspondents and scheduled for December 10 (McKern letter to Deuel, October 31, 1932 [MPM]). Cole wrote to Guthe on November 18 (UC) regarding Guthe's (1932[8]) paper of October 24: "I am enclosing a letter relating to the archaeological scheme which we are to discuss when you come here on the 10th. I have tried to present a scheme somewhat more simple than the one you sent. Unless it is simple I fear no scheme will work." We were unable to locate a copy of the letter to which Cole refers, although we think the thrust of its contents is hinted at in materials produced by Cole (National Research Council 1937:39–42), Cole and Deuel (1937), and Deuel (1935a, 1935b). Guthe responded on November 23 (UC), noting that: "I read your archaeological scheme based upon McKern's outline. It is so nearly like McKern's scheme that I am sure an adjustment can be reached. Off hand, I do not like the suggestion of a locale and a site both, nor the use of the word 'culture' in association with the other terms. Those are details which can be straightened out on December 10th, without doubt." Cole wrote back to Guthe on November 30 (UC), stating,: "I am looking forward to your visit here on the tenth and I have no doubt that we will find a lot of material to discuss. Just had a nice note from McKern commenting on the outline I sent you. I am not set on any particular scheme but am anxious to have whatever we do result in something workable."

By early December 1932, before the "informal evening meeting" in Chicago, McKern had letters from Emerson F. Greenman (University of Michigan), Paul S. Martin (Field Museum of Natural History), Warren K. Moorehead (Phillips Academy [Andover, Massachusetts]), and Harold S. Colton (Museum of Northern Arizona), all of whom commented on Guthe's paper. McKern reported to Guthe in a December 6 letter (MPM) that "all [of these individuals are] favorable to the general plan and more or less favorable to the specific plan." He also told Guthe that he had written "a rather long letter to [Diamond] Jenness [National Museum of Canada] attempting to make clear our classificatory idea, modeled after the biological classificatory system, as based exclusively upon cultural similarity, independent of any consideration of the temporal factor, geographical distribution or evolutional sequence, citing parallel instances from the zoological classification to illustrate." Finally, McKern noted, that "I must admit that I can never be influenced to endorse anything related to the ethnological 'culture area' idea, which I believe has outlived its usefulness."

Two days later, in anticipation of the upcoming informal Chicago meeting, McKern wrote to Guthe again (MPM), this time to express his opinions on what promised to be "three controversial issues" at that meeting:

> First: I favor a system generally modeled after the biological classificatory system, based exclusively on cultural similarities, just as the biological system is based exclusively upon physiological similarities. For example, the biological groups "species," "genus," "family," "order," etc., absolutely disregard geographical distribution and the temporal factor. I hold that our system must also disregard these factors if it is to be simple and useful. We can not do better in this than to follow paleontological method.
>
> Second: If the above contention is to be accepted, it necessarily follows that our system must be divorced from the old ethnological culture-area idea, which is a culture-geographical complex with definite temporal limitations, and which, moreover, is basically incorrect in that it posits essential culture uniformity within an area. It stresses distribution rather than cultural similarity.
>
> Third: If all the data were at hand, our cultural groups would merge one into the other with so gradual an expression of growth and change that no hard and fast lines of demarcation could be established. Therefore, our classificatory system, like that of any study attempting to classify elements that change with time, must be arbitrary, the degree of arbitrariness to be determined only by the factor of usefulness, and usefulness over the entire interested field rather than locally. Whether we have four, five or six culture-types, then, must depend upon general needs throughout North America north of Mexico, rather than upon the possibly more limited immediate needs of the Wisconsin or Illinois areas. The fact that one district can not immediately use all of the types that are in conformity as major types and that are useful in other interested districts can not

be applied as a valid objection to the number of types in the proposed classificatory system. I could cite examples from the biological classification.

As far as we can determine, Guthe did not respond to this letter. McKern seldom cited "examples from the biological classification" in his publications or correspondence, and he did not describe the "paleontological method" of classification in much detail. His remarks under "First" and "Third" indicate he was well aware of how biological classifications were built in the 1920s and 1930s and what those classifications signified. In particular, McKern recognized (1) the incongruity of using static classes to categorize dynamic, evolving entities; (2) that the number of taxonomic categories or ranks—what he called "culture-types"—is arbitrary; and (3) that the classification had to be analytically useful, although he was silent on exactly what analytical usefulness he had in mind.

THE DECEMBER 10, 1932, INFORMAL MEETING IN CHICAGO

The "informal evening meeting" was held on December 10 in Chicago (Cole and Deuel 1937:34; McKern to Deuel, letter of October 31, 1932 [MPM]). Along with McKern, in attendance were Samuel A. Barrett (Milwaukee Public Museum), Fay-Cooper Cole (University of Chicago), Thorne Deuel (University of Chicago), James B. Griffin (University of Michigan), Carl E. Guthe (University of Michigan), and A. R. Kelly (University of Illinois) (Cole and Deuel 1937; Fisher 1997). We are unaware of any written transcript of this meeting, but letters written afterward indicate some of what transpired. McKern, for example, wrote to Guthe on December 17 (MPM): "In looking back at the meeting last week, I remain satisfied that we acted wisely in yielding to Cole's demand, supported by Kelly, for the term 'basic culture.' I don't like the term, and I shall continue to use the word 'culture' in a general rather than a specific sense, but the fact that we came to a unanimous decision on the entire system is of greater weight than the merits or demerits of any single term; at least that is my judgement on the matter. If the term proves objectionable, let the objection come from another source. I should like to hear your own personal reactions to that meeting and its results." That the terms designating the cultural taxa were such a contentious issue suggests that the participants either were searching for commonsensical terms that would not require explicit and particularistic definitions or were not fully aware of the fact that the terms designated particular ranked and nested classes. Because such units are strictly ideational, they could be given names such as A, B, C, and D; or 1, 2, 3, and 4; or even species, genus, family, and order without influencing either their empirical content or their epistemological status. The number of taxonomic categories and their names would not be resolved until late in 1935.

In his December 17 letter, McKern asked Guthe if he thought it advisable that McKern and Barrett publish two papers—"Ancient Aztalan" and "The Upper Mississippi Aspect for Wisconsin"—that were nearly ready for submission and that used the classificatory system and terminology. Guthe wrote to McKern on December 26 (MPM) that he should "go ahead with the idea" of publishing the papers. Other statements in Guthe's letter warrant mention:

> The general reaction on the part of those who have written us [about Guthe 1932[8]] is favorable to the principle involved. Actually, the objections, which are all of a minor nature, may be grouped under two heads; first, confusion concerning the smaller groupings, due in large measure to the terms we suggested for them, and second, technical objections to the particular groupings in the chart. Both of these groups of objections can be eliminated without changing the principles involved.
>
> The Chicago meeting brought out the importance of emphasizing the three major groups (Basic culture, Phase, and Aspect). I am convinced that we can put this idea across and have it accepted by the majority of the professionals. The change of name of the two smaller groups to focus and component certainly clarifies the conceptions we had in mind, and bids fair to bring additional adherents to the fold. However, even if these terms are not accepted in other areas, it does not ruin the idea. . . . Changes in terminology do not radically affect the scientific value of publications. . . . To repeat, I think the classificatory system of designating cultures, which you have proposed is definitely here to stay. There may be minor changes in terms and in the grouping of the various determinant-complexes, but I do not think there will be any change in the principle. . . .
>
> As for the Chicago conference, I was very happy over the result. I admit I had misgivings concerning Cole and Deuel, who, prior to the meeting, did not seem to get the idea of the smaller grouping, and seemed to be a bit too provincial in their attitude. However, as might have been expected, the opportunity to thrash things out, not only cleared the atmosphere of misunderstandings, but also served to place the whole idea upon a much sounder footing, especially from the

point of view of terminology. I fail to get very excited about the use of the word "culture." Much of my objection at the time of the meeting was due to a desire to draw out argument, and stimulate a careful analysis rather than have a somewhat hasty acceptance of the term. In spite of what you may feel, anthropologists do think in terms of "culture," and I think will continue to do so. However, the term should refer to a well-rounded, integrated system of living, with variations in different localities, very much like our present civilization or culture is "American," altho [*sic*] it differs in different parts of the country. I feel there is an excuse for the use of the term—the question is whether the professionals will learn to think of its specific meaning or will insist upon the use of a lax, generalized meaning.

Guthe apparently revised the classification system in light of the discussion at the December 10 meeting in Chicago and sent a copy to McKern, who commented at some length on that version in a letter to Guthe of February 8, 1933 (MPM):

> Generally, and in detail to a preponderating extent, I like the new text and hereby tender my endorsement of this latest result of your much-appreciated efforts. My adverse criticism boils down to one primary and two secondary items, as follows.
>
> The primary point involves our definition for the term "determinant complex." Throughout the text you have employed the term in the sense of a complex of traits involving shape, material, decorative techniques and decorative motifs for a given pottery determinant. This is what I, and some others, call a trait complex.
>
> The term as I have previously conceived and used it applies to a complex of determinants for a given cultural class. Thus, for the Effigy Mound aspect, such determinants as effigy-shaped burial mounds, flexed burials or bone reburials, grooved axes, a woodland type of pottery, stone fireplaces associated with burials, etc., would comprise the determinant complex for that cultural aspect. The term so used is comparable to the term "culture complex" excepting that it applies to all types of cultural classes rather than exclusively to the basic culture class. . . . I find that Deuel shares my idea in this. In any case, I believe that our little group is the first to have employed such a term for any purpose, and we certainly should come to an agreement on its definition.
>
> I have taken the liberty to "edit" the text sufficiently to illustrate

> my conception of the use of the term. I do not wish to be unreasonably stubborn about it, however, and I think that you will find me receptive to any counter-arguments you may present in support of your use of the term.
>
> Point Two. On Page 2, first paragraph, I question the accuracy of your use of the word "genetical." I still contend that paleontological classifications are made on the basis of morphological similarities; genetical-relationship determinations are secondary to and dependent upon morphological factors. The genetical relationship is, in instances, immediately recognized, due to morphological similarities, but whether or not these similarities indicate genetical relationship, the same morphological similarities would determine the classification. I fear that a large majority of our paleontologists would object to our statement that the genetical factor is of essential importance to fossil classification.
>
> Point Three. On Page 5, I do not see the need for the excommunication of the cultural classes "focus" and "component." Of all those who responded to our request for critical comment, there was but one man who did not have definite use for smaller classes such as these in his field of interest and experience. That man finally came around to accept their usage and now, according to Deuel, finds that he actually has need for them in his archaeological-survey-of-the-Mississippi-Valley project. . . . I have inserted a couple of suggested additions to somewhat dull the edge of the separating sword, if in your final opinion this brutal separation should stand. After all, any investigator who finds an occupation site has at least one component, whether or not he wishes to call it by that name, and if he finds two or more sites with identical cultural expressions, which is not an unusual occurrence in any field, Illinois included, he actually has a focus, whether or not he is an advocate of great caution in experimental terminology. The facts are actual; we are simply recommending names to facilitate the handling of established facts. Doesn't it strike you that way?

It must have struck Guthe that way, given the next circulated version of the MTM (McKern et al. 1933[10]). But before turning to it, reread McKern's second point in the quotation above. Again, McKern clearly knew what was going on in biological and paleontological classification in the 1920s and 1930s. Organisms were grouped together based on formal (phenotypic) similarity, as were fossils, and both sorts of groups were thought to be similar only *potentially* as a result of shared genetic heritage. Thus, genetics actually had little to do with the grouping or classification procedure itself. Genetic continuity would become the theoretical basis of the grouping only with the neo-Darwinian synthesis of the early 1940s. As well, McKern, like paleontologists of the time, seems to have been aware that formal similarity might *not* be a valid indication of "genetic" relationship; later (McKern 1939[15]), he would suggest such a relationship *could be hypothesized* on the basis of formal similarity. We do not think he misjudged paleontologists of the early twentieth century when McKern implied that they would object to the statement that "the genetical factor is of essential importance to fossil classification." This factor would not play an active role during the actual classification of organisms or fossils until Simpson (1944) incorporated it into paleontological theory. Similarly, it was not central to the *taxonomic* implications—the theory or basis of classification, in this case general "relationship"—of any classification of organisms or fossils.

Another issue worthy of highlighting is under McKern's third point. There he indicated that if an archaeologist "finds two or more sites with *identical* cultural expressions . . . he actually has a focus." This would become the recurrence criterion—that the validity of a focus depended on finding essentially the same set of traits distributed among multiple components. McKern's letter of February 8, 1933, was the first mention of this criterion. It would reappear in circulated and published versions of the method, but it would be overlooked by a number of other archaeologists. Its epistemological importance resided in the fact that it underscored the bottom-up procedure for building a cultural taxonomy. Logical division from the top down could produce terminal taxa with only one member each. Whether those terminal taxa were somehow valid could not be determined in such cases. The recurrence criterion demanded that each terminal taxon (focus) have more than one member component, and this, as McKern would make explicit later, served as an empirical warrant for the validity of those terminal taxa.

The final issue requiring comment is McKern's "primary point." The reason McKern disagreed with Guthe's definition of a determinant complex was that the latter had conflated determinant traits with traits in general. As McKern implied in the third paragraph, a determinant complex was definitive of a "given cultural class," and multiple associated determinants were synonymous with "culture complex." This seemingly innocent quibble over traits and their status as definitive criteria would be a constant source of confusion throughout the history of McKern's method and would contribute greatly to its never being used in the way he intended.

THE SECOND CIRCULATED VERSION: 1933

Guthe revised the text according to McKern's suggestions and sent the new version out as an NRC Circular Letter on April 4, 1933 (McKern et al. 1933[10]). Griffin (1943:327) stated that the manuscript was "based on McKern's original paper, to which were added the conclusions reached in Chicago and in the resulting correspondence, and it was sent to a number of archaeologists throughout the country for suggestions." The four-and-a-half-page manuscript was over the names W. C. McKern, Thorne Deuel, and Carl E. Guthe. Four taxonomic units—in ascending order of inclusiveness, focus, aspect, phase, and basic culture—had been agreed upon (Table 3.1). *Component* was the term applied to an empirical archaeological manifestation. As McKern et al. 1933[10]:4) defined it, a component was "the manifestation of a given culture at a single site." Components thus were the building blocks of the hierarchy, and the successively more inclusive units were listed in order with their definitions. Each of those definitions basically stated that the unit of concern comprised a "group" of the immediately subordinate units that shared a number of determinants. The number of determinants decreased and their generality increased as one read the list of units from focus to basic culture. Fewer determinants were shared as the units became more inclusive, and the determinants also became more general in nature. The key, then, was to establish determinants by the comparative analysis of components and thus work from the bottom up in building the taxonomy of archaeological materials. How determinants were in fact to be determined was unclear, a problem that was to plague the entire history of the method.

It is in the 1933 version of the MTM that reference was made not only to paleontological classification but also to linguistic classification. The third paragraph contains the pertinent sentences, where these other methods are used to warrant a purely formal classification. In particular, time and space are ignored by linguistic and paleontological systematics, so they should also be ignored by archaeological systematics. Linguists had been building taxonomies of languages for purposes of historical linguistics since the nineteenth century; they were studying language evolution and phylogeny (Sampson 1980). Paleontologists had been making similar studies of fossils classified in a taxonomic framework since the late nineteenth century (for example, Lull 1917; Matthew 1926, 1929, 1930). McKern et al.'s failure to mention this aspect of the disciplines they chose to legitimate their choice of classificatory method speaks loudly of the general abhorrence of anything evolutionary in the anthropology of the time (Lyman and O'Brien 1997). It also suggests that the method was simply a grouping technique for arranging archaeological phenomena according to their varying degrees of similarity. It was, simply put, phenetics.

A. V. Kidder appears to have been the first person to respond to the circular, sending Guthe a letter dated April 12, 1933 (MPM), a copy of which Guthe forwarded to McKern. McKern noted in a letter to Guthe on April 28 (MPM) that he was in receipt of the copy of Kidder's letter but had himself not yet received any responses to the April 4 circular letter. Kidder's letter is worth quoting in full:

> I have read the circular letter of April 4th regarding culture classification with much care, great interest, and complete approbation. I have tried applying it to the situation existing in New Mexico with the following, it seems to me, very satisfactory results:
>
> | | |
> |---|---|
> | Basic culture | Southwest |
> | Phase | Pueblo |
> | Aspect | Pueblo IV |
> | Focus | Rio Grande |
> | Sub-focus | Glaze |
> | Components | Glaze I, Glaze II, etc. |
>
> This seems to work admirably. As you suggest, extra terms may be incorporated, e.g., sub-focus, which is necessary to distinguish the Glaze-using pueblos from those to the north which used Biscuit ware. One would therefore speak of the Glaze sub-focus in discussing the culture in question. This is very much better than the old method of talking of the glaze area, or glaze region, as geographically the thing is not an entity, as Glaze and Biscuit sites more or less overlap on the Pajarito. And "Component" is an excellent word, it seems to me, for referring to minor divisions at a site. In the case of Pecos, it is, of course, interchangeable with period because the temporal relationships are known, but "component" will often be much safer where chronological work has not yet been done. I think I'll use these terms in the Pecos pottery book, explaining in the Introduction what they mean. It will be some months before I will get the thing finally together, so if your group makes any changes in the meantime, please let me know.

Kidder (1936b) did not use McKern et al.'s terminology, but he did have much to say about the somewhat similar classification system developed by Lyndon Hargrave, Harold Colton, and Harold Gladwin for the archaeology of the Southwest (see chapter 5).

Guthe responded to Kidder on April 18 (MPM) and, as might be expected, was pleased with Kidder's remarks, but he also noted an error in his use of the classification method and suggested how to fix it. Guthe also outlined why the terms *focus* and *component* came to be adopted:

> Your comments upon the culture classification brought great joy to this office. It means a good deal to have you agree with the general principles laid down and find that you can fit the suggestions made into the already accepted scheme of classification in the Southwest. I am particularly glad to notice that you approve of the word "component." It may interest you to know the details of the episode which brought into being the terms "component" and "focus." A small group of us, consisting of Cole, Deuel, Barrett, McKern, Kelly, Griffin, and myself, were sitting before a blackboard in a corner of the exhibit rooms of the Department of Anthropology at the University of Chicago. On the blackboard were a series of terms and concentric circles by means of which we were trying to come to some agreement. I had with me a list of synonyms taken from Roget's Thesaurus. This had been examined by the group during the course of the discussions. Finally, the insistence of Barrett brought to a head the consideration of these two terms of focus and component, and resulted in their adoption. I am not sure who first suggested these two words, but I feel definitely that Barrett's emphasis of their value was responsible for their adoption.
>
> It is perfectly clear that you have grasped the point of the article which McKern and the rest of us prepared. However, I am inclined to disagree with your use of the word component. According to the definition, a component occurs at only one site and therefore when you apply this term to a type of culture, such as Glaze I or Glaze II, you destroy the intended meaning of the word. I would be inclined to suggest that the term "focus" be applied to the Glaze periods generally, and "sub-focus" to Glaze I, II, etc. This necessitates a subdivision between Aspect and Phase for the more general Rio Grande group of communities. The word "variant" might be used for this intermediate class, although a number of synonyms would serve equally well. A group of synonyms from which you might choose a more satisfactory term is: structure, center, pattern, specific, commune, horizon, member, nucleus, version, sphere, domain. Otherwise, the table which you give fits into our scheme admirably. The term component would be used with the name of a specific site. . . .
>
> The chief difficulty in the adoption of this system of classification by practicing archaeologists will be found in establishing determi-

> nants and determinant complexes. We speak rather glibly of the difference between Pueblo I aspect and Pueblo II aspect and yet can we list definitively determinants by means of which these two aspects may be distinguished? A still more difficult problem will be to establish the determinants between the several basic cultures.

When McKern wrote back to Guthe on April 28, he noted, as had Guthe in his response to Kidder, that were Kidder to adopt the classification method in his book on Pecos pottery (Kidder and Shepard 1936), that method would be "established" in North American archaeology.

Emerson Greenman, curator of archaeology at the Ohio State Archaeological and Historical Society, wrote to McKern on May 17 (MPM), questioning the table that accompanied the circular letter, in particular why certain subordinate units were included within particular superior, more-inclusive units. In the process, Greenman implicitly underscored Guthe's point to Kidder: How are determinants identified? He also pointed out that "the whole problem is one of pigeon-holing. In order to be entirely consistent little holes must be left between some of the compartments, but that balls things up." Here Greenman revealed two things. First, empty classes—that is, ones without empirical members—were to be avoided. Such notions were common during that era (Dunnell 1986). Second, Greenman clearly did not understand that the classification was being built from the bottom up by grouping units into successively more-inclusive units. This procedure would not create empty classes because the units were being derived from empirical materials; the units literally were extensions of sets of associated artifacts variously grouped together, and thus empty classes were an epistemological impossibility.

McKern made two points in his response to Greenman (May 24, 1933 [MPM]). First, he emphasized that the table had been included "merely to illustrate how local classifications, whatever they might be, could be hung on the general framework of cultural types which we proposed." McKern et al. had not been trying to establish anything regarding what they thought about the prehistory of some area. Second, their main point was "to suggest a general classificatory framework whereby groups previously, indiscriminately called 'cultures' were to be classified according to type as foci, aspects, phases and basic cultures." McKern did not address either the issue of how determinants were to be determined or the issue of empty classes. Greenman (June 19, 1933 [MPM]) wrote back, thanking McKern for his letter and also making an interesting point. Greenman concurred with McKern that the use of the term *culture* was not good, particularly because in Greenman's view the term seemed to connote "human activities." Greenman suggested *series* as a "more scientific term" and one that "would indicate that the archaeologist is dealing with actual physical objects from which his inferences are drawn directly, uncontaminated by the mass of hypothetical laws which the ethnologists and sociologists have built up around the term culture." Greenman's suggestion fell on deaf ears; the term *series* never appears in any discussion or description of the taxonomic method, perhaps because during the 1930s *series* was coming to have explicit genealogical connotations (Lyman et al. 1997).

McKern wrote to Guthe on June 14 (MPM), thanking him for the copies of his correspondence with Winslow Walker (Bureau of American Ethnology)[1] and George C. Vaillant (American Museum of Natural History) regarding the McKern et al. circular letter. Although we did not find copies of these letters, McKern's remarks to Guthe reveal the gist of the contents of that correspondence:

> I utterly fail to understand the difficulty experienced by some of these chaps in their efforts to understand and specifically apply the classification method. I have submitted your last classification circular to a number of high school graduates, selected on the basis of possessing interest and average intelligence, with the idea of testing the lucidity of your statements. Perhaps this was not a very fair test, but the circular passed the test with an average of about 95 per cent. If these kids can understand this text, why do experienced field students have so much trouble with it? I hesitate to draw the conclusion suggested. One fact seems rather apparent; not a few of our archaeological students are without classificatory training, [and therefore] do not know the basic principles for any classification.
>
> A classification is necessitated because of the inability of the human mind to visualize large inclusive subjects in their entirety, a factor which renders it necessary to break up a subject into convenient pieces. If you will permit the figure, classification is a sort of mental mastication to facilitate easy digestion; the subject is taken in bites each of which may then be easily chewed up. Consequently, classification is in no sense natural, but purely arbitrary, and useful in direct ratio to its contribution to the convenience with which study materials may be handled. This being true it follows that, in order to be of maximum usefulness, a classification must be simple, fundamental

1. McKern referred to him as "William" Walker; our guess is that he meant "Winslow" Walker.

> and elastic. I believe that our proposed method complies entirely with these rules and purposes, and the only criticisms that I have heard attack our method on the basis of these very essentials, advocate changes in the direction of complexity, extrinsicality and rigidity.

In the second paragraph, McKern's "figure" was actually a metaphor, but in our view a poor one. On the one hand, it is true that a classification should allow the retrieval of information by knowing what each included class comprises irrespective of what it is called, and thus the classification allows "materials [to] be handled." That a classification should be arbitrary, on the other hand, is ambiguous. The classes can be arbitrary only with respect to some property inherent among the phenomena being classified or relative to some analytical purpose. McKern did not specify in his letter what the purpose of the classification method was, other than that it should be "useful." But useful for what? The criticisms of the classification to which McKern referred were misplaced. The units of the classification were *classes*—ideational units of measurement—and were flexible because their definitive criteria could be altered to fit the required measurement situation. Critics were viewing those units as *groups*, or empirical units, which *are* inflexible. That the units of McKern's classificatory method were flexible and thus could be shaped to fit any situation would be made more explicit in later versions of the MTM. That the particular nature of those units depended on the materials examined should have been clear to all commentators, but apparently it was not.

Of some interest is the next paragraph of McKern's June 14 letter to Guthe. There he not only expressed his opinion of what, five years later, Waldo Wedel (1938) would refer to as the *direct historical approach* but also gave it virtually the same name:

> I am glad that, in your letter to Walker, you properly sat upon the "direct historical" method as one which can be used independently in any field of natural history that includes interest in a pre-known or prehistoric period. That historical-method fad is gathering altogether too much headway with archaeological students. Its danger lies in the fact that it overemphasizes the importance of geographical location, and assumes cultural uniformity for materials found at a certain site with traditional or historical significance as to origin. A culture complex based solely upon site-association is, in my opinion, valueless, since a determinant complex must be established through its occurrence as a constant complex at several sites. Otherwise we have no logical right to assume that a given set of culture-indicative

> objects and data has a single cultural origin. This is made certain only by the occurrence of the same complex again and again at distinctly separate sites. Therefore, the direct historical method is useless unless its products are substantiated by the strictly analytical "determinant" method. How far would paleontologists have gotten if they had depended upon a "direct historical" method? To stay within our own field of thought, what would be the present status of European archaeology, or the prehistory of man, if research in these studies had been limited to working back from historical starting points?

McKern (1934[11]:10) perhaps was referring to some of the correspondence between Guthe and Walker when he later wrote about what "has been termed the direct-historical method." We suggest this because we have not found any published use of this term other than in McKern's correspondence and publications. McKern would get into an argument with Julian Steward about the relative values of the direct historical approach and the MTM nearly a decade later (chapter 5). In the quotation immediately above, however, he repeated many of the points regarding the "direct-historical method" raised by John R. Swanton at the National Research Council–sponsored Conference on Southern Pre-History History held in Birmingham, Alabama, in December 1932 (National Research Council 1932). Swanton was a Harvard-trained archaeologist-turned-ethnologist who spent his career with the Bureau of American Ethnology. His early work was on North American Indian languages, and although he continued to produce linguistical texts throughout his career (for example, Swanton 1919, 1940), he became better known for his ethnohistorical work. Swanton was sympathetic to the goals of archaeology and, important from the perspective of the direct-historical method, he could place individual Indian groups in specific places at particular times.

At the Birmingham conference, Swanton presented two papers in which he summarized the ethnohistory of southeastern Indian groups. He noted that ethnologists tended to classify human groups variously on the basis of "their physical characters, their languages, and their general culture" (Swanton 1932a:10); that language seemed to be "the most satisfactory method of classifying Indian tribes [but] that this is a cultural, not a biological, feature, and the same language may be adopted by people otherwise distinct, while biologically related tribes may acquire the use of unrelated languages" (Swanton 1932a:11); and that early recorders of Native American lifeways generally failed "to ascribe [ethnic identity to] native artifacts clearly" (Swanton 1932b:60). He therefore cautioned that assigning an ethnic or linguistic identification to an archaeological manifestation was slippery business at best. Yet he concluded with the statement that "it is important beyond all else for you archaeologists to tie your discoveries onto known tribes, after having done which you may trace them back into the mysterious past as far as you will, and your work will have more interest for you and for us all" (Swanton 1932b:74). The conference proceedings indicate that most participants were aware of the shortcomings of the direct-historical method (O'Brien and Lyman 2001), but it also is apparent that in their desire to convert the archaeological record into an ethnographic record they were willing to accept that incorrect ethnic and/or linguistic identifications might be made. The direct historical approach was the preferred method for the job (Lyman and O'Brien 2001a), but McKern clearly thought such a procedure was better left unattended.

Recall what McKern said in his June 14 letter to Guthe: "a determinant complex must be established through its occurrence as a constant complex at several sites." This recurrence-criterion feature, a crucial part of the MTM, would be repeated in later versions. Its significance resided in the fact that a larger unit could not be established on the basis of a single component. Others would later argue that a single component *was* sufficient and perhaps even preferable (see chapter 5). Guthe (1932[8]:1) had earlier said that similar components "may be found . . . but the identicality of [the] determinant traits" across those components would "not be widespread." In other words, multiple member components of a focus seemed to be unexpected, and when found those components would be similar but not identical, and they would be distributed over a limited geographic space. McKern et al. (1933[10]:3) were a bit more optimistic when they said that "it is very probable that two or more localities or sites will be found to contain almost identical determinant complexes." The key word was "almost," which was left unquantified.

What was the significance of recurrent (implying identical) or nearly identical components? For one thing, they demonstrated "the contemporaneous existence of several communities, all of which have a single culture in common" (McKern et al. 1933[10]:3). For another, according to McKern in his June 14 letter to Guthe, it permitted one to "assume that a given set of culture-indicative objects and data has a single cultural origin." This is the strongest statement of the phylogenetic implications of his taxonomic method that McKern ever made, but note that it is in a personal letter and that it concerns the relationships of components, not cultural taxa.

Harold S. Colton of the Northern Arizona Museum transmitted some thoughts on the classification method to Guthe, who forwarded them to McKern. After reading Colton's comments, McKern wrote to Guthe (June 30, 1933 [MPM]), noting that Colton misunderstood the concept of basic culture. Further,

> if such group names as Pueblo I, Pueblo II, etc., are to be employed in our classification, it should be clearly understood that the basis for the classification is culture complexes rather than temporal succession. This does not imply that the status of established chronological periods in the Southwest is to be questioned, but merely that our classification has nothing to do with temporal factors. And the reason for our insisting upon avoiding temporal and distributional factors, besides the involved complexity, is just as easily stated. We have been attempting to formulate a classificatory method that would apply equally to all archaeological provinces on the continent, a method that will prove useful in the formative period when classification can be so important a factor in keeping problems clearly outlined and so facilitating their solutions. . . . The Southwest is far ahead of us in available data, and has a classification of cultural sequence that will hold water. This is not true to a comparable extent in any other American province.
>
> I believe the two classifications, respectively based on culture and time, should remain separate, although one may contribute to the other, just as similar paleontological classifications have remained separate. A certain fossil form is classified purely on the basis of physical similarity as genus "x," species "y," regardless of the formation in which it occurs, but its occurrence in a certain stratum may demonstrate the fact that the formation is to be classified as "z" horizon of the Cambrian. The first classification is based upon physical type; the second, on temporal sequence.
>
> I believe it advisable to do the same thing in American archaeology, separating our cultural and temporal classifications, although one may contribute to the other. . . .
>
> There is little difference between this [paleontological] method and that suggested by Colton, excepting that we are not mixing the two classifications under a single intricate system. Colton seems, to some extent, to concede the desirability of keeping them separate. . . .
>
> I am considerably encouraged by the fact that Colton clearly understands our proposed system and seems willing to put it to the test.

> This classificatory method must sink or swim on its demonstrated usefulness, with the entire field, rather than a single province, in mind.

That Colton displayed a greater understanding than most archaeologists of what McKern and Guthe were attempting to do no doubt resided in the fact that he held a doctorate in biology. As we discuss in chapter 5, Colton was, along with Lyndon Hargrave and Harold Gladwin, attempting to adapt the Linnaean biological taxonomy for archaeological application in the Southwest. Guthe forwarded a copy of McKern's June 30 letter to Colton, along with his own comments on Colton's suggestions, and sent a copy of those comments to McKern (August 31, 1933 [MPM]). His remarks largely echoed those of McKern quoted above, but he also pointed out how the choice of determinants was critical because it influenced the resulting groups.

Guthe (August 31, 1933 [MPM]) also responded to comments from Henry B. Collins of the U.S. National Museum. In his letter to Collins, Guthe emphasized that different determinants had different "values" in the sense that a trait could be a determinant for a phase, for an aspect, or for a focus, noting in particular that "we need a clearer definition of the characteristics of the pottery to which we so blindly assign cultural names." The next day, Guthe responded to comments from Winslow Walker (letter from Guthe to Walker, September 1, 1933 [MPM]), noting that Walker's comments on the table in Guthe (1932[8]) confused "classes of cultures with those used as names of individual cultures." This problem was commonplace in Americanist archaeology at the time (Lyman et al. 1997). Guthe and McKern were using the terms *focus*, *aspect*, *phase*, etc., as ideational units—classes—of greater or lesser inclusiveness; the names they gave particular foci, aspects, phases, and so on were for empirical manifestations of these classes. Thus the units were like the units of biological taxonomy (Figure 3.1). The species, genus, family, order, and other units of biological taxonomy were taxa of different levels of inclusiveness. For example, the genus *Odocoileus* in North America includes at least two species (*O. virginianus* and *O. hemionus*), and the family Cervidae in North America includes several genera (*Odocoileus*, *Cervus*, *Rangifer*), each containing one or more species. The names of taxa are particular to sets of specimens; the taxonomic-unit names are classes that designate particular categorical ranks.

Because the particular foci, aspects, and other units in the table in Guthe (1932[8]) were classes and therefore had spatio-temporal distribu-

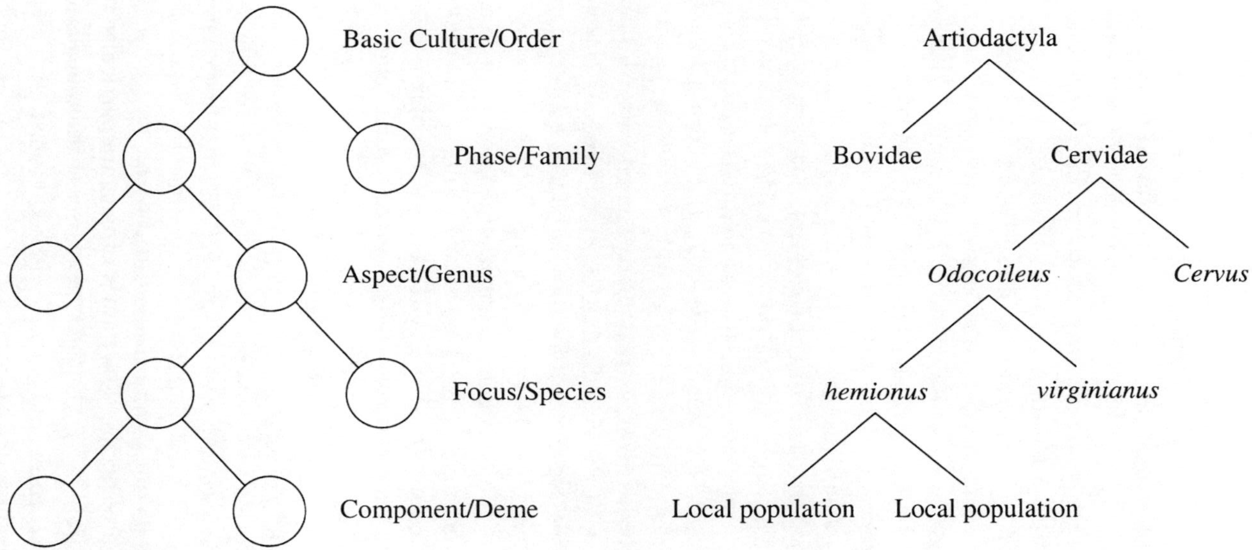

Figure 3.1. The similarity between W. C. McKern's system of taxonomic units *(left)* and the Linnaean biological taxonomy for the Class Mammalia, Order Artiodactyla *(right)*. Some taxa are omitted.

tions, some of their names included geographic (typically) or temporal designations (less often). Walker simply could not comprehend how this could be so if time and space were not used to help define the classes. Guthe was quite clear about this in his letter to Walker:

> The balance of your letter indicates a confusion in your mind between culture, space and time. It is impossible to define or characterize a culture in terms of either space or time, because neither of these are integral parts of a culture. Space and time are external forces having an influence upon a culture. An animal is not described, when it is said that it lived in New Mexico 10,000 years ago. Neither can one characterize a house by saying it was built in 1837 in Pennsylvania. Both these objects must be described by listing their several parts in such terms as to enable the student to distinguish them from similar parts in similar objects. The same is true of cultures, which must be defined in terms of their elements, so that we can distinguish between different cultural complexes. We cannot compare cultures until we know their similarities and differences. After cultures have been defined, then they can be *arranged* in both space and time.

Importantly, in his remarks to Walker (shared with McKern), Guthe also pointed out that the classification scheme "has been carefully developed so that phases, aspects, and foci may be added or combined or shifted in rank without upsetting the whole structure." This is precisely the benefit said to attend the Linnaean taxonomy (chapter 2). It is sufficiently flexible that all or some of the particular groups of one rank can shift in rank in light of new evidence. Further, a particular group of specimens comprising a component might change its focus membership, just as a deme in biology could, in the 1920s, change its species membership. The determinants used to specify the particular units of all ranks except the least inclusive—components were stratigraphically associated sets of artifacts—and the most inclusive—basic cultures were merely adaptive patterns—depended on the materials studied. Changing the samples studied would change the list of determinants, a point McKern recognized (see below), although its full significance escaped him.

On September 27 McKern (MPM) responded to a letter from Charles Keyes, director of the Iowa Archaeological Survey. McKern noted that the terms *focus*, *aspect*, *phase*, and so on had been agreed on by the participants in the December 10, 1932, informal meeting in Chicago, but other terms might be better, should such be suggested. The important thing, in McKern's view, was that the discipline "start out using some standardized set of terms." This would certainly have facilitated communication among archaeologists, just as the terms *species*, *genus*, *family*, and so on facilitated communication among biologists. They all knew more or less what they were talking about, although they might quibble over whether a particular species should be assigned to genus A or B. McKern noted that various particular units might imply certain spatial limits given their names, but that was an incorrect implication. McKern reminded Keyes that the term *Neanderthal* came from Germany, but specimens with this name were known in "western Asia." The results of applying the classification were subject to modification in light of new data. The important thing in McKern's view was that "the student will have to become familiar with arbitrary definitions, as is the case with any classificatory terms." What McKern meant by "arbitrary definitions" was that the definitive criteria of a taxonomic class were decided on by the analyst in light of the specimens under scrutiny. That is, contrary to Linnaeus's dictum that the genus gives the (definitive) characters, which implies that the taxa are natural and observable and thus discoverable, McKern held it to be the other way around—the definitive characters chosen by the archaeologist yield the taxa.

Archaeologists who responded to early versions of the MTM regularly confused the nested classes of progressively greater inclusiveness proposed by McKern et al. (1933[10]) with empirical units such as Basket Maker or Oneota. Harold Gladwin of Gila Pueblo, Arizona, wrote to Guthe on October 31, and Guthe responded on December 4, forwarding copies of Gladwin's letter and his response to McKern (MPM). That Gladwin confused ideational units and empirical units is apparent in one of his statements: "I have gone very carefully over the circular issued by yourself and Dr. McKern and I have come to the conclusion that any attempt to adopt a uniform method of designating cultural progress designed to cover both the Southwest and the Mississippi Valley must prove unsatisfactory to one of the two groups." Gladwin also disliked the terminology for the system of units. Guthe found himself yet again having to explain that the classification involved a method, not a result, and the terms used really did not matter as long as everyone used the same terms and units in the same way.

Some of the most interesting correspondence occurred when Deuel wrote to McKern on January 14, 1934 (MPM). After noting that there might be more than two basic cultures in the "eastern United States (east of the Mississippi)," Deuel remarked, "There seem to be some components that object to being squashed into either compartment,—more information [may] corroborate, or reverse this conclusion." McKern's January 25 response (MPM) is revealing:

I am not at all sold on the assumption that there are only two basic cultures east of the Mississippi. In fact, I shall be extremely surprised if additional basic cultures are not forthcoming, even on the basis of existing data. I am sure that Guthe shares my opinion in this; in fact, I believe that he has attempted to name several other cultures in a tentative classification.

You mention the difficulty encountered in attempting to assign certain components to a single focus. This sort of thing is to be expected, not only for components, but for foci, aspects and, conceivably, phases as well. This is due to the fact that our classification, like every other classification that has ever been devised, is purely artificial, not natural. That means that we should expect all degrees of intermediate manifestations which must be arbitrarily assigned to one side of the classificatory division line or the other, as the data seem to warrant. Since new data may change the apparent relationship criteria, it may be necessary, in instances, to change the classification from time to time in conformation with new information. This condition of affairs is true of all methods of classification, and is particularly noticeable in paleontology.

A number of things in McKern's statement warrant comment. First, biological taxonomists after 1859 had a theory that indicated that the systematist or classifier did not make taxa. Rather, taxa *existed* because they had been made by the natural process of Darwinian evolution and thus could be discovered. Biological classification was *natural* and not artificial *if*, and this is an extremely important if, one ignored the fact that evolutionary descent with modification comprised continuous change over time within a lineage. Within-lineage (vertical) variation was continuous, but between-lineage (horizontal) variation was discontinuous. Those who studied extant organisms had no trouble recognizing distinct taxa (for example, Mayr 1942), whereas those who studied the fossil record realized that the taxa they identified within a lineage were arbitrary sections of a continuum (for example, Simpson 1944, 1951). McKern's "intermediate manifestations" reflected the fact that evolution was continuous over time and, further, that *cultural* evolution was reticulate such that between-lineage differences were smeared. Thus, formal variation was continuous both horizontally and vertically. Assigning specimens to a particular class therefore demanded "arbitrary" assignment "to one side of the classificatory division line or the other" because the definitive criteria of the two sides were unclear. In a way, McKern was correct because he had identified what later was termed "the materialist paradox": How do we classify the continuously various phenomena of evolution with discontinuous units such as biological taxa (Dunnell 1995)?

McKern had the answer: Use ideational units (classes) as taxa. But because he was coming up with the definitive criteria for those units extensionally, his classes were preordained to blend together and give the appearance of transitional specimens. This relates to another thing to note in McKern's letter. His relationship criteria must denote determinants, and McKern was correct that these will change as the materials compared change. The determinants were extensionally derived and depended on the cultural units being compared. McKern cannot be faulted for any ambiguous wording, given when he was writing. Recall from chapter 2 that in the 1930s the typological species concept still had a strong grip on biological systematics and that this concept would not be replaced until the late 1930s. That concept resulted from the fact that definitive criteria of taxa were formal characters that were extensionally derived; the concept was an attempt, if only implicit, to deal with transitional specimens by assigning them the rank of terminal taxa.

The second circulated version of the MTM (McKern et al. 1933[10]) had considerable influence on Americanist archaeology. Earl Bell of the University of Nebraska was so impressed that he not only directed his students to use it (for example, Cooper 1936; Dunlevy 1936) but also reprinted much of that version (Bell 1936). Frank M. Setzler of the Bureau of American Ethnology wrote to McKern on February 3, 1934 (MPM), noting that: "Duncan Strong and I have been tremendously interested in the new archaeological classification. Both of us have given considerable thought to the matter but it seems that each time we were prepared to write you our reactions, either he or I left for the field." Strong would later respond to yet another version of the classification method.

THE THIRD CIRCULATED VERSION: 1934

McKern presented the next version of the MTM in May 1934 at the Central Section of the American Anthropological Association meeting in Indianapolis. That version was distributed in August (Deuel 1935a) as Circular No. 17 of the National Research Council's Committee on State Archaeological Surveys (McKern 1934[11]). It was reprinted in 1937 as an appendix to the NRC-sponsored 1935 Indianapolis Archaeological Conference proceedings (National Research Council 1937), where the method was the topic of considerable discussion (O'Brien and Lyman 2001). Before turning to that discussion, it is worth summarizing what was different in this new version and to review the correspondence McKern received in response to Circular No. 17.

The first obvious difference in the 1934 version is that it is considerably longer than the immediately previous version. McKern et al. (1933[10]) comprised 2,236 words, whereas the 1934 version (McKern 1934[11]) comprised 5,020 words. The 125 percent increase in length is not just the result of more elaborate discussion and detailed definitions. A considerable portion of the increase resulted from the inclusion of examples of determinants. McKern gave detailed lists of the pottery determinants of the Mississippi basic culture, the Upper Mississippi Phase of that basic culture, the Wisconsin Aspect of that phase, and the Mississippi Uplands Focus of that aspect in order to illustrate the increasing degree of specificity in such lists. McKern did not explain why he chose characters and character states of pottery to illustrate that the number of determinants decreases and the generality of those determinants increases as one read up the system of taxonomic units. We suspect his choice reflected two things. First, at the time, everyone acknowledged that pottery was a complex cultural trait that could be reduced to any number of finer-scale traits (what we would call characters or character states). In other words, pottery was an excellent choice for what McKern wanted to illustrate (see below). Second, it had been demonstrated time and again since about 1915 that were one to classify pottery in particular ways, all kinds of implications would be suggested, not the least of which was that time could be measured (Lyman and O'Brien 1999; Lyman et al. 1997; O'Brien and Lyman 1999b).

McKern (1934[11]) devoted a paragraph or two to determinant traits. His focus was on their scale. He noted that "the difference in complexity between objects such as simple bone awls and pottery vessels" presented a difficulty because whereas the first seemed to represent a single determinant, the latter could be conceived of as "comprising a number of determinants." Pottery "certainly is more culturally indicative than a pointed fragment of bone" because "single pottery traits" might be temper, handle shape, or surface treatment. Not only did McKern make it clear that determinants could be of varying scale, he seemed at least intuitively aware of the fact that *functional types* of artifacts such as bone awls were less "culturally indicative" than what had for several decades been termed *styles* or *stylistic types* (Lyman et al. 1997). Of equal importance for correct implementation of the method, McKern should have clarified how the determinant status of a trait was ascertained, but he did not. This would be a major topic of discussion the following year.

McKern added considerable length to the 1934 version by devoting a paragraph to the culture-area concept and several paragraphs to describing what he perceived to be shortcomings of the direct-historical method. With respect to the first, he noted that the geographic boundaries drawn by anthropologists were unknown to "American aborigines" and that no culture area was static throughout the history of human occupation of North America. With respect to the direct-historical method, McKern repeated the earlier cautions of Swanton (1932a, 1932b), noting that the method often resulted in the classification of an archaeological manifestation on the basis of linguistic and/or sociopolitical identity. He emphasized the fact that archaeological data comprise "material culture, and in no instance includes linguistic data" (McKern 1934[11]:1). His statements seem to have largely fallen on deaf ears, as archaeologists continue today to debate the validity of such classifications (for example, Hughes 1992; chapters and references in Terrell 2001).

In McKern's view, a linguistic or sociopolitical classification of archaeological material did "not ideally answer the needs of the archaeologist" (1934[11]:1). He did not explicitly identify the needs of the archaeologist but implied that a linguistic or sociopolitical classification of archaeological manifestations was equivalent to a paleontologist's "statement that *Elephas primigenius* [now *Mammuthus primigenius*] is the mammoth" (1934[11]:1). McKern's point seems to have been that it is unclear what such a result gains archaeology; the two terms he gave for a particular proboscidean are effectively synonyms. He emphasized that "archaeological classification must necessarily be based on criteria available to the archaeologist" (1934 [11]:2) and that the purpose of classification is to make it possible "for one student to describe phenomena in terms readily comprehensible to another student versed in the taxonomic method. It reduces a multiplicity of facts to simplicity and order, and supplies a standardized terminology without which students encounter difficulty in conversing on a common subject" (1934[11]:3). In other words, a useful classification will enhance communication because it serves as a good information storage-and-retrieval system (for example, Mayr 1995). Thus the terms *Mammuthus* and *mammoth* not only have internationally agreed-on meanings, they denote rather large, extinct proboscideans plus a host of other facts such as when they existed and where their remains might be found. But there is more to the classification than simply facilitating communication.

The differently ranked units—McKern identified the same four units (basic culture, phase, aspect, focus) as in the previous version (Table 3.1)—denoted different scales of relatedness such that "more inclusive parent cultures" (1934[11]:4) and "subdivision[s] of an even larger cultural order" (1934[11]:5) were recognizable. This means that the interpretive significance of the classification resides in its implications of relationships among cultural taxa, just as with the Linnaean taxonomy's implications for biological taxa in the 1930s. McKern did not explicitly state that those relationships included phylogenetic ones (he was more explicit in McKern 1939[15]) for the simple reason that "under the blending influences of diffusion and cultural growth by invention, there can be no hard and fast natural [cultural taxa]" (p. 9) equivalent to biological taxa. This statement echoed concerns raised by Kroeber (1923) as well as the hesitancy of biological taxonomists of the time. Nevertheless, based on earlier and later correspondence and published statements, McKern seems to have believed that a good taxonomic classification of cultural manifestations could in fact reveal *something* about the phylogenetic history of the included cultural units.

McKern received feedback on his 1934 statement. Strong wrote to McKern (September 24, 1934 [MPM]) that he had

> just finished re-reading your latest on taxonomy and agree heartily with all you say. As an objective approach to culture history some such system is obviously essential. The classification proposed for the Mid-west seems very promising and I am working over my Plain's data to see how they fit in. . . .
>
> As you know, my primary drive has been toward securing time perspective. As a tool in this attempt I have emphasized the difference between pseudo-history (based on tradition or general geographic location) and actual history (based on adequate documentation and exact geographic location). . . . As you point out, the two approaches, classificatory and true historic, must go hand in hand. The classificatory system organizes the entire field and the exact historic method, where applicable, forms a definite scientific bridge between the known and the unknown. In final analysis, it seems to me, archaeology must either be culture history or sterile antiquarianism, hence the necessity for obtaining time perspective will always be paramount.
>
> As I see the situation, the proposed taxonomic classification must be separated from only time sequence classification. Thus, in any study, there would be two tables or charts, one of objective relationship and another of time sequence, while the conclusion of the paper would serve to integrate the two. Is this your conception of the matter? One aspect of time, or at least historicity, could possibly be introduced into the taxonomic classification, i.e., in regard to the component, where the term historic, protohistoric or prehistoric, as the case might be, could be bracketed. In certain cases where tree rings apply this might be an actual date. Naturally in all cases, stratification and mixture at a site would lead to two or more components, or

> possibly one mixed component? I would appreciate your reactions toward this matter of time sequence in relation to taxonomy when you have a chance to write.

McKern provided his reactions in a letter to Strong on October 11 (MPM):

> I am entirely in sympathy with you in your attack on the problem of the temporal factor in cultural history, which I sincerely hope will result in a temporal taxonomic method serving to bridge the gap between the cultural classification and ethnological or known historic factors. Culture and time can not be treated in a single classification, but it does not follow that a temporal classification and a cultural classification can not be coordinated. Something in that line must be done; without a consideration of time sequence the archaeological picture loses all perspective.
>
> The closest parallel in method that comes to my mind is that employed in paleontology. A given fossil is biologically classified according to physical peculiarities, regardless of time horizon. A temporal classification follows, and the biological specimen, although classified as such independently, may serve as a marker for the particular temporal formation in which it occurs, or it may have little significance in the time scale, as the case may be.

McKern concluded by noting that he agreed "entirely" with Strong's suggestion that two charts—one showing "objective," or cultural, relationships and one showing time sequence—could be integrated in the conclusions.

McKern's 1934 version of the classification method was more polished and more detailed than previous versions, but it was still misunderstood by some, whereas others simply could not abide its lack of consideration of time and geographic space. Regardless, it was prompting much discussion of method in the midwestern and the eastern United States. This was exemplified by a conference held in late 1935.

THE INDIANAPOLIS ARCHAEOLOGICAL CONFERENCE OF 1935

In its efforts to improve the quality of archaeological research in the United States, the National Research Council's Committee on State Archaeological Surveys sponsored three meetings of professional and avocational archaeologists. The first was held in St. Louis in 1929; the second in Birmingham, Alabama, in 1932; and the third in Indianapolis in 1935 (O'Brien and Lyman 2001). It was at the last that McKern's method was discussed in some detail. Much of the discussion about the method was transcribed and published as part of the proceedings of that meeting (National Research Council 1937), and thus we have a detailed record of what a number of archaeologists thought about it. The discussions also reveal the contributions of others to what would be the final published version of the method (McKern 1939[15]). McKern attended the meeting in Indianapolis, and some of his comments included in the discussions are quite interesting. A sign of the importance of the proposed method in the view of the participants is found in the fact that McKern's 1934 version was included as an appendix (McKern 1937b) in the published proceedings of the conference, despite the fact that that version was modified during the course of the conference discussions.

Guthe (1937:5) laid out the purpose of the meeting in the preface to the mimeographed report that emanated from it:

> The conference was called for the specific purpose of discussing the technical problems relating to the comparative study of the archaeological cultures in the upper Mississippi Valley and Great Lakes region. Detailed descriptions of the results of the investigation of individual sites were not pertinent to the meeting. The group of delegates was purposely kept small in order to insure the freedom of informal discussion, and was confined to research students who were interested either in the archaeological problems of a restricted part of the area, or in the comparative significance of these problems with relation to similar ones in other areas.

Guthe touched on some of the "technical problems" related to the comparative study of archaeological cultures. In his view, the greatest need was for "a uniform methodology and a greater correlation" of the various investigations that had been taking place with increasing frequency over the previous decade (Guthe 1937:v). McKern (1937a:1) presented the opening paper at the conference and was explicit about such needs: "I can't discuss local Wisconsin problems without touching on general problems. These center around an inadequacy of analytical and systematic methods, and terminology. Our major problem is determining how to cooperate to mutual advantage with students of cultures similar to those in Wisconsin. We have great difficulty understanding each other because we do not do things in the same way, and lack a systematized terminology. My specific problems relate to cultural manifestations and their place in the classification."

When the Indianapolis conference was held, there had been few previous attempts to apply the taxonomic method, and most of these exemplified, technically, misapplications (for example, Deuel 1935a, 1935b), a topic we consider in more detail in chapters 4 and 5. Only McKern's (1934[11]) discussion of Wisconsin data illustrated a correct application. By *correct application* we mean (1) that the method and system of units were employed in the manner originally conceived by McKern, particularly the bottom-up construction of ever more-inclusive cultural units based on the identification of determinants, and (2) that a distinction was made between determinant traits and other, merely descriptive, traits.

At the time of the Indianapolis conference there were four levels of units in the classificatory method—basic culture, phase, aspect, and focus—the same four that were in McKern et al. (1933[10]). During the discussions at Indianapolis, Frank H. H. Roberts (U.S. National Museum) suggested dropping the term *basic culture* because of the confusion surrounding the term, and he suggested the term *base* be used in its place. Later in the discussions, Guthe brought this possibility up again and suggested as well that a new level, *pattern*, be inserted between *phase* and *base*. Pattern was a term that had been discussed for some time (Table 3.1), and its insertion into the hierarchy at Indianapolis created the five-tier system that appeared in the final version of the method (McKern 1939[15]).

It was a common misconception among those who were not part of the group that devised the MTM at the informal Chicago meeting of 1932 that *component* was the sixth, and lowest, *taxon* in the system. McKern and others consistently warned that this was not the case. Rather, a component was "the manifestation of a given culture at a single site" (McKern et al. 1933[10]:4) or "the manifestation of any given focus at a specific site" (McKern 1934[11]:4). This unit "serves to distinguish between a site which may bear evidence of several cultural occupations, each foreign to the other, and a single, specified manifestation at a site" (McKern 1934 [11]:4). In other words, components were the empirical units that were classified as members of particular foci, aspects, phases, patterns, and bases; the latter five units were the classificatory taxa—literally, the classes—comprising the system. This was a major stumbling block for many, and we wonder if McKern inadvertently contributed to the confusion with his example. Recall that in that example he focused on pottery, and in his discussion of how to classify that pottery he described a taxonomic classification. The parallels between biological classification of organisms into taxa and McKern's classification of artifacts into cultural taxa are also apparent in how organisms and artifacts themselves are classified (Figure 3.2). One begins with discrete organisms comprising a local population or deme, or with discrete artifacts comprising an archaeological component. Specimens of either sort are classified on the basis of their characters and character states into terminal taxa. But not just any set of specimens will do; the classified specimens must somehow comprise a unit larger than a discrete specimen. McKern was not very clear about this for several more years (see chapter 4). He was, during the middle 1930s, implying and illustrating by example what is shown in Figure 3.2. There is no clear indication in that figure of where taxa as classes start, and we think *this* contributed to the mistaken impression that components were taxa. There were other problems as well.

Those attending the Indianapolis conference had a difficult time deciding whether known cultural manifestations should be labeled as aspects or foci, and some were irritated that their favorite manifestation might lose its primacy. Take, for example, the following exchange:

> MCKERN: It seems to me that the majority of Hopewell traits are un-Woodland.
>
> DEUEL: Outside of Ohio, our Central Basin largely consists of Woodland characteristics, and there are a number of sites called Hopewell that have traits like Marksville [Avoyelles Parish, Louisiana] and others which cannot be placed.
>
> ROBERTS: Would you say that in your Central Basin, except for Ohio, you have about an equal division of Woodland and Mississippi traits? It seems to me that your separate Pattern here is Hopewell. You may find out that it is a northern extension of your southern pattern. Why not make the Pattern Hopewell?
>
> GUTHE: As a matter of convenience, what is there wrong in thinking in terms of Aspects and Phases? Include a Hopewell Phase under the Central Basin Pattern.
>
> MCKERN: Why can't we say an unnamed Pattern under which we get Hopewell?
>
> SETZLER: Why not use Hopewellian Phase instead of Hopewell?
>
> MCKERN: Hopewell is also a Component in itself. Use the Scioto Valley [Ohio] as Focus.
>
> SWANTON: . . . I thought it was understood that ethnological terms be excluded? (National Research Council 1937:61)

As in the Linnaean taxonomy, there were neither rules nor particular characters to consult when designating a taxon as a particular rank.

Try as they might, many of the participants couldn't shake their tendency to cling to subjective impressions of evolutionary relationships between various units, just as biologists of the time were grappling with the

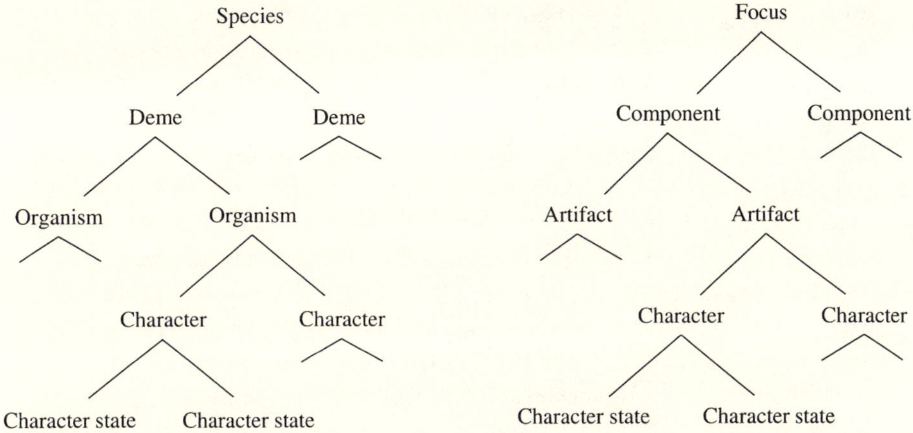

Figure 3.2. Alignment of a taxonomic classification of organisms and a taxonomic classification of artifacts. Compare this arrangement to the one in Figure 3.1.

Linnaean taxonomy. For example, Setzler stated, "I want a single Pattern called Mississippi, with all pottery-agriculture divisions listed under it." He then asked, "Can't you make your divisions under Phases instead of the Pattern?" (National Research Council 1937:60). Deuel realized what Setzler was getting at: "It seems to me what is bothering Setzler is the fact that he sees a genetic relationship between the Gulf cultures and the Mississippi cultures, which should be if the two are classified on the basis of their inherent traits" (National Research Council 1937:60). By "inherent traits" we suspect Deuel was referring to "determinant traits." Whether we are correct in our suspicion or not, the concept of determinant traits was the subject of considerable discussion.

McKern, perhaps inadvertently, started the ball rolling with respect to traits in his opening remarks: "A great problem is bound up with the classification of specific types of materials such as pottery, stone implements, bone, shell, etc. Some of these, such as pottery, are sufficiently complex to require a classification before they may be adequately described. Comparative research will be greatly facilitated by the use of a standard classification, which should be worked out as soon as possible" (McKern 1937a:2). Means of classifying pottery in particular were then under consideration and would see extended discussion in the next several years (for example, Colton and Hargrave 1937; Ford and Griffin 1938; Guthe 1934; Hargrave 1932). William S. Webb (University of Kentucky) was explicit when he asked, "How is one to know what a trait is?" (National Research Council 1937:54). James B. Griffin (University of Michigan) responded, "A good deal of the reliability of the traits an individual selects depends on his archaeological experience. . . . I [Griffin 1935] tried to separate things which I thought would be significant" (National Research Council 1937:54). Griffin noted that this separation sometimes involved, for example, using as a trait bone awls, other times turkey-metatarsal awls, and still other times notched turkey-metatarsal awls. Griffin's point related to scale, which McKern alluded to when he noted that pottery was so technologically complex as to warrant a classification separate from other, less complex, artifacts. McKern later remarked, "You have complex objects which comprise a group of traits, such as pottery, and you also have simple objects with perhaps only one trait" (National Research Council 1937:55).

William Ritchie (Rochester Museum of Arts and Sciences) stated that "there is a difference in trait determinants and link traits.[2] Bone awls are found all over the world. . . . I wouldn't say they attain diagnostic value. . . . Where is a beveled adze found except in our Archaic Algonkin, where it becomes a trait determinant? I say the link trait is the bone awls and the beveled adze is a determinant trait" (National Research Council 1937:54). McKern then remarked, "This is the difference between general and specific traits. It applies to the culture classification as a whole. A bone awl becomes a diagnostic trait for a specific division. When you come to an aspect of that phase, you have subvarieties of this same implement. The subvarieties are not determinants for the whole area, but for the smaller group. What you have to consider is the cultural significance of any trait—either as a link or a diagnostic trait. If its application is limited, it is a determinant for a smaller group" (National Research Council 1937:54–55).

After more discussion, Guthe asked, "How are we going to describe these traits? How to differentiate between the character of the traits? My suggestion is that we try to define a linked trait and a diagnostic trait. Can we define a diagnostic trait in general terms?" (National Research Council 1937:56).

McKern responded to Guthe's question: "A *diagnostic trait* is a trait which applies only to that class and is unique for that class. A *link trait* is one which ties it in with another group. We have what we are calling a diagnostic trait for a phase which is not found anywhere else. But within that phase, that diagnostic trait may become a link trait for a smaller group" (National Research Council 1937:56) (Figure 3.3a). Griffin agreed

2. The terms *link traits* and *linked traits* were used interchangeably throughout the 1930s. Because McKern (1939[15]) finally settled on *linked traits* in the final published manuscript, which became the most widely cited version of the MTM, we use it here unless *link traits* appears in a direct quotation.

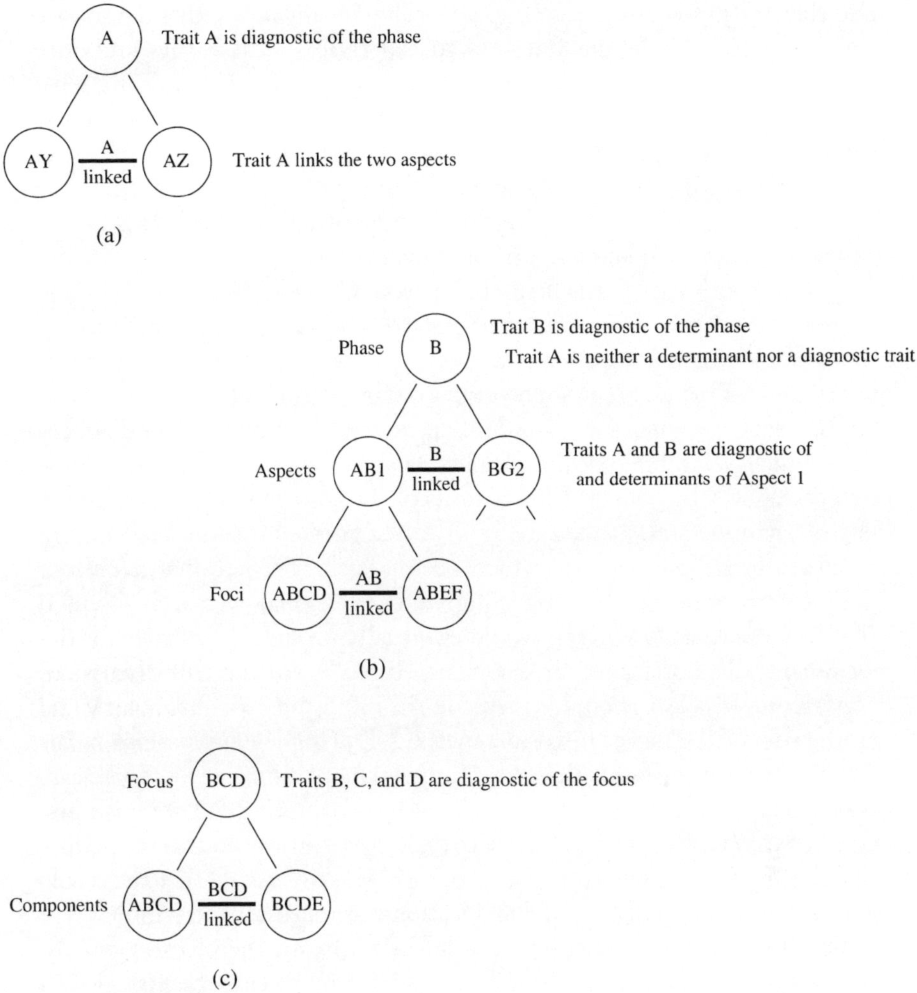

Figure 3.3. Three models of the status of a culture trait as determinant, diagnostic, or linked discussed at the 1935 Indianapolis Conference: (a) W. C. McKern's model; (b) James B. Griffin's model; (c) William Ritchie's model. Each circle represents a cultural taxon of some rank, and each capital letter represents a culture trait.

with this and remarked that "you might find traits in foci which would be linked traits between them but could not be determinant traits in the phase" (National Research Council 1937:57) containing those foci (Figure 3.3b). Ritchie then said, "Diagnostic traits of components form a focus and become link traits between components" (National Research Council 1937:57). We think Ritchie misspoke here, given his use of these terms elsewhere (Ritchie 1937, 1938). He probably meant to say that diagnostic traits of a focus hold the status of linked traits at the taxonomic rank of that focus's member components (Figure 3.3c). This is basically what McKern had said (Figure 3.3a). What they were all driving at was that the status of a trait depended on the particular position in the hierarchy in which the trait was being considered (Figure 3.3).

Guthe suggested that "a diagnostic trait of any culture class is one which occurs only in it and not in the culture class of the same order [category, rank] with which it is being compared" (National Research Council 1937:57). McKern suggested omitting "of the same order" because he thought one might compare a phase with a focus, which were units of different rank. This was true—one might compare units of different rank—but that such a comparison would influence the status of a trait as diagnostic or linked is, in biological taxonomy, false because that status should be influenced only by comparisons of units of the *same* rank. McKern at least intuitively understood this. Finally, Guthe suggested that a linked trait of a culture be defined as "one which occurs both in it and in the culture classes with which it is being compared" (National Research Council 1937:57). McKern (1939[15]) would eventually provide definitions for determinant, diagnostic, and linked traits, largely following this discussion.

McKern was clear about his views on the importance of chronology and on the role of the direct historical method. During the discussions at Indianapolis, he remarked, that "it is important to find stratified sites or, lacking these, to connect any sites revealing a primitive culture with history" (National Research Council 1937:7). Later in the course of the discussions, he elaborated on the latter point: "It seems to me that the whole purpose of our archaeological classification is to permit us to handle these materials conveniently until we can tie them in with the historic groups, but we can't force the issue. In the first place, I insist that the historic approach is a secondary method, for the simple reason that in a vast majority of cases, the first thing with which you come in contact is cultural debris, which cannot be related. As soon as you know you have a culture complex, other things being favorable, you have a chance to associate it with materials of some historic group. Until then, you have no right to assign it to a historical group. As a general thesis, the recurring complex method comes first, and then the direct historical method" (National Research Council 1937:53). McKern was correct in his assertion that the direct historical method depended on the similarity between a trait list or complex derived from an archaeological manifestation and that derived from a historically documented group (Lyman and O'Brien 2000, 2001a). He overstated his case, however, by characterizing the direct historical approach as a "secondary method." We think he meant that it should be applied second in order, after the recurring complex method. This would have been more accurate and less offensive phrasing to those who advocated the direct historical approach (see chapter 5).

Several individuals expressed concern over what exactly comprised the two generally agreed-on basic cultures (bases) then evident in the Midwest—Mississippi and Woodland (Deuel 1935a). Others suggested that the addition of a new categorical rank—pattern—would muddy the waters. Cole, who could not attend the conference due to illness, had transmitted a letter to the conference that was read by Guthe. The significance of some of Cole's remarks escaped the notice of those expressing their doubts about the standardization of classificatory method. Cole anticipated those doubts: "That the tentative classification set up at Pecos [in 1927] was one of the most important advances in southwestern archaeology is generally accepted. That it was not final is shown by the changes and modifications which have taken place. Now the surveys and excavations in southern Arizona indicate that further modifications must be made. It is not *necessary* that *a scheme be perfect to prove useful*" (National Research Council 1937:40).[3] McKern and Guthe had been making this point often in their correspondence with each other and with those who had commented on the earlier versions of the method, yet others seemed unable to grasp the notion.

Cole did something else in his letter. He wrote that to "fill in" the categorical units—foci, aspects, phases, basic cultures—"we should, *ideally*, excavate and describe such a number of sites in each area that we could clearly see all the relationships; then we should set up a *focus* or *foci*. These in turn would be placed in the larger groupings. But *practically*, if we wait for such data we will remain in the chaotic condition of 1930 for another generation" (National Research Council 1937:41). Cole was suggesting that to build an accurate classification of archaeological manifestations from the bottom up was impractical because that demanded a hundred-percent sample, something that was unattainable. There was, however, an alternative. Cole noted that "we have broad surveys; we are in a position to set up a tentative scheme of *basic cultures*, *phases*, *aspects*, and *foci*. We are justified in such action *if* we keep in mind that this is a tentative scheme. It is a scheme to be tested by evidence; it is to be changed, modified, or discarded at any time" (National Research Council 1937:41). It is

3. A copy of this letter, on file in the Special Collections of Regenstein Library, University of Chicago, indicates it was accurately transcribed in the NRC proceedings.

significant that Cole listed the units in order from the most general and inclusive to the most specific and least inclusive. What he was advocating was to build the classification from the top down. Enough was known to build large general units, just as Deuel (1935a, 1935b) had recently done (chapter 4), and then to divide those units into progressively smaller ones. As more data were generated, the division process would have to be checked and the units perhaps reconfigured, but that was acceptable in Cole's view.

Immediately following the reading of Cole's letter, Setzler remarked that he perceived two groups "approaching this classification problem from two extremes. One has attempted to start with the components and work out every single trait known at a single site and build up by careful comparison to the phase and basic elements. The other group starts with the basic cultures and works down to the components" (National Research Council 1937:42–43). He expressed preference for the bottom-up procedure. During the following discussion, McKern indicated that the top-down approach "illustrates the error in our method. You find one site with a very limited complex of traits, and you start out with a basic culture on this basis. We should be satisfied at this time to determine the focus, or component, then we may later determine the basic culture" (National Research Council 1937:46). What McKern characterized as an error rather nicely described the use of archetypes, or *Baupläne*. McKern's correct concern was whether these were in fact definable with any certainty. As his correspondence with Deuel (McKern to Deuel, letters of October 15, 1932, and January 25, 1934 [MPM]) indicates, he did not think such certainty existed. Others thought that perhaps McKern was completely ignoring the larger, more-inclusive categories of basic culture and phase. McKern assured them he was not: "I have perhaps overstressed the importance of starting in at the detailed end rather than the general. I didn't mean that we should entirely disregard the more general divisions. I simply meant that instead of starting there and working down, for the present we have a great deal less information about the higher divisions and should take our classifications tentatively. You can be much more absolute in your statement when you come to the detailed divisions. You should not place as much emphasis on the determinants of a culture we don't know, as on the details of a focus which we do know" (National Research Council 1937:47). Griffin seemed to side with McKern when he remarked, "We need a detailed site-by-site analysis to establish our foci and from them, our aspects and phases. It will be slow, tedious work, but the framework will be sound" (National Research Council 1937:49). Griffin knew of what he spoke because he had in fact just completed such a "slow, tedious" analysis (Griffin 1935; see chapter 4).

We suspect Cole brought up the distinction between top-down and bottom-up construction because the various early statements on the classificatory method were clearly predicated on the latter alternative. Deuel, however, had recently shown to Cole's satisfaction that the top-down procedure worked quite nicely and that it clearly maintained the definitive contents of the generally recognized units termed Woodland and Mississippi. It was not at all clear that the bottom-up procedure would do either. Recall that Deuel and Cole had both participated in the informal meeting of December 10, 1932, and thus knew what the classificatory method was all about and how it had originally been designed to work. Deuel even helped author the 1933 version of the method (McKern et al. 1933[10]). He would also make other, less well-known contributions to the method. But he also tested the top-down procedure. In chapter 4, we return to this and other contributions he made.

DISCUSSION

In his history of the development of the MTM, Griffin (1943:328) noted that in Guthe (1932[8]) "sites or groups of sites were called 'types of determinant complexes'" and that the grouping of sites was to be on the basis of similarity among traits and trait complexes. Here "the units themselves were determinant-complexes" said Griffin (1943:328–329). We agree with this reading of Guthe's manuscript. Griffin's (1943:329) reading of McKern et al. (1933[10]) suggested to him that "the units were characterized by certain traits which form a determinant-complex, and these special traits are called determinants because they segregate one division from another." We also agree with this assessment because McKern et al. (1933[10]:1) stated that determinants were "those particular traits among the known evidences of a material culture which, because of their individuality, serve to differentiate it from other cultures. These traits, or determinants, will differ in various cultures."

In Griffin's view, the 1932 version of the MTM emphasized similarities, whereas the 1933 version emphasized differences. In the 1932 version, Guthe (1932[8]:2) indicated that the "first and most important [consideration during the classification process was] the similarities of culture traits and complexes." McKern et al. (1933[10]:1) referred to the method as a "method of scientific grouping," similar to that used in linguistics and paleontology. In both, specimens are "primarily and essentially grouped according to their morphological similarities," and "the primary criteria of differentiation should be differences in the subject matter itself." Given these statements, we disagree with Griffin's assessment and find that there is no difference between the two versions. In both, grouping like with like in one pile and placing unlike in another pile was the recommended procedure.

Griffin (1943:329) suggested that McKern et al. took the approach of first recognizing "the largest and most general cultural divisions" and then "working from the top of the classificatory scale to the bottom, of deriving the specific cultural traits from the more general ones." Griffin indicated that McKern emphasized working from the top down because the method began with the most general division. Guthe (1932[8]:1) had written that because "in the archaeological field, our first contacts with cultures are, figuratively, at the tips of the branches rather than at the roots, [the] list of [cultural] types is begun with the smallest unit of cultural classification." Further, in characterizing geographically the results of applying the classification, Guthe (1932[8]:2) remarked that "the classification begins with the smallest geographic units and closes with the largest." This is clearly a bottom-up procedure. McKern et al. characterized the method as a grouping technique and listed the units from smallest, least inclusive to largest, most inclusive in their summary, suggesting a bottom-up procedure. However, they described the units in order from largest, most inclusive to smallest, least inclusive, noting that the former can be "subdivided" into the latter. This must be the source of Griffin's impression that the procedure was top-down. Slightly later, McKern (1934[11]) listed the units in top-down order, but in fact, when discussing how he used the method in Wisconsin, he described a bottom-up procedure.

Griffin (1943:330) believed that McKern (1934[11]) emphasized that "determinants were to be characteristic for the division which they served to identify and not traits differentiating one division from another," and Griffin argued that "this concept of determinant is at variance with that of [McKern et al. 1933[10]." We disagree with the first statement because McKern (1934[11]:6) characterized what he called *determinants* as suitable for "differentiation" of cultural "divisions," where a division was a particular taxonomic rank such as an aspect or focus. Further, McKern was more explicit here than virtually anywhere else, stating that "the character of a determinant will depend upon the type of cultural division for which it serves as a determinant" (1934[11]:6). The lower, less inclusive the rank, the more complex and specific were the determinants and the greater their number. In McKern's view this demanded that different kinds of artifacts, such as bone awls and pottery, each be organized in separate classifications such that simple artifacts provided perhaps one determinant, whereas complex artifacts provided multiple determinants. McKern (1934[11]:9) did "not believe that this is an overemphasis but that it fairly represents the value of pottery . . . as a culture indicator." McKern et al. noted that the smaller, less inclusive the cultural taxon, the more determinants one would expect. They also indicated that determinants would be quite general traits of basic cultures, but they did not mention that traits became more specific with the decreasing inclusiveness of the culture ranks. Thus we disagree with Griffin's assessment that McKern et al. (1933[10]) and McKern (1934[11]) were at variance with each other with respect to what a determinant comprised. Rather, the concept was simply more thoroughly developed in the latter and also was more explicit than in the former, just as might be expected during the evolution of an analytical method.

Griffin (1943:330) suggested that "the only demonstration of the use of traits at arriving at such a schematic arrangement was McKern's analysis of Upper Mississippi Phase pottery." The analysis to which Griffin refers is McKern's (1934[11]) discussion of Wisconsin materials. As far as we have been able to determine, Griffin was correct. This fact no doubt contributed to the regular failure of many so-called users of the method to follow its procedures faithfully. For example, it was in McKern's 1934 article that he first made clear what he termed the "recurring complex method," which he defined as "the comparative study of culture-indicative materials encountered at various sites, leading to the knowledge that a certain complex of culture traits, adhering together as a unit, occurs repeatedly at a number of sites" (1934[11]:10).

In McKern's view the recurring-complex method was important to the taxonomic method because the recurrence of a set of traits "typical for several sites" established "the fact that it is a true complex" (1934[11]:4). By "true complex" McKern meant that an idiosyncratic association of traits would not be expected to recur, nor would a mixture of the traits of two distinct cultures. A recurrent association of traits would indicate an internally homogeneous cultural unit of some scale—perhaps a tribe comprising multiple human groups, bands, or communities. Here McKern was wise because he emphasized, first, that criticisms leveled at the archaeologist's taxonomic method by ethnologists were aimed at the latter's "extraordinarily indefinite, inaccurate use of the term 'culture,' which for want of a more specific term, is made to serve a multitude of purposes for which it never was intended" (1934[11]:2). Second, McKern pointed out that ethnologists should temper their criticisms because they had nothing better to offer the needs of an archaeologist.

Interestingly, McKern et al. (1933[10]:3, 5) suggested that although archaeologists were interested in the "growth of cultures. . . . no implication of genetical relationship between communities is implied" by the results one might obtain from applying the taxonomic method. McKern's (1934[11]) so-called cultural affinities thus were of an ambiguous sort, just as they were in the biological taxonomy of the 1930s. McKern et al.'s (1933[10]:3) remark that "almost identical determinant complexes" among multiple components suggested "the contemporaneous existence of several communities" indicates that the measurement of temporal affinity was at least one initial goal of the taxonomy. The lack of a clear and explicit theoretical reason for the taxonomic method, together with allusions to linguistic, paleontological, and biological classifications, no doubt served to confuse the issue.

By the end of the 1935 Indianapolis conference, a number of issues with respect to McKern's proposed taxonomic method had been resolved. Importantly, it was clear that the status of a particular trait as a determinant or linked trait depended on the manner in which the trait was being used. The terminology for the cultural taxa had been firmed up to include the five ranks that would appear in the final published version of the method (Table 3.1). As well, McKern had produced in print the only example of applying the method that he ever would. Others earlier in the year had attempted to apply the method in one version or another. Sometimes they used the bottom-up construction procedure, other times they used the top-down procedure. Further, they did not always distinguish among determinant, diagnostic, and linked traits.

4
Subsequent Developments, 1935–1940

Shallow ideas can be assimilated; ideas that require people to reorganize their picture of the world provoke hostility. (J. Gleick 1987:38)

Prior to the December 6–8, 1935, Indianapolis conference, two individuals —Thorne Deuel and James B. Griffin—applied a version of the midwestern taxonomic method, although it is probably more correct to say that they misapplied it in various ways. Others would also apply the method in one form or another, but we reserve discussion of those applications for chapter 5. Here we focus on the Griffin and Deuel applications for several reasons. First, their efforts reveal ideas about the method that differ, to lesser and greater degrees respectively, from McKern's. Second, their efforts document why McKern was compelled to publish the final version of the method, which appeared in 1939. Deuel was a coarchitect of the MTM, but, as we will see, he never followed the blueprint. If one of the founders couldn't follow it, was it any wonder no one else could?

JAMES B. GRIFFIN AND THE FORT ANCIENT ASPECT: 1935

Griffin earned his doctorate from the University of Michigan in 1936 and continued his association with Carl Guthe's Ceramic Repository for the Eastern United States, which was housed in Michigan's anthropology museum. Griffin was present at the informal dinner meeting of December 10, 1932, in Chicago when early versions of the MTM (McKern 1932[7]; Guthe 1932[8]) were discussed. Further, he was aware of the circular letter of April 4, 1933 (McKern et al. 1933[10]), and of McKern's (1934[11]) presentation of a revised version of the method at the Central Section of the American Anthropological Association meeting in Indianapolis in May 1934. In March 1935 Griffin published a preliminary analysis of materials representing what was called the "Fort Ancient culture" of southern Ohio, northern Kentucky, and southeastern Indiana. In that piece he chose five sites "as the basis for a comparative study" (Griffin 1935:1). One of the goals of his study was to "determine whether these five sites might be considered an archaeological unit, and if so, where that unit could be placed in relation to more general, and more specific, cultures. Another aim is to ascertain whether there are smaller units within the Fort Ancient culture; in other words, do these five sites represent an essentially homogeneous group which cannot be divided, or do two or three sites have enough differences to warrant more than one cultural unit within the Fort Ancient group." Based on published reports for the five sites, plus personal examination of the collections from three of them, Griffin compiled trait lists for each, grouping the traits under six categories: stone artifacts, bone implements, bone ornaments, shell artifacts, burial traits, and miscellaneous traits. Pottery was deemed "a sufficiently complex subject to warrant separate consideration."

Griffin (1935) listed 123 nonpottery traits in chart form as to their presence or absence in each of the five collections. The data in that chart were converted to percentages of traits common to all five sites, common to any four sites, to any three sites, to any two sites, and to any one site. Griffin noted that "approximately forty percent [of the 123 traits] appear at all of the sites" and that "a substantial majority of the traits is present in at least four of the five sites." He then presented a series of charts, each of which summarized the proportion of traits in each of the six categories that were shared by each site and the total number of traits shared by each pair of sites. Griffin concluded that the distribution of traits across the sites suggested there were two smaller divisions into which the five sites could be sorted.

Pottery was characterized as comprising considerable variation in its empirical expression. Griffin listed various characters—temper, texture, hardness, surface finish, design, kind of handle, and shape of rim, lip, and body—and the various character states of each, such as shell or grit temper and body shapes of salt pan, bowl, or jar. Each character state was categorized as "abundant, medium, rare, or absent" for each site. On the basis of that chart Griffin (1935:3–4) concluded that "the division into at least two smaller units is accentuated." One site "seems to be intermediate between these two groups and to constitute, at least temporarily, a division by itself." Griffin then remarked, "If this analysis is considered in terms of McKern's system of culture classification, it will at once be apparent that these five sites have a substantial majority of their traits in common, and may therefore be called the Fort Ancient Aspect." He also noted that two sites that had "a preponderating majority of their traits in common, may be called a Focus" and that two other sites "belong to another Focus." He then noted that the "selection of determinants listed for the Fort Ancient Aspect, and for the two well-defined Foci within the Aspect, is based on the traits that are characteristic, first, of all the sites, and then of [each of the two foci]. Those traits that are present at all of the sites, or at four out of the five, may be taken as determinants of the Fort Ancient Aspect."

Griffin (1935:4) argued that the absence of various traits from several of the sites was a result of sampling error and cautioned that although he suspected that many of the determinants of the aspect would "also be determinants for the Phase and for the Basic Culture," those cannot be "chosen with any degree of accuracy until a number of Aspects have been compared in detail." Not surprisingly, he stated that the "only sound method of procedure by which to establish accurately Phase and Basic Culture determinants is to proceed from the most specific manifestations to the more general."

Griffin may have expressed preference for the bottom-up procedure of unit construction as the "only sound method," but in fact he had worked both from the top down and from the bottom up. He worked from the top down when he chose five sites that seemed to represent the Fort Ancient Aspect; had he not been working from the top down, he would have selected any number of sites irrespective of whether he thought they were members of the Fort Ancient taxon. Griffin worked from the bottom up when he was grouping the five sites into foci. His use of the relative frequencies of pottery traits to help him group sites into foci was relatively unique and was never part of the taxonomic method as developed by McKern. For example, in response to Griffin's (National Research Council 1937:54) remarks that he had used the relative frequencies of traits in his analysis, McKern (National Research Council 1937:55) argued, "I don't think you can say 75% means one thing, and 60% something else. We must take into consideration that we haven't a complete series. You must rule out the statistical method in the strict mathematical sense." Finally, Griffin (1935) listed what he thought were the determinants of the Fort Ancient Aspect and its two foci, but he did not mention that those determinants were a function of the sites he had studied. Ironically, he would later criticize Deuel for choosing sites/components thought to belong to a cultural taxon and then using the identification of the definitive traits of the taxon among those components as a legitimate test of the method.

Griffin (1937) published a brief paper on the Fort Ancient Aspect in the pages of *American Antiquity.* In it he summarized his earlier work and noted that there were now four foci included within the aspect, each of which was more internally homogeneous than any two of them were to each other. He summarized the geographic distribution of the Fort Ancient Aspect and then noted that several components appeared to be post-Columbian in age. Griffin then described what was known of the ethnic identity of groups in the area of the Fort Ancient Aspect and concluded that there was "one serious difficulty encountered in attempting to identify the Fort Ancient culture with" a particular ethnic group: "We simply do not know the nature of the material remains occurring at documented village sites of any of these peoples." Nevertheless, he suggested there were contacts between various of the "carriers of Fort Ancient culture [and] neighboring archaeological cultures." In Griffin's mind, then, archaeological cultures were in some sense equivalent to ethnographically documented units termed cultures.

We consider Griffin's (1943) later analysis of Fort Ancient in chapter 5. It is important here to be aware of his initial 1935 analysis of these materials because it represents one of the first detailed efforts to apply the method to archaeological materials. The same year that Griffin's analysis was published, two other applications were published, both of which contrast with Griffin's application and one of which received comment by Griffin. Thus we are provided with a unique glimpse of how two individuals thought of and applied the method during what we think of as the midpoint of its development. Contrasts between applications highlight that the method was a grouping procedure of classification that not only was incompletely developed and poorly understood but was void of a taxonomic (theoretical) basis.

THORNE DEUEL'S IDEAS

Seldom remarked in standard histories of Americanist archaeology are Thorne Deuel's contributions to the development of the classification method typically attributed to McKern. Deuel was a student of Fay-Cooper Cole's at the University of Chicago, beginning his work there in 1931 and earning his Ph.D. in 1935. He served as an assistant editor for *American Antiquity* from 1935 to 1939 (when McKern was editor) and as an instructor and research associate in anthropology at the University of Chicago from 1935 to 1937. He became director of the Illinois State Museum in 1938 and served in that capacity until 1963. Interestingly, Cole had offered McKern the director's job (Cole to McKern, October 3, 1930 [UC]), but

McKern turned it down (McKern to Cole, October 15, 1930 [UC]) and stayed at the Milwaukee Public Museum. Deuel corresponded regularly with McKern, and the two of them, together with Guthe, prepared the 1933 version of the MTM (McKern et al. 1933[10]). Subsequent to that contribution, Deuel's efforts can be divided into two parts—one involving the substantive research associated with his dissertation and one involving two unpublished papers he authored on the classification method. We consider these parts in turn.

Substantive Research

Most of Deuel's expertise with respect to the MTM came from his work with Cole, who chaired the anthropology department at the University of Chicago. In 1930 Cole initiated what was variously termed the "Archaeological Survey of the Mississippi Valley" (Deuel 1937c) or, more accurately, the "Pictorial Survey of Mississippi Valley Archaeology" (Deuel 1935a). The purpose of the project was to collect and provide "in one place a story in photographs and explanatory notes, of the various cultural manifestations in the Mississippi Valley, the Atlantic seaboard region, and the Western Plains" (Deuel 1937c:1). Deuel (1937c:6) wanted a set of data available for use by researchers and perhaps eventually to publish a volume comparable to Kidder's (1924) *An Introduction to the Study of Southwestern Archaeology.* One goal of the project was to produce albums of artifact illusrations and explanatory notes that would provide a "key by which particular sites can be culturally placed—their affiliations determined" (Anonymous n.d.:3). In other words, as Cole told Samuel Dellinger of the University of Arkansas (letter, February 18, 1933 [UC]), the project results would "allow us to illustrate in an album, type materials so that any person could quickly know what any particular culture is."

The project was initially undertaken in 1930 by Frank M. Setzler, who over the course of the first year compiled albums of notes and photographs of diagnostic artifacts for Ohio, Indiana, and Wisconsin (Deuel 1937c). Setzler accepted a position with the U.S. National Museum in the spring of 1931, at which time Deuel took over as director of the pictorial survey. Documents on file in the University of Chicago archives indicate funding for the survey was provided by the National Research Council, the Rockefeller Foundation, the University of Chicago's Social Science Research Committee, and the University of Chicago's anthropology department. Work continued into 1937. The collection compiled by Setzler and Deuel comprises more than 8,000 photographs and 2,700 pages of written documentation for fourteen states (Styles and Bade 1988). These materials are currently curated at the Illinois State Museum in Springfield.

When Deuel took over the project, he noted that "a method of classifying sites and materials was necessary to make [the project] practicable and render the results intelligible to students using the albums" of photographs and notes (Deuel 1937c:1–2). He also noted that a "method of classification of sites on the basis of the archaeological materials present was proposed about [the time he took over the survey] by W. C. McKern." This was the classification method Deuel used to organize the photographs, artifact drawings, and notes he acquired over the next several years (Styles and Bade 1988). His plan was to examine "materials from type sites in each state" in order to define and classify "cultures into patterns, phases, aspects, and foci" and to "establish at the University of Chicago the story in pictures of the variations in cultural manifestations" (Deuel 1937c:4–5). Deuel stated that the "analysis of type sites is followed by a comparison of traits and classification into foci in a manner analogous to the zoological system."

Deuel's knowledge of McKern's suggested classification method and his work on the pictorial survey had several visible results. He used the terms *component*, *phase*, and *basic culture* in the published version of the paper he presented at the 1932 Illinois State Academy of Science meeting and integrated the units of the first two categories into a suspected chronological sequence (Deuel 1933). He then published a paper summarizing some of the results of the survey in *American Anthropologist* (Deuel 1935a). In that paper he distinguished between two basic cultures—Mississippi and Woodland—and used the terms *determinant traits*, *diagnostic traits*, and *characteristic traits* but without definition. He cited McKern (1932[7]), McKern et al. (1933[10]), and McKern (1934[11]) and noted that the list of determinant traits for each basic culture was "tentative." That same year he completed his Ph.D. dissertation (Deuel 1935b), a portion of which became an appendix (Deuel 1937a) in Cole and Deuel's *Rediscovering Illinois*, which was published in 1937.

Deuel (1935a:429) speculated in the *American Anthropologist* paper that "the majority of those who have dealt with the broader aspects of Mississippi Valley archaeology have been struck by the fact that sites in the region show a tendency to group themselves into two large divisions on the basis of the artifacts, burials, and the circumstances of occurrence." His goal in writing the paper was to "outline our knowledge of these basic cultures in the light of a four year [pictorial] survey of the region." He noted that although the less-inclusive units—phases—of each basic culture differed among themselves, "fundamentally they have more in common than any one of them has with any phase" of the other basic culture. The bulk of his paper comprised a listing of the different traits of each basic culture, given in text, tabular, and figure form. The implication is that the listed traits were definitive of a unit, but this is debatable.

In his review of Deuel's article, Guthe (1936:250) pointed out that "[s]ince Mr. Deuel has not used the McKern method of classification nor the word 'determinant' in the sense that McKern defined it, his use of the terms 'Basic culture' and 'phase' is unfortunate in that it may lead the reader to assume that the article is based upon McKern's suggested taxonomic method of culture-type classification." How could Guthe make this statement, given that Deuel is listed as second author of McKern et al. (1933[10])? He could do it for the simple reason that Deuel in fact did *not* use the term *determinant* in the sense originally specified. Deuel merely listed what seemed to him to be traits that more or less characterized, but that were not necessarily definitive of, the Woodland and Mississippi basic cultures. As Guthe noted in his review, the "usefulness of McKern's method rests upon the degree to which it will be found to fit the actual conditions existing in components at single sites and whether or not these components can be grouped into foci, aspects and larger associations. Obviously, the only way in which this can be done is by a comparative study of the cultural manifestations of many individual components. It is impossible to characterize the determinants for a group of components, whether it be a focus or a basic culture, until we know the total trait content of each component" (Guthe 1936:249).

What Guthe was driving at, and what Deuel did not make clear, was that McKern sought to group similar manifestations on the basis of their determinants—their definitive traits—in the process building from the bottom up a classification of successively more-inclusive cultural units. Deuel was working on the pictorial survey in part to provide a key that others could eventually use to identify the cultural affiliation of various unknown archaeological manifestations. As a result he was building a classification from the top down through a process of dividing larger units into successively smaller, less-inclusive units. Some of the traits he listed were definitive of each of the units, but precisely which traits were definitive and which were merely descriptive had to be gleaned from close reading of his paper, together with making some leaps of faith.

Guthe pointed out the top-down nature of Deuel's effort clearly in a December 5, 1935, letter to Cole (UC). In it Guthe stated, "I do stand definitely on the other side of the fence concerning [Deuel's] method of application of this system. I grant you that the technique of setting up a working hypothesis defining basic cultures is theoretically sound. However, I do not feel that the actual facts at hand justify such a working hypothesis in the scientific sense at the present time. Thorne's grouping of materials is a statement of his own opinion as a result of his broad knowledge of the variability of materials in the Mississippi Valley. I do not think that it is a fair test or application of McKern's proposed system." Guthe was correct; it was *not* a fair test of the system of units because the method had been designed to work from the bottom up, not from the top down. The latter required the assumption that the large units were already well enough known to provide good starting points, something that McKern had argued against at Indianapolis in 1935 and that concerned Guthe as well. Despite the fact that Guthe made this point not only in his review of Deuel's article but also in his letter to Cole, who was Deuel's adviser at Chicago, Deuel (and Cole) ignored it.

Deuel's dissertation, completed in 1935, underscored the top-down nature of his procedure. In it Deuel (1935b:1) began by noting, more explicitly than McKern, that archaeologists had to that point in time indicated the "relationship of [a] site to others previously investigated [on the basis of] such a meagre proportion of traits, that the bond was not demonstrated if indeed it did exist." Further, "the degrees of likeness between sites naturally varied considerably but the same designation [name] was used to cover a wide range of somewhat similar cultural units, as well as those of a local group with practically identical traits." Identification of an archaeological manifestation as having a particular ethnic or linguistic affiliation seemed to Deuel to be unwarranted and empirically unjustifiable. Concentration on the "more artistic and spectacular or perfect [artifact] specimens" was, in Deuel's view, "in part responsible for the bewildering number of local 'cultures' that have arisen" and had resulted in "differences between sites often overshadow[ing] their likenesses and each discovery [being] hailed as a new 'culture.'" The pictorial survey had been initiated as a means of addressing those problems, and applying McKern's (1932[7]; McKern et al. 1933[10]) classification method to the data generated by that survey would serve to test the utility of the method. Such a test was the purpose of Deuel's dissertation.

Deuel (1935b:3) began at the top of the hierarchy, noting that the classification method he was going to test "begins with *basic cultures*, which are subdivided into *phases*, *aspects*, and *foci*." He apparently chose to begin with the large units for two reasons. First, Deuel noted that a *component* was "a localized and often incomplete expression of a local group," and he hand wrote at the bottom of the copy of his dissertation on file at the Illinois State Museum that "in determining the cultural complex of any unit (pattern, phase, etc.) communities as nearly complete as possible must be explored." Because the *pattern* unit was added to the scheme at the Indianapolis Conference in December 1935, after Deuel completed his dissertation, we suspect Deuel added that line when he was writing the paper he presented at the 1937 meeting of the American Association for the Advancement of Science (see below). The significance of the added sentence, plus the line in his dissertation that components were "often incomplete" expressions of a local group—what he would later (Deuel 1939[14]) term a community—is that Deuel was unwilling to decide on the basis of a single component which traits were determinants and thus comprised a focus. Others working elsewhere at the time (for example, Colton 1939) were not so hesitant (see chapter 5), but here Deuel was correct in his thinking about the workings of the method. A single component could *not* be used to define a focus, a point McKern (1934[11]:4) had made earlier when he noted that "a specific list of [determinant] culture traits [must be] found to be typical for several sites, [thereby] establishing through its recurrence the fact that it was a true culture complex." Perhaps Deuel did not use the recurrence criterion because various components did not group at the scale of foci or aspect.

The second reason that Deuel preferred to start with the larger units is found in the fact that previous investigators had "for a number of years . . . tended to group the better known cultural manifestations . . . in two major divisions based on the large number of similarities within these units, and the marked differences between them" (Deuel 1935b:6). These units were the basic cultures known as Woodland and Mississippi, and because they had been recognized by many individuals in many areas, their determinant traits seemed to be well established (for example, Deuel 1935a). Deuel's analytical protocol was, therefore, to assign components to one of these two extensionally derived basic cultures. The procedure he used was to decide which basic culture a particular component was a member of: "A majority of determinant complexes decides to which basic culture any component belongs" (Deuel 1935b:6). This is an identification process; the classification is applied from the top down and comprises a key. No units are built because they already exist.

Deuel (1935b) noted several important features of the method he used. First, he grouped "cultural elements or determinants" into four main "complexes": "(1) Ceremonial (including burial custom and objects presumably used on ceremonial occasions); (2) Economic and Artistic (relating chiefly to the material, such as stone, bone, shell, etc. used for implements and ornaments, and the relative excellence of technique in producing and decorating them); (3) Military and Hunting (dealing with weapon types); and (4) Pottery." Second, "each [trait] complex is given a weight of *one* except pottery which is accorded *two* on account of its numerous determinant traits." Third, he noted that the absence of some traits from various components seemed to be a result of "inadequate samplings," whereas other traits might be missing because not all traits diffuse in equivalent manners.

Deuel indicated that only those traits "considered diagnostic for the *focus* are used" to "determine *foci*" (Deuel 1935b:8). Therefore,

> while the determinants for the *basic culture* and *phase* are necessary to give the *focus* its setting in the larger scheme, they can be ignored when considering the various foci, for it is assumed that they are common to all. In other words basic determinants need not be considered for classifying the phase[s of the basic culture of which a phase is a part], phasic determinants [need not be considered] for the aspect[s of which an aspect is a part], and so on. Likewise traits which occur in only one *component* of a focus are not considered diagnostic [of that focus] nor are those which are strictly limited to local conditions or resources. Where traits occur generally throughout the components used in establishing foci, they are excluded as focal *determinants*. Such traits are considered as determinants of the aspect or larger units.

What Deuel was driving at in the first several sentences exemplifies the top-down nature of his classificatory procedure (Figure 4.1). Traits that characterize the large, inclusive units are assumed to be present in the less-inclusive units and thus need not be mentioned with respect to the definition of those smaller units. Further, the last two sentences of Deuel's discussion illustrate the keylike nature of his taxonomy: Attributes common to all T_j units are determinants of their member T_{j-1} units.

Deuel then listed the traits evident in some twenty-five sites, first "assigning" sites/components (he used both terms interchangeably) to one of the two basic cultures (the pattern unit not yet having been added to the scheme). The assignment—actually, it was an identification—was based on the traits held in common between a component and the basic culture. A component was assigned to (identified as a member of) the basic culture with which it shared the most traits. The procedure was then repeated for the next lower, less-inclusive taxon, and each component of a particular basic culture was assigned to a particular phase member of that basic culture. Deuel noted that to carry the procedure down the hierarchy such that components of particular phases could be identified as particular as-

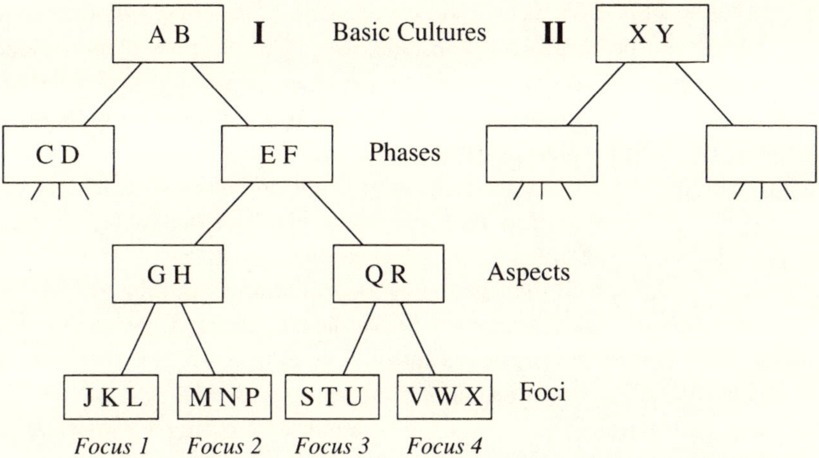

Figure 4.1. The top-down, keylike nature of Thorne Deuel's version of the midwestern taxonomic method. Note that although the definitive traits (capital letters) of each higher, more-inclusive taxon are not listed for the lower, less-inclusive taxa subsumed in them, they are assumed to be present. Thus, the complete list of determinant traits for Focus 1 would be ABEFGHJKL; for Focus 2, ABEFGHMNP; for Focus 3, ABEFQRSTU; and for Focus 4, ABEFQRVWX.

pects was difficult because of inadequate samples. He also stated that the less inclusive the unit, the smaller the geographic distribution of that unit: "Aspects usually extend over moderately extensive areas while foci are relatively small" (Deuel 1935b:32). Determinants were used throughout the procedure as definitive criteria of the various units within each taxonomic level. Deuel did this to identify a component as a member of a particular unit. How those determinants were chosen was never specified. He concluded by noting that if the abundance of only those traits that were unique to a focus were considered, "the likeness ratio of inter-group [component] pairs" was sufficiently high, whereas between-group ratios were sufficiently low, to suggest that he had legitimate foci.

Deuel published a brief version of his dissertation as an appendix to *Rediscovering Illinois* (Cole and Deuel 1937). He did two things there that warrant comment. First, he recognized the two methods of classification—working from the larger units downward or beginning with the smallest units and successively combining them into larger ones. He said that irrespective of which method was chosen, "there is one fundamental similarity in the approaches—the component or complex of traits at actual sites must form the basis of the classification" (Deuel 1937a:207). He also noted that he followed the top-down procedure, whereas Griffin (1935) had followed the bottom-up procedure. The second thing Deuel (1937a:208) did was to argue that "on the discovery of a community differing considerably from the nearest related ones, it is often impossible to define its focus. It is often possible and highly desirable, however, to indicate to which of the larger units the manifestation belongs." If it were unclear to which focus a component belonged, how was it possible to know which larger unit a manifestation belonged in? The answer resided in the approach Deuel used. If one started at the top and worked down, the first analytical pass placed components in the largest units. Lower taxa were defined by many specific traits, whereas higher taxa were defined by few general traits. What could be easier than using a few traits to pigeonhole a component? Further, for that kind of analysis, why make a distinction between diagnostic and determinant traits? Deuel certainly didn't, using them as synonyms and in the process ignoring all the hours of discussion at the Indianapolis conference.

Of considerable interest are Griffin's comments on Deuel's dissertation (manuscript on file, ISM). First, he liked Deuel's distinction between communities and components, noting that he preferred that "one base one's findings on communities and not on components." Deuel (1935b:3–4) had stated, "The total association of traits found in a single cultural level at a given site is called a *component*. A site may contain a number of *components* of the same or of different cultures. *Component* should not be confused with *community*. . . . [which] signifies the complete cultural manifestation of a local group; *component*, a localized and often incomplete expression of a local group. A burial mound or a temporary campsite would yield components but not communities." A *community*, then, was viewed as a taxon intermediate between a component and a focus in terms of inclusiveness. Second, Griffin pointed out that the use of negative traits—those absent from a component—if carried to the logical extreme of presence-absence for every trait, would "completely load the analysis."

Third, Griffin noted in several places that Deuel did not show how he arrived at the determinants he used, leaving the reader to assume that they were selected by subjective impression (see also Griffin 1943:332). Griffin in effect was saying that Deuel chose sites/components that represented a rather inclusive cultural taxon and then worked down through the taxonomic levels, dividing the sites into groups, then into subgroups, and so on until the least-inclusive taxa possible were reached. To do this Deuel had to know which sites to begin with because he knew the determinants of the most inclusive taxa before he began; he used those determinants to choose the sites he would consider. As we saw earlier, this is precisely what

Griffin (1935) did with the Fort Ancient sites. Either Griffin was not cognizant of the similarities of what he and Deuel had done, or what was good for Griffin was not good for Deuel. We suspect the latter and detail why in chapter 5.

In his review of Cole and Deuel (1937), Wilton M. Krogman of Western Reserve University, more a physical anthropologist than an archaeologist, remarked that "the student of North American archaeology has now at his command a text outlining method and procedure in careful and logical exactness" (Krogman 1937:677). Krogman liked the MTM, but he noted a potential weakness in it:

> The application of the taxonomic method to archaeology is an important advance in recovering order from chaos. Admittedly there have been far too many "cultures" based upon individual sites, and described by investigators whose knowledge of comparative data has been inadequate. A taxonomic framework, as it were, admits of classification in terms of inter-relationship. But herein lies a certain amount of danger; the tendency to fit facts into a previous general scheme; to give variants or minor deviations an equal rank with distinct elements. Classification cannot pay too much attention to detail, as, for example—to borrow an analogy from the field of zoology—where subspecific or even specific rank has been given to pelage differences which proved to be naught but seasonal changes. Again, it has been lately shown in the field of comparative myology that a basic similarity outweighs an adaptive change. These same rules must apply to archaeological taxonomy: elements in and of themselves do not have diagnostic value except as measured against the larger complex. (Krogman 1937:677–678)

Krogman was correct that "too much attention to detail" in zoology had resulted in the typological species concept, which at the time he was writing was being discarded. His comment on comparative myology—the study of the anatomy of muscles—was in reference to biological efforts in the 1930s and 1940s to understand the phylogeny of organisms by focusing on primitive (persistent) characters rather than on recently derived characters. If so, then a "classification in terms of inter-relationship" would seem to be one geared toward detecting phylogenetic affinities rather than just phenetic affinities. Given that Cole and Deuel (1937) incorporated temporal data in the form of stratigraphy into their analysis, Krogman was correct. He mused that the five terminal cultural taxa Cole and Deuel designated not only occurred in a temporal sequence but two of them were

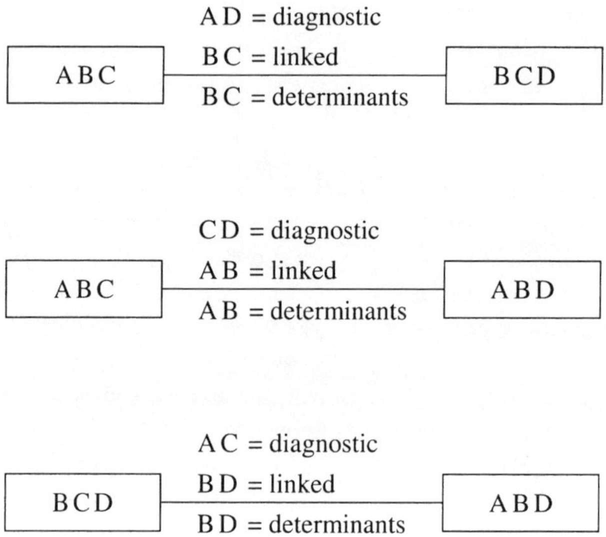

Figure 4.2. Three diagrams showing the influence of the units (rectangles) that are compared on the categorization of traits as diagnostic, linked, or determinant.

somewhat contemporaneous and two others "may have overlapped in time" (Krogman 1937:678).

What is even more important is McKern's impression of Deuel's efforts, as recorded in his review of *Rediscovering Illinois*. McKern (1938[13]) began his review by indicating that he did not think that Cole and Deuel's determinant traits were in fact determinants. Following the protocol discussed at the 1935 Indianapolis conference for distinguishing among the three kinds of traits, McKern (1938[13]:369) remarked, "That which is a diagnostic trait in one comparison may become a link trait in another, and it follows that there can be no complex of diagnostic traits, or determinants for a cultural division to be exhibited as standard in all comparisons." We consider this critical aspect of the classificatory method in some detail below. Here we point out that what McKern was getting at is illustrated in Figure 4.2, which shows that the status of a particular trait depends on the comparison being made. In McKern's view, Cole and Deuel should have known this, given their involvement with the MTM from the start. We suspect the reason they did not was that the bulk of *Rediscovering Illinois* rested on the analysis presented in Deuel's dissertation (Deuel 1935b) and in the paper that preceded it (Deuel 1935a). Both of those pieces were completed before the Indianapolis conference. Our suspicion is corroborated by McKern's (1938[13]) observation that Mississippi and Woodland were termed "basic cultures" by Cole and Deuel, despite the fact that the term was changed to "base" at the Indianapolis conference.

McKern (1938[13]:369) pointed out that Cole and Deuel's "objective" classifications of projectile points and pottery were "not the classificatory procedure originally advanced by the [devisers] of the taxonomic method employed, or in use by other advocates of the method." But McKern observed that Cole and Deuel's procedure nevertheless produced substantially the same results, despite the fact that only pottery and projectile points were used, whereas the original classificatory method had been designed to consider all artifacts of whatever scale. Cole and Deuel ignored large-scale traits such as house type, mound structure, and burial procedure, although they were included in the trait lists.

McKern noted that Deuel (1937a), in his appendix to *Rediscovering Illinois*, acknowledged that the procedure he had followed in his dissertation work was "an alternative" to the originally proposed method, but McKern couldn't help but use a metaphor for what he perceived that alternative to comprise. He chose, perhaps not surprisingly, biological classification to illustrate his point, describing the classification procedure that would result were Cole and Deuel to apply their alternative method to organisms. Were one to "identify various sub-varieties of grasshoppers" following that alternative, "one would put all the legs in one pile, the wings in another, and so on, without regard to which grasshoppers the various parts came from. . . . No doubt one could thus test the accuracy of the original associations, and in doing so actually determine the characteristic traits for each variety" (McKern 1938[13]:370). McKern's point was that the requisite associations were not apparent, or at least were not used, in Cole and Deuel's analysis. Further, McKern argued that "whereas pottery may in most instances offer more than any other subject in the way of culture indicators, it is extremely doubtful that its importance could ever warrant [cultural] classification primarily on a basis of pottery factors." This remark had little impact on the discipline because other workers (for example, Colton 1939; Ford 1938; Ford and Griffin 1938; Griffin 1943; Kidder 1936b) came to subscribe to exactly the opposite view—that classification of cultural manifestations largely or solely on the basis of pottery was sufficient because their primary interest was in the temporal sequence of cultural manifestations.

Not surprisingly, McKern was unimpressed with Deuel's preference for the top-down implementation of the taxonomy, and he stated that he would not cite the results as a recommendation for the continued use of the MTM. For McKern, foci were the natural starting points for implementing the classification method. Otherwise, he argued, the analyst's hand is forced. In Cole and Deuel's case, they had to choose between assigning a component to either the Woodland pattern or the Mississippi pattern; there was no possibility that a particular component might belong to an as-yet-unrecognized pattern. Here McKern astutely noted the difference between a top-down classification serving as an identification key and a bottom-up classification that seeks to group like with like into units of successively greater inclusiveness. In the case of the former, the (somehow predetermined) classes (sets of definitive criteria) yield the groups of empirical phenomena; in the latter, the groups yield the classes (Mayr 1969).

Despite these perceived weaknesses and flaws in Cole and Deuel's efforts, McKern (1938[13]:373, 374) concluded that the study "deserves the careful attention of all students of classification" because "this method for culture classification is in an experimental stage, as yet too immature to aspire to standardization." This raises the question of what Deuel thought of the method. This question is easily answered, given that he wrote a long letter in 1939 to Joseph R. Caldwell, then director of the Irene Mound excavations in Savannah, Georgia, and also authored two papers on the method after the Cole and Deuel volume had been published.

Correspondence with Joseph Caldwell

On January 31, 1939, Caldwell wrote to Deuel (ISM), noting that he had heard that "the McKern system has been amplified inasmuch as statistical percentages were used to modify the traits. I wish you would write me and verify this and also would you state just what you feel is implied by the statistics themselves." In asking for such verification, one of Caldwell's concerns was that by ignoring temporal differences between manifestations, "anachronistic percentages which will create a false impression as to the degree of correspondence between, let us say, culturally close but temporally separated manifestations" might result. Caldwell also recognized the materialist paradox when he noted that the "statistical statement of the attributes (I like the word better than traits) of a particular culture presents a static picture of that which is actually dynamic." Putting these two things—percentages and temporal change—together, Caldwell concluded, "If we allow the temporal factor, with its rider of cultural change, to slip in then the figures [percentages] will be thrown all the way to hell and gone and will not be representative of a culture but rather will be representative of a single culture plus an 'average' of its history and the figures won't be usable for our purpose." Caldwell added in a postscript that to avoid the problem he would prefer to "compare specific archaeological features representing short time periods rather than to compare site to site, wholesale. Later on, if we can get a series representing short-time intervals within sites, our site comparisons could be made with greater accuracy and understanding."

Deuel responded on April 9 (ISM). It is worth quoting most of his letter because of the points he made. We have added paragraph numbers in brackets and refer to them in the discussion that follows the letter:

> [1] As to the use of statistics in applying the classification: Just how far statistics will be employable is hard to say. However, this much should be said: in analyzing the components the frequencies of traits should be noted. Consequently, if a trait appears very few times in a number of components and not at all in others of the same focus, it will not be of value as a determinant although it may indicate contact with another cultural group (diffusional influences).
>
> [2] The McKern classification appears to me to be the best so far proposed since it emphasizes the importance of classifying culture on the basis of its content and *not* on some extraneous circumstance such as time, space, or some other relationship. This is in accord with the successful classifications in the other natural sciences of botany, zoology, palaeontology, linguistics, etc. However, I believe traits will have to be selected on the basis of their significance or fundamental importance. The lack of importance in certain traits and the considerable significance of others are easily discoverable; those that should be chosen as determinants, on the other hand, is not so clear.
>
> [3] The classificatory system, I believe, implies a genetic relationship though the exact degree of such relationship would not in general be shown by the position of a unit in it, any more than is the case in the biological taxonomies. The "crossing" of cultures (by diffusion) will perhaps be more common than hybridization in nature. Theoretically, it would seem that the diffused characters (traits) should be readily distinguishable. In some instances this is undoubtedly true. Diffusionist relationships might be shown between certain contemporary sites, of course, but between others the relationship would be genetic. For example, two components of the same focus may have "descended" from the same component, or from components of the same focus, or one component could conceivably have arisen from the other component in the same focus. For example, when a faction in Oraibi seceded from that town and set up a new village in another place, the villages were contemporaries and "identical" yet the new one was a descendant of the first.

[4] Temporal, spatial and other factors should always be considered where they can be of assistance. They should not however, be the criteria by which a component or cultural unit is classified or given a place in the taxonomic system. This should be done on a purely cultural basis, i.e., by determinant traits. Stratigraphy might definitely indicate which of two related cultures was the earlier and hence possibly the "parent" of the later. In zoology, the investigator determines certain animal remains to be those of an elephant from certain diagnostic physical traits, whether he lived in A.D. 1939 or around 25,000 B.C. whether found in Africa, Siberia, or in Illinois. He may not be able to tell which of two specimens is ancestral to the other, however. Of course, this is not determined by stratigraphy by zoologists but by the evolutionary theory of change, in regard to which scientists are not always in accord. In archaeology, the correct use of the classification will depend on how well the determinants are chosen. The "perfect" system will not be selected but will be worked out by trial and error just as is being done in zoology, botany, and palaeontology.

[5] Linnaeus put porpoises and whales among the fish yet Aristotle classed them properly as mammals. Nevertheless the former is rightly considered the Father of the Modern Botany & Zoological taxonomies because he classified the whole field (often merely compiling what others had worked out) and he used invariably the binomial taxonomic scheme, genus and species. . . .

[6] If there was imperceptibility of culture change in two components widely separated in time, I doubt that much of our "stratification" in America would assist us. If you can't tell it culturally, of what importance is a knowledge of temporal difference? Especially if you could not determine the length of the intervening interval whether months or centuries? You want too fine a measuring stick. Too fine distinctions as you may remember from mathematics and statistics may be without significance, carrying an interest in computation to eight decimal places in many computations.

[7] Why attributes instead of traits? I don't care which is used as long as you remember that you compare "habits of peoples" (not personal habits) as far as they can be defined or described from the investigation of more or less imperishable materials left behind and the tell-tale circumstances in which they occur. It is the habits, techniques, customs that we have to compare, not the mere material objects. A grooved axe for example signifies a technique of polishing and pecking stone in common with the like preparation for other ground stone objects,—it also signifies the custom of grooving for

hafting as well as a peculiar cross section. Moreover, it signifies a custom of its use as a cutting implement.

[8] Archaeologically you will scarcely be able to deal with the knee length skirt and the bustle (the bustle, however, is actually here now). A study of value would be the archaeology of present day culture based on materials that would remain 500 years and 5000 years from now, for a small village, of course.

[9] The fact that the classification reflects genetic factors (if it does) brings in the time factor of course. However, if you have to wait for the temporal factor before classifying (if it is made a criterion) one of two things will happen: (1) the time will be presumed to be the same as that for the first units classified or (2) very little organizing of the data will be done.

[10] You will have to elucidate your P. S. How the devil are you going to determine time periods and whether they are comparable in length? You are using too accurate an instrument to measure too great a mass—getting the weight of the earth in milligrams.

[11] You're darn right the McKern system can be made more effective. But be practical! Use it and find its short-comings.

A number of things in Deuel's letter warrant discussion. In the first paragraph, Deuel argued for paying attention to the frequency with which a trait occurs, noting that those that are infrequent would not serve well as determinants. This was an indication of weighting traits, but it was not the same criterion of weighting that was discussed at the 1935 Indianapolis conference, where traits were weighted as to their status as a determinant, linked, or diagnostic trait. Perhaps frequency of occurrence was what Deuel had in mind in paragraph 2, where he indicated that deciding which traits are significant and which are insignificant is not difficult. Perhaps in paragraph 3 he was getting at the distinction between frequently represented traits, which would signify relationships of descent, and rare traits, which would signify contact between two separate cultural lineages. The hybridization of cultures mentioned in paragraph 3 was a typical comment of the time (Lyman and O'Brien 1997), but it implies a 50/50 mixing of two gene lines, not the transmission of a single or a few traits (genes). This critical distinction of the scale of information exchange, regardless of source, continues to elude modern anthropologists (for example, Dewar 1995; Moore 1994) who maintain it is impossible to reconstruct prehistoric culture phylogeny.

Deuel's explicit statement about the evolutionary descent of one archaeological manifestation from another in paragraphs 3 and 9 is virtually unique. Most archaeologists of the time spoke merely of historical or cultural relationships rather than in terms of phylogenetic relationships (Lyman 2001; O'Brien and Lyman 1999b). In paragraph 3 Deuel revealed remarkable insight when he implied that the Linnaean taxonomy does not necessarily reveal degree of phylogenetic relationship, although it does reveal, in modern terms, phenetic affinity. That insight is also revealed in paragraph 4, where Deuel indicated that biologists of the time did not agree on the nuances of evolutionary theory.

In the absence of a universally applicable absolute chronometer such as radiocarbon dating, it is not too surprising that in paragraph 6 (see also paragraph 9) Deuel argued against the value of measuring periods of stasis and varying rates of culture change. Deuel responded to Caldwell's expressed preference for archaeological manifestations of short temporal duration as desiring "too fine a measuring stick" (paragraph 6). Deuel had noted in his 1937 paper for the American Association for the Advancement of Science (see below) that identical components must be considered contemporary, as McKern et al. (1933[10]) had, but this was a function of the classification. Deuel might have taken a different approach and noted that by definition a component represented a single occupation of a site (for example, McKern 1934[11]) and thus implied a relatively brief temporal span, but he did not, probably because the brevity of the time span was unknowable without an absolute chronometer.

Deuel's Statements on the Method

Deuel's only publications on the classificatory method were his 1935 paper in *American Anthropologist* and the extract of his dissertation that was included as an appendix in *Rediscovering Illinois.* He did, however, present two papers on the method at meetings of Section H (anthropology) of the American Association for the Advancement of Science. Both are rather insightful analyses of the method, and in them he repeated only a few of the points he made in his letter to Caldwell.

Deuel (1937b[12]) began the first paper by defining several critical terms. These included trait, complex, and determinant. Deuel defined *trait* as "a cultural habit of a group (whether or not it can be definitely described), which can be inferred from the form, appearance and conditions of occurrence of archaeological objects or features." In other words, a trait comprised a behavior inferred from empirical archaeological materials. We doubt McKern would have agreed because he tended to focus on the empirical rather than on the inferential. That Deuel defined a trait in terms of human behavior suggests that he held an ethnological or humanistic mind set, in which artifacts represent humans and their behaviors just as a bone represents an animal and its behaviors. This mind set echoed the age-old notion that "archeology is but prehistoric ethnology and ethnography" (Dixon 1913:558). The relegation of archaeology to stepson status within anthropology began in the late nineteenth century with John Wesley Powell and the founding of the Bureau of Ethnology (later the Bureau of American Ethnology).

Deuel (1937b[12]:2) defined *complex* as "a cluster of mutually related traits, as for example the agricultural complex." In other words, a complex was a set of functionally interrelated traits. He defined a *determinant* following McKern et al. (1933[10]) as a trait that "serves to unite certain sites or units together into a larger class, and to distinguish them from sites or equivalent units belonging to other classes" (Deuel 1937b[12]:2). He then distinguished between a *determinant series* and a *determinant complex.* The latter was the aggregate of determinants used to group units. That is, a determinant complex was the set of functionally interrelated traits that united the T_j classes of the taxonomy within the adjacent larger, more-inclusive class T_{j+1}. A *determinant series* was a "group of traits or complexes, not necessarily possessing any common or mutual relationship among themselves other than such association within equivalent units as determinants." In other words, a *determinant series* was the total set of determinants, irrespective of their independence or interdependence, that united the T_j classes of the taxonomy into the adjacent larger, more-inclusive class T_{j+1}. Deuel thus clarified and seemingly corrected his understanding of determinant traits. But Deuel took an additional step, one not taken by McKern, by making clear the classificatory significance of determinants. Deuel emphasized that a determinant series must comprise many traits and complexes to ensure against "independent invention." Clearly he was after not only phenetic relationships but also phylogenetic relationships.

Deuel followed McKern et al. when he suggested that two almost identical components were *assumed* to be contemporaneous, although they might not be. He also stated that the geographic distribution of archaeological materials was not considered during classification. But then he said something that McKern had only implied: The cultural units of the taxonomy represented "differing degrees of likeness" and "if based on an adequate number of traits or complexes still mean to us a genetic or developmental cultural relationship though more distant than that between components of a focus" (Deuel 1937b[12]:5). In short, Deuel was saying that similarity between archaeological manifestations rendered as determinants and linked traits was the result of cultural transmission and thus heritable continuity. He came back to this point later in the paper, reiterating that the McKern classification should "imply temporal, spatial and genetic relationships." In so doing, Deuel clearly had in mind something above and beyond a framework on which to hang various archaeological manifestations.

Deuel (1939[14]) began his second paper with a lengthy history of the McKern classificatory method, frequently quoting and citing Guthe (1932[8]) but particularly McKern et al. (1933[10]) and the discussions at the 1935 Indianapolis conference. He then turned to the criticisms of the method recently expressed by Clark Wissler (1938). Deuel (1939[14]:12) noted that Wissler incorrectly included component as one of the classes and pointed out that this unit was meant to be equivalent to a "zoological or biological . . . specimen." He also pointed out that Wissler equated traits with artifacts. Deuel lamented that error because it "leaves the implication that the system is based purely on the material objects found on a site without regard to the most ordinary observations." To Deuel, traits included human behaviors such as burying the dead in a flexed position. Deuel (1939[14]:7) admitted that for Wissler to make that error, there was "a weak point in the classification." Deuel noted that the weakness was that the definition of trait probably varied from person to person, so he defined it as "a cultural (not merely personal or individual) habit, custom or pattern of behavior, either simple or complex that is evidenced by archaeological remains, their association and such other cultural implications as the circumstances and conditions of their occurrence may reasonably suggest." This was basically the same definition he had given two years earlier (Deuel 1937b[12]), and it underscored yet again the ethnological mind set held by Deuel, if not by McKern and others involved with the classification.

Deuel (1939[14]) addressed a few other points raised by Wissler, but he quickly turned to a discussion of determinants, pointing out that the original definition (McKern et al. 1933[10]:1) had emphasized that because of their individuality, determinants served to differentiate among cultural units. Deuel (1939[14]:12) noted that McKern's (National Research Council 1937:56) definition of a diagnostic trait as one that pertained only to a particular "class, and is unique for that class" implied that such a trait "cannot occur as a trait in another unit" and that this "seems to deny the possibility of the diffusion of a determinant." In so doing, Deuel revealed his confusion regarding the precise nature of determinants as McKern saw them. Determinants are definitive criteria of a class; particular traits can be designated as determinants only if they are definitive of a class. On the one hand, diffusion might render a particular trait a non-determinant and perhaps make it a linked trait. On the other hand, that some traits might diffuse via transmission was irrelevant because, as McKern repeatedly emphasized, he was interested in determining the "relationships" between classes of archaeological cultures. At a minimum, diffusion between two cultural units indicated those units were in contact and thus had a particular kind of relationship above and beyond simple phenetic similarity. Diffusion did not preclude a trait from holding the status of a determinant, although it might.

That Deuel (1939[14]:12) misunderstood the role of determinants is further exemplified by his citing a number of comments from those who attended the 1935 Indianapolis conference as evidence that the MTM held "genetic implications." Reading those comments reveals that Deuel was correct with respect to the genetic implications, but the commentators were merely saying that if two archaeological manifestations held some traits—not necessarily determinants—in common, then they were somehow related, perhaps genetically (speaking metaphorically), perhaps culturally, or perhaps via diffusion. That formal similarity denoted some kind of relationship or affinity effected by transmission was the operational assumption of the 1920s through the 1950s (Rouse 1939; Willey 1953), but this notion was left undeveloped and was never considered in explicit theoretical terms (Lyman 2001).

Despite errors in his reasoning, it is unfortunate that Deuel's later statements on the classification method had such limited circulation. We found no evidence indicating that he shared either the 1937 paper or the 1939 paper with McKern. Deuel sent Guthe a copy of the 1939 paper, and Guthe commented on it in a letter of September 9 (ISM). Guthe pointed out that it was his understanding that "the concept of a 'determinant' does not imply that traits do not diffuse. It merely indicates that a particular trait actually was not subject to diffusion, and that this very fact gives it a diagnostic character." Guthe also emphasized that if Deuel were to pursue publishing the piece, and Guthe emphasized that "the article is one which is needed in our literature," then Deuel needed to "add a statement making clear that in [comparing the method with biological taxonomic procedures, Deuel was] referring only to the *method* of classifying data, and not making any inferences concerning the nature of the *content* of the two bodies of data (cultural and biological)." Despite these helpful—and in our view, accurate—comments, Deuel did not publish the paper. In the end, the paper that not only provided a formal name for the method but also had the widest circulation was authored solely by McKern and published in *American Antiquity* in 1939.

THE 1939 VERSION

McKern pointed out in the 1939 article that it was a revision of the 1934 paper (McKern 1934[11]) based on unpublished discussion, particularly discussion at the 1935 Indianapolis conference. After a brief synopsis of the history of the MTM, McKern (1939[15]:302) stated that "in most instances, we can not immediately bridge the barrier between pre-literate and historic or protohistoric cultural groups, and in many instances we can not reasonably hope ever to be able to do so." In other words, the direct historical approach was inapplicable in many cases, and even where applicable, such "ethnological classification does not satisfy archaeological requirements." Nor, in McKern's opinion, did "ethnologically conceived culture areas supply a basis for archaeological classification." Therefore, an alternative means "for culture classification in archaeology" was necessary. That alternative, in McKern's view, was applicable to "all cultural manifestations." Temporal and spatial variables were ignored, and the classification was "based upon the cultural factor alone," particularly "criteria available to the archaeologist." The classification would avoid "indefinite use of the word 'culture'" to denote manifestations of greatly varying size and was necessary because "chaos does not reduce itself to order without a plan. The accomplishments of science stand as a monument to planned orderliness." Clearly, McKern here, as he had since the early 1930s, fully appreciated the importance of systematics and classification as we defined them in chapter 2, but he was relatively circumspect about the taxonomic basis of the classification.

McKern (1939[15]:303) stated that as an archaeologist studies more and more materials distributed over successively larger areas, "he begins to observe evidence of cultural affinities, not only as regards specific complexes but involving distinctive types of complexes." Unfortunately, he never defined "cultural affinities." Nor did he make clear that his goal was to provide a common, standardized terminology that would allow communication among researchers and enhance the value of comparative analyses. Anticipating criticism from those who desired more data before classification began, McKern noted that "classification is nothing more than the process of recognizing classes, each class identified by a complex of characteristics." The term *recognizing* indicated that a class's empirical members were defined extensionally, thus the definitions were "constantly experimental, subject to such major and minor corrections as newly accumulating data may dictate." This indicates the basic method was one of grouping like with like (phenetics) and extracting definitive criteria from each resulting group.

McKern (1939[15]:304) also noted that given that cultural classes are recognized, sample adequacy was a real concern: "It is only in those instances in which sufficient data are available, quantitatively and qualitatively, to create a problem of cultural differentiation that classification can serve to any advantage." As we noted earlier, McKern used the word *arbi-*

trary in a variety of ways, one of them being to contend with the materialist paradox. But here, in 1939, McKern contradicted his previous discussions because he indicated that the particular members of each taxonomic level could be recognized. Although this could imply that he suspected the units were somehow real, we believe that what he was referring to was the fact that once definitive criteria for a taxon were established, those criteria could be used to recognize other empirical members of the taxon.

Turning to the terminology of the method, McKern defined three kinds of culture traits. Following Ritchie (1937) and discussions at the Indianapolis conference, McKern (1939[15]:305) defined a linked trait as one that was "shared in common by two manifestations." Diagnostic traits were those that were "found to occur in one manifestation and not in that with which it is compared, peculiar to the one manifestation in this comparison." Finally, determinants or determinant traits were diagnostic traits peculiar to and thus differentiated each of two manifestations in a particular comparison. That is, determinants depended on the comparison being made: "The term 'determinant' can only be employed as applied in a stated comparison." Because determinants were dependent on particular comparisons, "traits which are diagnostic and thus useful as determinants in one comparison may be linked traits in another comparison and, consequently, useless as determinants." McKern therefore emphasized that "there can be no truly valuable fixed list of determinants for any given culture class, serving as such in all possible comparisons." Comparisons of different manifestations would produce not only different sets of determinants but different groupings of manifestations. Such a method is akin to phenetics but without the statistical and mathematical measurement of similarity (see chapter 2). It is simply a grouping method, the results of which vary with the materials being grouped and the characters chosen.

The roles of determinant, diagnostic, and linked traits in rendering the method workable are illustrated in Figure 4.3. Notice that the status of a particular trait as linked, diagnostic, or determinant depends on the particular comparison being made (see also Figure 4.2). Figure 4.3 also shows how the simultaneous comparison of more than two T_j units results in the construction of a T_{j+1} taxon. This is accomplished by grouping members of T_j taxa on the basis of their linked traits that are used as determinants. Although McKern claimed otherwise when he argued that no final list of determinants could ever be written for a culture unit, determinants derived from the first several components ultimately provided the definitive criteria for identifying additional T_j members of a particular T_{j+1} culture taxon. In other words, the taxa were effectively extensionally derived classes, complete with definitive criteria rendered as determinants.

It is important to note that McKern (1939[15]) did not explicitly define

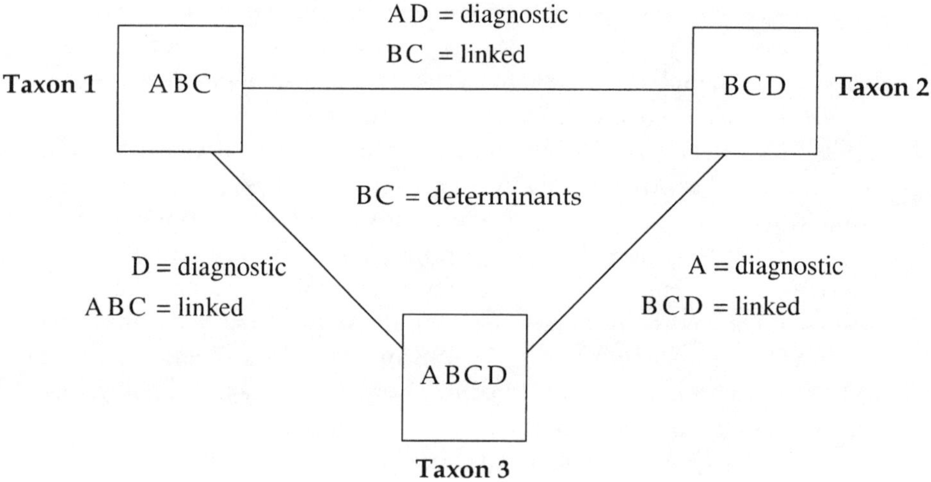

Figure 4.3. The analytical relations among diagnostic, linked, and determinant traits within the midwestern taxonomic method when three units (squares) are compared (compare with Figure 4.2). In this figure, a taxon can be of any category or level within the system of units (component, focus, aspect, or phase). Each capital letter designates a particular trait. Note that the status of a trait as diagnostic, linked, or determinant depends on the units compared. In this case, with three units, two of the four traits (B and C) are determinants of the taxon T_{j+1} that has the three illustrated taxa as members.

the term *trait*. We suspect, based on earlier discussions he had with Guthe, Deuel, and others, plus the literature of the time, McKern had in mind a "unit of observation . . . a unit of tribal culture" (Wissler 1923:50). Sapir (1916:29) had earlier used the term *element* as a synonym for trait and stated that "most cultural 'elements' are at least analysis complexes." Using our terms defined in chapter 2, a culture trait is an ideational unit—a class—useful for describing phenomena if not also for analyzing those phenomena. On the one hand, McKern (1939[15]:306) stated that "a simple type of artifact may serve as one element in a trait complex for one cultural division, and therefore may serve in some comparison as a determinant for that division." On the other hand, complex artifacts such as pottery raised the question of "whether it should be considered as a trait or as comprising a number of trait elements." Such complex artifacts were "important culture markers." The problem, in McKern's view, reduced to selecting "those trait details which have sufficient cultural significance to qualify them as culture determinants. This really implies a separate classification of the essential trait elements for any given complex cultural subject." This statement indicates he had changed his mind with respect to classification of artifacts in the year since he reviewed Cole and Deuel's *Rediscovering Illinois.* It also rather closely aligns his 1939 conception of a trait with the unit character concept of pheneticists—a more or less nonreducible, nonoverlapping analytical attribute used to group phenomena that share it.

McKern (1939[15]:307) stated that the larger, more-inclusive taxa comprised "for the most part traits that are in the nature of fundamental cultural trends. These fundamentals are quite different in character from the detailed material trait elements that are so important in determining highly specialized divisions." In other words, as one progressed up the taxonomy of cultural units to successively more-inclusive and general units, the definitive traits became more generalized. McKern suggested "horticulture might serve as a differentiating trait" among large-scale units, whereas "a peculiar motif in pottery decoration might serve as one determinant of a local specific division, but not as a determinant for the less specialized division under which it is classified, since it is peculiar to the local class." Thus, determinant traits of a large, inclusive unit "will be for the most part general in character and relatively few in number," whereas those of the successively lower, less-inclusive units "will be an enriched edition of the determinants for the immediately preceding, more general division, as altered to include greater detail, plus a considerable number of trait elements peculiarly characteristic of the more specialized division."

McKern (1939[15]:307) referred to the five culture units recognized by the method as "arbitrary divisions" that comprised a "taxonomic system." Beginning with the least-inclusive unit and progressing to the most inclusive, the units were focus, aspect, phase, pattern, and base. That these units each comprised groups was emphasized by McKern when he stated that "the manifestation of any given focus at a specific site is termed a *component* of that focus. This is in no sense an additional type of culture manifestation, one of the five class types; rather, it is the focus as represented at a site, and serves to distinguish between a site, which may bear evidence of several cultural occupations, each foreign to the other, and a single specified manifestation at a site." Components were the empirical units of the classificatory method. The other units were classlike groups of successively greater inclusiveness. By classlike groups we mean that the determinants of a focus or higher unit in the taxonomy are treated as definitive of the unit, but they depend on the manifestations polled and the comparisons made. Determinants of any given cultural taxon are extensionally derived. This critical distinction is shown in Figure 4.4.

McKern (1939[15]:308) reiterated and elaborated on the recurrence criterion he had first noted in 1934. A focus was a trait complex that has been "found to recur in characteristic purity and practical completeness at

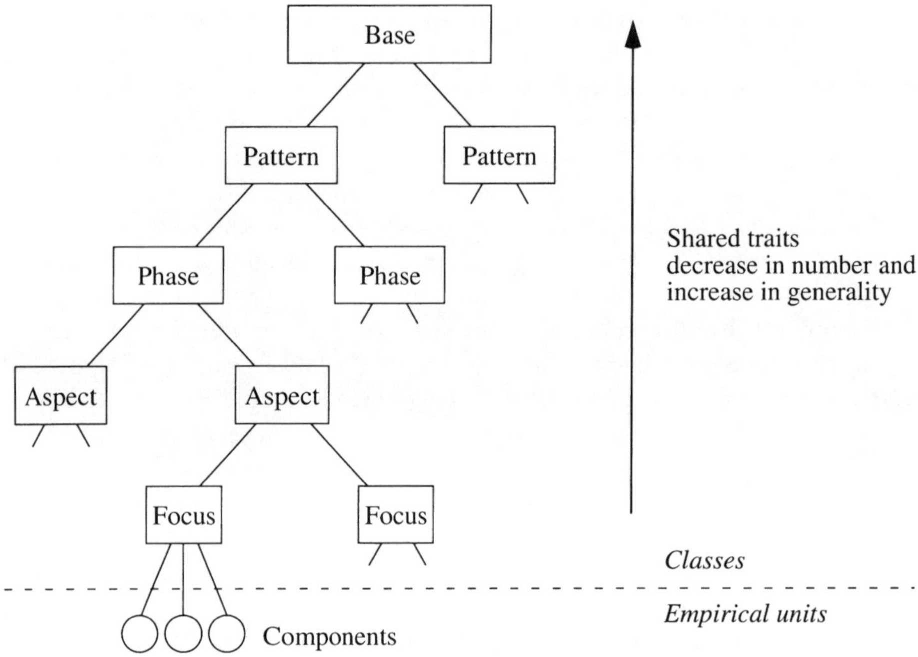

Figure 4.4. The system of units comprising the midwestern taxonomic method. Note that as one reads up the hierarchy from subordinate, noninclusive units to superior, inclusive units, determinant traits become fewer in number and more general in nature, and that only the components are empirical units.

[multiple] sites, to an extent suggestive of cultural identity." Thus, a focus could be specified only on the basis of multiple, virtually identical components. Further, a focus was "that class of culture exhibiting characteristic peculiarities in the finest analysis of cultural detail, and may in instances correspond closely to the local tribe in ethnology." We wonder if this phrase originated with Deuel's (1935a, 1935b, 1937a) discussions because this was the first explicit, if tentative, equation by McKern of an archaeological unit with an ethnological one. An aspect was a group of foci that were "very like each other"; that shared a "majority of the traits and trait elements"; and that "show marked dissimilarity to other compared foci" (McKern 1939[15]:308). All foci that were members of a particular aspect "share the somewhat less specific aspect trait units, but possess additional peculiarities in fine cultural detail." Thus the pottery of all foci members of an aspect might display red triangles, but the pottery of some member foci might have small, red triangles, whereas the pottery of other member foci might have large, red triangles.

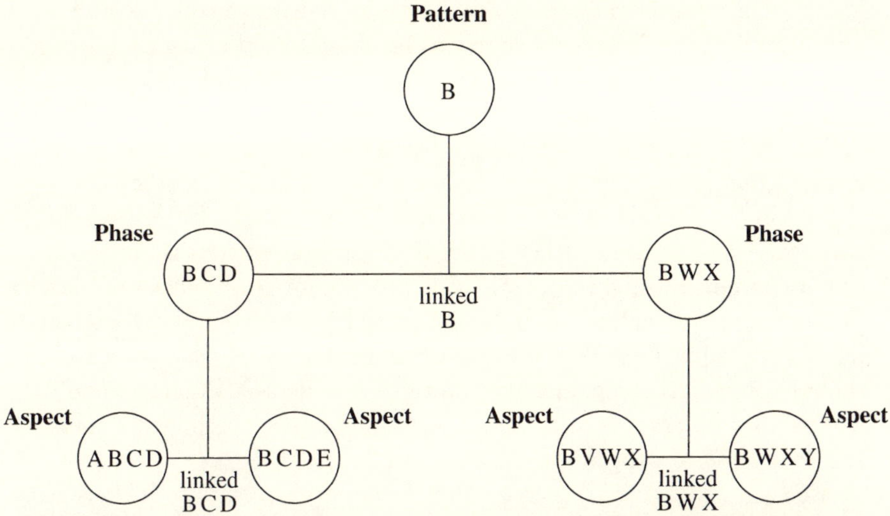

Figure 4.5. An example of how the determinant traits of a phase change, depending on whether they are derived from the member aspects of a phase or from comparison with another phase. Each circle represents a cultural taxon and each capital letter a trait. At the taxonomic level of phase, one phase comprises traits B, C, and D, and the other phase comprises traits B, W, and X. At the taxonomic level of pattern, only determinant B is definitive of the member phases of the pattern.

A phase was denoted by the still "more general character" of its determinant traits. In addition to this "qualitative factor," "a near majority of traits shared in common by compared aspects determine the phase, and these traits comprise the phase complex" (McKern 1939[15]:309). McKern emphasized that the "phase complex" was different from the "complex of determinants for the phase as specifically compared with another phase." That is, the phase complex as represented by T_{j+1} comprised its determinants based on its T_j members; it was a bottom-up construction. A determinant complex would differ when a phase was compared with another phase, as shown in Figure 4.5. A pattern comprised several phases that "share a small complex of broadly general traits, in contrast to other compared phases in which these traits do not occur." McKern indicated that "the traits used as determinants for the pattern will be such as deal with the cultural reflection of the primary adjustments of peoples to environment, as modified by tradition." These were in fact the diagnostic traits of each pattern, but McKern used the two terms—*determinant* and *diagnostic*—as synonyms when in fact they were nothing of the kind (Figure 4.2).

McKern (1939[15]) borrowed the concept of community from Cole and Deuel (1937:278), who had defined the term as a "complete cultural manifestation of a local group or as much of it as is determinable by archaeological exploration." Remember that in his dissertation Deuel (1935b:3–4) had defined a community as "the complete cultural manifestation of a local group." In suggesting the term perhaps Deuel had in mind a taxonomic unit—a class—intermediate between a component and a focus. However, we think this is unlikely because a component and a focus are archaeological manifestations, whereas a community is an ethnological concept. The purpose of the community unit/concept was to underscore that a component might not fully represent a community, nothing more. Deuel (1939[14]) was correct in his response to Wissler (1938) that a component was equivalent to a biological specimen. Several components each thought of as an incomplete community still renders a component equivalent to a single organism and renders several similar components equivalent to a deme of a species.

McKern (1939[15]:311) stated that "experience seems to demonstrate that absolute mathematical percentages in trait similarity can not be successfully employed to establish the class relationship between two compared manifestations." Recall that Deuel suggested in his April 9, 1939, letter to Caldwell that frequencies of each trait should be noted and that frequently represented traits were likely to be good determinants, whereas rare ones were not. Recall as well that Griffin (1935) had used such frequencies to identify determinants of the Fort Ancient Aspect. Deuel undoubtedly was aware of Griffin's analysis. McKern reasoned that because frequencies of traits depended on available samples, comparison of manifestations based on proportional frequencies was unwise.

Toward the end of the *American Antiquity* article, McKern (1939[15]: 312) made a statement that has been overlooked since the day he wrote it: "Relative grouping of cultural divisions by any such taxonomic method does not necessarily imply evolutionary relationship [although] a common historical origin may be suggested, but the implication should be considered as an indicator, guiding further research, rather than as proof in itself." This is somewhat contradictory: Implications of "evolutionary [phylogenetic] relaionships" were not inherent in the method, though implications of "common historical origin"—which is certainly phylogenetic—had to be tested. Here McKern followed paleontological procedure of the time in suggesting that an independent classification based on chronology be built so as to "establish or refute evolutionary sequence" (1939[15]:312). Unfortunately, he did not realize, as paleontologists a bit later would (for example, Simpson 1945), that mere historical continuity constitutes only a necessary test of "evolutionary," or phylogenetic, continuity; it does *not* constitute a sufficient test of heritable continuity. McKern (1939[15]:312) relied on the typical reason of the time for discarding a Darwinian model of cultural evolution: "Under the blending influences of diffusion, and the divergent tendencies involving cultural growth by invention, there can be no hard and fast natural division lines" between classificatory units, whether within a division or between divisions. In McKern's view, this fact rendered the "method of classification . . . arbitrary." Irrespective, McKern *never* said that those relationships could *not* be found in the classification. He was not as forceful as Deuel, who said that the MTM should be constructed to *show* such relationships, but McKern did not dismiss the subject out of hand. This reflects the nonexplicit and largely atheoretical nature of the concept of cultural affinities common within the discipline at the time (see chapter 1).

A 1940 POSTSCRIPT

The perceived significance of the MTM by those not directly involved in its construction is reflected by the fact that a short, somewhat simplified discussion of the method was solicited by the Archaeological Society of Delaware and published in its *Bulletin* in 1940. In that short piece, McKern (1940[16]:18) not only attempted to "correct certain important misconceptions of the way [the method] is supposed to work" but also stated the anthropological implications of trait complexes. A trait complex "may represent the customs and ways of living (culture) of a local group representing a single variety, or band, or Indians, sharing an identical lot of cultural habits." In making this statement, McKern tended to echo Deuel (1937b[12], 1939[14]) rather than his own earlier articles. McKern repeated the recurrence criterion for grouping components, although he did not use the term component and instead substituted another term: "If substantially the same traits are found to occur together repeatedly at site after site, one can be quite sure that this persistently grouped lot of traits is characteristic of a single culture. Such a repeatedly recurring series of traits is called a *culture complex*" (McKern 1940[16]:19). This was the first time McKern explicitly defined the term *culture complex*. In the 1939 article a culture complex comprised the traits characteristic of any culture unit in the system. Between the two statements, McKern contradicted his own admonition that a final and ultimate list of definitive criteria could not be written for a culture taxon. In the Delaware paper, McKern was saying such a list *could* be devised. It was called the culture complex. No wonder people were confused over how the method was supposed to work, particularly regarding the role of determinant, diagnostic, and linked traits.

From a historical perspective, the most important feature of the Delaware paper was McKern's inclusion of an ethnological warrant for the trait lists derived from components. As we noted in chapter 3, that a trait list recurred in component after component was thought to strengthen the ethnographic validity of the group of components as a focus when the latter was viewed as a society or tribe. But both the warrant and its strengthening agent were inferential and impossible to test in a nontautological manner. What still remained unspecified was how to determine if two or more artifacts were associated. The answer, of course, was to use some sort of depositional (empirical) unit—such as a stratum—that had visible boundaries in order to conclude that a set of artifacts contained items that were associated not only archaeologically but also in the culture represented.

DISCUSSION

What in 1939 became formally known as the midwestern taxonomic method was born in the mind of W. C. McKern in about 1930. By that time, Americanist archaeologists had come to something of an impasse over the means and terms used to describe and discuss assemblages of artifacts. The term *culture* was ubiquitous in the role of a grouping unit, but it varied tremendously in scope and meaning from one application to the next. According to McKern (1943[18]:313), "this vague and varying use of the word 'culture' to describe manifestations which were so unlike in scope and character, of which some were culturally correlative—but in different degree, while others lay wholly outside the specific field of relationship, led logically and necessarily to taxonomy."

The emergence of the culture-history paradigm in the 1920s and 1930s was heavily predicated on stylistic descriptions of artifacts because such descriptions allowed the measurement of time as a result of the homologous character of styles (Lyman et al. 1997, 1998; O'Brien and Lyman 1999b). As McKern (for example, 1934[11], 1939[15]) himself implied, stylistic traits—those that were "culturally indicative"—dominated the lower-level units in the taxonomic hierarchy, focus and aspect, whereas functional traits dominated the higher-level units. Thus it is not surprising that the focus, and to a lesser extent the aspect, were the most-used units, in that they allowed the identification of unique time-space positions. The phase unit proposed by Phillips and Willey (1953) that came to dominate Americanist archaeology in the 1960s was simply a modification of the focus to include explicit temporal and spatial parameters (see chapter 5).

The MTM is intimately associated with McKern and thus has been referred to as the McKern Taxonomic System (Cole 1943), the Midwestern

Taxonomic System (Brew 1946; Cole 1943; Lewis and Kneberg 1946), and the Midwestern System of Classification (Taylor 1948). But as McKern pointed out in his last revision of the method, it was the product of a consensus reached about a proposal originally made by him but which had been subjected to broad discussion. That discussion took place through personal correspondence among McKern, Guthe, and a host of others, as well as through meetings such as the informal Chicago meeting of December 1932 and the Indianapolis conference of 1935. Much of the correspondence and many of the discussions on the method diverted attention from the central issues that the method was designed to address—enhancing communication between archaeologists and searching for different degrees of cultural relatedness as denoted by the different categorical ranks making up the method. Those discussions resulted in McKern, Guthe, and Deuel constantly having to explain how the method worked.

In a real sense, parallel to those biologists who today use the term *Baupläne* to signify "the basic organizational plan common to higher taxa at the level of the phylum, order, or class" (Hall 1996:225), McKern's higher cultural taxa—base, pattern, phase—comprised basic body plans. A *Bauplan* comprises "a suite of characters that unites members at higher taxonomic levels" (Hall 1996:226)—precisely what the general determinant traits of McKern's higher-level units were supposed to do. McKern was thinking in terms of the affinities revealed between the various categories of cultural units his system of units designated, but he was hesitant to argue that those affinities might be genealogical or phylogenetic, no doubt because of the generally disciplinewide distaste for any such evolutionary connotation among cultural phenomena. Because of this, and because McKern developed no necessary and sufficient test for the evolutionary implications of the results of applying the method, we tend to think of the results as comprising what we call an affinity tree. The structure is hierarchical, and the included phenomena are affines based on their various degrees of formal similarity, but the other implications of affinity are unclear.

McKern (1939[15]) argued that no final list of definitive traits could be constructed, but he implied that it was possible to define culture classes based on a set of diagnostic traits, and he gave an example of such when he spoke of "Neanderthal man" (McKern 1934[11]:5). Such a class of fossils showed by example that a final, ultimate, and "truly valuable fixed list of determinants" *could* be extensionally derived. Finally, the fact that McKern (1938[13]:370) talked about identifying new members of various cultural taxa implied that one could in fact produce a fixed list of definitive criteria for cultural taxa. Hence, his discussions were contradictory. For the history of Americanist archaeology, the important thing to note is that archaeologists adopted the second stance, that cultural taxa could be defined on the basis of one or a few similar components, and then new members could be identified on the basis of the definitive criteria extensionally derived from the first component(s) polled. In short, the way the method was described was one thing, the way it was used was something else. As a result, many of the phases discussed today are the very constructs first proposed as foci of the MTM. This means that many of the archaeological units of prehistory are historical accidents that exist solely because particular assemblages were known when the method was applied in a given area. Further, various large-scale inclusive units such as "Archaic," "Woodland," and "Mississippian" originated as higher-level units in the method and were passed on to us through it.

The contributions of particularly Guthe and Deuel were such that they must be considered collaborators, if not codevelopers, of the MTM. In addition, Ritchie proposed the terms *linked* and *diagnostic* for the kinds of traits that appeared in the final version of the MTM (McKern 1939[15]). There were other individuals who had lesser roles, and still others who in asking questions and attempting to apply the method also had some influence on the method and how McKern described it after 1939. It is to those comments and applications that we turn next.

5
Applications, Comments, and Later Proposals

> Failure in science is more often a function of the lack of resolve than anything else. (D. Hull 1988:288)

McKern's initial statement on the classificatory method (McKern 1932[7]) was presented to a small group of archaeologists attending the May 1932 Illinois State Academy of Science meeting. Two of the authors of papers included in the proceedings of the meeting—Thorne Deuel (1933) and Richard Snodgrasse (1933)—used McKern's terminology, although their usage demonstrates they were unsure of what the terms actually meant. McKern's influence also was evident in Samuel Barrett's (1933) monograph on Aztalan, a large Mississippian site in Wisconsin. Barrett earned his doctorate in 1908 from the University of California and came to the Milwaukee Public Museum in 1909 as curator of anthropology. He began excavating Aztalan in 1919. Barrett worked there again in 1920, the same year he became director of the museum. In his monograph he mentioned the December 1932 Chicago meeting of "a small group" who sought to standardize terminology (Barrett 1933:370), and in his preface he thanked McKern for his "suggestions in respect to [cultural] comparisons." Barrett explicitly stated that he was seeking "affiliations" between the materials at Aztalan and cultures in other areas, and he used the various culture units—basic culture, phase, aspect, focus, and component—in his analysis.

Other archaeologists (for example, Cooper 1936; Ritchie 1936a, 1936b) in rather distant areas were influenced by later methodological statements (McKern et al. 1933[10]); McKern 1934[11]), which had wider distributions than the initial one. Misunderstanding was rampant, and some individuals published comments on what they perceived to be weaknesses or flaws in the method. McKern received the majority of criticism, and he responded—sometimes writing letters back, other times writing short articles for various journals, all in an effort to explain the classification method. By the early 1940s, Deuel and Carl Guthe—McKern's collaborators and strongest allies in the 1930s—were largely silent on the matter, although, as we will see, Guthe abandoned the unique protocol of the method in 1939 or 1940 in favor of a different one. Using the term loosely, support for the method came from others, all of whom modified the method to suit their own needs and priorities, thereby contributing to later confusion over how and why the method had been designed in the manner it had. We examine some of that confusion below.

APPLICATIONS

In outline, McKern's method was simple. The building blocks were components, which were assemblages of associated artifacts that represented the occupation of a place by a cultural group. Components were analytically rendered as trait lists. Similarity of trait lists, in turn, was used to assign components to a focus. Foci were also rendered as trait lists and similar ones grouped into an aspect. Determinants of an aspect were fewer and more general than those of foci. Aspects were analytically rendered into shorter lists of still more general traits, and similar aspects were grouped into a phase. The procedure continued through the pattern and base. McKern's (1939[15]) final revised description of the method was typical of the time. He described a classification procedure and defined the various units it comprised, yet he did not consider in any detail some of the most critical issues, such as how traits were to be defined, what *similarity* meant and how it was to be measured, or what *cultural relationship* or *affinity* meant in theoretical terms. Thus, a trait could be whatever the analyst wanted, similarity could be measured in different ways, and affinal taxa could be variously interpreted and explained. It was the obscure procedure of deciding whether a trait was a linked trait, a diagnostic trait, or a determinant that caused the most problems, prompting different solutions by different individuals.

William A. Ritchie in New York

Ritchie received his Ph.D. from Columbia University in 1944 and worked throughout his career principally in New York. In his early work (for example, Ritchie 1932a, 1932b) he, like everyone else, spoke of distinct cultures, but once he became familiar with the MTM he used the system of units to organize and structure his analysis. His 1937 paper, titled "Culture Influences from Ohio in New York Archaeology," was an early application of the terms *diagnostic traits* and *linked traits* in a widely circulated format. He used the term *determinant trait* (Ritchie 1936b) and *diagnostic trait* (Ritchie 1936a) a year earlier in less widely circulated venues, but he did not use them consistently.

Ritchie (1937:187) suggested that linked traits were "common to two or more possibly related [cultural units]" and that shared determinant traits served as evidence that archaeological manifestations were related. He pointed out in a footnote that future excavations and analyses would allow various traits to "be specifically allocated to foci already recognized and to others which must be created," suggesting that he was well aware of the extensional derivation of determinant, diagnostic, and linked traits. One of Deuel's students—Gretchen Cutter—protested that Ritchie had "violated the concept of a [cultural] base" (Cutter 1939:352) when he grouped one particular aspect without an agricultural economy with another aspect that had an agricultural economy. Cutter emphasized that "the McKern system is an empirical one" and that "the selection and weighting of particular traits" is a critical analytical step.

In a condensed version of his master's thesis, Ritchie (1938) again used the MTM to organize and structure data. He spoke of determinant traits and built his discussion largely around a number of aspects evident in New York. Ritchie summarized the prehistory of New York in a table in which he listed three patterns, three phases, five aspects, twenty-two foci, and a large number of components, many of which were generalized in the form "various sites." This generalization suggests Ritchie may have assumed all sites contained single components, but this is unclear. Interestingly, Hopewellian was listed as a phase with an unknown pattern affiliation, and Archaic was listed as a pattern with no phase or aspect members. Ritchie never defined the cultural units or categories he used, apparently assuming that everyone would know what they were and how they were related.

In his dissertation, which was published by the Rochester (New York) Museum, Ritchie (1944) used the direct historical approach, stratigraphic information, and the MTM. As might be expected, McKern (1945:140) was impressed with Ritchie's use of the method "as a means of conveniently organizing the otherwise chaotic variety of cultural manifestations." McKern noted that the classificatory method had "been employed only where need required" and had not been "an objective in itself." Ritchie used temporal data when available and identified cultures on the basis of the recurring complex method. McKern noted that the cultural taxa Ritchie described were not "sharply distinct, biologically exclusive and successive cultures," further noting that he was "impressed with the evidence of continuous change."

In his review of Ritchie's monograph, James B. Griffin (1945:407) argued that the MTM produced an "unfortunate result" because it emphasized traits that "serve to differentiate any unit from all other units," which "results in slighting the traits which connect units—particularly temporally successive units." The net effect, in Griffin's view, was the masking of transitional units, "the very items which are the most important in understanding the story of the cultural development of the people." Not surprising, particularly in light of his own recent work with the Fort Ancient culture (Griffin 1943; see below), Griffin (1945:407) stated that the "taxonomic and classificatory emphasis has served a useful purpose, but the well-recognized succession of cultures throughout the eastern United States invites the abandonment of attempts to complete the arbitrary taxonomic framework." By the early 1940s Griffin was a firm believer in whole cultures and the notion that over time whole cultures replaced other whole cultures (O'Brien and Lyman 1998).

Frederick Johnson (1944) was even less favorable toward Ritchie's work than Griffin was. Johnson pointed out that some of Ritchie's units comprised mixtures of distinct cultures and that some traits supposedly definitive of one unit were also present in other units. Johnson implied that typological similarity must be assumed to signify that the compared units were somehow related. He made several rather strong statements regarding his opinion of the method as used by Ritchie:

> The whole structure is largely the result of the devotion to method rather than a preoccupation with culture as an expression of human existence. Furthermore his classification depends upon that section of the method which is concerned with "diagnostic traits." It is difficult to understand how arbitrarily selected, specialized types of artifacts which occur in small numbers, and sometimes not at all, can be of great significance in establishing basic cultural relationships between units which are also found to possess a number of traits which are not comparable. Furthermore, when chains of these diagnostics, beginning with one set of types and ending with another, are used to indicate wide geographic distributions of nuclei it seems to me that the system is carried beyond the limits of credulity. . . .
>
> A feature of the book is the method which has been rigorously employed in an attempt to impose some order on the material brought to light. This is a full dress performance of the McKern Classification and Ritchie has brought into play practically every feature of the system which has ever been invented. . . . It seems that almost every time this Classification has been used in the manner exemplified by

> this book it has been refined or modified to meet the exigencies of the moment. Ritchie has continued this procedure. . . .
>
> Ritchie's use of the classification has brought out some of its advantages. One of the most important is that within limits it is an efficient method of arranging data so that it may be more easily comprehended. . . . Difficulty with the classificatory system is encountered in each case where the culture which forms part of some category has been modified by diffusion or even by internal evolution. In such cases the necessity for classification prevents the portraying of the amorphous character of culture. . . .
>
> . . . The continuity, changes and gradual evolution of culture in the northeast will never be fully brought out by any such system as Ritchie has employed. . . .
>
> . . . Are we interested only in the specimens and should we limit our endeavors to fitting them into a three dimensional picture puzzle? Or, on the other hand, are we interested in the artifacts as symbols of the existence of human beings? Ritchie's treatment of the material falls largely within the limits of the first query. (Johnson 1944: 533–535)

In Johnson's view, the "brutality of the Classification" Ritchie used obscured all the nuances of cultural evolution. This was the most damning criticism, as it identified the materialist paradox: How does one classify a dynamic, evolving entity such as a culture by using static units? The answer is to use theoretical units (classes) of measurement rather than empirical units. The problem of keeping one's measurement units—whether they be artifact types or cultural phases—distinct from the particular empirical expressions of those units is an old one (Lyman et al. 1997), and it continues to plague Americanist archaeology (O'Brien and Lyman 2000, 2002).

Lloyd Wilford in Minnesota

Lloyd Wilford, who worked at the University of Minnesota, received his Ph.D. from Harvard in 1937. In 1941 he published a paper in *American Antiquity* titled "A Tentative Classification of the Pre-Historic Cultures of Minnesota." As might be surmised from the title, he used the MTM to structure his observations. He, like Ritchie (1938), presented a table in which he summarized the "late prehistoric cultures of Minnesota" (Wilford 1941:232). That table included two patterns, each with a single phase. One phase comprised six aspects, six foci, and twenty-seven components; the other phase comprised a single aspect with three foci and an unclear number of components. Wilford noted that the "classification is only tentative, and primarily reflects regional differences without much depth of sequential relationships." He identified the few temporal differences between various manifestations but noted such data were limited and so emphasized the differences in geographical distributions of the manifestations. Wilford (for example, 1945, 1955) continued to use the MTM to organize his observations over the next fifteen years. He consistently failed to designate which traits were determinants, diagnostic, or linked, preferring instead to use statements like "trait A is *characteristic* or *typical* of culture taxon I." Such statements were scattered among other statements that can only be characterized as descriptive of various cultural taxa.

Waldo Wedel and William Duncan Strong on the Plains

Some historians (for example, Krause 1989) have stated that the MTM was used in early efforts to understand Plains prehistory (for example, Cooper 1936; Dunlevy 1936), but the only studies that came close to using McKern's taxonomic method properly were those by Wedel (1936) and Strong (1935). Wedel's monograph *An Introduction to Pawnee Archeology* was "a purely objective preliminary report on the archeology of the Pawnee" (Wedel 1936:ix). To that end, Wedel compiled a list of culture traits, particularly those having archaeological expression, from historical, ethnographic, and archaeological data. His goal was to produce "a reasonably accurate basis from which to work back into the unknown history of the tribe." He later would refer to this method as the direct historical approach (Wedel 1938). Strong's (1935) *An Introduction to Nebraska Archeology* was similar. He presented a summary table of the cultural taxa that consisted of two basic cultures, four phases, eight aspects, thirteen foci, and numerous components. The units were arranged in such a manner that time passed from the bottom to the top. Strong (1935) used some of Wedel's unpublished data and, as Wedel would do a year later, compiled trait lists for the Pawnee. Strong (1935:58, 59) described the traits he listed as "very characteristic" and "especially characteristic" of that group.

In a later work on the Pawnee, Wedel (1938) provided an excellent example of the direct historical approach that involved a simple comparison of trait lists for three cultures. Two cultures—the Lower Loup Focus and the Oneota Aspect—were archaeological units based on the taxonomic method, and one—Historic Pawnee—was ethnographic. The list contained 120 traits, of which the Historic Pawnee had 80, the Lower Loup Focus 82, and the Oneota Aspect 74. Wedel noted that all three culture units shared 39 traits, the Historic Pawnee and Lower Loup Focus shared 55 traits, the Historic Pawnee and Oneota Aspect shared 42 traits, and the

Lower Loup Focus and Oneota Aspect shared 48 traits. Based on these observations, Wedel stated that the "conclusion seems inescapable that the Lower Loup Focus stands in very much closer and more direct relationship *genetically* to the later historic Pawnee than to the contemporaneous Oneota peoples" (Wedel 1938:11 [emphasis added]). Such "genetic" connections were typical inferences in anthropology and archaeology of the first half of the twentieth century (for example, Boas 1904; Ford 1938; Griffin 1943; Lowie 1912; Wissler 1916), although the term *genetic* was used in a metaphorical sense to refer to relationships among cultural traits.

Strong (1940b:267) reviewed some of the Plains work that used the MTM and made an important observation: "The component is as basic to archaeology as knowledge of the local group is to ethnology or comparative sociology. Larger archaeological constellations, such as 'aspects' and 'phases,' will continue to change or merge, assuming higher reliability and greater social significance in strict accord with the increase of detailed knowledge of sites and components. But the site, once dug and reported on, remains a fixed and fundamental point in a changing conceptual structure. Hence, whatever obscures such basic data threatens the validity of the entire construct." Strong's take-home message was simple. Components were the empirical units of the MTM, and if they were not described in detail, the particular empirical representatives of the various taxonomic units would be unstable in terms of content and thus meaning.

William S. Webb, Thomas M. N. Lewis, and Madeline Kneberg in the Southeast

Webb (1939) compared trait lists for two sites he excavated in the Wheeler Basin of Alabama to trait lists extracted from publications on five other Alabama sites. There were thirty-six traits in all, and many of them were variously shared across all seven sites. On that basis, Webb called the trait group the "copper-galena complex" and indicated that "its homogeneity on these seven areas seems to justify setting it apart as distinctly different from other cultural complexes in the southeastern area, at least for the time being" (Webb 1939:191). He then compared this Alabama complex to trait lists from seven Hopewell sites in Ohio and found that "32 of the 36 traits of the Alabama complex are found on Hopewell sites, and not in any other well-developed complex" (Webb 1939:197). He concluded, "It seems possible to suggest in terms of the latest taxonomic method of classification that the copper-galena complex may be tentatively regarded as a manifestation of the Hopewell phase" (Webb 1939:201). Webb gave his Alabama copper-galena complex the name Copena (COPper-galENA) and presented the cultural taxonomy as basic culture: unknown; phase: Hopewellian; aspect: Southern; focus: Copena. He listed seven "diagnostic traits of the Copena Focus by which this manifestation is differentiated from Hopewell" (Webb 1939:201). A few years later, Webb and David DeJarnette (1942:302) assigned six components from six sites in the Pickwick Basin of Alabama to the Copena Focus because they shared a number of traits with the Wheeler Basin manifestations. Two other foci in other areas of the Pickwick Basin were recognized. Traits unique to each of those two foci were termed "diagnostic" traits, and those that were shared by them were said to be "common" and thereby formed a Pickwick Aspect (Webb and DeJarnette 1942:316–317).

The procedure Webb followed in both analyses was not exactly the protocol outlined by McKern. Rather, it was a procedure that many individuals used. Components that shared many traits, say more than 80 percent, were assigned to the same focus. As one progressed up the hierarchy to more-inclusive units, the proportion of shared traits decreased. Determinant, linked, and diagnostic traits were not consistently designated, nor did the traits themselves become more generalized as one progressed upward. As we will see later, this was to become the standard procedure by the late 1940s and early 1950s.

Lewis and Kneberg (1946) used the MTM in their analysis of the Hiwassee Island site in Tennessee. They referred to the "Midwestern taxonomic system" but did not reference any of McKern's articles. In their introductory chapter they simply stated that the "differentiation of cultures and their chronological sequence were worked out by an objective analysis prior to any attempt at historical reconstruction. The foci were established by trait comparisons, and components were recognized on the basis of traits with definite associations" (Lewis and Kneberg 1946:20). One must turn to an appendix to find a one-page statement on method; the other ten pages of that appendix were devoted to lists of traits (and their approximate frequencies) present or absent from each of the three foci they identified. In the appendix, Lewis and Kneberg (1946:169) acknowledged "McKern's criticism and advice."

The components recognized at Hiwassee Island were established on the basis of comparison with other sites in the region. Lewis and Kneberg (1946:169) had to do this because "Hiwassee Island is a typical example of multiple occupation where separation of two foci . . . is difficult." They did not distinguish among determinant, linked, or diagnostic traits, choosing instead merely to list all traits they considered and whether those traits were present or absent in the components at Hiwassee Island. At least two of the components were "stratigraphically sequent, but not separable in the sense that they represented two occupations," apparently because "the transitional period [between the two components] can hardly be called a component" (Lewis and Kneberg 1946:34). Our take on this is that Lewis and Kneberg had here encountered the materialist paradox. They were faced with a continuum, but they used discontinuous units (components) that were inferred to be temporally discrete and nonoverlapping occupations to carve up the continuum. The boundary between components was the transitional material.

In his review of Lewis and Kneberg, Jesse Jennings (1947:192) complained that "when a continuous flow of cultural traits can be seen to persist from period to period, the new periods being different in the possession of new traits, but retaining many old ones, the injection of a phase, focus, or pattern, before admitting a chronological and/or genetic relationship seems to serve no purpose beyond adding to the suspense." In Jennings's view, "forcing a clear, sharp stratigraphic sequence of cultures whose distant cultural equivalents are known, and whose chronological position is amply demonstrated, in[to] the [MTM's] classificatory pigeonholes is wasted effort." Comparing trait lists, demonstrating similarities and differences between such lists, showing their relative chronological positions, and thereby establishing the relationships of the lists "paid the historical debt [and is] what archaeology is expected to do." The MTM and its attendant hierarchy of cultural taxa was, in Jennings's view, unnecessary.

JULIAN H. STEWARD AND THE DIRECT HISTORICAL APPROACH

Philip Phillips reviewed Webb and DeJarnette's (1942) monograph on the Pickwick Basin. Phillips (1942:197) pulled no punches: "In spite of all that has been said to the contrary, I believe that [the stratigraphic and analytic (McKern) methods] cannot be harmonized, one must give way before the other." In the Pickwick monograph, according to Phillips, stratigraphy gave way to the MTM. The result was a "focus to end all foci." As Phillips noted,

> The stratigraphy plainly offered no opportunity for a break-down *that could be expressed by trait lists.* This is the important point. Your archaeologist unhampered by a classificatory bias, would find no trouble at all in breaking the series down into sequent periods, each marked by the appearance of a new type of material. Persistence of the older types would not bother him at all. But a unit in the McKern classification has to be set apart by differences, and if the differences

> are outnumbered by the similarities due to persistence then your classifier is helpless. . . .
>
> . . . [Evidence suggests the stratigraphy is mixed or disturbed, so the authors assume that] we are at liberty to reconstruct it. In this connection, the McKern Classification is highly recommended. (Phillips 1942:198, 200)

Steward (1944) would refer to Phillip's review when he similarly argued that any method for measuring time's passage in the archaeological record could not be reconciled or harmonized with the MTM. Steward earned his doctorate in 1929 from the University of California and worked for the Bureau of American Ethnology from 1935 to 1939. He wrote to McKern on December 9, 1939 (MPM), with some questions about the taxonomic method. We suspect he had just read McKern's (1939[15]) recently published version of the MTM. Steward asked the following:

> First, is there any possible modification of the taxonomic scheme that would make it possible to avoid the necessity of pigeon-holing complexes in such a way that relationships in more than one direction are obscured. While I know that you rule out any evolutionary implication, it is nonetheless comparable to biological schemes which fit evolutionary data. Yet we know that many cultures are in various degrees combinations of two or more rather different cultures. A case in point is Ritchie's treatment of the Iroquois whom he says have half Mississippi traits, half Woodland, yet whom he classes as Mississippi thus completely obscuring their equal relationship in the other direction.
>
> Another point is what relation the taxonomic scheme might have methodologically to the work being done by the University of California. In the California ethnographic surveys, like your upper Mississippi archeological materials, the initial raw data are element lists. These are then compared merely on the basis of associations. But the formula allows for mutual absences, which statisticians claim to be significant, and does not make comparisons solely on the basis of percentage resemblances. The resulting blocks of units (in this case tribes) having a high correlation are comparable to your archeological divisions. From this point on the treatment of the California data is irrelevant to your archeological problems. But I am wondering what would happen if your archeological components were treated by this statistical method and grouped into blocks according to strength of correlation. It is a lot of labor but wouldn't it rule out some of the

> inconsistent and careless application of your scheme? Or would it be worth the trouble?
>
> My last point is that it might be helpful if you would give a clear cut statement on whether you think the taxonomic scheme should be used where there is already history worked out. If archeological objective is first history, then the most significant categories of classification would seem to be, when possible, time and space. . . . Possibly you do not intend that a historical framework be scrapped.

Steward apparently did not grasp what McKern had written. McKern did not, for example, "rule out any evolutionary implication," as suggested by Steward. Rather, McKern emphasized that such an implication had to be tested with independent data. It was precisely because in his view cultural evolution could produce hybrid cultures that McKern demanded that any evolutionary implications be tested for temporal sequence. Steward's suggestion that a statistical method be used rather than, apparently, determinant, diagnostic, and linked traits would later be pursued by Kroeber (1940). Steward himself would pursue the historical theme a few years later.

McKern responded to Steward on December 15 (MPM), noting his (McKern's) background in paleontology:

> I remain obdurate on the matter of cultural classification for the Mississippi Valley region, based exclusively on the cultural factor. Incidentally, I have biological precedent for this. In paleontology, a subject in which I minored, classification is made on the basis of similarity alone. At least, that is the method employed by the vast majority of paleontologists and is the only correct one. In instances, forms that are remote in time sequence are closely related in the biological classification. Naturally, the evolutionary implication is much stronger in biology than it is in anthropology.

McKern went on to point out that time was important and that historical classification could be carried out parallel to the classification based on cultural traits. Steward responded with the following (MPM) on December 21:

> Were I to say anything about taxonomy, I should point out first that you are not strictly following the paleontological taxonomy. The categories are like any biological schemes but your materials are not. I mean that if you really followed it, your specimens would be classed,

> Genus, arrow points, Family, projectile points, etc. Actually, your materials are like the ecologist's assemblages of plants and animals, e.g., a mountain vegetation with certain pines, shrubs, etc. which biologists do not classify in a scheme with evolutionary implication, so far as I know. In fact, I should say that your scheme is merely a set of categories and that your means of placing complexes in the categories is the method. From this point of view, other methods of ascertaining which categories things belong in, such as Kroeber's might be workable. I am thinking especially of a way of basing similarities on negatives as well as positives. Whether categories of this kind would be more serviceable, I don't know. . . .
>
> I can't follow your advocation of parallel systems of classifying.

Several things in Steward's remarks warrant comment. First, Steward was correct that a classification method that employed a system of nested units of greater and lesser inclusiveness produced an architecture "like any biological scheme," but such a scheme has no necessary evolutionary implications. Second, McKern was classifying the equivalent of an ecologist's biota—Steward's "assemblages of plants and animals"—*if and only if* one viewed an artifact type or culture trait (Kroeber's and Steward's culture element) as equivalent in scale to a biological taxon. Thus, Steward noted that one could have the family projectile points, the genus arrow points (and perhaps also the genus dart points), and (we suspect) the species side-notched, corner-notched, basal-notched, and so on. Each individual projectile point of the genus arrow point and species side-notched could vary in numerous nondefinitive attributes from other members of that species. Finally, we suspect Steward could not "follow" the notion of "parallel systems of classifying"—one based on the form of trait, the other based on age—for two reasons. Not only did he believe types could be described so as to be temporally sensitive (Steward 1954) and thus have temporal positions (ages), but history was paramount in archaeology and thus to ignore it was unconscionable (Steward 1942, 1944).

As we saw in chapters 3 and 4, McKern was clear about his thoughts on the value of the direct historical approach. Steward, however, was a vocal advocate of that approach, arguing in particular that "if one takes cultural history as his problem, and peoples of the early historic period as his point of departure, the difference between strictly archaeological and strictly ethnographical interest disappears. Archaeology supplements the cultural picture drawn from historic documents and informant testimony. Ethnography explains archaeological materials in their cultural context. And where archaeology traces changes backward into the past, ethnography may trace them forward" (Steward 1942:341). Steward sought "valid theories which generalize data of cultural change, process, or dynamics" (Steward 1942:339), and archaeology provided the all important temporal data for writing such theories.

McKern (1942[17]:170) began his response to Steward's statement by pointing out that the direct historical approach and the MTM were not competitors, as implied by Steward, but rather that "each is intended to render a specifically different service." Both methods were "useful in advancing research towards its fundamental objectives"; the value of taxonomy resided in its providing a "systematic terminology to apply to historically unidentified culture manifestations." Without a loftier value, it is no surprise that Steward found McKern's method wanting. Similarly, when McKern stated that his method "indicate[s] similarity relationships" and "facilitates comparative studies between manifestations," one could easily have argued that other methods—Griffin's (1943), for example—did the same thing. McKern maintained that it was misguided to think that taxonomy "is an end in itself," but what was its purpose? In his last paragraph McKern (1942[17]:172) suggested "the historical and cultural objectives of archaeology . . . might be defined as ethnology projected into the past" and that his taxonomic method "actually implements the student to reconstruct an historical and cultural picture which may be integrated with and augment the time-limited concepts of the ethnologist." This was the goal that Americanist archaeologists had professed since the end of the nineteenth century (Lyman et al. 1997).

In his response to McKern, Steward (1944:99) made the point that "facts [or data] are totally without significance and may even be said not to exist without reference to theory. . . . [The] taxonomic method, seriation, or sequential ordering, has meaning only with reference to problems and theories." Pointing out that McKern agreed that the goal of archaeology was to "reconstruct histories," Steward wondered "in what manner historical reconstruction can be derived from taxonomic classifications. It is not obvious that the mere orderly arrangement of data in categories of similarity is a necessary or even useful step toward history." Steward then turned up the attack: "When classification employs categories comparable to those of biology, it may, in fact, actually obscure history. The danger of introducing biological concepts to cultural data has been recognized for years. Biological types fall into genera, families, and phyla that do not and cannot cross with one another, whereas associations of cultural elements continually fall apart and recombine in all sort of ways." This was an old argument (Lyman and O'Brien 1997), one based on the erroneous belief that because cultural evolution is sometimes reticulate, whereas biological evolution, at least as it applies to animals, is almost always cladogenetic, the latter cannot serve as a model of the former (for example, Boas 1904; Gladwin 1936; Kroeber 1923, 1931).

In Steward's (1944:99) view, McKern's cultural taxa forced the analyst to "pigeonhole cultural data in categories analogous to those of biology," and because a cultural manifestation had to belong to a single taxon, "there is no way in which to indicate its relationship to other groups, with which it may share a majority of its traits." Here Steward displayed a misunderstanding of the architecture of a taxonomic classification. The T_j taxa that are deemed members of a single T_{j+1} taxon are thought to be related, and their relationship is reflected by the fact that they are all members of the larger, more-inclusive taxon. The T_j taxa are inferred to be somehow related because they are similar, and that similarity results in their being placed in the same T_{j+1} taxon. Steward (1944) raised a question that he had raised in his earlier letter to McKern: How does one decide the correct category in which to place a manifestation if it shares an equal number of definitive attributes with two taxa? McKern (1942[17]) had already addressed this complaint by noting that such "transitional" forms were treated precisely as such. He might also have argued that not only would such a situation probably be rare, but if and when it did occur, one had but to recall two things: (1) determinant traits depended on the particular comparison being made and (2) no final list of determinant traits for any particular taxon of a given category—aspect, phase, pattern, or base—could ever be constructed (McKern 1934[11], 1939[15]). In this respect the MTM as presented by McKern was more explicit than any other subsequent method. As in biological taxonomy, classifying phenomena was a constant process of trial and error, given its goal of monitoring affinity. It did so by assessing the similarity of cultural manifestations and arranging those manifestations in a hierarchy of successively more-inclusive taxa. Ignoring for the moment Steward's accurate characterization of McKern's taxonomic method as atheoretical—a point to which McKern did not respond—Steward's comments begged another question. How did one measure similarity? A. L. Kroeber attempted to address this question directly through the use of statistical measures.

A. L. KROEBER AND THE QUANTITATIVE MEASUREMENT OF SIMILARITY

Kroeber wrote to McKern on January 29, 1936 (MPM), suggesting that "archaeologists have for some time been using the basic features of the [quantitative approach]" and that "statistical interpretations [may] give us [something] additional." The quantitative approach to which Kroeber referred was one he and his students had begun using in the 1920s (for example, Clements et al. 1926; Driver and Kroeber 1932). It involved the calculation of a quantitative measure of the similarity between two lists of culture traits based on the presence-absence of the traits. A typical inference was that the more similar the two lists, the stronger or greater the "historical connection" (Kluckhohn 1939a:352) between the cultures, although the weaknesses of making such an inference were clear (see Driver [1962], Golbeck [1980], and Kluckhohn [1939a] for histories and pertinent references). Thus Harold Driver (1962:17) could remark that "two or more researchers, working with correlation methods from the same corpus of data, are likely to show a high degree of agreement in the clusters of tribes or traits they discover, yet may differ considerably in the historical inferences drawn from the clusters." The patently phenetic nature of what Kroeber and his students were doing is obvious today, but it wasn't early in the twentieth century. Most anthropologists and archaeologists at the end of the nineteenth century were loath to apply quantitative methods to cultural data, and that feeling carried over well into the twentieth century. But given Kroeber's more positive view of such methods, it is not surprising that he would suggest that they could be applied to archaeological data.

Kroeber (1940:29) suggested that "statistical classification" could "(1) Check errors or oversights of 'intuitive' or inspectional interpretation. . . . (2) Present results with added clarity and incisiveness. . . . (3) Indicate minor revisions of classification. (4) Sometimes suggest the fact at work if a classification comes out conflicting or dubious at certain points." He emphasized that how the results of statistical classification were interpreted "in terms of cause or sequence is a subsequent and non-statistical matter." He pointed out that sample adequacy could influence results and that "more adequate samples" should be the ones used. Kroeber reanalyzed Griffin's (1935) Fort Ancient materials (see below) and noted that the results were a bit different from Griffin's, probably because Kroeber included only pottery traits, whereas Griffin used all traits. Kroeber's (1940:44) point was not to argue that Griffin's results were inaccurate but rather that "the main help that statistics promises is in arriving at an objective basis, instead of an essentially agreed basis, for the grouping of sites into foci, these into aspects, and so on down to bases, or whatever other categories may be demanded by the phenomena."

Two things had to happen before Kroeber's suggestion would be taken to heart about three decades later. First, anthropologists and archaeologists had to discard their misgivings about applying statistical techniques to cultural data. For example, Madeline Kneberg, a student of Fay-Cooper Cole's, responded to a letter from Cole on March 6, 1941 (MPM), pointing out that Kroeber's (1940) reanalysis of Webb's (1938) data was flawed because "the material which he used was not sufficiently accurate to begin with." How one could make subjective interpretations of such data but not analyze it statistically revealed the widespread misunderstanding of statistical procedures. Second, archaeologists had to learn statistical methods. Solving this problem was aided by increased access to inexpensive computing in the late 1960s and early 1970s. Kroeber (1952) and Driver (1962) suggested that in addition to these problems, changes in the focus of the discipline resulted more in benign neglect of quantitative methods than in criticism of them.

Despite the pointed recommendations of his adviser, as far as we know McKern never used any statistical technique for measuring the similarity of archaeological components. It is perhaps not surprising that McKern had little to say about quantitative efforts, given that various individuals (Champe 1936; Cooper 1936; Dunlevy 1936; Strong 1935; Webb 1939; Wedel 1936, 1938) were simply comparing and interpreting the percentages of traits shared by various manifestations. Such comparisons were commonsensical, readily understood, and did not require mathematical or statistical sophistication. Interestingly, a little-known and seldom remarked effort was made to standardize and quantify even this simplistic procedure. McKern *did* notice this effort, and he had something to say about it.

STANDARDIZING TRAIT-LIST COMPARISONS

John C. McGregor received his Ph.D. from the University of Chicago in 1946 and began working at the University of Illinois in 1948. He had served as assistant editor for the Southwest for *American Antiquity* from 1939 to 1941 and had published *Southwestern Archaeology* in 1941. His goal in writing the book was to fulfill a "need, often expressed by teachers, laymen, and students, for an organized framework upon which the individual interested in Southwestern archaeology may build" (McGregor 1941:vii). In the first couple of chapters McGregor outlined the history of archaeological research in the Southwest before turning to the concepts and methods used to structure his presentation. McGregor noted that Wissler's (1923) definition of a culture trait as a unit of tribal culture was "usable but hardly specific enough to explain definitely what a trait is" (1941:43). He suggested that there were "two types of traits: material, and non-mate-

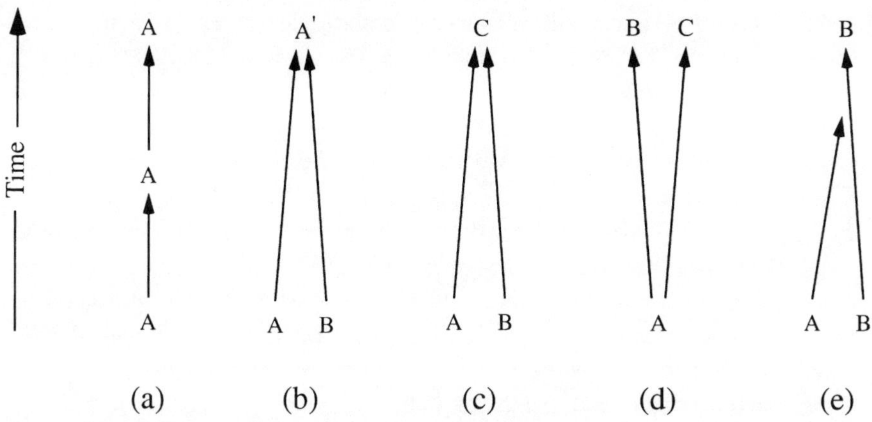

Figure 5.1. John McGregor's models of cultural change. Each capital letter denotes the culture or culture trait(s) under consideration: (a) lineal descent with no change; (b) fusional series in which B prompts change from A to A'; (c) fusional series in which A and B hybridize to form C; (d) divergence of A into B and C; (e) replacement of A by B (after McGregor 1941).

rial," where the former were "those things, or objects, used by man" and the latter were "mental attitudes, or customs." A culture, then, was "made up of all the material and non-material traits of the people," and McGregor emphasized that "any group of people, to be considered a distinct culture, must show a total aggregate of traits sufficiently distinct from that of any other people to set them definitely apart."

McGregor (1941:49) defined what he labeled *pure archaeology* "as the interpretation of the interrelationships of three kinds of phenomena: events, time, and space." He was more explicit than many archaeologists of the 1930s and 1940s when he observed that the problem that caused the archaeologist the most difficulty was the relationships among those three phenomena. He noted that the relationships were of two general kinds, characterized by five possibilities (Figure 5.1). The two general kinds were "developmental or 'genetic' series" and "non-genetic [or] replacement or competition series." McGregor used the term *genetic* in a metaphorical sense to describe cultural transmission within a cultural lineage. One possibility was a "developmental series," which comprised "lineal development, or chronological sequences, obviously a pure genetic series." A second possibility was what McGregor termed "fusional series," wherein "varying degrees of fusion or acculturation occur." A third possibility was "divergence, or splitting of a cultural sequence[, which] is usually a result of regional differentiation." A fourth possibility was "replacement of one series by another."

McGregor used *series* to mean a chronologically sequent group of phenomena, typically artifacts. He noted that some individuals in the Southwest, particularly those at the Museum of Northern Arizona (for example, Colton and Hargrave 1937), used the term to denote "that a number of types not only are related but that they are actually genetically related" (McGregor 1941:94). In other words, series was used as a synonym for a paleontologist's *lineage*. Whatever one thinks of McGregor's discussion of Figure 5.1, he accurately portrayed all possible phylogenetic modes of evolution relative to a lineage. The significance of this insight to McGregor's conceptualization of prehistory, then, should have carried over to his method of classifying archaeological materials.

McGregor reviewed the history and status of cultural classification in the Southwest, noting that the Pecos Classification of 1927 (Kidder 1927) had by the late 1930s undergone some revision. He then introduced what he labeled "a classificatory system for the Midwest," noting that it was "first proposed" in 1932 by McKern (McGregor 1941:60). McGregor noted that after discussion of the system at the 1935 Indianapolis conference, it became "more or less standardized" and that it "is based on a grouping by similarities of all the diagnostic culture traits of all the sites to be included in the comparison." He defined component, focus, aspect, phase, and pattern and noted that the "greatest single difficulty appears to be the identification of what are determinant traits," which he defined in a footnote as "recurring traits, or those traits which persistently recur in certain associations." McGregor cited no references by McKern, Deuel, or Guthe, but the source of his definition apparently resided in a

> conference held with Dr. Carl Guthe, one of the original sponsors of this classification, in which he finally suggested that all the available and comparable traits be considered, and that the divisions be based on the percentage of those traits which were found to be common to various sites. His suggestions are listed below.
>
> I. Component—85 percent or more of traits in common.
> II. Focus—65 to 85 percent of traits in common.
> III. Aspect—40 to 65 percent of traits in common.
> IV. Phase—20 to 40 percent of traits in common.
> V. Pattern—20 percent or less of traits in common. (McGregor 1941:60–61)

This meant that components that shared 85 percent or more of their traits should be grouped into the same focus; foci that shared 65 to 85 percent of their traits should be grouped into the same aspect; and so on.

McGregor (1941:62) remarked that Guthe's solution "would seem a much more specific and usable method of classification, for much of the variable human element would be removed with the absence of the necessity of determining what constitutes a diagnostic trait." Here McGregor was confusing determinant and diagnostic traits (Figures 4.2 and 4.3). As far as we can determine, McGregor's standardized percentages of traits necessary to designate a cultural taxon of a particular level were never used, although the basic concept if not the precise proportions of shared traits *was* used by many (see below). The interesting point from our perspective is that Guthe, by the time he talked with McGregor, had obviously given up on using determinant, linked, and diagnostic traits. The percentages of traits in common had never been a part of the MTM as originally formulated.

McKern (1944[19]) did not let McGregor's suggestions with respect to operationalizing the taxonomic method go unremarked. He pointed out that McGregor did not use the concept of "diagnostic culture traits" correctly, because the status of a trait as diagnostic of a culture complex depended on the comparisons being made (Figures 4.2 and 4.3). Second, a component was not a taxon and thus not a class. Rather, it was an empirical manifestation of a culture taxon. Third, culture taxa were not determined by the percentage of trait similarity "because culture traits do not have the same mathematical values—they are not quantitatively identical units in any mathematical sense" (McKern 1944[19]:445). In this respect McKern again underscored two critical points: (1) the taxonomy was built using a bottom-up procedure and (2) the building involved identifying "the recurrence of the same detailed [trait] complex at site after site." McKern argued that if this procedure was followed, "there remains no problem of type or degree of relationship." We suspect that although the "degree of relationship"—not quantitative similarity—may have been apparent to McKern, it was not to virtually anyone else. The basic protocol used by others was to compare trait lists and assess the similarities of those lists. A trait appearing in both lists was shared between units. McGregor attempted to get around the subjective assessment of taxonomic level and the difficulty of ascertaining a trait's status by standardizing how quantitatively similar two manifestations must be to qualify as members of the same focus, aspect, phase, or pattern. By not using the percentages McGregor suggested or some similar decreasing set of percentages, there was no way to decide to which higher taxon a particular component or lower taxon should be assigned. That the higher taxa would eventually be discarded in part because of this difficulty was anticipated by many of the applications of the MTM.

THE GRIFFIN SOLUTION

Perhaps the most significant contributing factor to Guthe's change of heart during his discussion with McGregor was that by the late 1930s Griffin had already used a method much like the one Guthe suggested to McGregor. Griffin had attended the 1935 Indianapolis conference and was aware of the changes to the method that originated there. He also was sensitized to the difficulties involved in distinguishing among determinant, linked, and diagnostic traits. We suspect for this reason that in his second analysis of Fort Ancient materials Griffin (1943:335) remarked that the "concepts 'determinant,' 'determinant trait,' 'determinant complex,' 'diagnostic,' 'diagnostic trait,' 'diagnostic complex,' and 'link traits' have not been seriously employed in this paper, partly because of the confusion and contradiction in the present use of such jargon and partly because there was no apparent need for such terms." Although Griffin's monograph was published in 1943, the analysis was completed early in 1939 (Griffin 1976). By that time Griffin had noticed that applications of the MTM varied considerably in terms of protocol. Although Griffin did not refer to the work of Deuel (1935a, 1935b, 1937a) and Cole (Cole and Deuel 1937) by name, we suspect he had precisely those efforts in mind when he commented on how some archaeologists working in the Mississippi Valley chose determinants: "A few 'determinants' are chosen from a small number of sites, and these same sites are then used to illustrate that the selected list recurs at these same sites" (Griffin 1943:338). Of course, this was not only what Cole and particularly Deuel did, it was what Griffin himself had done (Griffin 1935).

Recall that Griffin had expressed preference for the bottom-up procedure of building the classification, whereas Deuel (1935b, 1937a) preferred the top-down procedure. This might have been the root of the difficulty Griffin had with the method, but there may also have been some personal reasons that prompted Griffin's remarks. Guthe wrote to Cole on October 25, 1935 (UC), inquiring about the status of what eventually would be the volume on Illinois by Cole and Deuel (1937) and informing Cole that Griffin had told him (Guthe) that part of that book would contain a version of Deuel's dissertation, which discussed the Fort Ancient culture. Griffin (1935) had recently completed his own study of that culture, and

Guthe was concerned that the efforts of Deuel and Griffin had "resulted in substantial duplication of effort." Further, Guthe understood (no doubt from Griffin) that Deuel (1935b) did not refer to Griffin's (1935) effort. Cole responded on October 29 (UC) that "Deuel's thesis was not intended as a treatise on Fort Ancient or any other culture, but an attempt to test the classificatory system we helped set up." Cole also noted that he wished "Jimmy [Griffin] had made clear to me any feeling he had in this matter as I know we have no intention of infringing on the work of any one." Cole also indicated that he did not think Deuel had drawn on Griffin's work because at the time Deuel was writing, Griffin's piece had not yet been published. Further, Cole suggested to Guthe that the fact that Griffin and Deuel had worked independently, used more or less the same data, applied "somewhat different methods," and yet had come to "substantially the same result" was "fine." He assured Guthe that the published version of his and Deuel's book would "make direct reference to Jimm[y]'s methods and results but certainly [they] would not do so without his full consent." The pages referred to in the single index entry for Fort Ancient in *Rediscovering Illinois* contain no mention of Griffin (1935), although that reference is cited on page 208, where Deuel (1937a) emphasized that his and Griffin's methods differed.

Guthe wrote back to Cole on November 7 (UC), stating that if "the Fort Ancient culture was used to test the classificatory system largely because it was the best one as far as information was concerned, it seem[ed to Guthe] that any publication of such a test should include an explanation as to why Fort Ancient was used, namely, because of the work Griffin had done in organizing the material." Guthe agreed with Cole that no individual or institution should have a "monopoly on any single problem or region." But he also argued that "if progress is being made by an institution or individual on a given problem then the courtesy should be extended to allow them to complete what they have begun before somebody else tackles the problem." He emphasized that "due credit should be given to Griffin's report." To this Cole responded on November 12 (UC) with a reminder that "there is a long standing hostility between these two [Deuel and Griffin] which more or less colors whatever they do. I think it is up to us to give them each a good spanking and make them play the game for the benefit of archaeology as a whole. I like both of them very much, but they certainly indulge in a lot of foolishness." Guthe wrote back on November 23 (UC), apologizing for perhaps causing Cole some anxiety and agreeing that "personalities should [not] be dragged into the problem." Whether Cole or Guthe ever administered the "spankings" to Deuel and Griffin is unknown, but the fact that there was animosity between

Griffin and Deuel suggests that the latter's work on Fort Ancient was no doubt the former's inspiration for some of his remarks regarding how the MTM had been used in the Mississippi Valley.[1]

Guthe wrote the foreword to Griffin's 1943 monograph on Fort Ancient. In it he restated the thrust of his earlier letters to Cole when he remarked, "Every applicable research tool in anthropology and its related disciplines has been used [by Griffin]. The results and conclusions of the work of many colleagues have been incorporated into the study. It has been a pioneering effort, demonstrating one method which may be used in the synthesis of data from many sources" (Guthe 1943:v). That method bore little resemblance to the MTM. Griffin's list of what he called "characteristic" traits "does not comprise the Fort Ancient Aspect 'determinants,' as the term was defined in the original mimeographed statements on the classification, nor are they 'diagnostic traits' in the sense of that term in *Rediscovering Illinois*" (Griffin 1943:5). What, then, was Griffin doing in terms of method? First, he pointed out that "few cultural factors other than specific pottery types are peculiar to the Fort Ancient Aspect." Second,

> little or no attempt has been made to delimit either diagnostic traits or determinants that may be used in cultural comparisons to distinguish the Fort Ancient Aspect or any of its foci from all other cultural divisions. Instead, emphasis has been placed on establishing the Fort Ancient complex of traits. The focal and aspect traits have been listed in a separate table in order that the subjective element in their selection may be apparent. In any component which in the future is to be considered a part of the Fort Ancient Aspect a majority of the traits given in the aspect list should be present, provided the site has been fully excavated; and furthermore, the majority of the traits from the new site should be traits included in the Fort Ancient Aspect list. If the new site is to be classified in any one of the proposed foci, it should have, in addition, a majority of the traits characteristic of that particular focus, and, as its dominant pottery complex, the

1. The animosity between Griffin and Deuel was longstanding. In his retrospective examination of the history of midwestern archaeology, Griffin (1976:20) commented on Cole and Deuel's (1937) *Rediscovering Illinois*, noting in particular that to "regard the contributions of the book as the work of Cole and Deuel would be to ignore the milieu or cultural system in which the work was done; it was characterized by relatively free exchange of ideas, *piracy*, delays of publication and *failure to acknowledge significant contributions* (in other words, group intellectual activity, with the individuals whose names are on the publication receiving credit or blame for the development)" (emphasis added).

type or the types characterizing the particular division to which it is to be assigned. (Griffin 1943:5–6)

Griffin had not built a classification of Fort Ancient and its constituent parts that was subject to modification in the light of new evidence. He had, much like Deuel a few years earlier, established lists of traits that he believed were definitive of various cultural units and rendered them as a key that could be used to identify newly excavated materials. How did he do this? According to him, he chose Fort Ancient because there were lots of artifacts from many sites representing the culture, and those materials offered "a profitable field for comparisons of cultural and ceramic materials in light of the recently suggested McKern classification" (Griffin 1943:1). In other words, he already knew many of the constituent members—at least the sites—of the Fort Ancient taxon; he had earlier criticized Deuel for initiating his analysis in exactly the same manner. Although Griffin examined all artifacts and cultural traits, he gave "the most detailed consideration" to pottery because that kind of artifact had been "demonstrated" to be "the most important single factor in the interpretation of archaeological cultural relationships." To describe the pottery, he followed, with some modification, Guthe's (1934) suggestions and, as he had in 1935, Griffin (1943:4) compiled charts of pottery characteristics to determine "whether or not the pottery groups could be considered as relatively homogeneous units distinct from other groups" at Fort Ancient sites and non–Fort Ancient sites, respectively.

Griffin (1943) stated that his procedure followed that of Earnest A. Hooton (1930), a physical anthropologist who had created morphological types of skulls recovered from Pecos Pueblo, New Mexico. One first sorted specimens—skulls or pot sherds—into internally homogeneous groups. Such "morphological typing," as Griffin called it, was then tested via statistical analysis. If that analysis showed "that a relatively homogenous sample selected from a large heterogeneous assemblage is more characteristic of itself than it is of other selected samples or of the assemblage as a unit," then the types specified were valid. In our terms, the types and their definitive criteria were extensionally derived and comprised phenetic groups.

Once the pottery had been classified, the next step was to group sites into foci. Foci were recognized before the final trait lists for each focus were prepared and were "substantiated by, but are not derived from, the analysis" (Griffin 1943:5). Griffin's subjective impressions were confirmed by his analysis. Each focus showed "a close correlation between components." Griffin listed the traits characteristic of each focus as a unit within the Fort Ancient culture, the traits held in common between that focus and one other focus, and also the unique traits of any component. He then identified four foci and listed the traits characteristic of the Fort Ancient culture as a whole. Importantly, he noted that the characteristic traits included the majority of all traits as well as a majority of the traits characteristic of all Fort Ancient foci. He also noted that not all foci contained all of the characteristic traits of the aspect and that "there are few cultural factors other than specific pottery types which are peculiar to the Fort Ancient Aspect."

Donald Collier and George Quimby (1945) lamented that Griffin's study was not published earlier because if it had been it might have reduced later confusion by others over how the MTM was supposed to work. They also stated that the method was used as "merely a means by which Griffin ordered his data so that he would have an entity, definable as a whole or by parts, which he could manipulate for other desirable operations." Curiously, Collier and Quimby suggested Griffin's "use of the McKern classification most closely approaches what was intended by McKern (his views of 1935 and later)." We strongly disagree.

SOUTHWESTERN ALTERNATIVES

During the first decade of the twentieth century, "the concept arose of the development of cultures as the proper field for archaeological research in the Southwest" (Brew 1946:32). As in other areas of North America, prehistoric southwestern cultures were identified on the basis of such things as assemblages of artifacts, architectural features, and burial forms. Stratigraphic excavation provided the means by which culture change could be examined, and it became commonplace to associate all artifacts and features in a stratum and to refer to the conglomerate as an assemblage. By the mid-1920s it was apparent that if progress were to be made in understanding the development of cultures, some consensus had to be reached regarding artifact classification and cultural nomenclature.

A. V. Kidder hosted the first Pecos Conference at Pecos Pueblo, New Mexico, in 1927, the purposes of which included identifying fundamental problems of southwestern prehistory, formulating research plans, and producing a unified nomenclature (Kidder 1927). One product of the conference was the Basketmaker (now Anasazi)-Pueblo sequence. Opinion was unanimous at the conference that "the development of [southwestern] culture was essentially autochthonous" (Kidder 1927:489), meaning it was autonomous and its evolutionary novelty originated internally. In an attempt to establish "a basis for more precise definition of culture-stages [and] to arrive at agreement as to diagnostic culture-traits. . . . [p]ottery, it was agreed, is at the present time the most abundant, convenient and reliable criterion, and the cooking wares the simplest type for preliminary chronological determinations" (Kidder 1927:490). The various cultural periods were dichotomized as exhibiting such things as small versus large communities and the presence/absence of agriculture, pottery making, and craft specialization. As in those areas where the MTM was used, an aggregate of associated artifacts was rendered as a trait list said to represent a culture. Theoretical warrants for designating the boundaries of the aggregates were nonexistent and unnecessary because such sets of things were self-evident (stratigraphically) when encountered in the field.

There were two other important classificatory efforts, one spearheaded by Harold Gladwin of Gila Pueblo, Arizona, and the other by Harold Colton and Lyndon Hargrave of the Museum of Northern Arizona in Flagstaff. The classifications were more overtly biological than the MTM was, although elements of the latter were quickly incorporated.

Harold S. Gladwin

Gladwin, with the help of his future wife, Winifred Jones MacCurdy, established a field center, Gila Pueblo, in Globe, Arizona, in the 1920s. Gladwin had no formal training in archaeology, but he had been on a camping trip with Kidder in 1924 (Haury and Reed 1985). In 1930 he convened a small meeting of southwestern archaeologists for the purpose of creating a classification for Hohokam materials from southern Arizona in a manner similar to the way Pecos Conference workers were handling the archaeological record of the northern Southwest. Gladwin and Gladwin (1930:3)[2] noted in a report that grew out of that meeting that "new forms [of pottery were regularly] encountered which must either be shelved for future analysis or be granted recognition, to the extent of establishing the identity of the type, so that recurring instances can be noted." The discussants agreed that new types should not be described in terms of known cultures because the new types might signify previously unknown cultures; that using definitive criteria of known cultures would be misleading; and that temporal and comparative factors should not be used as these might require later modification. Using biological nomenclature as a guide, two criteria were chosen as definitive characteristics of pottery

2. The initial Medallion Papers issued from Gila Pueblo did not list the Gladwins as authors. Gladwin and MacCurdy married in 1933, at which time the earlier papers were altered with the addition of a glue-on patch to the front cover with their names on it as authors. Presumably they sent patches to libraries that had received their publications. Thanks to J. Jefferson Reid for clearing up that bit of confusion.

types: "a place where the type is known to occur, and its colour" (Gladwin and Gladwin 1930:4). Color, color combination, or surface treatment was chosen as the genus name, and geographic locality determined the specific name. Types such as "Tularosa Black-on-white" and "Kayenta Polychrome" (Gladwin and Gladwin 1930) show, however, that the genus and species designations were reversed in practice. Type names were not to have adjectives that denoted temporal position.

From this system of pottery classification emerged a "comprehensive scheme by which relationships and relative chronology could be expressed" (Gladwin and Gladwin 1934:8–9). Gladwin believed that all prehistoric groups in the Southwest had passed through the same cultural stages but at different times in different places. The system of nomenclature for cultures was hierarchical in structure and from bottom to top consisted of four units. Roots represented groups of people (Hohokam, Caddoan [subsequently labeled Mogollon], Basketmaker [subsequently labeled Anasazi], and Yuman [subsequently labeled Patayan and later Hakataya]; stems represented distinct geographic areas occupied by specific groups of people (San Juan stem of the Basketmaker root, for example); branches corresponded to small-scale "culture areas" (Chaco branch of the San Juan stem of the Basketmaker root) and represented "the various [cultural] developmental series [of phases] which have sprung from roots" (McGregor 1941:6); and phases were time-space-bound cultural variants within branches that contained characteristic features such as associated types of artifacts and architecture (Gladwin and Gladwin 1934:9–10). The Gladwin taxonomy of cultural units, then, was explicitly constructed to incorporate not only formal variation in artifact types but also variation in the geographic and temporal distributions of those types (Figure 5.2).

Gladwin (1936) saw similarities between his scheme and the MTM (McKern 1934[11]), but they were superficial. To highlight the similarities, Gladwin aligned the units of the two schemes as shown in Table 5.1. Gladwin and Gladwin (1934:10) originally stated that phases had "characteristic features," particularly pottery types. Gladwin (1936:258) later indicated that in the Southwest, "components have been listed in our Phases, but not named as such. This designation will be added in our next revised edition." In a later publication (Gladwin 1937), he indicated that phases were distinguished by types of architecture, by types of pottery, and less frequently by types of stone tools. It was here and only here where the similarity between Gladwin's taxonomy (Figure 5.2) and the MTM resided. On the one hand, McKern's units were merely groups of culture traits represented by artifact types that increased in generality as one read up the list. Temporal and spatial relationships were not part of the clas-

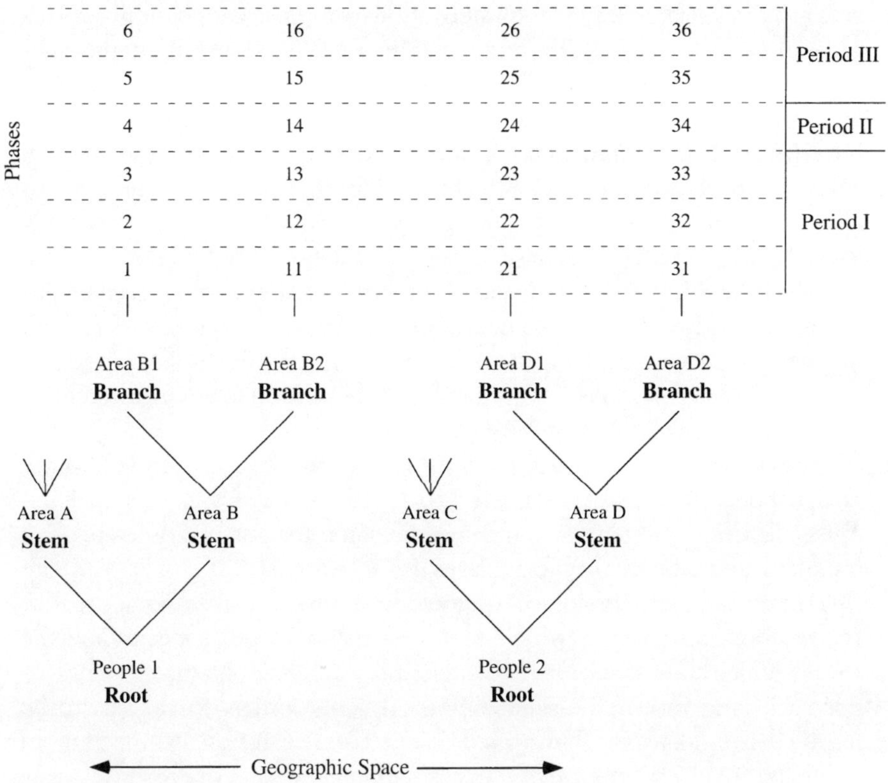

Figure 5.2. A model of Harold Gladwin and Winifred Gladwin's system of roots, stems, branches, and phases. Numbers designating phases are merely labels. Some branches and phases are omitted. Note that time as well as geographic space varies across the horizontal axis; time varies in the sense that designated periods may occur at different times within different branches. Time passes along the vertical axis only in portions of the graph containing phases.

Table 5.1. Harold Gladwin's Alignment of Archaeological Units Used in the Southwest with Those of the Midwestern Taxonomic Method

Southwest	Midwestern Taxonomic Method
Root	Basic culture
Stem	Phase
Branch	Aspect
Phase	Focus
(Unspecified unit)	Component

Source: Gladwin (1936).

sificatory criteria, and phyletic implications were merely possibilities that were to be tested. Gladwin's units, on the other hand, explicitly incorporated temporal and spatial positions as part of the classificatory criteria, and the inferred phyletic relations between the various units were built into the resulting graph. Those units were not nested in the same way that McKern's units were. His units were empirically based on common traits and increasing generality of those traits; formal similarity was the only variable considered. Gladwin's units were nested on the basis of common peoples inferred from shared spatiotemporal position and inferred evolutionary change over time. Gladwin's taxonomy was, then, much like a phylogenetic tree with the added variables of geographic space and ethnic identity. McKern (1944[19]) pointed out these fundamental differences, but no one seemed to take notice.

Shortly after his original formulation (Gladwin and Gladwin 1930, 1934) appeared in print, Gladwin (1936:258) noted that he felt that because the use of "a generic and a specific name for pottery types implied a biological analogy [that formulation] was a mistake. The idea is being carried too far along biological or zoological lines, and men do not realize the profound differences which exist between zoological species and the things which have been made by men and women. Zoological species do not cross and intergrade [and biological evolution] is so slow as to be hardly distinguishable." He argued that cultural evolution was much more rapid and involved "merging and cross-influences. . . . We are really dealing with [cultural] varieties rather than species, and, in consequence, there are bound to be a great many intermediate and transitional types." His skepticism was to be echoed for the next decade and ultimately resulted in the rejection of the biological model of evolution for the study of culture history (Lyman and O'Brien 1997). However, even as Gladwin was rejecting the biological model, two other southwestern archaeologists were going still farther with it.

Harold S. Colton and Lyndon L. Hargrave

Colton was a biologist by training, and Hargrave had been trained as an archaeologist but had a deep avocational interest in biology, particularly ornithology, and had spent most of his career working for and with Colton at the Museum of Northern Arizona in Flagstaff. Gladwin's writings, coupled with Colton and Hargrave's intellectual interests, probably contributed to the latter two adopting some of Gladwin's ideas even as Gladwin was abandoning them in the mid-1930s. But they also had their own particular notions about adopting and adapting the Darwinian model of biological evolution to archaeological problems.

Table 5.2. Lyndon Hargrave's Taxonomy of Southwestern Pottery

KINGDOM: Artifacts
  PHYLUM: Ceramics
    CLASS: Pottery
      ORDER: Basic combination of paste and temper
        WARE (FAMILY): Basic surface color after firing
          GENUS: Surface treatment
            TYPE or SUBTYPE: Description, comparison, distribution

Source: Hargrave (1932).

Hargrave (1932:7) noted that participants at the meeting at Gila Pueblo in 1930 "tentatively agreed to adopt a biological method in the classification of Southwestern pottery types" and that the results had been so "gratifying" that the "Museum of Northern Arizona decided to carry the biological method further, accepting that part which experience had shown would be applicable to inanimate objects such as pottery vessels." He went on to note that "absolute adherence to the method as applied by biologists is, of course, out of the question, but in the classification of [forty] pottery types included in this paper no major difficulty was encountered." His taxonomy is summarized in Table 5.2. Note that it contains two kinds of hierarchical arrangement. On the one hand, the kingdom, phylum, and class units are perfectly nested from least to most inclusive. On the other hand, the order, ware (family), genus, and type units are not nested as units of increasing inclusiveness. They are instead merely an ordering of characters, with surface treatment the least-inclusive character and paste and temper the most inclusive.

Hargrave (1932:9) suggested that "reliance for cultural affinity may be placed on sherds." Colton (1932:1) was even more explicit: "The classification has the following qualities: (1) it is roughly evolutionary; (2) it is based on fundamental structure, not on superficial surface details; (3) closely related types (in general) fall together." Hargrave (1932) described each pottery type in a top-down manner. He first listed the distinctive characters of an order, then those of a member ware, then of each member genus, then of each member type. He then went back up the hierarchy to another member genus of the first ware and worked his way back down. Hargrave also described each type's geographic and temporal distributions. In his words, the "classification is based upon the accepted biological method. Brief descriptions, stressing the importance of basic materials as fundamental criteria for identification, are given under each type mentioned, and discussions of major and minor divisions of the classification are given where it seemed advisable" (1932:32). He also noted that the classification results were not like those of biological systematics: "Many combinations of types and genera are possible in the manufacture of pottery vessels since the surface features of vessels are controlled by the whims of the maker and are not the results of natural laws. Such combinations we call hybrids" (Hargrave 1932:31). This no doubt was the source of Colton's (1932:1) comment that "it must be stressed . . . that this is not a 'natural' classification but is purely artificial. The very nature of the material presupposes this." Hybrids were rare at least in the animal world, so to have them among archaeological remains meant that the classification system applied to artifacts could not be natural but rather must be artificial.

Kidder (1936b:xxv) remarked that Hargrave's patterning of "archaeological upon biological taxonomy" was of "questionable desirability." Kidder's concern was that the "genetic relationships" implied by Hargrave's application of the classification system to his pottery types were tenuous:

> A ceramic or other cultural category, a group of the sort we are accustomed to call a type, is not an entity comparable to a biological species. Species, in the animate world, are kept pure by the infertility of hybrids. The laws of cultural genetics impose different and less tangible, though perhaps no less stringent, limitations. These laws cannot yet be formulated. The whole study of anthropology is, indeed, an attempt to discern their nature through observation of their operation. But certain things we already know: cultural crosses, far from producing sterility, often result in markedly increased virility; cultural parentage is not achieved by simple pair-mating, but may be the result of anything from parthenogenesis to the simultaneous or continuing interaction of many strains, each entering into the blend to a different degree. (Kidder 1936b:xxv)

What Kidder was driving at was what Colton had admitted: The classification system was "purely artificial" because no natural units akin to biological species were being designated by the system. However, this did not stop Colton and Hargrave from later drawing phylogenetic inferences from their pottery types.

A few years after Hargrave published his taxonomy, and a year before Kidder (1936b) published his opinion of that taxonomy, Hargrave and Colton (1935:50) wrote a longer statement regarding the phylogenetic implications of pottery types:

> Pottery types, like so many other things, are descended or derived from something older. Also, slight differences frequently occur in

> related geographic regions so that one can recognize differences and similarities in pottery types over a large area. Those types, generally obviously related because they were made by the same methods of manufacture, thus exhibit many similar characters of materials, surface treatment, and appearance, and are called WARES.
>
> Ware characters tell us many things of a fundamental nature about the people. If there are a number of related types found over a large area we know that this area was occupied by the same people; particularly so if houses, stone work, textiles, etc., were very similar. In some instances even the language spoken might be implied. Objectively we know that the people producing a certain ware in a given region used the same kind of materials, constructed their pottery vessels by the same methods, methods handed down from mother to daughter; and fired their vessels in a long established manner. Ware characters are thus fundamental and can be traced in time and space as peoples moved from one region to another. Type characters are less stable and reflect strongly minor time and space differences so that the time of certain movements of peoples may be determined when the life of a type can be told in years. Because types are more susceptible to change than are wares, in many geographic areas there are many types, each with a story of its own.

Hargrave and Colton (1935:50) listed eight rules of nomenclature for designating types, including that "the permanent name [of a type] must be binomial, i.e., a geographical name followed by a descriptive term" and that the name must not have a "comparative adjective" such as "proto" or "upper." These two particular rules echoed Gladwin and Gladwin's earlier procedure, and the two paragraphs quoted above explicitly provided a commonsensical warrant couched in Darwinian terms for the pottery taxonomies of Gladwin and Gladwin and of Hargrave. Hargrave and Colton made no mention of the other levels of the taxonomy specified by Hargrave, probably because they were preparing their upcoming handbook of pottery types (Colton and Hargrave 1937), where they altered the terminology and used only the three lowest units in Hargrave's taxonomy.

In their *Handbook of Northern Arizona Pottery Wares*, Colton and Hargrave (1937:2–3) defined *pottery type* as "a group of pottery vessels which are alike in every important characteristic except (possibly) form"; *pottery ware* as "a group of pottery types which has a majority of [the important] characteristics in common but that differ in others"; and *pottery series* as "a group of pottery types within a single ware in which each type bears a genetic relation to each other." The difference between type and ware resided in the number of attributes held in common among their members.

As in both the Linnaean taxonomy and Hargrave's earlier formulation, types (species) contained specimens that shared many attributes, and wares (genera) comprised several types that shared fewer attributes. A series was an entirely different matter because it comprised the interpretations given a particular set of types. Types and wares were units for the measurement of time and space because they were defined so as to have particular positions in the spatiotemporal continuum; series were units supposedly comprising a lineage of phyletically related types.

On the one hand, Colton and Hargrave did not indicate why particular characters or their particular states were selected for unit definition as opposed to others. Instead, they simply stated that the "proper" and "obvious" attributes were chosen. In commenting on Colton and Hargrave's classification, Paul Reiter (1938:490) saw it as "stimulat[ing] suspicion that the potters of northern Arizona must have been parsimoniously impeccable in their adherence to ceramic creeds." On the other hand, Colton and Hargrave were clear about the historical relatedness of the types. Their theoretical warrant for the phyletic interpretation of a series had been phrased earlier, in the long quotation above (Hargrave and Colton 1935). Although not developed at length, a series resulted from cultural transmission over time and space. But they went farther and distinguished among derived, collateral, and ancestral types and graphed their relations (Figure 5.3). Their unabashedly Darwinian-evolutionary model of pottery classification, however, was flawed because common sense underpinned the key notion—related forms were related because they were similar. In fact, it should have been the other way around—similar forms were similar because they were related (Simpson 1961:68–69).

Colton and Hargrave offered no explicit and detailed theoretical argument, nor did anyone else at the time, for the similarities being homologous, despite Kroeber's (1931) earlier procedural statement and Colton's own training in the biological sciences. Thus Reiter (1938:490) commented that he "was unable to find a single instance of proof of [the genetic relationships of pottery types]." James A. Ford (1940:264) noted that Colton and Hargrave had not considered "the utility of the types for discovering cultural history." Further, they had ignored the problem of selecting "a class of features [attributes] which will best reflect cultural influences [transmission via contact], and which in their various forms will be mutually exclusive, to serve as guides in the process" of determining ancestral-descendent relationships (Ford 1940:265). We think Ford, without using the term, was speaking of homologous similarity, but he too failed to make this clear. Colton and Hargrave provided no examples of the genetic relations of their types. Instead, they stated simply that genetic relations

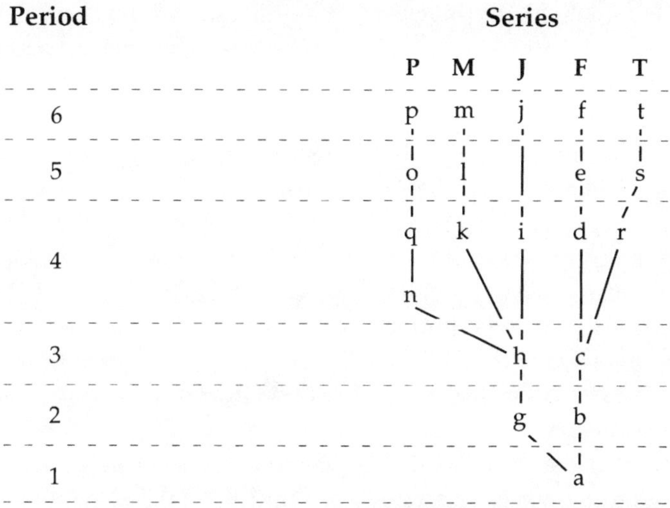

Figure 5.3. Harold Colton and Lyndon Hargrave's model of pottery evolution. Each column of letters represents a series. Type a is ancestral to all other types; type c is ancestral to types d, e, f, r, s, and t; type c is collateral to types d and r, and derivative from type b; types i, j, k, l, m, n, q, o, and p are related to each other through type h; types q and n are both ancestral to type o but collateral with each other and are derivative from types h, g, and a. That type c is collateral to types d and r, and types q and n are collateral to each other, is a function of where the horizontal lines designating period boundaries have been drawn.

among types were "obvious" and "clearly revealed" and that "definite evolutionary characters were recognized" (Colton and Hargrave 1937:2–3, 5).

The problem is this: To hypothesize that two sets of things are related in an ancestral-descendent fashion demands specification of how that relationship is generated. Colton and Hargrave provided no theoretical specification. Instead, they warranted their evolutionary inferences by reference to ethnographic data such as indigenous pottery will be made of local materials, changes in technology represent changes in "people," and styles of design diffuse (Colton and Hargrave 1937:xii). These suggestions were derived from Colton's observations of the behaviors of living Puebloan peoples and comprised empirical generalizations. This was typical of the time, but in fairness to Colton and Hargrave their efforts were more sophisticated than many of their contemporaries' efforts to construct an interpretive framework. They at least explicitly acknowledged the importance of cultural transmission and thus, by implication, heritable continuity.

Colton (1939:3) later followed Gladwin's lead, stating that his goal was to "outline the cultural units of Northern Arizona and show their relationships." Noting that the habits, customs, languages, social patterns, and material cultures of extant tribes all differed to similar degrees, he believed that by using archaeologically accessible material-culture traits, he could establish how closely related prehistoric cultural units were. Marked differences in material culture denoted distantly related (if at all) entities that "might loosely [be called] tribes" (Colton 1939:5). Conversely, similar material cultures denoted closely related tribes. Following McKern, the "characteristics that distinguish these 'tribes' are called determinants" (Colton 1939:5). Following Gladwin and Gladwin, a phase was "a fundamental unit in the culture of a human population of an area" made up of "contemporaneous prehistoric sites [the] determinants [of which show] great resemblances to one another"; "genetically related [phases] are grouped together into a branch [that represents] an Indian tribe" (Colton 1939:6).

For Colton, related branches made up a stem, and related stems constituted a root. Thus, unlike the MTM, which merely indicated phenetic relationships and only implied phyletic ones, Gladwin generally and Colton particularly offered a warrant of sorts for their groups of artifacts. This warrant rested on cultural transmission between ethnographic units such as tribes and peoples occupying different spatiotemporal loci, but it was not well developed and merely used evolutionary terms, the meanings of which were intuitively known to everyone. The use of evolutionary terms did not make it a theoretical system for determining ancestral-descendent relationships. Like the MTM, it did not address the fundamental problem of distinguishing between analogous and homologous similarity, nor did it specify how phyletic relations between artifact or culture types were to be determined.

Reviewers focused on Colton's phyletic interpretations rather than on his methods. Erik Reed (1940:190) thought Colton's scheme was a reasonable one: "The genetic and temporal approach seems more desirable in a region such as this where chronology is relatively well-known." Steward (1941:367) did not find it reasonable: "It is apparent from the cultural relationships shown in this scheme that strict adherence to a method drawn from biology inevitably fails to take into account the distinctively cultural and unbiological fact of blends and crosses between essentially unlike types. . . . It is true that cultural streams often tend to be distinct, but they are never entirely unmixed and often approach a complete blend. A taxonomic scheme cannot indicate this fact without becoming mainly a list of exceptions. It must pigeon-hole. . . . the method employed inevitably distorts true cultural relationships."

In a later statement, Colton (1942:34) explained that the scheme he had borrowed from Gladwin and used in his 1939 monograph was "a classification of prehistoric human groups" and *not* a classification of cultures. Colton (1942:264) indicated that "in the reconstruction of history two essential factors are required, the recognition of human social units by objective characters [determinants], and the construction of a time scale." He hinted at a theory of cultural transmission but did not elaborate. At the time, no one was talking about the transmission or inheritance of culture traits. Although Colton may have implicitly recognized the significance of what he was proposing, and certainly he possessed the requisite background in biology to have done so, his lack of exposition of transmission and inheritance mechanisms incorporated within a theory of cultural development failed to convince his contemporaries that what he was doing was warranted.

Clyde Kluckhohn (1939b:160) suggested that Gladwin's scheme was modified by Colton and Hargrave (1937; Colton 1939) by eventually "fusing it with McKern's" method. In our view, this was untrue. For one thing, Gladwin and McKern both demanded that multiple components were necessary to define a phase-focus unit. Colton argued a single component was all that was necessary. Colton (1939) did borrow the concepts of determinants, components, and foci from the MTM, and this was "a step in the right direction," according to Kluckhohn (1939b:160), who had been worried about determining which traits were diagnostic of cultural units. However, Colton did not use determinants in the way that McKern had originally envisioned. Determinants were supposed to be ascertained by comparative analysis of multiple components, which was impossible if one used but a single component.

As in the MTM, Colton's lower-level units—phases and branches—were distinguished largely on the basis of stylistic traits such as pottery designs, whereas his higher-level units—stems and branches—were based on technological and functional traits. This also typified the MTM. Confusion was compounded by Colton's lack of specification of the definitive criteria for membership in phase and branch units. Colton's system was largely a grouping method not unlike the MTM, in which definitive criteria for phases were extensional derivatives of all cultural manifestations occupying the same position in time. Thus, quite often, the definitive criteria of a phase were not distinguished from the unit members.

Precursors to a New Method

Given that Southwesternists had access to the temporal dimension via dendrochronology and stratigraphy, it is not surprising that the classification systems they used would serve as precursors to what was to replace the MTM in the 1950s. Gladwin and Gladwin (1934) used the term *phase* to denote cultural variations in time and space and suggested that phases be assigned geographic names. A few years later, Gladwin (1937:248) indicated that a phase was a unit of time of relatively brief duration and stated that it was unwise and "not safe to create a phase on [the basis of] only one component." In the 1930s a frequently represented pottery type was often used as the definitive criterion of a phase (for example, Gladwin 1943). Such types were ideational units that were extensionally defined and subsequently refined in the light of new evidence until they became index fossils that occupied very limited time-space positions (O'Brien and Lyman 1999b). Gladwin's (1943:28) statement that "there is nothing so convincing as repetition [of descriptions of multiple specimens] in establishing a type" leads one to suspect his units for discrete objects were extensionally defined classes. Phases and larger units were identified on the basis of "the presence or absence of various types of pottery" (Gladwin 1943:53), suggesting that these units were also extensionally defined classes.

Stratigraphic excavation allowed the definitive criteria of a phase to be extracted from the vertical, and thus time-sensitive, spatial units of archaeological sites. Either natural stratigraphic units or arbitrary levels provided sets of artifacts that were by definition temporally associated; from those assemblages could be extracted a list of traits, manifest as artifact types, that had demonstrably (after some trial-and-error refinement) limited temporal distributions. In turn, comparing these temporally diagnostic traits across the geographic space containing multiple sites allowed one to select those traits that were linked—held in common by multiple components—and those that could serve as determinants—distinguished by vertically superposed components. In light of the general conception that culture was akin to a continuously flowing braided stream of ideas (Lyman et al. 1997; O'Brien and Lyman 1998), the so-called stratigraphic revolution was, in the long run, more damaging than helpful (Lyman and O'Brien 1999; O'Brien and Lyman 1999b). True, it allowed the measurement of time, but it measured time in discontinuous chunks—strata or arbitrary levels—and reinforced the view that discrete cultures were manifest in the archaeological record. A demonstrably gradual, continuous evolution of pottery was cut up into stratigraphically documented chunks termed phases, which in turn were treated as culture units. Once temporal and spatial boundaries were set for ceramic types, other traits were imported to flesh out a phase description. The result was a mixing of various kinds of things, some that were clearly historical types and others that were variously descriptive, technological, and/or functional types (O'Brien and Lyman 1999b). Which traits were definitive and which merely descriptive typically went unanswered.

Colton (1939:9) used *component* in the same sense that McKern (1939[9]) did—"to indicate the presence of a focus in a large site where several foci are indicated." But he also equated a phase with McKern's focus: A phase-focus was "a fundamental unit in the culture of the human population of an area" (Colton 1939:6). A phase-focus unit was distinguishable from earlier or later units "by the differences in material culture traits, sometimes very slight" (Colton 1942:34). Kidder et al. (1946:9) later defined a phase as a "cultural complex possessing traits sufficiently characteristic to distinguish it for purposes of preliminary archaeological classification, from earlier and later manifestations of the cultural development of which it formed a part, and from other contemporaneous complexes." For Paul Martin et al. (1949:17), a phase referred to "an interval of time and to specific pottery types, bone and stone tool types, and house forms, all of which we have deliberately and arbitrarily set up as classifications." A few years later, Martin et al. (1952:30, 31) stated that "a phase is an artificial and chronological system superposed on man-made materials. . . . [W]e know that there is no break between phases and that phases are merely *arbitrary culture groups* set off in arbitrary units of time. . . . [A] phase may mean a moment, a span of centuries, a cluster of traits, or none of these; but rather an endless moving belt of progress—a continuum." Such musings would be reworked into a new system of units early in the 1950s. Before turning to that reformulation we need to consider a few commentaries on the MTM that took place in the 1940s, as that method was being eclipsed by a complete reworking of the phase-focus unit.

COMMENTS AND QUERIES

The 1939 version of McKern's classificatory procedure was his final published version. He published a shorter piece a year later (McKern 1940[16]) in which he summarized several of the critical points of the method, and he also felt compelled to publish a short clarification in 1943 (McKern 1943[18]). In this piece he devoted most of his discussion to two issues: Why the system of units comprised four classes (focus, aspect, phase, pattern) and what the "ethnological equivalents" of each were. He began by noting that the base unit had served little or no purpose and was generally omitted from classifications. With respect to the number of units, McKern indicated that psychology suggested the human mind automatically structures observations of a complex subject into a taxonomy and that the number of levels or categories of units should be determined based on utility.

Given that four units had been "apparent from several attempts at local classification before the problem of general taxonomy was attacked," that number was a "convenient" one to use (McKern 1943[18]:313).

In turning to the second question, that of ethnological equivalents of each taxon, McKern (1943[18]:314) responded with his own questions: "What are the definitions of these ethnological divisions? What is a tribe? What . . . are the divisions such as the Dakota or Chiwere, the Northern Plains or Central Eskimo, the Southwestern Culture Area?" He noted that particular tribes sometimes were sociopolitical units, sometimes cultural units, sometimes traditional units, sometimes linguistic units, and sometimes racial units. The net result was that some ethnological units were based on language, others on culture, and still others on other variables, and when a group was classified on the basis of more than one of those criteria, the results often conflicted. This was not a surprising conclusion given that his mentor's (Kroeber's) mentor, Franz Boas, had shown over the preceding several decades that race, language, and culture were largely independent of one another (various chapters in Boas 1940). McKern's method was consistently and always "concerned with varieties of culture as visualized from a comparative study of traits" (McKern 1943[18]:314). This was in part a result of the fact that one could not always identify the linguistic affiliation of an archaeological manifestation. Similarly, the geographic criterion was inapplicable to archaeological materials because prehistoric peoples had changed locations in prehistoric times.

Walter W. Taylor, who received his doctorate from Harvard in 1943 under the tutelage of Clyde Kluckhohn, voiced numerous criticisms of the MTM in his dissertation, later published by the American Anthropological Association as *A Study of Archeology* (Taylor 1948). He noted that the terms *trait complex* and *culture complex* as used by archaeological taxonomists did not follow standard usage. Citing anthropologist Ralph Linton (1936), Taylor argued that such a complex should comprise a set of functionally interrelated and interdependent units. Archaeologists had instead used the term *complex* merely to denote an aggregate of traits found within an archaeological manifestation. Citing Kluckhohn (1939c), Taylor pointed out that although similarities in lists of such units might denote historical relationships, this was difficult to accept given the absence of evidence for spatial and temporal propinquity of the lists. Next, Taylor pointed out that the presence-absence data given in trait lists masked important variation in the relative frequencies of traits, resulted in a failure to weight traits based on their importance, and therefore produced potentially "misleading" comparisons. Finally, Taylor argued that if one truly desired a "cultural taxonomy," then the taxa constructed by an archaeologist could not be simply lists of traits such as were produced by the MTM. Instead, those units must "reflect cultural relationships as they existed among actual, pre-existing human groups" (Taylor 1948:143). Trait lists were etic units, meaning that they had nothing to do with how a prehistoric toolmaker would classify an item, and these would not do: "What the archeologist is trying to do is to find some classification which will correspond most fully to what actually were the cultural relationships of human groups in the past" (Taylor 1948:146). Taylor alleged that although McKern professed otherwise, the taxonomic units of the "McKern system . . . are potentially representative of formerly existing units, cultural, linguistic, 'tribal,' ethnographic, etc." (Taylor 1948:140). Accepting this potentiality, the archaeologist should, in Taylor's (1948:145) view, "interpret his site in terms of the human group or groups which used it. This is nothing more or less than the construction of a cultural context for the site or its separable components. When this has been done and, if necessary, some definition made of the 'culture type,' then will come the time when comparative and taxonomic studies can profitably be initiated."

To McKern (1943[18]:315) a focus "may in instances correspond to a tribe, but fails to do so in other instances because the focus represents what is known of a cultural division whereas the tribe may represent a political, traditional, or other concept." Similarly, phases and patterns might correspond to smaller and larger culture areas, respectively, but this too did not seem to be a universal correspondence. McKern, then, was appropriately cautious with respect to converting archaeological data into something an ethnologist would recognize. He was going against the general grain of the discipline—one that was headed more and more in the anthropological direction. It was a mere ten years later that Philip Phillips (1953:246–247) penned the oft-quoted phrase "New World archaeology is anthropology or it is nothing." This was clearly what Taylor had in mind, and it would become the centerpiece of the next formulation of North American archaeological method.

THE WILLEY AND PHILLIPS PROPOSAL

By 1950 the MTM had been applied in numerous forms, few of which were true to what McKern envisioned. Determinant and linked traits typically were not identified; recurrent trait sets sometimes were referred to as diagnostic traits; various quantitative measures of similarity were used; and time and space were considered during classification. The ad hoc and piecemeal nature in which the method and its system of units were applied produced a situation in which just about any procedure of grouping components was acceptable, if only to its user. The only thing common to virtually all applications was the use of traits and lists thereof derived from artifacts and features. Philip Phillips and Gordon R. Willey made the next serious effort to build a model of classification units that could be used on a continental scale (Lyman and O'Brien 2001b). It had long been axiomatic in Americanist archaeology that typological similarity was an indicator of cultural relatedness. This was the reasoning behind McKern's development of the taxonomic method, and thus for many archaeologists a common or similar history for units judged to be similar was automatically implied. Phillips and Willey's model rested on this axiom, and it reflected in several ways the influence of the MTM.

Phillips and Willey (1953) discussed how to classify aggregates of artifacts and how to link those units to form regional chronologies. Their archaeological units included components, following McKern (1939[15]), and phases. The latter term was chosen over McKern's focus because Phillips and Willey, like Gladwin (1936), preferred the stronger temporal implication of phase. Thus they explicitly incorporated time in their archaeological units. Phillips and Willey went beyond the MTM in another way as well. They explicitly incorporated space in their scheme when they defined three spatial units—*locality* (often a site), *region*, and *area* (Phillips and Willey 1953:617). Further, Phillips and Willey (1953:621) were less hesitant than McKern to suggest that a component was approximately equivalent to an anthropologist's "'community,' [defined as] the maximal group of persons who normally reside together in a face-to-face association," and that a phase was approximately equivalent to a society. Phillips and Willey emphasized that the equations were hypothetical, but they also noted that they gave components and phases the aura of anthropological reality.

Following McKern, Phillips and Willey (1953:619) defined a component as "the manifestation of a given [phase] at a specific site." A phase was viewed as being temporally, spatially, and formally "sufficiently characteristic to distinguish it from all other units similarly conceived" (Phillips and Willey 1953:620). Components could be "combined into phases because analysis reveals cultural uniformity amounting to practical identity" (Phillips and Willey 1953:630). This implied the MTM's recurrence criterion. But unlike in the MTM, and instead following Colton (1939), a phase could be defined on the basis of a single component, although using multiple components was a better option. Again as in the MTM, the necessary and sufficient conditions for membership in a phase could be modified on the basis of newly discovered components.

Phases were classes (conceptual units) of components, and components were empirical manifestations of phases. One had to have a phase in order to identify its member components, but one needed components in order to write a phase definition. Thus a phase was extensionally derived just like a focus of the MTM. The difference was that not only were formal (phenetic) criteria used, so too were time and space used to help delimit a phase. A phase was to have a limited spatiotemporal distribution; no such explicit restriction attended the focus concept, although in practice most foci did have limited distributions.

For Phillips and Willey, as in the MTM, a component was the manifestation of a single occupation—a set of temporally, spatially, and behaviorally associated artifacts. The locations of the temporal and spatial boundaries of a component were dictated by stratigraphy. Stratigraphic boundaries were empirical and therefore did not require theoretical specification. Stratigraphic excavation produced collections of artifacts that were "segregated by layers of refuse and subdivisions thereof, in order that the succession of occupations may be determined" (Rouse 1953:59). This echoed earlier remarks (for example, Kroeber 1925; Wissler 1917) that a single, continuous occupation would occur in an unstratified deposit, whereas multiple, non-overlapping occupations would each occur in a separate stratum.

Phillips and Willey suggested that the conceptual units they termed *traditions* and *horizons* would allow one to correlate phases. *Horizon* was defined as "a spatial continuum represented by the wide distribution of a recognizable art style" and was viewed as being "useful in equating in time phases of culture widely separated in space" (Phillips and Willey 1953:625). In 1958, they defined a horizon in terms of what it signified: "a primarily spatial continuity represented by cultural traits and assemblages whose nature and mode of occurrence permit the assumption of a broad and rapid spread" (Willey and Phillips 1958:33). A horizon comprised numerous artifact types or traits, whereas a horizon style was a single artifact type or trait. *Tradition* was defined as "a major large-scale space-time-cultural continuity, defined with reference to persistent configurations in single technologies or total (archeological) culture, occupying a relatively long interval of time and a quantitatively variable but environmentally significant space" (Phillips and Willey 1953:628). This definition, too, was amended to read "an archaeological tradition is a (primarily) temporal continuity represented by persistent configurations in single technologies or other systems of related forms" (Willey and Phillips 1958:37).

Phillips and Willey (1953:630; Willey and Phillips 1958:41) used a single figure to illustrate how components, phases, traditions, and horizons all related to one another. We have modified and expanded this figure to illustrate those relations (Figure 5.4). Time and space are explicitly incor-

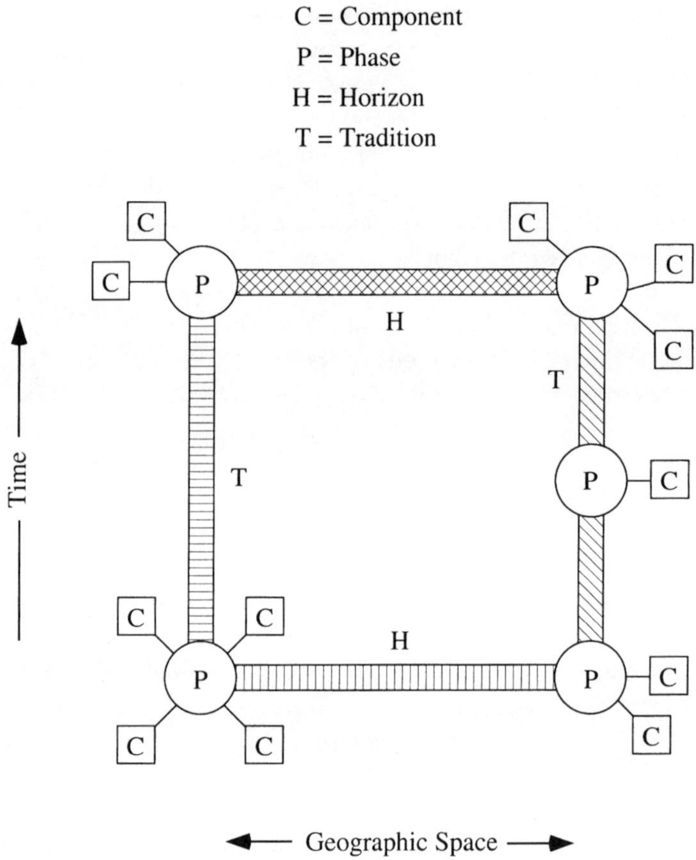

Figure 5.4. Philip Phillips and Gordon Willey's model of the interrelationships of components, phases, traditions, and horizons.

porated into the system of units, and phases are connected if not truly integrated with the horizon and tradition units. Unlike the MTM, Willey and Phillips clearly were attempting to monitor the phylogenetic histories and relationships of the prehistoric cultures designated by their phase units.

Horizons and traditions reflected cultural transmission over space and time, respectively (Rouse 1954, 1955), and provided the empirical warrants for discussing the historical development of cultures. They were "integrative" units that denoted "some form of historical contact," but the "contact" they denoted did *not* signify "phylogeny" (Willey and Phillips 1958:30). Willey's (1953:368) suggestion that "principles of continuity and change are expressed in the degrees of trait likeness and unlikeness which are the mechanisms of establishing the genetic lines binding the assemblages together" was metaphorical with respect to cultural transmission. But historical "relatedness," when couched in a temporal framework aimed at studying lines of cultural transmission (lineages) such as that envisioned by Willey and Phillips, cannot fail to be phylogenetic in the sense of Darwinian evolution's "descent with modification." The general abhorrence in anthropology and archaeology of anything Darwinian resulted in this contradiction (Lyman and O'Brien 1997).

Willey and Phillips (1955) also made a serious effort to align what was then known of the American archaeological record with a model of cultural evolution. That model was derived largely from Willey's contact with Julian Steward, who had proposed what would later be termed "multilinear cultural evolution" (Steward 1949, 1953, 1955). Willey and Phillips were appropriately cautious because they did not use the model strictly as an explanatory device but rather as an architectural structure on which to arrange the various prehistoric cultures according to their spatiotemporal distributions. To accomplish the arrangement, they designated five evolutionary stages of development—Lithic, Archaic, Formative, Classic, and Post-Classic—and used them as classes for identifying the historical-developmental level of the various prehistoric cultures in different areas.

McKern (1956) commented on the first version of Willey and Phillips's (1955) historical-developmental sequence, arguing that ecological factors, ethnological data, and historical information had not been sufficiently considered. Specifically, he "refuse[d] to accept the arbitrary allocation of early Northwest Coast culture to the Archaic as evidence that other Archaic cultures 'must have possessed' [Willey and Phillips 1955:791] similarly complex cultural developments" (McKern 1956:360). More significantly, he pointed out that contrary to Willey and Phillips's position, an agricultural economy was unnecessary to a sedentary life. McKern concluded that in their cultural-stage "taxonomy," Willey and Phillips had not done a very good job of establishing definitive criteria for each evolutionary stage. Willey and Phillips (1958) addressed the classification problem McKern identified by noting that they were merely attempting to determine if all known cultures could be arranged within their system of stages. We are unaware of any response by McKern to the second formulation of Willey and Phillips.

Much of what McKern and his MTM had failed to do was resoundingly dealt with by Willey and Phillips. Time and space were explicit and significant considerations. Archaeological manifestations rendered as phases had anthropological significance. The phylogenetic implications of horizon, tradition, and phase units were explicit. The higher-level units—aspect, pattern, and base—of the MTM were discarded, but so too were various strong parts of McKern's method. The most notable of these was the recurrence criterion, which demanded the comparison of multiple components and the clear specification of determinant, diagnostic, and linked traits. Instead, simple phenetic comparisons of trait lists were carried over into Willey and Phillips's method. The result was regular confusion over which traits were definitive of a phase and which were merely descriptive (Lyman et al. 1997). Similarly, after the mid-1950s McKern's insight regarding the materialist paradox was swept under the carpet and largely forgotten over the next thirty years.

DISCUSSION

The temporal dimension was explicitly not part of the classificatory criteria used by the MTM, and the method was criticized on this point. Steward (1942:339) noted that the method was flawed because it produced a "set of timeless and spaceless categories." In response, McKern (1942[17]) protested that he had merely set time and space aside for the moment in favor of form. He had *not* discarded them. Steward's (1944) rebuttal entailed two elements. First, he could not see how a taxonomic classification, which for him denoted branching evolution, could be forced onto cultural phenomena that not only branched or diverged through time but also converged to create a reticulate form of evolutionary descent. Second, Steward could not find any utility in the taxonomic method because it lacked any reference to theory.

Albert C. Spaulding, who had worked with McKern in the 1930s (Kehoe 1990), thought such criticisms were largely misplaced. Spaulding (1949:3) astutely pointed out that the MTM was "*a* taxonomic system, not *the* taxonomic system." According to Spaulding, the MTM was "intended to express judgments as to the degree of contact and cultural interchange which existed among the prehistoric communities." It was not, Spaulding argued, a method for determining relationships between cultural taxa but rather "simply a way of expressing the result of the determination." Thus, the method was not in conflict at all with other classifications of archaeological manifestations that might be built.

Phillips and Willey were in some ways more explicit than McKern, but in other ways they were equally ambiguous. For example, neither McKern nor Phillips and Willey discussed how artifacts were to be rendered into traits. They, along with most other archaeologists, simply compared artifact types. Typological similarity rather than trait-list similarity became the measurement device, but *why* the units—the types—comprising the measurement device were constructed the way they were went largely unremarked.

6
The Midwestern Taxonomic Method in Light of Biological Systematics

Tenacity is as essential as originality in science. (D. Hull 1988:288)

Looking back at the history of Americanist archaeology in 1961, William Haag (1961:19) observed that the midwestern taxonomic method "grew out of a dissatisfaction with the direct historical approach on the one hand, which could help archaeology to only a limited extent, and with ethnological and linguistic identifications [of archaeological manifestations] on the other. The apparent promise that this method would bring some greater measure of order led to its being widely interpreted as a genetic system more than a taxonomic one. That is, it seemed axiomatic that all manifestations having similar traits or a measure of similarity, were of common origin. . . . [L]ater users of the [method] drew sweeping relationships on the basis of cultural similarity." Haag noted as well that "the eventual fate of [the method exemplified] the destiny of a logical construct that proposes to meet virtually any conceivable situation." McKern would have disagreed with this evaluation. The MTM was *not* intended to "meet virtually any situation" of analysis and interpretation. Rather, it was intended to do two things. First, it was intended to provide a common terminology for a set of classificatory units that would enhance communication between archaeologists working in different areas. Second, it was intended to facilitate comparative analyses and thereby help archaeologists to decipher culture history and to determine "cultural affinities" (McKern 1939[15]: 303). Cultural relationships might be phylogenetic, but they might not be. They were, however, always phenetic because they were assessed simply on the basis of formal similarity. The fact that the method was used in variously modified forms by numerous researchers into the 1950s, the fact that the cultural units Mississippian and Woodland are still with us, and the fact that new cultural phases—foci with spatiotemporal coordinates—are identified yearly, suggests that the method has never completely died. Certainly we think Haag would not disagree that the *affinities*—of whatever kind—of archaeological materials were, throughout the twentieth century and still today, determined on the basis of shared traits or typological similarity—that is, phenetically.

Jesse Jennings and Edward Norbeck (1964:7) summed up the MTM in what we consider typical fashion:

> This system of classification of culture traits is identical in principle with the taxonomic scheme used by biologists in classifying forms of life. It consists of a series of increasingly large and generalized categories, beginning with the cultural inventory of a single level in the earth at a single site, which is called a "component." Two or more closely similar components form a "focus." Successively larger categories are called "aspect" and "phase." The most useful of these classes has been the focus. Cultural inventories similar enough to be classified together as a focus occur close together geographically, and the focus then denotes a local variety of culture of a geographical range that is defined to the extent that components have been revealed by archaeological excavation. When archaeologists have recognized a number of components (i.e., when they have excavated a number of sites having essentially the same cultural materials), the possibility of assigning the focus an assured placement in time is increased, since the stratigraphic positions of the components are ordinarily known and cross-checks are possible. Although opinion is divided regarding the usefulness today of the McKern classification, there is no doubt of its usefulness in the past. Application of the system in the 1930's and 1940's to the mass of unorganized data from the eastern two-thirds of North America resulted in almost instantaneous perception of both spatial and chronological relationships previously unnoticed in a century of study. As a tool for understanding, it was revolutionary and spectacularly successful, a fact to which its present reduced importance attests.

We characterized the preceding summary statement as typical because Jennings and Norbeck did not mention the important aspect of the method—the role of determinants and determinant complexes—and they only implied that "two or more closely similar components" were required to denote a focus. It also was typical because as Gordon Willey (1953) observed when characterizing Americanist archaeological method and theory of the mid-twentieth century, it was axiomatic to conclude that two archaeological manifestations were related because they were similar. McKern's determinant traits, diagnostic traits, and linked traits were neither distinguished nor recognized by Willey (1953), Phillips and Willey (1953), or almost anyone else who commented on how to determine cultural affinities among archaeological materials.

In yet another retrospective, James B. Griffin (1970:v) said the following about the MTM:

> This taxonomic device was designed to produce order within and between the large number of prehistoric complexes known at the time [early 1930s], all being referred to as "cultures." The method provided the framework for recognizing and demonstrating these different levels of relationships between these prehistoric manifestations and thus served as a valuable device for a period of years. Sites with a high degree of similarity were grouped together as a *focus;* foci which had a preponderating majority of their traits in common were called an *aspect;* one or more aspects which had a near majority of identical traits and other similarities were called a *phase;* and several phases could be regarded as belonging to a *pattern* if they shared a number of broad general traits. . . . Some parts of the methodology, terminology, and philosophy of this approach are still in use in defining the functioning of prehistoric societies, but the Midwest Taxonomic Method is no longer employed as a primary tool. It is not likely that another formal taxonomy will be developed.

Other classifications were in fact developed, such as Gladwin and Gladwin's, Colton and Hargrave's, and Willey and Phillips's. Only the first two were hierarchical in structure, but all were formal in the sense of specifying analytical units or concepts such as branches, series, wares, phases, horizons, and traditions. Some of these were variations of McKern's units.

Other archaeologists of the last half of the twentieth century also commented on the method, and we will turn to those comments later in this chapter. Before doing so, we return to the subject of chapter 2 and discuss the thoughts of a few early-twentieth-century biologists with respect to classification. Although McKern never referenced any biological literature in his various statements on the method, we may have found if not the precise book on which some of his reasoning was based, a book that contains at least some particular thoughts that influenced his conceptions of biological and archaeological taxonomy.

EARLY TWENTIETH-CENTURY BIOLOGICAL TAXONOMY

Recall that McKern minored in paleontology during his undergraduate education. Given that he earned his bachelor's degree in 1917, his textbooks would have been published that year or earlier. Richard Lull's (1917) *Organic Evolution* was typical of biological texts of the time, some of which McKern most certainly read. When Lull published his book, he was professor of vertebrate paleontology at Yale. Lull did not have much to say about biological taxonomy, but what he did say is interesting:

> [Organisms] may be grouped together for convenience of study in one of two ways: they may be classified taxonomically, according to actual blood relationships, or from the standpoint of their life conditions. . . . The adaptive response on the part of two unrelated organisms to similar environmental conditions may give rise to convergence, wherein organisms come to resemble each other so closely that they have sometimes been actually classed together. The distinction between convergent and homogeneous [homologous] organisms is often a matter of extreme difficulty.
>
> When the classification is based upon living organisms only, errors are also apt to occur, for groups of animals which to-day stand entirely isolated are shown to be related when their fossil ancestry is known. Zoological classification depends therefore in a measure upon Paleontology or the study of ancient life. (Lull 1917:29)

Lull clearly recognized that biological taxonomy could serve two analytical masters, but each required a different classification. The taxonomy could be constructed so as to reflect the phylogenetic, or blood, relationships of extant taxa, or it could be constructed so as to group organisms based on similarity of adaptation. If one desired the former, then data from the paleontological record were required. The difficulty with building a phylogenetic taxonomy concerned the distinction between analogous and homologous characters and character states. The problem of distinguishing between analogous and homologous characters and character states never arose in McKern's discussions. It should have arisen, given that A. L. Kroeber (1931) pointed it out early in the history of the development of McKern's method. Despite Lull's statement that making such distinctions was difficult, progress had been made by the early 1930s, and Kroeber was right on the mark when he pointed out the distinction to anthropologists. By the early 1930s even Lull was more optimistic. Lull (1931:42) repeated his earlier remark that "paleontology aids the systematist in his search for relationships which the modern animals could not possibly reveal," and he pointed out that for homologous organs, "the basic structure is the same in all, but variety of use has produced dissimilarity of form" and that this implied a "correspondence in origin." This was virtually the same wording that Kroeber (1931) used. McKern was either oblivious to these discussions, which we doubt, or, as we argued in chapter 3, he, like Kroeber (1923) and many other anthropologists of the 1920s and 1930s (see Lyman and O'Brien 1997), saw organic evolution as an inappropriate model for cultural evolution.

That a classification with a taxonomic structure might reveal relationships among the classified phenomena, and those affinities might be phylogenetic, was clear in a discussion that might have served as a major source of inspiration for McKern. The author of the discussion was James Johnstone, a British marine biologist. The relevant discussion appeared in Johnstone's (1914) *The Philosophy of Biology*, a book published during McKern's tenure as an undergraduate. Johnstone (1914:208) stated that the species is "a group of organisms all of which exhibit the same morphological characters. This sameness is not absolute, for the individuals composing the species may vary from each other with respect to any one character." In modern terms, species are polytypic because although individual members of a species will be similar, they will not be identical. This sounds like McKern's member components of a focus being practically but not completely identical. Most important, note that Johnstone's definition is a good one for the typological species concept and also that the method of grouping is phenetics.

Johnstone described the procedure for building a taxonomic classification of organisms:

> We can associate together groups of species in the same way that we associate together the individuals of the same species. There are certain morphological characters which are common to all the species in the category, but there are also differences between specific group and specific group, and these differences may be regarded as variations from the generic morphological type. All the Cats, for instance, have certain characters in common. . . . We postulate a feline type of structure, and we then regard the characters displayed by the cat, lion, tiger, leopard, etc., as deviations from this feline morphological type. Thus we establish the Family Felidae. But again we find that the Felidae together with the Canidae, and many other species of animals, also display common characters . . . and we express this

> resemblance by assembling all these families in one Order, the Carnivora. The Carnivores, however, are only one large group of Quadrupeds: there are many others . . . and all of these possess common characters. . . . We therefore group them all in the Class Mammalia. [The possession of an internal backbone by mammals and] Birds, Reptiles, Amphibia, and Fishes [results in our being] able to form a large category of animals—the Chordata—and this phylum is sharply distinguished from all other cognate groups. (Johnstone 1914:209–210)

Johnstone described a phenetic, bottom-up procedure of construction. The analyst starts with individual organisms, lumping together those that are most similar because they share the greatest number of characters, then lumping the resulting groups into more-inclusive and general groups on the basis of fewer, more-general characters, and so on until large, inclusive groups are reached. The definitive characters of the most-inclusive taxa are variously functional (carnivorous lifeway) and/or fundamental (presence of a backbone). All these comprise McKern's classificatory procedure without using the term *determinant*. The most convincing evidence that McKern in fact read Johnstone's book or one very similar is found in Johnstone's discussion of the purpose of biological classification. Johnstone (1914:289) stated that "it is convenient that we should express the results of biological investigation in schemes of classification, for only in this way can we reduce the apparent chaos of naturally occurring organic things to order, and state our knowledge in such a way that it can easily be communicated to others." This sounds exactly like McKern: Nature's chaos must be organized by classification in order for science to progress and its results to be communicable.

Another bit of evidence suggesting that McKern was influenced by Johnstone is found in the latter's argument that the biological taxonomy is an artificial construct rather than a reflection of nature's reality:

> We must always remember that the classifications of systematic biology are conceptual arrangements, depending for their precise nature on the point of view taken by their authors. The clear-cut distinctions that apparently separate phylum from phylum, class from class, order from order, and so on, do not really exist. There are no such categories of organisms in nature as genera, families, and the higher groupings. All that we can say exist naturally are the species, since all the organisms composing each of these groups are related together by ties of blood-relationship, and all are isolated from the or-

> ganisms composing other species by physiological dissimilarities which render the plants or animals of one species infertile with those of any other. . . . Our arrangements of plants and animals into systematic species and the higher groupings are convenient ways of symbolizing the results of morphological and physiological investigations, although they also indicate the main directions taken by the evolutionary process, but the manner in which they are stated in taxonomic schemes is always a more or less formal one. . . .
>
> [The] morphological schemata which we construct as diagnostic of phyla, or classes, or orders, etc., [do *not*] separate these groups from each other so clearly and unequivocally as our classifications suggest. (Johnstone 1914:289–291)

What Johnstone was driving at was that other than the species unit, which can be defined as reproductively isolated, the taxonomic units making up the Linnaean taxonomy are phenetic and thus arbitrary in terms of their number and their composition. This sounds like McKern, who argued that the recurrence criterion established the validity of his terminal taxa, yet also indicated that his terminal taxa—species for Johnstone, foci for McKern—were to a small degree arbitrary because of diffusion. Similarly, Johnstone's implication that the results of the classification "indicate [only] the main directions" of evolution, not its details, sounds like McKern. As McKern (1939[15]) indicated, the results of his classification might suggest phylogenetic relationships, but such implications had to be tested because they were by no means assured. Johnstone's last sentence is simply another way of making McKern's statement that there is no final and ultimate set of determinants for a culture taxon. This is because the status of a trait as a determinant (or linked, or diagnostic) trait depends on the comparisons being made. Johnstone (1914:292) made virtually this same point when he stated that "one does indeed see that a certain structural plan is characteristic of organisms belonging to each of the great phyla, while more detailed structural plans may be said to be characteristic of the subgroups. But minute morphological . . . investigation reduces almost to nothing the characters which are absolutely diagnostic of these various groups." Finally, Johnstone (1914:335) anticipated McKern's recognition of the materialist paradox, stating that "*the organism is a phase in an evolutionary flux*. Categories of organisms—varieties, species, genera, etc.—are fictions. They are arbitrary definitions designed to facilitate our description of nature. They are types or ideas. In constructing them we follow the method of the intellect, and we represent by immobility that which is essentially mobile and flows."

MODERN BIOLOGICAL TAXONOMY

A number of properties are shared by the MTM and phenetics. First, both focus on formal similarity without concern for kind of trait (homologous or analogous). Second, both are largely atheoretical with respect to why taxonomic units are built the way they are other than noting that the T_{j-1} members of T_j units are formally similar and that as taxonomic rank increases, the number of shared characters decreases. Third, phenetics considers unit characters—discrete (nonoverlapping), more or less nonreducible properties—and the MTM considers culture traits, which are also discrete, more or less nonreducible characters. Pheneticists define unit characters as "those that cannot be subdivided into logically or empirically independent characters" (Sokal 1966:110), but they recognize that it is logically impossible *not* to have character states that themselves have various states, save perhaps at the atomic level (Griffiths 1973). Using similar wording, Kroeber (1940:29) argued that a cultural trait could "usually be broken down into two or more traits," and Robert Ehrich (1950:471) noted that "if we regard the cultural trait as a cultural molecule, we find that it too can be atomized."

The fourth property shared by the MTM and phenetics is that both build a set of nested, increasingly inclusive units that pheneticists call *operational taxonomic units*—a term necessitated by the fact that phenetic taxa might not be those recognized by the Linnaean taxonomy. OTUs are artificial units, just as McKern emphasized that the cultural taxa of the MTM were artificial. Finally, both phenetics and the MTM produce results that have phylogenetic implications, but detecting such implications is not their analytical goal. Rather, the goal is to provide a set of members of each taxonomic level, the affinities of which are formal (phenetic) such that the resulting groups can be discussed. Pheneticists sometimes use their OTUs to infer phylogenetic history, just as some archaeologists other than McKern used a version of the MTM to infer phylogenetic history from the cultural taxa they constructed.

In the MTM the cultural taxa—focus, aspect, phase, pattern, base—to which assemblages are assigned are aggregates of artifacts and features. The taxa are groups that do not have any necessary temporal or spatial meaning. Such meaning has to be acquired independently of the technique. Groups are constructed phenetically—on the basis of the formal similarity of the aggregates. Quantitative measurements of similarity such as are done in modern phenetics are not attempted by the MTM. Kroeber suggested a way to measure similarity quantitatively, but his suggestion was not followed. Others, such as Griffin and Deuel, determined the percentage of traits shared between units, but they did not attempt to establish how similar was similar enough to comprise a particular taxonomic level. Rigid guidelines for determining this were suggested by McGregor, but no one followed them. One result was that the most-inclusive taxa were subjectively determined and thus eventually were discarded as largely inoperable.

Grouping methods merely describe a data set and assess formal similarities of subsets. The addition of new data requires that the whole system of units and their relations be recalculated. But the versions of the MTM that archaeologists applied proved quite usable. Why? Because those applications produced extensionally defined units that, once established on the basis of an initial analysis, were later used as classes. Initial inspection of a sample of components resulted in their being assigned to one or more foci and perhaps one or more higher-level units. Such assignments in turn resulted in the identification of traits common to all *and* limited to T_j members of the T_{j+1} unit. These traits initially held the status of linked traits that could be used as determinants for the T_{j+1} unit. They might be diagnostic traits at the T_{j+2} level, but they could also be linked and thus determinant traits (Figure 6.1). The status of a trait as determinant, linked, or diagnostic depended on the materials compared.

Once determinant traits at the T_{j+1} level had been derived, they served as definitive criteria for the identification of additional T_j members. As McKern (1939[15]:304) stated, "Classification is nothing more than the process of *recognizing* classes, each class identified by a complex of characteristics." Once a set of determinants has been derived for a T_{j+1} taxon, "any manifestation [at the T_j level] found to show this complex of [determinant] traits may be classified by definition" (McKern 1940[16]:19). This meant that the particular traits that met the conditions—they were present in all inspected units but in no others (determinants)—depended on the components polled. Thus the list could, and according to McKern was supposed to, change as knowledge of the archaeological record grew and more components were examined. The price paid was one of two kinds. Following McKern's argument literally meant that traits would change their status as new data were compared, and thus no ultimate list of determinants for any taxon could be written. The price to pay here was that definitive criteria of each taxon would be woefully unstable. Alternatively, the definitive criteria of the taxa were stable, but the price was that the definitive criteria of all cultural taxa were historical accidents of the assemblages known at the time the determinants were derived. Most archaeologists chose stable definitive criteria and lived with their accidents of history.

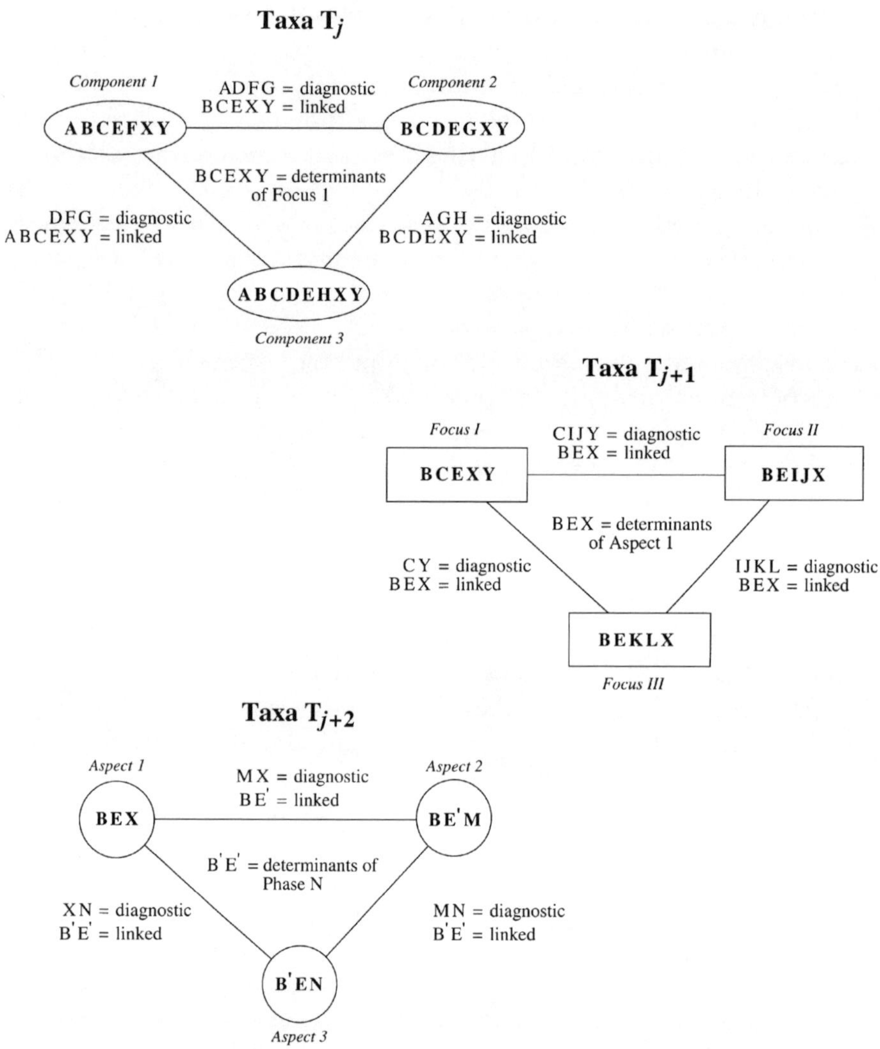

Figure 6.1. How to operationalize the midwestern taxonomic method. Capital letters represent culture traits; those without a prime indicate a specific form of a trait, and those with a prime indicate a general form of a trait. Note that as one progresses to taxa of rank T_{j+3} and greater (not shown), fewer traits and more general traits will comprise determinants of each particular taxon.

The advantage of the second alternative was that one's initial classification did not have to be changed after every field season. A little fine-tuning might take place, such as with Griffin's (1935, 1943) two-stage analysis of the Fort Ancient Aspect, but no major realignment of group boundaries or significant alterations of the definitive criteria (trait lists) of various cultural taxa was necessary. Choosing the second alternative no doubt contributed to the view that a single component was sufficient to provide the definitive criteria of a cultural taxon. The recurrence criterion emphasized by McKern was not used, or if it was, a focus might be proposed as a tentative unit until a second, similar component was found. Of course, this yet again begged the question of how similar was similar enough, but no one bothered to raise it in any serious fashion. One result was the relabeling in the 1950s of the MTM's focus unit as a phase, which added to formal similarity the criterion that components be spatiotemporally similar.

The MTM is a phenetic method. Because the nature of the culture traits used to build the taxa varied across the spectrum of homologous and analogous characters and also varied from specific unit characters to general fundamental characters, we view the results as comprising an affinity tree presented as a hierarchical classification. The included components and higher units are affines based on their various degrees of formal similarity. Other kinds of affinity are also implicated, such as phylogenetic relationships at low taxonomic levels and adaptational relationships at higher taxonomic levels, but this theoretical aspect of the method remained undeveloped and implicit.

EVALUATIONS BY OTHER ARCHAEOLOGISTS

Modern archaeologists have sometimes mischaracterized the MTM. A case in point is Alice Kehoe's (1990:34) statement that "cladistics is like McKern's Method in that it eschews all but one principle in ordering data (in cladistics, phylogeny; in McKern, a basically morphological similarity). Neither cladistics nor McKern's Method incorporate time or space criteria." The second sentence is correct, but the first is not on two counts. First, cladistics uses a particular kind of homologous character—synapomorphy (Figure 2.13). McKern made no distinction between analogous and homologous characters or between kinds of homologous characters. Second, cladistics orders phenomena based strictly on synapomorphies; phylogeny is *not* the empirical basis of an ordering (Brower 2000). Rather, phylogeny is the theoretical *explanation* for an ordering having the arrangement that it does (Kluge 2001).

Kehoe (1990:32) suggested that the various cultural taxa of McKern's taxonomic method were "ultimately determined by a worker's subjective judgment of the degree of similarity between components. . . . [But] the subjectivity inherent in the Method is negated by the public consensus. . . . Foci are like populations within a species, aspects correspond roughly to species, phases to genera, patterns to families in the Linnaean system, and bases to orders. . . . Like the Linnaean system, an ordering by the Midwestern Method was basically subjective, but carried a veneer of objectivity because real objects were adduced in argumentation to support a classification." These statements indicate a misunderstanding of not only the MTM but also the Linnaean system. The MTM was subjective only in the sense that two workers might compare different sets of traits manifest in multiple components. Assuming both workers chose the same set of traits, the same linked and determinant traits would result. Here, the MTM was more explicit than the Linnaean system. The former explicitly acknowledged that traits and their statuses depended on the manifestations compared, whereas the latter did not. Further, it should be clear that foci are nothing like "populations within a species" as alleged by Kehoe. Rather, foci are equivalent to species; they are taxa (classes), not empirical phenomena such as a population of organisms.

Richard Krause (1977:6, 1989:282) erroneously claimed that the MTM is "a six taxon, content-based taxonomic hierarchy." There are in fact only five taxa, although there are six units. Components are empirical and thus are not taxa. They are equivalent to populations of a species of organism (Figure 3.1). A group of multiple components categorized as a focus comprises the lowest, most-specific, and least-inclusive taxon—what is termed a *terminal taxon* by biologists. Krause argued that the method's units are ordered based on "set inclusion" of formal traits. In simple terms, "taxa are arranged so that each lower level unit is *a proper subset* of each higher level unit" (Krause 1977:6). This is true only if one ignores the fact that the larger and more general the taxon, the more general and the fewer its traits. As McKern (1934[11]) indicated, a basic culture could have pottery; a member phase of that basic culture could have pottery with various tempers; one of its member aspects might have mostly shell-tempered pottery; and one of that aspect's member foci might have exclusively shell-tempered pottery. Each terminal taxon T_j is literally a subset member of each T_{j+n} taxon, but this is only because the latter are denoted by more-general and fewer traits. In McKern's example, "for pottery alone, we have two determinants for the basic culture, nine for the phase, nineteen for the aspect, and twenty-six for the focus" (Krause 1977:9). In the final published version of the method, McKern (1939[15]:307) stated that "for the more specialized divisions . . . the determinants will be an enriched edition of the determinants for the immediately preceding, more general division, as altered to include greater detail, plus a considerable number of trait elements peculiarly characteristic of the more specialized division."

McKern did not have much in the way of temporal data and only a paucity of geographic data, and he was, by his own statements, following paleontological practice of considering only formal characters during classification. Krause argued that the set-inclusive logic of McKern's taxonomic method demanded that time and space not be considered. To illustrate why this is so, Krause (1977:7) presented a fictional example: "If Component A was occupied from 1700 to 1725, and Component B from 1720 to 1750, there would be only [six] years common to [both sets]. In other words, the logically legitimate duration of the focus would be calculated at [six] years. This solution would, however, make minimal empirical sense and lead to extreme difficulties in forming yet higher level taxa." Although true, Krause failed to recognize the role of determinant, linked, and diagnostic traits, whether formal, geographic, or temporal. If each of the six years shared by the two fictional components is treated as an independent trait, and each of the remaining forty-five years is as well, then only six of the total fifty-one annual traits (11 percent) are shared. Were such a low frequency of linked traits found among formal phenomena by McKern, we doubt he or anyone else would group the two manifestations together and give the six shared trait years 1720–25 the status of determinant traits. The same applies to geographic data and to temporal data such as that described by Krause.

Modern phenetics holds that taxa are *polythetic.* This means that each individual T_{j-1} member of taxon T_j has many characters, only a subset of which will be definitive of T_j. Further, not all T_{j-1} members of taxon T_j need display all definitive criteria of T_j to be identified as a member of T_j. Here is where McKern differed from modern pheneticists. His determinants were by definition shared by all T_{j-1} members of T_j. The fact that virtually all archaeologists who used the MTM failed to distinguish among determinant, linked, and diagnostic traits resulted in most cultural taxa being polythetic.

Bruce Trigger (1968:530) stated that the MTM "can now be seen as a highly formalistic misapplication of the taxonomic approach to the classification of archaeological cultures." This implies there is but one correct way to classify archaeological phenomena taxonomically and that McKern's way is not it. Trigger's characterization is problematic because he does not tell us what the correct application of the taxonomic approach comprises, let alone how it differs from McKern's approach. Trigger (1989:190) later suggested that foci and aspects "were defined" by "artifact types" recurring across multiple components. This is not what McKern said. Artifacts were classified in various ways, but they were used analytically as cultural traits that could vary markedly in scale, from the color of a design motif on a ceramic vessel to a form of projectile point to a burial pattern. McKern argued that the status of a trait as determinant, linked, or diagnostic depended on the comparisons being made. Thus, no ultimate list of determinants—definitive criteria—was possible. That McKern and others in fact *used* various criteria as definitive is a more accurate assessment. Trigger (1989:191) alleged that no attention was "paid to the fact that artifacts that were stylistically highly variable, such as pottery, often were divided into more types than were stone and bone ones." This is false. McKern worried about this regularly in his articles and even provided an argument (albeit weak) that such differential treatment of artifacts was legitimate. "The problem," McKern (1939[15]:306) wrote, "narrows down to the selecting, from the traits comprising a complex subject, those trait details which have sufficient cultural significance to qualify them as culture determinants."

Trigger (1989:191) stated that the "dendritic scheme [of the MTM] implied that cultures, like biological species, differentiated along irreversible paths, thereby ignoring convergence brought about by diffusion." This too is false. McKern (1939[15]:311) remarked that "under the blending influences of diffusion, and the divergent tendencies involving cultural growth by invention, there can be no hard and fast natural division lines" between his cultural taxa. McKern also explicitly downplayed the genealogical and phylogenetic implications of the taxonomy precisely because of the then-common view that cultural evolution, unlike biological evolution, was reticulate. Trigger (1989:192) also suggested that the MTM, "while struggling for classificatory objectivity and quantitative precision, perpetuated the pessimistic views about the Indians' capacity to change that had characterized American archaeology during the nineteenth century." McKern explicitly denied quantitative precision when he argued that we "must rule out the statistical method" (National Research Council 1937:55), and with the exception of McGregor's (1941) lone and ignored suggestion, there is no evidence of a struggle for "quantitative precision." Nor is there any evidence that McKern or anyone else who used the MTM or some version of it denied "the Indians [a] capacity to change." In fact, the numerous laments that the MTM ignored time directly and McKern's and others' implicit recognition of the materialist paradox contradict such a claim.

Finally, Trigger (1989:273) argued that the narrow "classificatory orientation of the Midwestern Taxonomic Method, and of chronological studies generally, suppressed a professional interest in the behavioral interpretation of archaeological data in North America." In our view this is at least partially incorrect because for one thing a cultural trait as viewed by McKern and especially by Deuel comprised evidence of human behavior. Further, McKern was concerned, as were others, that the manifestations comprising the archaeological record were not sets of frames in a motion picture. At best, those manifestations represented an incomplete and static record of past phenomena. Archaeologists assumed that archaeology was but prehistoric ethnography and that their job was to arrange artifacts in a chronological sequence so that they could track cultural lineages and processes. Of necessity, then, the first job had to precede the second.

Gordon Willey and Jeremy Sabloff (1993:123, 124) stated that the MTM is "probably best designated as [a] *genetic-taxonomic*" classification and that the set of cultural taxa it uses comprises a "genetic-taxonomic ladder." Neither characterization is accurate. McKern indicated only in passing that the taxonomy held phylogenetic implications. Further, the system of units comprised a hierarchy of nested taxa, not a "ladder," and most certainly not a progressive evolutionary ladder according to Alton Fisher. Willey and Sabloff (1993:124) were correct that "neither McKern nor the other proponents of the [MTM] were turning their backs permanently on space and time." As McKern said time and again, the MTM produced a set of formal (read: phenetic) cultural units whose temporal and spatial distributions could be summarized in a separate chart.

Robert Dunnell (2000) is virtually the only commentator who mentions the various trait statuses (determinant, link, diagnostic) and also gets the number of taxa (five) correct. He also points out that McKern never defined the term *trait*. Dunnell (2000:372) states that McKern sought "'natural' or 'real' groups without the influence of theoretical input." We disagree. Several times McKern was explicit that his classification produced artificial groups as opposed to natural groups. Further, he implied that manifestations would change group membership depending on the comparisons made, which suggests he did not view his groups as real or natural. Otherwise, there is no evidence suggesting that McKern based his classification on any theory, unless one considers phenetics to be theoretically informed, but even pheneticists indicate that it is not so informed. What he did do, and what seems to be the source of confusion, was to use the Linnaean taxonomy as a model for the MTM. Lack of knowledge of the implications of the Linnaean taxonomy as those were conceived in the first several decades of the twentieth century contributes to the confusion.

CONCLUSION

The MTM is an important part of the history of Americanist archaeology. Its gestation took place when archaeology was experiencing significant growing pains. Its early days witnessed the establishment of the Society for American Archaeology (Guthe 1967), three archaeological conferences sponsored by the National Research Council (O'Brien and Lyman 2001), and the heady days of the Works Progress Administration (Lyon 1996). The MTM comprised a phenetic technique. Archaeological manifestations were grouped based on their formal similarities manifest as shared cultural traits. Similar components were grouped into a focus; similar foci were grouped into an aspect; aspects that shared some traits were grouped into phases; phases that held a few general traits in common were grouped into patterns; and patterns that shared a couple of very general traits were grouped into a base. McKern's distinction among determinant, linked, and diagnostic traits was largely ignored by those who used the method, and some ignored the bottom-up method of unit construction. The practical result of such misapplications was that by about 1950 the method as originally designed by McKern had been abandoned. Most large, inclusive units were ignored, the focus was renamed a phase to incorporate time into the classification, and phases were linked based on units known as horizons and traditions. In our view, the interpretive result of these changes was that cultural units—phases—no longer were merely phenetically related. They instead were historically related, which meant they were *phylogenetically* related. The significant contribution of the MTM to the culture-history paradigm of Americanist archaeology was that it made archaeologists think about how they performed comparative analysis. That it failed to prompt them to think about theoretical matters caused the "cultural affinities" sought by McKern and his contemporaries to remain ambiguous in later classificatory models such as Phillips and Willey's. Those later models continue today, with those attendant ambiguities, to guide much archaeological research.

Previous commentators on the history of Americanist archaeology have tended to mischaracterize the MTM for three reasons. First, many of them have focused on how the method was described and applied by others rather than on McKern's original conception. Those descriptions and applications were clearly not of the sort McKern envisioned. Second, commentators usually have studied only the last programmatic statement (McKern 1939[15]). There is a wealth of detail not found there that resides in earlier and later statements published by McKern as well as in his correspondence. Finally, it should be abundantly clear that although McKern used as his model the Linnaean taxonomy as he knew it from coursework in paleontology, that taxonomy in the 1920s was not the same epistemologically nor ontologically as it was after about 1940. Previous commentators have failed to notice this. We have attempted to place our evaluation of the MTM and of McKern's reasoning within their proper historical context. In so doing, we think we have revealed why that method had a short, yet significant, life span within Americanist archaeology.

PART II
Historical Documents

A number of the papers presented here have been previously published, but several of them written in the early 1930s have not. In order to track the ontogeny of the midwestern taxonomic method, the papers should be read in chronological order. We have arranged the papers in that order based on when they were presented or published. All papers were retyped and edited. In order to enhance this part of the volume as a research tool, we include the original title (if any) and date of presentation or publication, and also indicate the original pagination in brackets. The source of the original from which the version printed here was taken is indicated in parentheses. Editing of the text involved (1) correcting spelling and punctuation errors, (2) omitting extraneous footnotes, (3) converting some footnotes and all citations to modern *American Antiquity* reference format, and (4) modernizing the spelling of some words. We also numbered the single figure and the single table that occur in these papers and wrote captions for each. Editorial changes beyond this are enclosed in brackets. References cited in the various manuscripts are listed at the end of the volume.

7
Culture Type Classification for Midwestern North American Archaeology

W. C. McKern

McKern, W. C. 1932. Culture Type Classification for Midwestern North American Archaeology. Paper prepared for presentation at the meeting of the Central Section of the American Anthropological Association. April.

Editors' Note: Although we have been unable to locate this first statement on what became known as the midwestern taxonomic method, it probably exists in some archive. We leave a space in its honor, with the hope that someone will pursue its whereabouts.

8
A Suggested Classification of Cultures

Carl E. Guthe

Guthe, C. E. 1932. A Suggested Classification of Cultures. Committee on State Archaeological Surveys, National Research Council. October 24. (Illinois State Museum Archives)
[1]

THE PROBLEM:

Archaeological evidence indicates the existence of culture relationship areas of greatly varying size, many of which show correspondingly varying degrees of cultural similarity in their component parts. The uncritical application of the term "culture" to a variety of types of determinant-complexes, ranging from the essentially simple to the specifically complex, has led to an improper and undefinable generalization of its meaning. This creates confusion between the several degrees of culture relationships and obscures the necessity for comparative research.

A system of classificatory terms is needed in order to distinguish between these various types of determinant-complexes.

TYPES OF DETERMINANT-COMPLEXES:

Since in the archaeological field our first contacts with cultures are, figuratively, at the tips of the branches rather than at the roots, this list of types is begun with the smallest unit of cultural classification.

A. The close association of objects indicating two or more material culture traits, in deposits of a single occupation or burial site, furnishes an imperfect estimate of the type of culture of those who used these objects. A single long-occupied site may contain two or more temporally related A-types.

B. The same A-type of complex may be found in more than a single site, but the identicality of its determinant traits will not be widespread. This B-type represents the culture of a single group who occupied several sites which now furnish identical material culture traits.

C. A comparative study of a number of B-types will almost invariably show slight differences between traits, but an essential and inescapable generic relationship, indicating the existence of minor local differences in material culture traits of a single group of people. By combining the traits of the several A-types involved, a more complete knowledge of a specific, phenomenal culture complex is obtained, which is apt to have a somewhat larger sphere of influence than the B-type of complex.

D. This type has been called a "basic culture," and is manifested over wide areas as a well-rounded complex of characteristic culture determinants, which, with the accumulation of detailed information, is found to be composed of a number of sub-groups of the character of the C-type.

[2] E. A comparison of data from neighboring fields with local data will, to an ever-increasing extent, permit the identification of still larger classes of cultures. Thus a number of D-types might be grouped on the basis of peculiar similarities into E-types, which would be larger cultural groups of far broader distribution, corresponding to the ethnological primary culture area.

F. Finally, the F-type of determinant-complex is the primary culture foundation, determined by a few fundamentals of widespread importance and influence, such as the agriculture-pottery complex.

It will be seen that two major considerations determine this classification of types of determinant-complexes. The first and most important is the similarities of culture traits and complexes. In the simpler types the emphasis is upon individual traits showing minor variations. As the types become more general, the minor variations are emphasized to less degree, and the number of traits increased, until in C-type the greatest number of traits are considered. Then, with a still decreasing interest in minor variations, the less essential traits and complexes are dropped until in the F-type only the broad fundamental determinants are used.

The second major consideration is geographical distribution which, however, is always secondary to the similarity of determinants. The classification begins with the smallest geographic units and closes with the largest.

The most difficult aspect of the problem is to choose terms which will serve adequately as descriptive "handles" for the several types, and still conform to a number of limiting considerations.

Table 8.1. The Relationship of Taxonomic Terms and Cultural Taxa

Northern Agriculture-Pottery			II		
			I		
	Mississippi	Upper Mississippi	——??——	Oneota	Iowa Sites
				Western Uplands	Midway
				Grand River	Walker-Hooper
				——??——	Fisher (Ill.)
				Lake Winnebago	McCauley
		——??——	——??——	Upper Republican	Sweetwater
				Historic Pawnee	
			Fort Ancient	(Several groups)	Sites in Ohio, Ind. and Kent.
			Iroquois	(Several groups)	Sites in Ontario, N.Y. and east
		Middle Mississippi	——??——	Aztalan	Aztalan
				Cahokia	East St. Louis
			——??——	——??——	F-34 (Lewistown)
		Tennessee-Cumberland	Gordon	Kentucky	Williams
				Tennessee	Gordon
					Fewkes
			Etowah	——??——	Cartersville
			——??——	Natchez	
		Lower Mississippi	Bluff Dwellers		
			Arkansas	Ouachita	
				Red River	
			Delta	(Several groups)	Sites along Miss. R. in Ark. and Miss.
	Woodland	Eastern Algonquian	——??——	III	
				II	Lamoka
				I	Lamoka
			——??——	Long Island	
			——??——	——??——	Safe Harbor
		Lake Michigan	——??——	——??——	Menomini Reserv.
			Effigy Mound	——??——	Kratz Creek
			Nebraska	——??——	Walker-Gilmore
		——??——	Hopewell	Scioto	Seip
					Turner
				——??——	Lewistown (Ill.)
				Michigan	Grand Rapids
				Iowa	
				Trempealeau	Nichols
	Gulf	——??——	Moundville		
			——??——	Urn Burial	
			Florida		
		——??——	Burnt Rock		
			Texas Coast		
	South Atlantic	——??——	Shell Mounds		
			Sand Mounds		

LIMITING CONSIDERATIONS:

1. *Simplicity.* Terms and classification should be comprehensive without being too involved.
2. *Elasticity.* The classification should be adaptable to needs arising from future discoveries and consequent corrections. Numerals and letters should be avoided.
3. *Intelligibility.* The terms should be readily comprehensible and easily adopted by the specialist and layman. English words would give the best results.
4. *Appropriateness.* The terms should not have dictionary definitions totally at variance with the newly applied technical significance.
5. *Clarity.* The terms should not have a common generalized meaning and should not seem to be dependent for full meaning upon another noun.
[3] 6. *Ambiguity.* False interpretations will be avoided by choosing words which are not now used as technical terms in any other classification in anthropology. This includes biological terms, of course.
7. *Comparisons.* Since the morphological, temporal and spatial relationships between the many determinant-complexes are as yet unknown, terms connoting such relationships should be avoided. That is, evolutionary, chronological and geographical terms would tend to restrict the meaning of the classification. Terms of this nature, as experience shows necessity, might be added later as modifying adjectives to the type name.

THE USE OF THE TERM "CULTURE"

Since the term "culture" refers to the complete set of traits and complexes used by a given group of people, and since the term has in actual usage become a vague one, it should be used to refer to the total group of complexes, without a specifying adjective, or at most with one of a generalized meaning. For example: "The rather simple culture illustrated by these specimens belongs to the 'Upper Mississippi Pattern,' although its 'Aspect' cannot be determined because of lack of data"; "The Hopewell 'Aspect' is identified with an artistic, essentially peaceful culture."

THE TABLE

Table 8.1 is an attempt to fit terms already in existence into the suggested scheme. It is obviously incomplete, and is in no way authoritative. It is presented merely as an added tool in studying the problem.

9
Local Types and the Regional Distribution of Pottery-Bearing Cultures

W. C. McKern

McKern, W. C. 1933. *Transactions of the Illinois State Academy of Science* 25:84–86.

[84]

Local Types and the Regional Distribution of Pottery-Bearing Cultures

by

W. C. McKern

Milwaukee Public Museum, Milwaukee, Wisconsin

This report sketches briefly late archaeological activities in Wisconsin with specific regard to pottery types, their distribution, and the extent to which they have helped establish our present opinions on the classification and distribution of cultures. Comparisons are attempted with neighboring and other related areas to show the indications of wider regional manifestations of local phenomena.

Collections of potsherds obtained from camp and village sites scattered throughout Wisconsin contain at least two easily distinguished types of pottery: (1) a rough, grit-tempered, cord-imprinted ware, named the Lake Michigan, and (2) a smooth, shell- or cell-tempered, incised ware, frequently equipped with loop-handles, named the Upper Mississippi. The first type is the more common and might be described as characteristic.

Lake Michigan culture.—The first intensive research in Wisconsin was concerned with the excavation of a compact group of effigy, conical, and linear mounds which were apparently the product of a single culture and are tentatively accepted as typical for the "Effigy Mound culture," probably a variant or subtype of the Lake Michigan culture. The pottery was rough, granular, low-fired ware, tempered with grit, decorated primarily with imprints from a cord-wrapped paddle, but with examples of a secondary intaglio ornamentation executed by means of cord-wrapped implements, or, more rarely, by means of incising or indenting, the forms varying slightly from a single *olla*-shaped pattern. The absence of indications of European contact (such as glass beads and implements of iron, brass, or silver) warranted the tentative conclusion that the culture flourished in a locally prehistoric period.

Habitation sites on the Menomini Reservation, a region long occupied by the Menomini Indians, yielded materials illustrative of a practically pure culture complex including the Lake Michigan pottery industry. The widespread prevalence of Lake Michigan pottery in Wisconsin may then reflect the equally widespread dominance of a basic culture largely common to the ancestors of the historic Algonkins of this province, comparable to the known historic dominance of the linguistic and cultural stock.

Aztalan culture.—The Aztalan culture complex, the second to be determined in Wisconsin, was encountered at the Aztalan village site in the south central part of the state and differs markedly from that of the Effigy Mound culture. Aztalan pottery is relatively superior. The tempering is generally of shell; the paste for the best grade of ware is thoroughly mixed and of uniform texture; surfaces are smooth; the hardness varies between a fairly soft utilitarian product and a finer ware of maximum hardness for a low-fired product; shapes are various including vessels with angular shoulders, hemispherical bowls, bird-effigy bowls, bowls with contracted rims, shallow platters, vessels with handled covers and gourd-shaped ladles; both vertically placed loop-handles and laterally directed tab-handles are represented; entire surfaces or certain limited surface areas are covered with a red paint or slip and are dyed black; the [85] best of the black ware is highly burnished; geometric intaglio patterns include both straight and curved linear motifs.

An original deposit at Aztalan illustrating the Lake Michigan culture had been so disturbed and mixed with other debris, due to cultivation, that the stratigraphic record has been lost, but a number of transitional potsherds that show mixed Aztalan and Lake Michigan influence illustrate lateral gradation and indicate that the two archaic groups were to some extent contemporary.

Upper Mississippi culture.—The third or Upper Mississippi culture was first encountered at a habitation site and associated group of low semispherical mounds. The pottery industry, which was well developed, was represented by many sherds and a number of entire vessels. This ware, illustrating the second most common pottery type found in the state, is characterized chiefly by such traits as shell tempering, flaky texture, light weight, smooth surfaces, roughly incised decorations employing a repetition of simple geometric motifs, shapes including hemispherical bowls, round-bottomed vessels often equipped with pairs of vertically placed loop-handles, beakers, and short-necked bottles. Simple undecorated rims and vertically notched rims are most common.

The most casual student may readily distinguish this pottery from Lake Michigan ware but plain sherds of the better quality may be at first confused with similar plain sherds of Aztalan pottery. Both are shell-tempered, smoothly surfaced, and of like texture, but rims, body shapes, and decorative motifs and treatments are distinctly different.

Later, three habitation sites on the Wisconsin banks of the Mississippi and three on the shores of Lake Winnebago supplied information for three variants which have been named, respectively, Grand River, Western Uplands, and Lake Winnebago.

Trempealeau culture.—The fourth distinct culture was first encountered in burial mounds and adjacent camp sites in Trempealeau County. The traits of the complex are distinct from those of the other cultures, although the pottery shows a pronounced similarity to that of the Lake Michigan culture. It is grit-tempered, has a granular structure, and not infrequently bears a primary surface decoration in intaglio effected by means of a cord-wrapped paddle, but the secondary decorative treatment is generally executed with a stamp or roulette, and the finer ware is smoothly surfaced, embellished in all known instances with an incised, cross-hatched outer rim, and radically departing in shape from the *olla*-form common to both the Lake Michigan and the utilitarian Trempealeau vessels.

Problems.—We have, then, four distinct cultures, of which close variants have been determined for the Lake Michigan and Upper Mississippi divisions. Our major problems are, briefly, who, when, and where. A general survey of historic Indian customs and a comparison of their culture traits with those known for the archaic groups convinces us only that we are dealing with the products of Indians; all the data cited indicates nothing more specific than a locally prehistoric time period for all four cultures; and available data regarding the geographical distribution, or center of distribution for each culture, are as yet meager.

Two courses of research will contribute to their solution: (1) continued field research of stratified sites that may supply information bearing upon time sequences, and (2) laboratory research to determine the cultural grouping of pure basic traits to form characteristic culture-indicative complexes, followed by a comparison of local data with those available from neighboring fields.

[86] The only stratified site investigated for Wisconsin gives evidence of an original Hopewell camp, probably contemporaneous with and later followed by Lake Michigan culture. The latter was finally contemporaneous with Upper Mississippi culture before disappearing to leave only Up-

per Mississippi culture. This time sequence applies only to the particular site studied and is not yet verified by findings at other sites.

A comparison of Lake Michigan and other pottery of the Woodland area makes it apparent that Lake Michigan ware, which is ascribed to some of the local Algonkins, is closely similar to so-called Algonkin pottery, which occurs over an area that extends from Iowa to the Atlantic coast. A closely parallel complex of pottery traits is known for some of the proto-historic and historic eastern Algonkins. The distribution of the ware, in so far as we know it, corresponds to the distribution of historic pottery-making Algonkins. These suggestive facts do not warrant the postulation that only Algonkins possessed the pottery industry, but tend to support conclusions that it was a culture-trait of some of the Wisconsin Algonkins. The question as to whether or not the builders of the effigy mounds, with their Lake Michigan type of pottery, were related to Algonkian progenitors can not be determined on the basis of pottery alone.

A comparison of the basic Upper Mississippi culture complex with culture-indicative data from other fields yields the information that closely parallel traits are recognized in Illinois (Langford 1927), Iowa (Keyes 1927), Minnesota, North Dakota, South Dakota, and Nebraska (W. D. Strong and E. Bell, personal communication).

The Aztalan culture finds its near parallel in the earlier of the two variants (A. R. Kelly, personal communication) represented in the Cahokia culture of Illinois. More distant comparisons serve to identify the Upper Mississippi and the Cahokia-Aztalan basic cultures as of Southeastern character and probably origin. There is reason to believe that both cultures are relatively late intrusions into the Woodland area.

The Trempealeau complex of traits is found to be extraordinarily like that of the Hopewell culture of Ohio. One of the most important of these trait similarities was that of pottery. Research in other states has revealed that the basic Hopewell culture was influential over an area extending from New York to Wisconsin and from Kentucky to Michigan. The place of the culture in the time sequence has been determined as relatively early for one Wisconsin site, as previously stated, and the tentative chronology for Illinois in Krogman's (1930) report also places basic Hopewell as relatively early in that state. However, accepting these chronological conclusions, it does not follow that basic Hopewell culture is to be identified with a definite time stratum wherever encountered; cultural relationship may involve cultural ancestors or descendants as well as a single cultural generation.

10
The Problem of Culture Classification

W. C. McKern, Thorne Deuel, and Carl E. Guthe

McKern, W. C., Thorne Deuel, and Carl E. Guthe. 1933. The Problem of Culture Classification. National Research Council Circular Letter. (National Research Council Archives, Washington, D.C.)

[1] Room 4019, Museums Building
Ann Arbor, Michigan
April 4, 1933
Dear Colleague:

This communication deals with the problem of culture classification on the basis of determinant complexes which was originally brought to your attention in my letter of October 24, 1932, and the accompanying manuscript on the subject. A number of thoughtful and worthwhile answers were received. A conference of six individuals was held in Chicago on December 10th to discuss the whole problem. The following suggestions resulted from this conference and a study of the replies obtained through correspondence. It is recommended that the original manuscript be kept before one during the following discussion.

This classification of cultures is based entirely upon the culture traits and complexes themselves, and an attempt is made to eliminate all other considerations. It is felt that a clearer appreciation of the comparative culture problems will be obtained through an analysis of the determinant complex for each culture. By the term "determinants," we refer to those particular traits among the known evidences of a material culture which, because of their individuality, serve to differentiate it from other cultures. These traits, or determinants, will differ in various cultures. In the Southwest, for example, the pottery shapes and decoration constitute highly practical determinants, and architecture is a close second. On the other hand, stone and bone implements are of little value as determinants because of their great similarity throughout the region and throughout the course of time. Yet in southern California, bone implements serve as excellent determinants. In the Mississippi Valley, cultural variations in pottery, in burial customs, and in the use of copper make these traits, among others, valuable determinants. The suggested classification seeks to distinguish between cultures and groups of cultures in terms of culture differences only; that is, by using only culture determinants as criteria.

It is important to understand that the geographical extent of a culture and its chronological relation to other cultures do not constitute criteria of differentiation in the classification. There are precedents in the fields of linguistics and paleontology for this method of scientific grouping. As we all know, languages are grouped together or separated on the basis of differences in language alone, and neither culture nor physical type have a classificatory significance. Similarly, in paleontological work, the fossils are primarily and essentially grouped according to their morphological similarities, and neither geographical location nor chronological position are the primary criteria for distinguishing types of fossils. To be sure, the temporal and geographical position of evidence in both language and paleontology are useful in supplementing the classification, but are not an integral part thereof. In this classification of cultures, when the grouping is according to associations or complexes, it is inevitable that some cultures will have geographical and possibly chronological relationships to others. As in linguistic and paleontological classifications, so in culture classification, the primary criteria of differentiation should be differences in the subject matter itself and not in its spacial or temporal associations.

[2] If this position is valid, it is next necessary to analyze the cultures in terms of cultural elements by means of which it will be possible to discover which of them are determinants and which have no classificatory significance. It should be emphasized that the problem deals with culture as a whole, and not with specific complexes or groups of traits. In other words, this classification does not interfere in any way with the suggested classification of pottery types made by Mr. Hargrave [1932], of the Museum of Northern Arizona, nor with the classification of stone implements sponsored by Dr. W. K. Moorehead [e.g., Peabody and Moorehead 1904]. There is a tendency on the part of some to think of culture in terms of a single trait complex. One of the primary reasons for this discussion is to emphasize the danger of such one-sided research.

If cultures are compared in the manner recommended, certain categories apparently will be agreed upon by all North American archaeologists. In the original manuscript [(Guthe 1932[8])], the most inclusive class, labeled F, was given the term "Base," and the one Base illustrated included all northern agriculture-pottery groups. Most archaeologists do not think in terms of this class, but confine their attention to the next smaller class because of the need for specialization. It is felt, therefore, that this so-called "Base" is academic and impractical at the present time, and should be entirely omitted.

Yet archaeologists do think in terms of larger groups of cultures, such as those found in the Southwest, the Mississippi Valley, the Great Plains, or the northeastern United States. The specialists interested in the archaeology of each of these general areas have already recognized differences in cultures. However, the lines of demarcation between the larger as well as the smaller groups of cultures are vague and difficult to define at present. The use of the following three classes should serve to clarify the comparative problems involved.

We recommend that the first and most widespread cultural group be called a "*basic culture.*" The criteria by which one basic culture should be differentiated from another consist of those fundamental or essential determinants which are recognized as constant within the basic culture, but as different from those in other basic cultures. It is evident that these determinant complexes would include a relatively small proportion of all the determinants within any given culture. They would deal with the primary adjustments of peoples to their immediate physical environments, and would include architectural adaptations as well as basic industrial patterns. Such basic cultures exist throughout the Southwest, the Mississippi Valley, and the Woodland area.

Clearly, each of these basic cultures may be divided into groups which are obviously different from one another in some respects. These might be termed "*phases*" of the basic culture. The members of each phase would be characterized by determinants possessed in common. They need not have a majority of determinants in common, provided that there be a significant number. For example, in the Southwest that group which has been given the name Hohokam is a different phase from that group known as Pueblo. In the Mississippi Valley, the Upper Mississippi phase is different from the Lower Mississippi phase.

[3] Furthermore, it is possible to subdivide these phases into several parts, without interfering with methods and conclusions already reached by our colleagues. As these divisions become more specific, it is clearly possible to increase the number of determinants which the members of each group have in common. It is also possible to use determinants which are not common to all the cultures within the larger groups. For example, determinants which may be used as criteria for defining a division of the Upper Mississippi phase of the larger Mississippi basic culture may not even exist in the Lower Mississippi phase. The term "*aspect*" is suggested

for the subdivisions of phases, and all groups of peoples having in common an approximate majority of determinants would constitute an aspect of a phase. For example, the several numerical stages of the Pueblo phase would be called aspects, such as the Pueblo III aspect of the Pueblo phase of the Southwestern basic culture.

These three terms are the specific recommendation of the little group, headed by McKern, which is attempting to clarify the comparative study of the preliterate cultures of North America. It is hoped that those who receive this communication will find it possible to adopt these terms and to agree to the criteria by which the several divisions have been determined. Because of the different degrees of knowledge concerning the more minute cultural variations within the several aspects of the basic cultures, and because of the variability of comparative problems in the different fields of research, it does not seem advisable at this time to recommend the general acceptance of further subdivisions in this classification. Yet subdivisions of aspects have already been developed by students of the several basic cultures. Those of the Southwest Basic culture are well known. In the Upper Mississippi phase of the Mississippi Basic culture, the aspects have also been subdivided for the purpose of local study.

However, the very nature of archaeological research almost requires the division of aspects into smaller culture groups, for the individual field archaeologist is primarily interested in the growth of cultures which are closely similar. His comparative studies tend to establish finer distinctions between determinant complexes than those used in establishing aspects. It is very probable that two or more localities or sites will be found to contain almost identical determinant complexes, thereby demonstrating the contemporaneous existence of several communities, all of which have a single culture in common. It should be possible, then, to establish a large number of determinants, common to all of these sites, by which this individual culture may be recognized. Such a condition constitutes a specialization, or a focus, of certain characteristics of a more inclusive culture, such as an aspect or phase. Therefore, the term "*focus*" is suggested to signify a group of communities which have a preponderating majority of determinants in common.

Yet the term "site" has a geographical, rather than a cultural, connotation and is therefore ambiguous. Depending upon the length of occupation of a site, the data obtained may or may not indicate changes in culture due to a variety of causes, such as passage of time, diffusion, or migration. It becomes necessary, therefore, to distinguish between the geographical site itself and the cultures which are represented by the materials found there. This evidence, [4] according to its quantity and quality, constitutes data by which the student may differentiate or associate the culture represented with similar data from the same or other sites. It is suggested that the term "*component*" be used to refer to the manifestation of a given culture at a single site. That is, a site may contain one or more components, each of which is a component of a larger class, such as a focus, phase, or aspect of a basic culture. The adjective attached to the word "component" would probably be the name of the site itself. A component, then, would be a localized, and usually incomplete manifestation at a single site, of a culture which may be shown to be related to a larger cultural class by an analysis of the determinants present in the component. The use of the word "component" will eliminate the confusion which now exists because of the lax use of the word "site" as synonymous with a given group of culture traits.

These two terms for subdivisions of phases are offered tentatively as suggestions. In some aspects and phases they will not be needed; in others, still further subdivisions will be required. The term component will always be useful to distinguish between a cultural record and a site.

Briefly, this suggested classification is based upon the following definitions:

> *Component:* A localized, and usually incomplete, manifestation at a single site of a culture which may be shown to be related to a larger cultural class by an analysis of the determinants present in the component.
>
> *Focus:* A group of communities which have a preponderating majority of determinants in common.
>
> *Aspect:* A group of communities which have an approximate majority of determinants in common.
>
> *Phase:* A group of communities which have a significant, but minor, number of determinants in common.
>
> *Basic Culture:* A group of communities which have in common a relatively small proportion of determinants dealing with the primary adjustments of peoples to their immediate physical environments.

It is essential that this classification be recognized as an experiment only. Whether or not it will prove practical will be determined by use of the scheme by archaeologists in their research. It is necessary that the classification be kept flexible and that the descriptions of the various classes be sufficiently general to permit adjustment to the local conditions. It should be noted that the geographic distribution of a class, although possibly suggested in its specific name, does not enter into the definition, and therefore can vary as experience and increased knowledge demand, without invalidating the definition. Similarly, temporal relationships do not enter into the definitions, and while they are bound to develop, as they have done in the Southwest, the resulting chronological adjustments will not affect the definitions. Yet, as in the study of languages and paleontology, both the spacial and temporal relationships will [5] assist the students of the subject in understanding the several classes of cultures described in this classification.

Objections may be raised because of the possibility of convergence of traits. Again, it should be understood that the definitions are objective, in the sense that they consider only the determinant complexes themselves, and that no implication of genetical relationship between communities is implied.

Finally, this classification permits the omission of any one or more of the classes. For example, a group of communities may be classified as one or more foci, but the determinant complexes known and used as criteria do not permit the grouping of these communities under either an aspect or a phase, but do enable the student to place them in a basic culture. The same situation may arise concerning aspects or phases.

McKern, Deuel, and Guthe, with the assistance of neighboring colleagues, have attempted to revise the original recommendation [(Guthe 1932[8]; McKern 1932[7])] in such a way that it will meet the suggestions and criticisms sent to McKern. We earnestly request that you give this matter serious consideration, and send your reactions to one of us.

W. C. McKern
Thorne Deuel
Carl E. Guthe

11
Certain Culture Classification Problems in Middle Western Archaeology

W. C. McKern

McKern, W. C. 1934. Certain Culture Classification Problems in Middle Western Archaeology. *National Research Council, Committee on State Archaeological Surveys, Circular* No. 17.
Reprinted as: W. C. McKern. 1937. Certain Culture Classification Problems in Middle Western Archaeology. In *The Indianapolis Archaeological Conference*, pp. 70–82. National Research Council, Washington, D.C. (Pagination is from the 1934 version; Illinois State Museum Archives)

[1]

Certain Culture Classification Problems
in Middle Western Archaeology
By W. C. McKern

During the past two years, a group of students with fields of interest representing practically the entire Mississippi Valley has been considering (1) the need for culture classification in North American archaeology and (2) the advisability of adopting a certain culture-type classificatory or taxonomic method submitted to them through the channels of the Committee on State Archaeological Surveys of the National Research Council. At present, thanks to the critical interest and cooperation of workers in all sections of the area involved, a revised method has been tentatively accepted by a sufficient number of these students to insure a thorough trial for it.

As a matter of fact, the method has been applied in classifying divisions previously apparent in several provinces, including Wisconsin, and it now seems appropriate to consider some of the problems encountered in these experiments. However, before attacking this phase of the subject, I wish to consider certain general aspects of the purposes and means of classification itself.

At the very beginning, something should be said of the need for cultural classification in archaeology. It may be advanced that we already possess an adequate taxonomic method. I have received such questions as this: Why call the cultural manifestation of the pre-literate Iroquois, Upper Mississippi, or any name other than Iroquois? In some instances we may have sufficient data to verify identification with a known historic group, such as the Iroquois. However, in most instances we cannot immediately bridge the gap between pre-literate and historic or proto-historic cultural groups; and in many instances we cannot hope ever to be able to do so. Yet we perceive that there are archaeologically collected data that warrant cultural segregation. The only taxonomic basis for dealing with all cultural manifestations, regardless of occasional direct historical links, is that of culture type as illustrated by trait-indicative materials and features encountered at former habitation sites. If in the future it becomes possible to name the historic ethnic group of which the pre-literate group is the progenitor, no confusion should result from the statement that, for example, Upper Mississippi Oneota is Ioway Sioux; no more so than from the statement that *Elephas primigenius* is the mammoth.

Aside from the inadequacy of the direct-historical method in supplying the archaeologist with a means of attachment to the ethnological classification, the latter, even if applicable, would not ideally answer the needs of the archaeologist. One ethnological classification divides the aborigines into linguistic stocks, which are first subdivided into more specific linguistic groups and, finally, into sociopolitical groups. The criteria for classification are social, primarily linguistic. The major portion of the data available to the archaeologist relates to material culture, and in no instance includes linguistic data. Consequently this ethnological classification does not satisfy archaeological requirements.

[2] It may be said that we have the ethnologically conceived culture areas to supply a basis for archaeological classification. However, these so-called culture areas involve two factors which the archaeologist must disregard in devising his culture classification if he is to avoid hopeless confusion; these are the spatial and temporal factors. First, the culture area attempts to define, or at least limit, geographical distribution. Unfortunately, the American aborigines did not always succeed in confining their cultural divisions within a continuous area or in keeping culturally pure an area of any important size. Second, the archaeologist considers the American Indians from the standpoint of all time, and certainly there can be no cultural areas devised which can include an unlimited temporal factor.

In brief, the archaeologist requires a classification based upon the cultural factor alone; temporal and distributional treatments will follow as accumulating data shall warrant. Moreover, the archaeological classification must necessarily be based upon criteria available to the archaeologist.

Any statement that the archaeologist has no need for a culture taxonomic method is in conflict with facts which all students of the subject must have encountered. One has only to consult the reports on research in almost any American province, particularly where identification with historically known groups has not been attempted, and note the indefinite use of the word culture to signify anything from the manifestation of a general pattern influential over an area a thousand or more miles in extent, to the highly specialized manifestation of a culture apparent at a cluster of closely localized sites. The confusion of unstandardized cultural terminology forces recognition of the need for simplifying the complexity of cultural data and concepts through the establishment of systematic order. In men's affairs, as should be particularly apparent at this time, chaos does not reduce itself to order without a plan. The accomplishments of science stand as a monument to planned orderliness.

Unlike the student of ethnology, the American archaeologist has not been influenced appreciably by the initial complexity of his subject to specialize in some certain aspect of that subject. He is more inclined to embrace in his studies all apparent aspects of his subject within the area available to him for investigation. As his problems lead toward comparative studies over wider areas, his conceptions of cultural manifestations take on broader interpretations. Starting with cultural differentiation, he begins to observe evidence of cultural affinities, not only as regards specific complexes but involving distinctive types of complexes. He lacks a specific terminology that is standard with his fellow students, by means of which he can clearly express his maturing concepts. He stretches old meanings to apply to his new needs and finds himself justly criticized, primarily by students limited to ethnological experience, for his extraordinarily indefinite, inaccurate use of the term "culture," which, for want of a more specific term, is made to serve a multitude of purposes for which it never was intended. Incidentally, the ethnologist should exhibit some hesitation in offering severe criticism, since he has nothing adequate to offer of a constructive nature that might aid the archaeologist in surmounting his difficulties.

The point is that the student of archaeology is greatly in need of a standardized culture scheme such as can be realized only through the medium of a taxonomic method.

[3] There are some who have hesitated to cooperate fully in this classificatory experiment on the grounds that the time for classification has

not yet arrived. They feel that we lack adequate information to warrant wholesale classification. With due respect for the caution exhibited in this attitude, I cannot but feel that this caution is based upon a false conception of the very nature and purpose of classification and a misunderstanding of the intentions of those endorsing the taxonomic method in question.

Classification is nothing more than the process of recognizing classes, each class identified by a complex of characteristics. At the present time we are all active in identifying cultural classes, no matter by what name we may call it, but we are not performing efficiently because we lack the necessary equipment. In the Encyclopedia Britannica, Dr. Abraham Wolf says: "Classification is one method, probably the simplest method, of discovering order in the world. . . . In the history of every science classification is the very first method to be employed." We have tried to get along without it too long. It is classification that makes it possible for one student to describe phenomena in terms readily comprehensible to another student versed in the taxonomic method. It reduces a multiplicity of facts to simplicity and order and supplies a standardized terminology without which students encounter difficulty in conversing intelligently on a common subject.

The adoption and use of a taxonomic method most certainly does not imply the immediate classification of all manifestations with apparent cultural significance. It is only in those instances in which sufficient data are available, quantitatively and qualitatively, to create a problem of cultural differentiation that classification can serve to any advantage. In some provinces little in the way of detailed classification can logically be attempted at this time; in other provinces much can be accomplished toward detailed classification; and in all provinces a taxonomic method should be adopted before any serious attempts are made at classification. Naturally, this method should be standard for the largest area possible. Following an agreement as to method, the actual classification should be a slow, deliberate procedure, constantly experimental, subject to such major and minor corrections as newly accumulating data may dictate, and to a maximum of constructive criticism and resulting improvement. Such is the history of any scientific classification. It is the method of classification to be employed, not any specific classification, that offers an immediate, initial problem for which a solution is now being attempted.

The method now in tentative operation is a simple one, based solely upon complexes of cultural factors. Time will not permit a comprehensive exposition of the method here; most of those who are directly interested in the subject are familiar with the details, which they indeed have helped to formulate. Four arbitrary divisions are made, differentiating between broadly influential types of manifestations and increasingly specialized, localized types.

The most general division is the *basic culture*, characterized by a few fundamental or essential determinants dealing with the primary adjustments of peoples to their immediate physical environments. Each basic culture is divisible into groups called *phases*, identified by complexes of important cultural limitations. As greater cultural detail is taken into consideration, a phase may be found to be manifested in readily distinguishable groups, all [4] sharing the phase determinants, but each exhibiting an important modicum of more specific traits peculiar to itself alone. These subdivisions of a phase are termed *aspects*. Similarly, aspects may be subdivided into *foci*, each focus exhibiting peculiarities in the final analysis of cultural detail. An additional term completes the taxonomic framework; the manifestation of any given focus at a specific site is termed a *component* of that focus. This is in no sense a fifth type of cultural manifestation; rather, it is the fourth division as represented at a site and serves to distinguish between a site which may bear evidence of several cultural occupations, each foreign to the other, and a single, specified manifestation at a site. Several components may be found to occur at a single site.

This method is comparable to a filing cabinet equipped with labeled drawers to facilitate the orderly arrangement of materials. I can best demonstrate its usefulness by example, illustrating from a field of my own experience, the Wisconsin field. Investigations at a large village site on the Grand River, in central eastern Wisconsin, produced a quantity of culture-indicative materials. These materials offered a variety of details not characteristically encountered at sites in general throughout the state but duplicated at several adjacent sites. Thus a specific list of culture traits was found to be typical for several sites, establishing through its recurrence the fact that it was a true culture complex. At the time, for lack of better terminology, the complex was said to characterize the Grand River culture.

Later, similar but not identical complexes were encountered in two other widely separated districts, one in the Mississippi uplands of the state and the other on the shores of Lake Winnebago. In each of these two districts a complex of detailed traits was found to occur at site after site, but the complex for each district exhibited strong peculiarities of its own. These data seemed to warrant the use of such terms as the Mississippi Uplands and Lake Winnebago cultures.

It was at once apparent, however, that all three cultures, so called, were closely related divisions of a more-inclusive parent culture, which we finally called the Upper Mississippi culture. Thus, we had an Upper Mississippi culture divided into three sub-cultures: the Grand River, Mississippi Uplands, and Lake Winnebago.

Comparative research soon demonstrated that similar manifestations were important in several adjacent states. There was a logically sound basis for including all of these manifestations within a single large cultural division, which tentatively retained the name Upper Mississippi culture. But the subdivisions in Wisconsin were more like each other than like some of the more distant manifestations. This seemed to require a further subdivision in recognition of a type of culture between the very general Upper Mississippi category and the specialized local divisions which had been named Grand River, Mississippi Uplands, and Lake Winnebago. We began to call this the Wisconsin Upper Mississippi culture. We now had the Upper Mississippi culture, represented in Wisconsin by the Wisconsin Upper Mississippi culture, of which three variants were known—the Grand River, Mississippi Uplands, and Lake Winnebago cultures.

[5] It was apparent from the first that this entire cultural manifestation was not characteristic of the Woodland area in which it so largely occurred, but that it was strongly reminiscent, in many important features, of certain southeastern area manifestations. A detailed comparison of traits seemed to demonstrate the fact that Upper Mississippi was but a subdivision of an even larger cultural order, which was most frequently referred to as the Mississippi culture.

The form of description with which I have been attempting to portray a decidedly complex cultural picture has produced an increasingly grotesque and unwieldy structure and will serve, I believe, to illustrate the need for specific terminology. However, when our taxonomic framework is applied, the picture clarifies and a modicum of order appears out of chaos, permitting the student to observe the identically same facts devoid of confusion. The most general division is the Mississippi basic culture, identified by a complex of fundamentals. The Mississippi basic culture is subdivided into a number of phases, including the Upper Mississippi phase. This phase is represented in a district including Wisconsin by at least one variant, the Wisconsin aspect. Another aspect is apparent in a district including Nebraska. These and other aspects will eventually be found to account for Upper Mississippi manifestations in Iowa, the Dakotas, Minnesota, Illinois, Indiana, Ohio, and in any other states where they are found to occur. In Wisconsin there are three known foci of the Wisconsin aspect: the Grand River focus, the Mississippi Uplands focus and the Lake

Winnebago focus. Each of these foci is represented by a number of known components (the occurrence of a focus at a single site), and additional components for the several foci are being discovered yearly.

To one unfamiliar with the status of archaeological information and problems in Wisconsin, such a term as "Grand River culture" is not intelligible; it is a title which carries with it no cultural conception whatever. On the other hand, such a term as "Grand River focus" categorically places in one's mind immediately the type of cultural manifestation referred to, and if "Wisconsin aspect of the Upper Mississippi phase" is added, the division at once takes its place in the culture scheme. Furthermore, one having had experience in some other division of the same phase is immediately in a position to review critically the data offered in substantiation of the classification submitted.

It will be noted that whereas the statement has been made that our taxonomic method is independent of the distributional factor, nevertheless certain geographical terms have been employed in the specific classification used here for purposes of illustration. However, these terms are used without a sense of geographical limitation. For example, a component of the Grand River focus might be encountered on the Fox River or outside Wisconsin. Such terms are convenient, rather than being distributional in any limiting sense, although they may indicate the place of original discovery. In a similar sense the geologist, without implication of geographical limits, speaks of the Niagara formation, which occurs not only in the Niagara Falls district but in Illinois, Iowa, Wisconsin, and elsewhere. In a similar sense, we speak of Neanderthal man, who has been found to have inhabited various districts remote from the Neanderthal of the Rhine province. In exactly the same sense, we speak of the Aurignacian culture in Africa, far from Aurignac, France. A culturally descriptive term might be considered more ideal, but reasonably short, practical terms that are truly descriptive of a culture complex are exceedingly difficult, in many instances utterly impossible, to devise.

[6] If later it can be established that the Mississippi Uplands focus, Wisconsin aspect of the Upper Mississippi phase, is culturally identical to primitive Ioway Sioux, that fact will in no way disturb the cultural classification but will serve to establish a point of contact between archaeological cultural and ethnological linguistic classifications, and thus give the archaeological division a historical import. Or, if it later develops that the Wisconsin aspect of the Upper Mississippi phase is a later manifestation than the Elemental aspect of the Hopewellian phase, this will furnish the basis for a temporal classification complementary to the cultural classification.

One of the most difficult problems is that of identifying the determinants for a cultural division, particularly those more specific divisions, the aspects and foci, in which cultural details are important criteria for differentiation. This difficulty is due partly to the difference in complexity between objects such as simple bone awls and pottery vessels. Culture criteria available to the archaeologist are demonstrated by culture-indicative materials, for the most part artifacts. A simple type of artifact may serve as one element in a trait complex for one cultural division, and therefore may serve as a determinant for that division. This may be the case with a simple type of bone awl. However, when a comparatively complex type of pottery is characteristic for a cultural division, the question arises as to whether it should be considered as a single determinant or as comprising a number of determinants. It certainly is more culturally indicative than a pointed fragment of bone. Single pottery traits, such as shell temper, loop handles, or cord-imprinted decoration, would seem to be at least as important as culture markers as a simple implement with a single differentiating trait. Thus, apparently, we may have a considerable variety of determinants exhibited by pottery alone. Probably other elements of cultural import will each supply more than a single determinant, as for instance, mound structure, burial methods, and house types.

The problem, then, narrows down to selecting, from the traits comprising a complex element, those traits having sufficient cultural significance to qualify as culture determinants. This implies a separate classification of the essential traits for any given complex cultural subject. For example, pottery should be classified under such essential heads as temper, texture, hardness, surface, color, shape, and decoration. Determinants in pottery for a cultural division could then be selected to cover these standard pottery traits. In the same way, the essential traits for burial methods and other complex subjects could be standardized through special classifications, with the result that the determinants for one cultural division would cover the same ground as, and carry similar weight to, those for another division of the same type.

However, the problem is not as simple as that. We have to deal with types of culture as different from each other as a basic culture and a focus. The basic culture is identified by determinants that express fundamental cultural trends. These fundamentals are quite different in character from the detailed material traits so important in determining highly specialized divisions such as foci. Thus, the character of a determinant will depend upon the type of cultural division for which it serves as a determinant. The presence of horticulture might serve as a determinant for some sedentary basic culture as distinct from a nomadic, hunting basic culture, but it could not serve to distinguish between two subdivisions of a horticultural basic culture. In the opposite [7] extreme, a specific motif in pottery decoration might serve as one determinant of a focus but not as a determinant for the aspect (or still less-specialized division), since it is peculiar to the focus.

One general axiom must guide the student in attacking this problem. Determinants must be characteristic for that division which they serve to identify. That being the case, determinants for a basic culture will be general in character and relatively few in number. For the more-specialized divisions, progressing from lesser to greater specialization, the determinants will be an enriched edition of the determinants for the immediately preceding, more general division, as altered to include greater detail plus a considerable number of specific traits peculiarly characteristic of the more specialized division. The focus determinants, for example, would be the aspect determinants made richer in detail and augmented by additional traits peculiar to the focus and exhibiting the greatest cultural detail apparent for the entire basic culture.

To exemplify, employing for the sake of simplicity a single form of cultural expression, pottery, two of the determinants for the Mississippi basic culture might be stated as: (1) manufacture and use of pottery vessels and (2) unamalgamated type of temper.

The Upper Mississippi phase of this culture is characterized by pottery determinants more or less in the nature of primary limitations, as follows:

Temper—shell, cell, grit, or crushed pottery.
Hardness—1 to 4, softer wares predominating.
Texture—fine to medium coarse.
Structure—compact and scaly to porous and flaky.
Natural color—grays, drabs, and dull terra cottas preponderating.
Surface—generally smooth, rarely rough or polished.
Thickness—walls ranging from medium thick to very thin.
Shape—simple variety of wide-mouthed jars and bowls.
Decoration—ornamentation in intaglio lines on outer surface between shoulders and rim.

A more detailed list of traits is required as determinants for the Wisconsin aspect of this phase, although it will be noticed that a few of the latter remain identically the same as for the phase:

Temper—preponderatingly shell.
Hardness—1 to 4, softer wares predominating.

Texture—fine to medium coarse.
Structure—compact and scaly to porous and flaky.
Natural color—grays predominating.
Surface—smooth to polished.
Thickness—walls thin for larger vessels, commonly to such an extent that exterior intaglio lines have produced pronounced corresponding interior cameo reliefs.
Shape—a. lips smooth and square or rounded.
b. rim angles ranging from horizontal flaring to secondary contracting.
c. neck, mere line of juncture between rim and body.
d. mouth broad.
[8] e. shoulders absent or round and unpronounced.
f. base round; conoidal base never characteristic.
g. handles either vertically placed loops in diametrically opposed pairs or similarly placed lugs; many vessels without handles.
Decoration—a. straight-lined patterns predominating.
b. notched or scalloped rims important.
c. absence of decoration by pigmentation.
d. motifs combined of geometric arrangements of lines and dots important.
e. curvilinear motifs rare.

The maximum in detail is required of pottery determinants for the focus. Those for the Mississippi Uplands focus of the Wisconsin aspect will serve to illustrate:

Temper—a. exclusively shell.
b. abundant temper most common.
Hardness—1 to 3.
Texture—fine to medium coarse, finer wares relatively rare.
Structure—flaky, porous wares predominating.
Natural color—varying slightly from gray to dull buff, light grays predominating.
Surface—characteristically smooth; pronouncedly smooth surfaces very rare; polished surfaces have not been encountered.
Thickness—2 to 12 mm, as thin as 4 mm in places in very large vessels.
Shape—a. for the most part simple variations of round-bodied, wide-mouthed jars with flaring rims.
b. square lips predominating.
c. rims most commonly broad with slight to pronounced flare; verti-

cal rims rising from contracting neck rare; rims with secondary contraction rising from contracting neck rare.
d. necks mere line of juncture between rim and body.
e. mouths invariably broad.
f. shoulders absent or but slightly apparent.
g. base invariably round.
h. handles round in cross section or broad, strap-like loops, the latter predominating; approximately one-third of vessels equipped with handles.
i. beakers and hemispherical bowls absent.
Decoration—a. present on majority of vessels.
b. intaglios preponderatingly incised, trailed, or indented.
c. patterns for most part carelessly designed and roughly executed.
d. curvilinear motifs absent.
e. repetition of a motif to form a symmetrical design rare.
f. combination of lines and dots very common as patterns.
g. corrugated, incised, or indented patterns on handles common.
h. notched or scalloped rims usual.
i. cord or other surface roughening does not occur.

[9] These series of pottery determinants are not submitted for close inspection as to their accuracy. As a matter of fact, some of the determinants, particularly for the more general divisions, are based upon rather meager information, and all are subject to correction. However, I believe they are sufficiently accurate to serve the illustrative purpose for which they are here presented.

Thus, for pottery alone, we have two determinants for the basic culture, nine for the phase, nineteen for the aspect, and twenty-six for the focus. These numbers have no mathematical significance but illustrate the numerical increase in determinants from the more general to the more specific divisions and serve to justify the acceptance of the classification itself. They also illustrate the minimum degree of detail which I believe should be recognized in selecting determinants. It should be remembered, of course, that pottery is but one factor in a cultural manifestation and should never serve alone to determine a classification.

In pottery I have purposely selected one of the more complex cultural subjects, since it offers a more difficult problem than some more simple product such as a projectile point. There are many subjects that may be adequately handled by a single determinant, discussed in increasing detail for each increasingly specific subdivision. It can be readily seen that a complex of determinants for any of the more specific cultural subdivisions may be composed of from thirty to forty percent of pottery traits. I do not believe that this is an overemphasis but that it fairly represents the value of pottery, when pottery is present, as a culture indicator.

This method of classification is arbitrary, like all other scientific taxonomic methods. Under the blending influences of diffusion and cultural growth by invention, there can be no hard and fast natural division lines. This absence of sharp lines of demarcation between classes applies equally to the subject matter of all natural sciences and cannot be advanced as a valid argument against classification. Our method is not nearly so arbitrary as the division of a continent into culture areas, which involves an inelastic temporal factor and a confusing and inaccurate distributional factor. The maximum degree of arbitrariness in our method is attained in the division of cultural manifestations into four rather than into some other number of culture types. The four divisions were finally agreed upon by the authors of this method as satisfying all apparent needs for major subdivision. With the means provided for subclassification into specific groups under these culture-type heads, the major requirements of remotely separate fields seem to be satisfied, as reported by specialists in those fields.

In applying any taxonomic method, there is always the danger that an unleashed enthusiasm may induce the classifier to attempt to make the facts fit the method. The lure of being methodical at all costs is a constant threat to the wholly profitable use of any method. It is well to bear constantly in mind the rule that the classification is, and forever must be, subservient to the facts. It is convenience and orderliness in handling archaeological data that is required of the classification, not a flawless, natural regimentation of the facts.

[10] Rather recently, it has become increasingly popular for American archaeologists to search out some site known or traditionally reputed to be one formerly occupied by a certain historic group of Indians and to examine data left there as illustrative of the former culture of that ethnic group. This has been termed the direct historical method. As a secondary method, employed to identify a known pre-literate cultural manifestation as that possessed by a historic ethnic group, this method has important value. But as a primary method employed to identify culturally data encountered for the first time, without comparing it with other data archaeologically important in that province, it is a method productive of inaccuracy and error.

Granting that it is established that the Iroquois, let us say, occupied a definitely known site in historic times, there remains the strong possibility that the same site was occupied previously by inhabitants possessing a culture, or cultures, foreign to that of the Iroquois. Consequently, there is the important question of precisely which of the various culture indicators present are attributable to the Iroquois. Even where clear-cut stratification is present, there is no way in which the student not previously acquainted with the value of traits as culture determinants can be certain that the culture detritus of any given stratum is not the result of cultural admixture. Such mixtures of culturally divergent materials often result from intermittent occupation of a site by culturally distinct groups or from the disturbance of deposits by human or natural agencies during or subsequent to occupation.

As a matter of fact, there is only one way in which the student can be certain that he is observing the products of a single cultural group in the culture detritus of a given site. This requires a knowledge that the traits found at this site belong to a culture complex definitely known to occur at other sites. Such information can develop only as the result of the use of the recurring complex method—the comparative study of culture-indicative materials encountered at various sites, leading to the knowledge that a certain complex of culture traits, adhering together as a unit, occurs repeatedly at a number of sites. Only when that information is available can the direct historical method be employed accurately to identify a previously established cultural division as a known historic division. The recurring-complex method alone can serve to determine a cultural division; subsequently, the direct historical method may serve to identify it historically.

The statements which I have made are admittedly controversial and have been presented in the hope of awakening critical thought on the subject of culture classification and of encouraging trial of a taxonomic method which, in the absence of some better method, promises to contribute materially toward introducing order into the existing chaotic status of culture concepts in middle North American archaeology.

May, 1934

12

Some Assumptions and Implications of the McKern Classification System

Thorne Deuel

Deuel, Thorne. 1937. Some Assumptions and Implications of the McKern Classification System. Paper presented at the meeting of the American Association for the Advancement of Science, Section H. Indianapolis. (Illinois State Museum Archives)

ABSTRACT

Most of the misunderstandings concerning the McKern system of classification fall under three headings: First, the basis on which the cultures are classified; second, the general assumptions underlying the classification; and third, the interpretation of the system.

Although the units refer to groups of sites having definite temporal and spatial distribution as well as relationships of a genetic nature, none of these are considered in classifying sites. The classification is based on groups of cultural traits alone and hence defines culture types.

Culture types archaeologically defined constitute in a measure ethnological types, and as such are subject to the same principles of persistence and change, contemporaneity and sequence, distribution and the like as are ethnologically determined culture types.

The classification implies contemporaneity of the focus only, and only in a very general way other types of relationships. The system, in addition, organizes the data for an attack on the other archaeological problems of time, space, and continuity.

Many of the misunderstandings and difficulties arising from attempts to employ the McKern system for the classification of cultural manifestations fall under three headings: First, the basis on which the cultures are classified; second, the general assumptions underlying the classificatory system; and third, the interpretation of the classification.

Before looking into these topics, it will be well to look over the principles suggested by those immediately interested in the proposed system soon after its inception. Quoting from one of several explanatory circular letters, "This classification of cultures is based entirely upon the traits and complexes themselves. . . . (It) seeks to distinguish between cultures and groups of cultures . . . by using cultural determinants as criteria. . . . The term 'focus' is suggested to signify a group of communities which have a preponderating majority of determinants in common" [(McKern et al. 1933[10]:1, 3)].

To make the succeeding discussion more intelligible, a definition of some of the terms seems in order, for example, *trait*, *complex*, *determinant*, *communities*, and *preponderating majority*.

A *trait* may be considered as a cultural habit of a group (whether or not it can be definitely described), which can be inferred from the form, appearance and conditions of occurrence of archaeological objects and features. *Complex*, as employed in this paper, signifies a cluster of mutually related traits, as for example the agricultural complex. A *determinant* is one of a number of associated traits that serve to unite certain sites or units together into a larger class, and to distinguish them from sites or equivalent units belonging to other classes.[1] In order to distinguish between complex as described here and such a group of associated determinants, it seems best to introduce a new term, *determinant series*, which may be defined as a group of traits or complexes, not necessarily possessing any common or mutual relationship among themselves other than such association within equivalent units as determinants. It should be emphasized here that the number of traits in a determinant series must be sufficiently large to exclude the possibility that their recurrence may be due to mere chance or independent invention.[2] A *community* refers to the complete cultural manifestation of a local group or as much of it as is determinable by archae-

1. In McKern et al. [(1933[10]:1)], determinants are defined as "those particular traits of a culture . . . which . . . serve to differentiate it from other cultures." The primary character of a determinant is rather its repetition in a determinant series (see below) which serves to *combine* units into larger groupings. This is in accord with present zoological method and characterizes actual practice in handling archaeological material under the McKern system in the Mississippi Valley region. Many trait differences between units do not constitute determinants at all.

2. For this reason single determinants or a complex such as pottery cannot be taken by themselves as diagnostic of a unit. This insistence on a determinant series consisting of numerous traits and complexes has the effect of making the cultural units more definite on the one hand, and of excluding certain transitional groups on the other. The same conditions produce similar results in the biological classification of species and should cause archaeologists no great concern.

ological investigation. A *preponderating majority* has been variously expressed. In one instance [(Guthe 1932[8]:1)] it has been called an "identity of determinants" and [McKern et al. (1933[10]:3)] suggest "almost identical determinant complexes" as an equivalent.[3]

I

We have a feeling in anthropology that cultures do not exist over long periods of time without readily distinguishable changes in traits. Hence, if the cultural traits in two components overlap to such a degree as to be "almost identical," they are assumed to be contemporaneous. McKern et al. (1933[10]:3) recognize this principle: "It is very probable that two or more localities or sites will be found to contain almost identical determinant complexes (i.e., determinant series), thereby demonstrating the contemporaneous existence of (the) several communities." Nevertheless, although we agree to the principle, time relationship is not a consideration in classifying (see note 4, below). If two sites, one of which had a lag of a thousand years or more, have a "near identity" of determinants, they would belong to the same focus.

Again, if we plot on a map all the localities over which equivalent culture units are distributed, a definite and limited region (or regions) is defined. (For obvious reasons, this does not constitute a culture area except in a very limited sense.) Yet geographical proximity or continuity has no direct effect upon the classification of cultural units. On the same hilltop, mounds and village sites may appear that represent several different patterns. Conversely, a component in Siberia having a preponderating majority of determinants in common with the Black Sand Component (Woodland) of Illinois, though it might evoke considerable skepticism, would—if satisfactorily demonstrated—be placed in the Black Sand focus of the Central Basin phase. Again we visualize a certain areal distribution when the Middle phase of the Mississippi pattern is mentioned, but the area itself is not taken into account when classifying any site found there.[4]

Turning now to units more inclusive than the focus, it is obvious that

3. *Complex* is used here in the sense of determinant series.

4. In certain cases, the archaeological data may be so scanty that classification on the cultural basis alone is not convincing. As examples might be cited a cemetery and an adjoining village site with few or no overlapping traits, yet actually segments of a single community, or components from a dry rockshelter and an open site of the same focus, having in the main as many contrasting as like traits. Here geographic proximity, chronology and other factors may be used to advantage in the identification. See Part II [of this chapter] below. Classification based on inadequate data must, of course, always be accepted with caution.

there is a successively smaller number of traits held in common as we pass to the aspect, phase, and pattern. These classes of differing degrees of likeness, if based on an adequate number of traits or complexes still mean to us a genetic or developmental cultural relationship though more distant than that between components of a focus. In other words, although we may conceive of two cultures arriving independently at one, two, or three simple adaptations to their surroundings, it is difficult to visualize dozens of identities arising wholly due to chance, or to the reaction of a common human structure to the same environment. We turn at once to diffusion, cultural continuity, isolation, trade, or to combinations of these factors. In a sense, the classification does rest fundamentally and generally upon just such assumptions, as I shall endeavor to bring out later on. This undoubtedly gives the classificatory system its apparent usefulness. Nevertheless, even while admitting that the *classificatory system* is founded ultimately on these postulates, the classifying process itself depends solely on the comparison of determinant series. Therefore, as stated or implied by the progenitors of the system, neither distribution, chronology, nor historical continuity directly determine the position of a cultural unit in the classification. As stated in the above-quoted principles and exemplified by present practice, the classification rests immediately on (1) typological identities, and hence on the similarities of the implied traits, and (2) on the recurrence of these in a sufficiently large series in each of the units compared to exclude the possibility of chance or parallel development. Briefly the classification of cultures under the McKern system is based immediately on cultural traits alone.

Diverging for a moment, it is generally conceded that, having made trait analyses of components, there are two technical approaches to the classification of cultures under this system, one proceeding by successive combinations into foci, aspects, and larger units, the other by combining the components into patterns by determinant complexes, and successively subdividing into phases and smaller units. Probably, in the end, no fundamental difference exists; on the one hand, the comparison of components and foci can be adequately checked only by careful comparison of all the traits appearing, and on the other, the smaller units cannot be identified as to pattern except on the basis of fundamental complexes.

Further thought in this direction shows the desirability of considering the base as well as the pattern even when grouping components into the smaller divisions. It has been suggested that one base be defined by sedentary living habits, pottery making, and an agricultural complex; a second by a nomadic or semi-nomadic life with hunting (and/or fishing) as the chief method of securing food [(National Research Council 1937:35–36,

38)]. When it is demonstrated that one local group had permanent houses, with a fairly large village community, pottery, and a maize complex, while another group had small camps with temporary shelters and subsisted chiefly by hunting, we know at once they do not belong to the same focus, aspect, phase, or pattern.

As a case in point, take the Hopewellian. Is it Woodland or Mississippi, or does it constitute a pattern by itself? In Illinois, Wisconsin, Iowa, and Indiana, Hopewellian units contain numerous Woodland elements and link up closely at the same time with Ohio Hopewellian. Certain traits in the Ohio manifestations bear a close resemblance, if they are not identical to some from the Marksville site in Louisiana. The Marksville "culture" on the other hand exhibits similarities to the Mississippi pattern which may have developed from it. The crux of the question as to the Hopewellian position may lie in the basal determinants. If it can be established that the Hopewellian groups had permanent dwellings and ceremonial buildings, cultivated the soil more or less intensively, producing maize and other crops in sufficient quantity to support relatively large village communities; whereas Woodland groups in general had temporary dwellings and depended for the most part on hunting and fishing, without agriculture, and hence existed in small camps, it would appear at once that Hopewellian, Marksvillian and Mississippi manifestations would belong to one base, Woodland to another. The classification on the basal level appears to be vital to the final organization of cultural units under this classificatory scheme.

II

Turning now to the assumptions inherent in the McKern system, we will do well to look again at the statement that the classification is determined solely by groups of cultural determinants. The result of classifying on such a basis is to set up a number of *culture types* of a specialized kind based upon traits implied by the archaeological data. Culture types insofar as they are thus defined include a section of the ethnological traits of a culture. As such we expect their occurrences, forms and variations to conform to certain principles, as for example:

1. A culture type does not persist without significant change except over limited time periods. Corollaries to this are (a) culture types exist over significant periods with little variation; and (b) communities that possess identical or nearly identical determinant series are contemporaneous.

2. A culture type has a tendency to occupy a continuous geographical area.

3. Culture types change and form new types through invention, environmental change or by contact with other groups through trade, migration and so on.

4. The above principles may be modified by interaction upon each other, by historical accident, or by other factors such as isolation, invasion, etc.

In brief, we may say that archaeological culture types, as defined by the McKern system, are assumed to be governed by the same principles of persistence and change, contemporaneity and sequence, distribution and the like as are the ethnologically determined culture types.

III

The third topic may be epitomized in the question: "To what degree does the organization of sites under the McKern classification imply temporal, spatial and genetic relationships?" The answer has largely been given above. It might be added that we may expect sites and other units (culture types) with the same or similar historic backgrounds, existing in the same region contemporaneously to be grouped under the same or adjacent units in the classification, and conversely, units with similar historical backgrounds but differing in time and region of appearance would lie in more widely separated units of the system. Also the less similar the immediate historical background, the greater the distance between units in the classificatory system. Hence, we can expect a unit of the McKern system to include other units more or less closely related in a historical continuum, in time, or in space or in all of them, but not in a *definite* chronological, distributional or historical capacity (except in the case of the components of the same focus). Such conclusions can be drawn only by a further study of the archaeological data themselves. These problems may be attacked and largely solved in some instances before any classifying into foci or other units has been made. Stratification, for example, solves at once the problem of temporal sequence for the components concerned, though the foci may be defined at some later time.

Summarizing, it may be said: (1) That the McKern classificatory system is based on cultural determinants alone and thus defines cultural types archaeologically. (2) That the same principles are assumed to govern these culture types that do those of ethnology. And (3), that the classification implies contemporaneity for the focus only. This, combined with the definition of culture types, organizes the data for an attack of other problems of time, space and continuity.

13

Review of *Rediscovering Illinois: Archaeological Explorations in and around Fulton County*

W. C. McKern

McKern, W. C. 1938. Review of *Rediscovering Illinois: Archaeological Explorations in and around Fulton County*, by Fay-Cooper Cole and Thorne Deuel. *American Antiquity* 3:368–374.

[368]

The patience of students in adjoining fields, awaiting a published report on the intensive investigations conducted in Illinois during the past twelve years, is finally rewarded in this carefully prepared work, which covers the results of research in Fulton County. Although the book deals specifically with a very limited area within the state, the reader will soon discover that cultural complexes and sequences treated in the text are of much wider import than the immediate locale of operations. The authors make no claim that these cultural and chronological manifestations will be found representative for the area outside that described, but the broader classifications, at least, are certainly based upon a much wider knowledge of data within the state, and throughout a field embracing many adjacent states. There is the plausible implication that these complexes and sequences may illustrate, fundamentally, and serve as an initial cross section of Illinois archaeology.

Specific factual and discursive presentations are preceded by a general introduction and an exposition of methods. The introduction consists largely of a popularized summary of purposes, problems and program, and correlates cultural and historical conclusions. This portion of the book is apparently intended primarily for the nonspecialist, although the inclusion of classificatory, survey, and other technical terminology will, I fear, prove a confusing element to an important number of amateur students. However, in all fairness, it should be said that these terms are fully defined and explained either in later chapters or in the excellent glossary which concludes the text.

The presentation of survey and excavation purposes and methods is exceptionally well done, and will no doubt serve the needs of the instructor to excellent advantage. The reviewer feels, however, that a false impression of the rigidity of excavation methods is created; methods that are nonelastic and cannot yield to the specific nature of the feature encountered. For example, the vertical-slicing technique is described without consideration of any alternative or deviation (p. 26), whereas the reviewer's experience has convinced him that technical methods are like tools: certain ones will prove most useful under certain conditions; certain others, under other conditions. Figuratively, all eating should not be accomplished with either a fork or a spoon; the field technique must be selected to meet the demands of the specific field. It is the reviewer's first-hand observation that the authors agree with this in practice if not in statement.

At this stage of development in archaeology for the eastern half of the United States, any positive treatment of culture classification cannot fail to stir up controversy. Of the authors' contribution to this subject, it should be [369] said initially that it is the most ambitious attempt to reduce field and laboratory data to lucid order in terms of culture that has ever been published for the Woodlands section of the Middle West, however deliberate and cautious may have been the course of its shaping.

The chapter opens with a brief history of the formulating of the taxonomic method, which is incorrectly referred to as a "classification of archaeological sites and materials of the Mississippi drainage" (p. 34). I should like to call to the authors' attention the omission of Dr. James B. Griffin's name from the list of those who participated in the original classificatory conference [(the informal meeting of December 1932)]. Moreover, inasmuch as the remainder of taxonomic divisions are accepted as endorsed at the Indianapolis Conference [of 1935], one wonders why no mention is made of that most generalized of all divisions, the "base." Although it is not employed in Illinois, it is a generally recognized class in the taxonomic scheme.

There follow lists of determinants for the two great culture patterns involved in the work: the Mississippi and Woodland, following a terminology which has been rather generally accepted. The advisability of including negative traits will be questioned by some. It is the reviewer's position that these, as given here and later in Appendix II, are trait complexes, not determinant complexes, since determinants are diagnostic traits in a comparison of two culture complexes. Consequently, that which is a diagnostic trait in one comparison may become a link trait in another, and it follows that there can be no complex of diagnostic traits, or determinants for a cultural division to be exhibited as standard in all comparisons.

Moreover, it is the reviewer's reaction that these trait complexes apply more accurately to certain phases, aspects, or foci in Illinois than to the more geographically comprehensive patterns.

The use of "Mississippi basic culture" (p. 38), an original term now in disuse, is probably due to an oversight.

Having presented these general views of the Woodland and Mississippi patterns, the task of classifying Fulton County manifestations is undertaken. Preceding the actual analytical study of materials, there is the expression of a preconceived conviction that the Woodland and Mississippi patterns are represented in Fulton County. "To test these convictions, also to obtain a purely objective view of all materials recorded, the larger cultural complexes, such as pottery and projectile points, were spread out and separated into types, without regard to place of occurrence or association with other objects" (p. 39). Although this is not the classificatory procedure originally advanced by the devisers of the taxonomic method employed [(McKern et al. 1933[10])], or in use by other advocates of the method, it is interesting to note that it produced substantially the same results. Of seven types of pottery objectively determined, a group of five related types turned out to have been found associated with similar complexes of Woodland-like materials. A sixth type occurred where no definite associations could be determined. Type 7 had Mississippi associations. Similarly, the projectile points fell into types with definite Mississippi and Woodland associations. Other types of artifacts were not present in sufficient quantity to lend themselves [370] to this objective method, and such traits as house type, mound structure, and burial procedure could hardly be handled conveniently in this manner. Actually, therefore, the method was employed only by analyzing traits represented by artifact types present in considerable quantity. The actual trait complexes for Fulton County manifestations listed elsewhere in the report must have been obtained largely by other means than this objective method.

The reviewer can only look upon this procedure as an interesting experiment. The more simple and direct method is that of analyzing materials from a site or community as such, comparing the list of traits so determined with similarly determined trait complexes from other sites or communities, and classifying on a basis of similarity or dissimilarity to establish foci. Comparisons of foci might serve to establish aspects, or more general classes. Naturally, since its determining traits are more general and fewer in number, previously identified patterns might be recognized almost immediately; their subdivisions, only after considerably more data were made available. Deuel (pp. 218–219) accurately outlines this method as an alternative for the one employed.

One is sorely tempted to draw a comparison with the biological classification. Employing this subjective method to identify various sub-varieties of grasshoppers, one would put all the legs in one pile, the wings in another, and so on, without regard to which grasshoppers the various parts came from, respectively. No doubt one could thus test the accuracy of the original associations and in doing so actually determine the characteristic traits for each variety.

The detailed descriptions of excavations are models of presentation, and serve to illustrate the technical care and precision with which the work was conducted. There is a cultural analysis accompanying the report for each site or community.

The six cultural divisions apparent from this research are discussed at some length by way of conclusions. These divisions are: Black Sand, Red Ochre, Central Basin, Hopewellian, Middle Mississippi, and Maples Mills. The authors admit the important part played by pottery in cultural determinations (p. 199), citing as justification a dearth of other materials at certain sites, and the fact that pottery possesses a number of diagnostic features. The absence of cultural data could hardly justify any classification, but the wholly tentative nature of any classification may warrant initial attempts on the basis of rather limited data. As regards the complexity of the subject of pottery, however, the fact that all cultural subjects possess a plurality of diagnostic features is slowly gaining recognition. A recent discussion with Cole substantiates his concurrence with this view. Whereas pottery may in most instances offer more than any other subject in the way of culture indicators, it is extremely doubtful that its importance could ever warrant classification primarily on a basis of pottery factors.

The assignment of these six divisions to class status in the classification is, in the reviewer's opinion, the weak department of the entire report. The Red Ochre manifestation can only be justified as a focus in the Woodland Pattern [371] on the strength of the data presented. How possibly could a class with the broad general features of a phase be determined from three closely associated sites in one county? As proposed and defined, these classificatory compartments are only to be employed as needed, and the data on Red Ochre available at the writing of this report are satisfactorily taken care of by the focus. Maples Mills apparently is also a Woodland focus. The Black Sand Focus is so designated. Foci are also recognized within the Central Basin, Hopewellian, and Middle Mississippi phases of Fulton County, although the authors, with their collective attention centered primarily upon patterns, and such immediate subdivisions of patterns as might be justified, appear to look upon the focus as the most remote and difficult of attainment of all classes, whereas the focus lies directly under their very feet, the logical starting point of classification. Deuel actually admits this position in Appendix I when he says "the component or complex of traits at actual sites must form the basis of the classification" (p. 207, fn 4).

On the same page, Deuel presents, as equally applicable, the two procedures of classification: (1) that which starts with the "largest unit" and works "downward"; and (2) that "beginning with the smallest units and successively combining them into larger ones." If the treatment of classifications in this work are representative of the No. 1 method, the apparent results would not be cited by the reviewer as a recommendation for the continued use of that method.

Hopewellian has been classified as a Woodland phase (p. 200). Apparently, pottery data serve primarily as a foundation for this stand, with general chipped-stone and burial traits serving to some extent. The trouble here again seems to be the technical viewpoint which induces the worker to start with the pattern, the most generalized cultural division, and work "down" toward the more specialized divisions, never fully arriving at the natural starting point, the focus. Thus, having to start with the pattern, one is confronted by the necessity of choosing between the two patterns identified for the Mississippi Valley: the Woodland and Mississippi; a manifestation must be assigned either to the Woodland or to the Mississippi pattern. Deuel reflects this attitude in his stated conclusion that Hopewellian must be Woodland since it is more like Woodland than it is like Mississippi (pp. 211–212). That this manifestation could possibly be a phase of some unidentified pattern, appears to be outside the range of Deuel's conception, due to this two-pattern limitation.

Deuel's stand on the Woodland category, not only for Fulton County manifestations of Hopewellian, but for the Trempealeau Focus as well, is rather difficult to analyze. He has established the fact for Fulton County, previously known for Hopewellian in general, that there are a number of linked traits in any comparison of Woodland manifestations. These are general traits such as would logically apply to a phase, and relate to pottery, chipped-stone, and burial procedure. However, Deuel's own Hopewellian complex, as given in Appendix II (p. 222), includes only five out of thirty-two listed traits that would [372] be generally accepted as characteristic of Woodland; and this is a very generous estimate. Are we to conclude that these five or less traits have greater diagnostic value than the twenty-seven or more traits that are not indicative of Woodland?

The argument that there is apparent cultural continuity exhibited in a series leading from Woodland (Central Basin Phase) to Hopewellian pottery (p. 200) does not apply. The taxonomic method is essentially based on cultural factors alone, yet here the factor of temporal succession is employed in support of the classification presented. Moreover, the temporal sequence is only apparent, in the nature of coinciding with the expected, and does not apply to traits other than ceramic. The fact is interesting, and should have been presented, but not in support of a purely cultural classification.

Table 1 of Appendix I lists pattern determinants for the Woodland and Mississippi patterns in a vertical series, and various Illinois and other Mississippi Valley components, with a few foci mixed in, in horizontal series, with tabulations to show similarities and dissimilarities warranting the classificatory assignments. With the Woodland group, on the basis of traits so listed, is the Trempealeau Focus. The twelve Woodland traits shared by Trempealeau, according to this table, include: burials predominantly flexed; grave goods, scarce or absent; grave goods chiefly of stone. Actually, Trempealeau Focus burials are never flexed, grave goods are the usual thing, and copper is present in a grave more commonly than stone. In addition, there are a number of burial traits, no less important or more detailed than those listed, which are characteristic for Trempealeau and not for Woodland. Similarly, throughout the table, important Trempealeau traits, which are also Hopewellian traits, and never Woodland traits, have been omitted. The reason for this is at once apparent: this is a table based on Woodland and Mississippi traits, and the Trempealeau traits referred to as omitted from the complex are neither Woodland nor Mississippi. The possibility of Hopewellian lying outside both of these patterns, although seriously considered by all other students of the Hopewellian Phase, is in no instance so much as mentioned in dismissal in this report.

There is much of interest in that portion of the Conclusions dealing with chronology. In all instances where stratigraphy is apparent Mississippi overlies Woodland. There is evidence that either the Black Sand or Red Ochre manifestations, both Woodland, are earliest in the picture; probably the former. In succession upwards come the Morton Focus (Woodland), the Hopewellian Phase, and finally, the Middle Mississippi Phase. There is, however, the possibility of late Woodland manifestations, including Maples Mills, being contemporaneous with Middle Mississippi. Much of this cultural stratigraphy parallels that indicated for related manifestations in adjacent areas of the Northern Mississippi province, although the Trempealeau Focus of Hopewellian appears to be nearer the bottom of the pile in Wisconsin. The summary of these chronological conclusions is presented in the form of a tentative cultural [373] history of Fulton

County which is brief but prophetic of future possibilities in Mississippi Valley archaeology.

A great deal that is pertinent to the entire presentation of facts and conclusions is contained in sixty-seven pages of appendices. These include: the Application of a Classificatory Method to Mississippi Valley Archaeology, by Deuel, which has been mentioned elsewhere in this review, and which deserves the careful attention of all students of classification; Diagnostic Traits of Woodland and Mississippi Units in Fulton County, separately listing several subdivisions; Details of Special Plates and Figures, strangely divorced from the illustrations described; and two final chapters by Neumann on human and faunal physical remains.

Deuel's presentation of the Upper Mississippi Phase will not satisfy students of the Oneota Aspect of that phase, which is represented in the discussion only by the Grand River Focus, and that under the cloud of "probable" (p. 216). Deuel's conception of the Mississippi Pattern seems to be decidedly unbalanced in favor of Middle Mississippi, and the Upper Phase appears to be based upon a knowledge of the Fort Ancient Aspect and a corresponding lack of accurate information on, or an unaccountable disregard for the Oneota. It is true that published reports on the Oneota are inadequate, but ample data had been made available to the author. This near omission is particularly unfortunate since the whole conception of an Upper Mississippi Phase had its origin from investigations of Oneota manifestations.

In Appendix IV, a preliminary study of the crania from Fulton County is contributed by Neumann. The results of this study are generally stated in the author's own words: "When we are confronted with the entire collection of skulls from Fulton County, the variability of the material is striking. In a number of individuals there appears a combination of racial characters, giving rise to types which are quite Australoid, Negroid, and even Caucasoid in appearance; but all of them possess characters generally associated with Mongoloids that speak for intensive intermixture." Neumann points out that this bears out Hooton's position that the American Indians can be classified as a single racial entity only if one admits the composite and exceedingly variable nature of that entity (pp. 261–262).

Certain physical types were found consistently associated with certain cultural manifestations. Moreover, "The apparent cultural continuity in pottery types running from Black Sand through the Central Basin to Hopewellian seems to be duplicated in the change in physical type" (p. 263).

Following is a thorough factual statement on the faunal remains, also by Neumann, based upon careful analysis, accompanied by a table showing varieties and occurrence; and an identification of shells by Baker.

Other appendices include: A list of county symbols used in the state survey; a well conceived and excellently executed glossary of terms employed; and an index.

Summarizing, the reviewer is impressed with the quantity of information [374] contained in this work; with the apparent purpose of the authors to produce a thorough and comprehensive report, both from a factual and a technological point of view; with the plentiful evidence of long tireless labors in field and laboratory devoted to the execution of this purpose; and with the general excellence of the product. If this review appears to contain a preponderance of adverse criticism, it is not intended to minimize the recognized value of the work as a whole, or the reviewer's lack of respect and admiration for the authors. Rather, it is one man's reaction specifically to the taxonomic methodology which holds such an important place in the report, and in the mind of the reviewer; presented with the full realization that this method for culture classification is in an experimental stage, as yet too immature to aspire to standardization; and offered with the hope that it will be accepted as wholly constructive in its purpose.

14
The McKern and Related Systems of Classification

Thorne Deuel

Deuel, Thorne. 1939. The McKern and Related Systems of Classification. Paper presented at the meeting of the American Association for the Advancement of Science, Section H. Alpine, Texas. (Illinois State Museum Archives)

In 1932 W. C. McKern of the Milwaukee Public Museum proposed that aboriginal archaeological remains in the Midwestern United States be classified on the basis of significant cultural traits, or "determinants" (McKern 1932[7]).

After sending out copies of a generalized plan [(Guthe 1932[8])] to many of the professional and amateur archaeologists in the United States, a conference was held in December of the same year at Chicago, participated in by the University of Chicago, Milwaukee Public Museum, University of Illinois and University of Michigan.

Subsequent to this meeting a second circular [(McKern et al. 1933[10])] was issued embodying the modifications suggested by mail or in the conference. In May 1934 McKern in the presidential address before the Central Section of the American Anthropological Association, presented a further exposition of the classification and the procedure to be used [(McKern 1934[11])]. In December, 1935, a second conference of archaeologists was called at Indianapolis to discuss common problems of classification. At this conference representatives were present from twelve leading institutions from the central and eastern United States. The discussions and findings of the conference were published early in 1937 [(National Research Council 1937)].

I now propose to show first what the originator and the advocates of this classificatory system advance as their aims, methods and interpretations, and secondly to discuss its strong and weak points in as unbiased a manner as is permitted one who is favorably impressed with its apparent value.

The basic principle underlying the McKern System as previously stated is the classification on the basis of determinants or cultural traits alone. [Guthe (1932[8]:2) states that] geographical distribution is made "the second major consideration (criterion) . . . which, however is always secondary to the similarity of determinants." [McKern et al. (1933[10]:1)] and all subsequent announcements insist that "this classification of cultures is based entirely upon the culture traits and complexes themselves," and that other criteria are not employed. The [classification] system "deals with cultures as a whole and not with specific complexes" [(McKern et al. 1933[10]:2)]. Its protagonists decry the tendency "to think of culture in terms of a single trait" [(McKern et al. 1933[10]:2)], such as pottery for example. The procedure is to "analyze the (components of the) cultures (into their) cultural elements by means of which it will be possible to discover which of them are determinants and which have no classificatory significance" [(McKern et al. 1933[10]:2)].

This brings us to the definition of determinants, by which "we refer to those particular traits among the known evidences of a material culture which, because of their individuality serve to differentiate it from other cultures" [(McKern et al. 1933[10]:1)]. The determinants include pottery shapes and decoration, architecture, bone implements (in southern California), and (in the Mississippi Valley) "variations in pottery, in burial customs, and in the use of copper" [(McKern et al. 1933[10]:1)]. At the Indianapolis Conference [(National Research Council 1937)], this is further emphasized and delimited. Determinants are indicated as of two orders, determinant trait and determinant complex or series.

It should be added that (excepting in Guthe 1932[8]) where geographical distribution is proposed as a secondary "consideration"), space, time, physical type, language, [and] politico-historical relationships are disregarded in classifying and do not constitute criteria. It is recognized that such factors are valuable in understanding cultures but they or any of them do not constitute criteria for classifying [(McKern et al. 1933[10]:1)].

The five categories or groups proposed for the System beginning with the highest include *base*, *pattern*, *phase*, *aspect*, and *focus*. The other terms used are *community* and *component*.

The *base* was originally defined as a "primary culture foundation," determined by a few fundamentals of wide-spread importance and influence, such as the agriculture-pottery complex [(Guthe 1932[8]:2)]. This category was omitted [by McKern et al. (1933[10])] but reinserted at the Indianapolis Conference [(National Research Council 1937)].

In 1935 two bases were indicated—the agricultural (pottery-agricultural-sedentary) and the nomadic (hunting-fishing) (National Research Council 1937:47, 59). It seems apparent that this unit is referred to in [McKern et al. (1933[10]:2)] in the statement: "It is evident that these determinant complexes would include a relatively small proportion of all the determinants within any given culture. They would deal with the primary adjustments of people to their immediate cultural environments and would include architectural adaptations as well as basic industrial patterns." The category base was omitted from the system by agreement at the Chicago conference in 1932. Nevertheless, a difference in the interpretation of the meaning of "basic culture," the most inclusive order at the time, appears to have existed, one group of those revising the system holding that the determinants of this unit were broad fundamental traits, whereas the others adhered to the idea that the term referred to the widely known Woodland and Mississippi units, the determinants of which seemed somewhat less generalized (National Research Council 1937:59). This circumstance was probably largely responsible for the unanimity of the acceptance of the category, *base*, at Indianapolis. Obviously the observation quoted refers to base rather than to pattern as now generally understood.

The base by implication consists of a number of patterns or unit divisions. The latter unit has not been delimited except as previously noted. Probably it would be agreed that the pattern is set off by a number of determinant complexes or series less fundamental and more numerous than those for the base but more generalized and fewer in number than those for phase.

"Clearly each of these (patterns) may be divided into groups which are obviously different from one another in some respects" [(McKern et al. 1933[10]:2)]. These are termed phases. "The members (units) of each phase would be characterized by the determinants possessed in common. They need not have a majority of determinants in common, provided that there be a significant number" [(McKern et al. 1933[10]:2)]. Upper and Middle phases of the Mississippi pattern are indicated as examples of this order [(McKern et al. 1933[10]:2)].

"Furthermore, it is possible to subdivide these phases into several parts" [(McKern et al. 1933[10]:3)] or units termed aspects. "All groups of peoples having an *approximate majority* of determinants in common would constitute an aspect" [(McKern et al. 1933[10]:2), emphasis added].

"The term focus is suggested to signify a group of communities which have a preponderating majority of determinants in common" [(McKern et al. 1933[10]:3)]. The determinants of each community (component?) will presumably be found to be "almost identical" [(McKern et al. 1933[10]:3)] with the others of the same focus, "thereby demonstrating the contemporaneous existence of the several communities" [(McKern et al. 1933[10]:3)]. The foci are, then, the units into which the next larger class, the aspect, can be divided.

"It is suggested that the term 'component' be used to refer to the manifestation of a given culture at a single site" [(McKern et al. (1933[10]:4)]. It is a localized, and usually incomplete manifestation "which may be shown to be related to a larger cultural class by analysis of determinants present" [(McKern et al. 1933[10]:4)]. The term *community*, not defined in [(McKern et al. 1933[10])], was probably employed as synonymous with component. Cole and Deuel [(1937:278)] gave their interpretation of community as "the complete cultural manifestation of a local group or as much of it as is determinable by archaeological exploration." It might be argued logically that archaeological investigation by present methods or any at this time conceivably possible can never recover a complete cultural manifestation and that there is no real difference between community and component in either degree or kind. This is particularly true since the designation *site*, on which the definition hinges, has no very exact connotation at present and it is doubtful if it can be limited more accurately. The term may signify a so-called "pure" site (one presumably having a single cultural manifestation with cemetery, village and workshop activities in evidence) as well as a single mound yielding components of three phases or patterns (itself a part of a larger group of mounds) or a compact group of mounds, village and cemetery remains showing several cultural occupancies.

This, then, sets forth the McKern system as it is described by its author, McKern, and its proponents. As Doctor Wissler [(1938)] is the only writer who has published a discussion of the proposed archaeological classification in some detail, I propose to consider the more important of his criticisms and give the position of the proponents of the system as already expressed in the published literature. This will include most of the criticisms and queries regarding the plan and its procedure.

To begin with, Dr. Wissler makes a careless summary of the categories and their definitions. Among several discrepancies, the inclusion of the component as one of the categories and the inference that the classification is based on artifact types alone are the most serious [(Wissler 1938:299)]. By analogy to the zoological or biological classification, the component represents the "specimen" to be classified and is not a category at all. In the second place the substitution of the term "artifacts" for "traits" as used by the advocates of the culture classification, is unfortunate to say the least. It leaves the implication that the system is based purely on the material objects found on a site, without regard to the most ordinary observations. Webster's New International Dictionary 1937 defines artifact as "a product of human workmanship, especially one of the simpler products of primitive art as distinguished from a natural object." It is doubtful if Dr. Wissler would consider customs like the burial of the dead in a flexed position, the practice of including pottery in graves, the incising of pottery, and similar traits of culture as artifacts or artifact types.

Indirectly, however, this does point to a weak point in the classification. It is assumed by the proponents of the plan that the meaning of the term trait is generally known. That every one dealing with culture has a more or less sharply defined idea of trait is obviously true but these ideas are widely different. As a suggestion for the purpose of argument, I propose that a trait of a community or component is a cultural (not merely personal or individual) habit, custom or pattern of behavior, either simple or complex, that is evidenced by the archaeological remains, their association and such other cultural implications as the circumstances and conditions of their occurrence may reasonably suggest. Thus a grooved axe presents a number of different traits such as (1) a customary general shape and cross section; (2) a manner of pecking and polishing stone; (3) the production and use of a groove presumably for hafting; and (4) its presumed use as a cutting tool somewhat in the same manner of a modern steel axe. These traits may have greatly varying significance.

A second objection to the system mentioned is the arbitrariness of the number of categories. The five orders or groups omit the highest order, *base*, from [Wissler's (1938)] list, though a published description of it appeared at least three months before his preface was written [and] were determined empirically as were the culture areas, or the orders in biological classifications [(Cole and Deuel 1937)]. That number seemed the fewest possible that were required. Attempts have been made to drop base and aspect but they appear to be needed, not only by one worker but by dozens who are using the system. Indeed, most of these workers would probably agree that if it seemed generally desirable to increase the number of categories or sub-groups or to drop one of them, no strong objection would be raised. At present five as the number of categories seems desirable.

There is another criticism that has a bearing on this same point. Dr. Wissler agrees that the components are realities, and (if I may be permitted to change the order in his statement) "that the significance of focus is clear enough" but the aspect is nebulous—here "our feet begin to leave the ground" [(Wissler 1938:300)]. I think the difficulty arises in this instance, first in an attempt to visualize theoretically the determinants without actually analyzing a series of components and organizing them into patterns, phases, and aspects as has been done by Griffin [(1935)] and Deuel [(1935a, 1935b)] independently of each other, and by somewhat differing procedures; secondly, it seems to be a criticism of a lack of provision for a definite procedure. This absence of a rigid method appears to me to be a strong point in favor of the classification at its present stage. McKern and those who have adopted the plan have suggested a general procedure but wisely left the detailed methods and the discovery of the determinants or determinant series open for other workers to develop and test. We have not advanced to the point of development in our taxonomy corresponding to Linnaeus in the biological taxonomies, perhaps, but Linnaeus used arbitrary criteria and they have long since been replaced in both zoology and botany by a so-called genetic system. Again this deliberateness may render revision necessary less frequently. McKern et al. [(1933[10]:2)] say "analyze the cultures in terms of cultural elements by means of which it will be possible to discover which of them are determinants and which have no classificatory significance." This of course, is general language but its import is quite clear. I don't think for a minute [that McKern et al.] thought by magic one would be able to pick out determinants but by dint of hard work in analyzing and testing component after component and focus after focus.

Another query might be considered here, as to whether this trial and error, or empirical method won't entail a great deal of subsequent revision. As McKern [(National Research Council 1937:44)] pointed out, the history of all scientific development has involved a constant changing in the terms and methods of classifying. This change still goes on today in the botanical, zoological and paleontological fields to mention only three.

To further quote Dr. Wissler [(1938:300)], "The champions of the above classification scheme have explicitly stated that neither chronology nor geography has a place in it." This exclusion is in accord with the biological and similar classifications; in zoology, for example, the remains of an *Elephas primigenius* are still *Elephas primigenius* whether they are found in Europe, Asia or North America and whether they lived 100,000 years or 10,000 years ago. Similarly, as pointed out by the proponents of the plan, although time, space, physical type, language, politico-historical and other relationships and factors are important for a better understanding of man and culture, the culture classification as such need not take them into consideration.

After reviewing the attempts in European archaeology to combine time and cultural content in the Stone Age cultural classification, it appears extremely doubtful that they can be united consistently in any comprehensive scheme covering wide distributions in time and space. If area and other factors are included also, the scheme as a taxonomic system becomes over-involved and valueless. Nevertheless, the use of a simple taxonomic system based on culture alone might in conjunction with other factors in limited areas produce valuable descriptive charts of chronological sequence, migration, diffusion, racial intermixture and so on. Peake and Fleure [(1927)] have done this very successfully for European areas in *Corridors of Time.*

Wissler [(1938:302)] observes that Parker and Ritchie's table of Classification of Aboriginal Cultures of New York State "as a whole is chronological." In this case, the arrangement of the patterns was made for the specific purpose of showing time sequence but that succession from earliest to latest is independent of and no part whatever of the classification on the basis of culture determinants. They might equally well have been arranged spatially or plotted geographically on a map. This would again be independent of their place in the classificatory system. However, to show the culture relationship of these units to those occurring in the Midwest for example, a different arrangement would appear, based on cultural determinants alone and only generally implying temporal and spatial distribution (Deuel 1937a), a partial expression of the archaeological taxonomic system. The fact that the "specimens" and orders of a limited area can thus be arranged in a time sequence or plotted to show geographical distribution demonstrates very nicely the flexibility of the system and the uses to which it may be put.

The present writer believes the description of determinants can be justly criticized on the ground that they are defined as the traits, "which because of their individuality, serve to differentiate it from other cultures" [(McKern et al. 1933[10]:1)]. It would seem more accurate to say they are the traits that serve to unite components or units in larger groups, in which the constituent units are more like each other than those of other groups. This is in line with present practice in botany (personal communication from G. D. Fuller, Professor of Plant Ecology, University of Chicago), zoology (personal communication from H. B. Ward, Professor of Zoology, University of Illinois) and genetics (Morgan 1925:44).

The uniqueness of the characters insisted on by Ritchie [(National Research Council 1937:54)], McKern, and Guthe [(National Research Council 1937:57)] may also constitute a point for criticism. "A diagnostic trait," says McKern [(National Research Council 1937:56–57)], "is a trait which applies (pertains) only to that class, and is unique for that class." As I interpret this statement, a diagnostic trait or determinant cannot occur as a trait in another unit. This seems to deny the possibility of the diffusion of a determinant. I doubt that many anthropologists would agree that determinants would fail to diffuse to groups in different cultural classes though determinants especially of the higher orders might tend to diffuse to a lesser degree.

A binomial (or trinomial) system of nomenclature similar to those in use in the biological taxonomies would be a convenient modification of the system. This will probably work out of itself as the classification goes on.

Lack of time prevents touching upon the genetic implications (if any) of the McKern system [(National Research Council 1937:41, 42, 44, 45, 48, 49, 61)] or of discussion of the methods of those putting it into practice [(see Cole and Deuel 1937; Deuel 1935b; Griffin 1935 for procedures used in classifying)].

SUMMARY

The advantages provided by the McKern classificatory system may be summarized as follows:

1. Classification has been found to be a convenient method of organizing data in the other natural sciences, even when the systems were more or less arbitrary. Classification is not an end in itself; it is a necessary starting point and furnishes a working tool. The McKern System presents a simple, direct plan of organization.

2. The foundation of the classification on the content itself, culture, is sound and is similar in this respect to the other taxonomic systems in the biological sciences.

3. The classification works reasonably well for those using the method and system, judging from published reports and papers by Parker and Ritchie [see Wissler (1938:301)], McKern [(1934[11])], Griffin [(1935)], Cole [(Cole and Deuel 1937)], Deuel [(1935a, 1935b)] and others. Its use has begun to produce an orderly arrangement among the formerly chaotic archaeological data in the Midwest and adaptable to the situation in New York. It promises to be usable in the Southwest and in the southeastern United States [(National Research Council 1937:38, 42–47)]. Many of the criticisms that are advanced against the classification seem due to unfamiliarity with the theory and use of the existing systems in botany and zoology or result from theoretical considerations that do not appear in practice.

4. The classificatory system facilitates the comparison of cultures in different areas through a standardization or coordination of methods in handling data.

5. The dependence of the system on culture determinants only permits

the classifying of components to be completed without waiting for temporal or spatial factors, linguistic, politico-historical, or other affiliations to become known. Thus the temptation to assume the nature of one or more of these on the basis of little or no evidence is removed. These relationships may be noted at any time without disturbing the classification.

6. The methods of procedure are only generally blocked out, permitting the use of the system over wide areas and divergent cultures. The system lends itself to revision. Care should be exercised on the part of those publishing that sufficiently complete data are presented so the reader may weigh the conclusions reached.

Whether or not the McKern classification is adopted, a similar simple system, based on the culture itself, should probably be adopted to aid in organizing archaeological research over wide areas. The McKern classification up to the present comes nearest to fulfilling these requirements.

15
The Midwestern Taxonomic Method as an Aid to Archaeological Culture Study

W. C. McKern

W. C. McKern. 1939. *American Antiquity* 4:301–313.

[301]

The Midwestern Taxonomic Method as an Aid to Archaeological Culture Study

W. C. McKern

In delayed response to a certain demand for a published statement covering the archaeological taxonomic method introduced in the northern Mississippi Valley area a few years ago and now tentatively employed in this, the northern Plains, and the Northeastern areas, it seems advisable to briefly set forth in this journal the essential framework for this method, and to include a revision of previously outlined but unpublished discussions relating thereto, in addition to a brief definition of certain problems involved in its application.

Although the present writer's name has been repeatedly associated with this method, it should be made clear that no single individual can be accurately held responsible for the final product. The relatively undeveloped original plan was revised by a self-appointed committee consisting of interested anthropologists representing the universities of Michigan, Chicago, and Illinois, and the Milwaukee Public Museum. A description of the taxonomic method tentatively endorsed by this group was prepared in mimeographed form and distributed (McKern et al. 1933[10]) for critical inspection to archaeological research students throughout the country. As a result of the constructively critical response to this action, certain details relating to terminology were altered. The general reaction to this revision was one of tentative acceptance, and it was considered the proper procedure to submit the method to trial by use.

At the Indianapolis Conference a change in the terminology for the classificatory divisions was adopted, creating a new division (base) at the generalized end of the frame (as was originally proposed but discarded), and substituting the term "pattern" for "basic culture" (McKern 1934[11], 1937b). The method as presented here follows the Indianapolis revision. [302]

THE NEED FOR CLASSIFICATION

Any adequate discussion of this or any other method relating to archaeological culture classification must logically follow some consideration of the need for culture classification in archaeology. It may be advanced that we already possess an adequate taxonomic method. I have received such questions as this: Why refer to the cultural manifestation of the pre-literate Iowa as the Upper Mississippi, or by any name other than Iowa? In instances we may have sufficient data to verify identification with some known historic group, such as the Iowa. However, in most instances we can not immediately bridge the barrier between pre-literate and historic or protohistoric cultural groups, and in many instances we can not reasonably hope ever to be able to do so. Yet we perceive that there are archaeologically collected data that warrant cultural segregation. The only taxonomic basis for dealing with all cultural manifestations, regardless of occasional direct historical tie-ups, is that of culture type as illustrated by trait-indicative materials and features encountered in former habitation sites. If at any time it becomes possible to name the historic ethnic group for which the pre-literate group is the progenitor, no confusion would result from the statement that, for example, Upper Mississippi Oneota is Chiwere Sioux; no more so than from the statement that *Elephas primigenius* is the mammoth.

Aside from the inadequacy of the direct-historical method to supply the archaeologist in every instance, and immediately, with means for attachment to the ethnological classification, the latter, even if applicable, would not ideally answer the needs of the archaeologist. One ethnological classification divides the aborigines into linguistic stocks, which are subdivided first into more specific linguistic groups and, finally, into socio-political groups. The criteria for classification are social, primarily linguistic. The major portion of the data available to the archaeologist relates to material culture, and in no instance includes linguistic data. Consequently, this ethnological classification does not satisfy archaeological requirements.

It may be said that we have the ethnologically conceived culture areas to supply a basis for archaeological classification. However, these so-called culture areas involve two factors which the archaeologist must disregard in devising his culture classification if he is to avoid hopeless confusion;

these are the spatial and temporal factors. First, the culture area attempts to define, or at least limit, geographic distribution. Unfortunately, cultural divisions of American aborigines did [303] not always succeed in confining themselves within a continuous area, or in keeping culturally pure an area of any important size. Second, the archaeologist considers the American Indian from the standpoint of all time, and, certainly, there can be no cultural areas devised to account for an unlimited temporal factor.

In brief, the archaeologist requires a classification based upon the cultural factor alone; temporal and distributional treatments will follow as accumulating data shall warrant. Moreover, the archaeological classification necessarily must be based upon criteria available to the archaeologist.

Any statement that the archaeologist has no need for a culture taxonomic method is in conflict with facts which all students of the subject must have encountered. One has only to consult the pre-classification reports on research in almost any American province (outside the Southwest, where a special classification has developed), noting the indefinite use of the word "culture" to denote anything from the manifestation of a general pattern influential over an area a thousand or more miles in extent, to the highly specialized manifestation of a culture apparent at a cluster of closely localized sites, and noting the confusion of unstandardized cultural terminology, to appreciate the need for simplifying the complexity of cultural data and concepts through the establishment of systematic order. In men's affairs, chaos does not reduce itself to order without a plan. The accomplishments of science stand as a monument to planned orderliness.

Unlike the student of ethnology, the American archaeologist has not been appreciably influenced by the initial complexity of his subject to specialize in some certain aspect of that subject; [he is] more inclined to embrace in his studies all apparent aspects of his subject within the area available to him for investigation. As his problems lead towards comparative studies over [a] wider area, his conceptions of cultural manifestations take on broader interpretations. Starting with cultural differentiation, he begins to observe evidence of cultural affinities, not only as regards specific complexes but involving distinctive types of complexes. He lacks a specific terminology that is standard with his fellow students, by means of which he can clearly express his maturing concepts. He stretches old meanings to apply to his needs, and finds himself justly criticized, primarily by students limited to ethnological experience, for his extraordinarily indefinite, inaccurate use of the term "culture," which, for want of a more specific term, is made to serve a multitude of specific purposes for which it never was intended.

[304] The point of all this is that the student of archaeology in the greater Mississippi Valley is greatly in need of a standardized culture scheme such as can be realized only through the medium of taxonomic method.

There are a few who have hesitated to cooperate fully in this classificatory experiment on the grounds of not being satisfied that the time for classification has yet arrived. They perceive that we lack adequate information to warrant wholesale classification. With due respect for the caution exhibited in this attitude, I can not but feel that this caution is based upon a false conception of the very nature and purpose of classification, and a misunderstanding of the intentions of those endorsing the taxonomic method in question.

Classification is nothing more than the process of recognizing classes, each class identified by a complex of characteristics. For many years, we have all been active in this business of identifying cultural classes, no matter by what name one may call it, but we have not performed with marked efficiency because we have lacked the necessary equipment. In the *Encyclopedia Britannica*, Dr. Abraham Wolf says: "Classification is one method, probably the simplest method, of discovering order in the world. . . . In the history of every science classification is the very first method to be employed." We have tried to get along without it overlong. It is classification that makes it possible for one student to describe phenomena in terms readily comprehensible to another student versed in the taxonomic method. It reduces a multiplicity of facts to simplicity and order, and supplies a standardized terminology without which students encounter difficulty in conversing intelligently on a common subject.

The adoption and use of a taxonomic method most certainly does not imply the immediate classification of all manifestations with apparent cultural significance. It is only in those instances in which sufficient data are available, quantitatively and qualitatively, to create a problem of cultural differentiation that classification can serve to any advantage. In some provinces little in the way of detailed classification can logically be attempted at this time; in other provinces much can be accomplished toward detailed classification; and in all provinces a taxonomic method should be adopted before any serious attempts are made at classification. Naturally, this method should be standard for the largest area possible. Following an agreement as to method, the actual classification should be a necessarily slow, deliberate procedure, constantly experimental, subject to such major and minor corrections as newly [305] accumulating data may dictate, subject to a maximum of constructive criticism and resulting improvement.

Such is the history of any scientific classification. It is the method of classification to be employed, not any specific classification, that offers an immediate, initial problem for which a solution is now being attempted.

PRELIMINARY TERMINOLOGY

Before describing the taxonomic system, certain details of involved procedure and related terminology should be explained and defined.

The word *determinant* is employed to denote any cultural trait when and as used as a marker for any specific cultural division. The term is in no sense synonymous with "trait."

In comparing any two culture manifestations, it may develop that certain traits are shared in common by two manifestations. Such traits, to follow Ritchie (1937:187), may be designated as *linked* traits. Traits found to occur in one manifestation and not in that with which it is compared, peculiar to the one manifestation in this comparison, are termed *diagnostic* traits (Ritchie 1937:187). It follows, by definition, that in any comparison of two manifestations only diagnostic traits can serve as determinants for either manifestation, since only traits peculiar to each of the compared culture varieties can be used to differentiate between them. It therefore follows that traits which are diagnostic and thus useful as determinants in one comparison may be linked traits in another comparison and, consequently, useless as determinants. Therefore, there can be no truly valuable fixed list of determinants for any given culture class, serving as such in all possible comparisons; the determinants for a hypothetical Culture A as compared with Culture B may be considerably different from the determinants for the same Culture A as compared with Culture C. The term "determinant" can only be employed as applied in a stated comparison.

In brief, all the traits characteristic for a given culture manifestation comprise the culture complex for that manifestation. However, in any comparison of this manifestation with another, made for purposes of classification, certain traits may be demonstrated as present in both complexes, and these linked traits, serving to show cultural similarity between the two culture variants, can not be employed as determinants in this comparison. Certain other traits, respectively peculiar to each [306] of the compared complexes and so serving to differentiate between them, are diagnostic traits and useful for culture determinants in this comparison. Other comparisons may produce an entirely new alignment of determinants.

USE OF TRAITS

One of the most difficult problems facing the classifier is that of identifying the determinants for a cultural division, particularly those more specific divisions in which cultural details are important criteria for differentiation. This difficulty is partly due to the difference in complexity between such an object as a simple bone awl and another such as a pottery vessel. Culture criteria available to the archaeologist are demonstrated by culture-indicative materials, for the most part artifacts. A simple type of artifact may serve as one element in a trait complex for one cultural division, and therefore may serve in some comparison as a determinant for that division. This may be the case with a simple type of bone awl. However, when a comparatively complex type of pottery is characteristic for one of the more specific cultural divisions, the question arises as to whether it should be considered as a trait or as comprising a number of trait elements. It certainly is more culturally indicative than a pointed fragment of bone. Single detailed pottery elements, such as shell temper, loop handles, or cord-imprinted decoration, would seem to be at least as important culture markers as a simple implement with a single differentiating trait. Thus, apparently, we may have a considerable variety of trait elements exhibited by pottery alone. Probably other subjects of cultural import in instances will each supply many, rather than a single trait; for instance, mound structure, burial methods, and house types. It may even seem advisable to recognize in the simplest of artifacts such distinct detailed traits as regards shape, material, and technique of fabrication.

The problem, then, narrows down to the selecting, from the traits comprising a complex subject, of those trait details which have sufficient cultural significance to qualify them as culture determinants. This really implies a separate classification of the essential trait elements for any given complex cultural subject. For example, pottery should be classified under such essential heads as paste, temper, texture, hardness, surface, color, shape, and decoration. Determinants in pottery for a cultural division in a specific comparison could then be selected to cover these standard pottery trait elements. In the same way, the essential detailed traits for burial method, and other complex [307] subjects could be standardized through special classifications, with the result that the determinants for one cultural division would cover the same ground as, and carry similar weight to those for another division with which it is compared. Simpler subjects would offer fewer but equally important trait details, or elements.

Our problem has also to deal with different types of culture, as different from each other as a broad basic type and a local specific type. The former is identified for the most part by traits that are in the nature of fundamental cultural trends. These fundamentals are quite different in character from the detailed material trait elements that are so important in determining highly specialized divisions. Thus, the character of a trait employed as a culture determinant will depend upon the type of cultural division for which it serves as a determinant. The presence of horticulture might serve as a differentiating trait for some sedentary division as distinct from a nomadic, hunting division, but it could not serve to distinguish between two subdivisions of a horticultural class. In the opposite extreme, a peculiar motif in pottery decoration might serve as one determinant of a local specific division, but not as a determinant for the less specialized division under which it is classified, since it is peculiar to the local class.

One general axiom must guide the student in attacking this problem. Traits or trait elements employed as determinants must be characteristic for that division which they serve to identify. That being the case, determinants for a *base* (see following taxonomic system), or even a *pattern*, will be for the most part general in character and relatively few in number. For the more specialized divisions, progressing from lesser to greater specialization, the determinants will be an enriched edition of the determinants for the immediately preceding, more general division, as altered to include greater detail, plus a considerable number of trait elements peculiarly characteristic of the more specialized division. For example, the *focus* determinants would be the *aspect* determinants made richer in detail and augmented by additional traits peculiar to the focus and exhibiting the greatest cultural detail apparent for the entire pattern.

TAXONOMIC SYSTEM

The method here under consideration is basically a simple one employing for its purposes complexes of cultural factors only. Five arbitrary divisions are made differentiating between specialized local types of culture manifestation and more general and broadly influential types.

[308] *Focus.* Starting at the site, as any investigator must, materials and associated data are collected which have cultural significance. Expressed in terms of culture traits, these data provide a trait complex for the site. If the complex of trait units so determined, or any important complex of trait units included therein, is found to recur in characteristic purity and practical completeness at other sites, to an extent suggestive of cultural identity, this recurring complex establishes the first of our class types, the *focus*.

A focus may be briefly defined as that class of culture exhibiting characteristic peculiarities in the finest analysis of cultural detail, and may in instances correspond closely to the local tribe in ethnology. It is dangerous, however, to define it as such.

The manifestation of any given focus at a specific site is termed a *component* of that focus. This is in no sense an additional type of culture manifestation, one of the five class types; rather, it is the focus as represented at a site, and serves to distinguish between a site, which may bear evidence of several cultural occupations, each foreign to the other, and a single specified manifestation at a site. In many instances several components, each at cultural variance with the other, may be found to occur at a single site.

Aspect. A comparison of established foci may supply evidence that certain foci are, on the one hand, very like each other, especially when certain of the more specific trait units are eliminated from consideration, and on the other hand, as a group, show marked dissimilarity to other compared foci. When this similarity of compared foci involves a preponderating majority of the traits and trait elements, the dissimilarity apparent for the greater part in considering the more detailed elements, these foci may be classified under the same *aspect*, the second class type. All foci in a given aspect share the somewhat less specific aspect trait units, but possess additional peculiarities in fine cultural detail. Thus, the type of decorative pattern on pottery might serve as an aspect determinant, shared by all the foci in that aspect, whereas the actual patterns employed might serve to differentiate one of these foci from another.

Phase. Similarly, like aspects may determine a *phase*, the third class type. As the classifier approaches the more generalized classes, cultural detail becomes less important to his purposes, and the traits that are shared by all aspects within the phase to make up the phase complex take on a more general character. For example, whereas actual decorative patterns on pottery may serve as focus determinants, and [309] less specific types of pattern decoration as aspect determinants, the trait of mechanical technique for ceramic ornamentation, shared by all its aspects, might be the most detailed trait of pottery decoration applicable to the phase. Or, the phase may be characterized by a general burial procedure, general pottery attributes, and general house-type features; whereas one aspect within a phase is differentiated from the other aspects as the result of a consideration of burials, pottery, and houses in somewhat greater detail. In addition to this qualitative factor, a near majority of traits shared in common by compared aspects determine the phase, and these traits comprise the phase complex. As previously demonstrated, it should be remembered that there is a difference between the phase complex, or any other class complex, and the complex of determinants for the phase as specifically compared with another phase.

Pattern. Several phases may be shown to share a small complex of broadly general traits, in contrast to other compared phases in which these units do not occur. Such a complex of traits determines that the phases identified thereby bear the relation to each other of belonging to the same *pattern*, the fourth class in the taxonomic frame. The traits used as determinants for the pattern will be such as deal with the cultural reflection of the primary adjustments of peoples to environment, as modified by tradition.

For example, the Mississippi Pattern, as compared with the Woodland Pattern, offers such determinants as (tentative list): characteristic extended inhumation; a pottery ware medium to fine in texture, prevailingly shell-tempered, characterized by incised, trailed or modeled decoration, offering relative variety in shape; basically triangular chipped-stone projectile points; secondary flaking superimportant over primary, to reduce thin flakes to a desired shape and size; ungrooved axes; relative superimportance of bone, antler, and shell as materials for a considerable variety of artifacts; sedentary territorial adjustment.

The Woodland Pattern, as compared with the Mississippi Pattern, offers such determinants as (tentative list): characteristic flex inhumation and/or secondary interments; a pottery ware characteristically grit-tempered, granular in structure, with intaglio surface ornamentation effected on soft unfired paste by means of cords and/or other indenting tools, prevailingly sub-concoidal in shape with simple shape variety; stemmed or notched chipped-stone projectile points and cutting implements; primary chipping superimportant over secondary, [310] to reduce thick flakes to a desired size and shape; grooved axes; semi-sedentary territorial adjustment.

Base. In addition to the diagnostic traits respectively employed as determinants for these two patterns, there are also certain broadly general linked traits shared by both; such as pottery, sedentary tendency, and, possibly, horticulture. On a basis of these similarities, if these patterns are compared, for example, with nomadic hunting patterns, the Mississippi and Woodland patterns may be classified together with the same *base*, the most general of the taxonomic divisions. The base is characterized by a few fundamentals, such as relate in the most general way to the food quest (horticulture, hunting, seed gathering), community order (camps, permanent villages), or possession of classes of products of outstanding cultural import (pottery, basketry). Hypothetical examples of the base might include such descriptively named divisions as: Horticultural-Pottery Base;

Nomadic-Hunting Base; Sedentary-Fishing Base; Seed-Gathering-Basketry Base.

To summarize briefly, the taxonomic frame consists of five major divisions: focus, aspect, phase, pattern, and base, progressing from localized detail to large general classes. The manifestation of a focus at any site is called a component of that focus. The method is comparable to a filing cabinet equipped with labeled drawers to facilitate the orderly arrangement of culture-indicative data.

RELATED PROBLEMS

Archaeological data at best offer a very incomplete cultural picture of the people under investigation, and great care should be taken to base classification upon as representative a mass of data as possible. The exploration of a burial site has been demonstrated in many instances to produce information more characteristic of burial customs of an ethnic group than of the complete culture. Similarly, data collected at a village site with no burials is deficient in that information on burial methods is lacking.

The error in classifying cultural divisions on a basis of site or component units, regardless of the limitations in character of such manifestations, i.e., whether burial, village, or other varieties of sites, may be corrected by a consideration of *communities* rather than components. This method of approach has been advanced by Cole and Deuel (1937:34, 278), [311] who define the community as "the complete cultural manifestation of a local group or as much of it as is determined by archaeological exploration." Any classification based, for example, on data collected exclusively at burial sites is subject to greater error, and is therefore less useful than if the determinants represent a community as manifest at both habitation and burial sites.

Experience seems to demonstrate that absolute mathematical percentages in trait similarity can not be successfully employed to establish the class relationship between two compared manifestations. This is largely due to the fact that a completed list of culture-indicative data for any culture group can never be made available, and that such lists as are available will be more inclusive for one community than for another with which it is compared. Moreover, the different character of the culture elements employed for determining separate classes, i.e., the generalized traits of a pattern as contrasted to the detailed trait units of a focus, serves to complicate any mathematical treatment of the problem; it is difficult to add apples and bushels of apples.

However, the quantitative similarity in culture indicators is decidedly serviceable in determining the classificatory place of a manifestation. After trait units for a community have been formulated as the result of field and laboratory research, and this trait list is compared with similarly prepared lists for other manifestations, it may be found that, culturally, the community complex is more similar to certain of the compared manifestations than to others. If the similarity should amount to a practical identity of these detailed trait elements, a focus would be indicated. If the similarity should amount to an important majority of the trait elements, at least aspect relationship would be indicated. Similarly, a comparison on a basis of more generalized traits in all probability would serve to identify pattern, possibly phase relationships.

It is not to be expected that a complete classification for any given work province can be made immediately. Classification will grow slowly under the most favorable conditions, and, in instances, will be delayed indefinitely. In all instances, the taxonomic method should be regarded as a tool to be used only when needed.

The growth of classification will not invariably be in logical sequence, from focus to base. After a focus has been determined, the classifier may fail for a time to find evidence of near cultural relationship and, lacking criteria indicating the proper aspect, or even phase, may assign the focus to a pattern before data indicative of the intervening [312] classes are made available; providing, of course, that the pattern complex has previously been defined.

The relative grouping of cultural divisions by any such taxonomic method does not necessarily imply evolutionary relationship. A common historical origin may be suggested, but the implication should be considered as an indicator, guiding further research, rather than as proof in itself. Cultural evolution can not be established by such a classification since time criteria, so essential to any study of directional growth, have no place in its determination; the method makes use of culture criteria only. A chronology independently constructed from available time criteria may later be determined as a parallel development and correlated with a culture classification to establish or refute evolutionary sequence.

Cultural distribution can only be portrayed on a basis of time, since distribution is not a fixed quantity for all time. Thus, any map devised to show the known distribution for a given culture division, such as the Upper Mississippi Phase, is a map of culture only; for any given time, it might offer a materially altered appearance.

In applying any taxonomic method, there is always the danger that an unleashed enthusiasm may induce the classifier to attempt to make the facts fit the method. The lure of being methodical at all costs is a constant threat to the wholly profitable use of any method. It is well to bear constantly in mind the rule that the classification is, and forever must be, subservient to the facts. It is convenience and orderliness in handling archaeological data that is required of the classification, not a flawless, natural regimentation of the facts required by the classification.

This method of classification is arbitrary, like all other scientific taxonomic methods. Under the blending influences of diffusion, and the divergent tendencies involving cultural growth by invention, there can be no hard and fast natural division lines. This absence of sharp lines of demarcation between classes applies rather equally to the subject matter of all natural sciences, and can not be advanced as a valid argument against classification. Our method is not nearly so arbitrary as the division of a continent into culture areas, which disregards an inelastic temporal factor and a confusingly mixed and unstable distributional factor. The maximum degree of arbitrariness in our method is attained in the division of cultural manifestations into five, rather than some other number of culture types. The five divisions were finally agreed upon by the authors of this method as satisfying all apparent [313] needs for major subdivision. With the means provided for ultimate subclassification into specific groups under these culture-type heads, if and when needed, the major requirements of remotely separate fields seem to be satisfied, as reported by specialists in those fields.

Although the space available here has not permitted for the taxonomic method adequate illustrations by example, it is hoped that the basic idea has been stated clearly, and that some of the most essential problems relating thereto have been defined. Admittedly, the value of such a method, and the ways for making it function to best advantage as discussed herein, are controversial subjects. However, in consideration of experience obtained as a result of a rather widespread trial of the method during the last six years, it appears to have contributed materially towards introducing order into the previously existing chaotic status of general culture concepts throughout the greater Mississippi Valley.

16
Application of the Midwestern Taxonomic Method

W. C. McKern

W. C. McKern. 1940. *Bulletin of the Archaeological Society of Delaware* 3:18–21.
[18]

APPLICATION OF THE MIDWESTERN TAXONOMIC METHOD

(*Editorial Foreword:* The author, who is Curator of Anthropology at the Milwaukee Public Museum, is one of America's prominent anthropological scholars. His name is associated with a classificatory, or taxonomic, system of indexing aboriginal cultures, which is in use in the Midwest and is now being applied in eastern areas.

In this article, prepared especially for the *Bulletin*, W. C. McKern discusses the midwestern method in simpler language than it has heretofore appeared. The Delaware Society is proud to offer this discussion for enlightenment of non-professional students everywhere. We consider it a notable contribution.

This article can not be hastily scanned. Its full meaning can be realized only by a careful digest of every word. Every true student will want to read and reread it.)

A certain amount of confusion over the application of the Midwestern Taxonomic Method has arisen, largely due to the bad example set by certain early experimental applications, and to the somewhat unnecessarily technical language employed in published descriptions of the method and its use. Since much of the unnecessarily technical language employed in the past has been my own, I may not be ideally suited to explain our method of classification, and to correct certain important misconceptions of the way in which it is supposed to work, in simplified language. However, I am willing to try.

Actually the method is quite simple, in spite of the efforts of some to introduce complexity into it. It is a proposal to group together, under common names, classes of cultural manifestations which show degrees of similarity. A complex of traits determined at a site may represent customs and ways of living (culture) of a local group representing a single variety, or band, of Indians, sharing an identical lot of cultural habits. Such a band might be illustrated in the historic period by the Mohawk Indians. This represents the most detailed class of cultural manifestation. In the comparative study of human culture as represented by materials found at archaeological sites, other degrees of similarity between manifestations are easily detected. More general traits appear to tie together groups of the detailed classes; and even more fundamental similarities tend to unite large general classes. Any comparative study of cultural data is greatly helped by such a systematic organization of the subject matter.

Although, like all other methods of classification, this method is arbitrary rather than natural, it is based wholly upon the one factor of cultural similarity and positively reflects any reality involved in cultural similarity.

Field investigation at any given site produces objects such as potsherds, implements and ornaments of stone, bone, horn, antler, shell, and the like; and information on the customs of the people such as burial procedure, ways of making things, house or wall types, food sources and variety, materials customarily employed, and other things relating to native life. From the information so assembled a list of *culture traits* may readily be shaped.

[19] This list of culture traits represents the former inhabitants of the site which is under investigation. It may represent a single cultural group occupying the site exclusive of any other group; or it may represent two or more distinctly separate cultural groups who occupied the site at different times. There may be no way immediately to discover which of these two possibilities is correct. Under ideal conditions, there may be present clear evidence that materials representing a relatively late occupation are resting upon materials previously deposited by an earlier, different group, with a distinct line of separation between the two deposits; but even this evidence does not conclusively prove that either the materials above this line of separation, or those below it, represent a single cultural group of people.

This problem is best solved by comparing the list of traits found at one site with similarly determined lists of traits from other, nearby sites. If substantially the same traits are found to occur together repeatedly at site after site, one can be quite sure that this persistently grouped lot of traits is characteristic of a single culture. Such a repeatedly recurring series of traits is called a *culture complex*.

If a comparative study of traits from various sites shows a practical identity between two or more sites (allowing for differences in quantity and the occasional absence of rare traits) the culture complex shared by these sites is that of a *focus*. When foci are compared, specifically similar foci determine an *aspect*. Certain aspects may be found to share important traits which bind them together in contrast to other aspects, thus determining a *phase*. Similarly, phases may bear resemblances which serve to unite them within a *pattern*.

Thus, a simple complex of fundamental traits binds together the entire pattern, to distinguish it from other patterns, and this culture complex is added to and enriched in greater and greater detail with the subdivisions of the pattern: phases, aspects, and foci, progressing from the more general to the more specific.

Once any one of these classes has been determined, and its essential culture complex known, any manifestation found to show this complex of traits may be classified by definition. For example, if materials found at a certain site define a series of culture traits which have already been described for the Woodland Pattern, the finder may at once conclude: this complex is already known and has been recorded for the Woodland Pattern; therefore, this manifestation is some variety of Woodland. Or he may go on to conclude: moreover, it is not only Woodland, but it has the more specific characteristics already determined for the Owasco Aspect, which would place it in the Northeastern Phase. The focus alone then would remain unidentified.

Suppose, however, that the traits discovered at a site appear to be a mixture of two known complexes, and still persists at site after site. The problem of placing such a cultural manifestation, apparently a mixture yet persisting as a focus complex, is not as difficult as might appear to be the case at first consideration. Cultural relationship is apparent, even though it does point in two different directions. The manifestation rests on the fence. The logical thing to do is to define it as intermediate between the two focus manifestations which it rather equally resembles. That places it definitely in relation to other foci in the classification.

[20] If, however, the complex indicates an admixture of closely related foci, but leans definitely closer to one of the similar focus complexes than to the other, it should be classified with the one it more closely resembles. It should constantly be borne in mind that our classification, like all other classifications, is arbitrary, and that separating lines are arbitrarily drawn. The purpose of the classification is that of organizing data for convenience in handling and the elimination of the element of confusion which arises with the constant accumulation of data. Taxonomy is purely a methodical procedure.

It may develop with subsequent research that a certain complex in the

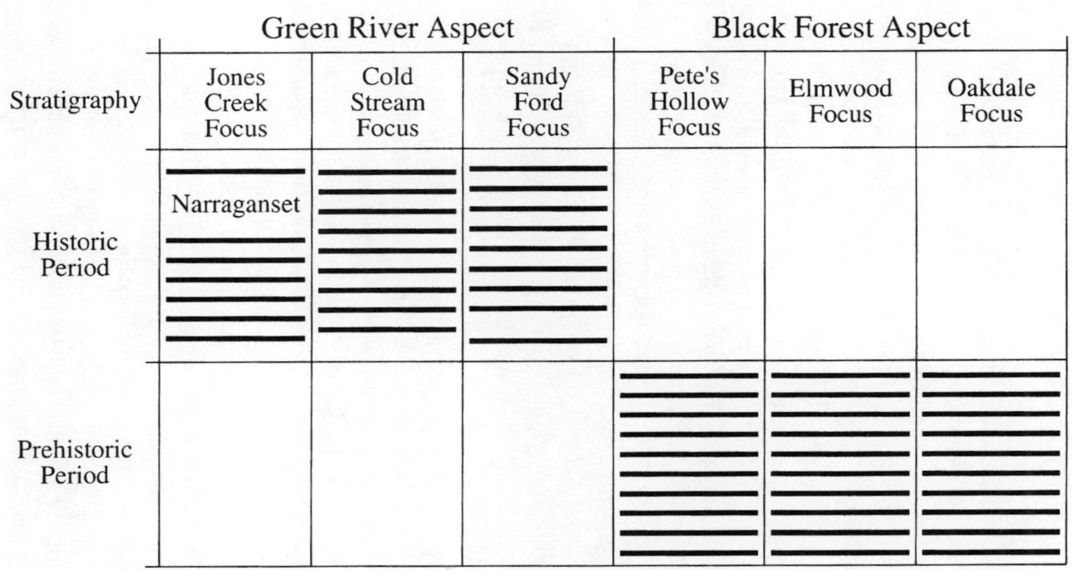

Figure 16.1. McKern's fictional example of how to integrate the units of the midwestern taxonomic method with temporal data and ethnographic data. Narraganset is a tribe, and each bold horizontal line represents a component or stratigraphic unit.

classification actually represents a certain tribe or linguistic division. However, this does not warrant the assumption that a focus invariably represents a tribe, or the aspect of a confederacy. Such interpretations must be demonstrated in each instance before they can justifiably be accepted.

Moreover, the matter of time sequence will have to be determined, wherever possible, independent of the taxonomic classification, and illustrated separately on a chart. For example, employing imaginary names: the Green River and Black Forest aspects may be determined as a result of comparing six foci, of which the Jones Creek, Cold Stream, and Sandy Ford foci determine the Green River Aspect, and the Pete's Hollow, Elmwood, and Oakdale foci determine the Black Forest Aspect. For the sake of simple illustration let us suppose that there is no apparent relationship between the two aspects. Later it becomes apparent that the Jones Creek Focus represents the Narraganset tribe, and that the Black Forest Aspect, including all its foci, wherever represented in stratified formations, occurs below the manifestations of the Green River Aspect. A chart might indicate these various facts in the manner shown in Figure 16.1.

There has been a certain amount of confusion over generalized traits, such as the manufacture and use of pottery, and detailed traits, such as incised straight-lined decoration on pottery. This confusion arises from the [21] idea that certain classes in the classification are to be determined by generalized traits, and certain others by specific traits, sometimes designated as "trait elements." I do not believe that arbitrary rules of this nature can apply. The types of traits characteristic of any cultural manifestation are the types actually found present in that manifestation, regardless of their generalized or specific nature. It has been observed repeatedly that the more general, widely inclusive cultural classes are to an important extent characterized by generalized traits, but this fact does not warrant the conclusion that such characteristics must invariably be encountered. The correct procedure is that of determining the traits present for any manifestation, regardless of their complexity or simplicity, and classifying on a basis of degree of similarity.

If the above attempt at a brief explanation of the essential nature of the method and its application does not wholly clarify the procedure, it at least may serve to bring into focus the parts which are not understood, and lead to specific questions on the subject. I shall gladly attempt to answer any questions which are fired in my direction.

Editor's Note: Questions pertaining to the Midwestern System should be addressed to this publication. Possibly enough questions will be forthcoming to warrant a supplementary article in which the author might make specific answers to each question.

17
Taxonomy and the Direct Historical Approach

W. C. McKern

W. C. McKern. 1942. *American Antiquity* 8:170–172.
[170]

TAXONOMY AND THE DIRECT HISTORICAL APPROACH

It seems apparent from Julian Steward's (1942) latest statement on "The Direct Historical Approach to Archaeology" that he still conceives of a basic conflict, or at least an inherent competition, between the direct historical and midwestern taxonomic methods, in spite of his initial statement to the contrary. He manifests a conviction that the latter is being overemphasized at the expense of the former. If his fears are well founded (and there are instances of malpractice which might be cited in support of his position), I should be among the first to join the crusade in defense of the direct historical "approach." However, in that case, his criticism should be directed against the culprits who are misusing methods rather than against any given method itself. Instead, Steward adopts the tone of one who sets to compare the respective values of two conflicting methods, to the glorification of one and the general degradation of the other.

Actually, not only is there no conflict between the two methods, as admitted by the author in his first paragraph (an admission which obviously is retracted in spirit throughout the major portion of the article), but the two methods can not be compared as to general value since each is intended to render a specifically different service. One might as well argue as to the relative value of a knife and a fork as general eating tools. Generally, they can not be compared, but, specifically, the fundamental purpose is best served by cutting the meat with the knife and conveying to the mouth the bite so prepared by means of the fork. Of course, the food may be eaten with a knife only, or even with the fingers, if one so chooses, but convenience is best served when both tools, as well as other tools, are employed to perform the complex act of eating. Archaeological research is a complex procedure which requires a variety of tools, each intended to serve a specific purpose. No single tool will perform all purposes equally well; we need every method which can be demonstrated as useful in advancing research towards its fundamental objectives.

The author's misconception of the intended purpose of taxonomy in archaeological methodology can best be illustrated by referring to his own words. For example, there is the statement: "[I]nterest in New York seems recently to have drifted away from problems of history to those of taxonomy" (Steward 1942:338). Perhaps the prodigal sons of the Empire State will choose to prepare their own answer to this accusation and I have no desire to steal their thunder, but I must say that I fail to see any necessity for a lessening of one interest to build up the other. I presume that one can recognize the need of a systematic terminology to apply to historically unidentified culture manifestations without losing interest in history or slowing down efforts to establish historical connections, direct or indirect, wherever possible. I have not noticed that such brakes have been applied in New York. The average human mind is perfectly capable of entertaining and promoting both programs at one time.

In demonstration of his conception of the relative usefulness of culture classification in archaeology, Steward (1942:339) reminds us that it is now becoming possible "to describe archaeological materials in terms of time and space," and concludes that "where history has already been blocked out, it is difficult to see what is gained by scrapping a scheme with historical terms and categories in favor of a non-historical one." I have heard of no proposal to "scrap" any procedure or terminology relating to the direct historical method. Taxonomy may be employed to apply arbitrary terms to manifestations, [171] and to indicate similarity relationships, where no historical connections are as yet feasible—in short, when the direct historical approach can not immediately be applied; and similar terms may be added to establish historical terms, without "replacing" them, in order to facilitate comparative studies between manifestations respectively of known and unknown historical connections. Parallel procedure in any science which has to deal with progression from the known to the unknown, and consequently of treating in instances the unknown as still historically unconnected with the known, is too common to require specific mention.

After picturing "archaeology" (no doubt referring to a conceived movement or faction which is not interested in ethnohistory) as considering itself other than a cultural science, the author remonstrates: "It is too often forgotten that problems of cultural origins and cultural change require more than ceramic sequences or element lists" (Steward 1942:339). There can be no quarrel with the statement, but its use in the presentation of his argument presupposes that the student who uses taxonomy is only interested in the systematic organization of his materials; that taxonomy, as employed by the prodigal sons of various other states in addition to New York, is treated as an end in itself. Actually, as proposed and correctly practiced, taxonomy in archaeology is no more an objective than are ethnohistoric demonstrations. Neither attains the goal of anthropological purpose; each contributes something towards a progression goal-ward. If there are those who have treated classification as an objective, they are subject to critical attack, but it should not be forgotten that there are those who have conceived ethnohistoric demonstrations, and even logical ethnohistoric assumptions, to be the final objective. In either case, those who have over-emphasized method are censurable; not the methods.

The author [(Steward 1942)] devotes some space to listing the unquestionable accomplishments of various investigators who have employed the direct historical method over a widespread area. To that list he might add Wisconsin, where McKern has tentatively identified two manifestations as prehistoric Winnebago and protohistoric Dakota, respectively. Strange as it may seem, these direct historical approaches were made in spite of the fact that the two manifestations also bore such taxonomic handles as "Lake Winnebago focus, Upper Mississippi phase," and "Clam River focus, Woodland pattern." Apparently neither procedure interfered with the other.

In regard to the citation of Strong's [(1935, 1936, 1940a)] valuable work in Nebraska, I should like to point out that he did a great deal there which was quite independent of any historical approach. As evidence in the extreme, just how does one employ the direct historical approach in regard to the cultural evidence of Level I, Signal Butte site? But we do not need such remote examples. Independent of any ethnohistoric interpretations, Strong has recognized cultural manifestations identified on a basis of purely cultural data, has defined them in terms of "element lists," and has supplied them with such arbitrary names as "Upper Republican," "Nebraska," and "Dismal River." Moreover, he has made comparative studies of these manifestations, involving the use of "ceramic sequences," to set up widespread cultural correlations. Only where known stratigraphy and ethnohistoric data warranted has he added conclusions relating to time and historical connections. If he had classified his culture groups according to a standard plan accepted by other workers in the same general field (which he did in so far as seemed profitable at the time), thus permitting them to visualize the cultural significance of these Nebraska manifestations in terms of local phenomena, the resulting taxonomic arrangement would not have interfered with or disturbed in any way the nature of his work, but it would immediately have called to the attention of other students in the general field the occurrence of the same phenomena and related problems in their respective provinces, and [172] might actually have hastened the clarification of problems regarding time and ethnohistorical connections.

Wedel (1940:343) has actually done this, greatly clarifying the picture of cultural variety and inter-cultural similarities throughout the central Great Plains, and yet this did not prevent him from attempting to show in the same publication, on a single chart, interrelationships involving culture, distribution, time, and ethnohistory, for the same area. Where is the conflict? In what manner did one treatment curtail or in any way alter the other? The taxonomic treatment did, however, serve two important purposes: (1) it enabled Wedel to graphically represent highly significant cultural similarities, in both local and widespread concept, where ethnohistorical interpretations were not as yet warranted, and to connect these manifestations typologically with those for which ethnohistorical interpretations have been made; and (2) it enabled other students in the same and marginal provinces to more readily correlate Wedel's data and conclusions with their own related phenomena, in terms of a common language.

A splendid example of how the two methods may serve cooperatively is offered in the progressive studies of a western subdivision of what has become known as the Upper Mississippi phase. Previous to any opportunity to apply the direct historical method, several easily recognizable varieties of what had long been known as the Upper Mississippi culture, and later classified as the Upper Mississippi phase, had become fairly well known in Wisconsin and Iowa. For convenience, as indicative of their apparent relatively close relationship, they were classified as several foci in the Oneota aspect of that phase. Rather late in the course of investigations, materials characteristic of one of these, the Orr focus, were found at sites historically reported to have been occupied by the Iowa division of the Chiwere Sioux, and with historic trade materials present in the graves. On the basis of this, the Orr focus was identified as protohistoric Iowa. Independently, materials characteristic for another of these manifestations, the Lake Winnebago focus, were found exclusively present at a site historically recorded as one of the old Winnebago village locations. These and additional corroborating data led Griffin to suggest that the Oneota aspect might correlate rather closely with the Chiwere Sioux. Whether or not the culturally similar Oneota manifestations can ever be exclusively ascribed to the ancestors of the Chiwere Sioux, the taxonomic correlation certainly has served to foster interest in involved historical problems, and to spur direct historical research in this field.

There is need for the direct historical approach, for taxonomy, and for any other methods which may prove useful, independently under limiting circumstances, and cooperatively where possible. It is true that ethnographic and historical studies "will overlap with and be tremendously facilitated by direct historical studies in archaeology" (Steward 1942:341), and in instances these will be aided rather than hindered by a taxonomic treatment of archaeological data. No one has stressed more than I the historical and cultural objectives of archaeology which, aside from method, might almost be defined as ethnology projected into the past. Taxonomy, no objective in itself, actually implements the student to reconstruct an historical and cultural picture which may be integrated with and augment the time-limited concepts of the ethnologist. The objectives of archaeology, no matter how far they may lead through historical interpretations to an increasing knowledge of cultural dynamics, will be approached with greater facility and accuracy if all helpful methods are employed. No single approach is adequate in scope to fill the bill.

18
Regarding Midwestern Archaeological Taxonomy

W. C. McKern

W. C. McKern. 1943. *American Anthropologist* 45:313–315.
[313]

REGARDING MIDWESTERN ARCHAEOLOGICAL TAXONOMY

Of certain questions which have arisen regarding the midwestern archaeological taxonomic method (erroneously called the McKern method) there are two, originating on the ethnological side of the imaginary fence, which, although asked repeatedly [for example, Wissler (1938:299–303)], have received scant attention and have prompted no published answers. These questions might be stated as follows: (1) what is the basis for the arbitrary division of culture into four types or classes (focus, aspect, phase, and pattern); and (2) what are these classes in terms of ethnological equivalents? Inasmuch as these questions involve the whole matter of cultural concept, and may reflect to some extent the feeling that ethnology and archaeology may be out of step on their march toward identical major objectives, I should like to submit this brief, pertinent discussion in evidence of a sincere effort to supply the erstwhile missing answers.

Four classes of culture, ranging from the most detailed to the most general, were selected as convenient arbitrary divisions, but specifically because that number satisfied demands which had been created by a lack of precise, orderly terminology in the existing midwestern field. That is to say, four divisions were apparent from several attempts at local classification before the problem of general taxonomy was attacked. Naturally, those interested in constructing a broad taxonomic frame on which to hang local classifications had no specific number of hooks in mind, but equipped the structure adequately to take care of all existing cultural categories. The form resulting from initial efforts actually proposed five classes, but the most general of these, the "base," was later eliminated; and although it was finally reinstated, it has served little or no purpose as yet and is generally omitted from discussion.

To cite a single example of how the four classes were determined, selecting the example from a field with which I am particularly familiar, research at many sites in Wisconsin had demonstrated the fact that the effigy mounds were manifestations of a distinct cultural division which became known as the Effigy Mound culture. However, the Effigy Mound sites of the Buffalo Lake region supplied abundant evidence that the culture here in its detail varied appreciably from the detailed culture apparent in, let us say, the Horicon Marsh district. Students began to speak of the Buffalo Lake culture, Horicon culture, and similar variants of the Effigy Mound culture, and to recognize the characteristic traits of each. Comparisons of these trait complexes with the evidence collected from the field at large soon demonstrated the cultural relationship of the Effigy Mound culture to a more general pattern of wide geographical distribution which had become generally known as the Woodland culture. But the Effigy Mound manifestation was comparatively more similar to certain other Woodland varieties first known in the region around Lake Michigan than to any of the remaining varieties within the general culture, and so there came into use the term: Lake Michigan culture.

This vague and varying use of the word "culture" to describe manifestations which were so unlike in scope and character, of which some were culturally correlative but in different degree, while others lay wholly outside the specific field of relationship, led logically and necessarily to taxonomy. Class names were selected to differentiate between a general culture scheme and the various degrees of culture within that scheme, as previously noted from studies of comparative data. Thus, the Buffalo Lake, Effigy Mound, Lake Michigan, and Woodland "cultures," for example, became the Buffalo [314] Lake Focus of the Effigy Mound Aspect of the Lake Michigan Phase of the Woodland Pattern.

In short, the choice of four classes was found to be practical in that they met classificatory requirements dictated by field and laboratory facts. The more far-reaching reasons underlying these factual requirements involve factors which may to some extent be ethnological, but which probably relate more importantly to psychology. In any case, the human mind, as demonstrated by mental varieties engaged in many fields of thought other than archaeology, including ethnology, appears to require a subdivision of any expansive subject field into often unnatural but always logical parts to facilitate examining the broader complexity in separate, simpler divisions, piece by piece; and that arrangement which adequately serves one mind seems to serve others in that field equally well. And so, the arbitrariness of taxonomy in one field parallels that in another. One might ask: why the particular number employed in the biological or any other taxonomic method? But a more proper question would be: does the particular number of type classes selected serve the taxonomic purpose to best advantage?

Inasmuch as arbitrariness is not an exclusive possession of midwestern archaeologists, I am tempted to respond to the second question: what is a focus, a phase, and so on, in terms comparable to those applied by ethnologists to type varieties of human society or culture—with the Yankee answer: what are the definitions of these ethnological divisions? What is a tribe? What, other than in terms of complexes of traits for each, are divisions such as the Dakota or Chiwere, the Northern Plains or Central Eskimo, the Southwestern Culture Area? Obviously in these cases we are not dealing primarily with political groups, although a tribe in instances may be such. Exclusive of certain "tribes," we are not considering social entities of any kind. Primarily we are concerned with varieties of culture as visualized from a comparative study of traits, whether associated with political or social entities or independent of them. Even the term "tribe," as constantly employed, may reflect a socio-political, cultural, or even traditional concept. The term has been applied to types of groupings as remotely alike as the Menomini and the Ojibwa. No one would suggest that the Ojibwa is a political group, and few would defend the statement that it is even an economic entity. In varying degrees it denotes linguistic or cultural similarities, and to an important extent it is purely traditional.

To complicate matters, the ethnological classification has been shaped largely on a basis of the single culture trait of language. If this were purely a linguistic classification as it probably is to a specialist in that field, its purpose would be clear and justifiable; but the study of the more geographically intact of such linguistic divisions has been made largely on a basis of the entire culture involved, and the divisions have come to be considered as cultural regardless of the linguistic terminology. However, when language and culture aside from language have been found to introduce conflicting elements into the classification, as is almost invariably true in the case of fundamental linguistic stocks, and equally true for many of their subdivisions, a culture-by-area terminology has been devised quite independent of language or languages spoken. Nevertheless, the more specialized, local divisions of culture continue to be known solely by their linguistic names regardless of cultural ties. Finally, such terms as "Eskimo" have racial as well as cultural and linguistic connotations.

This ethnological confusion has troubled archaeologists to a certain extent, since [315] they looked to ethnology for a pattern of terminology. The linguistic terms were entirely foreign to the nature and substance of archaeological data, and could be justifiably applied to archaeological manifestations only in some instances. The culture-area terms were not applicable since areal distribution usually involves overlapping, and invariably changes in time, whereas culture from the archaeological angle has a broad temporal perspective. Consequently, in field after field, archaeology has had to shape its own cultural taxonomy.

Considering these facts, the ethnologist is in a poor position to suggest that archaeological cultural terms should closely parallel his own mixed terminology. The *focus* may in instances correspond to a tribe, but fails to do so in other instances because the focus represents what is known of a cultural division, whereas the tribe may represent a political, traditional, or other concept. Similarly, the *aspect* may in instances conform to such groups as the Chiwere, Dhegiha, or Iroquois (Confederacy), but only in the sense and to the extent that these linguistically named divisions have cultural character.

The *phase* in instances closely parallels the initial subdivision of culture implied in a "culture area," although the areal limitation can not apply in archaeology, even where the culture is exclusive in the area, without a corresponding time limitation. For example, the historic Eskimo culture is generally conceived as including several cultural subdivisions any one of which, as the Central Eskimo, seems to bear a phase-like relationship to the whole culture. The prehistoric Eskimo picture, in the light of archaeologically produced data, offers more exact parallels.

The *pattern* is identical to the culture represented by the ethnological culture area, providing that the latter is based upon the true cultural factors and not upon selected data or devised for purposes of creating a simplified though inaccurate picture. For instance (and it is far from the only available instance), no archaeologist would or could intelligently use the term, "Southwestern culture"; although he would refer to the Southwestern area, in a geographical or historical sense, as a place where research has been conducted by a group of workers specially schooled in the facts and problems related to that field. The cultural picture in the Southwest, even for any single point in time, is not so uniform and simple as is implied in such a term.

Thus, the cultural divisions represented by the shelves in the midwestern taxonomic cupboard are difficult to visualize in terms of existing ethnologically conceived divisions because the archaeological divisions are based wholly on cultural factors, the only factors always and immediately available to the archaeologist, whereas the ethnological concepts are variously determined on a basis of culture, language alone, race, tradition, and geographical location at one point in time, or on varying mixtures of these factors. It is not my purpose here to present this contrast in methodology as a right-and-wrong comparison; it may simply illustrate certain fundamental differences in ethnological and archaeological approach. It is important, however, that such differences in method should be generally known, and that workers in each of the several branches of anthropology should possess a comprehensive understanding of the others' purposes, problems, and methods in order to permit a more intelligent cooperation toward approaching the larger objectives common to all.

19
An Inaccurate Description of Midwestern Taxonomy

W. C. McKern

W. C. McKern. 1944. *American Antiquity* 9:445–446.
[445]

AN INACCURATE DESCRIPTION OF MIDWESTERN TAXONOMY

For reasons best known to him, McGregor [(1941:60–62)] has included in his recent book on Southwestern archaeology a brief statement regarding the midwestern taxonomic method, although this method is not used in the Southwest. The statement is in error on several fundamental points, and it seems important to publish a correction just to keep the record straight.

First: the interpretation of "diagnostic culture traits" as traits which are standard for a culture complex in all cultural comparisons (McGregor 1941:61) is not in accord with the usual concept as employed in midwestern terminology. As originally proposed by Ritchie [(1937; see also National Research Council 1937:56–57)], and as previously pointed out in my review of Cole's and Deuel's *Rediscovering Illinois* [(McKern 1938[13]:369)], the diagnostic trait is determined by a specific comparison of two culture complexes, and applies only to a culture in that comparison. A trait which is diagnostic in one comparison may appear as a link trait in another, and so can not be generally diagnostic for a given culture complex in all comparisons.

Second: the *component* is not the most detailed, localized class of culture in the taxonomic frame (McGregor 1941:61–62). In fact, it is not a term designating any separate class of culture, but is the manifestation of a *focus* (the most detailed class) at a site. Culturally, the various components of a given focus are identical to each other and to that focus. The term is used to distinguish between a site, which may yield data representative of several distinct cultures, and the manifestation of a specific cultural focus at that site.

Third: classes in the taxonomic frame are not determined by percentages of trait similarity (McGregor 1941:62). Percentage identification was proposed in the early developmental period of experimentation and trial, but was never actually used, partly because culture traits do not have the same mathematical values—they are not quantitatively identical units in any mathematical sense—but primarily because this type of determinant was not needed. There has been no confusion over the allocation of a culture complex to its proper class. This is probably because taxonomy is resorted to only when circumstances require it; the problem is never that of classifying everything in sight. Classification starts with the focus, determined by the recurrence of the same detailed complex at site after site. There can be no question of the focal status if data are sufficient to warrant classification. Similarly, other foci are determined, and it may become clearly apparent in the course of comparative study that two or more foci are sufficiently alike to make practical their classification within the same aspect, that like aspects determine a phase, or that like phases determine a pattern. Once a pattern has been identified in terms of a complex of traits, a newly determined focus may immediately be recognized as within that pattern; the phase and aspect remain to be identified when accumulating data serve to indicate clearly the cultural relationship. In short, nothing is done until the type or degree of relationship is clearly apparent, and when this is apparent there remains no problem of type or degree of relationship.

The theoretical objection that it is difficult "to visualize the various divisions suggested" (McGregor 1941:61) is based probably upon the expectation that each of the type classes should correspond in character to some historically known type of social group: a local group, a tribe, or some other ethnological division of society or culture. Actually, the focus may sometimes parallel the tribe—depending upon the extent to which "tribe" is employed as a cultural term—and the other classes may sometimes parallel cultural divisions with such linguistic names as Iroquois or Chiwere, such ethno-geographic [446] divisions as Central Eskimo, or the cultural variety represented in such a term as "culture area." Yet there can be no prevailing parallel between these strictly cultural types in archaeology and such ethnological divisions, based, as they are, on language alone, culture, political economy, geographical distribution, or even race, or on combinations of these factors.

Moreover, the midwestern taxonomic divisions certainly do not essentially represent politico-economic groups of people, any more than such groups are represented by the culture-area or sub-culture-area concepts, or by such linguistic concepts as Ojibwa, Algonkin, Chiwere, or Sioux. Rather, they represent cultural adaptations of traditional habits and concepts, as modified by environment, invention, and diffusion, and subject to limitations of space and time, as manifested by culture-indicative data itemized as traits.

The objection that these archaeological classes can not be visualized in terms of historical groups of people would apply equally well, in parallel, to the divisions in any scientific classification. After all, try to visualize in natural group concept a species, a genus, or an order; or, for that matter, try to visualize the Chiwere in terms other than a complex of linguistic traits, or the northern Plains Indians in terms other than a complex of culture traits. The problem of visualizing cultural divisions has not materialized in the practice of classifying the archaeological varieties on the basis of the comparison of trait complexes. The problem is not one of visualizing culture-bearing groups of people, but one of convenient organization of qualitative and quantitative facts in order to facilitate further progressive research. The "variable human element" is not vitally involved where the actual demonstration of the occurrence of traits in a complex is observed and recorded repeatedly by numerous students.

It seems a bit extraordinary that McGregor (1941:62) apparently experiences no difficulty in visualizing the differences between roots, stems, branches, and phases in the Gladwin [and Gladwin (1934)] taxonomic method, none of which are determined on a percentage or similarly "exact" basis. The one fundamental difference between the midwestern and Gladwin methods is that the former employs the cultural factor alone, whereas the latter, theoretically, is based on cultural, temporal, and spatial factors, although actually classification is made repeatedly on cultural criteria alone before time and distribution can be determined.

References Cited

Anonymous

1989 Will Carleton McKern [obituary]. *Anthropology Newsletter* 30(1):4.

n.d. The Pictorial Survey of the Mississippi Valley: Its Aims, Methods and Results. Unpublished manuscript on file, Illinois State Museum, Springfield. [Probable author: T. Deuel]

Barrett, S. A.

1933 Ancient Aztalan. *Public Museum of the City of Milwaukee, Bulletin* 13:1–602.

Basile, J. J.

2000 McKern, William Carleton (1892–1988). In *Archaeological Method and Theory: An Encyclopedia*, edited by L. Ellis, pp. 349–350. Garland, New York.

Bather, F. A.

1927 Biological Classification: Past and Future. *Quarterly Journal of the Geological Society of London* 83:lxii–civ.

Bell, E. H.

1936 Introduction. In *Chapters in Nebraska Archaeology*, edited by E. H. Bell, pp. 5–9. University of Nebraska Press, Lincoln.

Bigelow, R. S.

1958 Classification and Phylogeny. *Systematic Zoology* 7:49–59.

Blackwelder, R. E., and A. Boyden

1952 The Nature of Systematics. *Systematic Zoology* 1:26–33.

Boas, F.

1898 A Precise Criterion of Species. *Science* 7:860–861.

1902 Some Problems in North American Archaeology. *American Journal of Archaeology* 6:1–6.

1904 The History of Anthropology. *Science* 20:513–524.

1932 The Aims of Anthropological Research. *Science* 76:605–613.

1940 *Race, Language, and Culture*. University of Chicago Press, Chicago.

Bock, W. J.

1973 Philosophical Foundations of Classical Evolutionary Classification. *Systematic Zoology* 22:375–392.

Borgmeier, T.

1957 Basic Questions of Systematics. *Systematic Zoology* 6:53–69.

Brady, R. H.

1985 On the Independence of Systematics. *Cladistics* 1:113–126.

Brew, J. O.

1946 Archaeology of Alkali Ridge, Southeastern Utah. *Peabody Museum of American Archaeology and Ethnology, Papers* 21.

Brower, A. V. Z.

2000 Evolution Is Not a Necessary Assumption of Cladistics. *Cladistics* 16: 143–154.

Buck, R. C., and D. L. Hull

1966 The Logical Structure of the Linnaean Hierarchy. *Systematic Zoology* 15:97–111.

Byers, D. S.

1939 Editorials. *American Antiquity* 5:1.

Cain, A. J.

1956 The Genus in Evolutionary Taxonomy. *Systematic Zoology* 5:97–109.

1958 Logic and Memory in Linnaeus's System of Taxonomy. *Proceedings of the Linnean Society, London* 169:144–163.

1959a Deductive and Inductive Methods in Post-Linnaean Taxonomy. *Proceedings of the Linnean Society, London* 170:185–217.

1959b The Post-Linnaean Development of Taxonomy. *Proceedings of the Linnean Society, London* 170:234–244.

1959c Taxonomic Concepts. *Ibis* 101:302–318.

Cain, A. J., and G. A. Harrison

1958 An Analysis of the Taxonomist's Judgement of Affinity. *Proceedings of the Linnean Society, London* 131:85–98.

Camin, J. H., and R. R. Sokal

1965 A Method for Deducing Branching Sequences in Phylogeny. *Evolution* 19:311–326.

Champe, J. L.

1936 The Sweetwater Culture Complex. In *Chapters in Nebraska Archaeology*, edited by E. H. Bell, pp. 249–299. University of Nebraska Press, Lincoln.

Clements, F. E., S. M. Schenck, and T. K. Brown

1926 A New Objective Method for Showing Special Relationships. *American Anthropologist* 28:585–604.

Cole, F.-C.

1943 Chronology in the Middle West. *American Philosophical Society, Proceedings* 86:299–303.

Cole, F.-C., and T. Deuel

1937 *Rediscovering Illinois: Archaeological Explorations in and around Fulton County.* University of Chicago Press, Chicago.

Colless, D. H.

1967 An Examination of Certain Concepts in Phenetic Taxonomy. *Systematic Zoology* 16:6–27.

1970 The Phylogram as an Estimate of Phylogeny. *Systematic Zoology* 19: 352–362.

1971 "Phenetic," "Phylogenetic," and "Weighting." *Systematic Zoology* 20: 73–76.

Collier, D., and G. I. Quimby Jr.

1945 Review of "The Fort Ancient Aspect, Its Cultural and Chronological Position in Mississippi Valley Archaeology" by J. B. Griffin. *American Anthropologist* 47:142–146.

Colton, H. S.

1932 Foreword. In Guide to Forty Pottery Types from the Hopi Country and the San Francisco Mountains, Arizona, by L. L. Hargrave, p. 1. *Museum of Northern Arizona, Bulletin* 1.

1939 Prehistoric Culture Units and Their Relationships in Northern Arizona. *Museum of Northern Arizona, Bulletin* 17.

1942 Archaeology and the Reconstruction of History. *American Antiquity* 8:33–40.

Colton, H. S., and L. L. Hargrave

1937 Handbook of Northern Arizona Pottery Wares. *Museum of Northern Arizona, Bulletin* 11.

Cooper, P.

1936 Archaeology of Certain Sites in Cedar County, Nebraska. In *Chapters in Nebraska Archaeology,* edited by E. H. Bell, pp. 11–145. University of Nebraska Press, Lincoln.

Cutter, G. F.

1939 Northeastern Classification. *American Antiquity* 4:352.

Darnell, R.

2001 *Invisible Genealogies: A History of Americanist Anthropology.* University of Nebraska Press, Lincoln.

Darwin, C.

1859 *On the Origin of Species by Means of Natural Selection, or, the Preservation of Favoured Races in the Struggle for Life.* Murray, London.

Deuel, T.

1933 Cultural Sequence in Fulton County. *Illinois State Academy of Science, Transactions* 25:96–97.

1935a Basic Cultures of the Mississippi Valley. *American Anthropologist* 37: 429–445.

1935b *The Application of a Classificatory Method to Mississippi Valley Archaeology.* Ph.D. dissertation, University of Chicago, Chicago.

1937a The Application of a Classificatory Method to Mississippi Valley Archaeology. In *Rediscovering Illinois*, by F.-C. Cole and T. Deuel, pp. 207–219. University of Chicago Press, Chicago.

1937b Some Assumptions and Implications of the McKern Classification System. Paper presented at the annual meeting of the American Association for the Advancement of Science, Section H, Indianapolis.

1937c Untitled manuscript on the Archaeological/Pictorial Survey of the Mississippi Valley. Unpublished manuscript on file, Illinois State Museum, Springfield.

1939 The McKern and Related Systems of Classification. Paper presented at the annual meeting of the American Association for the Advancement of Science, Section H, Alpine, Texas.

Dewar, R. E.

1995 Of Nets and Trees: Untangling the Reticulate and Dendritic in Madagascar's Prehistory. *World Archaeology* 26:301–318.

Dixon, R. B.

1913 Some Aspects of North American Archaeology. *American Anthropologist* 15:549–566.

Driver, H. E.

1962 The Contribution of A. L. Kroeber to Culture Area Theory and Practice. *Indiana University Publications in Anthropology and Linguistics, Memoir* 18:1–28.

Driver, H. E., and A. L. Kroeber

1932 Quantitative Expression of Cultural Relationships. *University of California, Publications in American Archaeology and Ethnology* 31:211–256.

Dunlevy, M. L.

1936 A Comparison of the Cultural Manifestations of the Burkett (Nance County) and the Gray-Wolfe (Colfax County) Sites. In *Chapters in Nebraska Archaeology*, edited by E. H. Bell, pp. 147–247. University of Nebraska Press, Lincoln.

Dunnell, R. C.

1971 *Systematics in Prehistory.* Free Press, New York.

1980 Evolutionary Theory and Archaeology. *Advances in Archaeological Method and Theory* 3:35–99.

1986 Methodological Issues in Americanist Artifact Classification. *Advances in Archaeological Method and Theory* 9:149–207.

1995 What Is It That Actually Evolves? In *Evolutionary Archaeology: Methodological Issues*, edited by P. A. Teltser, pp. 33–50. University of Arizona Press, Tucson.

2000 Midwestern Taxonomic System. In *Archaeological Method and Theory: An Encyclopedia*, edited by L. Ellis, pp. 371–372. Garland, New York.

DuPraw, E. J.

1964 Non-Linnaean Taxonomy. *Nature* 202:849–852.

Ehrich, R. W.
1950 Some Reflections on Archaeological Interpretation. *American Anthropologist* 52:468–482.

Eldredge, N., and M. J. Novacek
1985 Systematics and Paleobiology. *Paleobiology* 11:65–74.

Engstrom, M. D., J. R. Choate, and H. H. Genoways
1994 Taxonomy. In Seventy-Five Years of Mammalogy (1919–1994), edited by E. C. Birney and J. R. Choate, pp. 179–199. *American Society of Mammalogists, Special Publication* No. 11.

Ereshefsky, M.
1994 Some Problems with the Linnaean Hierarchy. *Philosophy of Science* 61: 186–205.
1997 The Evolution of the Linnaean Hierarchy. *Biology and Philosophy* 12: 493–519.
2001 *The Poverty of the Linnaean Hierarchy: A Philosophical Study of the Biological Taxonomy.* Cambridge University Press, Cambridge.

Fagan, B. M.
1997 *In the Beginning*, 9th ed. Longman, New York.

Fisher, A. K.
1988 Obituary: Will Carleton McKern. *Wisconsin Archeologist* 69:207–209.
1997 Origins of the Midwestern Taxonomic Method. *Mid-Continental Journal of Archaeology* 22:117–122.

Ford, J. A.
1938 *An Examination of Some Theories and Methods of Ceramic Analysis.* Unpublished Master's thesis, Department of Anthropology, University of Michigan, Ann Arbor.
1940 Review of "Handbook of Northern Arizona Pottery Wares" by H. S. Colton and L. L. Hargrave. *American Antiquity* 5:263–266.

Ford, J. A., and J. B. Griffin
1938 Report of the Conference on Southeastern Pottery Types. Mimeographed. Reprinted in *Newsletter of the Southeastern Archaeological Conference* 7(1):10–22.

Gilmour, J. S. L.
1937 A Taxonomic Problem. *Nature* 139:1040–1042.
1940 Taxonomy and Philosophy. In *The New Systematics*, edited by J. S. Huxley, pp. 461–474. Clarendon Press, Oxford.
1951 The Development of Taxonomic Theory since 1851. *Nature* 168:400–402.

Gladwin, H. S.
1936 Methodology in the Southwest. *American Antiquity* 1:256–259.
1937 Conclusions. In Excavations at Snaketown, I: Material Culture, by H. S. Gladwin, E. W. Haury, E. B. Sayles, and N. Gladwin, pp. 247–269. *Medallion Papers* No. 25.
1943 A Review and Analysis of the Flagstaff Culture. *Medallion Papers* No. 31.

Gladwin, W., and H. S. Gladwin

1930 A Method for the Designation of Southwestern Pottery Types. *Medallion Papers* No. 7.

1934 A Method for the Designation of Cultures and Their Variations. *Medallion Papers* No. 15.

Gleick, J.

1987 *Chaos: Making a New Science.* Penguin, New York.

Golbeck, A. L.

1980 Quantification in Ethnology and Its Appearance in Regional Culture Trait Distribution Studies (1888 to 1939). *Journal of the History of the Behavioral Sciences* 16:228–240.

Gould, S. J.

1991 The Disparity of the Burgess Shale Arthropod Fauna and the Limits of Cladistic Analysis: Why We Must Strive to Quantify Morphospace. *Paleobiology* 17:411–423.

Grayson, D. K.

1983 *The Establishment of Human Antiquity.* Academic Press, New York.

Griffin, J. B.

1935 An Analysis of the Fort Ancient Culture. *Ceramic Repository for the Eastern United States, Notes* No. 1. Ann Arbor, Michigan.

1937 The Chronological Position and Ethnological Relationships of the Fort Ancient Aspect. *American Antiquity* 2:273–276.

1943 The Fort Ancient Aspect, Its Cultural and Chronological Position in Mississippi Valley Archaeology. *University of Michigan, Museum of Anthropology, Anthropological Papers* No. 28.

1945 Review of "The Pre-Iroquoian Occupations of New York State" by W. A. Ritchie. *American Antiquity* 10:401–407.

1970 Foreword. In *Hiwassee Island,* by T. M. N. Lewis and M. Kneberg, pp. v–vii. University of Tennessee Press, Knoxville.

1976 A Commentary on Some Archaeological Activities in the Mid-Continent 1925–1975. *Mid-Continental Journal of Archaeology* 1:5–38.

Griffiths, G. C. D.

1973 Some Fundamental Problems in Biological Classification. *Systematic Zoology* 22:338–343.

1974 On the Foundations of Biological Systematics. *Acta Biotheoretica* 23: 85–131.

Guthe, C. E.

1932 A Suggested Classification of Cultures Prepared by the Committee on State Archaeological Surveys, National Research Council, October 24. Manuscript on file, Milwaukee Public Museum.

1934 A Method of Ceramic Description. In Standards of Pottery Description, by B. March, pp. 1–6. *University of Michigan, Museum of Anthropology, Occasional Contributions* No. 3.

1936 Review of "Basic Cultures of the Mississippi Valley" by T. Deuel. *American Antiquity* 1:249–250.

1937 Preface. In *The Indianapolis Archaeological Conference*, pp. v–vii. National Research Council, Washington, D.C.

1943 Foreword. In The Fort Ancient Aspect, by J. B. Griffin, pp. v–vi. *University of Michigan, Museum of Anthropology, Anthropological Papers* No. 28.

1967 Reflections on the Founding of the Society for American Archaeology. *American Antiquity* 32:433–440.

Haag, W. G.

1961 Twenty-Five Years of Eastern Archaeology. *American Antiquity* 27:16–23.

Hall, B. K.

1996 *Baupläne*, Phylotypic Stages, and Constraint: Why There Are So Few Types of Animals. *Evolutionary Biology* 29:215–261.

Hargrave, L. L.

1932 Guide to Forty Pottery Types from the Hopi Country and the San Francisco Mountains, Arizona. *Museum of Northern Arizona, Bulletin* 1.

Hargrave, L. L., and H. S. Colton

1935 What Do Potsherds Tell Us? (Wares, Types, and Rules of Priority). *Museum of Northern Arizona, Museum Notes* 7(12):49–51.

Haury, E. W., and J. J. Reid

1985 Harold Sterling Gladwin, 1883–1983. *The Kiva* 50:271–283.

Hennig, W.

1950 *Grundzüge einer Theorie der phylogenetischen Systematik*. Deutscher Zentralverlag, Berlin.

1966 *Phylogenetic Systematics*. University of Illinois Press, Urbana.

Herskovits, M. J.

1926 The Cattle Complex in East Africa. *American Anthropologist* 28:230–272, 361–388, 494–528, 633–664.

Hintze, J. L.

1999 *NCSS 2000 Statistical System for Windows*. Number Cruncher Statistical Systems, Kaysville, Utah.

Hooton, E. A.

1930 *The Indians of Pecos Pueblo*. Yale University Press, New Haven, Connecticut.

Hughes, R. E.

1992 California Archaeology and Linguistic Prehistory. *Journal of Anthropological Research* 48:317–338.

Hull, D.

1965 The Effect of Essentialism on Taxonomy: 2000 Years of Stasis. *British Journal for the Philosophy of Science* 15:314–326; 16:1–18.

1970 Contemporary Systematic Philosophies. *Annual Review of Ecology and Systematics* 1:19–54.

1988 *Science as a Process*. University of Chicago Press, Chicago.

Huxley, J. S. (editor)
1940 *The New Systematics.* Clarendon Press, Oxford.

Jennings, J. D.
1947 Review of "Hiwassee Island" by T. M. N. Lewis and M. Kneberg. *American Antiquity* 12:191–193.

Jennings, J. D., and E. Norbeck
1964 Introduction. In *Prehistoric Man in the New World,* edited by J. D. Jennings and E. Norbeck, pp. 1–10. University of Chicago Press, Chicago.

Johnson, F. A.
1944 Review of "The Pre-Iroquoian Occupations of New York State" by W. A. Ritchie. *American Anthropologist* 46:530–535.

Johnstone, J.
1914 *The Philosophy of Biology.* Cambridge University Press, Cambridge.

Kay, P.
1971 Taxonomy and Semantic Contrast. *Language* 41:866–887.

Kehoe, A. B.
1990 The Monumental Midwestern Taxonomic Method. In The Woodland Tradition in the Western Great Lakes: Papers Presented to Elden Johnson, edited by G. E. Gibbon, pp. 31–36. *University of Minnesota, Publications in Anthropology* No. 4.

Keyes, C. R.
1927 Prehistoric Man in Iowa. *The Palimpsest* 8:222–224.

Kidder, A. V.
1924 An Introduction to the Study of Southwestern Archaeology, with a Preliminary Account of the Excavations at Pecos. *Papers of the Southwestern Expedition, Phillips Academy,* No. 1. Yale University Press, New Haven, Connecticut.
1927 Southwestern Archaeological Conference. *Science* 66:489–491.
1936a Speculations on New World Prehistory. In *Essays in Anthropology,* edited by R. Lowie, pp. 143–152. University of California Press, Berkeley.
1936b Introduction. In *The Pottery of Pecos,* vol. II, by A. V. Kidder and A. O. Shepard, pp. xvii–xxxi. Yale University Press, New Haven, Connecticut.

Kidder, A. V., J. D. Jennings, and E. M. Shook
1946 Excavations at Kaminaljuyu, Guatemala. *Carnegie Institution of Washington, Publication* 561.

Kidder, A. V., and A. O. Shepard
1936 *The Pottery of Pecos,* vol. II. Yale University Press, New Haven, Connecticut.

Kluckhohn, C.
1939a On Certain Recent Applications of Association Coefficients to Ethnological Data. *American Anthropologist* 41:345–377.
1939b Discussion. In Preliminary Report on the 1937 Excavations, Bc 50–51, Chaco Canyon, New Mexico, edited by C. Kluckhohn and P. Reiter, pp. 151–162. *University of New Mexico, Bulletin* 345.

1939c The Place of Theory in Anthropological Studies. *Philosophy of Science* 6:328–344.

Kluge, A. G.

2001 Parsimony with and without Scientific Justification. *Cladistics* 17:199–210.

Knox, E. B.

1998 The Use of Hierarchies as Organizational Models in Systematics. *Biological Journal of the Linnean Society* 63:1–49.

Krause, R. A.

1977 Taxonomic Practice and Middle Missouri Prehistory: A Perspective on Donald J. Lehmer's Contributions. *Plains Anthropologist Memoir* 13:5–13.

1989 Toward a History of Great Plains Systematics. *Plains Anthropologist* 34:281–292.

Kroeber, A. L.

1923 *Anthropology.* Harcourt Brace, New York.

1925 Handbook of the Indians of California. *Bureau of American Ethnology, Bulletin* 78.

1931 Historical Reconstruction of Culture Growths and Organic Evolution. *American Anthropologist* 33:149–156.

1940 Statistical Classification. *American Antiquity* 6:29–44.

1952 *The Nature of Culture.* University of Chicago Press, Chicago.

Krogman, W. M.

1930 Paper presented at the annual meeting of the Central Section, American Anthropological Association, Milwaukee.

1937 Review of "Rediscovering Illinois" by F.-C. Cole and T. Deuel. *American Anthropologist* 39:677–678.

Langford, G.

1927 The Fisher Mound Group. *American Anthropologist* (n.s.) 29:153–205.

Lewis, T. M. N., and M. Kneberg

1946 *Hiwassee Island: An Archaeological Account of Four Tennessee Indian Peoples.* University of Tennessee Press, Knoxville.

Linton, R. B.

1936 *The Study of Man: An Introduction.* Appleton–Century, New York.

Lowie, R. H.

1912 On the Principle of Convergence in Ethnology. *Journal of American Folk-Lore* 25:24–42.

Lull, R. S.

1917 *Organic Evolution: A Text-Book.* Macmillan, New York.

1931 *Fossils: What They Tell Us of Plants and Animals of the Past.* University Society, New York.

Lyman, R. L.

2001 Culture Historical and Biological Approaches to Identifying Homologous Traits. In *Style and Function: Conceptual Issues in Evolutionary Archaeology,* edited by T. D. Hurt and G. F. M. Rakita, pp. 69–89. Bergin and Garvey, Westport, Connecticut.

Lyman, R. L., and M. J. O'Brien

1997 The Concept of Evolution in Early Twentieth-Century Americanist Archaeology. In Rediscovering Darwin: Evolutionary Theory in Archeological Explanation, edited by C. M. Barton and G. A. Clark, pp. 21–48. *American Anthropological Association, Archeological Papers* No. 7.

1999 Americanist Stratigraphic Excavation and the Measurement of Culture Change. *Journal of Archaeological Method and Theory* 6:55–108.

2000 Chronometers and Units in Early Archaeology and Paleontology. *American Antiquity* 65:691–707.

2001a The Direct Historical Approach and Analogical Reasoning in Archaeology. *Journal of Archaeological Method and Theory* 8:303–342.

2001b Introduction. In *Method and Theory in American Archaeology*, by G. R. Willey and P. Phillips, edited by R. L. Lyman and M. J. O'Brien, pp. I-1–I-78. University of Alabama Press, Tuscaloosa.

Lyman, R. L., M. J. O'Brien, and R. C. Dunnell

1997 *The Rise and Fall of Culture History.* Plenum, New York.

Lyman, R. L., S. Wolverton, and M. J. O'Brien

1998 Seriation, Superposition, and Interdigitation: A History of Americanist Graphic Depictions of Culture Change. *American Antiquity* 63:239–261.

Lyon, E. A.

1996 *A New Deal for Southeastern Archaeology.* University of Alabama Press, Tuscaloosa.

Martin, P. S., J. B. Rinaldo, and E. Antevs

1949 Cochise and Mogollon Sites, Pine Lawn Valley, Western New Mexico. *Fieldiana: Anthropology* 38:1–232.

Martin, P. S., J. B. Rinaldo, E. Bluhm, H. C. Cutler, and R. Grange Jr.

1952 Mogollon Cultural Continuity and Change: The Stratigraphic Analysis of Tularosa and Cordova Caves. *Fieldiana: Anthropology* 40:1–528.

Matthew, W. D.

1926 The Evolution of the Horse: A Record and Its Interpretation. *Quarterly Review of Biology* 1:139–185.

1929 On the Phylogeny of Horses, Dogs, and Cats. *Science* 69:494–496.

1930 The Pattern of Evolution. *Scientific American* 142:192–196.

Mayr, E.

1942 *Systematics and the Origin of Species.* Columbia University Press, New York.

1959 Darwin and the Evolutionary Theory in Biology. In *Evolution and Anthropology: A Centennial Appraisal*, edited by B. J. Meggers, pp. 409–412. Anthropological Society of Washington, Washington, D.C.

1965a Classification and Phylogeny. *American Zoologist* 5:165–174.

1965b Numerical Phenetics and Taxonomic Theory. *Systematic Zoology* 14: 73–97.

1969 *Principles of Systematic Zoology.* McGraw-Hill, New York.

1981 Biological Classification: Toward a Synthesis of Opposing Methodologies. *Science* 214:510–516.

1982 *The Growth of Biological Thought: Diversity, Evolution, and Inheritance.* Harvard University Press, Cambridge, Massachusetts.

1995 Systems of Ordering Data. *Biology and Philosophy* 10:419–434.

Mayr, E., and P. D. Ashlock

1991 *Principles of Systematic Zoology,* 2nd ed. McGraw-Hill, New York.

McGregor, J. C.

1941 *Southwestern Archaeology.* Wiley, New York.

McKern, W. C.

1922 Functional Families of the Patwin. *University of California, Publications in American Archaeology and Ethnology* 13:235–258.

1923 Patwin Houses. *University of California, Publications in American Archaeology and Ethnology* 20:159–171.

1924 Paradoxes of the Tongan Islands. *Milwaukee Public Museum, Yearbook* 4:131–156.

1929 Archaeology of Tonga. *Bishop Museum Bulletin* 60. Honolulu.

1931 Wisconsin Pottery. *American Anthropologist* 33:383–389.

1932 Culture Type Classification for Midwestern North American Archaeology. Paper prepared for presentation at the annual meeting of the Central Section of the American Anthropological Association, Ann Arbor.

1933 Local Types and the Regional Distribution of Pottery-Bearing Cultures. *Illinois State Academy of Science, Transactions* 25:84–86.

1934 Certain Culture Classification Problems in Middle Western Archaeology. *National Research Council, Committee on State Archaeological Surveys, Circular* No. 17.

1935 Editorial. *American Antiquity* 1:1–2.

1936 Editorial. *American Antiquity* 1:177–180.

1937a Wisconsin. In *The Indianapolis Archaeological Conference*, pp. 1–2. National Research Council, Washington, D.C.

1937b Certain Culture Classification Problems in Middle Western Archaeology. In *The Indianapolis Archaeological Conference*, pp. 70–82. National Research Council, Washington, D.C.

1938 Review of "Rediscovering Illinois: Archaeological Explorations in and around Fulton County" by F.-C. Cole and T. Deuel. *American Antiquity* 3:368–374.

1939 The Midwestern Taxonomic Method as an Aid to Archaeological Culture Study. *American Antiquity* 4:301–313.

1940 Application of the Midwestern Taxonomic Method. *Archaeological Society of Delaware, Bulletin* 3:18–21.

1942 Taxonomy and the Direct Historical Approach. *American Antiquity* 8:170–172.

1943 Regarding Midwestern Archaeological Taxonomy. *American Anthropologist* 45:313–315.

1944 An Inaccurate Description of Midwestern Taxonomy. *American Antiquity* 9:445–446.

1945 Review of "The Pre-Iroquoian Occupation of New York State" by W. A. Ritchie. *American Anthropologist* 47:140–142.

1956 On Willey and Phillips' 'Method and Theory in American Archaeology.' *American Anthropologist* 58:360–361.

McKern, W. C., T. Deuel, and C. E. Guthe

1933 On the Problem of Culture Classification. NRC Circular Letter of April 4, 1933. National Research Council Archives, Washington, D.C.

Meltzer, D. J.

1983 The Antiquity of Man and the Development of American Archaeology. *Advances in Archaeological Method and Theory* 6:1–51.

1985 North American Archaeology and Archaeologists, 1879–1934. *American Antiquity* 50:249–260.

1991 On "Paradigms" and "Paradigm Bias" in Controversies over Human Antiquity in America. In *The First Americans: Search and Research*, edited by T. D. Dillehay and D. J. Meltzer, pp. 13–49. CRC Press, Boca Raton, Florida.

Michener, C. D., and R. R. Sokal

1957 A Quantitative Approach to a Problem in Classification. *Evolution* 11: 130–162.

Moore, J. H.

1994 Putting Anthropology Back Together Again: The Ethnogenetic Critique of Cladistic Theory. *American Anthropology* 96:925–948.

Morgan, T. H.

1925 *Evolution and Genetics.* Princeton University Press, Princeton, New Jersey.

National Research Council

1929 Report of the Conference on Midwestern Archaeology, Held in St. Louis, Missouri, May 18, 1929. *National Research Council, Bulletin* 74.

1931 The Vermillion Conference. *Committee on State Archaeological Surveys, Circular* No. 9. Washington, D.C.

1932 *Conference on Southern Pre-History.* Washington, D.C.

1937 *The Indianapolis Archaeological Conference.* Washington, D.C.

O'Brien, M. J., J. Darwent, and R. L. Lyman

2001 Cladistics Is Useful for Reconstructing Archaeological Phylogenies: Paleoindian Points from the Southeastern United States. *Journal of Archaeological Science* 28:1115–1136.

O'Brien, M. J., and R. L. Lyman

1998 *James A. Ford and the Growth of Americanist Archaeology.* University of Missouri Press, Columbia.

1999a The Bureau of American Ethnology and Its Legacy to Southeastern Archaeology. *Journal of the Southwest* 41:407–440.

1999b *Seriation, Stratigraphy, and Index Fossils: The Backbone of Archaeological Dating*. Kluwer Academic/Plenum Press, New York.

2000 *Applying Evolutionary Archaeology: A Systematic Approach*. Kluwer Academic/Plenum Press, New York.

2002 The Epistemological Nature of Archaeological Units. *Anthropological Theory* 2:37–57.

O'Brien, M. J., and R. L. Lyman (editors)

2001 *Setting the Agenda in American Archaeology: The National Research Council Archaeological Conferences of 1929, 1932, and 1935*. University of Alabama Press, Tuscaloosa.

O'Brien, M. J., R. L. Lyman, Y. Saab, E. Saab, J. Darwent, and D. S. Glover

2002 Two Issues in Archaeological Phylogenetics: Taxon construction and Outgroup Selection. *Journal of Theoretical Biology* 215:133–150.

Overstreet, D. F.

1999 Will C. McKern. *Wisconsin Archeologist* 80:63–67.

Padian, K.

1997 The Rehabilitation of Sir Richard Own. *BioScience* 47:446–453.

1999 Charles Darwin's Views of Classification in Theory and Practice. *Systematic Biology* 48:352–364.

Panchen, A. L.

1994 Richard Owen and the Concept of Homology. In *Homology: The Hierarchical Basis of Comparative Biology*, edited by B. K. Hall, pp. 21–62. Academic Press, San Diego.

Peabody, C., and W. K. Moorehead

1904 The Exploration of Jacobs Cavern. *Phillips Academy, Department of Archaeology, Bulletin* No. 1.

Peake, H. J. E., and H. J. Fleure

1927 *The Corridors of Time* (10 vols.). Oxford University Press, Oxford.

Phillips, P.

1942 Review of "An Archaeological Survey of Pickwick Basin in the Adjacent Portions of the States of Alabama, Mississippi, and Tennessee" by W. S. Webb and D. L. DeJarnette. *American Antiquity* 8:197–201.

1953 American Archaeology and General Anthropological Theory. *Southwestern Journal of Anthropology* 11:246–250.

Phillips, P., and G. R. Willey

1953 Method and Theory in American Archaeology: An Operational Basis for Culture-Historical Integration. *American Anthropologist* 55:615–633.

Popper, K. R.

1968 *The Logic of Scientific Discovery*. Harper and Row, New York.

Reed, E. K.

1940 Review of "Prehistoric Culture Units and Their Relationships in Northern Arizona" by H. S. Colton. *American Antiquity* 6:189–192.

Reiter, P.

1938 Review of "Handbook of Northern Arizona Pottery Wares" by H. S. Colton and L. L. Hargrave. *American Anthropologist* 40:489–491.

Ridley, M.

1993 *Evolution.* Blackwell Science, Cambridge, Massachusetts.

Ritchie, W. A.

1932a The Algonkin Sequence in New York. *American Anthropologist* 34: 406–414.

1932b The Lamoka Lake Site: The Type Station of the Archaic Algonkin Period in New York. *New York State Archaeological Association, Researches and Transactions* 7(4).

1936a New Evidence Relating to the Archaic Occupation of New York. *New York State Archaeological Association, Researches and Transactions* 8(1).

1936b A Prehistoric Fortified Village Site at Canandaigua, Ontario County, New York. *Rochester Museum of Arts and Sciences, Research Records* No. 3.

1937 Culture Influences from Ohio in New York Archaeology. *American Antiquity* 2:182–194.

1938 A Perspective of Northeastern Archaeology. *American Antiquity* 4: 94–112.

1944 The Pre-Iroquoian Occupations of New York State. *Rochester Museum, Memoir* No. 1.

Ritvo, H.

1997 *The Platypus and the Mermaid and Other Figments of the Classifying Imagination.* Harvard University Press, Cambridge, Massachusetts.

Rouse, I. B.

1939 Prehistory in Haiti: A Study in Method. *Yale University Publications in Anthropology* No. 21.

1953 The Strategy of Culture History. In *Anthropology Today,* edited by A. L. Kroeber, pp. 57–76. University of Chicago Press, Chicago.

1954 On the Use of the Concept of Area Co-tradition. *American Antiquity* 19:221–225.

1955 On the Correlation of Phases of Culture. *American Anthropologist* 57: 713–722.

Sampson, G.

1980 *Schools of Linguistics.* Stanford University Press, Stanford, California.

Sapir, E.

1916 Time Perspective in Aboriginal American Culture, a Study in Method. *Canada Department of Mines, Geological Survey, Memoir* 90.

Sharer, R. J., and W. Ashmore

1993 *Archaeology: Discovering Our Past,* 2nd ed. Mayfield, Mountain View, California.

Shenefelt, R. D.

1959 Taxonomic "Descriptions." *Science* 130:331.

Simon, H. A.

1962 The Architecture of Complexity. *American Philosophical Society, Proceedings* 106:467–482.

Simpson, G. G.

1944 *Tempo and Mode in Evolution.* Columbia University Press, New York.

1945 The Principles of Classification and a Classification of Mammals. *American Museum of Natural History, Bulletin* 85.

1951 The Species Concept. *Evolution* 5:285–298.

1959 Anatomy and Morphology: Classification and Evolution: 1859 and 1959. *American Philosophical Society, Proceedings* 103:286–306.

1961 *Principles of Animal Taxonomy.* Columbia University Press, New York.

Sneath, P. H. A.

1957 The Application of Computers to Taxonomy. *Journal of General Microbiology* 17:201–226.

Sneath, P. H. A., and R. R. Sokal

1973 *Numerical Taxonomy.* Freeman, San Francisco.

Snodgrasse, R. M.

1933 Notes on the Archaeology of Jo Daviess County. *Illinois State Academy of Science, Transactions* 25:87–88.

Sokal, R. R.

1966 Numerical Taxonomy. *Scientific American* 215(6):106–116.

1974 Classification: Purposes, Principles, Progress, Prospects. *Science* 185: 1115–1123.

Sokal, R. R., and J. H. Camin

1965 The Two Taxonomies: Areas of Agreement and of Conflict. *Systematic Zoology* 14:176–195.

Sokal, R. R., J. H. Camin, F. J. Rohlf, and P. H. A. Sneath

1965 Numerical Taxonomy: Some Points of View. *Systematic Zoology* 14: 237–243.

Sokal, R. R., and P. H. A. Sneath

1963 *Principles of Numerical Taxonomy.* Freeman, San Francisco.

Spaulding, A. C.

1949 Cultural and Chronological Classification in the Plains Area. *Plains Archaeological Conference Newsletter* 2(2):3–5.

Stearn, W. T.

1959 The Background of Linnaeus's Contributions to the Nomenclature and Methods of Systematic Biology. *Systematic Zoology* 8:4–22.

Stevens, P. F.

1980 Evolutionary Polarity of Character States. *Annual Review of Ecology and Systematics* 11:333–358.

Steward, J. H.

1929 Diffusion and Independent Invention: A Critique of Logic. *American Anthropologist* 31:491–495.

1941 Review of "Prehistoric Culture Units and Their Relationships in Northern Arizona" by H. S. Colton. *American Antiquity* 6:366–367.

1942 The Direct Historical Approach to Archaeology. *American Antiquity* 7:337–343.

1944 Re: Archaeological Tools and Jobs. *American Antiquity* 10:99–100.

1949 Cultural Causality and Law: A Trial Formulation of the Development of Early Civilizations. *American Anthropologist* 51:1–27.

1953 Evolution and Process. In *Anthropology Today*, edited by A. L. Kroeber, pp. 313–326. University of Chicago Press, Chicago.

1954 Types of Types. *American Anthropologist* 56:54–57.

1955 *Theory of Culture Change: The Methodology of Multilinear Evolution.* University of Illinois Press, Urbana.

Stewart, T. D.

1949 The Development of the Concept of Morphological Dating in Connection with Early Man in America. *Southwestern Journal of Anthropology* 5:1–16.

Strong, W. D.

1935 An Introduction to Nebraska Archeology. *Smithsonian Miscellaneous Collections* 93(10).

1936 Anthropological Theory and Archaeological Fact. In *Essays in Anthropology Presented to A. L. Kroeber*, edited by R. H. Lowie, pp. 359–368. University of California Press, Berkeley.

1940a From History to Prehistory in the Northern Great Plains. In Essays in Historical Anthropology of North America, pp. 353–394. *Smithsonian Miscellaneous Collections* 100.

1940b Review of "Chapters in Nebraska Archaeology" edited by E. H. Bell. *American Antiquity* 5:266–268.

Styles, B. W., and M. J. Bade

1988 The University of Chicago Photograph File. *The Living Museum* 50: 19–22.

Sylvester-Bradley, P. C. (editor)

1956 *The Species Concept in Palaeontology.* The Systematics Association, London.

Swanton, J. R.

1919 A Structural and Lexical Comparison of the Tunica, Chitimacha, and Atakapa Languages. *Bureau of American Ethnology, Bulletin* 68.

1932a The Southeastern Indians of History. In *Conference on Southern Pre-History*, pp. 5–20. National Research Council, Washington, D.C.

1932b The Relation of the Southeast to General Culture Problems of American Pre-history. In *Conference on Southern Pre-History*, pp. 60–74. National Research Council, Washington, D.C.

1940 Linguistic Material from the Tribes of Southern Texas and Northeastern Mexico. *Bureau of American Ethnology, Bulletin* 127.

Szarski, H.

1949 The Concept of Homology in the Light of the Comparative Anatomy of Vertebrates. *Quarterly Review of Biology* 24:124–131.

Taylor, W. W.

1948 A Study of Archeology. *American Anthropological Association, Memoir* 69.

Terrell, J. E. (editor)

2001 *Archaeology, Language, and History: Essays on Culture and Ethnicity.* Bergin and Garvey, Westport, Connecticut.

Thomas, D. H.

1998 *Archaeology,* 3rd ed. Harcourt Brace, Fort Worth, Texas.

Thompson, W. R.

1952 The Philosophical Foundations of Systematics. *The Canadian Entomologist* 84:1–16.

Trigger, B. G.

1968 Major Concepts of Archaeology in Historical Perspective. *Man* 3:527–541.

1989 *A History of Archaeological Thought.* Cambridge University Press, Cambridge.

Valentine, J. W., and C. L. May

1996 Hierarchies in Biology and Paleobiology. *Paleobiology* 22:23–33.

Van Riper, A. B.

1993 *Men among the Mammoths: Victorian Science and the Discovery of Human Prehistory.* University of Chicago Press, Chicago.

Webb, W. S.

1938 An Archaeological Survey of the Norris Basin in Eastern Tennessee. *Bureau of American Ethnology, Bulletin* 118.

1939 An Archaeological Survey of the Wheeler Basin on the Tennessee River in Northern Alabama. *Bureau of American Ethnology, Bulletin* 122.

Webb, W. S., and D. L. DeJarnette

1942 An Archaeological Survey of Pickwick Basin in the Adjacent Portions of the States of Alabama, Mississippi, and Tennessee. *Bureau of American Ethnology, Bulletin* 129.

Wedel, W. R.

1936 An Introduction to Pawnee Archeology. *Bureau of American Ethnology, Bulletin* 112.

1938 The Direct-Historical Approach in Pawnee Archeology. *Smithsonian Miscellaneous Collections* 97(7):1–21.

1940 Culture Sequence in the Central Great Plains. In Essays in Historical Anthropology of North America, pp. 291–352. *Smithsonian Miscellaneous Collections* 100.

Wilford, L. A.

1941 A Tentative Classification of the Prehistoric Cultures of Minnesota. *American Antiquity* 6:231–249.

1945 Three Villages of the Mississippi Pattern in Minnesota. *American Antiquity* 11:32–40.

1955 A Revised Classification of the Prehistoric Cultures of Minnesota. *American Antiquity* 21:130–142.

Willey, G. R.

1953 Archaeological Theories and Interpretation: New World. In *Anthropology Today*, edited by A. L. Kroeber, pp. 361–385. University of Chicago Press, Chicago.

1999 Foreword. In *Measuring the Flow of Time: The Works of James A. Ford, 1935–1941*, edited by M. J. O'Brien and R. L. Lyman, pp. vii–xiv. University of Alabama Press, Tuscaloosa.

Willey, G. R., and P. Phillips

1955 Method and Theory in American Archaeology, II: Historical-Developmental Interpretation. *American Anthropologist* 57:723–819.

1958 *Method and Theory in American Archaeology.* University of Chicago Press, Chicago.

Willey, G. R., and J. A. Sabloff

1993 *A History of American Archaeology,* 3rd ed. Freeman, New York.

Wissler, C.

1916 The Genetic Relations of Certain Forms in American Aboriginal Art. *National Academy of Sciences, Proceedings* 2:224–226.

1917 *The American Indian.* McMurtrie, New York.

1923 *Man and Culture.* Crowell, New York.

1938 *The American Indian,* 3rd ed. Oxford University Press, New York.

Wray, G. A.

1999 The Origin of Animal Body Plans: A Study in Evolutionary Developmental Biology. *Paleobiology* 25:139–143.

Index